The Handbook of Communication Skills

The ever increasing importance of interpersonal skills both to personal well-being and to effectiveness in professional practice is reflected in the burgeoning research literature on skilled communication. *The Handbook of Communication Skills* is recognised as one of the foremost texts in this area, and this updated and expanded new edition will be welcomed by practitioners and theorists alike.

In response to the increasing demand for information on dimensions of interviewing, a section on 'Interviewing contexts' has been included, with chapters on the key interviewing contexts of selection, helping and appraisal, as well as the exciting new field of cognitive interviewing. In addition, a chapter on 'Relational communication' has been included since this is one of the areas of most rapid growth in social psychology and communication.

The Handbook of Communication Skills represents the most significant single contribution to literature in this domain, and has chapters by world leaders in their particular fields. It will be of continued interest to researchers and students in psychology, as well as the vast range of people in the 'interpersonal professions'. As such, the *Handbook* is used in a wide variety of contexts, from theoretical mainstream communications modules on degree programmes to vocational courses in health, business and education.

Owen D. W. Hargie is Professor of Communication at the University of Ulster, and has an international reputation in the study of skilled communication. He has written over one hundred articles and book chapters, and has co-authored and edited ten books, including *Social Skills in Interpersonal Communication* (3rd edn, 1994), with C. Y. M. Saunders and D. A. Dickson, and *Professional Interviewing* (1992), with R. Millar and V. Crute.

Praise for the first edition:

The Handbook of Communication Skills

Second edition

Edited by
Owen D. W. Hargie

London and New York

In memory of my late father, Ernest Hargie

First edition published 1986
by Croom Helm
Reprinted 1989, 1991 (twice), 1993
by Routledge

Second edition published 1997
by Routledge
11 New Fetter Lane, London EC4P 4EE

Simultaneously published in the USA and Canada
by Routledge
29 West 35th Street, New York, NY 10001

Typeset in Times by Florencetype Ltd, Stoodleigh, Devon
Printed and bound in Great Britain by
TJ Press (Padstow) Ltd, Padstow, Cornwall

British Library Cataloguing in Publication Data
A catalogue record for this book is available from the British Library.

Library of Congress Cataloguing in Publication Data
The handbook of communication skills/edited by Owen Hargie.
    p. cm.
    Includes bibliographical references and index.
    1. Interpersonal communication. 2. Communication–Psychological
aspects. 3. Interviewing. I. Hargie, Owen.
BF637.C45H284   1997
302.2—dc20   96-7560

ISBN 0-415-12325-9 (hbk)
ISBN 0-415-12326-7 (pbk)

Contents

List of figures	vii
List of tables	viii
Notes on contributors	ix
Editorial introduction	1

Part I Background

1 Communication as skilled performance   7
Owen D. W. Hargie

2 Interpersonal communication: a theoretical framework   29
Owen D. W. Hargie

Part II Core communication skills

3 Non-verbal behaviour as communication   67
Richard M. Rozelle, Daniel Druckman and James C. Baxter

4 Questioning   103
Jim Dillon

5 Reinforcement   134
Len Cairns

6 Reflecting   159
David A. Dickson

7 Explaining   183
George Brown and Madeleine Atkins

8 Self-disclosure   213
Charles H. Tardy and Kathryn Dindia

9 The process of listening   236
Robert N. Bostrom

10 Humour and laughter   259
Hugh C. Foot

Part III Specialised contexts

11 Asserting and confronting   289
   Richard F. Rakos

12 Interacting in task groups   320
   Arjaan P. Wit and Henk A. M. Wilke

13 Negotiating and bargaining   339
   Ian E. Morley

14 Relational communication   358
   Colin T. C. Hargie and Dennis Tourish

Part IV Interviewing contexts

15 The selection interview   385
   Rob Millar and Mary Gallagher

16 The helping interview: a cognitive-developmental approach   409
   Sandra A. Rigazio-DiGilio and Allen E. Ivey

17 The appraisal interview and the performance evaluation interview 430
   Henk T. Van der Molen and Frits Kluytmans

18 The cognitive interview   451
   Amina Memon

Part V The training context

19 Training in communication skills: research, theory and practice 473
   Owen D. W. Hargie

   Name index   483
   Subject index   498

Figures

2.1 Welford's model of the human sensory-motor system   30
2.2 Argyle's motor skill model   31
2.3 Extended model of interpersonal interaction   32
2.4 Maslow's hierarchy of human needs   33
2.5 Categories of social behaviour   40
2.6 Impossible figure   45
4.1 Classroom and psychotherapy contexts   104
4.2 Courtroom and news contexts   107
4.3 Interrogation and polling contexts   109
4.4 Medical and personnel contexts   112
13.1 The space of possible bids   340
13.2 Two-person two-choice matrix game   342
16.1 The developmental sphere   424

Tables

2.1 The process of attribution 48
3.1 Transmission of messages 78
5.1 Characteristics of positive and negative reinforcement 139
7.1 The polar contrasts of scientific and personal understanding 189
7.2 Planning strategies and performance skills in explaining 193
7.3 High- and low-scoring explanations 196
7.4 Effective structuring moves in explaining 199
7.5 Health improvement: processes and outcomes 203
9.1 Intercorrelations of various sections of the National Teacher Examination 246
9.2 Factors generated by intercorrelations of ETS 'communication skills' assessments 246
9.3 Percentages of news headlines correctly recalled as a function of visual format and modality 248
9.4 Recall of news as a function of presentation modality 249
9.5 Recognition scores 250

Notes on contributors

Madeleine Atkins was Head of the Department of Education and is now Dean of the Faculty of Education at the University of Newcastle. Her main research interests are in interactive learning skills and the impact of new technologies on learning. She has written texts, articles and reviews of teaching, learning and assessment in higher education. She has also been involved in vocational training in General Practice and the training of hospital doctors. Dr Atkins has acted as a consultant to many national bodies in the UK, including the Department for Education and Employment and the Higher Education Quality Council.

James C. Baxter is Professor of Psychology at the University of Houston. He received his PhD in psychology from the University of Texas at Austin. His primary research interests are in person perception, self-presentation and personality theory.

Robert N. Bostrom is Professor of Communication at the University of Kentucky, Lexington. His books include *Listening Behavior*, *Persuasion*, *Communicating in Public* and *Communication for Everyday Use*. His edited texts include *Communication Competence* and the *ICA Yearbooks, Volumes 7 and 8*. His research has appeared in such various publications as *Human Communication Research*, *Communication Monographs*, the *Journal of Communication* and the *Journal of Religious Humanism*. He lives on a farm in Woodford County, Kentucky, and is currently at work on a new book on communication research methods.

George Brown is currently visiting Professor of Education at the University of Ulster. He was Reader in University Teaching Methods at the University of Nottingham and National Co-ordinator of Academic Staff Development for the UK Committee of Vice Chancellors and Principals. His research interests are in the fields of higher education and classroom teaching, and he has published widely on lecturing, teaching and assessment, staff development, and medical and dental education. He is co-author of the influential book *Effective Teaching in Higher Education*. Dr Brown has acted as a consultant for numerous bodies including the UK Higher Education Funding Council, British Council, UNESCO, WHO, and the World Bank.

Len Cairns is Professor and Head of the School of Education at Monash University in Victoria, Australia. He is a graduate of the University of New South Wales, University of Sydney (MEd and PhD) and the University of Arizona (MEd). He has researched and published extensively in teacher education and is a Fellow and past President of the Australian Teacher Education Association. Recently, he has specialised in the area of language and learning, adding a different dimension to his earlier work in social psychology and education where his interests were in interpersonal perception, unobtrusive measures and microteaching.

David A. Dickson is Head of the Social Skills Centre at the University of Ulster, Jordanstown. After reading psychology and philosophy at Queen's University, Belfast, he obtained a masters degree in education from the New University of Ulster and a PhD from Ulster Polytechnic. He is an Associate Fellow of the British Psychological Society, holding Chartered status, and a member of the International Communication Association. His main areas of interest are in interpersonal communication, particularly in the health and caring fields. He has published numerous articles, chapters and books in these areas. His books include *Rewarding People: The Skill of Responding Positively*, *CST for Health Professionals: An Instructor's Handbook* and *Social Skills in Interpersonal Communication*.

J. T. ('Jim') Dillon holds advanced degrees in history and education, and a PhD from the University of Chicago. His books on questioning include *The Practice of Questioning*, *Questioning and Teaching*, *Questioning and Discussion* and *Using Discussion in Classrooms*. Other recent books are *Deliberation in Education and Society*, *Personal Teaching* and *Jesus as a Teacher*. He is Professor of Education at the University of California.

Kathryn Dindia is an Associate Professor in the Department of Communication at the University of Wisconsin Milwaukee, where she has taught for fifteen years. She received her PhD in Speech Communication from the University of Washington in 1981. She has published articles and book chapters on self-disclosure, communication and relationship maintenance and sex-differences in communication behaviour. Most recently, she published a book chapter entitled 'Self-disclosure, self-identity, and relationship development: A transactional/dialectical perspective' in the revised edition of *Handbook of Personal Relationships*.

Daniel Druckman is currently Principal Study Director at the National Research Council in Washington, DC and Senior Contract Professor of Conflict Management at George Mason University in Fairfax, VA. He received a PhD in social psychology from Northwestern University in Illinois, USA. In addition to nonverbal communication, his primary interests are in the areas of interparty conflict resolution, negotiations, nationalism, political stability and modelling methodologies, including simulation. He has published numerous articles, books, and book chapters on these topics. He has also written, with Rozelle and Baxter, *Nonverbal Communication: Survey, Theory, and Research* and, most recently, co-edited two volumes, *Learning, Remembering, Believing: Enhancing Human Performance* and *Enhancing Organizational Performance*, both published by the National Academy Press. He received the 1995 Klineberg prize from the Society for the Psychological Study of Social Issues for his work on nationalism.

Hugh C. Foot is Professor and Head of the Psychology Department at the University of Strathclyde, Glasgow. He is a Fellow of the British Psychological Society and Honorary Editor of *The Psychologist*. His publications include two books on humour and laughter – *Humour and Laughter: Theory, Research and Applications* and *It's a Funny Thing,*

Laughter and he has written over twenty articles and book chapters on this topic. He also co-organised the first International Conference on Humour and Laughter held in Cardiff in 1976. His other research interests include child pedestrian behaviour and children's collaborative learning.

Mary Gallagher is a Lecturer in the School of Behavioural and Communication Sciences at the University of Ulster. She obtained her undergraduate degree in human communication in 1983 from the Ulster Polytechnic, followed in 1987 by her DPhil in the field of counselling psychology from the University of Ulster. She worked as a researcher in the field of adolescent needs before taking up her present position. Her research interests include interviewing and counselling and she has published articles in journals such as *Counselling Psychology Quarterly, British Journal of Guidance and Counselling* and *Counselling.*

Colin T. C. Hargie is Lecturer in Communication at the University of Ulster. He is a graduate of Queen's University, Belfast and the University of Ulster, with undergraduate and postgraduate qualifications in sociology, counselling and education management. He has considerable experience in the organisation and development of outreach adult education programmes. He was responsible for establishing and running the Employee Development Programme at the Ford Motor Company in Belfast. His research interests include interpersonal and organisational communication with a special focus on relational development. He has published a large number of book chapters and articles in journals such as *Innovation and Learning in Education, Research in Education* and *The International Journal of Education Management.*

Owen D. W. Hargie is Professor of Communication at the University of Ulster. His special area of interest is in the study of interpersonal and organisational communication, fields in which he has published ten books (including *Social Skills in Interpersonal Communication, Professional Interviewing, Auditing Internal Communications: A Handbook, Looking Into Community Pharmacy* and *CST for Health Professionals: An Instructor's Handbook*), and over ninety book chapters and journal articles. He is also Editor for the book series *International Series on Communication Skills* published by Routledge. He acts as a consultant on communication for numerous public and private sector organisations.

Allen E. Ivey is a Distinguished Professor in the APA-accredited Counseling Psychology Program at the University of Massachusetts. He is nationally and internationally known for his over thirty years of work with *Microskills* and for his construction of *Developmental Therapy*, having published over two hundred articles and twenty-two books on these topics. He is well known for providing cutting edge, non-pathological and pragmatic helping frameworks that have spawned research and theory construction for two generations. Dr Ivey is currently involved in explicating the intercultural implications of *Developmental Therapy*. Additionally, he serves as the Editor of the *Counseling and Development Book Series* of *Teachers College Press.*

Frits Kluytmans is Associate Professor in the Faculty of Social Sciences at the Open University, the Netherlands. He is responsible for the development of course material for distance education in the fields of personnel and organisation, and has published numerous articles and books in this area. His books include *Human Resources Management, Leerboek*

Personeelsmanagement (*Handbook of Personnel Management*) and *Gespreksvoering: Vaardigheden en Modellen* (*Dialogues: Skills and Models*).

Amina Memon is Lecturer in Psychology at the University of Southampton. Her research areas include the validity of laboratory studies of memory and the theoretical principles derived from them in relevant contexts. She has conducted extensive research on the difficulty of forensic interviewing techniques such as the cognitive interview. Dr Memon has a background in cognitive and social psychology. Her publications include key journal articles on eyewitness memory and on the cognitive interview. She has also contributed to numerous edited volumes and collaborated with leading researchers from Britain, Germany and North America, in the field of eyewitness memory.

Rob Millar is a Lecturer in the School of Behavioural and Communication Sciences at the University of Ulster. He obtained his undergraduate degree in psychology in 1974 and then worked as a careers officer for three years, before joining Ulster Polytechnic in 1978. His DPhil in psychology was obtained from the University of Ulster. His research area is in the field of occupational psychology and organisational communication. He was senior author of *Professional Interviewing* (Routledge) and has published numerous research articles in journals such as *British Journal of Guidance and Counselling*, *Work and Stress* and *British Journal of Educational Psychology*.

Henk T. Van der Molen is Professor of Psychology in the Faculty of Social Sciences at the Open University in The Netherlands. In 1995 he became the President of the Dutch Psychological Association (Nederlands Instituut van Psychologen, NIP). He has published a large number of articles and books on communication skills training and is a specialist in research into the effectiveness of programmes in this field. He is co-author of *Personal Conversations: Roles and Skills for Counsellors*, *Gesprekken in Organisaties* (*Professional Conversations in Organisations*), *Methodiek van Gesprekstraining* (*Methodology of Communication Skills Training*) and *Gespreksvoering: Vaardigheden en Modellen* (*Dialogues: Skills and Models*).

Ian E. Morley is Senior Lecturer in Psychology at the University of Warwick. His research interests include social psychology, negotiating, leadership and group performance. For over twenty years he has been writing extensively on aspects of bargaining and negotiating, and is co-author of two major books: *The Social Psychology of Bargaining* and *A Social Psychology of Organizing*.

Richard F. Rakos is Professor and Chair of the Psychology Department at Cleveland State University. He is a behaviour therapist who has published widely in the areas of assertion, behavioural self-management, behaviour analysis of social systems and societal phenomena and law and psychology. His publications in assertiveness include numerous articles in scientific journals, book chapters, an audio-cassette training programme and the book *Assertive Behavior: Theory, Research and Training*. Professor Rakos teaches graduate courses in clinical interviewing, behaviour therapy, and ethical and legal issues for therapists. He also maintains a small but active private practice.

Sandra A. Rigazio-DiGilio is an Associate Professor in the COAMFTE-accredited Marriage and Family Therapy Program at the University of Connecticut, and holds a joint appointment in the Department of Psychiatry. She has published extensively on a systemic translation of Developmental Therapy – *Systemic Cognitive-Developmental Therapy and Systemic Cognitive-Developmental Supervision.* Dr Rigazio-DiGilio serves on the AAMFT Board of Directors, as an Associate Editor of the *Counseling and Development Book Series* of *Teachers College Press*, and as an Associate Editor for the *Journal of Mental Health Counseling.*

Richard M. Rozelle is Professor of Psychology and Dean of the College of Social Science at the University of Houston. He received his PhD in social psychology from Northwestern University. His research interests include impression formation and management, attitude –behaviour change, bargaining behaviour, behavioural medicine, organisational climate and programme evaluation.

Charles H. Tardy is Professor of Speech Communication at the University of Southern Mississippi. He received his PhD from the University of Iowa. He has published widely, including editorship of *A Handbook for the Study of Human Communication* and numerous articles in major journals such as *American Journal of Community Psychology*, *Communication Monographs, Communication Research, Journal of Language and Social Psychology, Human Communication Research* and *Southern Communication Journal.* His current research on physiological responses to the production of self-disclosive speech is being funded by a grant from the National Institutes of Health.

Dennis Tourish is a Lecturer in Communication at the University of Ulster. He holds a primary degree in Human Communication and an MSc in Health and Social Services Management. He has research interests in various aspects of interpersonal communica- tion. He has also carried out research into how communication between management and other sections of organisations is assessed, how such assessments are used to facilitate changes in relationships and how such changes are evaluated. He has published widely in a range of journals such as *Human Relations, Counselling Psychology Quarterly* and *Health Services Management Research.*

Henk A. M. Wilke is Professor of Social and Organisational Psychology at the University of Leiden, The Netherlands. His has published several books (including *Group Performance*) and numerous articles on research and theory in the area of cognitive social psychology (e.g., social comparison of attitudes and abilities, group polarisation, group identification) and group dynamics (e.g., coalition formation, bargaining, leadership, task performance, co-operation versus competition).

Arjaan P. Wit is Assistant Professor of Social and Organisational Psychology at the University of Leiden, The Netherlands. His academic interests and publications are in research, theory and practice in the area of co-operation versus self-interested behaviour in mixed motive situations such as small task groups, organisations or even society at large (e.g., evaluating programmes of public education on environmental concern).

Editorial introduction

As society develops and becomes more complex, there has evolved the need for a greater number of what Ellis (1980) termed 'interpersonal professionals' who spend a large part of their working lives in face-to-face interaction with others. Such professionals include doctors, teachers, speech therapists, physiotherapists, occupational therapists, social workers, psychologists, psychotherapists, nurses, careers advisers, counsellors and business executives, to name but a few. Historically, the training of many of these professionals focused almost entirely upon the acquisition of specialised knowledge. More recently, however, the centrality of interpersonal communication in their work has been recognised and catered for in training.

Competence in most types of profession involves the effective implementation of three main sets of skills: first, cognitive skills which refer to the knowledge base of the profession, that which characterises it and sets it apart from others; second, technical or manipulative skills which are inherent within a profession – a surgeon must be able to utilise a scalpel skilfully, a nurse must be able to dress a wound and a surveyor needs to know how to use a theodolite; third, social or communication skills, including the ability of the individual to interact effectively with others in the professional context.

Traditionally, the education and training of most professional groups placed emphasis upon the former two sets of skills at the expense of interpersonal skills. This is somewhat surprising, given that it has long been recognised that the ability to communicate effectively is essential for success in many walks of life. McCroskey (1984, p. 260), in emphasising this fact, pointed out that: 'The importance of competence in communication has been recognized for thousands of years. The oldest essay ever discovered, written about 3000 BC, consists of advice on how to speak effectively. This essay was inscribed on a fragment of parchment addressed to Kagemni, the eldest son of Pharaoh Huni. Similarly, the oldest extant book is a treatise on effective communication. This book, known as the *Precepts*, was composed in Egypt about 2675 BC by Ptah-Hotep.' It can thus be argued that scholarship in the field of communication has been going on for some five thousand years!

In the first edition of this book, it was pointed out that the study of communication had been largely overlooked in the education and training of many professional groups. In the intervening decade much has changed. Communication as a social science discipline has developed at a very rapid pace. There has been a huge growth in communication research and theory, as evidenced by the number of journals and books now devoted to this discipline. This has been paralleled by a concomitant large increase in the number of students undertaking undergraduate and postgraduate degree programmes in this field

(Hargie, 1992). A significant proportion of this work has been at the interpersonal level, including the study of professional interaction. Almost without exception, those involved in the training of professionals now recognise the necessity for neophytes to become competent communicators.

Given the importance of effective communication, it is reasonable to expect that professionals should have knowledge of, and expertise in, communication skills. Indeed, as noted by Ellis and Whittington (1981, p. 41), 'All but the most isolated occupations demand interaction with others at times, but some jobs have skilled interaction as a primary focus'. Therefore, it is hardly surprising that in the past few years increasing attention has been devoted to the study of social skills in professional contexts. In 1981, Hargie and Saunders listed a total of sixteen separate professions wherein programmes of training in interpersonal communication had been implemented and evaluated in the literature. It is true to say that this list has since expanded considerably, and that every profession now incorporates an element of study and training in the sphere of interpersonal communication as part of the curriculum. The extent of this training will depend upon the degree of interaction inherent in the job.

Increasing attention has also been devoted to the entire spectrum of socially skilled interaction. The fairly obvious observation that some individuals are more socially skilled than others has led to carefully formulated and systematic investigations into the nature and functions of social skills. Ellis and Whittington (1981) identified three discrete contexts within which such investigations have taken place: *Developmental* where the concern is with the development of socially skilled behaviour in children; with how, and at what stages, children acquire, refine and extend their repertoire of social skills; *Remedial* where the focus of attention is upon those individuals who, for whatever reason, fail to develop an adequate repertoire of social skills. Investigators are interested in attempting to determine the nature and causes of social inadequacy, and in ascertaining to what extent social skill deficits can be remediated; and *Specialised* where attention is devoted to the study of interpersonal skills in professional encounters. Most professions necessitate interaction of a specialised nature either with clients or with other professionals. Therefore, it is important to chart the types of communication skills which are effective in professional situations.

It is with the latter context that this book is concerned. Research into specialised social skills has developed rapidly, and the decade since the publication of the first edition of this handbook has witnessed a vast amount of investigation. This text now brings together much of this research to provide a comprehensive study of those communication skill areas central to effective interpersonal functioning in a range of professional contexts.

Although it is difficult to sectionalise communication, for the purpose of analysis the book is divided into four main sections. Part 1 sets the book in context by providing a theoretical framework for the study of communication as a form of skilled activity. The concept of communication as skilled performance is examined (Chapter 1), and a theoretical model of interpersonal communication as skill is fully delineated (Chapter 2). Part 2 then focuses upon eight core communication skills, namely non-verbal communication, questioning, reinforcement, reflecting, explaining, self-disclosure, listening, and humour and laughter. While these are not entirely mutually exclusive (for example, aspects of non-verbal communication are relevant to all of the other chapters), each chapter deals with a discrete and important component of communication.

In Part 3, the focus moves from key skills which are relevant across many situations to an analysis of interpersonal communication in four specialised and widely researched contexts. This section therefore incorporates an examination of central dimensions inherent in situations where assertion and confrontation are required (Chapter 11), a synopsis of factors which impinge upon the individual working in a task group (Chapter 12), negotiating and bargaining encounters (Chapter 13) and pivotal elements inherent in the development, maintenance and dissolution of relationships (Chapter 14).

Part 4 is then devoted to the study of a range of four interviewing contexts. The importance of interviewing was succinctly summarised by Millar *et al.* (1992, p. 183) who pointed out that 'The interview is a ubiquitous activity. Everyone will have had the experience of being interviewed at one time or another, and an increasing number of people are required to play the role of interviewer in a professional capacity. For this latter group, a knowledge of the nature of interviewing can make an important contribution to effective practice'. This is an apt justification for the inclusion of this section in the present text. While it is beyond the scope of the present text to include chapters on all types of interview, the main forms of interview relevant to most professionals are included, namely the selection interview (Chapter 15), the helping interview (Chapter 16), the appraisal interview (Chapter 17) and the cognitive interview (Chapter 18).

The final chapter then provides an overview bringing together the main issues arising from the study of communication skills.

The information about interpersonal communication provided in this book should be regarded as providing resource material. How these resources are applied will depend upon the personality of the reader and the situation in which any interaction occurs. It is impossible to legislate in advance for every possible social context, and decisions about what approach could best be employed can only be made in the light of all the available background information. As such, this book certainly does not provide a preordained set of responses for given situations. Rather, it offers a selection of communication perspectives which should both inform the reader and facilitate the interactive process.

This book provides reviews of research, theory and practice pertaining to a range of key skills and dimensions of communication. As such, it offers valuable information which can be used to reflect upon, refine and extend one's own personal style and pattern of interaction. At the same time, it should be recognised that the coverage of interpersonal skills is not intended to be exhaustive, since there are specialised skills relevant to particular contexts (e.g., 'breaking bad news' in the medical sphere) which could not be covered in a text of this nature. Furthermore, research in the field of social interaction is progressing rapidly and it is anticipated that other general skills will be identified as our knowledge of this area increases. Finally, although the aspects contained in this book are presented separately, in practice they overlap, are interdependent and often complement one another. However, for the purposes of analysis and evaluation it is valuable to identify separately those elements of communication which seem to 'hang together', and thereby attempt to understand and make sense of what is a complex field of study.

REFERENCES

Ellis, R. (1980) 'Simulated Social Skill Training for the Interpersonal Professions', in W. Singleton, P. Spurgeon and R. Stammers (eds), *The Analysis of Social Skill*, Plenum, New York.

—— and Whittington, D. (1981) *A Guide to Social Skill Training*, Croom Helm, Beckenham.
Hargie, O. (1992) *Communication: Beyond the Crossroads*, University of Ulster, Jordanstown.
—— and Saunders, C. (1983) 'Training Professional Skills', in P. Dowrick and S. Biggs (eds), *Using Video*, John Wiley, Chichester.
McCroskey, J. (1984) 'Communicative Competence: The Elusive Construct', in R. Bostrom (ed.),*Competence in Communication: A Multidisciplinary Approach*, Sage, Beverly Hills.
Millar, R., Crute, V. and Hargie, O. (1992) *Professional Interviewing*, Routledge, London.

Part I
Background

1 Communication as skilled performance

Owen D. W. Hargie

INTRODUCTION

Any analysis of interpersonal communication is inevitably fraught with difficulties, since the process involves a large number of interrelated factors. This means that in order to make sense of, and systematically investigate, social encounters, it is necessary to employ an interpretive framework with which to study this area. In fact, a large number of alternative frameworks has been developed for this purpose. For example, interpersonal encounters have been conceptualised variously as a kind of joint economic activity or social exchange in which both sides seek rewards and try to minimise costs, which may be in the form of money, services, goods, status, love or affection (Kelley and Thibaut, 1978; Sletta, 1992); as transactional episodes during which individuals play roles akin to acting as either parent, adult or child, and respond to others at one of these three levels (Berne, 1975); and as analogous to dramatical performances in the theatre, in that everyone has a role to play with expected lines – some play more prominent roles than others, the actors behave differently 'front stage' as opposed to 'back stage', there are various 'props' in the form of furniture and fittings, there is a storyline and all of this changes from one 'play' to the next (Hare and Blumberg, 1988).

These are just three of the approaches which have been developed as templates for the analysis and interpretation of interpersonal communication. In this chapter and in Chapter 2 another approach will be presented, namely the perspective that social behaviour is a form of skilled performance, and that it is therefore meaningful to compare socially skilled behaviour (such as interviewing or negotiating) with motor skill behaviour (such as playing tennis or operating a machine). Further pursuing this analogy, it is argued that the models and methods successfully employed for some hundred years in the study of motor skill can usefully be applied to the analysis of social skill. The validity of this comparison, and the accompanying implications for the study of interpersonal behaviour, will be investigated here.

This chapter is therefore concerned with an examination of the nature of skill, and in particular with the perspective that interpersonal communication can be conceptualised as skill. In order to evaluate this perspective, it is necessary to relate the history of the study of social skill directly to the study of motor skill, since it was from the latter source that the concept of communication as skill eventually emerged. The extent to which this analogy can be pursued is then discussed, together with an analysis of the nature of social skill *per se*. So overall, this chapter provides a reference point for the entire book, by delineating the nature, and defining features, of social skill.

MOTOR SKILLS

The study of perceptual-motor skills has a long and rich tradition within psychology. Such skills, which involve co-ordinated physical movements of the body, are widely employed in human performance and include, for example, eating, walking, writing, riding a bicycle or playing golf. Welford (1968) traced the scientific study of motor skill back to 1820, when the astronomer Bessel investigated differences between individuals performing a task that involved the recording of star-transit times. However, direct psychological interest in the nature of motor skill really began with studies by Bryan and Harter (1897) into the learning of Morse code, followed by studies on movement by Woodworth (1899), and investigations by Book (1908) into the learning of typewriting skills. Since these early studies, the literature on perceptual-motor skill has become voluminous, and indeed this area remains an important focus of study for psychologists.

Numerous definitions of motor skill have been put forward. Marteniuk (1976, p. 13) stated that 'a perceptual-motor skill refers to those activities involved in moving the body or body parts to accomplish a specified objective', while Kerr (1982, p. 5), in similar vein, iterated that 'a motor skill is any muscular activity which is directed to a specific objective'. These definitions emphasise the goal-directed nature of skilled behaviour, which is regarded as intentional, rather than as chance or unintentional. As Whiting (1975, p. 4) pointed out: 'Whatever processes may be involved in *human* skill learning and performance, the concern is with *intentional* attempts to carry out motor acts, which will bring about predetermined results.'

A further distinction has been made between innate behaviour, such as breathing and coughing, and learned behaviour. For behaviour to be regarded as skilled it must be behaviour which has been learnt. This feature is highlighted by a number of theorists. Thus, motor skill was defined by Knapp (1963, p. 4) as 'the learned ability to bring about predetermined results with maximum certainty', while Magill (1989, p. 7) noted that skills 'all have in common the property that each needs to be learned in order to be properly executed'.

Other aspects of skilled performance were covered by Cratty (1964, p. 10) who described motor skill as 'reasonably complex motor performance ... (denoting) ... that some learning has taken place and that a smoothing or integration of behavior has resulted'. Skilled behaviour is therefore more complex than instinctive or reflexive movements, and consists of a hierarchy of smaller component behaviours, each of which contributes in part to the overall performance. In this respect, Summers (1981, p. 41) viewed skilled performance as requiring 'the organization of highly refined patterns of movements in relation to some specific goal'. More recently, and following a comprehensive review of the features of motor skill, the definition proffered by Proctor and Dutta (1995, p. 18) was that 'Skill is goal-directed, well-organized behavior that is acquired through practice and performed with economy of effort'.

As these definitions indicate, while there are commonalities, different theorists tend to emphasise different features, such that Irion (1966, p. 2), in tracing the history of research into motor skills, concluded: 'The field of motor skills does not suffer from a lack of variety of approach. Indeed, the approaches and methods are so extremely various that there is some difficulty in defining, in a sensible way, what the field of motor skills is.' Robb (1972, p. 1) in discussing the acquisition of motor skill, reached a similar conclusion, stating that

'The problems associated with how one acquires skill are numerous and complex. For that matter, the term *skill* is itself an illusive and confusing word'.

However, Welford (1958, p. 17) summarised the study of this field as being encapsulated in the question: 'When we look at a man working, by what criteria in his performance can we tell whether he is skilled and competent or clumsy and ignorant?' In other words, the basic distinction to be made is between skilled and unskilled behaviour, although, in fact, these two concepts represent opposite ends of a continuum of skilled performance, with individuals being more or less skilled in relation to one another. In his investigations into the nature of skill, Welford (1958) identified three main characteristics:

1 They consist of an organised, co-ordinated activity in relation to an object or a situation and, therefore, involve a whole chain of sensory, central and motor mechanisms which underlie performance;
2 They are learnt, in that the understanding of the event or performance is built up gradually with repeated experience;
3 They are serial in nature, involving the ordering and co-ordination of many different processes or actions in sequence. Thus, the skill of driving involves a pre-set repertoire of behaviours which must be carried out in temporal sequence (put gear into neutral, switch on ignition, and so on).

SOCIAL SKILLS

Given the vast amount of attention which has been devoted to the analysis and evaluation of motor skill performance, it is rather surprising that it was some considerable time before psychologists began to investigate seriously the nature of social skills. Welford (1980) attributed the growth of interest in this field to the initial work of Crossman. In a report on the effects of automation on management and social relations in industry, Crossman (1960, p. 53) noted that a crucial feature in the work of the operator of an automatic plant was the ability 'to communicate easily with his fellows, understand their points of view and put his own across. In other words, they must exercise *social skills*. As yet no serious attempt has been made to identify or analyse these skills further'. Crossman subsequently contacted Michael Argyle, a social psychologist at the University of Oxford, and together they carried out a study of social skill, explicitly designed to investigate the similarities between human–machine and human–human interactions. In this way, the first parallels were drawn between motor and social skills.

In 1967 Fitts and Posner, when discussing technical skills, emphasised that 'Social skills are also important. In particular, man must learn to communicate with others and must acquire the complex social patterns of his group' (p. 1). In the same year, Argyle and Kendon published a paper in which they related the features of motor skill, as identified by Welford, directly to the analysis of social skill. They proposed a definition of skill as comprising 'an organized, coordinated activity, in relation to an object or a situation, that involves a chain of sensory, central and motor mechanisms. One of its main characteristics is that the performance, or stream of action, is continuously under the control of the sensory input ... (and) ... the outcomes of actions are continuously matched against some criterion of achievement or degree of approach to a goal' (Argyle and Kendon, 1967, p. 56). While recognising some of the important differences between motor and social performance, they argued that this definition could be applied in large part to the study of social skill.

The intervening years since the publication of Argyle and Kendon's paper have witnessed an explosion of interest in the nature, function, delineation and content of socially skilled performance. However, quite often researchers and theorists in this area have been working in differing contexts, with little cross-fertilisation between those involved in clinical, professional and developmental settings. The result has been a plethora of different approaches to the analysis and evaluation of social skill. Therefore, it is useful to examine the existing degree of consensus as to what exactly is meant by the term 'social skill'.

In one sense, this is a term which is widely employed and generally comprehended, since it has already been used in this chapter and presumably understood by the reader. Indeed, the terms 'communication skill', 'social skill' and 'interpersonal skill' have entered the lexicon of everyday use. For example, many job advertisements stipulate that applicants should have high levels of social, or communication, skill. In this global sense, social skills can be defined as the skills employed when communicating at an interpersonal level with other people. This definition is not very illuminating, though, since it describes what social skills are *used for* rather than what they *are*. It is rather like defining a bicycle as something which gets you from one place to another! Attempts to provide a more technical, insightful definition of social skill proliferate within psychology. It is useful to examine some of these definitions in order to ascertain the extent to which common elements emerge.

DEFINITIONS OF SOCIAL SKILL

In reviewing this field, Phillips (1978) concluded that a person was socially skilled according to 'The extent to which he or she can communicate with others, in a manner that fulfils one's rights, requirements, satisfactions, or obligations to a reasonable degree without damaging the other person's similar rights, satisfactions or obligations, and hopefully shares these rights, etc. with others in free and open exchange' (p. 13). This definition emphasises the macro elements of social encounters, in terms of reciprocation between participants, and focuses upon the outcome of behaviour rather than the skills *per se* (although Phillips also noted that 'knowing how to behave in a variety of situations' is part of social skill). A similar approach was adopted by Combs and Slaby (1977, p. 162) who defined social skill as 'the ability to interact with others in a given social context in specific ways that are socially acceptable or valued and at the same time personally beneficial, mutually beneficial, or beneficial primarily to others'.

Although again highlighting *outcome*, this definition differed from that of Phillips in that it is less clear about to whom the skilled performance should be of benefit. Both definitions view social skill as an *ability* which the individual may possess to a greater or lesser extent. Spitzberg and Cupach (1984, p. 41) linked ability to performance when they pointed out that 'skills may be considered as abilities focused on goal accomplishment whether the goal is as specific as speaking without a trembling voice or is as general as learning to manage the greeting ritual in a variety of contexts'. A similar focus has been put forward by other theorists. Spence (1980) encompassed both the outcome or goals of social interaction and the *behaviour* of the interactors when she defined social skills as 'those components of social behaviour which are necessary to ensure that individuals achieve their desired outcome from a social interaction' (p. 9). In like vein, Kelly (1982, p. 3) stated: 'social skills can essentially be viewed as behavioral pathways or avenues to an individual's goals.' Ellis (1980, p. 79) combined both the goal-directed nature and the interactive component when he pointed out that 'By social skills I refer to sequences of individual behaviour which are integrated in some way with the behaviour of one or more others and which measure up to some pre-determined criterion or criteria'.

Other definitions, while focusing upon behaviour, have included the concept of positive or negative reactions (reinforcement) by the other person as an element of skilled behaviour. Thus Libet and Lewinsohn (1973, p. 304) defined social skill as 'the complex ability to maximize the rate of positive reinforcement and to minimize the strength of punishment from others'. The problem with this definition is that it does not address the social dimension of behaviour and, as Curran (1979) pointed out, an adroit boxer beating his opponent in the ring, while receiving the adulation of the crowd, could be regarded as socially skilled using these rather general terms of reference. More specific aspects of situational features were noted by Cartledge and Milburn (1980, p. 7) who viewed social skills as 'behaviors that are emitted in response to environmental events presented by another person or persons (for example, cues, demands, or other communications) and are followed by positive environmental responses'.

Several theorists have restricted their definitions to the behavioural domain. Rinn and Markle (1979) conceived of social skill as a repertoire of verbal and non-verbal behaviours, as did Wilkinson and Canter (1982, p. 3) who stated that: 'Verbal and nonverbal behaviour are therefore the means by which people communicate with others and they constitute the basic elements of social skill.' Curran (1979), in discussing definitional problems, actually argued that the construct of social skill should be limited to motoric behaviour. He based his argument on the fact that the behavioural domain is still being charted and that this task should be completed before expanding the analysis into other domains. However, this emphasis on behaviourism would not be acceptable to many of those involved in research, theory and practice in social skills, who regard other aspects of human performance (such as cognition and emotion) as being important, both in determining behaviour and understanding the communication process.

A final defining feature was recognised by Becker *et al.* (1987, p. 9) who highlighted the fact that 'To perform skillfully, the individual must be able to identify the emotions or intent expressed by the other person and make sophisticated judgments about the form and timing of the appropriate response'. Thus, the skilled individual needs to take cognisance of the others involved in the encounter. This involves perceptual acumen and perspective-taking ability, together with a capacity to mesh one's responses meaningfully, and at apposite moments, with those of others.

An analysis of these definitions reveals a remarkable similarity with the position relating to motor skill, in that there are common elements across definitions, but no uniform agreement about the exact nature of social skill. Phillips (1980, p. 160) summed up the state of affairs which still pertains regarding attempts to define social skill: 'The simple facts about all social skills definitions are these: they are ubiquitous, varied, often simple, located in the social/interpersonal exchange, are the stuff out of which temporal and/or long-range social interactions are made, underlie and exemplify normative social behaviour and, in their absence, are what we loosely call psychopathology.'

However, Furnham (1983) has not regarded the lack of consensus in social skills definitions as a major problem, pointing out that while there also exists no agreed-upon definition of psychology, this has not retarded the development of the discipline. Indeed, progress in all areas is a cycle in which initially less precise terms are sharpened and redefined in the light of empirical enquiry. Furthermore, social interaction is such a rapidly changing, complex process involving a labyrinth of impinging variables, that an understanding of even a small part of the process can be difficult to achieve. It is hardly surprising, therefore, that definitions of what constitutes social skill have proliferated within the literature. Any definition, however all-embracing, must, of necessity, be a simplification. This is not to say that global definitions are without value: at the very least, a definition sets parameters as to what should be included in the study of social skill and so acts as a guideline as to what should constitute legitimate investigation in this field.

Michelson *et al.* (1983) identified six main elements as being central to the concept of social skills, namely that they: (1) are learned; (2) are composed of specific verbal and non-verbal behaviours; (3) entail appropriate initiations and responses; (4) maximise available rewards from others; (5) require appropriate timing and control of specific behaviours; and (6) are influenced by prevailing contextual factors.

These six elements constitute the core dimensions of social skill. A socially skilled individual will have acquired the ability to behave in an appropriate manner in any given situation, and to relate meaningfully with others. Actual judgements of skill are based upon overt behavioural performance, so that it is possible for someone to be *au fait* with the requirements needed to function successfully in a social context, in terms of being able to describe these requirements, and yet still fail to put this knowledge into practice (through, for example, a high level of anxiety). Such an individual would not be described as socially skilled.

Given the above parameters, the definition adopted in this book is that social skill is *the process whereby the individual implements a set of goal-directed, interrelated, situationally appropriate social behaviours which are learned and controlled.* This definition emphasises six main features of social skills.

Process

While behaviour is a key aspect of skill, it is in turn shaped by a range of other features. As such, motoric behaviour represents the overt part of an overall process in which the individual pursues goals, devises implementation plans and strategies, continually monitors the environment, considers the position of others involved in the encounter, responds, estimates the likelihood of goal success and adjusts future behaviour accordingly (these elements of skilled performance will be fully discussed in Chapter 2).

One of the process dimensions which has attracted considerable attention within the interpersonal communication literature is the notion of competence. Indeed, Spitzberg and Cupach (1984, p. 11) argued that 'Competence is an issue both perennial and fundamental to the study of communication'. Some theorists have conceptualised skill as being subsumed by competence. For instance, Ridge (1993) defined competence as the ability 'to choose a strategy, then select among skills appropriate to that context and employ these skills' (p. 1), given that 'a strategy is a plan derived from a context that determines which skills to apply' (p. 8). Thus, competence is regarded as the ability to choose appropriate strategies and implement these in terms of skilled performance. Konsky and Murdock (1980, p. 86) adopted a similar position when they argued that 'competency has two dimensions – knowledge and skill. *Knowledge* includes our awareness and under-standing of the numerous variables which affect human relationships. *Skills* involve the ability to pragmatically apply, consciously or even unconsciously, our knowledge'.

However, it is also possible to argue that skill subsumes competence. Thus, the *Chamber's English Dictionary* defines skill as 'aptitudes and competencies appropriate for a particular job'. In this way, the skilled soccer player or the skilled negotiator would be regarded as highly competent in many separate facets of the process in which they are engaged. Likewise, it makes sense to describe someone as 'competent but not highly skilled' at performing a particular action.

Given that the terms 'skill' and 'competency' are often used interchangeably, it is hardly surprising that Phillips (1984, p. 25), in examining definitional issues, concluded that 'Defining "competence" is like trying to climb a greased pole. Every time you think you have it, it slips'. For example, the definition proffered by Yoder *et al.* (1993, p. 54), that 'Communication competence is the ability to choose among available communicative behaviors so that interpersonal goals may be successfully accomplished during an encounter while respecting the goals of others' could equally be a definition of skill. Argyle (1994) also viewed the two as closely linked when he defined social competence as 'the possession of the necessary skills, to produce the desired effects on other people in social situations' (p. 116). In reviewing this area, Hargie and Morrow (1994) concluded that competence requires that the individual possesses a repertoire of communication skills, has a predisposition towards communicating with others and has the opportunity to communicate. So interpersonal competence encompasses behaviour, attitude to others and circumstances.

In essence, the terms 'skilled' and 'competent', when applied to the interpersonal domain, both indicate that the individual is equipped with the range of social skills required to perform effectively. Skills *per se* are processes of which behaviours are the surface mani-festations, in turn determined and driven by a whole array of cognitive, affective and perceptual activities.

Goal-directed

Socially skilled behaviours are goal-directed and intentional. They are selected by the indi-vidual in order to achieve a desired outcome, and are therefore purposeful as opposed to unintentional. The importance of goals has long been recognised within psychology. McDougall (1912), for example, claimed that a key characteristic of human behaviour was its purposeful, goal-directed nature. In defining this term Miller *et al.* (1994, p. 171) stated that 'a goal is, simply, something that an individual wants or desires to attain because it is rewarding in its own right'. Dillard (1990) proposed a similar definition of goal, while highlighting the fact that as well as achieving new end states, the maintenance of a present, desirable state of affairs may be one of our prime objectives.

Four main theories for explaining and predicting goal-directed intentions and behaviours have been proposed (Bagozzi and Kimmel, 1995). The *theory of reasoned action* purports that behaviour is determined directly by one's intentions to carry it out, and these are in turn influenced by one's attitudes (positive or negative) towards the behaviour and by perceived social pressure to perform it. The *theory of planned behaviour* extends the former theory by adding the notion of perceived behavioural control as an important predictor of intention and action. Perceived behavioural control refers both to the presence of facilitating situational conditions and to feelings of self-efficacy (personal confidence in one's ability to execute the behaviour successfully). The *theory of self-regulation* emphasises the centrality of motivational commitment, or desire, to act (this aspect will be further discussed in Chapter 2). Finally, the *theory of trying* interprets goal-directed behaviour within three domains – trying and succeeding, trying but failing, and the process of striving *per se*. This theory stresses the importance of personal attitudes to success and failure as predictors of intentions and actions, as well as attitudes to the process involved *en route* to the goal. For example, one may decide not to try to lose weight because of a personal belief that one would fail anyway, or because the process of dieting and exercising is not viewed as desirable. The frequency and recency of past behaviour are also seen as important. Thus, one is likely to be less hesitant about asking a member of the opposite sex for a date if one has had a lot of dates (frequency), the last of which was two days ago (recency), than if one has only ever dated three people and the last date was ten years ago.

In essence, however, the decision to pursue particular goals seems to be determined by two main factors, namely the attractiveness of goal attainment and the strength of belief that the goal can be achieved (Weldon and Weingart, 1993). In their comprehensive analysis of the nature, role and functions of goals as regulators of human action, Locke and Latham (1990) demonstrated how goals both give incentive for action and act as guides to provide direction for behaviour. They reviewed studies to illustrate that: (1) people working towards a specific, difficult goal outperform those working with no explicit goal; (2) performance level increases with goal difficulty (providing the person is committed to the goal); and, (3) giving people specific goals produces better results than do vague goals (such as 'do your best').

A distinction needs to be made between long-term and short-term goals. Actions are generally driven by short-term, immediate goals, although the long-term or superordinate goal will be taken into account (Von Cranach *et al.*, 1982). In order to achieve the long-term goal, a number of short-term goals will need to be devised and executed, and these in turn guide our moment-by-moment behaviour. Sloboda (1986) used the term 'goal stacks' to refer to a hierarchy of goals through which one progresses until the top of the stack is reached. He also noted that in real life we not only pursue one set of goals, but rather seek many disparate goals, and as a result, it is sometimes difficult to keep all of them in mind. However, at any time, we can never be working directly on more than one or two of them. The stereotypical absent-minded professor is probably trying to work on too many goals and so forgets some of them. Likewise, most people have had the experience of going to a room for something and upon arrival thinking 'What did I come here for?'!

Skilled behaviour is hierarchically organised with larger goal-related tasks comprising smaller component sub-units. For example, a personnel officer may want to appoint an appropriate person for a job vacancy (long-term goal). In order to do so, there is a range of sub-goals which must be carried out – advertising the position, drawing up a shortlist of candidates, interviewing each one, and so on. These sub-goals can be further subdivided. At the interview stage the chief goal will be to assess the suitability of the candidate, which, in turn, involves sub-goals including welcoming the candidate, making introductions and asking relevant questions. The short-term goals therefore provide a route to the achievement of the long-term goal.

Another aspect of skilled action is that goals are usually subconscious during performance. The skilled footballer is not consciously aware of his objectives when running with the ball, but these will nevertheless govern behaviour. When shooting on goal, the footballer does not consciously think 'I must lift back my left foot, move my right foot forward, hold out my arms to give me balance, etc.' The essence of skill is the subconscious processing of such behaviour-guiding self-statements. In the same way, the socially skilled individual does not have to think consciously 'I want to show interest so I must smile, nod my head, engage in eye contact, look attentive and make appropriate responses'.

Langer *et al.* (1978) termed behaviour which is pursued at a conscious level as *mindful* and behaviour carried out automatically as *mindless*. More recently, Burgoon and Langer (1995, p. 108), in analysing these constructs, illustrated how in skilled performance when 'communication activity is intentional, guided by goals and plans that reflect choice making and flexible thinking, it can be characterized as mindful'. On the other hand, a lack of skill may entail mindless behaviour, since this involves limited information processing, a lack of awareness of situational factors and rigid behaviour patterns.

Part of skill is the ability to act and react quickly at a subconscious level. An extreme example was given by Argyle (1983, p. 57) who reported a lecturer who claimed the ability to 'arise before an audience, turn his mouth loose, and go to sleep'! In discussing the role of the unconscious, Brody (1987) made the distinction between being aware and being aware of being aware. He reviewed studies to illustrate how stimuli perceived at a subconscious level can influence behaviour even though an individual is not consciously 'aware' of the stimuli (this issue is further explored in Chapter 2). At the stage of skill learning, such conscious thoughts may be present, but these become more subconscious with practice and increased competence. An example given by Mandler and Nakamura (1987, p. 301) is that 'the pianist will acquire skills in playing chords and trills and in reading music that are at first consciously represented, but then become unconscious. However, the analytic (conscious) mode is used when the accomplished artist practices a particular piece for a concert, when conscious access becomes necessary to achieve . . . changes in the automatic skills'.

Boden (1972, p. 264) described behaviour carried out to achieve a conscious goal as 'under the direct control of the self; it is being actively attended to; it is guided by precise foresight of the goal; and it is open to introspection in the sense that its component features are discriminable (and verbally describable)'. The individual will be aware of particular behaviours and of the reasons why they are being employed, will have planned to carry them out and will be able to explain and justify the behaviours in terms of the goals being pursued. A young man who has arranged a date with a young woman may plan, for example, a sequence of behaviour in order to achieve a particular goal and be aware of his goals as he carries out his dating behaviour.

Thus, if person A is skilled and wishes to persuade person B to do something, this may be achieved by using some combination of the following techniques: smiling, complimenting B, promising something in return, emphasising the limited opportunity to take advantage of a wonderful offer, using logical arguments to show the advantages of the recommended action, highlighting the dangers of doing otherwise, or appealing to the moral/altruistic side of B (Hargie *et al.*, 1994). These behaviours are *directed* towards the *goal* of successful influence over B's behaviour.

Interrelated behaviour

Social skills are defined in terms of identifiable units of behaviour which the individual displays, and actual performance is in many ways the acid test of social skill. In recognising the centrality of behaviour, Millar *et al.* (1992, p. 26) pointed out: 'Judgements about skill are directly related to behavioural performance. We do not judge soccer players on their ability to discuss the game or analyse their own performance, but rather we regard them as skilful or not based upon what they do on the field of play. Similarly, we make judgements about social skill based upon the behaviour of the individual during social encounters.' Noel Coward once said of his singing that he couldn't do it although he knew how to! A key aspect of skilled performance, therefore, is the ability to implement a smooth, integrated behavioural repertoire.

In a sense, all that is ever really known about others during social interaction is how they actually behave. All kinds of judgements (boring, humorous, warm, shy, and so on) are inferred about people from such behaviours. As mentioned earlier, skilled behaviour is hierarchical in nature with small elements such as changing gear or asking questions combining to form larger skill areas such as driving or interviewing, respectively. This view-point has guided training in social skills, whereby the emphasis is upon encouraging the trainee to acquire separately smaller units of behaviour before integrating them to form the larger response elements – a technique which has long been employed in the learning of motor skills (this issue of skills training is further discussed in Chapter 19).

Socially skilled behaviours are interrelated in that they are synchronised and employed in order to achieve a common goal. Skill therefore involves a co-ordinated meshing of behaviour, since 'skill is said to have been acquired when the behavior is highly integrated and well organized' (Proctor and Dutta, 1995, p. 18). The car driver needs simultaneously to operate the clutch, accelerator, gear lever, brakes, steering wheel and light switches. Similarly, someone wishing to provide reward to another will concurrently use head nods, eye contact, smiles, attentive facial expressions and statements such as 'That's very interesting'. These latter behaviours are all interrelated in that they are indicative of the skill of rewardingness (Dickson *et al.*, 1993). Conversely if someone does not look at us, yawns, uses no head nods, yet says 'That's very interesting', these behaviours would be contradictory rather than complementary and the person would not be using the skill of rewardingness effectively. Someone adopting such a pattern of mixed response over a prolonged period would be judged to be low in social skills. People who always act in a socially incompetent fashion would be deemed to be socially unskilled regardless of the depth of theoretical knowledge they may possess about interpersonal behaviour. In discussing this issue, Roloff and Kellerman (1984, p.175) asserted that 'competence is a judgment that a person's behavior corresponds to certain standards of performance. In the case of communication competence, the focus is upon the evaluative judgment of a person's verbal and nonverbal behavior'.

Bellack (1983, p. 34) highlighted how such behaviours need to be viewed as a whole when making judgements about competence, pointing out that in social presentation:

the elements combine to form a gestalt. The contribution of any one element varies across respondents, observers, behaviours and situations. . . . Intermediate levels of many responses may play little role in forming the gestalt, while extremes may have dramatic impact. Similarly, non-context elements (e.g. posture, inflection) may be of secondary importance when consistent with verbal content, but they may dramatically alter the meaning of a response when they are discordant.

Situationally appropriate

The importance of contextual awareness for the effective operation of motor skill has long been recognised. Welford (1976, p. 2), for instance, pointed out that 'skills represent paticular ways of using capacities in relation to environmental demands, with human beings and external situations together forming a functional "system"'. Likewise, Ellis and Whittington (1981, p. 12) asserted that a core feature of skill was 'the capacity to respond flexibly to circumstances'. For behaviour to be socially skilled it must therefore be contextually appropriate, since behaviours which are apposite when displayed in one situation may be unacceptable if applied in another. Singing *risqué* songs, telling 'blue' jokes and using crude language may be appropriate at an all-male drinking session following a rugby game. The same behaviour would, however, be frowned upon if displayed in mixed company during a formal meal in an exclusive restaurant! It is essential, then, to be able to decide which behaviours are appropriate to certain situations. Simply to possess the behaviours is not enough. A tennis player who has a very powerful serve will not be deemed skilful if the ball is always sent directly into the crowd. Similarly, being a fluent speaker will be of little value if the speaker always monopolises the conversation, talks about boring or rude matters, or does not listen to others when they speak. Skills must therefore be targeted to given people in specific settings. Different forms of reward are appropriate for young children, teenagers and adult members of the opposite sex; for some of these groups statements such as 'You're a clever little girl', 'You have really grown up' and 'I find you very attractive' will be more apposite than they would be for others.

The influence of situational factors plays an important part in determining the behaviour of people during interpersonal encounters. Magnusson (1981) argued that such factors are important for three reasons: first, we learn about the world and form conceptions of it in terms of the situations which are experienced; second, all behaviour occurs within a given situation and so can only be fully understood through a knowledge of contextual variables; and third, a greater knowledge of situations increases our understanding of the behaviour of individuals.

There is firm evidence to indicate that certain behaviours are situationally determined. For example, Hargie *et al.* (1993) carried out a study of effective communication skills in community pharmacy, in which they videotaped 350 pharmacist–patient consultations. They found that certain skills which were commonly employed when dealing with 'over the counter' items were not employed by the pharmacist when handling prescription-related consultations. For instance, the skill of suggesting/advising, which was defined as 'the offer of personal/professional opinion as to a particular course of action, while simultaneously allowing the final decision to lie with the individual' (p. 84), fell into this category. Examples of this skill recorded by Hargie *et al.* included: 'I think you'd be better taking the adult Meltus because it just thins the phlegm and then you cough it up yourself'; 'Have you tried an inhalation at all? Sometimes it can help.' When dealing with prescription items, it would seem that suggestions or advice are not given, probably because these patients have already been advised by their doctor and the pharmacist may not wish to appear to intervene.

Individuals skilled in one context may not be skilled in another. For example, an excellent mid-fielder in soccer may be a terrible goalkeeper. Likewise, experienced teachers have been shown to have some difficulties in making the transition to being skilled school counsellors (Hargie, 1988). In essence, the more similarity there is between the requirements of situations, the more skills are likely to transfer. A professional tennis player is likely to be good at other raquet sports such as badminton or squash; in the same way, a good car salesperson is likely to be successful in other similar selling contexts.

One similarity between motor and social skill is that they are both sequential in nature. Thus, the skill of driving involves a pre-set sequence of behaviours which must be carried out in the correct order. In social interaction there are also stages which tend to be followed sequentially. For instance, Morris (1971) identified the following sequence for courtship: eye to body; eye to eye; voice to voice; hand to hand; arm to shoulder; arm to waist; mouth to mouth; hand to head; hand to body; mouth to breast; hand to genitals; genitals to genitals. This sequence is obviously different from the motor skills sequence in that it is not always necessary to go through all of these steps, depending upon the situation and the person involved. Elements may be removed if, for example, the first meeting is at a dance or if the other person is willing.

In most social situations a certain sequence of behaviour is expected. Checking into a hotel usually involves interacting in a set way with the receptionist, being shown to your room and giving a tip to the porter who delivers your cases. Likewise, when going to the doctor, the dentist or church, there are sequences of behaviour which are expected and which can be more or less formalised, depending upon the setting. In the case of the former, the sequence would be:

1 Patient enters the surgery;
2 Doctor makes a greeting;
3 Patient responds and sits down;
4 Doctor seeks information about the patient's health;
5 Patient responds and gives information;
6 Doctor makes a diagnosis;
7 Doctor prescribes and explains treatment;
8 Doctor makes closing comments;
9 Patient responds, stands up and leaves the surgery.

This sequence will also be expected by the patient who would be most unhappy if the doctor moved straight from (1) to (7) without going through the intervening steps!

It can be disconcerting and embarrassing if one is in a situation where the behaviour sequence deviates from what is expected or has not been learned (for example, attending a church service of a different religious denomination). In such situations, however, we will usually cope and, unlike the sequence of behaviours in, for example, driving a car, these social behaviours are *expected* rather than *essential*. It is only in certain rituals or ceremonies that a pre-set sequence is essential (for example, weddings in church) and responses are demanded in a fixed temporal order.

Social skills are usually more fluid and individualised than most motor skills in that people can, and do, break the sequential 'rules' without necessarily being social failures.

In this sense, social skills are more open and free-flowing than many motor skills. Different people will employ different combinations of behaviours (often with equal success) in professional contexts. This process is referred to as *equifinality* (Curran *et al.*, 1984), whereby the same goal can be achieved through the implementation of differing strategies which will have alternative behavioural approaches (or, in everyday parlance, 'There is more than one way to skin a cat'!). However, what does seem to be the case is that there are common stages in social episodes (e.g. opening, discussion, closing), but the behaviours used within each stage will vary from one person to another.

Therefore, 'knowing' the social situation is an important aspect of social skill, in order to relate behaviours successfully to the context in which they are employed. Further aspects of the situational context will be explored in Chapter 2.

Learning

The fifth aspect of the definition is that social skills are comprised of behaviours which can be learned. All social behaviour is learned; we know that if children are reared in isolation they do not develop normal interactive repertoires and do not acquire a language. Indeed, there is evidence to indicate that the degree of deprivation of appropriate learning experiences from other humans will differentially affect the social behaviour of individuals (Messer, 1995). Thus, children from socially deprived home backgrounds are more likely to develop less appropriate social behaviours, whereas children from culturally richer home environments tend to be more socially adept.

Bandura (1971) developed a social learning theory which posited that all repertoires of behaviour, with the exception of elementary reflexes (eye blinks, coughing, etc.), are learned. This social learning process involves the *modelling* and *imitation* of significant others, such as parents, peers, pop stars, siblings and teachers. The individual observes how others behave and then follows a similar behavioural routine. By this process, from an early age, children may walk, talk and act like their same-sex parent. At a later stage, however, they may begin to copy and adopt the behaviour of people whom they see as being more significant in their lives by, for example, following the dress and accents of peers regardless of those of parents. The second major element in social learning theory is the *reinforcement* of behaviours which the person displays. As a general rule, people tend to employ more frequently those behaviours which are positively reinforced or rewarded, and to display less often those behaviours which are punished or ignored.

This is not to say that there are not innate differences in individual potential, since some people are more naturally talented than others in specific areas. While most behaviours are learned, it is also true that people will have different aptitudes for certain types of performance. In this way, although it is necessary to learn how to play musical instruments or how to paint, some may have a better 'ear' for music or 'eye' for art and so will excel in these fields. Likewise, certain individuals have a 'flair' for social interchange and will find interpersonal skills easier to learn and perfect. However, in all skill performance, practice is essential for improvement. In the words of Aristotle, 'If you want to learn to play the flute, play the flute'. As we shall see in Chapter 2, however, feedback on performance is vital to the learning of skills. In this sense, it is not practice alone which makes perfect, but practice, the results of which are known, understood and acted upon, which improves skill.

Cognitive control

The final element of social skill, which is also a feature of social learning theory, is the degree of cognitive control which the individual has over behaviour. Thus, a socially inadequate individual may have learned the basic behavioural elements of social skill but may not have developed the appropriate thought processes necessary to control their utilisation. If a social skill is to have its desired effect, then the timing of its implementation is a crucial consideration. Behaviour is said to be skilled only if it is employed at the opportune moment. For example, smiling and saying 'How funny!' when someone is relating details of a sad personal bereavement would certainly not be a socially skilled response. Indeed, saying the right thing at the wrong time is a characteristic of some social inadequates. Learning *when* to employ socially skilled behaviours is every bit as important as learning *what* these behaviours are, *where* to use them and *how* to evaluate them. Parks (1994, p. 591) aptly summarised the elements of competent communicative control: 'To be competent therefore we must not only "know" and "know how" we must "do" and "know that we did".' In his discussion of the notion of interpersonal competence, Parks highlighted the importance of hierarchical control theory, which conceives of personal action as a process controlled by nine linked and hierarchical levels. From lower to higher these levels are as follows.

Level 1: intensity control

This is the level just inside the skin involving sensory receptors, muscle movements and spinal responses. Damage at this basic level can have serious consequences for communication. For example, impairments to vision, hearing or to the vocal chords can dramatically impede interpersonal ability.

Level 2: sensation control

Here, the sensory nuclei collected at Level 1 are collated and organised into meaningful packages. The ability to portray a certain facial expression would be dependent upon activity at this level.

Level 3: configuration control

The basic packages developed at Level 2 are, in turn, further organised into larger configurations which then control movements of the limbs, perception of visual forms and speech patterns. The ability to decode verbal and non-verbal cues occurs at this level.

Level 4: transition control

This level further directs the more basic configurations into fine-grained responses, such as changing the tone of voice, pronouncing a word or using head nods at appropriate moments. Transition control also allows us to recognise the meaning of such behaviour in others.

Level 5: sequence control

At this level, we control the sequence, flow, intensity and content of our communications. The ability to synchronise and relate our responses appropriately to those with whom we are interacting, and to the situational context, is handled at this level. Thus, judgements of the extent to which someone is socially skilled can begin to be made at this sequence control level.

Level 6: relationship control

Here the individual judges and makes decisions about larger sets of relationships (cause–effect; chronological, etc.), so that appropriate strategies can be implemented to attain higher-order goals. For example, the ability to encode and decode deceptive messages would be controlled at this level. Likewise, longer-term tactics for wooing a partner, negotiating a successful business deal or securing promotion at work, will all involve relational control.

Level 7: programme control

At this level, schemas or programmes are developed to predict, direct and interpret communication in a variety of contexts. Existing circumstances will then be compared with previous knowledge and experience. In this way, conceptual schemas are used to facilitate the process of decision-making. A schema is a cognitive structure which is developed after repeated exposure to the same situation, and which provides the person with a store of knowledge and information about how to behave in this context (Edwards and McDonald, 1993). Schemas contain 'scripts' which have been learned and are readily available for enactment as required. By adulthood, we will have developed thousands of schemas to deal with a wide variety of people across a range of situations, such as checking-in at an airport, shopping at the supermarket, or giving directions to a stranger on the street.

It would seem that our implementation of schemas is guided by inner speech. Johnson (1993) in examining this field, identified three main characteristics of inner speech. First, it is egocentric and used only for our own benefit, in that the producer and intended receiver of the speech is one and the same person (oneself). Second, it is silent and is not the equivalent of talking or mumbling to oneself out loud. Third, it is compressed, containing a high degree of semantic embeddedness, so that single words have high levels of meaning. Johnson used the analogy of a shopping list to explain the operation of inner speech. When going to the supermarket we just write *bread*, *biscuits*, *soap*, etc. on a list. In the supermarket when we look at the word *bread* we know that we want a small, sliced, wholemeal loaf made by 'Bakegoods' and we select this automatically. In a similar fashion, as we enter a restaurant, inner speech reminds us of 'restaurant' and releases the schema and script for this situation, thereby enabling us to activate 'restaurant mode'. Other actions within the restaurant will also be guided by inner speech (e.g. 'ordering', 'complimenting', 'paying', or 'complaining').

One of the reasons why it can be difficult for us to deal with new situations is that we have not developed relevant schemas with which to operate smoothly and effectively therein. In any profession, learning the relevant schemas and scripts is therefore an important part of professional development. An experienced teacher will have developed a large store of classroom-specific schemas, such as 'class getting bored' and 'noise level too high', each with accompanying action plans – 'introduce a new activity', 'call for order'. These schemas are used both to evaluate situations and to enable appropriate responses to be made. In this way, experienced teachers will be able to cope more successfully than novices. The same is true in other professions. Experienced doctors, nurses, social workers, or salespeople will likewise have developed a range of work-specific schemas to enable them to respond quickly and confidently in the professional context. This ability to respond rapidly and appropriately is, in turn, a feature of skilled performance. Thus, the skilled professional has the cognitive ability to analyse and evaluate available information and make decisions about how best to respond, and will also have formulated a number of contingency plans which can be implemented immediately should the initial response fail.

Level 8: principle control

Programmes must be related directly to our guiding principles or goals and these, in turn, control their implementation. In this sense, we have to create programmes which are compatible with our goals. However, as Parks (1994) pointed out, 'unsuccessful behavior often occurs because individuals lack the necessary programming to actualize their principles' (p. 603). This is particularly true of novel situations or when one is confronted by unexpected events, for which programmes have not been fully developed. In summarising problems at this level Heath and Bryant (1992, p. 220) noted how 'Control includes the ability to interact in ways that affect relationships and execute programs of action in search of goals. During communication, persons may have to improvise if their initial plans fail'.

Level 9: system concept control

At the very top of this hierarchy is our system of idealised self-concepts. These drive and control our principles, which in turn determine programmes, and so on. Someone whose idealised self-concept included being a 'trustworthy person' would then develop principles such as 'Always tell the truth' and 'Fulfil one's obligations'. Further down the hierarchy, at the programme control level, schemas would, in turn, be formulated to enable these principles to be operationalised across various contexts.

SOCIAL SKILLS AND MOTOR SKILLS

From the above analysis of social skill, it is obvious that there are similarities and differences between social skills and motor skills. The main similarities include the goal-directed or intentional nature of behaviour, the fact that it is learned, that skill is identified as a set of synchronised behaviours and that cognitive control is necessary for success. Sloboda (1986) used the acronym FRASK to describe the five central elements of skilled performance as being Fluent, Rapid, Automatic, Simultaneous and Knowledgeable. The similarities between social and motor skill can be highlighted by examining each of these features.

Fluency

In the form of a smooth almost effortless display, fluency is a feature of skilled performance. Compare, for example, the international ice-skater with the person making a first attempt to skate on the ice rink. Likewise, experienced television interviewers make what is a very difficult task look easy. Fluency subsumes two factors. First, the overlapping of sequential events in that the preparations for action B are begun while action A is still being performed. Thus, a car driver will hold the gear lever while the clutch is being depressed, while an interviewer will prepare to leave a pause when coming to the end of a question. Second, a set of actions is 'chunked' and performed as a single unit. For instance, skilled typists need to see the whole of a word before beginning to type it and only then is a full set of sequenced finger movements put into operation as a single performance unit. In a similar way, the greeting ritual – smiling, making eye contact, uttering salutations and shaking hands or kissing – is performed as one 'unit'.

Rapidity

This is a feature of all skilled action. The skilled person can 'sum up' situations and respond swiftly, with the result that performance becomes smoother and more fluid. In one study of chess players, Chase and Simon (1973) showed novices and grandmasters chessboards on which were placed pieces taken from the middle of an actual game. After viewing the board for five seconds, they were asked to reconstruct the game on a blank board. On average, novices correctly replaced four out of twenty, whereas masters replaced eighteen out of twenty, pieces. Interestingly, in a second part of this study when the subjects were shown a board on which the pieces were placed in a way that could not have resulted from an actual chess game, masters performed no better than novices. Thus, rapidity was related to chess *playing*. Socially skilled individuals develop a similar ability in relation to specific contexts – for example, interviewers will know how to deal with a vast array of interviewee responses. This ability to respond rapidly means that skilled individuals appear to have more time to perform their actions and as a result their behaviour seems less rushed.

Automaticity

Skilled actions are performed 'without thinking' or automatically. We do not think about how to walk or how to talk – we just do it. Yet, in infancy both skills took considerable time and effort to acquire, and in cases of brain injury in adulthood both may have to be relearned. The other feature of automaticity is that skill once acquired is in a sense mandatory, in that a stimulus triggers our response automatically. When a lecture ends the students immediately get up from their seats and walk to the exit. Likewise, as we pass someone we know we look, smile and say 'Hello, how are you?', get a reciprocal gaze, smile and the response 'Fine, thanks. And yourself?', give the reply 'Good!' and both parties walk on without having given much thought to the encounter.

Simultaneity

This is the fourth dimension of skill. The components of a skilled activity are executed conjointly: for example, depressing the clutch with a foot, changing gear with one hand

and steering the car with the other while looking ahead. Furthermore, because of the high degree of automaticity it is often possible to carry out an unrelated activity simultaneously. For example, experienced drivers carry out all sorts of weird and wonderful concurrent activities, not least of which include talking on the car telephone, operating a radio cassette, eating, drinking, shaving, reading, or applying make-up. Equally, the driver can engage in the social skill of carrying on a deep philosophical discussion with passengers while travelling at high speed on the motorway.

Knowledge

As discussed earlier, knowledge is important. Skill involves not just having knowledge but actually applying it at the appropriate juncture. Knowing that the green traffic light turning to amber means get ready to stop is not sufficient unless acted upon. Similarly, a doctor may know that a patient question is a request for further information, but may choose to ignore it so as to shorten the consultation as part of a strategy of getting through a busy morning schedule.

Thus, the FRASK process applies to both social and motor skill, although the analogy between these two sets of skill is rejected by some theorists. For example, Plum (1981) argued that the meaning of 'good' tennis playing can be easily measured by widely agreed criteria such as accuracy and points scored, whereas the meaning of social acts cannot be so judged. However, the skilled negotiator can also be judged upon specified outcomes (percentage pay increase, price of goods, and so on). Plum further argued that good motor skill equals success, yet good social skill is purely subjective; for example, what is judged as an act of empathy by one person could be viewed as an insensitive intrusion by someone else. Again, similar disputes exist regarding motor skill operators. At soccer games the author has often debated vigorously with fellow spectators whether a forward was attempting to shoot or pass, whether a goal was the result of a great striker or a terrible goalkeeper, and whether the mid-fielder was capable of playing at national level or incapable even of playing for the club side. Equally, it is agreed that often the most skilful sides do not win the trophies – if they are lacking in fitness, determination and work-rate, or have not had 'the luck'.

Both Plum (1981) and Yardley (1979) have iterated that social skills are unique in that only the people involved in interpersonal interaction understand the real meaning of that interaction. This is certainly true in that no one can experience exactly what another person is experiencing. However, the same is also true of motor skill operators. Television commentators frequently ask sportsmen following a competition, 'What were you trying to do at this point?' or 'What was going through your mind here?' as they watch a video-replay of the action. This is to gain some further insight into the event, and how it was perceived by the participants. While such personal evaluations are important, so too are the evaluations of others. When people are not selected at job interviews, do not succeed in dating, or fail teaching practice, their personal perspective does not help. In such situations they are usually regarded as lacking in skill, just as is the youth who fails to get picked for a sports team or the car driver who fails the driving test.

Another argument put forward by Yardley (1979) is that social skills are not goal-directed in the same way as motor skills. She opined that few individuals could verbalise their superordinate goals during social interaction and that, furthermore, social interaction is often valued in its own right rather than as a means to an end. Again, however, these arguments can be disputed. It seems very probable that negotiators, if asked, could state their superordinate goals during negotiations, while a doctor would be able to do likewise when making a diagnosis. Furthermore, although social interaction is often valued *per se*, it is likely that individuals could give reasons for engaging in such interactions (to share ideas, pass the time, avoid loneliness, and so on). In addition, motor skill operators often engage in seemingly aimless activities, as when two people on the beach kick or throw a ball back and forth to one another, for which they would probably find difficulty in providing superordinate goals.

What is true is that there are gradations of skill difficulty: opening a door is a relatively simple motor action to which we do not give much thought, while using a head nod during conversation is similarly a socially skilled behaviour to which we do not devote much conscious attention. On the other hand, piloting a jumbo jet or defending a suspected murderer in court are more complex skills requiring a great deal of planning and monitoring.

So, while there are numerous similarities between social and motor skills, there are also four key differences.

1 Social interaction, by definition, involves other people, whereas many motor skills, such as operating a machine, do not. The goals of the others involved in interaction are of vital import. We not only pursue our own goals, but also try to interpret the goals of the other person. If these goals concur, this will facilitate social interaction, but if they conflict, interaction can become more difficult. Closer parallels can be drawn with social skills where motor skill operation involves the participation of others. Thus, an analogy can be drawn between a game such as tennis and a social encounter such as negotiating. Both 'players' make moves, try to anticipate the actions of their 'opponent', try to score 'points' and win the 'game'.

2 Feelings and emotions have been shown to be important in interpersonal interaction (Crawford *et al.*, 1992), in that the way we feel will affect the way others are perceived and responded to. Furthermore, we often care about the feelings of other people, but rarely worry about the feelings of machines. The concept of 'face' is important here, in that we are concerned with the self-esteem both of ourselves and of those with whom we are interacting. Face in this sense refers to the social identities which we present to others – it is the conception of who we are and of the identities we want others to accept of us. In arguing that maintaining or saving face is an underlying motive in all social encounters, Cupach and Metts (1994, p. 4) highlighted how in most circumstances, 'when any person's face is threatened during an interaction, all participants are motivated to restore it because not doing so leaves them open to the discomfort and embarrassment that arises'.

3 The perceptual process is more complex during interpersonal encounters. There are three forms of perception in social interaction: first, we perceive our own responses (we hear what we say and how we say it, and may be aware of our non-verbal behaviour); second, we perceive the responses of others; third, we enter the field of *metaperception*, wherein we attempt to perceive how the other person is perceiving us and to make judgements about how others think we are perceiving them.

4 Personal factors relating to those involved in social interaction will have an important bearing upon the responses of participants. This would include the age, gender and

appearance of those involved. For example, two members of the opposite sex will usually engage in more eye contact than two males.

These differences between social and motor skill will be further discussed in Chapter 2. Although there are differences between motor and social skills, it would appear that there are enough similarities to allow useful parallels to be drawn between the two, and to employ methods and techniques used to identify and analyse the former in the examination of the latter. In this way, interpersonal communication can be viewed as a form of skilled behaviour.

OVERVIEW

This chapter has examined the core elements of skilled performance as identified in the analysis of perceptual-motor skill, and has related them directly to the analysis of social skill. While certain differences exist between the two sets of skills, there are also a number of features of skilled performance which are central to both, namely the intentionality, learning, control and synchronisation of behaviour. The realisation that such similarities exist has facilitated a systematic and coherent evaluation of social or communication skill. This has resulted in concerted efforts to determine the nature and types of communication skill in professional contexts, and guided training initiatives to encourage professionals to develop and refine their own repertoire of socially skilled behaviours. However, both of these facets are dependent upon a sound theoretical foundation. This chapter has provided a background to such theory, and this will be extended in Chapter 2, where an operational model of interpersonal skill in practice will be delineated.

REFERENCES

Argyle, M. (1983) *The Psychology of Interpersonal Behaviour* (4th edn), Penguin, Harmondsworth.
—— (1994) *The Psychology of Interpersonal Behaviour* (5th edn), Penguin, London.
—— and Kendon, A. (1967) 'The Experimental Analysis of Social Performance', in L. Berkowitz (ed.), *Advances in Experimental Social Psychology: Volume 3*, Academic Press, New York.
Bagozzi, R. P. and Kimmel, S. K. (1995) 'A Comparison of Leading Theories for the Prediction of Goal-directed Behaviours', *British Journal of Social Psychology*, 34, 437–61.
Bandura, A. (1971) *Social Learning Theory*, General Learning Press, New Jersey.
Becker, R. E., Heimberg, R. G. and Bellack, A. S. (1987) *Social Skills Training for Treatment of Depression*, Pergamon, New York.
Bellack, A. S. (1983) 'Recurrent Problems in the Behavioural Assessment of Social Skill', *Behaviour Research and Therapy*, 21, 29–41.
Berne, E. (1975) *What Do You Say After You Say Hello?*, Corgi, London.
Boden, M. (1972) *Purposive Explanation in Psychology*, Harvard University Press, Cambridge, MA.
Book, W. (1908) *The Psychology of Skill*, University of Montana, Studies in Psychology, Vol. 1 (republished 1925), Gregg, New York.
Brody, N. (1987) 'Introduction: Some Thoughts on the Unconscious', *Personality and Social Psychology Bulletin*, 13, 293–8.
Bryan, W. and Harter, N. (1897) 'Physiology and Psychology of the Telegraphic Language', *Psychological Review*, 4, 27–53.
Burgoon, J. K. and Langer, E. J. (1995) 'Language, Fallacies, and Mindlessness-Mindfulness in Social Interaction', in B. R. Burleson (ed.), *Communication Yearbook: Vol. 18*, Sage, Thousand Oaks.
Cartledge, G. and Milburn, J. (1980) *Teaching Social Skills to Children*, Pergamon Press, New York.
Chase, W. and Simon, H. (1973) 'The Mind's Eye in Chess', in W. Chase (ed.), *Visual Information Processing*, Academic Press, New York.

Combs, M. and Slaby, D. (1977) 'Social Skills Training with Children', in B. B. Lahey and A. E. Kazdin (eds), *Advances in Clinical Child Psychology*, Plenum Press, New York.

Cratty, B. (1964) *Movement Behavior and Motor Learning*, Lea & Febiger, Philadelphia.

Crawford, J., Kippax, S., Onyx, J., Gault, U. and Benton, P. (1992) *Emotion and Gender: Constructing Meaning from Memory*, Sage, Newbury Park.

Crossman. E. R. (1960) *Automation and Skill*, DSIR Problems of Progress in Industry, No. 9, HMSO, London.

Cupach, W. and Metts, S. (1994) *Facework*, Sage, Thousand Oaks.

Curran, J. (1979) 'Social Skills: Methodological Issues and Future Directions', in A. Bellack and M. Hersen (eds), *Research and Practice in Social Skills Training*, Plenum Press, New York.

—— , Farrell, D. and Grunberger, A. (1984) 'Social Skills Training: A Critique and Rapprochment', in P. Trower (ed.), *Radical Approaches to Social Skills Training*, Croom Helm, London.

Dickson, D. A., Saunders, C. Y. and Stringer, M. (1993) *Rewarding People: The Skill of Responding Positively*, Routledge, London.

Dillard, J. (1990) 'The Nature and Substance of Goals in Tactical Communication', in M. Cody and M. McLaughlin (eds), *The Psychology of Tactical Communication*, Multilingual Matters, Clevedon.

Edwards, R. and McDonald, J. L. (1993) 'Schema Theory and Listening', in A. Wolvin and C. Coakley (eds), *Perspectives on Listening*, Ablex, Norwood, NJ.

Ellis, R. (1980) 'Simulated Social Skill Training for Interpersonal Professions', in W. T. Singleton, P. Spurgeon and R. Stammers (eds), *The Analysis of Social Skill*, Plenum Press, New York.

—— and Whittington, D. (1981) *A Guide to Social Skill Training*, Croom Helm, London.

Fitts, P. and Posner, M. (1967) *Human Performance*, Brooks-Cole, Belmont.

Furnham, A. (1983) 'Research in Social Skills Training: A Critique', in R. Ellis and D. Whittington (eds), *New Directions in Social Skill Training*, Croom Helm, Beckenham.

Hare, A. P. and Blumberg, H. H. (eds) (1988) *Dramaturgical Analysis of Social Interaction*, Praeger, New York.

Hargie, O. (1988) 'From Teaching to Counselling: An Evaluation of the Role of Microcounselling in the Training of School Counsellors', *Counselling Psychology Quarterly*, 1, 75–83.

—— and Morrow, N. (1994) 'Pharmacist–Patient Communication: The Interpersonal Dimensions of Practice', in G. Harding, S. Nettleton and K. Taylor (eds), *Social Pharmacy: Innovation and Development*, The Pharmaceutical Press, London.

—— , Morrow, N. and Woodman, C. (1993) *Looking Into Community Pharmacy: Identifying Effective Communication Skills In Pharmacist–Patient Consultations*, University of Ulster, Jordanstown.

—— , Saunders, C. and Dickson, D. (1994) *Social Skills in Interpersonal Communication* (3rd edn), Routledge, London.

Heath, R. L. and Bryant, J. (1992) *Human Communication Theory and Research: Concepts, Contexts and Challenges*, Lawrence Erlbaum, Hillsdale, NJ.

Irion, A. (1966) 'A Brief History of Research on the Acquisition of Skill', in E. A. Bilodeau (ed.), *Acquisition of Skill*, Academic Press, New York.

Johnson, J. (1993) 'Functions and Processes of Inner Speech, in Listening', in A. Wolvin and C. Coakley (eds), *Perspectives on Listening*, Ablex, Norwood, NJ.

Kelley, H. H. and Thibaut, J. W. (1978) *Interpersonal Relations: A Theory Of Interdependence*, John Wiley, New York.

Kelly, J. (1982) *Social Skills Training: A Practical Guide for Interventions*, Springer, New York.

Kerr, P. (1982) *Psychomotor Learning*, CBS College Publishing, New York.

Knapp, B. (1963) *Skill in Sport*, Routledge & Kegan Paul, London.

Konsky, C. W. and Murdock, J. I. (1980) 'Interpersonal Communication', in J. Cragan and D. Wright (eds), *Introduction to Speech Communication*, Waveland Press, Prospect Heights, Illinois.

Langer, E., Blank, A. and Chanowitz, B. (1978) 'The Mindlessness of Ostensibly Thoughtful Action', *Journal of Personality and Social Psychology*, 36, 635–42.

Libet, J. and Lewinsohn, P. (1973) 'The Concept of Social Skill with Special Reference to the Behavior of Depressed Persons', *Journal of Consulting and Clinical Psychology*, 40, 304–12.

Locke, E. A. and Latham, G. P. (1990) *A Theory of Goal Setting and Task Performance*, Prentice Hall, Englewood Cliffs, NJ.

McDougall, W. (1912) *Psychology: The Study of Behaviour*, Williams & Norgate, London.

Magill, R. (1989) *Motor Learning: Concepts and Applications* (3rd edn), W. C. Brown, Iowa.

Magnusson, D. (ed.) (1981) *Towards a Psychology of Situations*, Lawrence Erlbaum, Hillsdale, NJ.

Mandler, G. and Nakamura, Y. (1987) 'Aspects of Consciousness', *Personality and Social Psychology Bulletin*, 13, 299–313.

Marteniuk, R. (1976) *Information Processing in Motor Skills*, Holt, Rinehart & Winston, New York.

Messer, D.J. (1995) *The Development of Communication: From Social Interaction to Language*, John Wiley, Chichester.

Michelson, L., Sugai, D., Wood, R. and Kazdin, A. (1983) *Social Skills Assessment and Training with Children*, Plenum Press, New York.

Millar, R., Crute, V. and Hargie, O. (1992) *Professional Interviewing*, Routledge, London.

Miller, L. C., Cody, M. J. and McLaughlin, M. L. (1994) 'Situations and Goals as Fundamental Constructs in Interpersonal Communication Research', in M. Knapp and G. Miller (eds), *Handbook of Interpersonal Communication* (2nd edn), Sage, Thousand Oaks.

Morris, D. (1971) *Intimate Behaviour*, Cape, London.

Parks, M. R. (1994) 'Communication Competence and Interpersonal Control', in M. Knapp and G. Miller (eds), *Handbook of Interpersonal Communication* (2nd edn), Sage, Thousand Oaks.

Phillips, E. (1978) *The Social Skills Basis of Psychopathology*, Grune & Stratton, New York.

—— (1980) 'Social Skills Instruction as Adjunctive/Alternative to Psychotherapy', in W. Singleton, P. Spurgeon and R. Stammers (eds), *The Analysis of Social Skills*, Plenum Press, New York.

Phillips, G. M. (1984) 'A Competent View of "Competence"', *Communication Education*, 33, 25–36.

Plum, A. (1981) 'Communication as Skill: A Critique and Alternative Proposal', *Journal of Humanistic Psychology*, 21, 3–19.

Proctor, R. W. and Dutta, A. (1995) *Skill Acquisition and Human Performance*, Sage, Thousand Oaks.

Ridge, A. (1993) 'A Perspective of Listening Skills', in A. Wolvin and C. Coakley (eds), *Perspectives on Listening*, Ablex, Norwood, NJ.

Rinn, R. and Markle, A. (1979) 'Modification of Skill Deficits in Children', in A. Bellack and M. Hersen (eds), *Research and Practice in Social Skills Training*, Plenum Press, New York.

Robb, M. (1972) *The Dynamics of Motor Skill Acquisition*, Prentice-Hall, Englewood Cliffs, NJ.

Roloff, M. and Kellerman, K. (1984) 'Judgments of Interpersonal Competence', in R. Bostrom (ed.), *Competence in Communication*, Sage, Beverly Hills.

Sletta, O. (1992) 'Social Skills as Exchange Resources', *Scandinavian Journal of Educational Research*, 36, 183–90.

Sloboda, J. (1986) 'What is Skill?', in A. Gellatly (ed.), *The Skilful Mind: An Introduction to Cognitive Psychology*, Open University Press, Milton Keynes.

Spence, S. (1980) *Social Skills Training with Children and Adolescents*, NFER, Windsor.

Spitzberg, B. and Cupach, W. (1984) *Interpersonal Communication Competence*, Sage, Beverly Hills.

Summers, J. (1981) 'Motor Programs', in D. Holding (ed.), *Human Skills*, John Wiley, New York.

Von Cranach, M., Kalbermatten, U., Indermuhle, K. and Gugler, B. (1982) 'Goal-directed Action', *European Monographs in Social Psychology*, 30, Academic Press, London.

Weldon, E. and Weingart, L. (1993) 'Group Goals and Group Performance', *British Journal of Social Psychology*, 32, 307–34.

Welford, A. (1958) *Ageing and Human Skill*, Oxford University Press, London (reprinted 1973 by Greenwood Press, Connecticut).

—— (1968) *Fundamentals of Skill*, Methuen, London.

—— (1976) *Skilled Performance: Perceptual and Motor Skills*, Scott, Foresman & Co., Glenview, Illinois.

—— (1980) 'The Concept of Skill and its Application to Performance', in W. Singleton, P. Spurgeon and R. Stammers (eds), *The Analysis of Social Skill*, Plenum, New York.

Whiting, H. (1975) *Concepts in Skill Learning*, Lepus Books, London.

Wilkinson, J. and Canter, S. (1982) *Social Skills Training Manual*, John Wiley, Chichester.

Woodworth, R. S. (1899) 'The Accuracy of Voluntary Movement', *Psychological Research Monograph Supplement* 3, No. 3.

Yardley, K. (1979) 'Social Skills Training: A Critique', *British Journal of Medical Psychology*, 52, 55–62.

Yoder, D., Hugenberg, L. and Wallace, S. (1993) *Creating Competent Communication*, W. C. Brown, Iowa.

2 Interpersonal communication: a theoretical framework

Owen D. W. Hargie

INTRODUCTION

This chapter explores in greater detail the analogy between motor skill and social skill, as discussed in Chapter 1. In particular, it examines the central processes involved in the implementation of skilled behaviour and evaluates the extent to which a motor skill model of performance can be operationalised in the study of interpersonal communication. An extended model of interpersonal interaction, based upon the skills paradigm, is presented. This extended model is designed to account for those features of performance which are peculiar to social encounters.

THE MOTOR SKILL MODEL

Several models of motor skill, all having central areas in common, have been put forward by different theorists. A good example of this type of model is the one presented by Welford (1965), in the shape of a block diagram representing the operation of perceptual motor skills, in which the need for the co-ordination of a number of processes in the performance of skilled behaviour is highlighted. As shown in Figure 2.1, this model represents the individual as receiving information about the outside world via the sense organs (eyes, ears, nose, hands, etc.). A range of such perceptions is received, and this incoming information is held in the short-term memory store until sufficient data have been obtained to enable a decision to be made about an appropriate response. Such a decision is facilitated by using information already retained in the long-term memory store. Having sifted through all the data from these sources, a response is then carried out by the effector system (hands, feet, voice, and so on). In turn, the outcome of this response is monitored by the sense organs and perceived by the individual, thereby providing feedback which can be used to adjust future responses. Thus, a golfer will observe the position of the ball in relation to the hole, the lie of the land between ball and hole and prevailing weather conditions. All of this information is held in short-term memory and compared with information from long-term memory regarding previous experience of similar putts in the past. As a result, decisions are made about which putter to use and exactly how the ball should be struck. The success of the putt will be observed and used to guide future decisions.

Argyle (1972), in noting the degree of similarity which seemed to exist between motor and social skill, applied this model to the analysis of social skill (Figure 2.2). His model was a slightly modified version of Welford's, in which the flow diagram was simplified by

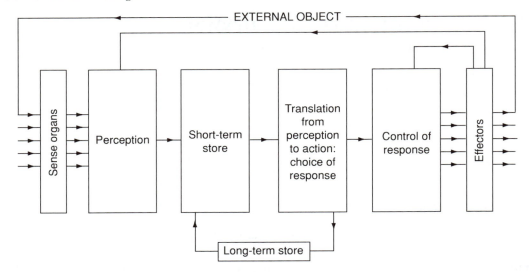

Figure 2.1 Welford's model of the human sensory-motor system

removing the memory store blocks, combining sense organs and perception, control of responses and effectors, and adding the elements of motivation and goal. An example of how this model can be applied to the analysis of motor performance would be when someone is sitting in a room in which the temperature has become too warm (motivation), and is therefore wanting to cool down (goal). This can be achieved by devising a range of alternative plans of action (translation), such as: opening a window, removing some clothing or adjusting the heating system. Eventually, one of these plans will be carried out: a window is opened (response), and the situation monitored. Cool air then enters the room, making the temperature more pleasant (change in outside world). This change in temperature will be perceived by the individual and the goal deemed to have been achieved. Another goal will then be pursued.

A simple example of the application of this motor skill model to a social context would be a female meeting a member of the opposite sex whom she finds very attractive (motivation), and wanting to find out his name (immediate goal). To do so, various plans of action can be translated (e.g. ask directly; give own name and pause; ask someone to effect an introduction), and carried out – for example, the direct request: 'What's your name?' (response). This will then result in some response from the other person: 'Norris' (change in the outside world), which she will hear while also observing his non-verbal reactions to her (perception). She can then move on to the next goal (e.g. follow up, or terminate, discussion).

At first sight, then, it would appear that this motor-skill model can be applied directly to the analysis of social skill. But there are several differences between these two sets of skills which are not really catered for in the basic motor-skill model. In fact, many of these differences were recognised by Argyle (1967) in the first edition of *The Psychology of Interpersonal Behaviour* when he attempted to extend the basic model to take account of the responses of the other person in the social situation, and of the different types of feedback which accrue in interpersonal encounters. However, this extension did not really succeed and was dropped by Argyle in later editions.

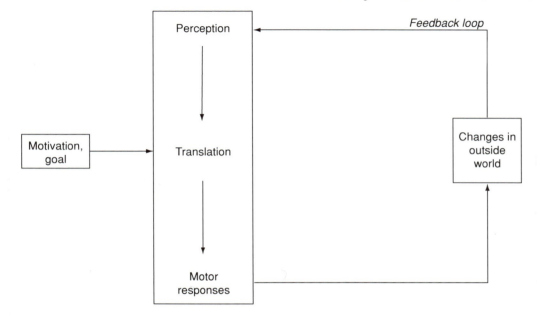

Figure 2.2 Argyle's motor skill model

Subsequently, few attempts were made to expand the basic model to account for the interactive nature of social encounters. Pendleton and Furnham (1980), in critically examining the relationship between motor and social skill, did put forward an expanded model, albeit applied directly to doctor–patient interchanges. Furnham (1983) later pointed out that, although there were problems with this interactive model, it was a 'step in the right direction'. In the first edition of the present book, a model was presented which built upon the Pendleton and Furnham extension, in an attempt to cater for many of the special features of social skill. This model was subsequently revised and adapted by Dickson *et al.* (1989), Millar *et al.* (1992) and Hargie *et al.* (1994). These revised models all accounted for the differences between social and motor performance as discussed in Chapter 1.

However, it is difficult to devise a model which would provide an in-depth representation of all the facets of interpersonal interaction. Such a model would be extremely complicated and cumbersome. As a result, a relatively straightforward, yet robust, extension has been produced. This model, as illustrated in Figure 2.3, takes into account the goals of both interactors, the influence of the person–situation context, and the fact that feedback comes from our own as well as the other person's responses. In addition, the term 'translation' has been replaced by 'mediating factors', to allow for the influence of emotions, as well as cognitions, on performance, and the reciprocal relationship between goals and mediation is also recognised. This model can best be explained by providing an analysis of each of the separate components.

GOALS AND MOTIVATION

As discussed in Chapter 1, a key feature of skilled performance is its goal-directed, intentional nature. The starting point in this model of social interaction is therefore the goal

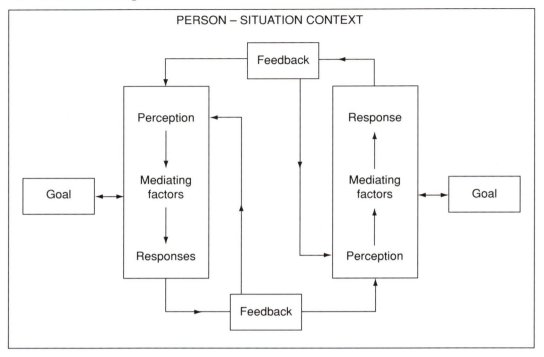

Figure 2.3 Extended model of interpersonal interaction

being sought by the individual, and the related motivation to achieve it. Carlson (1990, p. 404) described motivation as 'a driving force that moves us to a particular action . . . . Motivation can affect the *nature* of an organism's behavior, the *strength* of its behavior, and the *persistence* of its behavior'. The motivation which an individual has to pursue a particular goal is, in turn, influenced by needs. There are a number of needs which must be met in order to enable the individual to live life to its fullest possible extent. Psychologists have posited various categorisations of needs, but the best known hierarchy of human needs remains the one put forward by Maslow (1954), as exemplified in Figure 2.4.

At the bottom of this hierarchy, and therefore most important, are the physiological needs which are essential for the survival of the individual, including the need for water, food, heat, and so on. Once these have been met, the next most important needs are those connected with the safety and security of the individual, including protection from physical harm and freedom from fear. These are met in society by various methods, such as the establishment of police forces, putting security chains on doors, or purchasing insurance policies. At the next level are needs for belonging and love – the desire for a mate, wanting to be accepted by others and to avoid loneliness or rejection. Getting married, having a family or joining a club, society or some form of group, are all means whereby these needs are satisfied. Esteem needs are met in a number of ways through, for instance, occupational status, achievement in sports or success in some other sphere. At a higher level is the need for self-actualisation, by fulfilling one's true potential. People seek new challenges, feeling the need to be 'stretched' and to develop themselves fully. Thus, someone

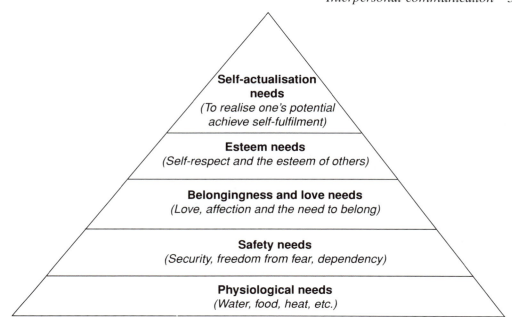

Figure 2.4 Maslow's hierarchy of human needs

may give up secure salaried employment in order to study at college or set up in business.

Maslow argued that only when the more basic needs have been achieved does the individual seek higher needs. The person who is suffering from hunger will usually seek food at all costs, even risking personal safety, and is unlikely to worry about being held in high esteem. At a higher level, someone deeply in love may publicly beg a partner not to leave, thereby forgoing self-esteem. However, it should be recognised that this hierarchy does not hold in all cases. Needs can also be influenced directly by individual goals: take the example of political prisoners who starve themselves to death in an attempt to achieve particular political goals. But, for the most part, this hierarchy of needs holds true, and the behaviour of an individual can be related to existing level of need. Similarly, people can be manipulated either by promises that their needs will be met or by threats that they will not be met. Politicians promise to meet safety needs by reducing the crime rate and improving law and order; computer dating firms offer to meet love needs by providing a partner; while company management may threaten various needs by warning workers that if they go on strike the company could close and they would lose their jobs.

Note that one of the processes which occurs during social encounters is the search for *uncertainty reduction* (Berger, 1987). We want to know what others think of us, what relationship we will have with them, what is expected of us, what the rules of the interaction are, and so on. In other words, we have a need for high predictability about the behaviour of ourselves and others, and we are happier in familiar situations with low levels of uncertainty about what to expect and how to behave.

A final aspect worthy of mention here is that Maslow's hierarchy applies to Western culture, but not to all cultures. As will be discussed later in the chapter, in some Eastern cultures 'belongingness' plays a central role in terms of need, in that being fully accepted by one's peers may represent the core state for which the individual is striving (McLaren, 1994).

Theories of motivation

There are three main theories of motivation which have been put forward to explain human behaviour. The earliest of these, 'drive theory', purported that humans possess drives which are activated and energised by the need to attain certain goals. When we are hungry, it is argued, we have a drive to behave in such a way as to obtain food; when we are cold we are driven to seek heat, and so on. Drive reduction is said to occur when the goal of the drive is attained, and this results in a pleasant internal state. While drive theory satisfactorily accounts for much human behaviour, it does not explain some behaviours, like going on frightening rides at an amusement park, climbing a mountain or bungee jumping. In these cases drives are increased rather than decreased. Furthermore, drive theory tends to over-emphasise internal states while failing to take account of the influence of external events and stimuli. Someone who is not initially hungry may be tempted to eat by the sight of cakes in a café window. In this instance, the cakes can be seen as an incentive to eat.

As a result, an alternative theory of motivation, 'incentive theory', was postulated, underlining the importance of external incentives as motivation for behaviour. Incentive is activated through anticipation of a desired goal. A central tenet of this theory is that we seek positive incentives and avoid negative ones. Thus, when hungry, food would be a positive incentive and approached. On the other hand, the sight of a very boring individual would be a negative incentive and so avoided. Bindra and Stewart (1971, p. 9), in recognising the importance of both theories, pointed out that 'any goal-directed action is instigated by a central motivational state, which itself is created by an interaction within the brain between the neural consequences of bodily organismic states ("drives") and neural consequences of environmental incentives ("reinforcers")'.

Arousal is an important element of drive (where it is viewed as being caused by deprivation) and incentive (where it is regarded as the result of external stimuli) theories. A recognition of the central role of arousal led to a third theory of motivation, 'arousal theory', wherein motivation is seen as being one among a number of causes of arousal (others being environmental factors such as noise and other people; novel events; drugs). The 'optimum level hypothesis' purports that level of arousal has a direct effect upon behaviour, in that when we are under- or over-aroused our performance is adversely affected. Someone who is extremely nervous about speaking in public will usually perform poorly, as will the person who couldn't care less about the speech. Optimum performance occurs when there is a moderate degree of arousal.

Arousal levels vary from one person to another. Some people need a high level of stimulation and become bored easily, whereas others prefer a minimum amount of stimulation to perform effectively. Individual levels of arousal can influence the behaviour of the individual in many ways, ranging from type of job to choice of marriage partner. Those with low levels of arousal will prefer safe, quiet jobs, whereas others with high levels of arousal need occupations in which danger and excitement are prevalent. The level of arousal which can be tolerated is also affected by the time of day; lower levels are required early in the morning and increase throughout the day. A knowledge of the effects of arousal on performance should be recognised by many professionals. Teachers may need to increase the arousal level of pupils during the first class of the day, whereas they may have to decrease arousal in the first class after lunch, in order to encourage concentration. Similarly, doctors and dentists often deal with people in high states of arousal and should pay attention to environmental stimuli (waiting room, surgery) and their own behaviour, in an effort to reduce this arousal. A dentist who is clearly nervous will certainly serve to increase the arousal level of the patient!

Motivation is therefore important in determining the goals which we seek in social inter-action. Indeed, traditionally, motivation has been defined as 'the process by which behavior is *activated* and *directed* toward some definable goal' (Buck, 1988, p. 5). Our behaviour, in turn, is judged on the basis of the goals which are being pursued. However, judgements about an individual's goals can prove inaccurate and we can be deceived by others in terms of the reasons for their behaviour. Someone may be friendly with us in order to obtain extraneous benefit, rather than for the sake of any friendship or liking for us. In other words, there may be an ulterior motive for behaviour. Nevertheless, judgements about the goals of others, based upon their responses to us, are frequently made and are generally accurate. This is why we are surprised or shocked if we discover that someone who was trusted as having honourable goals turns out to have deceived us by having hidden goals. In certain cases, judgements about the goals of behaviour are of crucial importance: for example, when a courtroom jury has to decide whether a killing by a defendant was accidental or pre-meditated.

As the model outlined in Figure 2.3 illustrates, both parties to an interaction have goals. Goal conflict may occur where goals being pursued by both sides do not concur, or where there is internal inconsistency in goals. Informing a good friend of an annoying habit, while maintaining the same level of friendship, would be one example of the latter. Encounters such as this obviously require skill and tact. Yet we know little about how to ensure success in such encounters. As noted by Knapp *et al.* (1994), despite a great deal of interest in the subject of goal-directed action, relatively little work has been carried out to investigate the process whereby communicators negotiate intentions. Thus, we know that we have goals and that those with whom we interact also have goals, but for relationships to develop, ways must be found of successfully negotiating mutual goal achievement. As Kreps and Kunimoto (1994, p. 37) put it: 'All relationships are based on the development and maintenance of *implicit contracts*, mutually understood agreements to meet one's, often unspoken, expectations for the other.' But how and in what ways does the explicit or implicit negotiation of these goals directly or indirectly impinge upon the actual process of communication?

Goals, and our motivation to pursue them, therefore play a vital role in determining behaviour. Once appropriate goals have been decided upon, these have an important bearing on our perceptions, behaviour and on the intervening mediating factors.

MEDIATING FACTORS

The term 'mediating factors' refers to those internal states, activities or processes within the individual, which mediate between the feedback which is perceived, the goal which is being pursued and the responses that are made. As Millar *et al.* (1992, p. 39) noted, 'It is now widely recognised that significant intervening processes occur within the individual which mediate between perception of the stimulus and the execution of a response'. These processes influence the way in which people and events are perceived, and determine the capacity of the individual to assimilate, process and respond to the social information received during interpersonal encounters. It is at this stage that the person makes decisions about the likelihood of goals being achieved, given the existing situation, and then decides upon an appropriate course of action. There are two core mediating factors, namely cognition and emotion.

Cognition

Although, as highlighted by O'Keefe and Lambert (1993, p. 68), 'There is substantial controversy in cognitive science concerning the fundamental design of the architecture of cognition', it is clear that cognition plays a very important role in skilled communication. This is because 'it is in the mind that intentions are formulated, potential courses of action considered, and efferent commands generated' (Greene, 1988, p. 37). But what do we mean by cognition? One definition is that it is 'all the processes by which the sensory input is transformed, reduced, elaborated, stored, recovered and used' (Neisser, 1967, p. 4). This definition encompasses the main functions of cognition which involves *transforming*, or decoding and making use of the sensory information which is received. To do so, it is often necessary to *reduce* the amount of information which is attended to, in order to avoid overloading the system. Conversely, at times it is necessary to *elaborate* upon minimal information by making interpretations, judgements or evaluations (e.g. 'He is not speaking to me because I have upset him').

Some of the information will be *stored* either in short-term or long-term memory. While there is debate about the exact nature and operation of memory, there is considerable evidence to support the existence of these two systems (Bentley, 1993). Short-term memory has a limited capacity for storage, allowing for the retention of information over a brief interval of time (no more than a few minutes), while long-term memory has an enormous capacity for storage of data which can be retained over many years. Thus, information stored in short-term memory will quickly be lost unless it is transferred to the long-term memory store. For instance, we can usually still remember the name of our first teacher at primary school, yet a few minutes after being introduced to someone for the first time we may well have forgotten their name. One theory which has been put forward to account for memory is that we use a process of *context-dependent coding*. Remembering occurs by recalling the context of the original event. When we meet someone we recognise but cannot place, we try to think where or when we met that person before – in other words, we try to put the individual into a particular context. A similar process occurs in social situations, whereby we evaluate people and situations in terms of our experience of previous similar encounters. Information that is stored can be *recovered* or retrieved to facilitate the processes of decision-making and problem-solving.

However, while some thoughts are purposeful and goal-oriented, other cognitive activity may be disordered, less controlled and more automatic, or involuntary, in nature. The extent to which such erratic thoughts determine the main direction of mental activity varies from one person to another, but is highest in certain pathological states, such as schizophrenia, where a large number of unrelated thoughts may 'flood through' the mind.

Socially skilled individuals have greater control over cognitive processes and use these to facilitate social interaction.

Snyder (1987) demonstrated how those high in social skill have a capacity for monitoring and regulating their own behaviour in relation to the responses of others – a system he termed *self-monitoring*. This process of regulation necessitates an awareness of the ability level of the person with whom one is interacting and of the 'way they think', since, as Wessler (1984, p. 112) pointed out, 'in order to interact successfully and repeatedly with the same persons, one must have the capacity to form cognitive conceptions of the others' cognitive conceptions'. Such *metacognition* is very important in forming judgements about the reasons for behaviour. However, as with many of the processes in skilled performance, there is an optimum level of metacognition, since if overdone 'all of this thinking about thinking could become so cumbersome that it actually interferes with communication' (Lundsteen, 1993, p. 107). In other words, it is possible to 'think oneself out of' actions.

The socially skilled individual has an ability to 'size up' people and situations more rapidly, and respond in a more appropriate fashion, than the person who is low in social skills. Such an ability is dependent upon the capacity to process cognitively the information received during social interaction.

Emotion

The importance of mood and emotional state in the communication process and the part they play in characterising our relationships with others have been clearly recognised (Parkinson, 1995). This central role played by the affective domain in interpersonal encounters was aptly summarised by Metts and Bowers (1994, p. 508) as follows: 'Emotion is a fundamental, potent, and ubiquitous aspect of social life. Affective arousal forms a subtext underlying all interaction, giving it direction, intensity, and velocity as well as shaping communicative choices. Emotion is also one of the most consequential outcomes of interaction, framing the interpretation of messages, one's view of self and others, and one's understanding of the relationship that gave rise to the feeling.'

Differing theoretical perspectives exist concerning the nature and cause of emotion and, indeed, 'The best way to define emotion has long been a vexing problem for both research and theory' (Gallois, 1993, p. 4). An early viewpoint put forward by James (1884) was that emotions were simply a category of physiological phenomena resulting from the perception of an external stimulus. Thus, James argued, when you see a bear, the muscles tense and glands secrete hormones to facilitate escape – as a result fear is experienced. However, this view was undermined by later research which demonstrated that patients who had glands and muscles removed from the nervous system by surgery nevertheless reported the feeling of affect. More recent theorists have emphasised the link between cognition and emotion, and highlighted two main elements involved in the subjective experience of the latter: first, the perception of physiological arousal; and, second, the cognitive evaluation of that arousal to arrive at an emotional 'label' for the experience (Berscheid, 1983).

However, differences persist about the exact nature of the relationship between cognition and emotion. Some argue that a direct causal relationship exists between cognitive and affective processes, with the latter being caused by the former (Mathews, 1993). Within this model, irrational beliefs would be seen as causing fear or anxiety, which, in turn, could be controlled by helping the individual to develop a more rational belief system. This perspective is regarded by others as being an oversimplification of what is viewed as a more complex relationship between cognition and affect (Forgas, 1994). It is argued that emotional states can also cause changes in cognition, so that an individual who is very angry may not be able to 'think straight', while it is also possible to be 'out of your mind' with worry. In this sense, there does seem to be a reciprocal relationship, in that the way people think can influence how they feel and vice versa.

Cognition has been conceptualised as comprising two main dimensions: *analytic cognition* which is rational, sequential and reason-oriented; and *syncretic cognition* which is more holistic and affective in nature. Chaudhuri and Buck (1995), for example, found that differing types of advertisement evoked different forms of cognitive response in recipients. Thus, advertisements which employed product information strategies strongly encouraged analytic cognition and discouraged syncretic (or affective) cognition, whereas those using mood arousal strategies had the converse effect. There may be individual differences in cognitive structure, in that with some people analytical thought may drive central processes, while others are more affective in the way they think. Also, it is likely that when interacting with certain people, and in specific settings, affective cognition predominates (e.g. at a family gathering), whereas in other contexts analytic cognition is more likely to govern our thought processes (e.g. negotiating the price of a car with a salesperson in a garage showroom). More research is required to investigate the exact determinants of these two forms of cognition.

Emotion itself has been shown to have three main components: first, the direct conscious experience or feeling of emotion; second, the physiological processes which accompany emotions; and third, the observable behavioural actions which are used to express and convey them. Izard (1977, p. 10), in noting these three processes, pointed out that 'virtually all of the neurophysiological systems and subsystems of the body are involved in greater or lesser degree in emotional states. Such changes inevitably affect the perceptions, thoughts and actions of the person'. As a result, the individual who is in love may be 'blind' to the faults of another and fail to perceive negative cues, while someone who is very depressed will be inclined to pick up negative cues and miss the positive ones. Similarly, a happy person will display signs of happiness by smiling, being lively and joining in social interaction, while a sad person will adopt a slouched posture, flat tone of voice and will generally avoid interaction with others.

Emotional states are, therefore, very important both in terms of our perception of the outside world and how we respond to it. The importance of the affective domain is evidenced by the vast array of words and terms used to describe the variety of emotional states which are experienced. Averill (1975) carried out an investigation in which he identified a total of 558 discrete emotional labels, ranging from 'abandoned' and 'abashed' to 'zealous' and 'zestful'. In other studies, Bush (1972) accumulated a total of 2,186 emotional adjectives in English, while Clore *et al.* (1987) found 255 English terms referring to core emotions. The fact that we have a very large number of terms to describe emotional states is one indication of the importance of this domain. However, as Shaver *et al.* (1987) illustrated, there would seem to be six basic emotion categories – love, happiness, surprise, anger, sadness and fear. Within each of these basic emotions, Shaver *et al.* found a range of sub-categories, so that, for example, 'love' contains *inter alia* 'affection' and 'lust', while 'sadness' subsumes 'embarrassment' and 'shame'. There are also behaviours associated with the expression of these emotions, so, for instance, love can involve kissing, hugging and extensive mutual gaze.

While some emotions seem to be expressed in a common fashion across cultures (interest, joy, surprise, distress, disgust, anger, shame and fear), there are also significant differences between cultures. For example, Levy (1974) reported that the Tahitian language had no word to signify anything comparable to a sense of guilt. Also, there is still a great deal of debate over exactly how many basic emotions exist, and what to call them once they are identified (Orton and Turner, 1990). In addition, the factors which provoke emotion differ across cultures, although in general terms, 'Positive emotions can be seen as produced by stimuli representing ... achievement of goals, satisfaction of motives, realization of response tendencies, acquisition of incentives. Negative emotions can be seen as the result of stimuli representing mismatch with any of the above' (Frijda, 1986, p. 265).

While emotion and cognition are the two main aspects focused upon in this chapter, there are other related mediating factors which influence how we process information. This was highlighted by Miller *et al.* (1994, p. 187) who noted that 'individuals also enter into situations with preexisting experiences, beliefs and knowledge, resources, emotional tendencies, and so forth, all of which may not only affect what situation we enter but how we color and construe the current situation and make subsequent behavioral choices'. In this sense, 'communication phenomena are surface manifestations of complex configurations of deeply felt beliefs, values and attitudes' (Brown and Starkey, 1994, p. 808). Thus, our values, attitudes and beliefs affect our perceptions, actions, cognitions and emotions. The devout Christian may view the death of a close relative as an act of God and a cause for celebration, since the deceased has 'gone to a better place', while the atheist may regard this as a time of sorrow at the termination of a life. Our political, moral and religious beliefs and values therefore influence our actions and reactions to others. These also influence our attitudes towards other people, which, in turn, will affect our thoughts, feelings and behaviour during social encounters.

Our attitudes are affected not only by our beliefs and values, but also by previous experiences of the person with whom we are interacting, as well as by our experiences of similar people. All of these factors come into play at the decision-making stage during interpersonal encounters. For the most part, this process of translating perceptions into actions takes place at a subconscious level, thereby enabling faster, smoother responses to be made. Just as the skilled car driver does not have to think consciously about depressing the clutch and putting the gear lever into neutral, so the skilled counsellor does not have to think consciously about encouraging his or her client to speak freely. As highlighted in Chapter 1, a feature of skilled performance is the ability to operate at this subconscious level, while monitoring the situation to ensure a successful outcome.

RESPONSES

Once a goal and related action plan have been formulated, the next step is to implement this plan in terms of social responses. It is the function of the response system (voice, hands, face, etc.) to carry out the plan in terms of overt behaviours and it is at this stage that skill becomes manifest. Social behaviour can be categorised as in Figure 2.5.

Thus, an initial distinction can be made between linguistic and non-linguistic behaviour. Linguistic behaviour refers to all aspects of speech, including the actual verbal content (the words used), and the paralinguistic message associated with it. Paralanguage refers to the way in which something is said (pitch, tone, speed, volume of voice, accent, pauses,

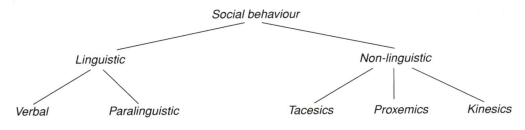

Figure 2.5 Categories of social behaviour

speech dysfluencies, etc.). Non-linguistic behaviour involves all of our bodily communication and is concerned with the study of what we do rather than what we say. It can be divided into three main dimensions. Tacesics is the systematic study of bodily contact – in other words, what parts of the body we use to touch one another, how often, with what intensity, in which contexts and to what effect. Proxemics is the systematic study of the spatial features of social presentation – that is, the social distances we adopt in different settings, how we mark and protect personal territory, the angles at which we orient towards one another and the standing or seating positions we take up. Kinesics is the systematic study of body motion – that is, the meanings associated with movements of the hands, head and legs, the postures we adopt, our gaze and our facial expressions. These aspects of social behaviour are discussed fully throughout the remaining chapters of this book, with Chapter 3 being devoted to the study of non-verbal communication.

One important aspect of individual behaviour is the concept of style, defined by Norton (1983) as 'the relatively enduring pattern of human interaction associated with the individual' (p. 19) involving 'an accumulation of "microbehaviors"... that add up to a "macrojudgment" about a person's style of communicating' (p. 38). Norton identified nine main communicative styles, each of which can be interpreted as a continuum, as follows:

1   *Dominant/submissive.* Dominant people like to control social interactions, give orders and be the centre of attention; they use behaviours such as loud volume of voice, interruptions, prolonged eye contact and fewer pauses to achieve dominance. At the opposite end of this continuum, submissive people prefer to keep quiet, stay out of the limelight and take orders;

2   *Dramatic/reserved.* Exaggeration, storytelling and use of non-verbal communication are techniques used by dramatic individuals who tend to overstate their messages. The other end of the continuum is characterised by the reserved type of person who is more quiet, modest and prone to understatement;

3   *Contentious/affiliative.* The contentious person is argumentative, provocative or contrary, as opposed to the agreeable, peace-loving, affiliative individual;

4   *Animated/inexpressive.* An animated style involves making use of hands, arms, eyes, facial expressions, posture and overall body movement to gain attention or convey enthusiasm. The converse here is the dull, slow-moving, inexpressive person;

5   *Relaxed/frenetic.* This continuum ranges from people who do not get over-excited, always seem in control and are never flustered, to those who are tense, quickly lose self-control, get excited easily and behave frenetically;

6 *Attentive/inattentive.* Attentive individuals listen carefully to others and display overt signs of listening such as eye contact, appropriate facial expression and posture. Inattentive individuals, on the other hand, are poor listeners who do not make any attempt to express interest in what others are saying;

7 *Impression-leaving/insignificant.* The impression-leaving style is characterised by flamboyant individuals who display a visible or memorable style of communicating and leave an impression on those whom they meet. They are people who, for example, wear loud clothes, have unusual hair styles or a controversial interactive manner. The opposite of this is the insignificant individual who 'fades into the fabric' of buildings, is non-controversial and dresses conservatively;

8 *Open/closed.* Open people talk about themselves freely, are approachable, unreserved, unsecretive, frank and conversational. At the opposite end of this continuum are closed individuals who reveal no personal information, are secretive, loath to express opinions and 'keep themselves to themselves';

9 *Friendly/hostile.* This style continuum ranges from the friendly person who will smile frequently, be happy, very rewarding and generally non-competitive, to the hostile person who is overtly aggressive, highly competitive and very unrewarding.

Most people can be evaluated overall in terms of these continua, although style of communication can also be affected by situations. A dominant teacher in the classroom may be submissive during staff meetings, while a normally friendly individual may become hostile when engaging in team sports. Nevertheless, there will be elements of style which will endure across situations, and these will have a bearing on a number of facets of the individual. For example, someone who tends to be dominant, frenetic, inattentive, or hostile will probably not make a good counsellor. Similarly, a very dominant person is unlikely to marry someone equally dominant.

As discussed in Chapter 1, much of the behaviour that one displays is learned through a process of modelling and imitation of significant others. Various behaviours will be tried out, until eventually the individual evolves a personal style of communication. A similar process occurs when the neophyte enters a new profession, resulting in a professional style of interacting. Much of this text is devoted to an analysis of a wide array of responses in terms of skills, styles and strategies. However, in order to respond appropriately it is necessary to be aware of available feedback during communication.

FEEDBACK

'Feedback' is a term derived from cybernetics (the study of automatic communication and control in systems), which is the method of controlling a system by reinserting into it the results of its past performance. This concept of feedback as a control process operates on the basis that the output of a system is 'fed back' into the same system as additional input, which, in turn, serves to regulate further output (Annett, 1969). In this way, a thermostat on a central-heating system acts as a servomechanism, automatically feeding back details of the temperature into the system which then regulates heating output. One important difference between this mechanistic view and its application to the interpersonal domain is that humans actively interpret feedback. Thus, what was intended by the sender to be positive feedback may be misconstrued by the receiver as negative. Likewise, feedback from others may be ignored altogether.

Nevertheless, once a response has been carried out, feedback is available to determine its effects and enable subsequent responses to be shaped in the light of this information. In order to perform any task efficiently, it is necessary to receive such feedback so that corrective action can be taken as required. As Sloboda (1986, pp. 32–3) put it: 'Feedback of one sort or another is essential to all skill acquisition. One cannot improve unless one has ways of judging how good present performance is, and in which direction change must occur.' Thus, sighted individuals would find it very difficult to ride a bicycle, make a cup of coffee, or even walk along a straight line in the absence of visual feedback. In inter-personal encounters feedback allows people 'to monitor their progress toward the goal and adjust their behaviour when monitoring suggests that the goal will not be met' (Locke and Latham, 1990, p. 329).

Within the sphere of social interaction, we receive feedback from the reactions of other people towards us, as messages are received and transmitted from person to person in a continuous return loop. At the same time, the transmitting person is receiving self-feedback which provides information about performance (see Figure 2.3). For example, if we ask a question which we immediately perceive to be poorly worded, we may rephrase the question before the listener has had an opportunity to respond to the initial one. High self-monitors will more readily access such information and by so doing control the images of self they project to others. It is on the basis of self-perception over time that we form a view about our own personality. We develop self-schemata regarding the type of person we believe ourselves to be, and our self-concept in turn influences the way in which encounters with others are perceived and interpreted.

During communication, as the number of channels open for messages to be transmitted varies, so also does the potential for feedback. A written message denies any immediate interactional feedback, while a telephone limits the visual feedback but enhances the paralinguistic channel. In situations where we are interacting with someone who is not giving us 'much feedback' we are generally ill at ease since we are not sure how we are 'being received'. One extreme example of lack of feedback which most people find some-what disconcerting occurs when we telephone someone and unexpectedly have to interact with an answering machine instead of the required person – in many instances the caller hangs up without leaving any message.

Fitts and Posner (1973) delineated the three main functions of feedback. First, it can provide motivation to continue with a task – if the feedback suggests the possibility of a successful outcome. In this way, feedback gives information about performance. A sales-person who believes the customer is showing interest would be more motivated to try to clinch a sale. Second, it offers knowledge about the results of behaviour. Whether the sale is successful or not will help to shape the salesperson's future sales attempts – to change or to replicate the same approach. Third, feedback can act as a form of reinforcement from the listener, encouraging the speaker to continue with the same type of messages. So, during an interaction, feedback in the form of comments such as 'I fully agree' or 'Great idea!', and non-verbal behaviours including smiles and head nods, are overt positive reinforcers (see Chapter 5).

What is referred to as *backchannel behaviour* has been shown to be a key form of feedback. This allows the listener to feed back information (agreement, disagreement, interest, involvement, etc.) to the speaker on an ongoing yet unobtrusive basis, in the form of vocalisations ('m-hm', 'uh huh'), head movements, posture, eye movements and facial expressions. The skilled speaker engages in *track-checking behaviour* by monitoring these backchannel cues to assess whether the message is being understood, accepted, and having the intended impact, and to make adjustments to the delivery as necessary. Research findings indicate cross-cultural differences in type and degree of backchannel behaviour, and also show that judgements of communicative competence are higher where interactors display similar levels of backchannel behaviour (Kikuchi, 1994).

During conversations an important signal of willingness to listen is eye contact. In most (though not all) societies, the listener looks more at the speaker than vice versa. The eyes also help to regulate turn-taking in conversation, control and provide feedback to the speaker and, if listener gaze decreases, the speaker may speak with greater emphasis, inquire if the other person is interested, and eventually, if positive feedback is still denied, will cease interaction.

In interpersonal communication we are bombarded by a constant stream of sensory stimulation in the form of noises, sights, smells, tastes and tactile sensations. While bodily olfaction has a very important communicative function which can affect the relationships we develop with others (Serby and Chobor, 1992), in Western society our bodily odours are often camouflaged by the application of various types of artificial scents. During social encounters we therefore receive most perceptual information through the eyes and ears and, to a lesser extent, through tactile senses. Indeed, we receive such a barrage of sensory input that it is necessary for the individual to filter out some of the available stimuli, to deal more effectively with the remainder. As noted by Witkin (1993, p. 35), this 'Selective processing is of prime importance to the listener, since otherwise he would be totally overwhelmed'. In this sense, a selective perception filter is operative, and its main function is to filter a limited amount of information into the conscious mind, while storing the remainder at a subconscious level. For example, in a lecture context, students are bombarded by stimuli in terms of the voice of the lecturer, the noises made by other students, the pressure of their feet on the floor or their backside on the seat, the hum of an overhead projector, the feel of a pen, and so on. If the lecturer is very stimulating, then much of the other stimuli will be filtered out, whereas if the lecturer is boring then one's aching backside may become a prime focus of attention.

Unfortunately, vital information from another person may be filtered out during social interaction and less important cues consciously perceived. One reason for this is that humans are not objective animals since our 'Beliefs tell us what to listen to, how to filter incoming information' (Thompson, 1993, p. 158). Thus, from all the social stimuli available to us, we may focus upon less relevant stimuli and miss important verbal or non-verbal signals. The difference between feedback and perception is that while there is usually a great deal of feedback available, it may not be consciously perceived. It is crucial that professionals learn to make appropriate use of the feedback available during interactions with clients, by perceiving the central messages and filtering out peripheral ones.

PERCEPTION

Our perceptions provide us with information concerning our environment, in terms of physical objects, events and other people. Roth and Bruce (1995, p. 13) described perception as 'how we make sense of all the information we receive from the world via our senses', while Hinton (1993, p. ix) stated that 'Interpersonal perception is all about how we decide what other people are like and the meanings we give to their actions'. This latter type of perception is commonly referred to as 'person perception', which 'not only involves the judgments we make about people as objects (tall, bald, wearing brown shoes, etc.) but is primarily concerned with the impressions we form of people as people (impulsive, religious, tired, happy, anxious and so on)' (Warr and Knapper, 1968, p. 3). The centrality of person perception was emphasised by Cook (1979), who argued that the way people perceive one another directly determines their behaviour during interaction.

One of the most common observations made concerning the nature of humans is that 'people are all different'. They differ in terms of physical characteristics such as height, weight and colour. They differ in sex, socio-economic status, cultural inheritance, educational attainments, peer group influences and personality traits. People also differ in the way they perceive the world around them, and 'read' the same situation in differing ways. In this sense, reality for each individual is socially constructed from the way in which incoming information is perceived and interpreted. In order to understand why and how people differ in this way, we need first to understand some of the factors which influence the perceptual process.

Roth (1976) identified four important elements of perception. First, our perceptions enable us to structure and organise the world into an acceptable order to give it meaning. Thus, we respond to people as people, rather than as a series of different shapes and colours. Second, we integrate a number of perceptual cues in order to make judgements. During social encounters the verbal and non-verbal signals received are combined to produce an overall perceptual message. When we meet people we notice their dress, body shape, age, sex, verbal and vocal messages, and so on, and integrate all of this information into a meaningful whole. Third, we make associations and causal links between perceptions: if we see a brick being hurled at a window we expect the glass to shatter, and attribute this breakage to being caused by the impact of the brick. Similarly, if we shout at someone who then begins to cry, we assume that our behaviour has caused the tears. Fourth, we attribute stability and constancy to our perceptions. For example, as people walk away from us, they actually 'appear' to be getting smaller, but we do not believe that they are slowly shrinking and interpret the decreased size as being a result of distance. Constancy and stability in the behaviour of other people are also looked for and we are surprised if they deviate markedly from the way we expect them to behave.

Perceptual ability is influenced by the familiarity of incoming stimuli. Bentley (1993) illustrated how knowledge is a set of associated concepts, such that new information is learned by building connections to the existing cognitive network. Consequently, if incoming material is difficult to understand, it will be harder to assimilate and conceptualise. Within social interaction such elements as a common understandable language, recognised dialect and phrasing, influence perceptual capacity. So our speed of perception would drop if someone were to use technical terms with which we were unfamiliar or spoke at too fast a rate. Likewise, if the non-verbal signals do not register as understandable, or are distracting, then our perceptual reception is hampered. In either situation, we may selectively filter out the unfamiliar or unacceptable and thus receive a distorted or inaccurate message.

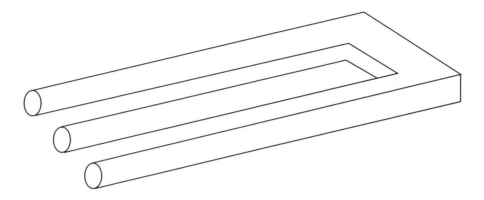

Figure 2.6 Impossible figure

Accuracy

There is a great deal of evidence to indicate that we are often inaccurate in our perceptions and can be deceived in terms of what we appear to see (Jones, 1990). For example, a series of bulbs lit in quick succession will seem like the flowing movement of light. Another example of how perception can be distorted is shown in the 'impossible object' in Figure 2.6. This object is meaningful if we look at either end of it, but when viewed in its entirety it is, in fact, an optical illusion. Likewise, in person perception one can be deceived by appearances – for instance, family and friends are often shocked when someone commits suicide without seeming to be at all unhappy.

Perceptions are also influenced by context, so that the symbol '1' will be seen as a number in the first sequence and as a letter in the second sequence below.

    1 – 2 – 3
    G – 1 – H

In the same way, our perceptions of people are influenced by the interactional context. Millar *et al.* (1992) argued that everyone makes mistakes in perception and this is not necessarily catastrophic. They use a tennis analogy, pointing out that while even world-class players make unforced errors, the important aspect is that they are more often accurate and can assimilate information more rapidly, than less skilled players. Skilled interactors will likewise swiftly process incoming data and make fewer perceptual errors than less socially skilled people.

The primacy and recency effects also play an important role in perception. The *primacy effect* refers to the way in which information perceived early in an encounter can influence how later information is interpreted. In this way, initial impressions of people we meet for the first time influence how we respond to them, despite the fact that such impressions can be misleading. Important decisions, such as whether or not to give someone a job, can be highly influenced by the first impressions of the candidate gleaned by the interviewer. The *recency effect* refers to the way in which the final information received can affect our judgements. For example, in a sequence of employment interviews the final candidate is more readily remembered than those interviewed in the middle of the sequence. The importance of the opening and closing stages of interaction have been reviewed by Hargie *et al.* (1994) who described them as structured, formalised sequences during which there is a greater opportunity to accentuate important points or create an effective impact on others. It is not surprising, therefore, that parents take care to teach children, from a very young age, how to employ the greeting and parting rituals.

Labelling

The process of labelling is used during person perception to enable people to be categorised more readily. Labels are related to aspects such as age, physical appearance, sex, race, mode of dress, as well as non-verbal and verbal behaviour. Judgements and inferences are made according to the 'picture' received. Labelling is influenced by past experience, expectations and interpretation of the situation. It also arises from the need to classify and categorise others, and to simplify incoming information, which would otherwise become unmanageable.

One type of label is that of the social *stereotype*. 'Stereotype' is a term which originated from the print process and referred to a plate which repeatedly printed the same image. In similar vein, a 'psychological stereotype is a fixed impression of a group of people' (De Vito, 1994, p. 66). Once a person is identified as belonging to a particular group, the characteristics of that group tend to be attributed irrespective of actual individual characteristics. In this way, set patterns of behaviour are anticipated in those belonging to specific groups. Thus, a person belonging to a professional group is likely to evoke a set of behavioural expectations: police officers will be associated with one set of expectations, while nurses will be associated with a different set. The stereotype an individual holds of a professional group will tend to influence how the behaviour of any particular member of that group is perceived and interpreted.

As Fiedler (1993, p. 349) pointed out, 'perceptions and judgements of people not only reflect the objectively available stimulus information but also to a considerable extent the judge's own inferences or stereotypical expectations'. For example, Fyock and Stangor (1994) carried out a meta-analysis of twenty-six studies which had investigated how people remembered information about particular social groupings. They found that stereotypes tended to be maintained 'through memory biases that favour processing of information that is consistent with existing expectations about real social groups' (p. 339). In other words, we are more likely to remember information which is consistent with our existing stereotype for any group. A related process here is the *confirmation bias*, which refers to the way in which, through a process of perceptual accentuation, we tend to make an initial judgement about another person early in an encounter and then seek out information which will accentuate and confirm this first evaluation.

Expectations can directly influence both the behaviour of the individual and the outcomes of interaction. This *interpersonal expectancy effect*, which has been shown to be operative in a range of professional contexts, including health, business, education, social research and the courtroom (Blanck, 1993), can be either positive or negative. For instance, if we are given positive information about someone we then form positive expectations and respond accordingly. In this way, a self-fulfilling prophecy can occur, in that we actually encourage the anticipated response. The effects of expectations upon behaviour can also be negative. For example, if we believe that people from a particular racial background are aggressive, when we meet someone of that race we are more likely to behave in a way which anticipates aggression, thereby provoking a more aggressive response and so confirming our original beliefs.

In one famous study, teachers were informed by researchers that they had identified certain children (whose names were actually selected at random) as being 'late bloomers' who would start to show improvements at a later stage. At follow-up, it was found that these pupils had indeed performed at a higher level than their peers. One hypothesis was that the expectations of teachers affected the amount of attention and reward they gave to the late bloomers, and this in turn resulted in the improved performance of pupils, who were keen to fulfil the perceived exectations of the teacher (Rosenthal and Jacobson, 1992). Other studies in classrooms have shown that teacher expectations can influence (in descending order of effect magnitude) their impressions of pupils, the grades they award, the resulting performance of pupils on objective tests and their actual IQ levels (Blanck, 1993).

Theories of perception

There are two main theories of perception, namely intuitive and inference. Intuitive theories regard perception as being innate, purporting that people instinctively recognise and interpret the behaviour and feelings of others. There is some evidence to support the existence of such an innate capacity. It has been found, for example, that monkeys reared in isolation are able to recognise and respond to the emotions displayed by other monkeys. Furthermore, humans blind from birth are able to display facial expressions of emotions (albeit of a more restricted range as compared to sighted people), and a number of such expressions seem to be common across different cultures. However, although there may be elements of emotion which are perceived intuitively, it is unlikely that many of the perceptual judgements people make are innate (for example, warm, intelligent, sophisticated). Such detailed judgements are culture-specific and dependent upon learning.

If perception were innate and instinctive, then we should be very accurate in our perceptions. Yet this is patently not the case. It has also been demonstrated that it is possible to improve perceptual abilities, thereby supporting the view that there is a degree of learning involved. Thus, while intuition plays a role in our perceptions of others, it cannot account for the entire process. The second theory purports that judgements of others are based on inferences made as a result of past experiences. An example of how such inferences are arrived at is: fat people are usually happy (generalisation based upon past experience); this woman is fat (this person is perceived as fitting the generalisation); therefore she is probably happy (inference).

Bruner and Tagiuri (1954) charted the importance of what they referred to as *implicit personality theories* which influence the judgements people make about others. These theories are dependent on three types of inference rules. *Identification rules* involve the perception of overt cues (dress, shape, physical appearance) in order to identify and 'place' people in certain ways. *Association rules* enable people to be associated with a certain set of beliefs or stereotypes, once they have been categorised and identified as belonging to a particular group. *Combination rules* involve the combination of a number of cues in order to allow an overall picture to be built up. Thus, perceptual judgements are made as the result of the identification, association and combination of a range of cues. Through this process, we develop categories with which to describe others, and hold certain beliefs about which categories 'hang together'. In this way, if we were told that someone was compassionate, we might expect other qualities to be displayed (e.g. sympathetic, kind, generous). This can lead to what is termed *logical error*, where, for instance, the belief may have been developed (perhaps based on past experience) that intelligent people are always honest and that person A being intelligent must therefore also be honest (Hinton, 1993). There are also *central traits*, the presence of which induce a range of other judgements. In particular, the traits 'warm' and 'cold' have been shown to be central, in that once a judgement of someone is made on the warm–cold continuum, other positive or negative judgements respectively tend to be inferred. Thus, warm people are perceived as sociable, popular, happy, good-natured and humorous (Dickson *et al.*, 1997).

It would seem, therefore, that both intuition and inference play a part in person perception. The innate perception of certain basic emotions in others is probably important for the survival of the individual, but in a complex society, learned inferences enable us to recognise and interpret a range of social messages, and respond to these more readily.

Attribution

One key feature of interpersonal communication is the way in which we attribute causes to the actions of both self and others. There are three main variables involved in attribution: (1) Consistency – how often is the behaviour displayed by this person in this situation?; (2) Distinctiveness – does the person display this behaviour in other similar situations?; (3) Consensus – do other people display similar behaviour in this context?

An important distinction here is whether we view behaviour as being primarily the result of situational or dispositional factors. Thus, in Table 2.1, Mr X who makes a large donation at a charity function may be seen as trying to impress others present (external attribution) or as being a very generous person (internal attribution). When interpreting motives for such single behaviours we employ discounting and augmenting strategies. For example, if no one else made a large donation and we later discovered that Mr X had made several less public donations to other charities, we would be more likely to discount the situational explanation and make a personal attribution (row 2 in Table 2.1). Furthermore, if we then learned that in order to make these donations Mr X lived a very frugal personal lifestyle, this would augment the dispositional attribution. Another influencing factor here is the

Table 2.1 The process of attribution

	Consistency	Distinctiveness	Consensus	Probable attribution
1	*High*. He always gives large sums to this charity.	*High*. He seldom gives to other charities.	*High*. Everyone else gave a large sum.	To this particular charity.
2	*High*. He always gives large sums to this charity.	*Low*. He gives generously to other charities.	*Low*. No one else gave a large sum.	To this particular person.
3	*Low*. He has never given a large sum to this charity before.	*High*. He seldom gives to other charities.	*Low*. No one else gave a large sum.	To the situation or circumstances.

extent to which the person has control over the behaviour. For example, if Mr Y, whom we knew to have recently been made bankrupt, did not give any money to the charity, we may imply that this was because he had no money to give. On the other hand, if he nevertheless gave a large sum we might then attribute his bankruptcy to poor financial ability.

What is known as the *fundamental attribution error* refers to the process whereby we tend to over-emphasise dispositional causes and under-estimate the impact of situational aspects when interpreting the behaviour of others. Furthermore, the presence of a *self-serving bias* means that when interpreting our own failures we are much more likely to emphasise external factors, but when explaining personal success we tend to highlight internal causes (e.g. a maths exam may be failed because of a poor teacher, or passed because of a flair for the subject). Conversely, other people's failures are more likely to be attributed solely to dispositional aspects.

Person perception, therefore, is concerned with the impressions people form of one another and how interpretations are made concerning the behaviour of others. It is concerned with the 'external' world coming into contact with the 'internal' world of expectations, hopes, fears, needs, memories, etc. The more socially skilled individual possesses greater perceptual ability than someone who is less socially adept. To be effective in social interaction it is necessary to be sensitive to relevant social feedback, in terms of the verbal and non-verbal behaviour being displayed both by oneself and by others. If such perceptions are inaccurate, then decisions about future responses will be based upon invalid information, and the resulting responses are therefore likely to be less appropriate.

Perception is the final central process involved in the dyadic (two-person) model of social interaction, as outlined in Figure 2.3 and, together with the processes of motivation and goal, mediating factors, response and feedback, comprises the core of such interaction. However, in order to attempt to comprehend the nature of interpersonal communication fully, we must take into account two other aspects, namely personal and situational factors, which impinge upon, and influence, such communication.

THE PERSON-SITUATION CONTEXT

In their review of models of communication, Heath and Bryant (1992, p. 57) noted how 'Early process models exhibited little awareness of the impact context has on communication. But researchers quickly became aware of the role context plays. The context of each communication event shapes it'. In this sense, communication is embedded in a context and interactive messages can only be fully understood by taking cognisance of the situation (S) in which they occur. At the same time, the person (P) side of the equation is very important. In his detailed analysis of the field of personality, Phares (1988, p. 26) concluded that 'Situations alone do not determine behavior. People bring with them to every situation something of themselves. This "something" is what makes each person different from all others. Therefore, every situation is interpreted, analyzed, filtered, and perceived based on the unique set of past experiences, learnings, and biological qualities of each individual'. It is, therefore, necessary to study interpersonal communication within the parameters of what Hargie *et al.* (1994) termed the 'person-situation context'.

The *person-situation debate* within psychology has produced three perspectives. Personologists purport that behaviour is mainly a feature of inner personality traits;

situationalists argue that it is primarily a function of the setting in which people find themselves; while interactionists hold that behaviour is a product of P x S. In reviewing research into this debate, Argyle (1994, p. 102) concluded: 'The overall results are very clear: persons and situations are both important, but P x S interaction is more important than either.'

Person factors

Personality

An important part of this equation is the person; and indeed the concept of personality and the role it plays in determining behaviour has long occupied the minds of social scientists. While recognising that there are many differing perspectives on personality, and hence varying definitions, Mischel (1993, p. 5) defined it as 'the distinctive patterns of behavior (including thoughts and emotions) that characterize each individual's adaptation to the situations of his or her life'.

One common unit of analysis in the study of personality has been that of traits. It is argued by trait theorists that whether we are co-operative or competitive, extroverted or introverted, dominant or submissive, dependent or independent, and so on, will influence both how we interpret and respond to situations. While many inventories have been developed to measure a plethora of such characteristics, there is considerable debate regarding the exact number of traits, or factors, which can be charted reliably. Kline (1993) identified what he termed the 'big five' as extroversion, neuroticism (or anxiety), toughmindedness, conscientiousness and open-mindedness, whereas Cattell (1995) has argued strongly for the validity of his '16PF' inventory which identifies sixteen such factors. Traits can be viewed as representing naturally occurring goal tensions within individuals. For example, extroversion–introversion represents the tension between wanting to meet and socialise with others on the one hand and the desire to have peace and quiet and be alone on the other. It would seem that while traits are not universally reliable in predicting behaviour they are most useful in predictions of individual behaviour across similar situations (Miller *et al.*, 1994).

However, there is no clear indication about what exactly the determinants of personality are. Although a combination of hereditary and prenatal factors is contributory, experiences in infancy and early childhood seem to play a vital shaping role. Furthermore, while personality is relatively stable, it can and does change as a result of experiences throughout the lifespan. We need to interact with others for a period of time before making judgements about their personality. Yet, even before we actually talk to others, we make a number of inferences about them based upon 'how they look'. Such judgements can markedly affect the goals we pursue, our motivation to open an interaction, the way in which we perceive the actions of others and how we respond to them. Therefore, it is necessary to take account of those aspects of the individual which are immediately visible, namely gender, age and appearance.

Gender

During social interaction we tend to respond differently to, and have differing expectations about, the behaviour of people depending upon whether they are male or female. This is not culture-specific, since 'All known cultures specify that male–female is a fundamental distinction ... (and) ... associate men and women with different sets of characteristic features and with different sets of behavioural expectations' (Eckes, 1994, p. 107). From an early age, sexual differences are signalled by the ways in which infants are dressed, and responded to, by adults. These gender stereotypes proliferate in child rearing, with children being reminded of gender role expectations in phrases such as 'Big boys don't cry' or 'That's not very lady-like'. Such practices inevitably contribute towards later differences in behaviour, and expectations thereof. However, the extent to which gender differences in behaviour are innate or learned remains unclear, although it is likely that both nature and nurture play a part in shaping later gender response patterns (Jacklin, 1992).

In Western society, males are more likely to be viewed positively if they are regarded as being competent, assertive and rational, with the ideal American male being one who is silent, strong, controlled and logical; females are generally more likely to be highly valued if they display traits such as gentleness, warmth and tact (Mader and Mader, 1993). With ongoing emphasis upon equal opportunities, and the growing numbers of women entering what were formerly regarded as male professions, it will be interesting to note to what extent such values persist. A high degree of gender segregation exists within the labour market and this seems to be very resistant to change (Scott, 1994).

Differences have been reported in studies of non-verbal behaviour, with some of the common trends being that women smile more frequently, require less interpersonal space, gesture less, touch and are touched more, use a greater number of head nods and engage in more eye contact but stare less than males (Hughes, 1994). In addition, there is strong evidence that women are much more skilled than men at both encoding and decoding non-verbal behaviour (Borisoff and Merrill, 1991).

Gender variations have also been reported in several aspects of language (Swann, 1992; Mader and Mader, 1993), with women using more of the following:

- Tag questions ('... isn't it?', '... don't you think?');
- Compound requests ('If you wouldn't mind, could you open that door?' rather than 'Open that door');
- Hedges or qualifiers ('perhaps', maybe', 'somewhat');
- Disclaimers ('I'm no expert on economics, but ...', 'I may be mistaken, however ...');
- Intensifiers ('truly', vastly', 'such');
- Fillers ('like', 'you know', 'ummm').

However, in their analysis of this area, Giles and Street (1994) highlighted the fact that there are many inconsistencies in the findings of studies into gender differences in verbal and non-verbal behaviour, concluding that 'when differences do exist, they likely reflect sex-preferential tendencies rather than sex-exclusive tendencies' (p. 113). In other words, some females *choose* to behave in what is regarded within their particular culture as a feminine style. This is probably because males or females who deviate markedly from their expected sex role behaviour are likely to encounter problems during social interaction. In this sense, the study of gender needs to take account of not only biological make-up but also psychological make-up. As a personality factor, gender can be divided into the following four categories:

	High femininity	**Low femininity**
High masculinity	Androgynous	Masculine
Low masculinity	Feminine	Indeterminate

In this way, a *feminine* female is likely, in various situations, to behave differently from a *masculine* female. Research bearing such psychological gender characteristics in mind will be more fruitful in charting actual behavioural variants of performance.

Age

The age of those with whom we interact will also influence our behaviour and expectations (Aiken, 1994). Although people often attempt to camouflage their actual age, this is one dimension of others which we can usually estimate with a high degree of accuracy (Hargie and Dickson, 1991). Generally, mature professionals are often viewed as being more competent, whereas the newly qualified professional may find difficulty in inspiring confidence in clients. In this way, expectations are held about others based upon age. The neophyte professional may be regarded as 'still wet behind the ears'; an older person wearing trendy fashions may be seen as an 'old fool' or 'mutton dressed as lamb'; while 'Act your age!' is an instruction given to even very young children.

A problem age for most people appears to be late adolescence and early adulthood, when the individual is still developing a self-image, going through the transition from childhood into adulthood, trying to establish a career and position in society, searching for a mate or coping with the demands of a young family. It is at this stage that problems such as drug addiction, schizophrenia and anorexia nervosa tend to be most prevalent.

There is increasing research into patterns of interpersonal communication in older adulthood, which has shown that, despite the often publicised problems of the elderly, there are both positive and negative interactional aspects to the ageing process (Hummert *et al.*, 1994). Indeed, Gergen and Gergen (1981, p.486), in considering research in this field, concluded that 'The greatest life satisfaction is experienced by individuals who are approximately seventy years old. Although satisfaction declines after the age of seventy, it never reaches the low experienced by people in their twenties and thirties'.

However, following a review of this area, Snyder and Miene (1994, p. 64) concluded that 'attitudes about the elderly are more negative than those about younger people'. Snyder and Miene identified four positive and eight negative research stereotypes of the elderly as follows:

> **Positive**   John Wayne conservative; liberal matriarch/patriarch; perfect grandparent; sage.
> **Negative**   Despondent; mildly impaired; severely impaired; vulnerable; shrew/curmudgeon; recluse; nosy neighbour; bag lady/vagrant.

The possession of negative stereotypes of the elderly can lead younger adults to adopt a speech style which has been variously described as 'secondary baby talk', 'elderspeak', or 'patronising speech'. This pattern includes the presence of simplification strategies (e.g. slower delivery, low grammatical difficulty), and clarification strategies (e.g. increased volume, deliberate articulation). Such patterns, as well as being demeaning, may actually have negative effects on the self-identity of the elderly persons to whom they are directed and, with the 'frail elderly', upon their attitudes towards illness (Taylor, 1994).

Appearance

The physical appearance of others, in terms of body size, shape and attractiveness, also affects our behaviour and expectations. As Stewart *et al.* (1979) illustrated, people are judged upon their appearance from a very early age, so that nursery school children have been shown to exhibit an aversion to chubby individuals and a greater liking for physically attractive peers.

Attractiveness is a very important feature in social encounters. A range of research studies has shown that individuals who are rated as attractive are seen as being more popular, intelligent, friendly and interesting to talk to. They have also been found to receive higher grades in school, date more frequently, be more likely to secure employment and earn more when in work, and are less likely to be found guilty in court. While they are also seen as more vain, materialistic and likely to have extramarital affairs, it remains the case that 'on the whole, we seem to equate beauty with goodness' (Saks and Krupat, 1988, p. 256). Ratings of physical attractiveness are fairly consistent across variations in age, gender, socio-economic status and geographical location. Aronson (1988) argued that cross-cultural agreement about ratings of attractiveness have been influenced by popular culture, with children being raised on a diet of Disney cartoon characters, Ken and Barbie dolls, scream-dream pop stars and TV soaps. There are clear features of attractiveness therein, such as the females as portrayed by Cinderella or Snow White with small faces, clear complexions, thin figures and large eyes. It is not surprising, then, that research has shown cross-cultural agreement regarding facial features of attractiveness in young adult females as including larger eyes relative to size of face, higher cheek bones and thinner jaw, as well as shorter distance between nose and mouth and between mouth and chin (Perret *et al.*, 1994). The male physique rated as attractive by females includes being tall, slim, with medium-thin lower trunk and medium-wide upper trunk, having small buttocks, thin legs and a flat stomach (Argyle, 1988).

Cook (1977, p. 323), in an analysis of interpersonal attraction, pointed out: 'In most but not all relationships people look for someone who is attracted to them. ... A relatively unattractive or unpopular person who tries to make friends with – or a sexual partner of – someone much more attractive or popular is likely to suffer a rebuff.' One example of this is the finding that we tend to marry those at the same level of physical attractiveness as ourselves. However, more recent research and theory into the study of attraction has emphasised how initial judgements of attractiveness can be tempered by psychological, sociological, contextual and relational influences (Duck, 1995). As such, attractiveness involves more than physical features and is not just 'skin deep'. For instance, a physically unattractive professional may be successful and popular with clients by developing an empathic interactive style coupled with a competent professional approach.

Physique can also influence how others are perceived and reacted to. Some tentative conclusions can be gleaned from research findings in this area: ectomorphs (thin figure) tend to be seen as tidy, quiet and tense; mesomorphs (muscular) as strong, healthy, adventurous and forceful; and endomorphs (fat) as warm-hearted, agreeable, good natured, sympathetic and dependent on others (Richmond *et al.*, 1991). While it is clear that we do make judgements about people on the basis of their body shape, studies reporting these findings have tended to concentrate on extreme stereotypes, and do not really consider variations of these types. For example, a female with large breasts but a slim waist would not necessarily provoke the stereotype of an endomorph. Height is another significant element, particularly in relation to judgements of males. Taller men tend to achieve more in our society in terms of occupational indices such as promotion and salary, and social indices such as dating. Furthermore, higher status males tend to be viewed as taller in direct proportion to their status (regardless of actual height). While research evidence in relation to the effects of height of females is rather scanty, it does seem that, for many women, being tall is often regarded as a deficit, since 'short men and tall women have problems in date or mate selection ... when adolescent boys are worried about their height, they are worried by their shortness, whereas adolescent girls who worry about height are concerned by their tallness' (Stewart *et al.*, 1979, p. 215).

Although one of the prime functions of clothes is to protect the wearer from cold or injury, dress also serves a number of social functions (Hargie *et al.*, 1994). The importance of social signals conveyed by apparel is evidenced by the amount of money spent on fashion wear in Western society. This is because in many situations, it is very important to 'look the part'. Indeed, people spend a great deal of time in stores choosing clothes which will 'suit them' and allow them to send the appropriate messages to others. Dress provides us with information concerning the wearer's gender, group membership, individual identity, personality, status and occupation. Most professionals have either a formal or informal uniform, which often facilitates identification (for example, the nurse in hospital), or one that is chosen as a symbol of professional image (the businessman's three-piece suit).

Socially skilled people devote time and effort to the selection of appropriate apparel for interpersonal encounters in order to project a suitable image. We carefully 'dress up' for important occasions such as selection interviews or first dates. In addition, we also carefully select other embellishments including 'body furniture' (rings, bangles, necklaces, brooches, ear-rings, watches, hair ribbons or bands), spectacles, and make-up, to enhance our overall personal image. Since so much attention is devoted to the choice of dress, it is hardly surprising that we make judgements about others based upon this feature. In terms of impression management, it is patently advisable to dress with care! Eicher and Kelley (1972), in a study of high school girls, found that it was dress first, then personality, then common interests that influenced decisions about pursual of friendships. Therefore, it would appear that the way we dress can act as a powerful signal, providing information to others about the types of people we are.

The situation

Argyle *et al.* (1981, p. 3), in defining a social situation as 'the sum of the features of the behaviour system, for the duration of a social encounter', identified several core features.

Goal structure

As noted earler in this chapter and in Chapter 1, goals represent a central aspect of skill. The goals which we seek will be influenced by the situation in which we are interacting, while, conversely, the goals we pursue also help to determine the situations in which we choose to interact. Thus, in the surgery the doctor will have goals directly related to dealing with patients. However, if the doctor has a 'social' goal of finding a mate, social situations in which available members of the opposite sex are likely to be encountered will be sought.

In this way, goals and situations are intertwined. Most professional contexts have specific goal structures comprising primary goals and related secondary goals. A doctor wishing to make a diagnosis (primary goal) will have to obtain a set of answers to structured questions (secondary goals). A knowledge of the goal structure for any situation is an important aspect of skilled performance.

Roles

In any given situation, people will play, and be expected to play, different roles, which carry with them sets of expectations about behaviour, attitudes, feelings and values. Thus, a doctor is expected to behave in a thorough, caring fashion, to be concerned about patients' health and to treat their problems in confidence. A central feature of training in any profession is that the trainee is expected to learn in detail the duties associated with the role of that particular profession. We will, of course, play different roles from one situation to another – for example, from that of manager at work to parent or spouse at home. We can also play more than one role in the same situation: if we are entertaining friends at home we may be expected to play the roles of host, spouse, friend and parent. The roles of those involved will affect both the goals and behaviour of participants. For example, a teacher will behave differently, and have different goals, when teaching pupils in the classroom, attending a staff meeting at lunch-time, or having an interview with the Principal about possible promotion.

Rules

Social interaction has been likened to a game, involving rules which must be followed if a successful outcome is to be achieved. The main difference is that games involve explicit rules whereas, for the most part, social interaction involves implicit rules (although in more formal interactions, such as debates, there may be explicit rules). Examples of breaking the implicit rules would include refusing to answer any questions at all at a selection interview, singing loudly in the cinema, or wearing a bathing suit to church. Professionals must not only be aware of the rules of the situations which they encounter, but also of how to deal with clients who break them (for example, pupils misbehaving in the classroom). One interesting general rule to do with the use of time is that higher status people expect those of lower status to wait for them, but not vice versa. For instance, in the health context Frankenberg (1988) illustrated how consultants expect lower status professionals and patients to wait but do not expect to be kept waiting themselves.

Repertoire of elements

Different types of behaviour will be more or less appropriate in different situations and, therefore, it is important for professionals to develop a range of behavioural repertoires. By developing as wide a repertoire as possible, the professional will more readily cope with a variety of clients. So in one situation fact-finding may be crucial and the skill of questioning will be central, while in another situation it may be necessary to explain carefully certain facts to a client. These behavioural repertoires are usually sequential in nature (see Chapter 1, p. 18).

Concepts

A certain amount of conceptual information is necessary for effective participation in any given situation. In order to play the game of poker, one must be aware of the concepts of 'full house', 'flush' and 'run'. Similarly, a patient visiting the dentist may need to be aware of the concepts of 'filling', 'crown' or 'bridge'. However, a common error which many professionals make is to assume that patients are familiar with concepts when, in fact, they are not. Most professionals have developed a jargon of specific terminology for various concepts, and must ensure that it is either avoided or fully explained when dealing with clients.

Skills and difficulties

The nature of the task being performed is another central consideration: if it is simple and pleasant then it can be executed with ease, but is likely to cause difficulties if it is unpleasant or complex. Within any particular profession there will be some tasks which are more difficult than others, and certain professional situations will cause particular difficulties that require specific skills. Dealing with aggressive clients, counselling terminally ill patients and their relatives, teaching children with learning disabilities, or making a formal business presentation, are all situations which require detailed preparation, in terms of the difficulties that these situations present and the skills and strategies appropriate for handling them.

Language and speech

There are linguistic variations associated with social situations, with some requiring a higher degree of language formality than others. Giving a lecture, being interviewed on television or chairing a committee meeting all usually involve a more formal, deliberate, elaborated use of language than, for example, having a chat with a friend over coffee. Equally, changes in tone, pitch and volume of voice change across situations: there are vocal patterns associated with evangelical clergymen addressing religious gatherings, barristers summing up in court and sports commentators describing ball games. Professionals need to develop and refine their language and speech to suit a particular context.

Physical environment

The nature of the environment will influence the behaviour of individuals. Humans, like all animals, feel more secure on 'home territory' than in unfamiliar environs. Thus, a social worker will tend to find clients more at ease in their own homes than in the office, whereas the social worker will probably be more comfortable in the latter situation. People also tend to feel more comfortable, and therefore talk more freely, in 'warm' environments (soft seats, concealed lights, carpets, curtains, pot plants). The physical layout of furniture is also important in either encouraging or discouraging interaction. The organisation and preparation of the physical environment is, therefore, a feature of situations which professionals should consider in relation to interactions with clients.

Culture

One key contextual dimension pertains to cultural milieu. Few aspects of the communication process have attracted as much attention within the past decade as the study of culture. Bantz (1994, p. 183) explained the reason for this interest as being that 'With a richer comprehension of culture and its relationship to communication (and communication research), we will more adequately understand communication as practiced in our world'. Culture can be defined as 'a pattern of meanings (beliefs, attitudes, values) that influence the way a specific group of people interact and relate to one another' (Mader and Mader, 1993, p. 361); it is 'a *set of values* which are shared by a group . . . . The values are learned by members of the group, and hence taught by other members' (Mead, 1990, p. 14). Thus, culture is passed down from one generation to another and, while not static, is a stable system within which people negotiate identity and relationships (Fitch and Sanders, 1994). Furthermore, in discussing the problems of communication in a multicultural society, Ivey (1994, p. 12) highlighted how 'any group that differs from the "mainstream" of society can be considered a subculture', and the actions of individuals will be more readily understood in the light of subcultural influences.

A common broad distinction made is between *collectivist* and *individualistic* cultures. Eastern cultures (e.g. Japan, China, Korea) tend to be collectivist and *high-context*, in that much of the communicative meaning is implicit and attached to relationships and situations rather than to what is said. The style of communication is more indirect and self-concealing, with the result that verbal messages can be ambiguous. These cultures foster an *interdependent self* with high value placed upon external features such as roles, status, relationships, 'fitting in', being accorded one's proper place, being aware of what others are thinking and feeling, not hurting the other's feelings and minimising imposition when presenting requests (Kim, 1994). Time is conceived as being subservient to duties, relationships and responsibilities.

Western cultures (e.g. USA, UK, Canada, Germany, Norway) are *low-context*, with an emphasis upon open, direct communication with explicit meaning, so that verbal messages tend to be clearer, more complete, specific and pointed. There is a discomfort with ambiguity, and anxiety when meaning depends upon something other than the words uttered. These cultures encourage the development of an *independent self* that is bounded, unitary, stable and detached from social context, with a consequent focus upon internal abilities, thoughts and feelings, expressing oneself and one's uniqueness, and being 'up front'. Goals tend to be more personal and instrumental, and time is seen as paramount – being viewed as akin to a commodity which can be 'spent', 'saved', 'invested' or 'wasted'.

Collectivist cultures therefore inculcate a 'We' identity as opposed to an 'I' identity in individualist cultures. This can be illustrated by comparing the Korean proverb, 'Better to die rather than to live in dishonour/disgrace', with the American saying, 'Give me liberty or give me death'. When asked what they look for in possible marriage partners, 'respondents from individualist societies tend to stress the personality of a desired mate, whereas those from collectivist cultures are more likely to mention such socially valued characteristics as a greater earning potential or social status' (Goodwin, 1995, p. 74). Put another way, an American is likely to ask 'What does my heart say?' and a Chinese 'What will other people say?' Cultural differences have also been found in style of request, between direct forms ('Close that window'), indirect forms ('It's getting cold') and those in between

('Would it be OK to have the window closed?'). Kim and Wilson (1994), for example, found that American undergraduates considered the direct style as the most effective way of making a request whereas Korean undergraduates rated it as the least effective strategy. Furthermore, the American sample saw clarity as a key dimension of successful requests while Koreans viewed clarity as counter-productive to effectiveness. The potential for cross-cultural collisions in requesting is obviously high!

Cultural differences have also been charted in the workplace (Pepper, 1995). Japanese firms are often an extension of the family to which employees are very loyal and in return receive high levels of job security. In Britain, more focus is placed on personal career, which may entail company-hopping. As a result, British companies are more loath to spend money on training than their Japanese counterparts, as this may be a wasted investment. Also, managers in Britain are reluctant to become involved in the personal lives of employees, whereas the same restriction does not hold in Japan (Tayeb, 1994).

However, Singelis and Brown (1995) pointed out that while cultural experiences influence the development of self-image, notions of individualistic and collectivist persons are prototypes at opposite ends of a continuum. They noted how 'studies demonstrate that these two selves coexist to varying degrees within individuals . . . both exist as tendencies of a greater or lesser intensity' (p. 358). Thus, at different times, in different situations, and with different people, we may adopt either an individualistic or a more collectivist style of communicating.

As a more general concept, Brown and Starkey (1994) described culture as a pattern of meanings inherited from the past which provides a means for interpreting the present. Culture in this sense refers to the traditional way of behaving in any particular context. Brown and Starkey illustrated how when 'the culture' of an organisation changes employees no longer have a template for interpreting the present and so uncertainty increases. At such times of change, staff need as much information as possible to help them to 'read' current trends.

The relationship between the individual and the impinging culture is crucial. As noted by Ivey (1994, p. 12) 'individuals differ as much as or more than do cultures. You will want to attune your responses to the unique human being before you'. Ivey and Authier (1978), in recognising the importance of what they termed the cultural-environmental-context, highlighted the role of *cultural expertise* which they defined as the ability 'to communicate with a maximum number of individuals within a particular cultural setting' (p. 224). An example of cultural expertise is contained in the old adage 'When in Rome do as the Romans do'. It also necessitates the development of a knowledge and understanding of the cultural and sub-cultural norms, beliefs, values and responses of those with whom we are interacting. Being a skilled person includes the possession of a high level of cultural expertise.

OVERVIEW

The model described in this chapter has been designed to account for the central facets of interpersonal interaction. It will be apparent from this review that interaction between people is a complex process. Any interpersonal encounter involves a myriad variables, some or all of which may be operative at any given time. Although each of these has been discussed in isolation, it should be realised that in reality many occur simultaneously. Communication is, in this sense, *transactional* in that: 'We encode and send messages while we are decoding and receiving other messages. We are not sources, then receivers, then sources, then receivers. We are both participants involved in a communication event – affecting and affected by one another, functioning continuously and simultaneously' (Rhodes, 1993, p. 225). People in social encounters are therefore interdependent, and as information is perceived it is immediately dealt with and responded to, on an ongoing basis, so quickly that we are not usually aware that these processes are occurring. A key feature of skilled performance is that we behave for the most part at this subconscious level.

Given the number of factors which influence the behaviour of individuals during social interaction, it is extremely difficult to make judgements or interpretations about the exact reasons why certain behaviours are, or are not, displayed. Indeed, Stephen (1994) urged communication scholars to take cognisance of historical and societal variables, since the study of interpersonal interaction is an ongoing journey in which, across time and cultures, differing patterns of behaviour need to be mapped. The model as presented in this chapter provides a systematic structure for analysing human behaviour. It has taken account of the key processes involved in interpersonal communication, namely the goals which people pursue, and their motivation to pursue them; the cognitive and affective processes which influence the processing of information; the feedback available during social encounters; the perception of this feedback; personal and contextual factors; and the social responses which people make.

While some of the features of the extended model of interpersonal interaction (Figure 2.3) are the same as those contained in the motor skills model (Figure 2.2), there are also differences. In particular, the reciprocal nature of social interaction, the role of emotions, the nature of person perception and the influence of the person–situation context, are more impactful during social, as opposed to motor, skill performance. However, it can be argued that the analogy between motor and social skills has proved to be useful in providing a basic foundation upon which to build a theoretical framework for interpreting interpersonal interaction.

The extended model also illustrates how communication breakdown can occur at any of the interrelated stages. For instance, an individual's *goals* may be unrealistic or inappropriate, or communicators may have competing, irreconcilable goals. At the *mediation* level, the person may suffer from *disordered thought processes*, may have underdeveloped schemas, or may be lacking in emotional empathy. Problems may also occur because inappropriate *responses* are used, or because the person has poor *perceptual* acumen and cannot make use of available *feedback* from others. Breakdown may be a factor of the *person–situation* axis, due to cultural insensitivity, or inappropriate personality characteristics (e.g. someone who is highly neurotic is unlikely to be a good counsellor). The model has also been shown to provide a valuable template for research investigations which have been carried out in the fields of health care (Skipper, 1992), negotiation (Hughes, 1994), and counselling (Irving, 1995).

The main focus in this chapter has been upon the application of the main interactive processes involved in dyadic interaction. When more than two people are involved, although the same processes apply, interaction becomes even more complex and certainly much more difficult to represent diagrammatically. Despite the increased complexity (in terms of differing goals, motivation, and so on), a knowledge of these central processes will facilitate attempts to understand, and make sense of, the behaviour of the individual in both group or dyadic interaction.

REFERENCES

Aiken, L. R. (1994) *Aging: An Introduction to Gerontology*, Sage, Thousand Oaks.

Annett, J. (1969) *Feedback and Human Behaviour*, Penguin, Harmondsworth.

Argyle, M. (1967) *The Psychology of Interpersonal Behaviour*, Penguin, Harmondsworth.

—— (1972) *The Psychology of Interpersonal Behaviour* (2nd edn), Penguin, Harmondsworth.

—— (1988) *Bodily Communication* (2nd edn), Methuen, London.

—— (1994) *The Psychology of Interpersonal Behaviour* (5th edn), Penguin, London.

——, Furnham, A. and Graham, J. (1981) *Social Situations*, Cambridge University Press, Cambridge.

Aronson, E. (1988) *The Social Animal* (5th edn), W. H. Freeman, New York.

Averill, J. (1975) 'A Semantic Atlas of Emotional Concepts', *JSAS Catalogue of Selected Documents in Psychology*, 5, 330.

Bantz, C. (1994) 'Editor's Note', *Communication Monographs*, 61, 183.

Bentley, S. C. (1993) 'Listening and Memory', in A. Wolvin and C. Coakley (eds), *Perspectives on Listening*, Ablex, Norwood, NJ.

Berger, C. (1987) 'Communicating Under Uncertainty', in M. Roloff and G. Miller (eds), *Interpersonal Processes: New Directions In Communication Research*, Sage, Newbury Park.

Berscheid, E. (1983) 'Emotion', in H. Kelley, E. Berscheid, A. Christensen *et al.* (eds), *Close Relationships*, W. H. Freeman, New York.

Bindra, D. and Stewart, J. (eds) (1971) *Motivation* (2nd edn), Penguin, Harmondsworth.

Blanck, P. D. (ed.) (1993) *Interpersonal Expectations: Theory, Research and Applications*, Cambridge University Press, Cambridge.

Borisoff, D. and Merrill, L. (1991) 'Gender Issues and Listening', in D. Borisoff and M. Purdy (eds), *Listening in Everyday Life* , University of America Press, Maryland.

Brown, A. and Starkey, K. (1994) 'The Effect of Organizational Culture on Communication and Information', *Journal of Management Studies*, 31, 807–28.

Bruner, J. and Tagiuri, R. (1954) 'The Perception of People', in G. Lindzey (ed.), *Handbook of Social Psychology*, Addison-Wesley, Reading, MA.

Buck, R. (1988) *Human Motivation and Emotion* (2nd edn), John Wiley, New York.

Bush, L. E. (1972) 'Empirical Selection of Adjectives Denoting Feelings', *JSAS Catalogue of Selected Documents in Psychology*, 2, 67.

Carlson, N. R. (1990) *Psychology* (3rd edn), Allyn & Bacon, Boston.

Cattell, R. B. (1995) 'The Fallacy of Five Factors in the Personality Sphere', *The Psychologist*, 8, 207–8.

Chaudhuri, A. and Buck, R. (1995) 'Affect, Reason and Persuasion Advertising Strategies that Predict Affective and Analytic-cognitive Responses', *Human Communication Research*, 21, 422–41.

Clore, G. L., Ortony, A. and Foss, M. A. (1987) 'The Psychological Foundations of the Affective Lexicon', *Journal of Personality and Social Psychology*, 53, 751–66.

Cook, M. (1977) 'The Social Skill Model and Interpersonal Attraction', in S. Duck (ed.), *Theory and Practice in Interpersonal Attraction*, Academic Press, London.

—— (1979) *Perceiving Others*, Methuen, London.

De Vito, J. (1994) *Human Communication: The Basic Course* (6th edn), HarperCollins, New York.

Dickson, D. A., Hargie, O. D. W. and Morrow, N. C. (1989) *Communication Skills Training for Health Professionals: An Instructor's Handbook*, Chapman & Hall, London.

—— (1997) *Communication Skills Training for Health Professionals* (2nd edn), Chapman & Hall, London.

Duck, S. (1995) 'Repelling the Study of Attraction', *The Psychologist*, 8, 60–3.

Eckes, T. (1994) Features of Men, Features of Women: Assessing Stereotypic Beliefs about Gender Subtypes', *British Journal of Social Psychology*, 33, 107–23.

Eicher, J. and Kelley, J. (1972) 'High School as a Meeting Place', *Michigan Journal of Secondary Education*, 13, 12–16.

Fiedler, K. (1993) 'Constructive Processes in Person Cognition', *British Journal of Social Psychology*, 32, 349–64.

Fitch, K. and Sanders, R. (1994) 'Culture, Communication, and Preference for Directness in Expression of Preferences', *Communication Theory*, 4, 219–45.

Fitts, P. and Posner, M. (1973) *Human Performance*, Prentice-Hall, London.

Forgas, J. P. (1994) 'The Role of Emotion in Social Judgments: An Introductory Review and an Affect Infusion Model', *Journal of Social Psychology*, 24, 1–24.

Frankenberg, R. (1988) '"Your Time or Mine?" An Anthropological View of the Tragic Temporal Contradictions of Biomedical Practice', *International Journal of Health Services*, 18, 11–34.

Frijda, N. (1986) *The Emotions*, Cambridge University Press, Cambridge.

Furnham, A. (1983) 'Research in Social Skills Training: A Critique', in R. Ellis and D. Whittington (eds), *New Directions in Social Skill Training*, Croom Helm, Beckenham.

Fyock, J. and Stangor, C. (1994) 'The Role of Memory Biases in Stereotype Maintenance', *British Journal of Social Psychology*, 33, 331–43.

Gallois, C. (1993) 'Prologue', *Journal of Language and Social Psychology*, 12, 3–12.

Gergen, K. and Gergen, M. (1981) *Social Psychology*, Harcourt Brace Jovanovich, New York.

Giles, H. and Street, R. L. (1994) 'Communication Characteristics and Behavior', in M. Knapp and G. Miller (eds), *Handbook of Interpersonal Communication* (2nd edn), Sage, Thousand Oaks.

Goodwin, R. (1995) 'Personal Relationships Across Cultures', *The Psychologist*, 8, 73–5.

Greene, J. O. (1988) 'Cognitive Processes: Methods for Probing the Black Box', in C. H. Tardy (ed.), *A Handbook for the Study of Human Communication*, Ablex Publishing Co., Norwood, N.J.

Hargie, O. and Dickson D. (1991) 'Video-mediated Judgements of Personal Characteristics Based upon Nonverbal Cues', *Journal of Educational Television*, 17, 31–43.

Hargie, O., Saunders, C. and Dickson, D. (1994) *Social Skills in Interpersonal Communication* (3rd edn), Routledge, London.

Heath, R. L. and Bryant, J. (1992) *Human Communication Theory and Research: Concepts, Contexts and Challenges*, Lawrence Erlbaum, Hillsdale, NJ.

Hinton, P. R. (1993) *The Psychology of Interpersonal Perception*, Routledge, London.

Hughes, K. (1994) 'An Investigation into Nonverbal Behaviours Associated with Deception/Concealment during a Negotiation Process', DPhil. thesis, University of Ulster, Jordanstown.

Hummert, M. L., Wiemann, J. W. and Nussbaum, J. F. (1994) *Interpersonal Communication in Older Adulthood: Interdisciplinary Theory and Research*, Sage, Thousand Oaks.

Irving, P. (1995) 'A Reconceptualisation of Rogerian Core Conditions of Facilitative Communication: Implications for Training', DPhil. thesis, University of Ulster, Jordanstown.

Ivey, A. (1994) *Intentional Interviewing and Counseling: Facilitating Client Development in a Multicultural Society* (3rd edn), Brooks/Cole, Pacific Grove.

—— and Authier, J. (1978) *Microcounseling: Innovations in Interviewing, Counseling, Psychotherapy and Psychoeducation*, C. C. Thomas, Springfield, Illinois.

Izard, C. E. (1977) *Human Emotions*, Plenum Press, New York.

Jacklin, C. N. (ed.) (1992) *The Psychology of Gender: Vols 1–4*, Edward Elgar, Cheltenham.

James, W. (1884) 'What is Emotion?', *Mind*, 4, 188–204.

Jones, E. E. (1990) *Interpersonal Perception*, W. H. Freeman, New York.

Kikuchi, T. (1994) 'Effects of Backchannel Convergence on a Speaker's Speech Rate and Track-checking Behavior', paper presented at the Annual Conference of the International Communication Association, Sydney, 11–15 July.

Kim, M. (1994) 'Cross-cultural Comparisons of the Perceived Importance of Conversational Constraints', *Human Communication Research*, 21, 128–51.

—— and Wilson, S. R. (1994) 'A Cross-cultural Comparison of Implicit Theories of Requesting', *Communication Monographs*, 61, 210–35.

Kline, P. (1993) *Personality: The Psychometric View*, Routledge, London.

Knapp, M., Miller, G. and Fudge, K. (1994), 'Background and Current Trends in the Study of Interpersonal Communication', in M. Knapp and G. Miller (eds), *Handbook of Interpersonal Communication* (2nd edn), Sage, Thousand Oaks.

Kreps, G. L. and Kunimoto, E. N. (1994) *Effective Communication in Multicultural Health Care Settings*, Sage, Thousand Oaks.

Levy, R. (1974) 'Tahiti, Sin and the Question of Integration Between Personality and Sociocultural Systems', in R. A. Le Vine (ed.), *Culture and Personality*, Aldine, Chicago.

Locke, E. A. and Latham, G. P. (1990) *A Theory of Goal Setting and Task Performance*, Prentice Hall, Englewood Cliffs, NJ.

Lundsteen, S. W. (1993) 'Metacognitive Listening', in A. Wolvin and C. Coakley (eds), *Perspectives on Listening*, Ablex, Norwood, NJ.

McFall, A. (1982) 'A Review and Reformulation of the Concept of Social Skills', *Behavioural Assessment*, 4, 1–3.3.

McLaren, M. (1994) 'Hofstede Revisited: New Zealand Culture as Revealed in a Series of Critical Incidents', paper presented at the Annual Conference of the International Communication Association, Sydney, 11–15 July.

Mader, T. E. and Mader, D. C. (1993) *Understanding One Another: Communicating Interpersonally*, W. C. Brown, Madison, Wisconsin.

Maslow, A. (1954) *Motivation and Personality*, Harper & Row, New York.

Mathews, A. (1993) 'Biases in Processing Emotional Information', *The Psychologist*, 6, 493–9.

Mead, R. (1990) *Cross-Cultural Management Communication*, John Wiley, Chichester.

Metts, S. and Bowers, J. (1994) 'Emotion in Interpersonal Communication', in M. Knapp and G. Miller (eds), *Handbook of Interpersonal Communication* (2nd edn), Sage, Thousand Oaks.

Millar, R., Crute, V. and Hargie, O. (1992) *Professional Interviewing*, Routledge, London.

Miller, L. C., Cody, M. J. and McLaughlin, M. L. (1994) 'Situations and Goals as Fundamental Constructs in Interpersonal Communication Research', in M. Knapp and G. Miller (eds), *Handbook of Interpersonal Communication* (2nd edn), Sage, Thousand Oaks.

Mischel, W. (1993) *Introduction to Personality* (5th edn), Harcourt Brace Jovanovich, Fort Worth.

Neisser, U. (1967) *Cognitive Psychology*, Appleton-Century Crofts, New York.

Norton, R. (1983) *Communicator Style: Theory, Application and Measures*, Sage, Beverly Hills.

O'Keefe, B. and Lambert, B. (1993) 'Managing the Flow of Ideas: A Local Management Approach to Message Design', *Communication Yearbook*, 18, 543–82.

Orton, Y. A. and Turner, T. J. (1990) 'What's Basic About Basic Emotions?', *Psychological Review*, 97, 315–31.

Parkinson, B. (1995) *Ideas and Realities of Emotion*, Routledge, London.

Pendleton, D. and Furnham, A. (1980) 'A Paradigm for Applied Social Psychological Research', in W. Singleton, P. Spurgeon and R. Stammers (eds), *The Analysis of Social Skill*, Plenum Press, New York.

Pepper, G. L. (1995) *Communicating in Organizations: A Cultural Approach*, McGraw-Hill, New York.

Perret, D. I., May, K. A. and Yoshikawa, S. (1994) 'Facial Shape and Judgements of Facial Attractiveness', *Nature*, 368, 239–42.

Phares, E. J. (1988) *Introduction to Personality* (2nd edn), Scott, Foresman & Co., Glenview, Illinois.

Rhodes, S. C. (1993) 'Listening: A Relational Process', in A. Wolvin and C. Coakley (eds), *Perspectives on Listening*, Ablex, Norwood, NJ.

Richmond, V. P., McCroskey, J. C. and Payne, S. K. (1991) *Nonverbal Behavior in Interpersonal Relations*, Prentice-Hall, Englewood Cliffs, NJ.

Rosenthal, R. and Jacobson, L. (1992) *Pygmalion in the Classroom*, Irvington, New York.

Roth I. (1976) *Social Perception*, Open University Press, Milton Keynes.

Roth I. and Bruce, V. (1995) *Perception and Representation: Current Issues* (2nd edn), Open University Press, Milton Keynes.

Saks, M.J. and Krupat, E. (1988) *Social Psychology and its Applications*, Harper & Row, New York.

Scott, A. (1994) *Gender Segregation and Social Change*, Oxford University Press, Oxford.

Serby, M. and Chobor, K. (eds) (1992) *Science of Olfaction*, Springer, New York.

Shaver, P., Schwartz, J., Kerson, D. and O'Connor, G. (1987) 'Emotion Knowledge. Further Exploration of a Prototype Approach', *Journal of Personality and Social Psychology*, 52, 1061–86.

Singelis, T. M. and Brown, W. J. (1995) 'Culture, Self and Collectivist Communication: Linking Culture to Individual Behavior', *Human Communication Research*, 21, 354–89.

Skipper, M. (1992) 'Communication Processes and their Effectiveness in the Management and Treatment of Dysphagia', DPhil. thesis, University of Ulster, Jordanstown.

Sloboda, J. (1986) 'What is Skill?', in A. Gellatly (ed.), *The Skilful Mind: An Introduction to Cognitive Psychology*, Open University Press, Milton Keynes.

Snyder, M. (1987) *Public Appearances Private Realities: The Psychology of Self-monitoring*, Freeman, New York.

—— and Miene, P. (1994) 'Stereotyping the Elderly: A Functional Approach', *British Journal of Social Psychology*, 33, 63–82.

Stephen, T. (1994) 'Communication in the Shifting Context of Intimacy: Marriage, Meaning and Modernity', *Communication Theory*, 4, 191–218.

Stewart, R., Powell, G. and Chetwynd, S. (1979) *Person Perception and Stereotyping*, Saxon House, Farnborough.

Swann, J. (1992) *Girls, Boys and Language*, Basil Blackwell, Oxford.

Tayeb, M. (1994) 'Japanese Managers and British Culture: A Comparative Case Study', *The International Review of Human Resource Management*, 5, 145–66.

Taylor B. C. (1994) 'Frailty, Language, and Elderly Identity: Interpretive and Critical Perspectives on the Aging Subject', in M. L. Hummert, J. W. Wiemann and J. F. Nussbaum (eds), *Interpersonal Communication in Older Adulthood: Interdisciplinary Theory and Research*, Sage, Thousand Oaks.

Thompson, B. (1993) 'Listening Disabilities: The Plight of Many', in A. Wolvin and C. Coakley (eds), *Perspectives on Listening*, Ablex, Norwood, NJ.

Warr, P. and Knapper, C. (1968) *The Perception of People and Events*, John Wiley, London.

Welford, A. (1965) 'Performance, Biological Mechanisms and Age: A Theoretical Sketch', in A. Welford and J. Birren (eds), *Behavior, Aging and the Nervous System*, C. C. Thomas, Illinois.

Wessler, R. (1984) 'Cognitive-Social Psychological Theories and Social Skills: A Review', in P. Trower (ed.), *Radical Approaches to Social Skills Training*, Croom Helm, Beckenham.

Witkin, B. R. (1993) 'Human Information Processing', in A. Wolvin and C. Coakley (eds), *Perspectives on Listening*, Ablex, Norwood, NJ.

Part II
Core communication skills

3 Non-verbal behaviour as communication

Richard M. Rozelle, Daniel Druckman and James C. Baxter

In this chapter, we survey a large cross-disciplinary literature on non-verbal communication. After placing the study of non-verbal behaviour in historical perspective, we highlight the major approaches that have guided scientific explorations. Non-verbal communication can be understood best in relation to the settings in which it occurs. Settings are defined both in terms of the varying roles taken by actors within societies and the diverse cultures in which expressions and gestures are learned. Based on an example of research conducted in a laboratory-simulation of international politics, we develop implications for the themes and techniques that can be used to guide analyses of behaviour as it occurs *in situ*.

NON-VERBAL BEHAVIOUR IN PERSPECTIVE

In recent years, it has become increasingly recognised that investigators in a field of inquiry – any field – bring personal perspectives and figurative comparisons to bear on their work. Such perspectives have been called paradigms, metaphors, or fundamental analogies, and their influence has been thought to be pervasive. Indeed, both philosophers and working scientists acknowledge the value and necessity of such processes in the realm of creative thought (Glashow, 1980; Koestler, 1964; Leary, 1990; Oppenheimer, 1956; Pepper, 1942).

Examples of this phenomenon abound. For instance, in psychology Gentner and Grudin (1985) undertook a review of a sample of theoretical contributions to the field published in *Psychological Review* between the years 1894 and 1975. From the sixty-eight theoretical articles they reviewed, they were able to identify 265 distinct mental metaphors. They defined a mental metaphor as 'a nonliteral comparison in which either the mind as a whole or some particular aspect of the mind (ideas, processes, etc.) is likened to or explained in terms of a nonliteral domain' (p. 182). These metaphors were all introduced by their contributors as ways of understanding the field. They were often based on explicit comparisons, such as James' 'stream of consciousness', but also were frequently based on subtly implied, extended comparisons only identifiable from broad sections of text. Gentner and Grudin identified four categories of analogy which characterised the period – spatial, animate-being, neural and systems metaphors – and found clear trends in metaphor preference and rates of usage over time.

Such an examination of the field of psychology is illuminating and provocative. Recognising that the use of different metaphors places different aspects of the field in relief and interrelation, and introduces different explanatory and predictive emphasis, one can identify remarkable shifts in the ways in which psychologists have thought about their subject matter. For example, the recent emphasis on systems metaphors suggests a focus on lawfully constrained interaction among elements where organisation, precision and mutuality of influence are stressed. Predictions are complex but specific, analysis is multifaceted and hierarchic. Fundamentally, such metaphors are thought to be constitutive of the subject matter we study (Gibbs, 1994; Soyland, 1994).

A number of contemporary cognitive scientists extended the analysis of metaphor and other linguistic forms (tropes), showing that they abound in everyday usage (even beyond scientific and creative discourse) and clearly reflect the presence of poetic aspects of mind (Gibbs, 1994; Jaynes, 1976; Lakoff, 1993; Lakoff and Johnson, 1980; Ortony, 1993). Linguistic forms such as metaphor, metonymy, irony and related expressions, point to our fundamental ability to conceptualise situations figuratively (e.g. non-literally) and transpose meaning across domains. Indeed, such complex processes are assumed to occur essentially automatically and unconsciously (Gibbs, 1994). Although such analyses have focused on linguistic expression, both oral and written, the role played by non-verbal aspects of language does not seem to have been examined explicitly.

Non-verbal behaviour as communication

A comparable examination of contributions to the field of non-verbal behaviour may be meaningful. To this end, it is interesting to note that attention has been directed at the meaningfulness of gesture and non-verbal behaviour since earliest recorded Western history (cf. Aristotle's *Poetics*; *Rhetoric*). According to Kendon (1981), Classical and Medieval works on rhetoric frequently focused on the actual conduct of the orator as he delivered his speech. They occasionally defined many forms of particular gestures and provided instructions for their use in creating planned effects in the audience.

At least as early as 1601, gesture as a medium of communication co-ordinate with vocal and written language was recognised by Francis Bacon (1884; 1947). He suggested that 'as the tongue speaketh to the ear, so the hand speaketh to the eye' (quoted in Kendon, 1981, p. 155). Subsequent analyses, inspired by Bacon's proposal, were undertaken to examine chirologia (manual language) as both a rhetorical and natural language form (Bulwer, 1644/1974). During the eighteenth and nineteenth centuries, scholars argued that emotional expression and gesture, the so-called 'natural languages', surely provided the foundation for the more refined and artificial verbal symbolic communication (e.g. Lavater, 1789; Taylor, 1878). Spiegel and Machotka (1974) have identified a collateral history in dance, mime and dramatic staging beginning in the late eighteenth century. Body movement as communication has been an analogy of broad and continuing interest.

In examining the focus on non-verbal behaviour as communication, a number of somewhat different analogies can be identified. Darwin (1872) focused on facial behaviour as a neuromuscular expression of emotion, vestiges of the past and informative of an inner affective state. A number of investigators have extended this approach and elaborated the *affective expression* metaphor (e.g. Ekman, 1992a; Ekman *et al.*, 1972; Izard, 1971; Tomkins, 1962, 1963; Woodworth and Schlosberg, 1954). In delineating bodily movement, gesture, vocalisation and particularly facial movement as expressive of affect, an emphasis is placed on the rapid, automatic, serviceable, universal aspects of behaviour. Indeed, consciousness, intention and guile are ordinarily not central to such an analysis, although experiential overlays and culturally modified forms of expression are of interest. In examining how readily people recognise affective displays in others (Ekman and Oster, 1979; Hager and Ekman, 1979; Matsumoto, 1996; Triandis, 1994) or how rules of expression are acquired (Cole, 1984), an emphasis is placed on the plastic nature of neuromuscular form.

A related metaphor comparing non-verbal actions, especially accidents and parapraxes to a *riddle* or *obscure text*, has been employed by psychodynamic investigators. Indeed, Freud (1905/1938, 1924) argued that such actions are usually meaningful and can often be recognised as such by a person. At the same time, Freud acknowledged that people frequently deny the significance of gestural-parapraxic actions, leaving the analyst in a quandry with respect to the validity of interpretation. Freud offered a number of interpretive strategies, including articulation with the person's life context and delayed verification as approaches to this problem.

In dealing with the problem of denial, Freud seems to have foreshadowed the more recent concerns about the questions of consciousness and intention in determining expressive actions. In any event, Freud's approach to the investigation of non-verbal behaviour as communication appears to have taken the analogies of the riddle or perhaps the obscure text which can be made meaningful by the application of accepted interpretive (for example, hermeneutic) principles. Many psychoanalytic investigators have utilised the broad interpretive analysis of behavioural text (Deutsch, 1952, 1959; Feldman, 1959; Schafer, 1980). Feldman's examination of the significance of such speech mannerisms as 'by the way', 'incidentally', 'honest', 'before I forget', 'believe me', 'curiously enough' and many others provides an illustration of the fruitfulness of regarding speech and gesture as complex, subtle, multi-levelled communication.

Certainly, the reliance on an affective expression as opposed to an obscure text analogy places the process of communication in different perspectives. In the first instance, the automatic, universal, perhaps unintended and other features identified above are taken as relevant issues, while the articulation with context, uniqueness, obfuscation and necessity of prolonged scholarly examination by trained and skilful interpreters are equally clearly emphasised by the behaviour as riddle analogy.

A third approach to the behaviour as communication analogy has been provided by the careful explication of non-verbal behaviour as *code* metaphor. Developed most extensively by Birdwhistell's (1952, 1970) analogy with structural linguistics and the Weiner *et al.* (1972) comparison with communication engineering, the central concern rests with the detailed, molecular examination of the structure of the code itself, modes (that is, channels) of transmission and accuracy-utility of communication. Conventional appreciation is essential to accuracy and efficiency, as auction applications, stock and commodities trading, athletic coaching, and social-political etiquette and protocol applications may attest (Scheflen and Scheflen, 1972). Levels of communication (for instance, messages and meta-messages), channel comparisons, sending and receiving strategies and accessibility of the intention–code–channel–code–interpretation sequence as an orderly, linear process are all designed to emphasise the systematic, objective and mechanistic features of the metaphor (Druckman *et al.*, 1982). Indeed, the utilisation of non-verbal behaviour as meta-message is very informative, if not essential, in distinguishing ironic from literal meaning.

However, the boundaries of the particular variations in the 'behaviour as communication' analogies which have been identified are fuzzy, and the explicit categories of the metaphors as employed by particular investigators are difficult to articulate fully. Yet the three variations of the communication analogy seem valid as the history and current invest-igation in non-verbal behaviour as communication is examined. In this spirit, a fourth general communication metaphor can also be identified – non-verbal behaviour as *dramatic presentation*.

While this analogy clearly descends from mime, dance and dramatic stage direction (Poyatos, 1983; Spiegel and Machotka, 1974; Stanislavski, 1936), the approach has been most skilfully developed by Goffman (1959, 1969), Baumeister (1982) and DePaulo (1992) as both expressive form (that is, identity and situation presentation) and rhetorical form (that is, persuasion, impression management and tactical positioning). The particularly fruitful features of this analogy appear to be the crafted, holistic, completely situated, forward-flowing nature of expression, with emphasis on recognisable skill, authenticity and purpose. Strategy, guile and deception are important aspects of this analogy, and subtlety and complexity abound (Scheibe, 1979; Schlenker, 1980).

Non-verbal behaviour as style

Although the 'non-verbal behaviour as communication' analogies hold historical prece-dence in the area, two additional analogies can be identified: non-verbal behaviour as *personal idiom* (Allport, 1961; Allport and Vernon, 1933) and non-verbal behaviour as *skill* (Argyle, 1967, 1969; Argyle and Kendon, 1967; Hargie *et al.*, 1994).

Allport introduced the important distinction between the instrumental aspects of action and the expressive aspects, the latter being personalised and stylistic ways of accomplishing the tasks of life. Comparisons with one's signature, voice or thumb print are offered. This perspective emphasises holism, consistency and configural uniqueness, while de-emphasising complexity, skill and authenticity. Demonstrations of the application of the analogy have been offered (certainly among the ranks of the stage impressionists, if not scientific workers), but the richness and fruitfulness of the metaphor have not yet been fully exploited.

Perhaps the most inviting metaphor of non-verbal behaviour has been the emphasis on skilled performance. The fruitfulness of the analogy of acquired skills as a way of thinking about non-verbal behaviour has been recognised for some time (Bartlett, 1958; Polanyi, 1958). However, its extension to non-verbal behaviour has been rather recent (Argyle, 1967; Argyle and Kendon, 1967; DePaulo *et al.*, 1985; Friedman, 1979; Hargie *et al.*, 1994; Knapp, 1972, 1984; Rosenthal, 1979; Rosenthal *et al.*, 1979; Snyder, 1974). The analogy has directed attention to the expressive or sending (encoding) and interpretive or receiving (decoding) aspects of non-verbal exchange, and has begun to highlight aspects of face-to-face interaction not investigated hitherto.

The skilled performance analogy

Since the introduction of the skilled performance metaphor is somewhat recent in the area of non-verbal behaviour analysis, it might prove useful to attempt to explicate some of the categories of such an analogy. As Bartlett (1958) pointed out, in the general case and in every known form of skill, there are acknowledged experts in whom much of the expert-ness, though perhaps never all of it, has been acquired by well-informed practice. The skill is based upon evidence picked up directly or indirectly from the environment, and it is used for the attempted achievement of whatever issue may be required at the time of the performance. Examples of such performance would include the sports player, the operator engaged at the work-bench, the surgeon conducting an operation, the telegrapher deciphering a message, or the pilot controlling an aeroplane (see Chapter 1).

Initial examination of the comparison suggests a number of important features of skilled performance (for more detailed analysis of these see Chapters 1 and 2) which are relevant to the investigation of non-verbal behaviour. First, skilled performances usually imply complex, highly co-ordinated motor acts which may be present in unrefined form at the outset of training, but in many cases are not, and which only emerge gradually with training and development. Thus, final performances may be quite different from untutored performances. Also, the recognisability of individuality in the crafting of skilful expression seems clearly implied. A second feature of such performance is that it is based on perceptually differentiating environmental properties or conditions often unrecognised by the untutored. A quality of 'informed seeing' or 'connoisseurship' develops which serves to guide and structure refined action.

A third feature of skilled performances is their dependence on practice, usually distributed over extended periods of time (see Druckman and Bjork, 1991). The importance of combinations of both practice and rest as aids in acquiring desired performance levels and the occurrence of marked irregularities in progress during the attainment of desired levels is recognisable, as are the influences of age and many physical condition factors (Bilodeau, 1966). A fourth important feature of skilled performances is their persistence and resistance to decay, interference and effects of disuse. While comparisons are difficult, the general belief is that skilled actions remain viable after verbal information has been lost to recovery. A fifth area of importance is the general assumption that individuals vary in the extent to which they display refined performances. A sixth characteristic of skilled actions is that they are ineffable, acquired best by modelling and described only imprecisely by linguistic means. Finally, the expression of skilled performances usually entails the incorporation of internalised standards of the quality of expression. Performers can recognise inadequacies or refinements in their performance, which serve to guide both practice and performance styles.

The development of the skilled performance metaphor in the investigation of non-verbal behaviour as expression seems to have suggested several areas of development and possible advance in the field. Training strategies, individual differences, the role of practice, the importance of performance feedback and internalised criteria of achievement represent a few areas of investigation of non-verbal behaviour implied by this analogy which have not been fully exploited to this point.

THE SCIENTIFIC STUDY OF NON-VERBAL BEHAVIOUR

Literature dealing with non-verbal behaviour as communication has increased dramatically in volume and complexity, particularly during the last several decades. Wolfgang and Bhardway (1984) listed 170 booklength volumes published during the previous hundred years that contained non-verbal communication materials, the vast majority of which had appeared within the last fifteen years. Today's electronic databases attest to the health and continued development of the field. One recent search of the area, covering the last eight years, yielded over three hundred books and chapters on the subject of non-verbal behaviour as communication.

The topic is usually presented with two different emphases: (1) a theoretical-research orientation and (2) an application-demonstration orientation. Because of its relation to the subtle and interpretative aspects of communication, there is a tendency on the part of popular lay texts to emphasise application without a balanced presentation of the theory and research which examines validity and reliability aspects necessary for proper understanding of non-verbal behaviour as one form of communication. Indeed, an interesting piece in this vein appeared on the Internet recently, providing an extended discourse on the psychological meaning of the handshake. While fascinating, and probably face valid, no recognisable empirical data accompanied the analysis.

The challenge of the present chapter is to discuss non-verbal behaviour as a communication skill, while maintaining the scientific integrity needed to evaluate critically the degree to which application is appropriate for any particular reader. It is hoped that the reader will assume a critical, scientific perspective in treating non-verbal behaviour as a meaningful yet complex topic for research and application.

Behavioural dimensions

Knapp (1972) suggested seven dimensions which describe the major categories of non-verbal behaviour research as related to communication, and are useful for placing this chapter in perspective. The first category is kinesics, commonly referred to as 'body language', and includes movements of the hand, arm, head, foot and leg, postural shifts, gestures, eye movements and facial expressions. A second category is paralanguage and is defined as content-free vocalisations and patterns associated with speech such as voice pitch, volume, frequency, stuttering, filled pauses (for example, 'ah'), silent pauses, interruptions and measures of speech rate and number of words spoken in a given unit of time. A third category involves physical contact in the form of touching. Another category is proxemics which involves interpersonal spacing and norms of territoriality. A fifth category concerns the physical characteristics of people such as skin colour, body shape, body odour and attractiveness. Related to physical characteristics is the category of artefacts or adornments such as perfume, clothes, jewellery and wigs. Environmental factors make up the last category and deal with the influences of the physical setting in which the behaviour occurs: a classroom, an office, a hallway, or a street corner.

There are numerous examples in the literature that detail these categories, either individually or in combinations (Argyle and Cook, 1976; Duncan and Fiske, 1977; Ekman *et al.*, 1972; Harper *et al.*, 1978; LaFrance and Mayo, 1978; Mahl and Schulze, 1964), and the reader is referred to these for detailed discussion. This chapter will present these categories in various combinations as they pertain to non-verbal behaviour as a communication skill. It is important to stress that non-verbal behaviour is dependent upon all of these factors for meaningful communication to take place. Some of these categories are covered in the theoretical and empirical presentation; others are not, but are nevertheless important and should always be considered as part of the 'universe' comprising non-verbal communication.

Setting and role influences on non-verbal behaviour

One of the major problems in focusing on the interpretation of non-verbal behaviour is to treat it as a separate, independent and absolute form of communication. This view of the topic is much too simplistic. The meaning of non-verbal behaviour must be considered in the context in which it occurs. Several types of contextual factors will be used to guide this discussion of non-verbal communication and the behaviours associated with it.

One involves the environmental setting of the behaviour. Both the physical and social aspects of the environment must be described in sufficient detail to assess possible contributing factors to non-verbal behaviour as meaningful communication. For example, the furniture arrangement in an office can be a major factor influencing the non-verbal behaviours exhibited therein. Body movements are different depending upon whether the person is sitting behind a desk or openly in a chair. The proximity and angle of seating arrangements have been shown to serve different functions during interaction and to affect such behaviour as eye contact, gazing and head rotation (Argyle and Dean, 1965; Manning, 1965).

Non-verbal behaviour may have very different meanings when exhibited on the street than, say, in a classroom. Background noise level in a work setting may produce exaggerated non-verbal communication patterns that would have very different meaning in a more quiet setting such as a library. The influence of ecological factors on behaviour has become an increasingly important focus in the study of human behaviour (McArthur and Baron, 1983; Stokols and Shumaker, 1981; Willems, 1985). Most research in non-verbal communication dealing with physical-environmental factors has focused on interpersonal spacing, proxemics and cultural differences in interaction patterns (Baxter, 1970; Collett, 1971; Hall, 1966).

The social climate of the environment is also an important factor in the consideration of non-verbal behaviour (Jones *et al.*, 1985). Research has demonstrated that different behaviours are produced in stressful versus unstressful situations (Rozelle and Baxter, 1975). The formality of a setting will determine the degree to which many non-verbal behaviours are suppressed or performed. Competitive versus co-operative interaction settings will also produce different types, levels and frequencies of non-verbal behaviours. These are just several examples of factors affecting the communicative meaning of non-verbal behaviour. The reader is encouraged systematically to survey factors that may be of importance in more personally familiar settings.

Non-verbal behaviour as communication: process and outcome factors of the interaction episode

Many communication models as applied to non-verbal behaviour have concentrated on the interpersonal level and have not elaborated to the same degree the role and situational levels of communication. An important distinction in viewing non-verbal behaviour as communication is that between the *encoder* and the *decoder*. The encoder is analogous to an actor or impression manager, producing and 'sending' the behaviours to be interpreted. The decoder is analogous to an observer 'receiving' the presented behaviours and interpreting them in some fashion. Within the context of the encoder–decoder distinction, a major concern is that of intention and whether intended and unintended messages obey the same rules and principles of communication (Dittmann, 1978).

Ekman and Friesen (1969) have provided two general classifications for behavioural messages. The first is the 'informative act' which results in certain interpretations on the part of a receiver without any active or conscious intent on the part of the sender. Thus, an individual's non-verbal behaviour is unintentionally 'giving off' signals that may be either correctly or incorrectly interpreted by a decoder (Goffman, 1959). The important point is that an impression is being formed without the encoder's knowledge or intention. A second classification is termed the 'communicative act'. In this case, the encoder is intentionally attempting to send a specific message to a receiver. A difficulty lies in distinguishing varying degrees of conscious intent as opposed to 'accidental' or non-specifically motivated behaviour. Extreme examples of communicative behaviours intended to convey such emotions as anger, approval or disagreement are usually described in the literature (for example, Jones and Wortman, 1973). Similarly, informative acts such as fidgeting and gaze aversion are presented as examples of informative behaviour indicating unintended guilt, anxiety or discomfort.

As will be discussed later in this chapter, role and situational considerations can lead to gross misinterpretations of what is considered 'informative' or 'communicative' behaviour on the part of both encoder and decoder in an interaction. Most interactions among people involve less extreme emotion and a complexity of intentions. Also, many social interactions involve changing roles between encoder and decoder as the participants take turns in speaking and listening (for example, Duncan, 1969; Jones and Thibaut, 1958).

A useful model dealing with the issues of social influence in non-verbal communication was presented by MacKay (1972). The distinction is made between two types of non-verbal signals exhibited by the encoder: (1) goal-directed, and (2) non-goal-directed. The receiver or decoder then interprets either of these signals as being (3) goal-directed or (4) non-goal-directed. Thus, the signal and the interpretation may be similar: (1) goal-directed signal being interpreted as goal-directed; (2) non-goal-directed signal being interpreted as non-goal-directed, or dissimilar; (3) goal-directed signal being interpreted as non-goal-directed; and (4) non-goal-directed signal being interpreted as goal-directed. When considering goal-directed signalling, MacKay's model assumes that the encoder is behaviourally attempting to communicate a specific internal state or presence and that the intended communication has a desired effect on the encoder. If, in the encoder's judgement, the intended effect has not been achieved, the goal-directed, non-verbal behaviour is modified to achieve the desired effect. Therefore, the encoder actively evaluates the reaction of the decoder and proceeds accordingly.

Requiring communicative behaviour to be explicitly goal-directed, with an immediate adjustment on the part of the encoder depending upon the decoder's response, limits the number of behaviours that can be considered communicative. In typical conversations, many non-verbal behaviours become automatic responses and are performed at low levels of awareness or involve no awareness at all. What was once a specifically defined goal-directed behaviour becomes habitual and is no longer a product of conscious intention. The degree to which non-verbal behaviours involve varying levels of awareness then becomes difficult to determine.

Another consideration for the understanding of non-verbal communication is whether or not the encoder and decoder share a common, socially defined signal system. Weiner *et al.* (1972) argued that this is a crucial requirement for communication to occur, regardless of the degree to which any behaviour is intentional. This represents a limited perspective on what is considered communication. One of the more pervasive problems in the use of non-verbal behaviour in the encoding and decoding process is when a common system is *not* shared and misinterpretation of behaviour results. Certain encoded behaviours may

Communication - sending messages.

have unintended effects, especially when contextual factors such as cultural, role and spatial factors are inappropriately considered during an interaction. The misinterpretation of behaviour that results can lead to profound consequences and must be considered a type of communication *per se*.

APPROACHES TO NON-VERBAL BEHAVIOUR AS COMMUNICATION

Ekman and Friesen

Perhaps the most useful model of non-verbal communication that encompasses these issues (but does not resolve them) is one originally presented by Ekman and Friesen (1969). They began by distinguishing between three characteristics of non-verbal behaviour: (1) usage, (2) origin and (3) coding.

Usage refers to the circumstances that exist at the time of the non-verbal act. It includes consideration of the external condition that affects the act, such as the physical setting, role relationship and emotional tone of the interaction. For example, the encoder and decoder may be communicating in an office, a home, a car, or a street. The role relationship may involve that of an interviewer–interviewee, therapist–client, supervisor–employee, husband–wife or teacher–student. The emotional tone may be formal or informal, stressful or relaxed, friendly or hostile, warm or cold, competitive or co-operative. Usage also involves the relationship between verbal and non-verbal behaviour. For instance, non-verbal acts may serve to accent, duplicate, support, substitute for or be unrelated to verbal behaviours.

Usage is the characteristic Ekman and Friesen chose to employ in dealing with awareness and intentionality on the part of the encoder, as discussed previously. In addition, usage involves external feedback which is defined as the receiver's verbal or non-verbal reactions to the encoder's non-verbal behaviours as interpreted by the encoder. This does not involve the receiver's actual interpretations of the sender's behaviour, but is only information to the sender that his or her non-verbal behaviours have been received and evaluated. Finally, usage also refers to the type of information conveyed in terms of being informative, communicative or interactive. Informative and communicative acts have been discussed. Interactive acts are those that detectably influence or modify the behaviour of the other participants in an interaction. Thus, these three information types involve the degree to which non-verbal messages are understood, provide information and influence the behaviour of other people.

The second characteristic of non-verbal behaviour discussed by Ekman and Friesen is its origin. Some non-verbal behaviours are rooted in the nervous system, such as reflex actions; other non-verbal behaviours are commonly learned and used in dealing with the environment: for example, human beings use their feet for transportation in one form or another. A third source of non-verbal behaviour refers to culture, family or any other instrumental or socially distinguishable form of behaviour. Thus, we adopt idiosyncratic behaviours when driving a car, we eat in a certain manner and groom ourselves in various ways. Social customs dictate non-verbal patterns of greeting one another, expressing approval or disapproval and apportioning appropriate distances from each other depending upon the type of interaction involved.

The third characteristic of non-verbal behaviour is coding, that is, the meaning attached to a non-verbal act. The primary distinction is between *extrinsic* and *intrinsic* codes.

Extrinsically coded acts signify something else and may be either arbitrarily or iconically coded. Arbitrarily coded acts bear no visual resemblance to what they represent. A thumbs-up sign for signalling that everything is OK would be an arbitrarily coded act since it conveys no meaning 'by itself'. An iconically coded act tends to resemble what it signifies, as in the example of a throat-cutting movement with a finger. Intrinsically coded movements are what they signify. Playfully hitting a person, say on the upper arm, is an intrinsically coded act in that it is actually a form of aggression.

Employing usage, origin and coding as a basis for defining non-verbal behaviour, Ekman and Friesen went on to distinguish among five categories of behavioural acts.

Emblems

These are non-verbal acts that have direct verbal translation and can substitute for words, the meaning of which is well understood by a particular group, class or culture. Emblems originate through learning, most of which is culture-specific, and may be shown in any area of the body. Examples include waving the hands in a greeting or frowning to indicate disapproval. Ekman *et al.* (1984) found substantial regional, national and intranational variation in these displays, leading them to suggest compiling an international dictionary of emblems. Differences have also been found in the way cultures interpret emblems: cultures studied include the Catalans in Spain (Payrato, 1993), Dutch interpretations of Chinese and Kurdish gestures (Poortinga *et al.*, 1993), and Hebrew speakers in Israel (Safadi and Valentine, 1988).

Illustrators

These are movements that are tied directly to speech and serve to illustrate what is verbalised. Illustrators are socially learned, usually through imitation by a child of a person he or she wishes to resemble. An example of an illustrator is holding the hands a certain distance apart to indicate the length of an object.

Regulators

These non-verbal acts serve to regulate conversation flow between people. Regulators are often culture-specific and may be subtle indicators to direct verbal interaction such as head nods, body position shifts and eye contact. Because of their subtle nature, regulators are often involved in miscommunication and inappropriate responses among people of different cultures or ethnic backgrounds. This will be examined in greater detail when the authors' police–citizen research is described (see p. 82f.).

Adaptors

These are object or self-manipulations. The specific behaviours are first learned as efforts to satisfy bodily needs, usually during childhood. In adult expression, only a fragment of the original adaptive behaviour is exhibited. Adaptors are behavioural habits and are triggered by some feature of the setting that relates to the original need. There are three types of adaptors: (1) self-adaptors such as scratching the head or clasping the hands;

(2) alter-adaptors which may include protective hand movements and arm-folding intended to protect oneself from attack or to represent intimacy, withdrawal or flight; and (3) object adaptors, which are originally learned to perform instrumental tasks and may include tapping a pencil on the table or smoking behaviours.

Affect displays

These consist primarily of facial expressions of emotions. There is evidence that people from different cultures agree on their judgements of expressions for the primary emotions but disagree on their ratings of the intensity of these expressions (Ekman, 1994, 1993, 1992a, 1992b; Matsumoto and Ekman, 1989; Ekman *et al.*, 1987; Ekman and Friesen, 1986). However, these expressions are usually modified and often hidden by cultural display rules learned as 'appropriate' behaviour. Thus, affect displays may be masked in social settings in order to show socially acceptable behaviour. It may be the case that the events that elicit emotions vary from culture to culture but the particular facial muscle movements triggered when a given emotion is elicited may be relatively universal.

The non-verbal characteristic-category system of Ekman and Friesen has provided a useful means of analysing and organising non-verbal behaviours used in communication and is readily applicable in describing processes of information and expression-exchange in normal, social interactions. Extended use of the system has focused on a number of significant topic areas, among which could be cited many investigations into the relationships between genuine and recalled emotion and facial expression (Ekman, 1992a, 1993; Ekman *et al.*, 1990), and the utility of the system in distinguishing honest and authentic expressions from the deceptive and dissembling (Ekman, 1992a; Ekman and O'Sullivan, 1991; Ekman *et al.*, 1991; Hyman, 1989). Perhaps one of the most promising findings to emerge from this literature is the recognition of a particular smile, 'The Duchenne Smile', which seems to be a reliable indicator of genuine enjoyment and happiness. Moreover, this facial profile seems to be quite resistant to staging and dissimulation (Ekman, 1993).

Dittman

Another way of organising non-verbal acts in terms of their communicative nature, is by focusing on the 'communication specificity' and channel capability of message transmission. These concepts have been presented by Dittman (1972, 1978) as part of a larger model of the communication of emotions and are an important aspect of using non-verbal behaviour as a communication skill. Dittman focused primarily on four major channels of communication: (1) language; (2) facial expression; (3) vocalisations; and (4) body movements. These four channels can be discussed in terms of their 'capacity', defined as the amount of information each may transmit at any given moment. Channel capacity can be described along two dimensions: (1) communication specificity (communicative-expressive) and (2) information value (discrete-continuous). Table 3.1 summarises the relationships among the four communication channels and the two dimensions of information conveying potential or capacity.

The closer a channel is to the communicative end of the continuum, the more discrete its information value will be in terms of containing distinguishable units with identifiable meanings (for instance, words). The more discrete a communication is, the greater the

Table 3.1 Transmission of messages

Channel of communication	Channel capacity	
	Specificity	Information value
Language	Communicative	Discrete
Facial expression		
	⇑	⇑
Vocalisations		
Body movements	Expressive	Continuous

communication specificity it will usually have. These channels have the greatest capacity for conveying the largest number of messages with a wide variety of emotional meaning.

Channels at the other end of the capacity dimension are described as being relatively more expressive and continuous. For example, foot movements or changes in posture are more continuous behaviours than are spoken words, and are more expressive than specifically communicative in their emotional content. These channels have a lower capacity for conveying information regarding how a person is feeling. Facial expressions and vocalisations (paralanguage) may vary in their capacity to convey emotional expression depending on their delivery, the role the person is playing, the setting of the behaviour and whether the decoders are family, friends or strangers.

Dittman also discussed the degree to which a message varies in intentional control on the part of the encoder, and awareness on the part of the decoder. Intentional control refers to the degree to which an encoder is in control of allowing his or her emotions to be expressed. Level of awareness refers to a decoder either being aware of, repressing or not noticing a message being sent by an encoder.

The most useful contribution by Dittman to the non-verbal communication area is his analysis of channels of communication. A major challenge in non-verbal behaviour research is to examine the degree to which single versus multiple channels of transmission provide more meaningful communication in human interaction.

Mehrabian

An influential approach that uses multiple non-verbal categories and attempts to organise them in terms of three dimensions is that of Mehrabian (1972). These dimensions, described as social orientations, are *positiveness*, *potency* and *responsiveness*. Positiveness involves the evaluation of other persons or objects that relate to approach-avoidance tendencies, usually described in terms of liking. Non-verbal behaviours associated with positiveness represent 'immediacy' cues such as eye contact, forward-lean, touching, distance and orientation.

Potency represents status or social control and is demonstrated through 'relaxation' cues of posture such as hand and neck relaxation, sideways-lean, reclining angle and arm–leg position asymmetry. Responsiveness is expressed through 'activity' cues that relate to orientating behaviour and involve the relative importance of the interaction participants. Such non-verbal behaviour as vocal activity, speech rate, speech volume and facial activity are indices of responsiveness. Mehrabian's system of non-verbal expression is thus organised into (1) dimensions, (2) associated cues and (3) specific non-verbal indicators of the cues.

Mehrabian's system places non-verbal behaviour in socially meaningful contexts and is especially useful for non-verbal behaviour as a communication skill. The dimensions of non-verbal behaviour can be applied equally to encoding or decoding roles and are supported by numerous experimental results. For example, data collected by Mehrabian and others indicate that the positiveness dimension, with its immediacy cues, is primarily concerned with deceptive or truthful communication. The potency dimension, as expressed by relaxation cues, is useful in understanding situations where social or professional status is salient, such as military rank, corporate power, teacher–student relations and therapist–client interaction.

The responsiveness dimension, as expressed by activity cues, relates to persuasion, either as intended (encoding) or perceived (decoding). Thus, Mehrabian organised a complex set of non-verbal behaviours into manageable proportions, which are readily testable and applicable to social situations experienced daily, particularly by professionals whose judgement and influence are important to those with whom they communicate.

Patterson

A more recent attempt to organise non-verbal behaviour into basic functions or purposes of communication is presented by Patterson (1983, 1988). He argues that as social communication, non-verbal behaviour is only meaningful when considered in terms of an exchange of expressions between participants in an interaction. It is this relational nature of behaviours that must be considered and requires sensitivity to the behavioural context each person constructs for the other (1983), or for third parties viewing participants in a primary relationship (1988). The basic functions of non-verbal behaviour are related to the management (both interpretation and presentation) of those acts primarily involved in social interaction.

There are seven basic functions suggested: (1) providing information; (2) regulating interaction; (3) expressing intimacy; (4) expressing social control; (5) presentation function; (6) affect management; and (7) facilitating service or task goals. Non-verbal behaviour is best considered as 'co-ordinated exchanges' and configurations of multi-channel combinations as related to the seven functions. Thus, presenting non-verbal behaviour in terms of separate channels (for instance, facial expressions, arm movements, paralanguage, and so on), does not properly emphasise the interdependent and co-ordinated relationship among channels that are meaningfully involved in the functions. This configural approach is important for application to the development of communication skills.

The information provision function is considered to be most basic and is seen primarily from an impression formation or decoder perspective. When observing an encoder's (actor's) behaviour patterns, the decoder may infer aspects of the encoder's acquired dispositions, temporary states, or the meaning of a verbal interaction. Facial cues are emphasised (Ekman and Friesen, 1975) usually to infer emotional expressions. However, other channels of non-verbal behaviour such as the postural, paralinguistic and visual are also important in formulating the impression.

The function of regulating interaction deals with the development, maintenance and termination of a communicative exchange. These non-verbal behaviours are usually 'automatic' or operate at low levels of awareness. Two types of behaviour are involved in regulating interactions: the first are structural aspects that remain relatively stable over the course of an interaction and include posture, body orientation and interpersonal distance; the second is dynamic and affects momentary changes in conversational exchange, such as facial expression, gaze, tone and pitch of voice and change in voice volume (Argyle and Kendon, 1967; Duncan, 1972). Both the information and regulating functions are 'molecular' in form and represent communicative aspects of more isolated and specific non-verbal behaviours.

The last five functional categories represent broader purposes of communication and are molar descriptions of more extended interactions. These are of greater importance in understanding and predicting the nature of non-verbal acts during an interaction. Intimacy refers to liking, attraction or, generally, the degree of 'union' or 'openness towards another person'. Extended mutual gazing into another's eyes, closer interpersonal spacing and mutual touching are examples of communicating intimacy.

Social control functions to persuade others and establish status differences related to the roles of the interaction participants. Examples of non-verbal behaviours involved in social control are gaze patterns and touch to clarify status differences; and eye contact, direct body orientation and vocal intonation to attempt to persuade someone to accept another's point of view. Much of the authors' research relates to this function and will be discussed later in the chapter.

The presentational function of non-verbal behaviours is managed by an individual or a couple to create or enhance an image, and is typically aimed not so much at the other partner as it is at others outside the direct relationship. Some authors have identified these processes as 'tie-signs' (Goffman, 1971) or 'withness cues' (Scheflen and Scheflen, 1972). Holding hands, standing close and sharing a common focus of attention are frequent examples. Such behaviours occur more often in the presence of others. The affect management function focuses on the expression of strong affect by demonstrative processes such as embracing, kissing and other forms of touching associated with strong positive affect; or embarrassment, shame, or social anxiety, as in instances of decreased contact, averted gaze and turning away from the partner.

The service-task function involves non-verbal behaviours that are relatively impersonal in nature. Role and situational factors are particularly important here since many of the same non-verbal behaviours involved in intimacy are also present in service-task functions. A good example is close interpersonal spacing and touching behaviour on the part of a physician towards a patient or between hairdresser and customer. The distinguishing feature of service-task behaviours is that they function to service the needs of individuals.

Patterson (1995) has attempted to expand his functional conception of social process maintenance by conceptualising a dynamic, multi-staged, parallel processing model of non-verbal communication. The model encompasses four classes of factors, each containing multiple processes: (1) determinants (biology, culture, gender, personality); (2) social environment (partner, setting); (3) cognitive-affective mediators (interpersonal expectancies, affect, goals, dispositions, cognitive resources, attentional focus, cognitive effort, action schemas); and (4) person perception and behavioural processes (impression formation, actor behaviour). In the broadest sense, the model attempts to describe the complex demands entailed in simultaneously initiating and monitoring interactive behaviour. It is generally recognised that if non-verbal behaviour is discussed separately by channel, it is primarily for organisational clarity; any one channel should not be considered at the exclusion of others in either managing or interpreting social behaviour. This, of course, results in a more complex task in using non-verbal behaviour as a communication skill, yet it places the topic in a more appropriate perspective *vis-à-vis* communication in general.

Patterson's functional approach to non-verbal behaviour is similar to Mehrabian's in its application to social-communicative processes. Both stress the importance of the multi-channel use of configurative aspects of non-verbal communication. However, Patterson provides a broader framework in which to view non-verbal behaviour in role- and setting-specific conditions, by emphasising the degree of overlap in multi-channel expression among the functions and the importance of interpreting these expressions in light of the psychological, social and environmental context.

The complexity of the task of communicative and self-presentational uses of non-verbal behaviour has been reviewed by DePaulo (1992). She examined the difficulties of communicating intended messages and emotional states through non-verbal channels. Two factors received particular emphasis. Non-verbal behaviour is more accessible to others in an interaction than it is to the actor. This makes self- (or relationship) presentational refinements and monitoring difficult for the actor and access direct and figural for others. Second, it is never possible to 'not act' by non-verbal channels. While one can fall silent verbally, one can never become silent non-verbally. These two features of non-verbal behaviour *vis-à-vis* speech highlight the significant and problematic nature of non-verbal behaviour as communication.

NON-VERBAL COMMUNICATION IN CONTEXT

This chapter has stressed that non-verbal behaviour, as a communication skill, is most usefully understood when discussed in role- and setting-defined contexts. With the possible exception of facial expressions subject to display rules, non-verbal communication cannot be discussed adequately by presenting principles that have universal application. Perhaps a useful way of presenting research results as applied to communication skills is to provide a sampling of findings in selected contexts. At present, research on non-verbal communication is incomplete and asks more questions than it provides answers, yet it is hoped that the reader will better appreciate scientific attempts to study this communication skill meaningfully.

In his review, Knapp (1984) discussed the relevance of non-verbal behaviour to communication in general and suggested several assumptions from which the research can be viewed. Among these are that human communication consists primarily of combinations of channel signals such as spatial, facial and vocal signals operating together. Another assumption is that communication is composed of 'multi-level signals' and deals with broader interpretations of interactions such as general labelling (for example, a social or professional encounter) and inferences about longer term relationships among the inter-actants. His last assumption is most crucial for the present discussion since it points out the critical importance of context for generating meanings from human communication encounters.

Setting and role applications

A major limitation of much non-verbal behaviour research is that it is conducted in a laboratory setting devoid of many of the contextually relevant environmental and social features present in real life interactions (Davis, 1984; Druckman *et al.*, 1982; Knapp, 1984). This is a serious problem in attempts to generalise techniques of impression management and processes of impression formation to specific role-defined settings (such as the psycho-therapeutic or counselling session), health professional–patient interactions, the employment interview and police–citizen encounters. Professionals in these areas have a special interest in non-verbal behaviour. Accurate and effective communication is crucial to accomplishing the purposes of the interaction. One series of studies conducted over a number of years is illustrative of setting- and role-defined research and reveals the importance of the interplay among the categories of kinesics, paralanguage, proxemics, physical characteristics, adornments and environmental factors mentioned earlier as describing major categories of non-verbal behaviour.

The specific role-defined setting was that of a standing, face-to-face police–citizen interaction. In the initial study (Rozelle and Baxter, 1975), police officers were asked to indicate the 'characteristics and features they look for when interacting with a citizen while in the role of a police officer'. They were also asked to indicate cues they used in forming these impressions of the citizen. These cues or information items were classified as either behavioural (that is, the other person's verbal and non-verbal behaviour) or situational (that is, aspects of the environment, such as number of other people present, inside a room or on the street, lighting conditions).

The officers were asked to compare a 'dangerous' versus 'non-dangerous' situation. Under conditions of danger, the officers indicated a broadened perceptual scan and were more likely to utilise behavioural (mainly non-verbal) and situation-environmental cues (for instance, area of town, size of room, activities on the street) in forming an impression of the citizen. Under the non-dangerous conditions, the officers concentrated almost exclusively on specific facial and vocal cues, eye contact, arm and hand movements, dress and behavioural sequences such as body orientation and postural positions. Under these less stressful conditions, police officers indicated an impression formed that described the citizen primarily in terms of dispositional characteristics (i.e. guilty, suspicious, deceptive, honest, law-abiding).

Dispositional causes of observed behaviour are contrasted with situational causes such as attributing one's behaviour to momentary discomfort or confusion, crowding, responding to another's actions or other events in the immediate environment. Thus, in the more typical police–citizen interaction, which is non-stressful for the police officer (for instance, obtaining information from a witness to an accident or crime), the officer focused predominantly on the citizen's non-verbal behaviours and dispositional attributions, rather than situational attributions, to explain the citizen's behaviour (for example, guilty or innocent).

Actor and observer bias in explaining non-verbal behaviour

An important feature of impression-management (encoding) and formation (decoding) processes deals with differences arising out of the perspectives of the interaction participants (Jones and Nisbett, 1972; Ross and Nisbett, 1991). In most role-defined interactions, the person in the encoding role is considered to be the actor, whereas the decoder is the observer. It has been proposed that unless otherwise trained or sensitised (Watson, 1982), observers over-emphasise dispositional qualities in inferring the causes of the actor's behaviour, while ignoring the more immediate situational factors related to the observed behaviour. Actors, on the other hand, usually over-emphasise situational factors at the expense of dispositional ones in explaining their own behaviour.

Rozelle and Baxter (1975) concluded that police officers see themselves as observers, evaluating and judging the behaviours of the citizen with whom they are interacting. As a result, the officer makes predominantly dispositional interpretations, ignoring situational causes of the observed behaviour. It is of particular importance to note that in this type of face-to-face interaction, the officer is probably one of the more distinguishable features of the situation and the officer's behaviour is an important situational determinant of the citizen's behaviour. Thus, the officer under-estimates or ignores personal behaviour as a contributing, situational determinant of the citizen's behaviour. This can lead to misinterpretations of behaviour, particularly when judgements must be made on the basis of a relatively brief, initial encounter. It should also be noted that the citizen may be misinterpreting his or her own behaviour in terms of reacting to the situation, including the officer's behaviour; thus, non-verbal cues are not 'managed' properly to avoid expressing or concealing appropriate behaviour for desired evaluation on the part of the officer. Other types of role-defined interactions resemble this condition in various degrees.

Interpersonal distance, roles and problems of interpretation

A more dramatic example of how this observer bias can lead to clear, yet inaccurate, interpretations of behaviour was obtained when the category of proxemics was included in the police–citizen interaction. Based on his observations of North American behaviour in a variety of settings, Hall (1959, 1966) proposed four categories of interpersonal distance that describe different types of communications in face-to-face interactions:

1 Intimate distances in which interactants stand from 6 to 18 inches from each other. Types of interactions expressing intimacy are 'love-making and wrestling, comforting and protecting';
2 Personal distances of 1.5 to 4 feet which usually reflect close, personal relationships;
3 Social or consultative distances of 4 to 7 feet that are typical of business and professional–client interactions;
4 Public distances that range from 12 to 20 feet and involve public speaking in which recognition of others spoken to is not required. *only during question period.*

Hall (1966) stipulated that these distances are appropriate only for North American and possibly Northern European cultures and that other cultures have different definitions of interpersonal spacing.

A study by Baxter and Rozelle (1975) focused on a simulated police–citizen interview between white male undergraduates at a North American university and an interviewer playing the role of a police officer questioning the student-citizen about various items in his wallet. The interview consisted of four 2-minute phases in which the distance between the officer and citizen was systematically varied according to Hall's first three distance classes.

For both the experimental and control groups, the role-played officer stood 4 feet away from the student during the first 2-minute phase. At the beginning of the second 2-minute phase, the officer casually moved within 2 feet (personal distance) of the subject for both groups. For the experimental group only, the intimate or 'severe crowding' condition (due to the inappropriate distances for the roles being played) occurred during the third 2-minute phase: the officer moved to an 8-inch nose-to-nose distance from the subject, and then returned to the 2-foot distance during the fourth 2-minute phase. The 2-foot distance was maintained throughout phases two, three and four for the control group. The police interviewer was instructed to maintain eye contact during all phases of the interaction. The student was positioned next to a wall which prevented him from moving back or escaping during the crowding condition.

The non-verbal behaviours exhibited by the subjects during the crowding condition were consistent with typical reactions of people experiencing inappropriate, intimate, interpersonal spacing. As the subject was increasingly crowded during the interview, his or her speech time and frequency became disrupted and disorganised, with an uneven, staccato pattern developing. Eye movements and gaze aversion increased, while few other facial reactions were displayed. Small, discrete head movements occurred, and head rotation/ elevation movements increased. Subjects adopted positions to place their arms and hands between themselves and the interviewer, and there was a noticeable increase in hands-at-crotch positioning. Brief rotating head movements increased, while foot movements decreased.

These non-verbal behaviours were produced by a situational manipulation (that is, crowding) but were strikingly similar to those emphasised by Rozelle and Baxter's real police officers as the described behaviours indicating dispositional characteristics of guilt, suspicion and deception. Officers in the earlier study specified facial and vocal cues, arm and hand behaviour, posture and body orientation; they related non-verbal behaviours as being particularly reliable indices of these dispositions. At that time, the training course (at the police academy) required of all officers included instructions to stand close to the citizen and maintain maximal eye contact during such an interview. Thus, reliance on non-verbal behaviour has, in this role-specific setting, a high probability of miscommunicating intention, motivations and other dispositions from actor to observer. The observer, by not properly including his or her own behaviour as a significant part of the situation influencing the actor's non-verbal behaviour, inaccurately forms an impression of the actor in a highly reliable and confident manner.

Cultural influences

The important role played by cultural differences in non-verbal behaviour is suggested from several directions. Early studies by Watson (1970) and by Watson and Graves (1966) have shown differences in gazing behaviour, space behaviour, body orientations and touching behaviour among members of different cultures (also see Jourard, 1966; Shuter, 1976). More recent studies by Ekman and his colleagues distinguished the universal from the culturally-specific sources for expressions of emotion (e.g. Ekman and O'Sullivan, 1988). While the underlying physiology for the primary emotions may be universal, the actual expression elicited is subject to cultural and situation-determined display rules as we discussed above. Display rules serve to control an expression or to modify certain expressions that would be socially inappropriate or would reveal deception.

Klopf *et al.* (1991) showed that the Japanese subjects in their study perceived themselves to be less immediate – indicated by less touching, more distance, less forward-lean, less eye contact, and oriented away from the other – than their Finnish and American subjects.

These variations may reflect cultural differences in rules dealing with intimacy (Argyle, 1986). Anecdotal reports also suggest distinct patterns of expression for Japanese negotiators – in the face (immobile, impassive), the eyes (gaze away from others), the mouth (closed), the hands (richly expressive gestures) and synchronous movements in pace, stride and body angle with other members of a group (March, 1988). Understanding preferred non-verbal expressions may be a basis for communicating across cultures as Faure (1993) illustrated in the context of French–Chinese negotiations. They may also reveal the way that members of different societies manage impressions (Crittenden and Bae, 1994).

Sub-cultural differences in interpersonal spacing preferences have been examined in several observational studies (Baxter, 1970; Thompson and Baxter, 1973; Willis, 1966). In general, African Americans tend to prefer interacting at greater distances and at more oblique orientations than Anglo-Americans, who in turn prefer greater distances and more indirection than Mexican Americans. Indeed, the Thompson and Baxter study demonstrates that African, Anglo- and Mexican Americans, when interacting in intercultural groups in natural contexts, appear to 'work towards' inconsistent spacing arrangements through predictable footwork and orientation adjustments. A subsequent study by Garratt *et al.* (1981) trained Anglo-American police officers to engage in empirically determined 'African American nonverbal behaviour and interpersonal positioning' during an interview with African American citizens. These interviews were contrasted with 'standard' interviews conducted by the same officers with different African American citizens. Post-interview ratings by these citizens showed a clear preference for the 'trained' policeman, along with higher ratings in the areas of personal, social and professional competence. A similar study with comparable results had been carried out previously by Collett (1971) with trained English interviewers interacting with Arab students.

Differences were also found between African American and white American subjects in gazing behaviour. The African American subjects directed their gaze away when listening and towards the other when speaking (LaFrance and Mayo, 1978). Similar patterns of gaze behaviour were found as well in other societies (Winkel and Vrij, 1990). Preliminary evidence obtained by the authors of this chapter suggest that the differences in gaze may reflect differences between sub-cultural groups in felt stress.

A few studies have investigated cultural factors in deceptive enactments. Comparing Chinese experimental truth-tellers to liars, Cody *et al.* (1989), Yi Chao (1987) and O'Hair *et al.* (1989) found that only speech errors and vocal stress distinguished between the groups. Other paralinguistic variables were related more strongly to question difficulty. Like the Americans in the studies reviewed by DePaulo *et al.* (1985), the Chinese liars (compared to the truth-tellers) experienced more difficulty in communicating detailed answers to the questions that required effort. Both the liars and truth-tellers were brief in communicating negative feelings, smiling frequently and suppressing body and hand movements. With regard to Jordanian subjects, Bond *et al.* (1990) found that only filled pauses distinguished between the liars and truth-tellers: the Jordanians expressed more filled pauses when lying than when telling the truth. Compared to a comparable sample of Americans the Jordanian subjects (liars and truth-tellers) displayed more eye contact, more movements per minute and more filled pauses. However, both the American and Jordanian subjects used similar, inaccurate non-verbal cues (avoiding eye contact and frequent pauses) judging deception by others. (For a review of other cross-cultural studies, see Druckman and Hyman, 1991.)

While suggestive, these studies are not sufficient probes into the cultural dimensions influencing non-verbal behaviour. None of them describes the way people from different cultures feel when they violate a social taboo, for example, or attempt to deceive or exploit an interviewer. While the studies are informative, they do not illuminate the psychological states aroused within cultures that give rise to the kind of 'leakage' which may be used to examine complex intentional structures in different cultural groups. Based on their review of deception research, Hyman and Druckman (1991) concluded that: 'detection of deception would be improved if one could anticipate the sorts of settings that constitute social transgression or a guilt-producing state for particular individuals (or cultures)' (p. 188).

Some research implications

Building on the idea of cultural display rules, investigations designed to discover the situations which produce guilt for members of different cultural groups would be helpful. Situations that produce guilt are likely to vary with an individual's cultural background and experience. When identified, these situations could then be used as settings for enacting scripts that involve either deception or truth-telling by subjects from those cultures. The enactments should reveal the non-verbal behaviours which distinguish deceivers and truth-tellers within the cultural groups. These behaviours would be culturally-specific 'leaked' cues.

Following this approach, such studies could be implemented in stages. First, interviews would be conducted to learn about a culture's 'folk psychology' of deception (see Hyman and Druckman, 1991). Respondents would be asked about the kinds of lies and lying situations that are permissible versus those that are taboo within their culture. Second, experimental deception vignettes would be presented for respondents' reactions in terms of feelings of guilt, shame and stress. The vignettes can be designed to vary in terms of such dimensions as whether the person represents a group or her/him self, the presence of an audience during the interview, and the extent to which he or she prepared for the questions being asked. Analyses would then suggest the dimensions that influence feelings of guilt or shame for each cultural group. Preliminary findings on sub-cultural groups, obtained by the authors of this chapter, showed differences in stress for members of different cultural groups and less guilt felt by respondents in all cultural groups when they were in the role of group representative compared to non-representative. (See also Mikolic *et al.* (1994) for evidence on the disinhibiting effects of being in groups.) Third, the information gathered from the interviews could provide the bases for more structured experimental studies designed to discover those non-verbal behaviours that distinguish between liars and truth-tellers (the leakage cues) for each of several cultural groups. These cues could then be used for diagnostic purposes as well as for the development of training modules along the lines of work completed by Collett (1971), Costanzo (1992), Druckman *et al.* (1982), Fiedler and Walka (1993), and Garratt *et al.* (1981).

Non-verbal behaviour in professional settings: a sample of research findings

Although the police–citizen encounter was brief, and involved rather extreme situational-proxemic variations with only a moderate amount of verbal exchange, it has elements similar to many professional interactions. For example, the actor-observer distinction could be applied to the employment interview. In such an interaction, the interviewer could be considered the 'observer' or decoder evaluating the verbal and non-verbal acts of the interviewee who is the 'actor' or encoder.

In the authors' experience with the professional interview setting, the interviewer often makes an important, job-related decision regarding the interviewee based on dispositional attributions occurring as a result of behaviour observed during a 30-minute interview. Although the employment interview may be a typical experience for the interviewer during the working day, it is usually an infrequent and stressful one for the interviewee. This could increase the observer-dispositional bias, actor-situational bias effect. The interviewer, in the role of observer, proceeds 'as usual', while the interviewee reacts in a sensitive manner to every verbal and non-verbal behaviour of the interviewer. Unaware that the very role of the interviewer is an important, immediate situational cause of the interviewee's behaviours, the interviewer uses these same behaviours to infer long-term dispositional qualities to the interviewee-actor and may make a job-related decision on the basis of the impression formed. Thus, from a non-verbal communication perspective, the impression formed is, to varying degrees, inadvertently encoded by the interviewee-actor, and possibly misinterpreted in the decoding process on the part of the interviewer (the employment interview is discussed in detail in Chapter 15).

This miscommunication process may be particularly important during the initial stages of an interaction, since expectancies may be created that bias the remaining interaction patterns. Research indicates that first impressions are important in creating expectancies and evaluative judgements (and sometimes diagnoses) of people in interviewing, counselling, teaching, therapeutic and other professionally role-related interactions. Zajonc (1980) stated that evaluative judgements are often made in a fraction of a second on the basis of non-verbal cues in an initial encounter. Others have shown that a well-organised judgemental impression may be made in as little as four minutes. People who are in professional roles such as interviewing, counselling and teaching should constantly remind themselves of the influence they have on clients' non-verbal behaviour and not to rely on 'favourite' non-verbal behaviours as flawless indicators of dispositional characteristics.

Knowledge of potential effects of verbal and non-verbal behaviour can be useful in impression management techniques to create more effective communication in face-to-face interactions. For example, in a simulated employment interview setting, Washburn and Hakel (1973) demonstrated that when applicants were given a high level of non-verbal 'enthusiasm' by the interviewer (for instance, gazing, gesturing and smiling), the applicants were judged more favourably than those given a low level of interviewer enthusiasm. Another study showed that when candidates received non-verbal approval during an employment interview, they were judged by objective observers to be more relaxed, more at ease and more comfortable than candidates who received non-verbal disapproval from the interviewer (Keenan, 1976).

Impression management strategies may also be utilised by the interviewee. For example, the American Psychological Association gives specific suggestions, based on research, to graduate school applicants on how to communicate non-verbally favourable qualities during an interview (Fretz and Stang, 1982). Research studies generally show that such non-verbal behaviours as high levels of gaze, combinations of paralinguistic cues, frequent head movement, frequent smiling, posture, voice loudness and personal appearance, affect impressions formed and evaluative judgements made by employment interviewers (Forbes and Jackson, 1980; Hollandsworth *et al.*, 1979; Young and Beier, 1977). Caution should be advised before applying these specific behaviours, since qualifying factors have been reported. For example, one study reported that if an applicant avoids gazing at the interviewer, an applicant of high status will be evaluated more negatively than one of low status (Tessler and Sushelsky, 1978). Evidently, gaze aversion was expected, on the part of the interviewer, from a low-status applicant but not from a higher status one. Status differences and associated non-verbal behaviours have also been recognised in the military setting where physical appearance such as uniform markings clearly identify the ranks of the interactants (Hall, 1966).

This brief sampling of empirical results provides impressive evidence for the importance of non-verbal behaviour in managing and forming impressions in role-defined settings. However, these results also reveal that non-verbal behaviour in the form of kinesics interacts with other non-verbal categories such as proxemics, paralanguage, physical characteristics and environmental factors. Although this creates a rather complex formula for applications, all of Knapp's seven dimensions are important to consider in developing communication skills in the various contexts of role-defined interactions that one experiences.

AN EXAMPLE OF RESEARCH AND APPLICATION: INTERNATIONAL POLITICS

In this section, a programme of research will be briefly presented that illustrates an attempt to identify systematically certain non-verbal behaviours associated with specific intentions of the communicator (encoder), and to then apply these findings to develop better skills in interpreting (decoding) observed behaviour of others (Druckman *et al.*, 1982). The context selected for this research is international politics. This is an area that encompasses a broad range of situational, cultural, personal and social factors and thus attempts to deal with the complexity of non-verbal expression and interpretation. It is also an area which contains elements similar to a variety of everyday experiences encountered by a broad range of people in professional and social interactions.

Laboratory research

The initial research project involved a role-playing study in which upper-level university students were instructed to play the role of a foreign ambassador being interviewed in a press conference setting. A set of pertinent issues was derived from United Nations transcripts and presented to the subjects in detail. After studying the issues, subjects were randomly assigned to one of three intention conditions which directed them to express their country's position on the issues in either an honest, deceptive or evasive fashion. Examples of honest, deceptive and evasive arguments and discussion points were presented to the subjects to help prepare them for the interview.

A formal 15-minute videotaped interview was conducted between the 'ambassador' and a trained actor playing the role of a press interviewer. An informal 7-minute post-interview discussion was also videotaped in which the subject was asked to be 'him/herself' and discuss his or her activities at the university. It is important to note that the subject-ambassadors were not aware that the purpose of the study was to assess non-verbal behaviour exhibited by them during the interview. Thus, the study dealt with 'informative' rather than consciously controlled 'communication' acts as described by Ekman and Friesen (1969) and discussed by Dittman (1978). Also, the interviewer was unaware of whether the subject was in the honest, deceptive or evasive intention condition. Ten subjects served in each of the conditions. The videotaped interviews were coded by an elaborate process involving 200 student volunteers carefully trained reliably to observe specific channels of non-verbal behaviour patterns produced by subjects in the honest, deceptive and evasive conditions.

Research findings

Among the detailed results presented by Druckman *et al.* (1982), several general findings are appropriate for this discussion. One set of analyses revealed that honest, deceptive and evasive subjects could be classified accurately solely on the basis of their non-verbal behaviours. Using ten non-verbal behaviours (for instance, head-shaking, gaze time at interviewer, leg movements, and so on), 96.6 per cent of the subjects were classified correctly as being honest, deceptive or evasive. In another segment of the interview, three non-verbal behaviours (for instance, leg movements, gaze time at interviewer and object-fidgeting) were accurate in 77 per cent of the cases in detecting honest, deceptive or evasive intentions of the subject.

These computer-generated results were in striking contrast to another set of judgements produced by three corporate executives selected on the basis of their experience and expertise in 'dealing effectively with people'. These executives viewed the tapes and then guessed if the subject had been in the honest, deceptive or evasive condition. Results indicated that the experts correctly classified the subject-ambassadors in only 43, 30 and 27 per cent of the cases, respectively. Thus, even 'experts' would appear to benefit from further training and skill development in interpreting non-verbal behaviours – and actually may be in special need of such training (DePaulo *et al.*, 1985).

Another set of analyses revealed significant shifts in non-verbal behaviour patterns when the subject changed from the ambassador role to being 'him/herself' during the informal post-interview period. Generally, subjects showed more suppressed, constrained behaviour when playing the role of ambassador: for example, significantly fewer facial displays, less head nodding, fewer body swivels and less frequent statements occurred during the interview than in the post-interview period. It would appear that the same person displays different patterns and levels of non-verbal behaviour depending upon the role that is being communicated. Also, different patterns of behaviour occurred in the three 5-minute segments of the formal interview. Thus, even when a person is playing the same role, different behaviours emerge during the course of an interaction. These may be due to factors of adaptation, stress, familiarity, relaxation, or fatigue.

Yet another set of analyses using subjects' responses to a set of post-interview questions indicated that certain patterns of non-verbal behaviours were related to feelings the subject had during the interview (for example, stress, relaxation, confidence, apprehension), and that these patterns were related to the intention condition assigned to the subject. Evasive and honest subjects displayed behaviours indicating involvement, while evasive and deceptive subjects displayed non-verbal indication of stress and tension. Subjects in all three conditions displayed behaviour patterns related to expressed feelings of confidence and effectiveness.

Training the decoder

Even though the results of this study were complex, they were organised into a training programme designed to improve the observer's ability to distinguish among honest, deceptive and evasive intentions of subjects playing this role. Four training programmes were presented to different groups of decoders and represented four types of instruction, ranging from general (a global lecture and an audio-only presentation) to specific information (a technical briefing and inference training) regarding non-verbal indicators of intention. Results showed that accuracy of judgement in distinguishing between honest, deceptive and evasive presentations improved as the specificity and applied organisation of the instructional materials increased. The strategy used for inference training was shown to be especially effective (see Chapter 5 in Druckman *et al.*, 1982, for details).

Strategies for interpreting non-verbal behaviour: an application of experimental results

The studies reviewed above support the assumption that gestures, facial expressions and other non-verbal behaviours convey meaning. However, while adding value to interpretation in general, an understanding of the non-verbal aspects of behaviour may not transfer directly to specific settings. Meaning must be established within the context of interest: for example, the non-verbal behaviour observed during the course of a speech, interview or informal conversation.

Building on the earlier laboratory work, a plan has been developed for deriving plausible inferences about intentions and psychological or physical states of political leaders (see also Druckman and Hyman, 1991). The plan is a structure for interpretation: it is a valuable tool for the professional policy analyst; it is a useful *framework* for the interested observer of significant events. In the following sections, themes and techniques for analysis are discussed, and the special features of one particular context, that of international politics, is emphasised.

Themes for analysis

Moving pictures shown on video or film are panoramas of quickly changing actions, sounds and expressions. Just where to focus one's attention is a basic analytical problem. Several leads are suggested by frameworks constructed to guide the research cited above. Providing a structure for analysis, the frameworks emphasise two general themes, namely focusing on combinations of non-verbal behaviours and taking contextual features into account.

While coded separately, the non-verbal behaviours can be combined for analysis of total displays. Patterns of behaviours then provide a basis for inferences about feelings or intentions. The patterns may take several forms: one consists of linear combinations of constituent behaviours, as when gaze time, leg movements and object-fidgeting are used in equations to identify probable intentions; a second form is correlated indicators or clusters, such as the pattern of trunk swivels, rocking movements, head-shaking and head nodding shown by subjects attempting to withhold information about their 'nation's' policy; another form is behaviours that occur within the same time period as was observed for deceivers in the study presented above – for example, a rocking/nodding/shaking cluster was observed during interviews with deceptive 'ambassadors'.

Patterned movements are an important part of the total situation. By anchoring the movements to feelings and intentions, one can get an idea of their meaning. But there are other sources of explanation for what is observed. These sources may be referred to as context. Included as context are the semi-fixed objects in the setting (for instance, furniture), the other people with whom the subject interacts and the nature of the discourse that transpires. The proposition that context greatly influences social interaction/behaviour comes alive in Rapoport's (1982) treatment of the meaning of the built environment. Constraining influences of other people on exhibited expressions are made apparent in Duncan's (1983) detailed analyses of conversational turntaking. Relationships between verbal statements and non-verbal behaviour are the central concern in the analyses of stylised enactments provided by Druckman *et al.* (1982). Each of these works is a state-of-the-art analysis. Together, they are the background for developing systems that address the questions of *what* to look for and *how* to use the observations/codes for interpretation. Highlighted here is a structure for interpreting material on the tapes.

It is obvious that the particular intention–interpretation relationships of interest vary with particular circumstances. Several issues are particularly salient within the area of international politics. Of interest might be questions like: What is the state of health of the leader (or spokesman)? To what degree are statements honestly expressive of true beliefs (or actual policy)? How committed is the person to the position expressed? How fully consolidated and secure is the person's political position?

Knowing where to focus attention is a first step in assessment. A particular theme is emphasised in each of the political issues mentioned above. Signs of failing health are suggested by incongruities or inconsistencies in verbal and non-verbal behaviours, as well as between different non-verbal channels. Deception is suggested by excessive body activity, as well as deviations from baseline data. Strong commitment to policy is revealed in increased intensity of behaviours expressed in a variety of channels. The careful recording of proxemic activity or spatial relationships provides clues to political status. Biographical profiles summarise co-varying clusters of facial expressions and body movements. Each of these themes serves to direct an analyst's attention to *relationships* (for health indicators and profiles), to *particular non-verbal channels* (for deception and status indicators), or to *amount* as in the case of commitment.

Knowing specifically what to look at is the second step in assessment. Results of a number of experiments suggest particular behaviours. These provide multiple signs whose meaning is revealed in conjunction with the themes noted above. Illustrative indicators and references in each category are the following.

Health indicators

1 *Pain*: furrowed brow and raised eyelids; change in vocal tone and higher pitch (Ekman and Friesen, 1975);
2 *Depression*: hand-to-body motions, increased self-references and extended periods of silence (Aronson and Weintraub, 1972);
3 *Irritability*: more forced smiling (McClintock and Hunt, 1975), fewer positive head nods (Mehrabian, 1971);
4 *Tension*: increased spontaneous movement (Mehrabian and Ksionzky, 1972), faster eyeblinking, self-adaptive gestures (for body tension) (McClintock and Hunt, 1975);

5 *Stress*: flustered speech as indicated by repetitions, corrections, use of 'ah' or 'you know', rhythm disturbances (Baxter and Rozelle, 1975; Kasl and Mahl, 1965), abrupt changes in behaviour (Hermann, 1979), increased eye movements and gaze aversion in an otherwise immobile facial display, increased head rotation/elevation, increased placement of hands in front of the body (Baxter and Rozelle, 1975);
6 *General state*: verbal/non-verbal inconsistencies where different messages are sent in the two channels (Mehrabian, 1972).

Deception indicators

1 *Direct deception*: speech errors as deviations from baseline data (Mehrabian, 1971), tone of voice (DePaulo *et al.*, 1980), fidgeting with objects, less time spent looking at the other than during a baseline period, patterns of rocking, head-shaking and nodding movements varying together (co-ordinated body movements) (Druckman *et al.*, 1982);
2 *Indirect deception (evasion)*: more leg movements during periods of silence (when subject feels less assertive), frequent gazes elsewhere especially during periods of stress, frequent head-shaking during early periods in the interaction, increasing trend of self-fidgeting throughout the interaction (Druckman *et al.*, 1982; McClintock and Hunt, 1975).

Commitment to policies

1 *Commitment*: increased use of 'allness' terms (Hermann, 1977), increased redundancy, more trunk swivels, more time spent looking at (versus looking away from) the other (Druckman *et al.*, 1982);
2 *Persuasiveness (impact on others)*: increased intensity in voice, increased object (other) – focused movements (Freedman, 1972), more facial activity and gesturing, increased head nodding, fewer self-manipulations, reduced reclining angles (Mehrabian, 1972; Washburn and Hakel, 1973);
3 *Credibility (impact on others)*: sustained gazing at short distances (Exline and Eldridge, 1967; Hemsley and Doob, 1975), relaxed vocalisations (Addington, 1971)

Political status

1 *Relative status*: non-reciprocated touching, eye contact at closer distances for higher status members, more frequent use of words suggesting distance from people and objects (Frank, 1977), hand and neck relaxation, sideways-lean, reclining posture, arm–leg position asymmetry (Mehrabian, 1972);
2 *Changes in status*: increased physical distance from colleagues (Dorsey and Meisels, 1969), increased signs of psychological withdrawal from situations (outward-directed gestures, changed postures) for reduced status (Mehrabian, 1968), more frequent appearances at state functions for enhanced status.

Techniques for analysis

Whereas patterns of non-verbal behaviour are the basis for interpretation, it is the separate behaviours which are the constituents of the displays. A first step is to code specific, well-defined movements and expressions. Advances in technique make possible the efficient coding of a large variety of behaviours. Particularly relevant is a sub-set of non-verbal behaviours chosen on the basis of high reliability, as determined by independent coders, and importance, in terms of distinguishing among intentions and emotional states. Included in this list are the following: gaze time at interviewer or other person, leg movements, object-fidgeting, speech errors, speaking frequency, rocking movements, head nodding, illustrator gestures and foot movements. These are some of the movements or vocalisations coded directly from videotapes of laboratory subjects (experiments cited above) and world leaders.

Efficiency is gained by training coders to be channel specialists. Small groups are trained to focus their attention on one channel – vocalisations, eyes, face, body, legs, or spatial arrangements. Frequencies are recorded for some measures (for instance, leg movements); for others, the coder records time (for example, gaze at interviewer, speaking time). Further specialisation is obtained by assigning the different groups to specific segments of the tapes. Such a division of labour speeds the process, increases reliability and preserves the coders for other tasks. A set of twenty-five non-verbal behaviours shown by subjects in thirty, 20-minute tapes was coded in about three weeks, each individual coder contributing only 2 hours of effort.

The procedures define a coding scheme or notation system for processing video material. Computer-assisted analysis would facilitate the transforming of non-verbal measures into profiles of selected world leaders. Here, one becomes more interested in characteristic postures or movements than in particular psychological or physical states. The emphasis is on idiosyncratic styles of leaders, conditioned as they are by situational factors. Using the non-verbal notation system, these behaviours can be represented as animated displays. Recent developments in computer graphics and virtual reality technologies expand the range of programming options (Badler *et al.*, 1991). They also contribute tools for the creative exploration of movement and expression control, such as manipulating the display to depict styles in varying situations (Badler *et al.*, 1993).

The list of behaviours is one basis for structuring the analysis. Another basis is a more general category system that encompasses a range of situations, purposes and verbal statements, as well as types of displayed non-verbal behaviours. Sufficient footage in each category makes possible the tasks of charting trends, making comparisons and developing profiles. It also contributes to inventory management: systematic categorising and indexing of materials aids in the task of retrieving relevant types from archival collections. Multiple measurements provide alternative indicators that may be useful when all channels are not available to the observer (such as leg and foot movements for a speaker who stands behind a podium, eye movements for an actor seen from a distance). They also provide complementary indicators, bolstering one's confidence in the inferences made. And, for the time-sensitive analyst, a manageable sub-set of non-verbal behaviours can be identified for 'on the spot' commentary.

Systematic comparisons

Focusing on the individual foreign leader, the non-verbal indicators can be used to build profiles. It is evident that such an approach emphasises Allport's (1961) concept of morphogenic analysis and stresses the analogy of expressive behaviour as personal idiom.

This strategy of systematic comparison is designed to increase an analyst's understanding of his 'subject'. This is done by tracking the displays exhibited by selected individuals across situations and in conjunction with verbal statements.

Comparisons would be made in several ways: (1) examine deviations from baseline data established for each person (for instance, speech errors); (2) compare non-verbal displays for the same person in different situations (for example, within or outside home country; formal or informal settings); and (3) compare displays for different types of verbal statements (for example, defence of position, policy commitment). These analyses highlight consistencies and inconsistencies at several levels – between situations, between verbal and non-verbal channels, and within different non-verbal channels. They also alert the analyst to changes in non-verbal activity: being aware of changes from a baseline period would give one a better understanding of relatively unique expressive behaviour. Further analysis consists of comparing different persons in similar situations or dealing with similar subject matter.

The value of these comparisons is that they contribute to the development of a system of movement representation similar to the notation and animation systems described by Badler and Smoliar (1979). Extracted from the data are sets of co-ordinated movements which may change over time and situations. The co-ordinated movements can be represented in animated graphic displays. Illuminated by such displays are 'postural' differences within actors across time and between actors. When associated with events and context, the observations turn on the issue of how the feelings and intentions which are evoked by different situations are represented in body movement. When compared to displays by actors in other cultural settings, the observations are relevant to the question: What is the contribution of culture to observed non-verbal displays? (See our discussion above on cultural influences.)

Several analytical strategies enable an investigator to get to know his subject or group. Each strategy formalises the idea of 'following a subject around'. Extended coverage provides an opportunity to assemble baseline data for comparisons. It also permits execution of within-subject analytic designs for systematic comparison of displays observed in different situations and occasions, as well as when addressing different topics. These strategies enable an analyst to discriminate more precisely the meaning of various non-verbal displays.

Extensive video footage makes possible quite sophisticated analyses of leaders' behaviours. Relationships are highlighted from comparisons of responses to questions intended to arouse varying levels of stress. Profiles are constructed from the combinations of expressions and movements seen over time. Predictive accuracy of the form 'Is this person telling the truth?' is estimated from behaviours coded in situations where a subject's intentions are known, namely does the sub-set of behaviours discriminate between an honest, evasive and deceptive statement? Contributing to an enhanced analytical capability, these results reduce dependence on notation systems developed in settings removed from the critical situations of interest. They would also contribute information relevant to time-sensitive requests.

Time-sensitive requests

Demand for current assessments often place the analyst on the spot, being frequently asked to provide interpretations without the benefits of penetrating analysis, extensive video footage or hindsight. Indeed, these are the conditions often present for both technical specialist and layman. Scheibe (1979) noted that the informed observer (whom he calls the 'sagacious observer') relies on good memory for past characteristic patterns and astute observation of departure from the 'typical'. Under these conditions, notation systems are especially useful. They provide the analyst with a structure for focusing attention on relevant details. Determined largely on the basis of what is known, the relevant details are part of a larger coding system whose validity is previously established. Serving to increase the analyst's confidence in personal judgements, the codes (relevant details) highlight where to focus attention and what to look at. Examples include the following.

Abrupt changes   Readily detectable from limited data, abrupt changes may take the form of incongruities between different non-verbal channels (face and body) or increased intensity of behaviours expressed in a number of channels. The former may be construed as signs of failing health; the latter often indicates a strong commitment to policies.

Leaks   Regarded as signs of deception, leaks take the form of excessive activity in one channel (body) combined with reduced activity in another (face) (Ekman and Friesen, 1974). Based on a 'hydraulic model' analogy, the concept of leakage describes the consequences of attempts by a subject to control facial expressions during deception – to wit, the poker face.

A study designed by the authors was intended as a test of the leakage hypothesis. Subjects in one condition were asked to control their facial expressions during a deceptive communication; those in another condition were asked to control their body movements. Both conditions were compared to an earlier session where subjects were not instructed to control expressions or movements during deception. More body movements in the 'control-face' condition and more facial expressions in the 'control-body' condition than in the earlier session would support the leakage hypothesis. Although the results did not support this hypothesis, they did reveal less overall animation for deceivers in both conditions, supporting the findings obtained by DePaulo *et al.* (1985) showing behavioural inhibition for motivated liars. (See Druckman and Hyman, 1991, for further details.)

Micro-momentary expressions (MMEs)   Regarded as universal expressions, MMEs are the muscle activities that underlie primary emotions (happiness, sadness, surprise, anger, fear, disgust, interest) and information-processing stages (informative seeking, pre-articulation processing, response selection). With the aid of special instrumentation, workers have been able to identify quite precisely the muscle clusters associated with particular emotions (Ekman *et al.*, 1980) or processing stages (Druckman *et al.*, 1983; Karis *et al.*, 1984).

Illustrated above are the kinds of observations that can be used for inferences from limited data; for example, behaviours that change quickly (MMEs) or obviously (incongruities), and those that occur within the time frame of a statement (leaks). However, useful as these indicators are, they are only a part of the story: missing are the cultural and contextual influences that shape what is observed. These influences are discovered through careful analysis of leaders' behaviour in the settings of interest (see the example of videotape analysis of an international conference discussed in Rozelle *et al.*, 1986).

OVERVIEW

Considering the large number of full-length books and articles published on non-verbal behaviour, the present chapter has only provided an up-to-date sampling of the literature on this important form of communication. (For an earlier review, see Rozelle *et al.*, 1986.) Beginning with an organisational overview and historical perspective, the discussion covered general issues, theoretical and methodological frameworks, and provided some specific examples of research findings and applications. As the chapter has demonstrated, there is a wealth of information generated from scientific inquiry which reveals the significant impact of non-verbal behaviour on communication; yet this body of knowledge is incomplete and often complex.

The authors have argued that non-verbal behaviour, as a communication skill, is meaningful only if the context of behaviour is taken into account. Incomplete or narrow perspectives regarding others' or one's own behaviour may lead to misinterpretation of actions observed or performed. On the other hand, careful and reliable applications of non-verbal behaviour can enrich and enlighten one's understanding and control of communication in a variety of situation, role and cultural settings.

In addition to further experimental work and replication of results, one direction for future research may be to study, in greater detail, the accomplishments and strategies of performers and interpreters of non-verbal behaviour. For example, when considering non-verbal behaviour as skilled performance, aspects of style, expertise and expression are stressed. The ways in which such crafted performances are accomplished and their effects assessed should aid in the training and development processes as well as in directing future experimental research. However, regardless of the specific approach, non-verbal behaviour must be examined rigorously by a variety of laboratory and field perspectives such as those discussed in this chapter. Understanding is furthered and applications become possible when attempts are made to synthesise results obtained from the use of a variety of methods and frameworks. The achievements made to date hold promise for significant progress in basic and applied research on this important form of communication.

REFERENCES

Addington, D. W. (1971) 'The Effect of Vocal Variation on Ratings of Source Credibility', *Speech Monograph*, 35, 242–7.
Allport, G. (1961) *Pattern and Growth in Personality*, Holt, Rinehart & Winston, New York.
—— and Vernon, P. (1933) *Studies in Expressive Movement*, Macmillan, New York.
Argyle, M. (1986) 'Rules for Social Relationships in Four Cultures', *Australian Journal of Psychology*, 38, 309–18.
—— (1967) *The Psychology of Interpersonal Behaviour*, Penguin, London.
—— (1969) *Social Interaction*, Aldine-Atherton, New York.
—— and Cook, M. (1976) *Gaze and Mutual Gaze*, Cambridge University Press, New York.
—— and Dean, J. (1965) 'Eye-Contact, Distance and Affiliation', *Sociometry*, 28, 289–304.
—— and Kendon, A. (1967) 'The Experimental Analysis of Social Performance', in L. Berkowitz (ed.), *Advances in Experimental Social Psychology*, Academic Press, New York.
Aristotle (1927) *Poetics*, W. Heineman, London.
—— (1991) *The Art of Rhetoric*, Penguin, London.
Aronson, H. and Weintraub, W. (1972) 'Personal Adaptation as Reflected in Verbal Behaviour', in A. W. Siegman and H. Pope (eds), *Studies in Dyadic Communication*, Pergamon, New York.
Bacon, F. (1884) *The Essays*, Lee and Shepard, Boston.
—— (1947) *The New Atlantis*, Russell F. Moore, New York.

Badler, N. I. and Smoliar, W. W. (1979) 'Digital Representation of Human Movement, *Computing Surveys*, 11, 19–38.

Badler, N.I., Barsky, B. A. and Zeltzer, D.(eds) (1991) *Making the Move: Mechanics, Control, and Animation of Articulated Figures*, Morgan Kaufman Publishers, San Mateo, CA.

Badler, N.I., Phillips, C. B. and Webber, B. L.(1993) *Simulating Humans: Computer Graphics Animation and Control*, Oxford University Press, New York.

Bartlett, F. (1958) *Thinking: An Experimental and Social Study*, Basic Books, New York.

Baumeister, R. (1982) 'A Self-presentational View of Social Phenomena', *Psychological Bulletin*, 91, 3–26.

Baxter, J. C. (1970) 'Interpersonal Spacing in Natural Settings', *Sociometry*, 33, 444–56.

—— and Rozelle, R. M. (1975) 'Non-verbal Expression as a Function of Crowding During a Simulated Police–citizen Encounter', *Journal of Personality and Social Psychology*, 32, 40–54.

Bilodeau, E. (ed.) (1966) *Acquisition of Skill*, Academic Press, New York.

Birdwhistell, R. (1952) *Introduction to Kinesics*, Foreign Service Institute, Washington DC.

—— (1970) *Kinesics and Context*, University of Pennsylvania Press, Philadelphia.

Bond, C., Omar, A., Mahoud, A. and Bonser, R. (1990) 'Lie Detection Across Cultures', *Journal of Nonverbal Behavior*, 14, 189–204.

Bulwer, J. (1644/1974) *Chirologia*, Southern Illinois University Press, Carbondale. Ill.

Cody, M., Lee, W. and Chao, E. (1989) 'Telling Lies: Correlates of Deception Among Chinese', in J. Forgas and J. Innes (eds), *Recent Advances in Social Psychology: An International Perspective*, McGraw-Hill, New York.

Cole, P. (1984) 'Display Rules and the Socialisation of Affect Displays' in G. Ziven (ed.), *The Development of Expressive Behaviour: Biology-Environment Interactions*, Academic Press, New York.

Collett, P. (1971) 'Training Englishmen in the Nonverbal Behaviour of Arabs', *International Journal of Psychology,* 6, 209–15.

Costanzo, M. (1992) 'Training Students to Decode Verbal and Nonverbal Cues: Effects on Confidence and Performance', *Journal of Educational Psychology*, 84, 308–13.

Crittenden, K. S. and Bae, H. (1994) 'Self Effacement and Social Responsibility: Attribution as Impression Management in Asian Cultures', *American Behavioral Psychology*, 37, 653–71.

Darwin, C. (1872) *The Expression of Emotion in Man and Animals*, John Murray, London.

Davis, M. (1984) 'Nonverbal Behaviour and Psychotherapy: Process Research', in H. Wolfgang (ed.), *Nonverbal Behaviour: Perspectives, Applications, Intercultural Insights*, C. J. Hogrefe Inc., New York, pp. 203–29.

DePaulo, B. (1992) 'Nonverbal Behavior as Self-Presentation', *Psychological Bulletin*, 111, 203–43.

——, Zuckerman, M. and Rosenthal, R. (1980) 'Detecting Deception: Modality Effects', in L. Wheeler (ed.), *Review of Personality and Social Psychology*, Vol. 1., Sage, Beverly Hills.

——, Stone, J. I. and Lassiter, G. D. (1985) 'Deceiving and Detecting Deceit', in B. R. Schlenker (ed.), *The Self in Social Life*, McGraw-Hill, New York.

Deutsch, F. (1952) 'Analytic Posturology', *The Psychoanalytic Quarterly*, 21, 196–214.

—— (1959) 'Correlations of Verbal and Nonverbal Communication in Interviews Elicited by Associative Anamnesis', *Psychosomatic Medicine* 21, 123–30.

Dittman, A. T. (1972) *Interpersonal Messages of Emotion*, Springer, New York.

—— (1978) 'The Role of Body Movement in Communication', in A. W. Siegman and S. Feldstein (eds), *Nonverbal Behaviour and Communication*, Lawrence Erlbaum, Hillsdale, NJ.

Dorsey, M. A. and Meisels, M. (1969) 'Personal Space and Self Protection', *Journal of Personality and Social Psychology*, 11, 93–7.

Druckman, D. and Bjork, R. A.(eds) (1991) *In the Mind's Eye: Enhancing Human Performance*, National Academy Press, Washington, DC.

Druckman, D. and Hyman, R., (1991) 'Hiding and Detecting Deception', Chapter 9 in D. Druckman and R. A. Bjork (eds), *In the Mind's Eye: Enhancing Human Performance*, National Academy Press, Washington, DC.

Druckman, D., Rozelle, R. and Baxter, J. (1982) *Nonverbal Communication: Survey, Theory, and Research*, Sage, Beverly Hills.

Druckman, D., Karis, D. and Donchin, E. (1983) 'Information-processing in Bargaining: Reactions to an Opponent's Shift in Concession Strategy', in R. Tietz (ed.), *Aspiration Levels in Bargaining and Economic Decisionmaking*. Springer-Verlag, Berlin.

Duncan, S. D. (1969) 'Nonverbal Communication', *Psychological Bulletin*, 72, 118–37.

—— (1972) 'Some Signals and Rules for Taking Speaking Turns in Conversation', *Journal of Personality and Social Psychology*, 23, 283–92.

—— (1983) 'Speaking Turns: Studies in Structure and Individual Differences', in J. M. Wiemann and R. P. Harrison (eds), *Nonverbal Interaction*, Sage, Beverly Hills.

—— and Fiske, D. W. (1977) *Face to Face Interaction: Research, Methods, and Theory*, Lawrence Erlbaum, Hillsdale, NJ.

Ekman, P. (1974) 'Detecting Deception From the Body or Face', *Journal of Personality and Social Psychology*, 39, 228–98.

—— (1975) *Unmasking the Face: A Guide to Recognizing Emotions from Facial Clues*, Prentice-Hall, Englewood Cliffs, NJ.

—— (1992a) 'Facial Expression of Emotions: New Findings, New Questions', *Psychological Science*, 3, 34–8.

—— (1992b) 'Are There Basic Emotions?', *Psychological Review*, 99, 550–3.

—— (1992c) *Telling Lies: Clues to Deceit in the Marketplace, Politics and Marriage*, Norton & Company, New York.

—— (1993) 'Facial Expression and Emotion', *American Psychologist*, 48, 384–92.

—— (1994) 'Strong Evidence for Universals in Facial Expressions: A Reply to Russell's Mistaken Critique', *Psychological Bulletin*, 115, 268–87.

—— and Friesen, W. V. (1969) 'The Repertoire of Nonverbal Behavior: Categories, Origins, Usage, and Coding', *Semiotica*, 1, 49–98.

—— (1974) 'Detecting Deception from the Body or Face', *Journal of Personality and Social Psychology*, 39, 228–98.

—— (1975) 'The Repertoire of Nonverbal Behaviour: Categories, Origins, Usage and Coding', *Semiotica*, 1, 49–98.

—— (1986) 'A New Pan-Cultural Facial Expression of Emotion', *Motivation and Emotion*, 10, 159–68.

Ekman, P. and Oster, H. (1979) 'Facial Expression of Emotion', in M. Rosenzweig (ed.), *Annual Review of Psychology*, Annual Reviews Inc., Stanford, CA, 527–54.

Ekman, P. and O'Sullivan, M. (1988) 'The Role of Context on Interpreting Facial Expressions: Comment on Russell and Fahr (1987)', *Journal of Experimental Psychology, General*, 117, 86–8.

—— (1991) 'Who Can Catch a Liar?', *American Psychology*, 46, 913–20.

Ekman, P., Friesen, W. V. and Ellsworth, P. (1972) *Emotion in the Human Face*, Pergamon, New York.

Ekman, P., Friesen, W. V. and Ancoli, S. (1980) 'Facial Signs of Emotional Experience', *Journal of Personality and Social Psychology*, 39, 1125–34.

Ekman, P., Friesen, W. V. and Bear, J. (1984) 'The International Language of Gestures', *Psychology Today*, May, 64–9.

Ekman, P., Friesen, W. V., O'Sullivan, M., Chan, A. *et al.* (1987) 'Universals and Cultural Differences in the Judgments of Facial Expressions of Emotion', *Journal of Personality and Social Psychology*, 53, 712–17.

Ekman, P., Davidson, R. and Friesen, W. (1990) 'The Duchenne Smile: Emotional Expression and Brain Physiology', *Journal of Personality and Social Psychology*, 58, 342–53.

Ekman, P., O'Sullivan, M., Friesen, W., and Scherer, K. (1991) 'Face, Voice, and Body in Detecting Deception', *Journal of Nonverbal. Behaviour*, 15, 125–35.

Exline, R. V. and Eldridge, C. (1967) 'Effects of Two Patterns of a Speaker's Visual Behavior Upon the Perception of the Authenticity of His Verbal Message', paper presented at the meeting of the Eastern Psychological Association, Boston.

Faure, G. O. (1993) 'Negotiation Concepts Across Cultures: Implementing Non-verbal Tools', *Negotiation Journal*, 9, 355–9.

Feldman, S. (1959) *Mannerisms of Speech and Gestures in Everyday Life*, International Universities Press, New York.

Fiedler, K. and Walka, I. (1993) 'Training Lie Detectors to Use Nonverbal Cues Instead of Global Heuristics', *Human Communication Research*, 20, 199–223.

Forbes, R. J. and Jackson, P. R. (1980) 'Nonverbal Behaviour and the Outcome of Selection Interviews', *Journal of Occupational Psychology*, 53, 65–72.

Frank, R. S. (1977) 'Nonverbal and Paralinguistic Analysis of Political Behaviour: The First McGovern-Humphrey California Primary Debate', in M. G. Hermann (ed.), *A Psychological Examination of Political Leaders*, John Wiley, New York.

Freedman, R. (1972) 'The Analysis of Movement Behaviour During the Clinical Interview', in A. W. Siegman and B. Pope (eds), *Studies in Dyadic Communication*, Pergamon Press, New York.

Fretz, B. R. and Stang, D. J. (1982) *Preparing for Graduate Study in Psychology: Not for Seniors Only!*, American Psychological Association, Washington, DC.

Freud, S. (1905/1938) 'Psychopathology of Everyday Life', in A. A. Brill (ed.), *The Basic Writings of Sigmund Freud*, Modern Library, New York.

—— (1924) *A General Introduction to Psychoanalysis*, Doubleday, Garden City.

Friedman, H. (1979) 'The Concept of Skill in Non-verbal Communication: Implications for Understanding Social Interaction', in R. Rosenthal (ed.), *Skill in Non-verbal Communication: Individual Differences*, Oelgeschlager, Gunn & Hain, Cambridge, MA.

Garratt, G., Baxter, J. and Rozelle, R. (1981) 'Training University Police in Black-American Nonverbal Behaviours: An Application to Police–Community Relations', *Journal of Social Psychology*, 113, 217–29.

Gentner, D. and Grudin, J. (1985) 'The Evolution of Mental Metaphors in Psychology: A 90-year Perspective', *American Psychologist*, 40, 181–92.

Gibbs, R. (1994) *The Poetics of Mind*, Cambridge University Press, New York.

Glashow, S. (1980) 'Toward a Unified Theory: Threads in a Tapestry', *Science,* 210, 1319–23.

Goffman, E. (1959) *The Presentation of Self in Everyday Life*, Doubleday Anchor Books, Garden City.

—— (1969) *Strategic Interaction*, University of Pennsylvania Press, Philadelphia.

—— (1971) *Relations in Public*, Basic Books, New York.

Hager, J. C. and Ekman, P. (1979) 'Long-distance Transmission of Facial Affect Signals', *Ethology and Sociobiology*, 1, 77–82.

Hall, E. T. (1959) *The Silent Language*, Doubleday, New York.

—— (1966) *The Hidden Dimension*, Doubleday, New York.

Hargie, O., Saunders, C. and Dickson, D. (1994) *Social Skills in Interpersonal Communication*, Routledge, London.

Harper, R. G., Weins, A. N. and Matarazzo, J. D. (1978) *Non-verbal Communication: The State of the Art*, John Wiley, New York.

Hemsley, G. D. and Doob, A. N. (1975) 'Effect of Looking Behavior on Perceptions of a Communicator's Credibility', paper presented at the meeting of the American Psychological Association, Chicago, Ill.

Hermann, M. G. (1977) 'Verbal Behaviour of Negotiators in Periods of High and Low Stress', in M. G. Hermann (ed.), *A Psychological Examination of Political Leaders*, Free Press, New York.

—— (1979) 'Indicators of Stress in Policymakers During Foreign Policy Crises', *Political Psychology*, 1, 27–46.

Hollandsworth, J. G., Jr., Kazelskis, R., Stevens, J. *et al.* (1979) 'Relative Contributions of Verbal, Articulative, and Nonverbal Communication to Employment Decisions in the Job Interview Setting', *Personnel Psychology,* 32, 359–67.

Hyman, R. (1989) 'The Psychology of Deception', in M. Rosenzweig and L. Porter (eds), *Annual Review of Psychology*, 40, 133–54.

Hyman, R. and Druckman, D.(1991) 'A Broader Concept of Deception', Chapter 10 in D. Druckman and R. A. Bjork (eds), *In the Mind's Eye: Enhancing Human Performance*, National Academy Press, Washington, DC.

Izard, C. (1971) *The Face of Emotion*, Appleton-Century Crofts, New York.

Jaynes, J. (1976) *The Origin of Consciousness in the Breakdown of the Bicameral Mind*, Houghton Mifflin Co, Boston.

Jones, A. P., Rozelle, R. M. and Svyantek, D. J. (1985) 'Organizational Climate: An Environmental Affordances Approach', unpublished manuscript, University of Houston, Texas.

Jones, E. E. and Nisbett, R. E. (1972) 'The Actor and the Observer: Divergent Perceptions of the Causes of Behaviour', in E. E. Jones, D. E. Kanouse, H. H. Kelly *et al.*(eds), *Attribution: Perceiving the Causes of Behaviour*, General Learning Press, Morristown, NJ.

Jones, E. E. and Thibaut, J. (1958) 'Interaction Goals as Bases of Inference in Interpersonal Perception', in R. Taguiri and L. Petrullo (eds) *Person Perception and Interpersonal Behaviour*, Stanford University Press, Stanford, CA.

Jones, E. E. and Wortman, C. (1973) *Ingratiation: An Attributional Approach*, General Learning Press, Morristown, NJ.

Jourard, S. (1966) 'An Exploratory Study of Body-accessibility', *British Journal of Social and Clinical Psychology*, 5, 221–31.

Karis, D., Druckman, D., Lissak, R. *et al.* (1984) 'A Psychophysiological Analysis of Bargaining: ERPs and Facial Expressions', in R. Karrer, J. Cohen and P. Tueting (eds), *Brain and Information: Event-Related Potentials*, Annals of the New York Academy of Sciences, Vol. 425, New York Academy of Sciences, New York.

Kasl, S. V. and Mahl, G. F. (1965) 'The Relationsips of Disturbances and Hesitations in Spontaneous Speech to Anxiety', *Journal of Personality and Social Psychology,* 1, 425–33.

Keenan, A. (1976) 'Effects of Nonverbal Behaviour of Interviewers on Candidates Performance', *Journal of Occupational Psychology*, 49, 171–76.

Kendon, A. (1981) 'The Study of Gesture: Some Remarks on its History', in J. N. Deely and M. D. Lenhart (eds), *Semiotics* (1983), Plenum Press, New York.

Klopf, D. W., Thompson, C.A., Ishii, S. and Sallinen-Kuparinen, A. (1991) 'Nonverbal Immediacy Differences Among Japanese, Finnish, and American University Students', *Perceptual and Motor Skills*, 73, 209–10.

Knapp, M. L. (1972) *Nonverbal Communication in Human Interaction*, Holt, Rinehart & Winston, New York.

—— (1984) 'The Study of Nonverbal Behaviour vis-à-vis Human Communication Theory', in A. Wolfgang (ed.), *Nonverbal Behaviour: Perspective, Application, Intercultural Insights*, C. J. Hogrefe Inc., New York.

Koestler, A. (1964) *The Act of Creation*, Hutchinson, London.

LaFrance, M. and Mayo, C. (1978) *Moving Bodies: Nonverbal Communication in Social Relationships*, Brooks Cole, Monterey, CA.

Lakoff, G. (1993) 'The Contemporary Theory of Metaphor', in A. Ortony (ed.), *Metaphor and Thought* (2nd edn), Cambridge University Press, New York.

—— and Johnson, M. (1980) *Metaphors We Live By*, University of Chicago Press, Chicago.

Lavater, J. (1789) *Essays on Physiognomy*, Vol. 1, John Murray, London.

Leary, D. E. (1990) *Metaphors in the History of Psychology*, Cambridge University Press, New York.

McArthur, L. Z. and Baron, R. M. (1983) 'Toward an Ecological Theory of Social Perception', *Psychological Review*, 90, 215–38.

McClintock, C. C. and Hunt, R. G. (1975) 'Nonverbal Indicators of Affect and Deception', *Journal of Applied Social Psychology*, 1, 54–67.

MacKay, D. M. (1972) 'Formal Analysis of Communicative Processes', in R. A. Hinde (ed.), *Nonverbal Communication*, Cambridge University Press, Cambridge.

Mahl, G. F. and Schulze, G. (1964) 'Psychological Research in the Extralinguistic Area', in T. H. Sebeok, A. S. Hayes and M. C. Bateson (eds), *Approaches to Semiotics*, Mouton, The Hague.

Manning, P. (ed.) (1965) *Office Design: A Study of Environment*, Rockliff Brothers Ltd, Liverpool.

March, R. M. (1988) *The Japanese Negotiator: Subtlety and Strategy Beyond Western Logic*, Kodansha International, Tokyo.

Matsumoto, D. (1996) *Culture and Psychology*, Brooks Cole, Pacific Grove.

—— and Ekman, P. (1989) 'American–Japanese Cultural Differences in Intensity Ratings of Facial Expressions of Emotion', *Motivation and Emotion*, 13, 143–57.

Mehrabian, A. (1968) 'Relationship of Attitude to Seated Posture, Orientation and Distance', *Journal of Personality and Social Psychology*, 10, 26–30.

—— (1971) 'Nonverbal Betrayal of Feeling', *Journal of Experimental Research in Personality*, 5, 64–73.

—— (1972) *Nonverbal Communication*, Aldine, Chicago.

—— and Ksionzky, S. (1972) 'Categories of Social Behaviour', *Comparative Group Studies*, 3, 425–436.

Mikolic, J. M., Parker, J. C. and Pruitt, D. G. (1994) 'Escalation in Response to Persistent Annoyance: Groups vs. Individuals and Gender Effects', unpublished manuscript, State University of New York, Buffalo.

O'Hair, D., Cody, M. J., Wang, X. and Yi Chan, E. (1989) 'Vocal Stress and Deception Detection Among Chinese', paper presented at the annual meeting of the Western Speech Communication Association, Spokane, Washington, DC.

Oppenheimer, R. (1956) 'Analogy in Science', *American Psychologist*, 11, 127–35.

Ortony, A. (1993) *Metaphor and Thought* (2nd edn), Cambridge University Press, New York.

Patterson, M. L. (1983) *Nonverbal Behaviour: A Functional Perspective*, Springer, New York.

—— (1988) 'Functions of Nonverbal Behavior in Close Relationships', in S. Duck (ed.), *Handbook of Personal Relationships: Theory, Research and Interventions*, John Wiley, New York.

—— (1995) 'A Parallel Process Model of Nonverbal Communication', *Journal of Nonverbal Behavior*, 19, 3–29.

Payrato, L. (1993) 'A Pragmatic View on Autonomous Gestures: A First Repertoire of Catalan Emblems', *Journal of Pragmatics*, 20, 193–216.

Pepper, S. (1942) *World Hypotheses*, University of California Press, Berkeley.

Polanyi, M. (1958) *Personal Knowledge*, Routledge & Kegan Paul, London.

Poortinga, Y. H., Schoots, N. H. and Van de Koppel, J. M. (1993) 'The Understanding of Chinese and Kurdish Emblematic Gestures by Dutch Subjects', *International Journal of Psychology*, 28, 31–44.

Poyatos, F. (1983) *New Perspectives in Nonverbal Communication*, Pergamon, New York.

Rapoport, A. (1982) *The Meaning of the Built Environment: A Nonverbal Communication Approach*, Sage, Beverly Hills.

Rosenthal, R. (ed.) (1979) *Skill in Nonverbal Communication: Individual Differences*, Oelgeschlager, Gunn & Hain, Cambridge, MA.

—— , Hall, J., DiMatteo, M. *et al.* (1979) *Sensitivity to Nonverbal Communication: The PONS Tests*, Johns Hopkins University Press, Baltimore, MD.

Ross, L. and Nisbett, R. (1991) *The Person and the Situation*, McGraw-Hill, New York.

Rozelle, R. M. and Baxter, J. C. (1975) 'Impression Formation and Danger Recognition in Experienced Police Officers', *Journal of Social Psychology*, 96, 53–63.

Rozelle, R. M., Druckman, D. and Baxter, J. C. (1986) 'Nonverbal Communication', in O. Hargie (ed.), *A Handbook of Communication Skills*, Croom Helm, London.

Safadi, M. and Valentine, C. A. (1988) 'Emblematic Gestures Among Hebrew Speakers in Israel', *International Journal of Intercultural Relations*, 12, 327–61.

Schafer, R. (1980) 'Narration in Psychoanalytic Dialogue', *Critical Inquiry*, 7, 29–53.

Scheflen, A. E. and Scheflen, A. (1972) *Body Language and Social Order*, Prentice-Hall, Inc., Englewood Cliffs, NJ.

Scheibe, K. (1979) *Mirrors, Masks, Lies, and Secrets*, Praeger, New York.

Schlenker, B. (1980) *Impression Management*, Brooks Cole, Monterey, CA.

Shuter, P. (1976) 'Proximics and Tactility in Latin America', *Journal of Communication*, 26, 46–52.

Snyder, M. (1974) 'Self-monitoring of Expressive Behaviour', *Journal of Personality and Social Psychology*, 30, 526–37.

Soyland, A. (1994) *Psychology as Metaphor*, Sage, Thousand Oaks.

Spiegel, J. and Machotka, P. (1974) *Messages of the Body*, Free Press, New York.

Stanislavski, C. (1936) *An Actor Prepares*, Theater Arts Books, New York.

Stokols, D. and Shumaker, S. A. (1981) 'People in Places: A Transactional View of Settings', in John H. Harvey (ed.), *Cognitive, Social Behavior and the Environment*, Lawrence Erlbaum, Hillsdale, NJ.

Taylor, E. G. (1878) *Research Into the Early History of Mankind*, John Murray, London.

Tessler, R. and Sushelsky, L. (1978) 'Effects of Eye Contact and Social Status on the Perception of a Job Applicant in an Employment Interviewing Situation', *Journal of Vocational Behaviour*, 13, 338–47.

Thompson, D. and Baxter, J. (1973) 'Interpersonal Spacing of Two Person Cross Cultural Interactions', *Man–Environment Systems*, 3, 115–17.

Tomkins, S. (1962) *Affect, Imagery, and Consciousness: The Positive Affects, Vol. 1*, Springer, New York.

—— (1963) *Affect, Imagery and Consciousness: The Negative Affects, Vol. 2*, Springer, New York.

Triandis, H. C. (1994) *Culture and Social Behavior*, McGraw-Hill, New York.

Washburn, P. V. and Hakel, M. D. (1973) 'Visual Cues and Verbal Content as Influences on Impressions Formed after Simulated Employment Interviews', *Journal of Applied Psychology*, 58, 137–41.

Watson, D. (1982) 'The Actor and the Observer: How are their Perceptions of Causality Divergent?', *Psychological Bulletin*, 92, 682–700.

Watson, O. M. (1970) *Proxemic Behavior: A Cross-Cultural Study*, Mouton, The Hague.

—— and Graves, T. D. (1966) 'Quantitative Research in Proxemic Behavior', *American Anthropologist*, 68, 971–85.

Weiner, M., Devoe, S., Runbinow, S. and Geller, J. (1972) 'Nonverbal Behaviour and Nonverbal Communication', *Psychological Review*, 79, 185–214.

Willems, E. P. (1985) 'Behavioral Ecology as a Perspective for Research in Psychology Research', in C. W. Deckner (ed.), *Methodological Perspectives in Behavioral Research*, University Park Press, Baltimore, MD.

Willis, F. N. (1966) 'Initial Speaking Distance as a Function of Speakers' Relationship', *Psychonomic Science*, 5, 221–2.

Winkel, F. W. and Vrij, A. (1990) 'Interaction and Impression Formation in a Cross-Cultural Dyad: Frequency and Meaning of Culturally-Determined Gaze Behavior in a Police Interview Setting', *Social Behavior*, 5, 335–50.

Wolfgang, A. and Bhardway, A. (1984) '100 Years of Nonverbal Study', in A. Wolfgang (ed.), *Non-verbal Behaviour: Perspectives, Applications, Intercultural Insights*, C. J. Hogrefe Inc., New York.

Woodworth, R. and Schlosberg, H. (1954) *Experimental Psychology*, Holt, Rinehart & Winston, New York.

Yi Chao, E. (1987) 'Correlates and Deceit: A Cross-Cultural Examination', Unpublished PhD thesis, University of Southern California, CA.

Young, D. M. and Beier, E. G. (1977) 'The Role of Applicant Nonverbal Communication in the Employment Interview', *Journal of Employment Counseling*, 14, 154–65.

Zajonc, R. B. (1980) 'Feeling and Thinking: Preferences Need No Inferences', *American Psychology*, 35, 151–75.

4 Questioning

Jim Dillon

Nothing would seem easier or more straightforward than asking a question and getting an answer. Indeed, everyone asks and answers questions as an everyday occurrence. Yet how can we use questions skilfully in situations of professional practice? First, we will review the remarkable diversity of questioning in eight fields of practice. We will see the diverse workings of question–answer, not only in different contexts but also in diverse, even contrary, ways. Next we will examine the elements of questioning – the assumptions behind the question, the question asked, and the answers given. Here we will see how the various aspects of questioning can actually be manipulated this way and that to various purposes and circumstances. We come to appreciate that using everyday questions will not work in professional practice, while borrowing successful questioning techniques from some other field will only frustrate our particular purposes and circumstances. In the conclusion to the chapter we will see a practical scheme of action plus a principle to guide our practice of questioning.

THE DIVERSITY OF QUESTIONING

To see at a glance how questioning differs in various fields, let us look at a sort of slide-show of practices. The cartoons in Figures 4.1–4.4 give us a snapshot of typical questioning practices in eight different fields. As we click off the series of slides, we will first notice the differences among the various fields. But as we look more closely at each slide, we discover remarkable differences in question–answer practices even within one and the same field.

Education and psychotherapy

The first slide in our show (Figure 4.1) pictures questioning in a classroom and in a psychotherapy session. These caricatures make plain that the questioning in the two situations is distinctly different, to the point where teachers and therapists (or counsellors and social workers) could probably not use the same questioning techniques or approaches. What is not so evident – indeed, what is missing – is the counter-practice where, one would imagine, it is the questing student and patient who are seen to be the ones asking the questions. However, they do not ask questions. Neither do the clients in most other professional contexts. In general, it is the professional who asks the questions; the clients only give answers.

Classroom

Psychotherapy

Figure 4.1 Classroom and psychotherapy contexts

The classroom cartoon (Figure 4.1) depicts a situation that is familiar to most of us. For that precise reason we might not perceive how very peculiar it is as question–answer communication. Looking at the cartoon we can see three intriguing features. First, we see that the teacher has the answer as well as the question. The students are supposed to have the answer and then to give it to the teacher who already has it and who therefore has no need of it. Second, there is one questioner and many respondents; and while there may well be many answers, there is only one answer that counts, the one that the teacher already has before putting the question. That answer, like the question, does not derive from the cognition of the participants in the exchange but resides, as shown in the cartoon, in the books that they hold almost at arm's length from self. A third feature is even more remarkable and it is peculiar to classroom question–answer. The teacher punctuates the question with an exclamation point, while students punctuate their answer with a question mark.

Although these features are typical of classroom questioning, the cartoon in Figure 4.1 does not show us the whole picture. No cartoon could. The classroom may be a single place, perhaps thought to be a rather simple place at that, but it is actually a complex of multiple contexts and processes, involving various kinds of questioning. What the cartoon shows is the questioning typical of recitation episodes. There is also classroom discussion, involving distinctly different question–answer processes. Studies of classroom recitation and discussion (Dillon, 1988, 1994) reveal that the two processes differ in a range of characteristics, such as kinds of questions asked, answers given and evaluations supplied. For instance, in recitation, the teacher is the primary speaker, speaking mainly in questions, whereas in discussion the teacher uses far fewer questions and students speak half or more of the time. Discussion has fewer, longer, slower exchanges involving a mix of student and teacher statements and questions, reflecting matters on which participants do not have a good or sure answer. The answer to discussion questions is not predetermined as in recitation; various students might appropriately have various answers; and instead of being evaluated only by the teacher's 'right/wrong' the answers are evaluated by all participants' 'agree/disagree'.

From this classroom case we can begin to appreciate that there can actually be diverse practices of questioning within one and the same field, in addition to the diverse practices between one field and another. The practical lesson to learn is how to use questions and answers according to our particular purposes in the particular circumstances of our practice.

It would be wrong to copy and to apply questioning techniques from other fields, or to think that any given technique could be recommended for use in diverse fields. We would bumble as well by using the same questioning technique in two different circumstances within one and the same field of practice – such as recitation and discussion episodes in a classroom. Purposes and circumstances vary even in this one room; the practice of questioning should vary accordingly.

The conclusion to draw is a principle of practice, not a set of techniques or a style or approach to questioning. The principle requires us *to discipline our questioning behaviour in favour of serving a professional purpose in particular circumstances of practice*. This principle can be applied to any field.

The cartoon therapy session in Figure 4.1 shows a one-to-one situation by contrast to the classroom mob scene. Yet, contrary to what we might imagine, it shows no question–answer communication going on. The therapist does not really have the question himself; it does not figure in his cognition or almost in his very speech; and he does not need to obtain the answer. Rather, the therapist is shown offering or suggesting the question to the patient. The perplexed patient may well speak the answer out loud, even while facing the therapist, but he is not giving the answer to the therapist, and he might be construed as not even speaking to the therapist. The patient actually speaks the answer to self and for self. So much does the questioning in psychotherapy differ from the questioning in classrooms that we can see by a glance at Figure 4.1 that it would be absurd for a therapist to use the same questioning techniques as the teacher. But, as noted for the case of classrooms, there are yet further differences within the field of psychotherapy itself.

The various schools or styles of psychotherapy use questions in distinctly different, even opposite, ways. In 'rational-emotive' therapy (Ellis, 1977) the therapist is supposed to take a questioning stance rather than making declarative statements. In 'client-centred' or non-directive therapy (Rogers, 1951) the therapist is not supposed to ask any questions at all but instead to use declarative statements, along with fillers or encouragers ('hmm-mm') and sympathetic silences. In 'eclectic' styles of therapy (Long *et al.*, 1981) the therapist is supposed to use questions at certain times and not to use questions at other times. Analysis of published transcripts of these therapies (Dillon, 1990) shows the rational-emotive therapist using nothing but questions, the client-centred therapist using everything but questions and the eclectic therapist using questions half of the time.

Oddly enough, patients or clients do not ask questions. Whatever the school of therapy, the therapists are not supposed to answer a client's question (for various reasons, such as avoiding client dependency). If the therapist is to make any response to a question, it should be to sustain the client's inquiry.

The variegated case of psychotherapy shows us as clearly as can be that there is no *one* such thing as the use of questions in psychotherapy, and that as a consequence there cannot be *any* best questioning technique, style, or approach. What, then, would constitute skilful questioning in this field? The only answer is a principle of practice: skilful questioning in this and other fields would be *that use of questions which serves to purpose in this circumstance.*

Law and journalism

Our second slide (Figure 4.2) shows a further pair of diverse practices, a courtroom examination and a television news interview. One interesting feature here is that, although many question–answers are heard, they are not being exchanged between questioner and answerer. Yet there is a great deal of question–answer communication, only with a third party.

The cartoon lawyer (Figure 4.2) already has the answer to the question being put to the witness. The witness too already has the answer, and is constrained by law to give it. Interestingly, the witness is not permitted to ask questions, only required to give answers. Although the witness faces the attorney while answering, the answer is not given to the attorney who, although having asked the question already has the answer; rather, the answer is given to the jurors who, although not knowing the answer, have not asked the question. Hence, in spite of the manifest fact that many questions are being asked and many answers are being given, no question–answer communication is transpiring between questioner and answerer.

Lawyers use questions in a range of contexts, not all of them within a courtroom. Outside of the courtroom they ask questions in interviews, depositions and rehearsals of witnesses. Within the courtroom they ask questions in trials and non-trial proceedings such as preliminary hearings. Within the trial, they ask questions in episodes of direct examination and cross-examination. Thus, there are multiple contexts for questioning even within the courtroom, and still further within a trial. And the features of questioning differ in distinct ways in the various contexts.

The questioning even varies as used by the lawyer within a trial proceeding, according to whether the attorney acts for the prosecution or for the defence, and whether it is during direct or during cross-examination. Detailed study of a murder trial (Woodbury, 1984) reveals that the questioning varied systematically according to questioner and

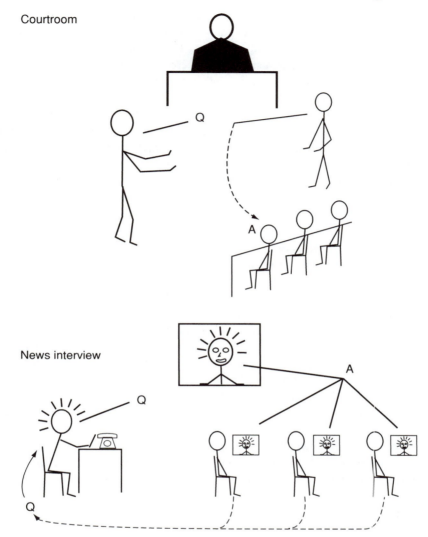

Figure 4.2 Courtroom and news contexts

episode. For instance, although the majority of all questions were yes/no type, there were many more less-controlling, 'wh'-type questions on direct examination than on cross-examination, and more by the prosecuting attorney than by the defence attorney. More yes/no questions were asked on cross- than on direct examination and more by the defence than by the prosecution. On direct examination, the prosecutor asked more 'wh'-questions than yes/no questions, and on cross-examination asked more yes/no than 'wh'-questions. The defence attorney asked more yes/no questions than the prosecutor did; more yes/no questions on cross-examination than on direct examination and more yes/no than 'wh'-questions on both direct and cross-examination. While both the prosecution and the defence asked more prosodic or intonated types of yes/no questions on cross-examination than on direct examination, the prosecutor used four times the prosodic questions on cross-examination as he did on direct examination, while the defence asked four times as many as the prosecution did in both episodes. The prosodic type of yes/no question is especially suitable to the defence, especially on cross-examination.

In sum, the use of questioning varies in each role, during each episode, with each witness and in each proceeding in or out of courtrooms. As a consequence, we cannot imagine that any one practice could describe such a thing as the lawyer's use of questioning, nor can we possibly recommend any one questioning technique or style, for no single one could serve various purposes and circumstances. Finally, it may startle us to learn that the best court-room questioners do not ask questions off the cuff; they have prepared their questions well in advance, and they have gone to the lengths of writing the questions down, arranging them in suitable order, and even pre-testing and rehearsing the questions before approach-ing the witness (Kestler, 1982). This is a good example for questioners in other fields, even though they would be mistaken to copy the lawyer's questioning techniques.

The caricature of a television news interview (Figure 4.2) pictures another complicated question–answer scheme. The sober and neutral yet celebrated journalist puts a pointed question, and the beaming celebrity respondent – a politician or other public figure, for example – happily provides an elaborate answer. This looks like it could be a straight-forward question–answer exchange but our cartoon shows us that it is nothing of the sort. Far from it: no communication at all is taking place between the questioner and the respondent. Three remarkable features begin to strike us. In the first place, the answer archetypically does not respond to the question. Second, the answer is not given to the questioner, even though the politician may be facing the journalist. Third, the party to whom the answer is given has not asked the question and is not even present in the interview. To the short, pointed question of the journalist an impressively grand, filigreed and non-responsive answer is animatedly spoken by the politician to a scattered and passively watching public which has not asked the question. The journalistic conceit runs that the journalist asks questions on behalf of the public's right to know. Today's media marvels permit these question–answer theatrics to be performed in front of an absent audience by celebrated actors who not only do not perform in front of the audience but not even in face of each other, while at the same time the marvel of their question–answer routine permits an answer to be played neither to the questioner nor to the question.

Studies of BBC radio and television news interviews (Harris, 1989; Jucker, 1986) show that the typical interview is short, only a few minutes long, and that question, answer and next question follow one another within less than half a second's lapse. Despite those rapid moves and despite the fact that the great majority of the questions are yes/no or either/or types, the respondent manages to speak three to four times more than the ques-tioner, often enough not in response to the question. Despite the journalist's follow-up and probing questions, the respondent continues to give vague answers, and to answer some unasked questions of his/her own choosing.

How odd it would be for us to think – as we might perhaps have thought before thinking twice about it thanks to our little cartoons – that clinical therapists, courtroom cross-examiners, or classroom teachers might try to use the same approach to questioning as television news interviewers use. Everything about purposes and circumstances differs. Yet the journalism manuals (Metzler, 1988) offer some good advice. They urge print and

Figure 4.3 Interrogation and polling contexts

broadcast journalists to define their purpose beforehand and to prepare the questions, anticipating possible answers; then to listen to the answers and afterwards to evaluate the interview. Practitioners in any field could well follow this advice.

Interrogation and polling

In fields of journalism and law, we saw that the respondent gives the answer not to the questioner but to a third party who is not asking the question and who may be present (courtroom) or not (newsroom) in the exchange. Now in our third slide of diverse practices of questioning (Figure 4.3) we can see that it is the questioner who brings the answer to a third party who is not present in either case and who may be asking the question (polling) or not (interrogation). Another remarkable difference is that there is no special place or room required for the putting of questions in criminal interrogation and opinion polling. Unlike the case with courtrooms, classrooms, newsrooms and consulting rooms, pollsters and interrogators can ask their questions anywhere the respondent may be found, out in the field and not in any prescribed or formalised setting.

On the whole, the prize for the best questioning goes to interrogators. The academic honours for knowing most about questioning and being the best prepared for using questions goes to opinion pollsters. Yet we can see at a glance that they do not use the same techniques – and neither should we! It would be foolhardy for us to copy their techniques and apply them to our purposes in our circumstances of practice.

Indeed, these two fields not only use different techniques, but some of their techniques are plain contradictory. Interrogators deliberately avoid using precise terms and vocabulary, while pollsters toil to cast their questions in ever so precise and correct terms. Survey researchers laboriously test their questions for standardised, accurate and patent assumptions, while interrogators freely insert into their questions wrong and hidden assumptions and false information. Both of them are good questioners but they use opposite techniques. It would be foolish for an interrogator to put fussily correct questions to a suspect, and foolish for a pollster to put vague, imprecise questions to a respondent. Why? Because neither question would then serve to purpose in circumstance. For example, the questioners would not get factual, reliable information in answer.

The cartoon interrogator (Figure 4.3) does not quite have the question from his/her own cognition, and particularly does not care what the answer is, so long as it is factual. The criminal interrogator holds up the question to the suspect or informant; the hapless suspect is seen reluctantly to let go of the answer, just dropping it, as it were; and the interrogator brings the answer to a third party for judgement. Hence, what may at first appear to be a one-to-one question–answer communication actually takes place in three steps, not two, involving three distinct parties, each of whom takes one of the steps. By contrast, in classrooms and some other settings such as medical clinics, it is the questioner who judges the answer. But the interrogator must not judge the answer or the respondent, for otherwise the purpose of interrogation would be foiled.

The caricature in Figure 4.3 does not represent the extraordinary diversity of circumstances and people involved in interrogation, more diverse than in any other field of questioning. In questioning all of these people, the manuals (Buckwalter, 1983; Yeschke, 1987) stress that the interrogator should exhibit human relations qualities akin to a counsellor, such as being non-judgemental and non-adversarial, trustworthy, considerate, and so on. Indeed, one manual is entitled *The Gentle Art of Interviewing and Interrogation* (Royal and Schutt, 1976). Why is that? The purpose is to obtain factual, truthful information about some criminal matter; the respondent has that information and the questioning has to be such as to obtain it. All manner of people may be interrogated, not just the archetypical tight-lipped criminal; and *everyone* who is interrogated may, for any of a dozen understandable reasons, withhold information or give non-factual information. Accordingly, the proper style of interrogation is patient and persistent questioning – and listening.

Amazingly, the two most common faults of inexperienced interrogators are failure to ask the question that the informant actually has crucial information on, and failure to listen carefully to the answers that are given. Good interrogators prepare by outlining the matter under investigation, identifying possible topics and writing down on paper the questions to ask about each topic. In fact, they should spend more time preparing the questions than they do in asking them (Buckwalter, 1983).

Opinion polling or survey and market research is no more of a one-to-one communication setting than interrogation is, yet not in the same way. The cartoon (Figure 4.3) shows some notable differences. Here there are many respondents, as there are in classrooms, but one respondent at a time; and here there is a third party, unlike classrooms but like courtrooms and interrogations. And here, unlike any other field, there are many questioners, all asking the same question; and many respondents – 1,000 or more – each giving different answers! The people who are putting the questions do not hold the question as their own cognition – they may simply be hired and trained to ask the question; and they do not care what the answer is, so long as it is reliable. The cartoon pollsters are seen to bring the answers back to a beaming third party, someone who has actually asked the big Question in favour of which the little questions have been put by other people, and someone who not only wants to have the answers but actively desires to know the variety of answers that come to the question.

Here, surely, is a strange case of question–answer communication. Pollster and respondent have never met and they remain anonymous throughout – even the responses remain confidential. Neither the question nor the answer serves the cognition or needs of either the questioner or the answerer. They are strangers asking and answering questions for some unknown purpose on behalf of some unknown party. Another point of distinction is that the questions are written, although posed and answered orally. When pollsters and survey researchers pose a question, they are actually either reading it or reciting it from memory. Above all, the written question has been carefully formulated and pre-tested to be as exact as possible.

It is no problem at all to ask and to answer questions. It is easy to ask people questions, but surprisingly hard to get reliable answers from them. People routinely guess, distort and lie, even when responding to simple questions about their library card, favourite soft drinks, television shows, opinions, etc. On that account, the experts advise laboriously preparing the questions, extensively testing them in the field, and then putting them in a non-judgemental manner (Sudman and Bradburn, 1982). A classic text (Payne, 1951) gives a checklist of 100 points for wording a question, and an example of reformulating a question forty times. Two researchers (Schuman and Presser, 1981) report over 200 experimental studies on questions that they personally have conducted in national surveys. Taking the example of this field, practitioners in most fields would be well advised to prepare and to write out the questions to ask orally.

Health care and personnel work

Our final slide (Figure 4.4) pictures a medical interview and a personnel interview, two situations of one-to-one question–answer communication. Both show the respondent in a subordinate status. The physician/director is in charge, and judges the quality of patient/ applicant by the answers. But we will not be surprised to learn that these are two very different circumstances of questioning. The physician typically asks many, quick, closed questions, while the personnel director asks fewer, more leisurely and open ones; and

Medical
interview

Personnel
interview

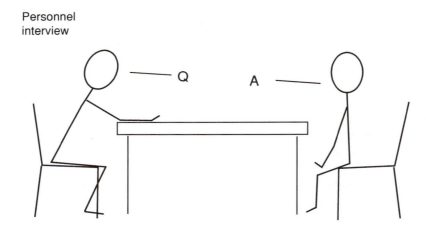

Figure 4.4 Medical and personnel contexts

whereas the patient is scarcely permitted to ask more than a question or two, if any at all, the applicant may actually be invited to ask questions.

In medical interviews, the physician speaks primarily in questions and the patient speaks primarily in answers. For instance, in a study of doctors in family practice (West, 1983), the doctors asked 91 per cent of the questions. Patients, like students in classrooms, sense that they are not supposed to ask questions of the doctor; it is more socially permissible to ask questions of a nurse, pharmacist, or lesser health professional. The great majority of physicians' questions are narrow/closed, by contrast to broad/open, and they are of a biomedical/technical character, by contrast to psychosocial or lifestyle questions (West,

1983; Wooliscroft *et al.*, 1986). The doctor puts chains of rapid yes/no or multiple-choice questions, with the next question overlapping the patient's last answer.

Much the same, to a lesser degree, can be seen in other health care contexts even where the patient can ask some questions. Recent studies of consultations in community pharmacies (Morrow *et al.*, 1993) reveal that the pharmacists asked twice the questions that the client did, all but a few of them closed questions, mainly yes/no type. Virtually none of the pharmacist's utterances were affective or psychosocial in character. When a client did attempt such an exchange over the problem, the pharmacist replied, 'Well, that's two spoonfuls three times a day' (p. 93).

It is strange to see doctors and teachers using questions almost in the way that courtroom cross-examiners do. What professional purposes are being served by this style of questioning? The routine practice of question–answer in medical interviews depends on a view of physicians as applied-scientific collectors of biotechnical data elicited from an ignorant, ideally passive object responding to the stimuli of the questioning. The questions bear on objective, physical features that are conceived to be standardised properties of all patients, while the appropriate answers are to be brief, objective and specific, precisely in terms of the questions as posed. Alternative practices would include asking open-ended questions as well, tied into the patient's narrative; listening with minimum interruption and allowing full, elaborated answers; and using the patient's terms in subsequent questions (Mishler, 1984).

In the cartoon personnel interview (Figure 4.4), the questioning may appear at first to resemble that in the medical interview. But a second look or a moment's reflection should convince us of the impending personnel disaster if the same kind of questioning were to be used. The cartoon employer – the personnel director or job recruiter – asks questions of the employee/applicant in order to form an appreciation or judgement as to suitability and performance at work. That would not appear to differ in significant respects from the evaluative purpose for which a physician might put questions to a patient. Yet several important differences in questioning practice need to follow, such as a more leisurely and more conversational exchange; an exploration of psychosocial, affective and lifestyle topics along with technical employment ones; and a more active, dynamic participation by the respondent in the interview.

Some typical practices in employment interviews have been revealed in a series of studies (Babbitt and Jablin, 1985; McComb and Jablin, 1984; Tengler and Jablin, 1983). Over the 30-minute session, the recruiter talks for about two-thirds of the time, the applicant for one-third. The recruiter asks a good number of questions, an average of twenty-one questions for the 30 minutes, yet this frequency is nothing like the several questions per minute put to breathless respondents in clinics, courtrooms and classrooms. By contrast to the overwhelming proportion of closed questions in these other contexts, only something over half of the recruiter's questions are closed (55 per cent), and more of them are follow-up questions (59 per cent) versus primary or new topic questions. The applicant speaks longer in response to the open and follow-up questions.

Two other features stand out in these employment interviews. First, the recruiter uses various verbal techniques apart from questions, including statements, verbal encouragers and silences. In fact, the recruiters on average used more statements (thirty-two) than questions (twenty-one) in the 30-minute interview. Second, the applicant too asked questions and in significant number or proportion – an average of eleven questions to the recruiter's twenty-one. The applicant's questions sought job information, the recruiter's opinions and clarification. Moreover, the recruiter actively invited questions from the applicant. These questions also serve to purpose in this circumstance, for recruiters find them useful for assessing the applicant's personality dynamics, for example, and the kind of information to provide to an applicant whom they are trying to recruit. Indeed, questions from the applicant are ranked third among twelve factors influencing a recruiter's decisions.

Plainly enough, we can see that the questioning practices typical of physicians, teachers and attorneys would foil the purposes of a personnel interview. Once again we come to appreciate that no one approach to questioning and no one set of questioning techniques can possibly serve to purpose in the diverse circumstances of professional practice. Each field and practitioner requires a special practice of questioning suitable to purpose in circumstance.

ELEMENTS OF QUESTIONING

In order to figure out just which practices might better serve to purpose in this or that circumstance, we would do well to study the elements of questioning and learn how they can operate this way and that. There are only a very few elements of questioning, yet it is amazing to see how many ways they can be turned to diverse purposes and circumstances.

Questioning is made up of three ordered elements. In the centre there is the *question* itself; after the question there are *answers*; and before the question there are *assumptions*. Each element is composed of an act plus a sentence, such as (1) the act of asking plus (2) the question that is asked. We will examine these three elements in turn – the assumptions made behind the question, the question asked, the answers given – studying in detail how in each case the act and the sentence involved (e.g. asking the question) can be manipulated in various ways to make the questioning serve either one purpose or another, in a variety of circumstances.

That is the kind of thing to learn about questioning – not some technique or some style that is suitable only for some singular purpose in some special field of practice, but the elements that make up questioning wherever it is used, so that we can skilfully turn these elements to our particular purposes and circumstances. One of the most useless things to learn is a set of practical techniques. The chances are that the techniques will not work in your field, first of all, and moreover almost certainly will not work to the diverse purposes and circumstances of your own practice. In other words, the most practical thing to learn about questioning is not some technique but an *understanding* of what questioning is and how it works.

Assumptions behind the question

Behind the question that is asked there are two kinds of assumptions which, because they are prior, are called *pre*suppositions and *pre*sumptions. The first kind of assumption is a logical property of the question-sentence; the second is a pragmatic property of the act of uttering that sentence. Thus, when a person asks a question, he/she is communicating something in addition to the question being asked; he/she communicates also what he/she is assuming by (1) the question and (2) the act of asking it – the presuppositions and presumptions.

Presuppositions

Informally put, presuppositions are those sentences which (express propositions that) are entailed by the question-sentence. For a question to be valid, its presuppositions must be true. Then it can be validly answered. If the presuppositions are not true the question cannot be truly answered. Any answer, then, to a question with not-true presuppositions – whether false or indeterminate, or not known to be true or false – itself reassumes that non-true supposition that the question pre-assumes. The question will be answered either way, and the presuppositions affirmed. We have to know whether our question is being validly answered and our presuppositions truly affirmed. Hence we need to know our presuppositions.

Linguists and logicians are the ones who can tell us what presuppositions are. Although their analyses are formidable, for some reason their examples are funny. Here are two favourite examples. The question 'Is the King of France bald?' presupposes that: (a) there is a present king of France; (b) the king is either bald or not-bald. The question 'Have you stopped beating your wife?' presupposes that: (a) you have a wife; (b) you used to beat her; (c) either you have stopped beating her or you are still beating her.

Logicians also supply sprightly names for questions that fail on various presuppositional grounds. Consider these three types (from Belnap and Steel, 1976):

1 *Trivial* – the answer is already known. 'Are these words written in English?';
2 *Foolish* – the question is known to have no true answer. 'Which of the following exist: unicorns or chimeras?';
3 *Dumb* – the question has no direct answer whatsoever. 'What are at least three truths from among the following: A and B?'

The implication for practice is that we should know the presuppositions and their truth. We should be able to answer to ourselves two analytic questions: (1) What does the question presuppose?; and (2) Is that which it presupposes known to be true? If we cannot answer these, then we cannot know the meaning and worth of the respondent's answer.

The implication is not that we should ask only questions that are true, but that we should know the truth of the questions we ask. Some questioners knowingly ask questions with false presuppositions or with interdeterminate ones. The following is an example of a deliberately false yet serviceable presupposition: An interrogator who believes that a criminal suspect is lying about being at a concert at the crucial hour in question may make up a fictitious event and then ask a question that presupposes the truth of this falsity, for example, 'How did you react when the tuba player had a heart attack?' (Buckwalter, 1983). Whatever the answer, it will prove to be false because it affirms the truth of the false presupposition. Cross-examiners, by contrast, may insert a *true* or indeterminate presupposition into a question in order that, whatever the answer, it be affirmed as true. 'Did you ever get those brakes fixed on that truck?' In that way, the adversarial witness unwittingly testifies to something that damages his/her case, for the presupposition is now admitted into evidence.

Presumptions

This second kind of prior assumption (again, in our informal terms) attaches not to the question-sentence but to the act of uttering it. For a question to be valid, its presuppositions must be true. For the act of asking to be genuine or sincere, its presumptions must be true – that is, they must accurately describe the conditions that hold in the question-situation.

When a person asks a question, he/she communicates his/her belief in certain conditions that obtain. These conditions describe such states as knowing the answer, desiring the answer, believing that there is an answer and one true answer, and estimating that the respondent can and will supply the answer. The respondent is invited to presume likewise or, at least, to believe that the questioner so presumes. For example, here are the presumptions describing what is called the *standard* question-situation. These are not standard in any field of question–answer practice, but every field will show some variation of each of these presumptions.

The first or primary presumption is that the questioner believes that the presupposition(s) to the question is or are true. It may be false, but no matter; asking the question presumes its truth (i.e. commits the speaker to it as true, or expresses the speaker's belief that it is true). The analytic question for us and our respondent to answer here is: Does the questioner believe that the question's presuppositions are true?

The 'standard' presumptions may be variously enumerated and formulated. One formulation (Dillon, 1988) holds that the person who asks a question asseverates and communicates these eight attitudes:

1 *Ignorance*. I am in a state of not-knowing, and I realise that I do not know;
2 *Perplexity*. I am experiencing perplexity (puzzlement, uncertainty, etc.) as a consequence of not-knowing;
3 *Need*. I feel a necessity to know;
4 *Desire*. I aspire to know;
5 *Belief*. I commit myself to the truth of the question (I believe that its presuppositions are true, its words are as I intend them, etc.);
6 *Faith*. I am confident that the unknown is knowable;
7 *Courage*. I venture to face the unknown and its consequences both within myself and the world;
8 *Will*. I resolve to undertake to know.

These are the presumptions of standard inquiry, as when a student or scientist raises a question about the subject matter being studied. But hardly any questioner in fields of practice holds to these particular presumptions.

To understand the role of presumptions, all we need do is to go down the list of 'standard-inquiry' presumptions and compare each one to our own field of practice. For example, cross-examiners know the answers to the questions they ask. Their practice positively requires them not to ask a question to which they do not know the answer. The rule of thumb runs, 'Never ask a question unless you already know the answer'. Media interviewers may not care what the answer is, nor whether it be true or not, rather that *an* answer be given that is of a certain quality – revealing, quotable, etc.

Interrogators of criminal suspects and reluctant witnesses or informants will at times communicate by their questioning that they already know the answer, whereas in truth they are trying to find it out. The suspect is to believe in a condition that the interrogator believes not to hold in the question–answer situation. Thus, the suspect comes to believe, 'This person already knows more than I thought, I might as well confess'. The interrogator who asks a question with a deliberately false presupposition ('How did you react when the tuba player had a heart attack?'), is involved in a situation with these presumptions:

1 The suspect might believe in the truth of the question's presupposition, and the interrogator knows it to be false;
2 The interrogator does not believe that there exists any true answer, and the suspect presumes that some answer must be true (but which one?);
3 The suspect wants to give the true (correct, right) answer, but the interrogator does not want any true answer at all, rather a false one is sought;
4 The investigator doesn't care what the answer is, any answer will do because all answers will be false.

The implication for practice is that the questioner should know just which conditions are being presumed, both by questioner and respondent, and how accurately these presumptions describe the situation. Then the questioning can be pursued with skill.

The question asked

This second element too has two parts, the question-sentence and the act of uttering it. Of all the various aspects, we will examine only the formulation of the question and the manner of its expression.

Formulation of the question

Formulation refers to the verbal form in which the question is couched. The major point about the formulation of a question is that it defines the kind of answer possible and it affects several characteristics of the eventual answer given. We will examine selected aspects of the question's formulation, namely its vocabulary and structure.

It is obvious that the wording of a question affects the answer. But the very *choice* of words can influence the answer, as survey researchers have continually demonstrated. For example, more than twice as many Americans will not 'allow' speeches against democracy as will 'forbid' them (Schuman and Presser, 1981). Many more people are willing to add a law to the Constitution regarding term limits than are willing to change the Constitution; more think it desirable to balance the national budget than think it not undesirable; and more people usually support the President's policy on X than the policy on X. Similarly, investigators find that their choice of words affects the readiness of suspects to reveal information. They *avoid* using correct, precise terms like 'murder', 'steal', 'rape' and they ask about 'shoot', 'take', 'sex'. Virile types admit having sex with a woman but will deny raping her. Tough guys don't assault and batter, they fight somebody. Thieves take but don't steal, murderers do it but don't kill, suspects are involved rather than being guilty and they will tell you about it but they won't confess their crime (Buckwalter, 1983).

The choice of words also affects answers about ordinary things that ordinary people have just seen. An observed person is reported to be 10 inches taller in answer to 'How tall?' than to 'How short?', and a movie 30 minutes longer for 'How long?' than for 'How short?' Eyewitnesses to traffic collisions give systematically higher estimates of speed when asked 'How fast were the cars going when they contacted/hit/smashed?' – 31/34/41 mph (Loftus, 1979). What is more, the wording of the question can influence people to give true answers about non-existent things. A long tradition of psychological experiments has shown that people will testify to events that never took place, and aver having seen objects that were not present in the scene before them. They do so unwittingly via answering questions that assert that event or object in the wording of the question. The simplest case is for the question to denote, by 'the' instead of 'an', an object that was not present in the observed scene. For example, three times as many college students answered 'yes' as 'no' to questions about their instructor's non-existent moustache, spectacles, accent and lisp. In our view, we attribute this result not merely to words but to the *presuppositions* marked by the wording. For example, in the question 'Did you detect his/a southern accent?' (Davis and Schiffman, 1985), the first question presupposes the existence of X, while the second does not. Here we see again that answers affirm the presuppositions and we see that respondents tend to agree with the presuppositions in the course of answering in terms of the question.

In general, respondents find it easier – even more desirable – to go along with the question as posed rather than to dispute it and complicate the exchange. Once having been so agreeably incorrect in their answer, respondents then base their answers to subsequent questions upon the truth of the false presupposition that they had affirmed in their previous answer. In that way their 'eyewitness' testimony can build fiction upon fiction. Eyewitnesses asked the 'smashed' (vs. 'contacted') version of the question, 'How fast were the cars going when they . . .?' tend to answer yes to the subsequent question, 'Did you see any broken glass?', when no broken glass existed at the scene they had witnessed (Loftus, 1979).

We note that these witnesses are not making up answers. They are searching their memory for information that is indeed truly remembered. But it is false information. It is traceable to the false presupposition, the truth of which they had affirmed in agreeably answering the prior question. It is a false answer truly given. In that way, we return to the usefulness for the questioner of knowing the presuppositions to questions, for on them will depend the content and the worth of the answer. The value of question–answer does not turn on its truth/falsity but on its suitability to purpose in a particular circumstance of practice. True answers can be worthless, as also false answers truly given.

As for structure, the syntactic structure of a question circumscribes the set of possible answers and it influences the answers actually given. We shall examine only the working of alternative questions and compare them to various questions without alternatives.

Alternative questions

These are structured so as to specify the alternatives or choices in answer. The two most useful points about alternatives are that questioners rarely specify them correctly (e.g. stating the wrong ones or too few), and that the number and kind of alternatives in the question affect the content and worth of the answer. Both the number and the content of alternatives affect the answers. For example, shoppers report having tried more new products, and having suffered more headaches, when asked 'How many – One? Five? Ten?' than for 'One? Two? Three?' (Loftus, 1982). A series of experiments (Schuman and Presser, 1981) has demonstrated particularly interesting effects of changing the alternatives in four different ways. The results are useful for learning how to formulate such questions in practice.

Don't know As a result of adding a 'don't know' or 'no opinion' alternative to the basic agree–disagree question, an average of 22 per cent more respondents (in nineteen experiments) shifted from agree or disagree to don't know.

Counter-argument Adding a consideration for the negative or opposite view in the question resulted in a shift of 8 per cent of respondents to the negative. Without such a consideration, respondents tend to agree with the proposition in the question. A general way to provide balance is, 'Some people think X, some people think not-X, which do you think?' or 'X because of A, and not-X because of B; X or not-X?'

Middle term Adding a logical middle term resulted in a shift of 15 per cent more respondents to the middle alternative. For example, 'strict, lenient, or about right?' instead of 'strict or lenient?' In one striking case, fully 42 per cent of the people described themselves as 'middle of the road' in politics when that term was added to the 'conservative/liberal' alternative in question; as a consequence, the conservatives immediately plunged from 58 per cent of the population to only 33 per cent, while the liberals fell from 30 per cent to 20 per cent. Political poll-takers know how to frame the questions to obtain the results they want.

Placement Whatever its content – no matter what it says – the last-listed of two or three alternatives was chosen by 10 per cent more respondents than when this very same alternative was in first or second place. For example, when asked if divorce should be made easier to obtain, more difficult, or stay as it is, 10 per cent more respondents chose 'more difficult' when that was the last alternative (vs. when it was the second), and 12 per cent more chose 'as it is' when that was last (vs. second).

The implication for practice is to appreciate the workings of alternatives and then manipulate them according to purpose. Far from benefiting from added alternatives, some purposes may require avoiding them altogether. For example, lawyers are advised to avoid questions that offer alternatives (Kestler, 1982). The witness might choose one of the two proffered alternatives instead of giving yet a third which would be more damaging; and on cross-examination there is no point to giving a choice: 'Pin the witness down to the answer you want' (p. 75).

Open/closed questions

These questions are structured without and with specified alternatives. One form of question permits respondents to bespeak their own ideas in their own words, whereas the other form specifies ideas and words for them to choose. Both types constrain the response but in differing ways. For example, asked about what they most prefer in a job, only half as many people volunteered 'a feeling of accomplishment' as did select it from the alternatives. Good pay was mentioned by as many respondents in both cases, but it was the least frequently chosen alternative and the most frequently volunteered answer. Fully 60 per cent of the responses to the open question fell outside of the five alternatives in the closed question (Schuman and Presser, 1981).

What is to be made of these differences? The implication for practice is to recognise that different answers are given to the two forms of question, and that the answers given to the one form may not even be given *at all* to the other form. The significance is that the questioner who asks closed questions may be specifying categories of thought that are unrepresentative of what respondents think, with the result that respondents confirm our own frame of reference without our even realising it.

Narrative/directive questions

These are structured so as to permit the respondent to speak at some length about personal knowledge of a topic, or to direct the answers point for point. For example, a witness might be asked 'And then what happened?' and afterwards be asked about specific points mentioned or omitted. The difference in the answers has long been known. One of the oldest experiments (Yamada, 1913) had students read a geographical description of South America, and then asked a free-narrative question ('What do you know about the surface of South America?') followed by a series of twenty-four specific questions from the reading. On average, the students made three times more errors in answering the specific questions, even incorrectly answering about points that they had correctly reported during their narrative answer. Apart from the accuracy of the answer, there is the matter of its completeness or the exhaustiveness of detail. A number of studies (Loftus, 1979) have found that answers to the free-narrative or open question are the most accurate but least complete; answers to the controlled-narrative or specific questions are less accurate and more complete; while answers to multiple-choice or alternative questions are the least accurate and the most complete.

The implication for practice is obviously that each of the different types of question has advantages and disadvantages. Investigators, for example, are advised to interview co-operative witnesses by first asking a free-narrative question, then a series of specific questions about the points mentioned; next to ask some cross-questions to re-examine or to verify selected points; and lastly to ask some open, summary questions to see if anything important has been left out. But that is not the case when faced with a reluctant witness; then the interrogator is to use patient, persistent, probing questions (Buckwalter, 1983). Another practical implication is to prepare our questions with care, to formulate them in writing and to arrange them in some order – all beforehand. What is more, practitioners in some fields are advised to test the formulation of the questions before using them in practice.

Nothing looks as effortless and spontaneous as the facile questioning by lawyers, journalists, teachers and the like seen on television or experienced in real life. Are the questions effective to purpose? Is the questioning skilful? That depends not only on the formulation of the question but also on the manner of expressing it.

Expression of the question

Formulation refers to the question-sentence; expression refers to the act of putting the question. Here we shall note only two aspects – the flow of questions and the attitude expressed in the questioning. These are enough to show the necessity of adopting a manner of questioning suited to particular purpose.

Flow of questioning

Flow refers to such things as the frequency, rate and sequence of questions asked. The most useful generalisation is that people don't like to be asked a lot of questions, especially at a fast pace. According to purpose, then, the practitioner would adjust the flow of questioning. One would think that where the purpose is to stimulate respondents' expressivity or to enhance their understanding, the questioning would be deliberate, measured and calm. And, where the purpose is to get respondents to disclose information that they do not wish to give, the questioning would be fast, urgent and hectic. Yet that is not the case, at least not in classrooms and interrogations.

Ever since the very start of research into classroom questioning (Stevens, 1912), observers have noted that teachers ask a great number of questions at a markedly high rate – too fast for pupils to think, let alone to express their thoughts. The average lapse of time between the pupil's answer and the teacher's next question has been measured at less than one second (Rowe, 1974). What purposes are served by this fast, continuous questioning? One of the purposes seems to be to maintain control over social and verbal behaviour in the classroom. But this manner of questioning cannot serve other purposes such as the enhancement of pupils' cognitive, affective and expressive processes.

Interrogators too can be seen to use this manner of questioning – in police dramas and Second World War movies. But in practice, as far as is known, their manner of questioning is advisedly measured and calm, the questions being asked in a conversational tone, in a smooth, lower, relaxed voice (Buckwalter, 1983). The interrogator is to *avoid* all rapid-fire questions and rushing any answers, to wait for the full answer, and to give the respondent the opportunity to qualify it. What purpose is served? The intended purpose is to obtain true, factual information from someone who is reluctant to disclose it. Rapid, rough questioning seems to frustrate this purpose; better to use persistent yet patient questioning, with a pause before and after the question.

For some reason, physicians use a manner of questioning similar to that popularly thought to be used by interrogators but not actually used by them, and identical to that actually used by teachers but seemingly not expected to be used by them. In doctor–patient interviews, the doctor speaks almost nothing but questions, asks numerous, response-constraining questions (yes/no, multiple-choice), at a staccato pace with incursions into patient turns, and with scarcely a pause between the patient's answer and the doctor's next question – as little as one-tenth of a second (West, 1983). What purposes are being served, and which ones frustrated, by this questioning? Cross-examiners also use rapid-fire questioning, but advisedly so. It is relentless and intimidating, keeping the witness under pressure and off-balance, while enforcing a subordinate status (Kestler, 1982). The purpose is to give the witness no time to think, and no opportunity to formulate the answer carefully. 'There should be no gap between questions which would allow the witness time to think' (p. 46). As the classic manual put it, 'He cannot invent answers as fast as you can invent questions' (Wellman, 1903, p. 68).

As these four cases show, the flow of questioning differs in various practices, as do the purposes that are served *and* that are not served by the manner of questioning in a given practice.

Regarding the *attitude* expressed in the questions, the practitioner may ask him or herself, 'Just what am I questioning *for*?', and then adopt an attitude of questioning which achieves that purpose. There is no one attitude to adopt, and no point in adopting the attitude of successful questioners in other circumstances. The only useful generalisation is that people find it threatening or somehow diminishing to be asked questions. A threatening manner is conducive to some purposes but not to others, even in the same situation. The questioner must be clear both as to what the purpose is and which purposes are being served by the manner of questioning. For instance, one purpose in a classroom might be to stimulate student thought, and in a personnel interview, to get the applicant to talk about him or herself; yet the teacher's questioning may serve rather the purpose of social and verbal control, and the interviewer's may cause the respondent to talk less and less with each successive question. There is a therapeutic purpose in psychoanalysis that the analyst's questioning might not only not serve but actually contravene, both by reinforcing such things as dependency and defensiveness in a patient and by serving the therapist's pregenital desire to master and dominate in the relationship (Olinick, 1954).

Such are the purposes that are exactly appropriate, on the other hand, in cross-examination. But they are quite inappropriate to interrogation and they are ruinous to survey interviewing. Interrogators and interviewers must deliberately adopt a non-judgemental manner of questioning, the first because they need all true information, the second because they need all reliable responses. The two cases form a surprising pair, for respondents in an opinion poll are not coerced into answering the questions and seemingly stand to lose nothing by answering them correctly, whereas suspects are in a coercive situation where they can lose a great deal by giving truthful answers. Yet survey respondents give distorted answers to innocuous questions about everyday matters. To avoid such distortion to the extent possible, interviewers must not only formulate their questions in a certain manner but also ask them in a non-judgmental way, conveying neither approval nor disapproval to the respondent.

Interrogators too, oddly enough, must ask questions in a non-judgemental manner. What the interrogator needs is truthful information; others, later, will make the judgements. Far from being judgemental, the attitudes and qualities to be exhibited by the interrogator include being understanding, considerate, sympathetic, empathic, concerned, gentle, kind, courteous, tactful, reasonable, fair, honest, warm, respectful, friendly. It is this manner of questioning, rather than the Hollywood-like opposite, that more likely induces a person who is fraughtfully implicated in a bad situation to tell the truth. The suspect comes to believe something like, 'The truth is the best solution to my predicament; this is someone I can trust, and who will understand. I can explain.' By contrast, a judgemental, superior, threatening or intimidating style of questioning seems to confirm the person's initial reluctance to disclose what is known. If people in an opinion poll have trouble averring that they do not hold a library card or that they prefer this opinion over that, we can imagine the difficulty of confessing to murder, rapine and mayhem.

In short, there is no one form of question and no one manner of asking questions that is known to have one given effect, even in given situations. What, then, are the types of questions that should be used? What strategies of questioning should be pursued? These are pressing questions in practice, and they are best answered by the practitioner in particular circumstances. The most practical approach to take is to look not so much at questions and questioning as to answers and answering. Knowing all about answers is the best way to know which questions to ask.

The answers given

Like the other elements of questioning, this one consists of a sentence and an act, or answer and answering. We will speak rather of response and responding. For it turns out that, of all the things that people may say and do when asked a question, the very *least* is to give an answer. We will examine types of responses and strategies of responding.

Types of responses

It may help to appreciate at the outset that most responses are not answers and that the defining characteristic of an answer is not 'something said in response to a question'. For, although answers are indeed responses to a question, so also are all manner of other things. We will say that 'answer' is not a thing but a *notion*, and in large part a pragmatic one. It describes a certain character that we attribute to a given sentence such that we conceive of that sentence as being of the kind, 'answer', when following upon a given question, and that same sentence as 'non-answer' when following upon some other question or no question at all. What, then, makes a sentence an answer? That is not an easy question and so far no one has a good answer to it. We can approach this question by considering the variety of responses that can be given. First, there are replies that follow a question but are non-responses; next there are responses that are non-answers; and last, answer-responses.

Non-responses

Nothing at all may follow upon a question, or nothing remotely connected with it, or nothing appropriately connected. Speech wildly unrelated to the preceding question is a non-response. Speech that is somehow related is a response. An utterance may be coherently related to a preceding question by grammatical and lexical cohesion, such as reference, substitution, ellipsis; and/or by prosodic, semantic and pragmatic agreement (Stenstroem, 1984).

Non-answer responses

Most responses are non-answers. The questioner may well want an answer of some particular type and may fancy that the other person is required to give an answer, but all that seems to be required is that the person give a response. All manner of non-answer responses can be given.

   Completion of invitation, ellipsis, interruption, emotion and *clarification* are among the types of non-answer responses found in the conversations of a married couple (Churchill, 1978). Not only were the non-answers given by the respondent, they were also accepted or tolerated by the questioner. The questioner apparently applies two tests to what follows upon the question: (1) Is it recognisable as a response?; (2) If not, can the non-compliance be explained away?

   Excuses are any responses that explicitly indicate either inability or unwillingness to answer (Johnson, 1979). But respondents rarely indicate an unwillingness to answer. Students will camouflage unwillingness as inability ('I don't know'), while teachers choose to infer inability rather than face what all parties suspect is an unwillingness to answer.

Evade and *disclaim* are appropriate responses, although not answers, because they relate coherently to the questioning act, although not to the question sentence (Stenstroem, 1984). A respondent may evade with 'You know that' or 'What a stupid question'; disclaim by 'I don't know' or 'I don't want to tell you'; and do either by saying 'How should I know?'

Non-answers of four types characterise the responses of public officials in broadcast news interviews (Greatbatch, 1986). First, the respondent can *claim inability* or make an excuse for lack of information, saying 'I don't know', or 'until I see the report, study the case', or yet 'I'm not at liberty to say'. Or the respondent can *reject the question*, denying its relevance or its presupposition. Asked whether he liked the Prime Minister, one official responded, 'Well, I think in politics, you see, it's not a question of going about *liking* people or not, it's a question of *dealing* with people, etc.' Asked whether local authorities should be forced to sell nationalised assets, the official responded by denying the presupposition: 'Well, they're not being forced to sell.'

A third type of non-answer is to *repeat the question*, reasserting the presupposition or even the very utterance. Asked what Cabinet job he foresaw for a political rival, the respondent replied: 'Of course, if he is elected he will be offered some job in the Cabinet, and I'd be very happy to do that, and I hope that that will occur.' The presupposition of that question stated, 'There will be a job for X', and the non-answer stated, 'There will be a job for X'. Finally, the respondent may *refuse to answer*. Most of the time the refusal is covert; the respondent talks on the topic but not to the question: 'Well, let me first say that . . .'. Overt refusals are commonly softened with polite formulas: 'Well, that's a matter I wouldn't want to comment on.'

Answer-responses

There remains the class of responses which are answers. A variety of definitions have been proposed and a variety of types distinguished. Sociolinguists, for example, have defined 'answer' as those responses that fulfil the logical or substantive expectations of the question (Johnson, 1979). Logicians, on the other hand, have viewed answers as those responses that are appropriate from the questioner's point of view (Harrah, 1985). We shall have to bear in mind that answers are imperfectly understood as relating now to the questioner, now to the question and now to the questioning.

To the question, 'Is glass a liquid at 70° F?' logicians (Belnap and Steel, 1976) say that: a *just-complete* (or direct) answer is, 'Glass is a liquid at 70° F'; and a *complete* answer (implies direct answer) is 'Glass is a liquid at 70° F, and China is populous.' To the question, 'Was she wearing the green dress, the emerald bracelet, or both?': an *eliminative* answer (negation of partial answer implies denial of some direct answer) is 'She wasn't wearing green' or 'emeralds'; and a *corrective* answer (implies denial of every direct answer) is, 'She was naked'.

More generally, logicians (Harrah, 1985) distinguish replies that are: *sufficient*, comprised of the set of indicated replies plus wanted replies (a sub-set of indicated) plus corrective replies (negate the presupposition or core assertion of the question); and *relevant*, comprised of full replies (imply the sufficient) and partial replies (implied by the sufficient).

With these lists in hand we can ask ourselves, what are the kinds of answer that I am after, and what kinds am I actually getting? For answers relate not only to the logic and syntax of the question but also to the knowledge and purposes of the questioner.

Conclusive answer

A reply to a question constitutes a conclusive answer to it if and only if it brings about the truth of the desideratum in question, making it the case that the questioner conclusively knows that X in question–answer (Hintikka, 1983). 'Charles Dogdson' is no conclusive answer to 'Who wrote *Alice in Wonderland*?' unless the questioner also knows Lewis Carroll. The criterion of conclusiveness describes answers in relation to the knowledge-state of the questioner.

Significant answer

An answer is significant when it is both informative and useful to the questioner in that situation in which the question is asked. For a simple example, consider how informative and useful 'Paris' is as an answer to the question, 'Where is the Eiffel Tower?' asked on the streets of Paris. To be both informative and useful, the answer must take into account the knowledge and purposes of the questioner in the question-situation (Grewendorf, 1983).

Interesting answer

An interesting answer denies the truth of some part of the routinely but weakly held assumption-ground of the audience that hears it. The answer is interesting not because it tells us some truth that we did not already know, but some truth which we already know is wrong (Davis, 1971). For example, what seem to be assorted, heterogeneous phenomena are in reality composed of a single element: Freud proposed that the behaviours of children, primitives, neurotics and adults in crowds, as well as dreams, jokes and slips of the tongue and pen, are all various manifestations of the same instinctual drives. To give an interesting answer is another matter than giving a correct answer, for the audience can reject the answer's value while affirming its truth. Much depends on the audience, such as advocates and opponents on an issue, or experts and laypersons. Experts will find interesting an answer that strikes laypersons as obvious, for it denies expert assumptions while affirming lay ones. A boring answer tells experts that what they think is true is true. In general, an answer that is not interesting is either obvious, absurd, or irrelevant.

Influential answers

The related concept of influential answers turns on how much influence each of the conceivable answers to a question can be expected to have (Cronbach, 1982). The valence of the answer is related to the values of the audience. For instance, on the issue of using Laetrile for cancer treatment, a positive answer will have great effect on unbelievers but a negative one will leave enthusiasts unmoved. As a general principle, answers may be assessed by the degree to which they promise to reduce uncertainty *and* to exert leverage. We might consider the socio-political as well as cognitive positions of those who will receive the answer. Otherwise our great effort to obtain reliable results, meaningful and true and good ones, could eventuate in the frustrated offer of a useless answer.

Fallible answers

We have to cope with the many respects in which answers are commonly deficient. Direct, complete answers can be incorrect. The answer may be a lie. The answer may be non-veridical even when the respondent is answering truly and genuinely. Medical patients may give full and forthcoming answers that are only partly informative and important. Survey respondents give distorted answers to commonplace questions. Informants in investigations and interrogations answer from their faulty perception, memory, understanding and knowledge, in addition to blinding prejudice. Eyewitnesses testify to events that never transpired, and they are positively certain of having seen them. Witnesses in courtrooms may be perjured, mistaken, incompetent, partisan, or otherwise prejudiced. With the exception of the outright liar, *all* of these respondents may be answering as best they can while giving woefully deficient answers.

We have no reason to expect that an answer, sound on all other counts of logic and linguistics, must also be an answer good and true. It can still fail on a dozen counts. We should know in advance what the answers are that might possibly come to our questions, and we should be able to see on the spot the kind of answer that is actually being given.

Strategies of responding

Just as was the case with responses and answers, so too there are many ways of responding without answering the question. Practitioners have to know these responding strategies in theory in order to spot and outmanoeuvre them in practice.

Evading

Evading is a routine strategy for responding to a question without answering it. There are any number of ways to evade a question. For instance, seven purposive devices have been identified for a woman to avoid answering a man's question, 'How old are you?' (Weiser, 1975). One device is to use selective ambiguity, taking the question another way. 'Don't worry, they'll let me into that bar.' Far more practised evading can be seen and heard in broadcast news interviews with politicians and other public figures who are renowned for giving evasive answers. They give off two simple linguistic signals whereby we can tell that they are evading the question (Jucker, 1986). The first is the parenthetic verb, especially: think, mean, suppose, imagine. In the following example, the official begins with 'I think' and uses two further 'I think' and one 'I suppose.'

> I think they've taken a lot of his advice and I think he's done a very good job. I think to some extent the Government has a regional policy and I suppose it's doing that at the moment.

Having been asked to criticise either the government or the expert in question, the respondent manages to praise both.

The other common signal is the particle or qualifier 'well'. It signals a lack of direct cohesion or relevance between answer and question, and a forthcoming lack of information in response. Asked whether the country might get better value for money out of the coal industry if it were in private hands, the Prime Minister responded: 'Well, I'm not talking, I'm not talking about denationalising the coal industry . . .'. The Prime Minister talked on without giving a statement of opinion as asked on the matter in question. Answers that do clearly state yes/no positions are rarely marked by 'well', whereas the hedged or less direct answers tend to be prefaced by 'well'. Fully 85 per cent of answers to 'wh'-questions that did not give the requested information were prefaced by 'well'; by contrast, 63 per cent of answers that did give the information were not prefaced by 'well' (Jucker, 1986).

Lying

Lying is the most satisfying strategy for the unwilling respondent. It is not an evasive strategy, for it directly answers the question. People routinely lie in answer to questions. Lying is even regarded as a right or a norm, especially in situations where the questions are asked by those of superior authority or status. But the most ordinary people in the most ordinary situations will lie; and when they are lying they usually get away with it because, as experiments have amply demonstrated, other people cannot tell any more than by chance whether the respondent is lying or telling the truth. One useful research finding is that *negative* probing makes liars appear to be more truthful (Stiff and Miller, 1986). Positive probes may relax the deceiver's effort. For example: 'It is pretty clear how you made such a notable improvement. What strategy caused the improvement?' (vs. 'It is hard for me to grasp how anyone could have improved this much'). Negative probes only increase the incentive to create an impression of truthfulness – to lie more effectively.

Stonewalling

Far from evading or lying, stonewalling is giving direct, correct answers to questions when and as asked. But the answers may be meaningless. A witness, for example, might answer just exactly as required but, if not asked or if not asked rightly, will not answer with the crucial knowledge held. The problem for the questioner is to ask *all* the right questions, each in *just* the right way, yet the questioner may not know enough to ask and be mistaken in what is known. Thus, the questions may be based on false presuppositions and mistaken presumptions which the stonewalling witness affirms to be true in the course of giving a perfectly direct and correct answer that only confounds or misleads the questioner. The questioner must press against the stone wall with a series of little, corrective questions pointed this way and that, each one yielding just one more tiny bit of information. For example, suppose an administrative official is called to a hearing about racial discrimination in the department's hiring practices, and suppose that no employment tests happened to be given during October.

How many minority candidates failed the test in October?
– None.
They all passed?
– No.
Well, how many passed, then?
– Zero.
Did any minorities even take the test?
– No.
Why not? How many candidates were there in all?
– Zero.

You mean, nobody even took the test?
– Right.
What, you do have a test, don't you?
– Yes.
And you give it regularly?
– Yes.
Did you give it in October?
– No.
All right, how about November? (etc.)

By contrast, a co-operative witness would have answered to the very first question, 'There wasn't any test in October'.

Co-operating

Co-operative responding consists of giving a corrective, indirect response rather than a correct, direct answer. It corrects the false presuppositions and mistaken presumptions entailed in the questioning, and it goes on to provide the supportive and/or suggestive information at issue. Giving a direct, correct answer is sometimes not helpful; co-operative answers are called for, especially in the frequent case of discrepancy in the mutual beliefs of questioner and answerer regarding the structure and content of the information. A co-operative answer is defined as 'both giving a truthful and informative response and "squaring away" the discrepancies in mutual beliefs discerned during the interaction' (Joshi, 1983, p. 237). For example, in the case where no linguistics courses had been offered:

Q: Which students got an F in linguistics in Autumn 1995?
A1: None.
A2: I don't know of any linguistics course in Autumn 1995.

The first answer is correct and direct but it is misleading. The second is corrective and indirect, co-operative and informative.

The principle of co-operative responding holds that not only must the respondent not give a false answer, but also must not permit the questioner to infer from the true answer something that the respondent knows to be false. The respondent must not only correct the questioner's assumptions but also supply additional information, supportive and suggestive, to make the answer *helpful* – both truthful and informative (Joshi, 1983).

Wonders never cease in the world of questioning, for machines have been designed to give co-operative responses. Some are natural-language question–answer systems such as PLIDIS (Berry-Rogghe *et al.*, 1980). PLIDIS has actually been used in the control of industrial water pollution in Germany. It is designed to give 'communicatively adequate answers' to busy officials who are expert about pollution but naive about question–answer systems. PLIDIS checks their questions and corrects their assumptions instead of mindlessly producing a correct but meaningless answer. For example, the question 'Did Brecht check the samples from Lauxmann in Stuttgart in 1996?' presumes that Brecht is entitled to collect samples. And it presupposes the existence of the person Brecht, the firm Lauxmann, the location Stuttgart, the time 1996, samples from 1996, firms in Stuttgart, a firm Lauxmann in Stuttgart, and samples from the firm Lauxmann in Stuttgart in 1996.

Should any of these be mistaken, PLIDIS will refrain from answering with a brute 'No' and will kindly rectify the question.

Withholding and concealing

These are by definition unco-operative strategies of responding. Many respondents do not disclose what they know, either intentionally concealing it or withholding it wittingly or not. It is a commonplace way to respond to questions. For but one example, in various types of investigations (criminal, insurance, industrial), both the innocent as well as the guilty may withhold or conceal information intentionally and unintentionally. Investigators question not only the tight-lipped criminal but also all manner of other people who for one reason or another may be hostile, reluctant, unco-operative, or just prejudiced about things. *Any* of these respondents may withhold or conceal information. Even friendly and co-operative witnesses still may not give information, for a dozen good reasons, such as protection of self or others and fear of becoming involved. The respondent may not even be aware of withholding information, by reason of ignorance of the legalities or other failure to recognise that what is known is relevant.

Withholding and concealing are not lying. They are indirect strategies of non-answering, whereas lying is giving direct but false answers. Withholding and concealing are probably best detected by assessing the situation as a whole, the set of answers to this point, and other verbal and circumstantial signals. Criminals and other duplicitous types are not the only ones to use these strategies. 'Nice people' too will withhold and conceal while responding. Indeed, for 'nice people' these may be the preferred strategies, for they permit them to avoid lying while still not telling of what they know. Just because we are asking the questions is no good reason for people to give us the answers. They know how to use plenty of other ways to respond.

Distorting

Distorting is the common strategy of giving inaccurate answers. Quite ordinary people give distorted answers to quite ordinary questions. They say more, or less, or differently than what they know. They are not lying. Often enough they distort unwittingly. It is up to the questioner to perceive the distortion. Wittingly or no, prejudice leads people to distort their responses, such as to questions asked in investigations of various kinds. Witnesses in courtroom examinations show bias for or against one side and version of events or the other. Even witnesses with no other interest in the case whatsoever are partisan to 'their' side (Wellman, 1903). They exaggerate or minimise the facts; they colour, slant and edit their answers.

Distorting is not limited to dramatic situations like courtrooms. In market surveys and opinion polls respondents commonly give distorted responses, even to questions about everyday things. For instance, people over-report socially desirable behaviour such as holding a library card and going to concerts; and they under-report socially undesirable behaviour such as being sick and out of work (Bradburn and Sudman, 1980). The general factors are whether the question is perceived to have a 'right/wrong' answer, and whether the questioner is anticipated to give approval/disapproval of the response or the respondent.

These apparently negative strategies of responding need not signify malicious or negative motives. They present a problem to the questioner but they solve a problem for the respondent. This becomes clear in the case of acquiescent responding, an apparently positive, but equally troublesome, strategy of responding.

Acquiescing

Acquiescing is to give an agreeable response, going along with what the questioner seems to be saying and demanding. It is not the same as co-operative responding; rather, it is closer to stonewalling. A co-operative response will not always be agreeable but will correct the question and questioner if they are mistaken. Stonewalling is to answer precisely in terms of the questions as posed, be they correct or incorrect. Acquiescent responding agreeably goes along with the demands of the question-situation, the formulation of the question, and the perceived view of the questioner. For instance, respondents in survey interviews tend to agree with what they think the interviewer is stating or thinking. They may say 'yes' to any statement whatsoever, even to two contradictory statements. People will agree that social conditions are more to blame than individuals for crime, and they will also agree that individuals are more to blame than social conditions (Schuman and Presser, 1981). They will readily respond in terms of the structure and form of the question regardless of their own opinion, knowledge, or behaviour. In that case, the answer tells nothing about the respondent but only confirms the questioner's frame of reference.

Acquiescence is a wonderful way for the respondent to solve several problems in the situation. The primary problem is being *a good respondent* (Sudman and Bradburn, 1974). Good respondents give answers as requested. If the respondents do not understand the question, if they have no knowledge of the matter or no opinion on it, a simple 'yes' will show them to be a good respondent while avoiding all the embarrassment of having to state 'I don't know' or 'I don't understand' and thus appearing unco-operative for not giving an answer. If the issue is controversial or if their stance on it seems different from that which they perceive the questioner or other informed people to hold, respondents can avoid being impolite and argumentative as well as misinformed by answering 'yes' or any other agreeable response. Finally, everyone knows that if they say 'no' or give some negative response they will be obliged by social convention to elaborate and to explain their disagreement. All of these entanglements can be avoided by answering agreeably. So respondents agreeably say 'yes' and let it go at that.

Acquiescing is all the more troublesome for the social fact that most questioners enjoy higher status, power and authority in the situation than do respondents. The social situation conduces to respondent acquiescence. Therefore, this seemingly positive and desirable strategy of responding might actually be the most negative one of all and the one most to be feared by the questioner. Much better to be faced with disagreeable respondents who will not go along with your questions but will give their own good answers.

The implication for practice is not some questioning strategy to counter the strategies of responding. Rather, it is simply to *listen to the answers*. A basic communication problem in question–answer situations is to get the respondent to give an answer and to get the questioner to listen to it. The overall implication is that questioning skill is not a matter of asking a specifiable set of questions in a specifiable set of ways. No type of question is a good or effective question to ask; no technique of questioning is a good or effective technique to use. Rather, good practice is an attribute of behaviour in context. Practice depends on knowing the elements of questioning and then manipulating them to purpose in circumstance.

CONCLUSION: THE PRACTICE OF QUESTIONING

Any of us who might be earnest about learning to use questions in professional practice are invited to take immediate steps towards the right practice of questioning. First, we shall have to side-step some attractive, easy avenues that will only lead us into the wrong direction. Above all, we have to stop asking questions in an everyday manner. Next, we should stop trying to imitate successful questioners in other fields. Last, we need to give up searching for techniques and strategies of questioning – not to mention tricks, gimmicks and trade secrets.

What we are left to figure out is which usage of questioning promises to serve to purpose and circumstance in our situation of practice. Study and understanding of the elements of questioning can help us to see the many possible uses of questions, but in the end we still have to act. Here we need a practical scheme of action. At the very least we need to take thoughtful action before, during and after asking questions – first preparing the questions to ask, next posing them and then pondering them.

1 *Prepare the questions.* What are the questions *for*? Which particular form of question should I ask? What possible answers might be given to the question?
2 *Pose the questions.* How should I put the question? What should I do with the answer?
3 *Ponder the question–answer.* How did the questions work? Which next questions might work better?

This scheme makes it plain that the professional practice of questioning is nothing like our everyday use of questions, instead requiring of us effortful thought and concentrated behaviour. The final part of the scheme brings us to make a new design on questioning: again we prepare the questions to ask, again we pose them, again we ponder them. That is the right use of questions. We discipline our questioning behaviour to serve professional purposes in our particular circumstances of practice.

REFERENCES

Babbitt, L. and Jablin, F. (1985) 'Characteristics of Applicants' Questions and Employment Screening Interview Outcomes', *Human Communication Research*, 11: 507–35.

Belnap, N. and Steel, T. (1976) *The Logic of Questions and Answers*, Yale University Press, New Haven, CT.

Berry-Rogghe, G., Kolvenbach, M. and Lutz, H. (1980) 'Interacting with PLIDIS, A Deductive Question Answer System for German', in L. Bolc (ed.), *Natural Language Question Answering Systems*, Hanser, Munich, 137–216.

Bradburn, N. and Sudman, S. (1980) *Improving Interview Method and Questionnaire Design: Response Effects to Threatening Questions in Survey Research*, Aldine, Chicago.

Buckwalter, A. (1983) *Interviews and Interrogations*, Butterworth, Stoneham, MA.

Churchill, L. (1978) *Questioning Strategies in Sociolinguistics*, Newbury, Rowley, MA.

Cronbach, L. (1982) *Designing Evaluations of Educational and Social Programs*, Jossey-Bass, San Francisco.

Davis, J. and Schiffman, H. (1985) 'The Influence of the Wording of Interrogatives on the Accuracy of Eyewitness Recollections', *Bulletin of the Psychonomic Society*, 23, 394–96.

Davis, M. (1971) 'That's Interesting!', *Philosophy of the Social Sciences*, 1, 309–44.

Dillon, J. T. (1988) *Questioning and Teaching: A Manual of Practice*, Routledge, London/Teachers College, New York.

—— (1990) *The Practice of Questioning*, Routledge, London.

—— (1994) *Using Discussion in Classrooms*, Open University Press, Milton Keynes.

Ellis, A. (1977) 'The Rational-emotive Facilitation of Therapeutic Goals', in A. Ellis and R. Grieger (eds), *Handbook of Rational-Emotive Therapy*, Springer, New York, 189–97.

Greatbach, D. (1986) 'Some Standard Uses of Supplementary Questions in News Interviews,' *Belfast Working Papers in Language and Linguistics*, 8, 86–123.

Grewendorf, G. (1983) 'What Answers can be Given?', in F. Kiefer (ed.), *Questions and Answers*, Reidel, Dordrecht, 45–84.

Harrah, D. (1985) 'The Logic of Questions', in F. Guenthner and D. Gabbay (eds), *Handbook of Philosophical Logic, Vol. II*, Reidel, Dordrecht, 45–84.

Harris, S. (1989) 'Questions in Political Broadcast Interviews', *Communication and Cognition*.

Hintikka, J. (1983) 'New Foundations for a Theory of Questions and Answers', in F. Kiefer (ed.), *Questions and Answers*, Reidel, Dordrecht, 159–90.

Johnson, M. (1979) *Discussion Dynamics*, Newbury, Rowley, MA.

Joshi, A. (1983) 'Varieties of Cooperative Responses in Question–Answer Systems', in F. Kiefer (ed.), *Questions and Answers*, Reidel, Dordrecht, 229–40.

Jucker, A. (1986) *News Interviews: A Pragmalinguistic Analysis*, Benjamins, Amsterdam.

Kestler, J. (1982) *Questioning Techniques and Tactics*, Shepard/McGraw-Hill, Colorado Springs, CO.

Loftus, E. (1979) *Eyewitness Testimony*, Harvard University Press, Cambridge, MA.

—— (1982) 'Interrogating Eyewitnesses – Good Questions and Bad', in R. Hogarth (ed.), *Question Framing and Response Consistency*, Jossey-Bass, San Francisco, 51–63.

Long, L., Paradise, L. and Long, T. (1981) *Questioning: Skills for the Helping Process*, Brooks/Cole, Monterey, CA.

McComb, K. and Jablin, F. (1984) 'Verbal Correlates of Interviewer Empathic Listening and Employment Interview Outcomes', *Communication Monographs*, 51, 353–71.

Metzler, K. (1988) *Creative Interviewing: The Writer's Guide to Gathering Information by Asking Questions* (2nd edn), Prentice-Hall, Englewood Cliffs, NJ.

Mishler, E. (1984) *The Discourse of Medicine: Dialectics of Medical Interviews*, Ablex, Norwood, NJ.

Morrow, N., Hargie, O., Donnelly, H. and Woodman, C. (1993) '"Why Do You Ask?" A Study of Questioning Behaviour in Community Pharmacist–Client Consultations', *International Journal of Pharmacy Practice*, 2, 90–4.

Olinick, S. (1954) 'Some Considerations of the Use of Questioning as a Psychoanalytic Technique', *Journal of the American Psychoanalytic Association*, 2, 57–66.

Payne, S. (1951) *The Art of Asking Questions*, Princeton University Press, Princeton, NJ.

Rogers, C. (1951) *Client-centered therapy*, Houghton-Mifflin, Boston.

Rowe, M. (1974) 'Wait-time and Rewards as Instructional Variables', *Journal of Research in Science Teaching*, 11, 81–94.

Royal, R. and Schutt, S. (1976) *The Gentle Art of Interviewing and Interrogation: A Professional Manual and Guide*, Prentice-Hall, Englewood Cliffs, NJ.

Schuman, H. and Presser, S. (1981) *Questions and Answers in Attitude Surveys: Experiments on Question Form, Wording, and Context*, Academic Press, New York.

Stenstroem, A.-B. (1984) *Questions and Responses in English Conversation*, Gleerup, Malmoe.

Stevens, R. (1912) 'The Question as a Measure of Efficiency in Instruction: A Critical Study of Class-Room Practice', *Teachers College Contributions to Education*, No. 48, Teachers College, New York.

Stiff, J. and Miller, G. (1986) '"Come to Think of it …" Interrogative Probes, Deceptive Communication, and Deception Detection', *Human Communication Research*, 12, 339–57.

Sudman, S. and Bradburn, N. (1974) *Response Effects in Surveys: A Review and Synthesis*, Aldine, Chicago.

—— (1982) *Asking Questions: A Practical Guide to Questionnaire Design*, Jossey-Bass, San Francisco.

Tengler, C. and Jablin, F. (1983) 'Effects of Question Type, Orientation, and Sequencing in the Employment Screening Interview', *Communication Monographs*, 50, 245–63.

Weiser, A. (1975) 'How Not to Answer a Question', in R. Grossman *et al.* (eds), *Papers from the 11th Regional Meeting of the Chicago Linguistic Society*, Chicago Linguistic Society, Chicago, 649–60.

Wellman, F. (1903) *The Art of Cross-examination* (4th rev. edn 1936), Macmillan, New York.

West, C. (1983) '"Ask Me No Questions": An Analysis of Queries and Replies in Physician–Patient Dialogues', in S. Fisher and A. Todd (eds), *The Social Organization of Doctor–patient Communication*, Center for Applied Linguistics, Washington, DC, 75–106.

Wooliscroft, J., Calhoun, J., Billiu, G., Stross, J., MacDonald, M. and Templeton, B. (1986) 'House Officer Interview Techniques: Impact on Data Elicitation and Patient Perceptions', paper presented at the annual meeting of the American Educational Research Association, San Francisco.

Woodbury, H. (1984) 'The Strategic Use of Questions in Court', *Semiotica*, 48, 197–228.

Yamada, S. (1913) 'A Study of Questioning', *Pedagogical Seminary Journal of Genetic Psychology*, 20, 129–86.

Yeschke, C. (1987) *Interviewing: an Introduction to Interrogation*, Thomas, Springfield, IL.

5 Reinforcement

Len Cairns

INTRODUCTION

The term 'reinforcement' is often used in a manner and with a meaning synonymous with reward, praise or encouragement or, even more broadly, feedback. As discussed in Chapter 2, in a social skills model of communication feedback is an important aspect which relates to how humans, when involved in communication, both give and receive feedback in that specific social situation and how this leads to development or change in the communication that is occurring.

It is important, at the outset of this chapter, that we clearly locate the theory and research relevance of the reinforcement notion within the social domain and relate the ideas to feedback within a social skills model of communication. In addition, the idea that reinforcement as a feedback element in communication will lead to increases in aspects of the behaviours being reinforced only has real significance if the reinforcers being examined have some real meaning to the players in the interaction. This means that the reinforcers must be contingently related and have some personal valence (power) and validity (meaning) for the individual. This aspect will be returned to later. It will be shown, in this chapter, that reinforcement is a key notion in a social skills model of communication and that many of the insights and ideas are relevant to the understanding of how humans do communicate.

In order for the phenomenon of reinforcement to have initial significance in this discussion of social communication, it is probably easiest to think of the idea that it is the after-effects of a person's communication response that lead to further communication or alteration in communication. The *after-effects* can be responses or feedback. The difference between these two terms is important for communication and the difference is often featured early in texts on the subject of communication (e.g. Taylor *et al.*, 1986, p. 9). A response in this context is meant to be *any* reaction to a sender's message, whereas feedback is meant to refer to those reactions which have some social meaning for the sender and are perceived as such and linked by the sender to the initial message. The important idea is that a response to a sent communication can only be feedback when the sender clearly perceives some reaction, whether in a face-to-face encounter or over the telephone or in writing.

In face-to-face communication there are both non-verbal and verbal aspects to feedback and reinforcement, ranging from the raised eyebrow (used effectively by Roger Moore in the James Bond movies and on television by Leonard Nimoy as Mr Spock in the *Star Trek* series), and through the shrug or nod of the head, to the tone of voice or the sarcastic note in a comment, or even the blunt expletive of dismissal.

In addition, in today's technology, much non-face-to-face feedback can also vary in time. Such feedback can occur in 'real time' or delayed time. The idea of delayed feedback in today's electronic age also has a number of different characteristics, particularly when compared with older notions of delayed feedback from around ten to twenty years ago. Included in the newer ideas is the point that a person may deliberately put a communication into a queue by using technology such as a telephone answering machine (or 'voice mail' as it is often referred to) or a computer e-mail set up to allow responses and interaction at a more personally convenient time. These aspects are relatively new to human communication and have introduced some interesting variations in the field. The way some of us use our answering machines to 'screen' telephone calls, for example, so as to decide with whom, when and under what conditions we might interact, is a feature of modern life which was neither necessary nor available in the past. It may be that the receiver who invokes such actions is attempting to avoid providing feedback, or is not wishing to engage in 'real time' communication because the feedback which might be provided to the message initiator may not be appropriate at this time. In very recent times some telephone users have actually begun to react quite forcefully to the implied feedback of the answering machine phenomenon by leaving strong, pointed messages ('I know that you are there. Pick up the 'phone!'). The range of reasons and possibilities for such behaviour is no doubt enough to fill a few years of research in a major university department. The recent advent of video-telephones and related technology has also raised some fascinating variations to ponder here.

CRITICISMS OF REINFORCEMENT

While we commonly talk of reinforcement in everyday language and we use the term 'feedback' frequently to describe reactions to what we say or do, the theory, research and study of communication is much more precise about these two terms. In addition, in the psychological literature, the term 'reinforcement' is defined in a way which reflects its most common derivation as a feature arising from operant psychology (Skinner, 1974). In this tradition, the term is usually defined as *a stimulus which when matched up with an emitted response (an operant action) increases the likelihood of that action being repeated.*

An example of this might be when a dog trainer stops at the kerbside and the dog being trained spontaneously sits at the edge. The trainer slips the dog a small piece of biscuit and pats it saying 'good dog'. It is highly likely that the dog will, in future, sit in this similar situation in anticipation of the desired reinforcement. This is particularly likely if the reinforcement event is repeated a few times subsequently. There are many examples of reinforcement around us in everyday life but most do not use basic drives such as hunger to underpin the 'satisfaction' element. In much of our human activity the value of the reinforcer is often something unique to us as humans. Such reinforcement is referred to as *conditioned reinforcement* and it usually involves some learned, social element (Kazdin, 1989).

A significant aspect of the notion of reinforcement as a core communication skill in a social skills model of communication lies in the term 'social'. As explained in Chapter 1, in this model, communication is regarded as social skill and the reinforcement which assists the ongoing aspects of that communication and its development is more precisely described as *social reinforcement*. What we mean when we use such a term is that the reinforcing effect of the stimulus is actually a socially important element. That is, the reinforcer has become something that will increase the likelihood of us repeating the behaviour it has been linked to by the nature of its significance to us in a social setting or situation. This concept differentiates the term from what is usually described as *primary reinforcement*, which refers to reinforcers which are related to primary, or unlearned aspects. Food and water are obvious examples of primary reinforcers.

Reinforcement, as mentioned above, has a history of being described as the foundation of the operant model of learning within the psychological theory and research field. The prominent twentieth-century psychologist, B. F. Skinner, has been the central figure in the writing and theory of the operant or behaviourist psychological movement (Skinner, 1974). This set of theories and research traditions has been extremely influential in the world of education, advertising and the treatment of behavioural disorders and, in addition, has pervaded a great deal of our everyday language and thinking. Probably, in the past hundred years, the two very different theorists and writers, Freud and Skinner, have influenced most what has been seen as the two basic elements of popular psychology. Often, those elements which are popularised have been twisted and debased elements of the actual theories which were originally propounded and this has led to many misconceptions and problems. It is important, in this chapter, that the reader is clear as to the behaviourist notion of reinforcement in the psychology literature and then sees the relationship to the notions of effective feedback within a social skills model of communication. There are common and important insights from the former to the latter and there are some elements which are not linked in the two uses of the term and the thinking.

In discussing the term 'reinforcement', it is common to argue that the idea is, and always should be, a straightforward behaviourist concept as outlined above, whereby a response is linked to a satisfying stimulus which reinforces the likelihood of the behaviour occurring again. However, this notion is far too simplistic in the field of communication between humans and ignores the greater degree of sophisticated understanding which has emerged over the past years. In addition, there is some degree of 'softening' of many writers' interpretation of the reinforcement notion in ways which reflect the development from neo-behaviourist and other influences in the 1980s and beyond into the 1990s.

It could be said, for example, that many of the theorists and writers who were heavily influenced by the behaviourist school of thought and research in the educational psychology area have, over the past few years, seriously modified their stance and their positions on many aspects of their work (Brown, 1994). That behaviourism has come under some serious reconsideration and appears to have a less central location as a key influential theoretical position does not destroy the area nor its credibility but, rather, has led to some serious redevelopments and repositioning.

Within the field of behaviour modification, which is the basic area where much of the applied research and fieldwork has occurred over the past twenty-five years in relation to reinforcement, there are a number of variations as to how the term and the idea of rein-forcement might best be discussed.

Kazdin (1989), as mentioned earlier, discussed two basic 'types' of positive reinforcers: *primary*, which he also calls 'unconditioned' (these cover such aspects as food and water as basic reinforcers which are with us from birth), and *secondary*, or 'conditioned' rein-forcers, which he describes as learned reinforcers (these cover such things as praise and grades at school). In a different, and much lighter treatment, Martin and Pear (1978) listed as the set of reinforcers available for consideration: 'consumable, activity, manipulative, possessional and social' (p. 22). This presentation, as part of a basic text aimed at a very broad market with 'no prior knowledge assumed about psychology or behavior modification' (p. xv) mixes some of the usual conceptualisations of the types of reinforcers with the modes of operation or delivery (activity, consumable, etc.). Such examples abound in the many texts from the 1970s era, when behaviour modification swept the medical and psychological courses around the globe. A more recent presentation on this aspect, which offers a very thorough and broad explanation, is that of Lieberman (1990), in which he differentiated between three types of reinforcement – primary, secondary and social – but pointed out that the latter, social reinforcement, could be said to be 'a blend of both primary and secondary reinforcers' (p. 171).

Finally, there is also the notion that there may be some form of continuum or even hierarchy of reinforcers and that those further up the 'ladder' are more sophisticated and learned reinforcers which may lead to a person 'self-reinforcing' behaviour through this upper level potency. MacMillan (1973, p. 113), writing in the schooling context, was one of the early advocates of such a series of possible levels where he hypothesised the following six elements:

1 Primary rewards – food and water;
2 Toys or trinkets;
3 Tokens or checks – with backups (toys or food);
4 Visual evidence of progress – graphs, letters, grades;
5 Social approval;
6 Sense of mastery – 'learning for the love of it'.

Such hierarchies, however, often fail to recognise that the nature of reinforcement relevance varies from one individual to another and so the levels are not invariant. MacMillan did acknowledge this aspect and presented his list as 'a tentative continuum'. It is perhaps reasonable to argue though that the two ends of such a continuum actually do represent significant differences and that Level 6 in MacMillan's list is a great deal more sophisticated as a response to reinforcement than the primary reinforcers at Level 1.

A further development of relevance to this presentation on the place of reinforcement in the social skills model of communication is the emergence in the 1970s and subsequent years of the social learning theory of Albert Bandura (Bandura, 1977). This theory argued that human learning involved a number of factors in addition to external reinforcement. Placing learning clearly in a social setting, social learning theory suggested that imitation, modelling, self-regulation and cognitive mediation were also important aspects of how and why we learn. As Kazdin (1989, p. 22) neatly summarised:

> Bandura has developed a social learning theory that encompasses various types of learning and the wide range of influences that each type entails. Thus, social learning approaches utilize elements of classical, operant, and observational learning to explain behavior. They integrate events in the environment and, to a much greater extent, cognitions (thoughts and beliefs, perceptions) about environmental events into a general framework that depends on different learning experiences.

While the Bandura developments contributed to some shifts and refinements in the field it was but one of a number of strands of development during the 1970s which came together to form and make what Hollin and Trower (1988) described as 'collective sense' and began the clinical social skills training tradition. The combination of the operant tradition with the social learning ideas of Bandura and the emergence in social psychology of the application of the motor-skill model to a social skills model (Argyle and Kendon, 1967; Argyle, 1969; Trower *et al.*, 1978; and later Hargie and McCartan, 1986 and Hargie *et al.*, 1994) all coalesced into a well-articulated model which employed the integration of the various theories and practices to explain and underpin treatment and action in a range of fields (see Chapters 1 and 2 for detailed analysis of this perspective). As will be discussed later in the following sections and in Chapter 19, in the field of education and more particularly teacher education, the advent of the microteaching approach (Allen and Ryan, 1969; Turney *et al.*, 1973, 1983; Hargie and Saunders, 1983) focused on a training and development approach which utilised many of the same theoretical conceptualisations.

A further element of key importance at this stage in clarifying the notion of reinforcement in this communication model is that of the contingent relationship between the behaviour (or in this case, the emitted communication) and the consequence of the behaviour which is necessary if the consequence is to be seen as reinforcement. The experimental literature in the behaviour modification field is full of discussions about the necessity for a contingent (i.e. definite linkage) relationship between the stimulus and the response in operant theory and practice if there is to be a reinforcing effect. The basic rule is that for some reaction to be positively reinforcing it must be valued as a response by the person to whom it is directed and the reaction must have some relationship to the behaviour or communication that it is aimed at reinforcing. This link is termed 'contingency'.

There are, in social skills terms, a number of different patterns of possible contingency relationships between communicators. As Trower *et al.* (1978) outlined, there are different sets of rules governing the sequence of individual utterances in different social situations. They described these as a set of four 'contingency' models based on the earlier work of Jones and Gerard (1967), and while not directly ascribed by either set of authors to an operant model, the Trower *et al.* text (1978, p. 29) clearly placed its discussion within the area as follows:

> Each episode has rules governing behaviour within it and an internal sequence which is highly predictable, and participants cooperate to perform it as a joint social act. They will agree to enact a particular episode if this is expected to be sufficiently gratifying for each of them, though there is some scope for negotiating the way the episode goes. Social performers try to bring about certain episodes, which will produce the responses they are seeking.

The four models presented are:

1 *Reactive contingency* which refers to the way two people in a conversation (say in a coffee break at work) actually respond to each other in a sequence and the conversation continues effectively;
2 *Asymmetrical contingency* which refers to the way two people may interact where the second person does not react to the first person's initiation as the second has an agenda or plan of his or her own which does not include this particular interaction (an example might be a speech);
3 *Mutual contingency* which describes the way each person reacts to the other but also has an individual plan. An example of this type of contingency might be a negotiation session, teaching or a therapy situation;
4 *Pseudo contingency* which refers to the situation where each person involved is not really responding or reacting to the other except in timing. This applies to rituals, play acting and other very structured situations.

Table 5.1 Characteristics of positive and negative reinforcement

	Positively valued stimulus	*Negatively valued stimulus*
Contingent application	Positive reinforcement	Punishment
Contingent removal	Response cost	Negative reinforcement

Finally, in this section, it is necessary to distinguish (albeit by way of a rather simplistic table) among the various terms in the field of behaviour modification which often lead to popular confusion. Of particular concern is the notion of *negative reinforcement* which is often used in popular discussions as if it was the application of some form of negative element such as a punishment to stop unwanted behaviour or to force other positive behaviour. The accompanying table presents a simplified model of the various components and their relationship as specified in an operant model.

In Table 5.1 it can be seen that positive reinforcement (usually just labelled reinforcement) is the contingent application of a positively valued stimulus. The notion of negative reinforcement, while still being reinforcing (that is, still leading to an increase in the likelihood of the behaviour being repeated), is actually the *removal* of a negatively valued stimulus. A famous example of this as offered by Skinner himself (1974, p. 51) is the removal of an 'ill-fitting shoe that is irritating your foot ... that act relieves the irritation and leads you to be likely to remove your shoe if you feel such an irritation again'.

Table 5.1 also attempts to clarify the difference between what is called *response cost* and *punishment* (some experts describe these two as 'punishment 1' and 'punishment 2' – e.g. Kazdin, 1989 – but this is probably too confusing and the 'response cost' notion has a far better clarity). For the purposes of this explanation, the term 'response cost' refers to the contingent removal of a positively valued stimulus. This might mean the withdrawal of positive reinforcers, or the denial of the opportunity to gain any positive reinforcement (as in 'time out' at school for misbehaviour in the classroom).

Punishment, as can be clearly seen from Table 5.1, refers to the contingent application of an aversive stimulus. Having something you do not like presented or done to you as a consequence of what you have done (or said) is the key concept to keep in mind. In general, our modern societies are less than supportive of the broad application of punishment between people and we have various legal sanctions against such behaviours. It is interesting, however, that in some societies, the legal sanctions to control and prevent further aberrant and abhorrent behaviours are often set up as punishment (e.g. caning, limb removal and execution).

REINFORCEMENT AND FEEDBACK

In most early communication models and conceptualisations, there have been approaches which have suggested that the simplest explanation of human communication, as in conversations, could be based on an 'S-M-C-R' model (after Berlo, 1960) or some variation thereon (Rogers and Agarwala-Rogers, 1976). In this type of presentation the S stands for source of the communication, the M is for the message sent, C is for the channel of communication and R is for the receiver. An important element in such models is that the receiver, once the message has been received, provides feedback to the sender. The idea of feedback in these models is that this feedback leads to continuation of the communication or some modification. There is two-way or *dyadic* communication occurring. Rogers and Agarwala-Rogers (1976, p. 13) defined the idea as follows:

> *Feedback* is a response by the receiver to the source's message. The source may take account of feedback in modifying subsequent messages: thus feedback makes communication a dynamic, two-way process. Feedback may be thought of as messages to the source conveying knowledge of the effectiveness of a previous communication. *Positive feedback* informs the source that the intended effect of a message was achieved; *negative feedback* informs the source that the intended effect of a message was *not* achieved.

Other publications and similar models over the years have also followed a similar pattern of defining and providing examples to explain the notion and nature of the concept of feedback within these models. Brooks (1981) described feedback as also having a 'regulatory effect upon the speaker' (p. 12), while studies by Verplanck (1955) and others by Stolz and Tannenbaum (1963) and Minkin *et al.* (1976) all examined aspects of conversational and laboratory manipulations of feedback and its effects on the message source within the broad parameters of these types of models of communication.

The social skills model, upon which this book rests, has led to some further refinements and developments. As stated above, the early development of this model by Argyle and his colleagues at Oxford had a particular feedback loop built into the model. In the Trower *et al.* (1978, p. 22) elaboration of the model there was an acknowledgement of the relationship between the social skills model and behavioural principles, in which they conceded that the term 'reinforcement' could be an optional term for feedback and also discussed the elements of 'rewardingness and control' exercised by people in communication interactions:

> People don't simply speak and mesh smoothly in conversation; they also reward and control each other. This brings in another aspect of the social skills model – motivation and planning – though the actual behaviour is executed often quite unconsciously at the 'translation' stage. During social interaction, participants behave with differing degrees of rewardingness and control. This has two effects – controlling the immediate behaviours of others, and affecting how much one is liked or disliked.

We now turn to a more explicit presentation of the argument in this chapter that the feedback element of the social skills communication model can be interpreted and examined as an example of reinforcement.

The position being presented starts with the notion of a communicator initiating a message to another person. In its simplest terms, this message, communication or utterance (depending on the mode of communication) is sent or transmitted to the receiver person. This is a simple I (initiator) to R (receiver) conceptualisation. In order to present and explain the idea of feedback as reinforcement in this conceptualisation, the behaviour of the receiver in response to the message is described as a *reaction*.

The receiver's reaction to a message in communication may be either one of a simple reaction or response (in the sense that it may not provide any real feedback to the initiator as mentioned at the outset of this chapter). Such a simple response may be non-verbal or verbal in face-to-face communication. It may be eye contact, proximity with some apparent attending behaviour, or a simple verbal 'yes', 'um' or 'uhuh' (these three are usually, in English, the most used initial reactions in conversation). What, in essence, these reactions are conveying is a 'message received' form of response which mostly has little or no feedback (as defined above) or reinforcement-type elements within it. It could be argued that these reactions, described as simple responses, are somewhat like neutral place-holders that indicate that the receiver of the communication is actually aware and able (and possibly willing) to participate in some interaction, but as yet the reaction is not of a type which provides feedback in a reinforcement sense.

For a reaction to be deemed to be reinforcement it is argued in this chapter that the following three characteristics are necessary:

1 *Personal validity* which refers to the way the message must have some real meaning of a valued sense to the persons involved. It should be a statement or a non-verbal message that is socially valid to the involved persons as some meaningful positive or negative element. For example, if the initiator of a message sends that message in English and the receiver, who understands it, replies in another language which the initiator does not understand, then there may not be any reinforcement at all unless there are accompanying non-verbal clues such as gesture or tone;

2 *Personal valence* which refers to the power within the message. Many messages in communication, while having factual and other content, may not carry much weight or power to have any effect on the recipient or any such intent from the initiator. The idea of valence in this context is that the message should, if it is to be seen as reinforcement, have some power or potency for the participants. This idea differs from validity in that the personal validity element relates to the meaning of the message while the valence refers to the power, the way some messages carry stronger effect and affect for people;

3 *Contingent relationship* which refers to the need for the reaction message to be contingently related to the initiation. Such contingency, it is argued, should be of the reactive or mutual type mentioned above. What this means is that there should be some mutual reaction and action sequence in a clear, ongoing link and/or there should be some mutuality in the understanding of the contingency.

The reaction of the receiver of a message is seen as reinforcement when these three elements are present. Such reinforcement may convey either *information* or *affect* and this could be either *real* (actual or explicit) or *implied* (particularly in the non-verbal sphere).

It is the absence of one or more of the three key elements mentioned above which often leads to some communications not actually 'working' as intended reinforcement. Take, for example, the teacher who uses praise such as 'good boy' or 'good girl' in the classroom as a message to a child intended as praise or encouragement for the completion of mathematics work. If this praise is not seen by the target receiver as having any personal validity or any personal valence then it is more a simple reaction and not legitimate feedback or reinforcement. The child is highly likely to ignore the comment and neither respond with any further communication nor feel reinforced.

In a more general example, a brief 'mm' on the telephone between two people will have the person to whom this is a reaction either asking for more specific feedback (and reinforcement) or attempting to 'interpret' the tone or pitch variations as non-verbal intent to gain validity and possible valence, or (and this is the most likely) interpreting this simple noise as acknowledgement that the listener is still on the line but that there is no other feedback or reinforcement in this exchange.

It is apparent that in communication the role of reinforcement is one that necessitates a close examination of the manner in which consequential behaviours (be they verbal or non-verbal) are presented to other individuals in interaction and how these behaviours are perceived by the parties involved.

REINFORCEMENT IN INTERPERSONAL COMMUNICATION

So far in this chapter we have defined, clarified and discussed the concept of reinforcement as an important element essential to the development and modification of interpersonal interaction and communication. In the sections to follow, the application of reinforcement in a variety of settings and applied fields of endeavour will be discussed. There has been much research and deliberation, along with criticism and controversy, about the place of reinforcement as a concept in education, language research, management and other spheres of applied work. This presentation attempts to examine briefly a number of significant aspects of the area and to provide the reader with adequate insights to explore this important concept.

Reinforcement and non-verbal communication

Chapter 3 presents a detailed account of the communication skill of non-verbal communication. In this section it is not intended that this area will be discussed again in a similar manner: readers are urged to examine the chapter on that skill carefully in relation to the aspects raised in this chapter. What follows is a brief explanation that relates the concept of reinforcement to non-verbal communication and puts the current discussion into perspective.

In communication both the non-verbal and the verbal aspects contribute to effective interaction. Both aspects are often forms of reinforcement as they function in the communicators' interaction. As Argyle described it in his classic 1975 volume, *Bodily Communication*:

> While one person is speaking, others may be listening; if so they send signals too, whether they realize it or not, and whether the speaker attends to these or not. The main back-channel signals are head-nods, short vocalisations, glances, and facial expressions, often in combination . . . . Back-channel signals may be: (1) 'listening behaviour', indicating attention and understanding; (2) feedback, for example agreement and approval; (3) imitation, matching the speaker's behaviour.

In an important study in 1977 Archer and Akert developed a new (then) technique to examine the relative significance or contributions of verbal cues and a combination of non-verbal and verbal cues to meaning in a conversation. Archer and Akert were concerned that earlier work by such researchers as Argyle in the UK and Birdwhistell and Mehrabian in the USA had argued that the verbal channel only contributed some 7 per cent of emotional meaning (Mehrabian, 1972) and that 'no more than 30 per cent to 35 per cent of the social meaning of a conversation or an interaction is carried by the words' (Birdwhistell, 1970). They developed what they called the Social Interpretations Test (SIT), a videotape of twenty 'unposed sequences of spontaneous behavior' to test a number of comparisons and gain some date on the effectiveness of 'full-channel' (verbal plus non-verbal) cues and verbal cues alone. They concluded that '(w)ords alone are not sufficient for accurate interpretations. Social interpretation in a wide variety of naturalistic situations is much more accurate when one has available both nonverbal and verbal cues than when one has only a verbal record of the interaction' (p. 449).

Trower *et al.* (1978, p. 22) put the matter of the feedback nature of the dual involvement of non-verbal and verbal cues in interaction in a succinct manner:

> *The feedback system.* A speaker needs intermittent, but regular, feedback on how others are responding, so that he can modify his utterances accordingly. He needs to know whether the listeners understand, believe, disbelieve, are surprised or bored, agree or disagree, are pleased or annoyed. This information could be provided by *sotto voce* verbal muttering, but is in fact obtained by careful study of the other's face: the eyebrows signal surprise, puzzlement, etc., while the mouth indicates pleasure and displeasure.

Many non-verbal elements such as eye contact, smiling and body orientation are frequently used in conversations and other face-to-face interactions as positive indications of both openness to communicate and reinforcement for continuation and reaction. Similarly, the deliberate and obvious avoidance of eye contact and the use of certain facial expressions or body movements in response to communication openings by an initiator could be described as a form of punishment in terms of the definitions presented in Table 5.1.

The significance of such elements of non-verbal communication as gaze, eye contact, gesture and body orientation in the initial, medial and closure stages of conversations has been discussed by researchers over the past twenty years (Argyle, 1967; Argyle and Cook, 1967; Cook, 1977). The argument in much of this research was that these elements were mostly low in the level of individual consciousness and somewhat regulatory in their application at the start and end of communication encounters. It could be argued, in this age, that with the greater publicity (and even direct training in some fields) over the past decade, a good many non-verbal cues are now more consciously manipulated by people in conversations, business, teaching and sales encounters (the advent of fast-food training in particular greeting styles, postures, smiles and verbal openings and follow-ups is a good example).

Certainly, there are great variations in personal perception of many non-verbal cues in society, and a number of which vary in meaning and potency across cultures. Not all convey the same meaning and not all that are seen as positive and even reinforcing in some cultures are seen in a similar vein in others. Some of the situation-specific behaviours have become so culturally embedded that they emerge as 'genres' or even rituals in which the nature of the feedback and/or reinforcement becomes lost. A good example of the way specific cultural situations and settings give rise to rule-governed behaviours and expectations (or 'genres' – socially derived sets of rules and expectations of form) can be found in such situations as the way a customer can summon a waiter in a restaurant in different cultures. In some, a subtle eye signal, move of the head or slight hand signal is seen as the more sophisticated and preferred mode. In others, a loud hiss is seen as appropriate. In still others, a click of the fingers is seen as neither rude nor too overt, but rather the norm, whereas in most Western cultures this is now seen as gauche behaviour to be avoided.

It is not surprising that the non-verbal communication area has developed to a degree where it is often discussed in terms as if it might be equivalent to a language by many writers (Argyle, 1975) or some aspects of it (kinesics) even described as 'body language' (Scheflen and Scheflen, 1972). Nor is it surprising that the notion of reinforcement has a strong and central place in the explanation of how those responses are learned.

It can be seen that many of the non-verbal cues utilised in conversations between people act very specifically as potential reinforcers within the considerations offered in this chapter.

Reinforcement and verbal communication

In most communication models and more particularly, in conversation models, the way there is some reciprocity and mutuality in the reinforcement and patterns of interaction becomes an area of extreme interest. Just as speakers in a conversation send feedback non-verbally by using head nods, smiles and eye contact to signal attention to the other speaker (Argyle, 1975), or if the signals have validity, valence and contingency, they may reinforce the other communicator to continue and develop interaction further, so too are there more complex and additional verbal reinforcers which signal meaning, acceptance, rejection, willingness to continue, and so on. There has been a range of research conducted that has examined reinforcement in such communication but it should be clear that there are two aspects to the discussion of reinforcement in this context.

The first refers to the way the actual feedback is seen as reinforcement within the communication. That is, the feedback loop meets the three elements mentioned above and that feedback between communicators serves as a reinforcement of the communication and ensuring continuation, development and interaction which is mutually gratifying as communication. The second usage of the term 'reinforcement' in this field of study and research is that which refers to the way positive verbal reinforcement is utilised as a learning or teaching tool within the social skills training of the communicators.

For example, one of the key elements of the social skills training approach has been to use verbal reinforcement (Donahoe and Driesenga, 1988) which is described as 'verbal praise and encouragement'. The content (i.e. the social skills being taught in many of these studies), also includes reinforcement itself as an element of the social skill of conversation. This aspect can cause some confusion when reading the material and when considering the overall case being asserted in this chapter.

An early study which employed reinforcement both as part of the verbal skills to be trained and within the training regime to develop the skill is that of Minkin *et al.* (1976). In a three-part study they set out to develop conversational skills in young female delinquents. In the initial stage they set out to identify the appropriate conversational target behaviours to be trained. They did this by asking 'normal' junior high school and college female students to hold conversations which they videotaped and then analysed to identify the conversational sub-skills. They then 'verified' the skills by having other students and community members rate the conversational skills evident in the videotapes. After this, they embarked on the training programme. They were interested to see if they could train the sample of females to increase their conversational behaviours as assessed by observers in beneficial, socially validated behaviours.

The socially validated conversational behaviours that were identified in the study were (1) 'conversational questions' and (2) 'positive conversational feedback'. The latter element of conversation was defined in behavioural terms in the tradition of behavioural psychology and in the manner that clearly showed the link with reinforcement. The study was quite successful in demonstrating that, in the training-centre environment, these two components (or skills) of conversation could be so behaviourally defined, observed and trained.

A later study in a similar vein was conducted by Kleitsch *et al.* (1983). Here the specific issue of previous studies occurring within laboratory, clinic or training-centre as opposed to real-life situations was addressed by attempting to improve the conversational interactions of four elderly socially isolated and retarded men. The procedures used involved quite natural social praise and conversation in language-learning groups. The results suggested that these procedures were not only effective in increasing the overall rate of the men's verbalisations, but also generalised to other situations.

It is in the area of teaching verbal communication that reinforcement aspects have been quite prominent and successful. There have been a number of studies, like those mentioned above, where people with skill and/or learning problems, or even psychiatric difficulties, have been 'trained' in conversational and other aspects of communication using reinforcement procedures or approaches based on a reinforcement (operant or behavioural psychology) approach. As cited earlier, some of the skills that were taught also often included providing feedback or reinforcing others as an aspect of effective communication.

Not all of the examples involve positive social reinforcement. Some of the research has applied aspects of negative reinforcement as described in Table 5.1. In an early and classic study using negative reinforcement, Heckel *et al.* (1962) used a loud noise projected through a speaker to increase conversation in a psychiatric therapy group. The noise commenced when the group was silent for more than a minute and only stopped when a member of the group broke the silence (thus conversation led to the withdrawal of the aversive stimulus – the loud noise – and that withdrawal acted as negative reinforcement for the verbal behaviour).

Another example of people showing that speech improvements and conversational skill increase by virtue of reinforcement interventions in research studies includes one involving a withdrawn psychiatric patient speaking louder and longer by utilising negative reinforcement where staff repeatedly nagged the patient if he did not speak louder and for longer periods. The withdrawal of the nagging when he did speak louder and longer was the negative reinforcement. In another study by Jackson and Wallace (1974), positive reinforcement, here implemented in the form of tokens and accompanying 'shaping' (gradual changes towards an expected target behaviour) was used to train a mentally retarded girl to speak louder than her previous barely audible level.

Such studies, which often took place with one or two subjects (who were usually patients in institutions), were reported frequently in journals of special education, behaviour disorders and therapy areas in the 1970s and 1980s. These approaches also have been extensively utilised in early schooling settings and special education facilities. While the approaches have been the subject of not inconsiderable controversy from time to time over the past twenty years, there is a large body of data pointing to test score gains and other effectiveness data where these methods have been employed (O'Leary and O'Leary, 1977; Rhine *et al.*, 1981; Kazdin, 1989).

One such set of materials and a subsequent teaching programme is that known as DISTAR. The acronym is the commercial name for the direct instruction model materials developed initially from the work of Wesley Becker, Siegfried Engelmann and Carl Bereiter. In subsequent years the materials and research involved a larger group of colleagues with Bereiter dropping out to some extent (Becker *et al.*, 1981). The materials involved three levels or sets of lessons in kit form for each of the three areas of curriculum – reading, arithmetic and language. Each kit included teacher-scripted lessons, was based on the operant psychology theory and featured strongly a lot of teacher-directed social reinforcement.

In the very large American federally funded research/experimental project entitled 'Follow Through' (which ran from 1967 until the early 1980s), the direct instruction model was one of many which set up twenty or so applications of their approaches in schools across America (Rhine *et al.*, 1981). These sites were to be exemplary applications of the materials and ideas competing with all the other approaches taking part in a giant study of various programmes of educating children in the basics in the early years of schooling. While with hindsight this might seem an incredibly misguided way to approach innovation and evaluation, that it occurred at all is quite remarkable. The two most successful programmes in the set of eight or more that were so pitted against each other (although there were constant attempts to argue that this was not the intent nor the design, it emerged in many minds as such) were the DISTAR project and the University of Kansas programme which was called the Behavior Analysis Model (Ramp and Rhine, 1981). Both models were based on the operant psychology approach and employed heavy use of reinforcement, particularly in teaching language and reading skills (Rhine, 1981).

Another programme and research study which has been reported more recently is that of the TALK Language Development Program which is a 'systematic behavioral program and technology that can be used to produce reliable increases in functional language, cognitive skills and developmental level in a wide variety of developmentally disabled preschool children' (Drash and Tudor, 1990, p. 179). This programme used positive reinforcement and a very behaviourally orientated approach to teach disabled children to talk and eventually converse. The appeal, according to the authors, in this approach was that it involved a standard technology for the analysis, reinforcement and recording of verbal behaviour and they presented data on its use and application across a range of children with disabilities. Drash and Tudor have applied their 'very successful' programme to 'normal infants' with some reported success as well. They concluded that it 'provides a systematic approach through which prevention of and recovery from language delay and functional retardation can for many preschool children become a practical reality' (p. 214).

Reinforcement obviously has been applied as a major aspect in the development of language and learning skills in a variety of situations and with a variety of people. That the skill is both an integral part of the conversational sequence between people and a major element in many studies of language and communication remediation and development is evident from even a cursory examination of the research literature. While there are many critics of the theory and others who decry the application studies (some of these will be mentioned in the conclusion of the chapter), it remains a major area of research and study in human communication.

REINFORCEMENT IN APPLIED SETTINGS

This section presents details of the application of the concept of reinforcement and derived work in applied settings.

Reinforcement in classroom communication

Reinforcement as a basic communication skill in the classroom has a long and powerful history. In fact, this teaching skill has been studied and focused on as a basic element of teaching and teacher education for many years (Cairns, 1973; Dunkin and Biddle, 1974; Arends, 1991). In addition, in the approach to teacher education known as 'microteaching' (Allen and Ryan, 1969; Turney *et al.*, 1973; McIntyre *et al.*, 1977; Brown, 1978) which rested on a paradigm derived from a behaviourist model and a sub-skills analysis of the teaching act, one of the key initial skills taught and trained in almost all interpretations of the model was the teacher's use of reinforcement. In addition, in more recent writing, Hollin and Trower (1988, p. 187) argued that 'micro teaching is a form of SST' (social skill training) and they detail the approach of Brown and Shaw (1986) as an exemplar.

Much of the earliest research in this tradition in the education domain examined the effect of teacher praise (and blame) on pupil achievement in the classroom. These studies tended to define teacher praise in a fairly general manner with little or no attention to contingency and reached conclusions from correlations between teacher praise and achievement such as, 'Praise has been found generally to have a facilitating effect on the performance of school children while blame has been found generally to have a debilitating effect on the performance of school children' (Kennedy and Willcutt, 1964, p. 331).

Studies after this era were largely of the behaviour modification type and focused on reinforcement more as a contingent and evaluative component of a teacher's communication with pupils rather than the more general concepts of non-contingent praise or blame. Research and practical applications in this area centred on how teachers communicated contingent praise and encouragement, mostly as verbal social reinforcement aimed at specific pupils and targeted to increase specific behaviours or improve classroom management by teachers (O'Leary and O'Leary, 1972, 1977; MacMillan, 1973; Sulzer and Mayer, 1972).

Among studies in this tradition have been those of Birnbrauer *et al.* (1965), in which attending behaviour to a reading task by eight retarded children was significantly increased by reinforcement procedures, and Broden *et al.* (1970), in which the teacher's attention was used to increase a pupil's attending behaviour. Other studies in this vein have examined the way teachers' reinforcement has been successfully manipulated to increase such pupil behaviours as passing arithmetic tests (Rosenfeld, 1972), verbally responding in class (Reynolds and Risley, 1968) and participation in class (Cormier and Wahler, 1971).

While there has been a good deal of advocacy for the significance of reinforcement as a teaching and classroom communication skill over the past two decades, there have been some points raised in the literature which have questioned a number of previously assumed aspects.

Brophy (1981) argued that much of the praise teachers use in the classroom is non-contingent and therefore not reinforcing. Further, he pointed out that pupils are often more attuned to the reinforcement variable than many teachers have given them credit for in the past. He even suggested that 'students also tended to reward teachers for their praise by responding very positively to it – smiling, beaming proudly and the like' (p.13). An additional point in Brophy's discussion was that teacher praise should meet four criteria if it is to be reinforcing: first, it should be specific in reference to the behavioural element that it is to reinforce; second, it should be clearly contingent upon the behaviour; third, it should be credible to the pupils involved; and fourth, it should be varied according to the teacher's understanding and knowledge of individual pupils. Brophy's criticisms and comments do provide a note of caution against the all too ready acceptance of the notion that all supportive and praise comments made by teachers (and others in similar social situations) are clear examples of reinforcement in the sense defined at the outset of this chapter.

One only has to watch a few episodes of the popular television series *The Simpsons* with one's own children to understand that many of the assumptions teachers have made about the manipulability of children and the reinforcing nature of some of the praise and encouragement teachers offer so overtly in the classroom are seen through by the now very sophisticated young children. Some of the cynicism of modern youth in the school context portrayed in movies and television programmes such as *Ferris Beuller's Day Off*, where the smart hero is often seen actually showing up the implausibility or out-of-touch nature of the teachers and in particular aspects, such as the teacher's attempts to use some aspects of verbal reinforcement, should be sobering for many educators. Nevertheless, the evidence for appropriate use and involvement appears to hold up reasonably well, even today (Alberto and Troutman, 1995).

Another criticism levelled against the idea and application of reinforcement has been that extrinsic rewards and incentives (reinforcers) may have a detrimental effect on the intrinsic motivation of pupils. That is, the child may come only to wish to perform a certain task or behaviour so as to gain the reinforcement and will thereby stop completing the behaviour when the reinforcement is not available or present (Schwartz, 1990). This notion was also raised by Brophy (1983) when he reiterated his earlier criticisms and added this as a new aspect based on the research reported by Lepper and Greene (1978). In a thorough review of the research studies in the area, Cameron and Pierce (1994) attend to this particular issue in detail. Their conclusion (p. 397), after a meta-analysis of some ninety-six studies in the field was that:

> The present findings suggest that verbal praise and positive feedback enhance people's intrinsic interest. This is an important finding. Most social interaction in business, education, and clinical settings involves verbal feedback from managers, teachers, and therapists. When praise and other forms of positive feedback are given and later removed, people continue to show intrinsic interest in their work. In contrast to recent claims made by Kohn (1993, p. 55), verbal praise is an extrinsic motivator that positively alters attitudes and behavior.

Recent developments and refinements of work in the field of behaviour modification have led to models and advocacy that has incorporated more of the cognitive psychology elements into a modified version of the traditional approaches. Some experts refer to this as 'cognitive behavior modification' (Finch *et al.*, 1993).

Reinforcement in the classroom is therefore an important element in the communication, interaction and teaching processes. It forms a key and integral part of the classroom communication system.

Reinforcement and social skills training

There have been many other areas where aspects of the reinforcement skill and related theory and practice have been applied. One such area in the clinical sphere is that known as social skills training (SST). This term is used to describe an approach originally developed and popularised by the Department of Experimental Psychology at the University of Oxford. As detailed in Chapter 1, an early article by Argyle and Kendon (1967) was the first to draw an analogy between the motor-skill model and a social skill model of behaviour and suggest that there was in this model 'a conceptual basis for understanding socially-skilled behaviour' (Hollin and Trower, 1988, p. 167).

Social skills training has, since its introduction in the late 1960s, developed into an internationally applied approach which has found many applications as a tool for therapy for patients in hospitals and other institutions who demonstrate social inadequacy problems.

The approach has, in more recent years, become more widely applied and developed (Curran and Monti, 1982; L'Abate and Milan, 1985; Hargie and McCartan, 1986; Hollin and Trower, 1988).

The basic elements of the social skills training model can be detailed as follows:

1 *Problem or skill specification.* The problem to be addressed and the identification of the social skills that are to be trained is carried out first;
2 *Didactic instruction.* The trainer presents the principles and what constitutes a competent performance of the skill;
3 *Modelling.* The trainer demonstrates the correct way to perform the response;
4 *Behavioural rehearsal or role-play.* The patient is helped to role-play the skills with instruction and assistance;
5 *Coaching.* The trainer gives instructions during the rehearsal;
6 *Feedback.* The trainer (and possibly others) provides feedback after the role-play to the patient about the performance;
7 *Verbal reinforcement.* The trainer uses praise and encouragement to reinforce the patient's behaviour;
8 *Generalisation.* Procedures such as self-monitoring and self-reinforcement are built in to help the patients generalise their new behaviours to natural situations;
9 *Homework.* The patient is given assignments to practise the new skills outside the training environment (based on Donahoe and Driesenga, 1988).

This basic set of elements is fairly consistently applied within the field. Hollin and Trower (1988) also described the social skills training model in very similar terms: 'The package of behavior-acquisition techniques used in SST has long been established and is comprehensively described in a number of texts (e.g. Trower *et al.*, 1978). The major components are instruction, modelling or demonstration, role-play practice and rehearsal, coaching and feedback and contingent reinforcement and homework.' As mentioned here, the training manual offered by Trower *et al.* (1978) was one of the first to set the aspects out clearly. They presented their model and training materials within a behavioural change context and made use of many of the same types of components defined as reinforcement in other fields. In subsequent writing there has been some debate as to whether this model tended to ignore the emotions and 'feeling side' of the social skills and whether there should be more cognitive consideration in the approach (Hollin and Trower, 1988). As these authors concluded in their review and critique of the field (1988, p. 172): 'In summary, there is some debate as to the relative effects of each component of training; and also whether cognitive and emotional therapies should be part of, or a separate type of, SST. However, there is little doubt that SST can be an effective means of changing behavior – a wealth of research papers testify to that fact. It is this success of the technique that has contributed to its widespread use and popularity.'

In his 1982 publication, Kelly presented a social skills analysis of intervention procedures for dealing with a much wider range of social and interpersonal problems. In addition, Kelly appeared to be more direct than his colleagues in the UK in acknowledging the central role of reinforcement. Kelly (1982, p. 5) put his position in the following terms:

All of the interpersonal skills that facilitate the building of relationships have in common with one another the fact that they increase the social attractiveness or reinforcement values of the person exhibiting them. Because others respond positively to individuals who are skilful in conversation, date-initiation, commendatory behavior or, in the case of children, prosocial-play skills, these competencies serve not only as avenues by which a person can initiate reinforcing relationships, but they also increase the likelihood that others will seek out further opportunities to interact with the individual.

Kelly offered suggestions for SST in the areas of conversational skills, date-initiation and other heterosocial skills, assertiveness training and job interview skills, as well as a section on SST for children. Within each of these areas Kelly included reinforcement components. In conversational skills he detailed 'reinforcing or complimentary components' (p. 141), which included 'verbalisations' that demonstrate that a person approves, concurs or understands what the other has said. In his other sections, Kelly clearly used a number of reinforcement components to develop and train social skills as well as involving a number of these as the actual social skills themselves. In his presentation of SST for children, Kelly was even more specific about the core skill of reinforcement which he described as 'praise' in the following way: 'the child who develops the ability of praising his or her peers will be an effective dispenser of reinforcement to them' (p. 219).

The wider applicability of the SST model can also be seen by a perusal of any of the major 'overview' works in this field of the past ten years (Curran and Monti, 1982; Trower, 1984; L'Abate and Milan, 1985; Hollin and Trower, 1986a, 1986b, 1988; Donahoe and Driesenga, 1988). Among the many areas of 'problems' that the techniques have been employed to work with individuals have been schizophrenia, mentally handicapped, anxiety and depression sufferers, alcoholics, people with eating disorders, relationship problems in marriage, drug abusers and people with work-related problems. Trainers have worked with and reported successes with children, adolescents, adults and the elderly as sub-groups in studies.

The generalisability of the training has been reported to stand up well within the clinical situation and, in the short term, in a number of the problem areas with chronic mentally ill patients, but there is less unequivocal data in the generalisation in other areas, particularly in relation to the issue of whether the newly acquired behaviours actually generalised to the natural environment (Hollin and Trower, 1988). In concluding their review of fifteen years of research evidence on SST, Donahoe and Driesenga (1988) pointed out that the generalisation issue was one of the key aspects which needed to be further addressed by research in the field.

The social skills training area can be seen, from this brief overview, to have involved the core skill of reinforcement in both the training procedures utilised by the approach and in many instances as one of the actual aspects of the social skills being trained.

Reinforcement and business communication and management

The field of business communication also has been one of the major sites for application of the notion of reinforcement as a core skill. In particular, the ideas have found applicability in the supervision and management of personnel. As early as 1979, Crane argued that 'the single most important aspect of communication is feedback. It is the reaction from those receiving a message that can be used by the sender to evaluate the message' (p. 77). More recently, George and Cole (1992), in the third edition of their widely used text, argued for the use of positive feedback as an explicit application of reinforcement theory: 'behavioral theorists such as B. F. Skinner have shown us how supervisors can use feedback, or *reinforcement*, to improve the performance of employees' (p. 148). The descriptions and examples given in many of the business communications courses offered in business schools at universities frequently show that the important element of feedback is couched in pure behavioural terms, which fits the definition of reinforcement. In some of the set texts for such courses the link is explicitly delineated; in others it is glossed over but is evident in the examples.

One such clear example should suffice to illustrate the point. Dwyer's large volume (over 700 pages) is one text cited and used in many business communication courses in Australian universities. In the 1993 (third) edition, she illustrated the use of effective feedback as follows: 'Open feedback is given for the right reasons to the right person at the right time in the right way. To recognise accomplishments reinforces behaviour which will lead to satisfactory performance, for example: "Alison, your immediate contact and follow-up by telephone of the complaint from Mayes Pty Ltd on late deliveries has led to an increase of 5% in next month's order from Mayes. Well done"' (p. 555).

Even a cursory reading of management and personnel practices handbook publications shows that communication is viewed as singularly important to supervision and management, and that within that communication topic, the concepts of feedback and reinforcement have been seen to be central. The skills have been advocated as useful procedures for enhancing supervisory or management responsibilities (McCarthy and Stone, 1986).

The systematic application of reinforcement techniques has been directly advocated as a means to manipulate management practices (Luthans and Kreetner, 1975). For example, McCarthy and Stone stated that 'in an organisational context, positive reinforcement can be used in behaviour modification to increase the frequency of desired responses among subordinates' (p. 260). In the early 1970s there were many reports of such aspects as increased productivity (Beecroft, 1976), improved work attendance, harmonious relationships between workers (Crane, 1979) and substantial cost cutting (*Psychology Today*, 1972). In more recent applications the two areas of training and leadership have shown a resurgence of the ideas and application of behaviour modification and operant thinking in the 1990s.

Some critics may have thought that the whole notion had either 'died out' as a fad of the 1970s or had been found wanting as an explanatory theory-into-practice set of notions. However, the emergence in the 1990s of the competency-based training and education movement in the UK, USA, New Zealand, Canada and Australia, in particular, has seen some rejuvenation of many of the arguments and issues, even if dressed in different clothes and even if defined and discussed as 'no longer the narrow, task-based concept that it once may have been interpreted in some countries a decade or two ago' (Harris *et al.*, 1995, p. 5). Nevertheless, it has been argued forcefully that the new wave competency-based approach to education and training reform has built definitions and approaches to the area which has 'extended' the original behaviourist ideas of the 1970s and added such aspects as knowledge and values to the idea. It is not the intention of this discussion to divert on to a tangential aspect of the debate and those who wish to examine the argument as to whether the current business, education and training developments in the competency-based approach are a resurrection of old behaviourist psychology ideas or a new interpretation may wish to follow up by reading Burke (1989), Latham (1989), Cairns (1992), or Harris *et al.* (1995).

The area of leadership, particularly in relation to business management and development, could be said to be one of the largest growth areas in the 1990s. Most bookshops, be they at airports or in central business districts, have a large section devoted to books on successful management and leadership strategies and case studies by international gurus of how they did it (e.g. Peters, 1987; Covey, 1990)!

It is fascinating how many of the approaches actually rely on and include aspects of reinforcement as one of the key variables. This appears so even if the basic philosophy of the approach, on the surface, is described as more humanistic and people-centred (Senge, 1992), which has often been argued as incompatible with the more behaviourist notions (Rogers, 1980). The application of behaviourist notions to leadership in the business education field has a long and strong history. In the mid-1970s the view was extremely overt that a manager or business leader was a manager of reinforcement contingencies (Sims and Szilagyi, 1975; Sims, 1977). While there were developments of other theoretical orientations derived from more humanistic schools of learning theory and motivation (Maslow, 1970; Rogers, 1980) as opposed to the Skinnerian operant tradition, the behaviourist ideas have still continued to be applied and developed by various advocates and experts. It is almost as if some of the basic notions of reinforcement (for example) have become so ingrained and generally accepted that they pervade, or are included as almost assumed truths in, many approaches.

In the 1980s there was a resurfacing, to some extent, of the overt attribution of leadership thinking, models and training, to the operant roots. Hunt (1984, p. 22), for instance, in a module on 'Leadership and Management Behavior', described what he called 'Leadership as Reinforcement' as one model of the process.

> The reciprocal exchange notion is also part of the *reinforcement* view of leadership. This view has its roots in Skinnerian learning theory. It is concerned with the effect that rewards and punishments can have in reinforcing particular behaviors .... The reinforcement view of leadership, though recent, has received a lot of attention. The most general finding is that contingent reward behavior is associated with higher levels of subordinate (follower) performance and dissatisfaction.

In a general overview of leadership in organisations, Bryman (1986) suggested that '(g)iven the prevailing focus within leadership research upon the leader and a group of subordinates, it is not surprising that the rewards that the former offers to the latter should attract attention' (p. 108). The interest and involvement of research and advocacy of the idea of the significance of reinforcement as a leadership skill, to enhance business, communication, supervision and staff development, then, has a quite strong and pervasive history of influence.

More recent approaches are emerging which, while arguing very strongly for organisations to embrace the notion of companies as 'learning organisations' with sensible approaches based on theory-into-practice rooted in the psychology of learners and learning theory, could not be said to be based upon nor really supportive of the operant model (Pearn *et al.*, 1995).

Another emerging trend of the 1990s in the business world has been a preoccupation with the idea of 'quality'. As one of the modern-day 'gurus' of the business reform movement, Charles Handy, has put it, '(q)uality, for instance, has become the new watchword of many organisations' (Handy, 1991, p. 114). The most significant model in the quality movement has been that termed the 'Total Quality Movement' (TQM) which is associated with the writing, research and advocacy of the late W. Edwards Deming (Deming, 1986; Mann, 1989). Deming is often credited with the initiation of the 'Japanese industrial miracle' (Geller, 1992) and then the American adoption of the TQM approach.

The significance of this aspect for the present discussion is that a number of experts in the operant psychology field have argued and presented analyses of how the behaviour modification and reinforcement-based traditions can be integrated with the TQM ideas (Mawhinney, 1992; Redmon, 1992). The argument presented by Mawhinney was that organisational behaviour management (the Skinnerian approach) could be related to the Deming TQM ideas in ways such as 'TQM should be much improved when effective and reliable contingencies of reinforcement support them' (p. 534). It remains to be seen to what extent this 'marriage' might succeed over time.

It is clear that the concepts discussed above have impacted strongly in the business, management and leadership areas. In addition to the quality movement and what has also been called the continuous improvement 'craze' (Harrington, 1991), there has been an argument that the key (at least in the USA) to greater international competitiveness (a goal that all modern countries seem to be hell bent on pursuing) is to improve the business processes of organisations. Harrington called this business process improvement (BPI) and in his presentation, in which he was critical of some of the previous TQM and other approaches, he still highlighted the importance of feedback and rewards. Harrington presented a different emphasis, one of improving the actual business process (all service processes that support production) rather than some of the traditional approaches to organisational improvement. However, in his summation, Harrington argued very forcefully for an inbuilt reward system as 'rewards and recognition are an essential part of the improvement process. They reinforce desired behavior and visually demonstrate management appreciation for a job well done' (p. 250).

Much has been made in this section of the application and significance of the ideas and procedures of reinforcement and operant thinking in the business and management world. There is little doubt that this application has been deliberate, overt and systematic. There is also no doubt that there are critics and those who object, question or challenge the whole basis and the notions involved. This aspect will be briefly examined in the conclusion to follow.

CONCLUSION

This chapter has examined the core communication skill of reinforcement and has detailed a number of applications of that notion across a wide range of applied fields from SST, through education and on to business and management.

While the reinforcement-based theoretical model of the way humans might communicate, learn and behave has led to an enormous body of research data and writing, there have been many critics who have voiced strong, and at times controversial, attacks on the Skinnerian behaviourist interpretation of communication and learning. Among the most vocal and prominent critics have been the influential writers and theorists, Noam Chomsky and Carl Rogers.

Chomsky, a linguistics scholar and regular commentator on other affairs, was particularly critical of the Skinnerian analysis of the way language develops, as well as being philosophically opposed to the behaviourist approach to the explanation of how humans develop and learn (Chomsky, 1959). Rogers, whose approaches to counselling and psychotherapy led to a sub-field of psychology known as Rogerian humanistic psychology, claimed that his 'struggle with behaviorist psychology' had been one of the major concerns and driving forces of his professional life (1980, p. 55). While Rogers acknowledged that Skinner's work was a 'creative achievement' of significance, he nevertheless could not accept the theory at its philosophical level and regarded the whole idea as repugnant and a manipulation of people.

There have been two areas of criticism of the operant reinforcement tradition which still raise considerable concern in the literature. First, there has been the argument that a reliance on the use and application of external (extrinsic) reinforcers may be detrimental to the internal or (intrinsic) motivation of individuals to complete tasks (Lepper *et al.*, 1973; Schwartz, 1990). Some of the discussion in this area, while raising the whole notion of external reinforcement and its efficacy, also centres on the possible differentiation between reinforcement and reward (Cameron and Pierce, 1994). The distinction in this argument is that by definition (as set out at the beginning of this chapter), the notion of reinforcement describes how a reinforcer is an event that increases the frequency of the behaviour that it is contingent upon, whereas a reward could be said to be a stimulus that is *assumed* to be positive but may not be in all cases. This is a rather fine distinction, but it forms a good deal of the basis for some of the discussions. Cameron and Pierce, in their extensive review of the research, concluded that verbal praise and feedback actually enhanced people's intrinsic motivation. However, they also found that other rewards and reinforcement left intrinsic motivation 'largely unaffected' (p. 398).

It is interesting that within the business area there has been a good deal of fairly recent debate about the incentive, reward and reinforcing aspects of pay, and other incentive schemes in achieving productivity and effective management. Kohn, writing in the *Harvard Business Review* in 1993, argued that incentives actually inhibited intrinsic motivation and were a form of 'bribe' that would not work. He offered a set of six reasons as to why he felt that rewards were not the management answer:

1 'Pay is not a motivator'. Taking his cue from this quote of Deming's, Kohn argues that increasing salaries does not lead to increased work;
2 Rewards punish. Here Kohn argued that rewards, because they are manipulative, have punitive effect. Not receiving an expected reward, said Kohn, is tantamount to punishment as well;
3 Rewards rupture relationships. Kohn suggested here that 'the surest way to destroy cooperation and, therefore, organisational excellence, is to force people to compete for rewards or recognition or to rank them against each other '(p. 58);
4 Rewards ignore reasons. Using rewards as the solution to managers' problems leads them to not bother with investigations of the actual causes;
5 Rewards discourage risk-taking;
6 Rewards undermine interest.

While Cameron and Pierce (1994) argued that their review showed quite clearly that Kohn's case was not supported by the majority of research studies, there is little doubt that there are many in society who would warm to Kohn's arguments.

Finally, the second aspect of some considerable reaction has been that relating to the way the movements within the education field (schooling reform, training reform, competency-based training and education, outcomes-based education) have all been underpinned by a behaviourist psychological view of the world of learning. While this basic assumption may be a long stretch of the bow, there is, nevertheless, a set of arguments which suggests that the philosophy and actual practices of much of the curriculum and teaching can be seen as an embodiment of behaviourist thinking. The argument follows the line that much of the direct instruction approach, which is an operant model in practice, relies on a simple and singular view of the learner and the learning/teaching process which utilises many teacher-scripted (or 'teacher-proof') packages or sets of teaching strategies and materials (Becker *et al.*, 1981; Hunter, 1982). These packages 'deskill' teachers and prevent real, authentic teaching and decision-making as a vital part of the professional process (Apple and Jungck, 1990; Romanish, 1991). This view, while frequently couched in evocative and emotional argumentation, needs to be read, reflected upon and accommodated. It should not be dismissed as yet another 'fringe whinge', which can be readily rejected.

OVERVIEW

This chapter began with a clarification of the reinforcement concept and then spent some time and space exploring the many different applications of the notion, the research in its support and the centrality of its place as a core communication skill. The perspective offered includes both an overview of the advocacy of the place of reinforcement in communication skills and a review of the many applications with some criticism reported to form the basis for a critical reflection on the analysis presented.

REFERENCES

Alberto, P. A. and Troutman, A. C. (1995) *Applied Behavior Analysis for Teachers*, Bobbs Merrill, Columbus, Ohio.
Allen, D. W. and Ryan, K. (1969) *Microteaching*, Addison-Wesley, Reading, MA.
Apple, M. W. and Jungck, S. (1990) '"You Don't Have to Be a Teacher to Teach This Unit:" Teaching, Technology, and Gender in the Classroom,' *American Educational Research Journal*, 27(2), 227–51.
Archer, D. and Akert, R. M. (1977) 'Words and Everything Else: Verbal and Nonverbal Cues in Social Interpretation', *Journal of Personality and Social Psychology*, 35(6), 443–49.
Arends, R. L. (1991) *Learning to Teach* (2nd edn), McGraw-Hill, New York.
Argyle, M (1967) *The Psychology of Interpersonal Behaviour*, Penguin, Harmondsworth.
—— (1969) *Social Interaction*, Methuen, London.
—— (1975) *Bodily Communication*, Methuen, London.
—— (ed.) (1981) *Social Skills and Work*, Methuen, London.
—— and Cook, M. (1967) *Gaze and Mutual Gaze in Social Interaction*, Cambridge University Press. London.
—— and Kendon, A. (1967) 'The Experimental Analysis of Social Performance', in L. Berkowitz (ed.), *Advances in Experimental Social Psychology, Vol. 3*, Academic Press, New York.
Bandura, A. (1977) *Social Learning Theory*, Prentice-Hall, Englewood Cliffs, NJ.
Becker, W. C., Engelmann, S., Carnine, D. W. and Rhine, W. R. (1981) 'Direct Instruction Model', in W. R. Rhine (ed.), *Making Schools More Effective: New Directions from Follow Through*, Academic Press, New York.
Beecroft, J. L. (1976) 'How Behavior Modification Improves Productivity at 3-M', *Training*, October, 65–83.
Berlo, D. K. (1960) *The Process of Communication*, Holt, Rinehart & Winston, New York.
Birdwhistell, R. L. (1970) *Kinesics and Context*, Ballantine Books, New York.
Birnbrauer, J. S., Bijou, S. W. and Wolf, M. (1965) 'Programmed Instruction in the Classroom', in L. P. Ullmann and L. Krasner (eds), *Case Studies in Behavior Modification*. Holt, Rinehart & Winston, New York.
Broden, M., Cruce, C., Mitchell, M. A., Carter, V. and Hall. R. V. (1970) 'Effects of Teacher Attention on Attending Behavior of Two Boys at Adjacent Desks', *Journal of Applied Behavior Analysis*, 3, 205–11.

Brooks, W. D. (1981) *Speech Communication*, W. C. Brown, Dubuque.

Brophy, J. E. (1981) 'Teacher Praise: A Functional Analysis', *Review of Educational Research*, 51(1), 5–32.

—— (1983) 'Classroom Organization and Management', *The Elementary School Journal*, 83(4), 265–85.

Brown, A. L. (1994) 'The Advancement of Learning', *Educational Researcher*, 23(8), 4–12.

Brown, G. (1978) *Microteaching: A Programme of Teaching Skills*, Methuen, London.

—— and Shaw, M. (1986) 'Social Skills Training in Education', in C. R. Hollin and P. Trower (eds), *Handbook of Social Skills Training: Vol 1. Applications Across the Life-Span*, Pergamon, Oxford.

Bryman, A. (1986) *Leadership and Organizations*, Routledge & Kegan Paul, London.

Burke, J. W. (1989) *Competency Based Education and Training*, The Falmer Press, London.

Cairns, L. G. (1973) 'The Skill of Reinforcement', in C. Turney, L. G. Cairns, G. Williams *et al.*, *Sydney Micro Skills. Series 1 Handbook*, Sydney University Press, Sydney.

—— (1986) 'Reinforcement', in O. Hargie, *A Handbook of Communication Skills*, Croom Helm, London.

—— (1992) 'Competency-based Education: Nostradamus's Nostrum', *The Journal of Teaching Practice*, 12(1), 1–32.

Cameron, J. and Pierce, W. D. (1994) 'Reinforcement, Reward and Intrinsic Motivation: A Meta-analysis', *Review of Educational Research*, 64 (3), 363–423.

Chomsky, N. (1959) 'A Review of B. F. Skinner's *Verbal Behavior*', *Language*, 35(1), 26–58.

Cook, M. (1977) 'The Social Skill Model of Interpersonal Attraction', in S. Duck (ed.), *Theory and Practice in Intrerpersonal Attraction*, Academic Press, London.

Cormier, W. H. and Wahler, R. G. (1971) 'The Application of Social Reinforcement in Six Junior High School Classrooms', ERIC ED 051 109.

Covey, S. R. (1990) *Principle-Centred Leadership*, Simon & Schuster, New York.

Crane, D. P. (1979) *Personnel: The Management of Human Resources*, Wadsworth, Belmont, CA.

Curran, J. P. and Monti, P. M. (eds) (1982) *Social Skills Training: A Practical Handbook for Assessment and Treatment*, Guilford, New York.

Deming, W. E. (1986) *Out of the Crisis*, Centre for Advanced Engineering Study MIT, Cambridge, MA.

Donahoe, C. P. Jr. and Driesenga, S. A. (1988) 'A Review of Social Skills Training with Chronic Mental Patients', in M. Hersen, R. M. Eisler and P. M. Miller (eds), *Progress in Behavior Modification, Vol. 23*, Sage, Newbury Park.

Drash, P. W. and Tudor, R. M. (1990) 'Language and Cognitive Development: A Systematic Behavioral Program And Technology For Increasing The Language And Cognitive Skills Of Developmentally Disabled And At-Risk Preschool Children', in M. Hersen, R. M. Eisler and P. M. Miller (eds), *Progress in Behavior Modification, Vol 26*, Sage, Newbury Park.

Dunkin, M. J. and Biddle, B. J. (1974) *The Study of Teaching*, Holt, Rinehart & Winston, New York.

Dwyer, J. (1993) *The Business Communication Handbook* (3rd edn), Prentice-Hall, Sydney.

Finch, A. J., Nelson, W. M. and Ott, E. S. (eds) (1993) *Cognitive-behavioral Procedures with Children and Adolescents: A Practical Guide*, Allyn & Bacon, Boston.

Geller, E. S. (1992) 'Editorial: Where's the Performance in Organizational Behavior Management?', *Journal of Applied Behavior Analysis*, 25(3), 519–23.

George, C. S. and Cole, K. (1992) *Supervision in Action: The Art of Managing* (3rd edn), Prentice-Hall, Sydney.

Handy, C. (1991) *The Age of Unreason*, Arrow Books, London.

Hargie, O. and McCartan, P. (1986) *Social Skills Training and Psychiatric Nursing*, Croom Helm, London.

Hargie, O. and Saunders, C. (1983) 'Training Professional Skills', in P. Dowrick and S. Biggs (eds), *Using Video*, John Wiley, London.

Hargie, O., Saunders, C. and Dickson, D. (1994) *Social Skills in Interpersonal Communications* (3rd edn), Routledge, London.

Harrington, H. J. (1991) *Business Process Improvement*, McGraw-Hill, New York.

Harris, R., Guthrie, H., Hobart, B. and Lundberg, D. (1995) *Competency-based Education and Training: Between a Rock and a Whirlpool*, Macmillan Education, South Melbourne.

Heckel, R. B., Wiggins, S. L. and Salzberg, H. C. (1962) 'Conditioning Against Silences in Group Therapy', *Journal of Clinical Psychology*, 18, 216–31.

Hollin, C. R. and Trower, P. (eds) (1986a) *Handbook of Social Skills Training: Vol. 1. Applications Across the Lifespan*, Pergamon, Oxford.

—— (1986b) *Handbook of Social Skills Training: Vol. 2 Clinical Applications and New Directions*, Pergamon, Oxford.

—— (1988) 'Development and Applications of Social Skills Training: A Review and Critique', in M. Hersen, R. M. Eisler and P. M. Miller, *Progress in Behavior Modification, Vol. 22*, Sage, Newbury Park.

Hunt, J. G. (1984) *Leadership and Managerial Behavior* (Modules in Management), Science Research Associates, Chicago.

Hunter, M. (1982) *Mastery Teaching*, TIP Publications, El Segundo, CA.

Jackson, D. A. and Wallace, R. F. (1974) 'The Modification and Generalization of Voice Loudness in a 15-year-old Retarded Girl', *Journal of Applied Behavior Analysis*, 7, 461–71.

Jones, E. E. and Gerard, H. B. (1967) *Foundations of Social Psychology*, John Wiley, New York.

Kazdin, A. E. (1989) *Behavior Modification in Applied Settings* (4th edn), Brooks/Cole, Pacific Grove, CA.

Kelly, J. A. (1982) *Social-Skills Training*, Springer, New York.

Kennedy, W. A. and Willcutt, H. S. (1964) 'Praise and Blame as Incentives', *Psychological Bulletin*, 62, 323–32.

Kleitsch, E. C., Whitman, T. L. and Santos, J. (1983) 'Increasing Verbal Interaction Among Elderly Socially Isolated Mentally Retarded Adults: A Group Language Training Procedure', *Journal of Applied Behavior Analysis*, 16(2), 217–33.

Kohn, A. (1993) 'Why Incentive Plans Cannot Work', *Harvard Business Review*, 71(5), 54–63.

L' Abate, L. and Milan, M. A. (eds) (1985) *Handbook of Social Skills Training and Research*, John Wiley, New York.

Latham, G. P. (1989) 'Behavioral Approaches to the Training and Learning Process', in Irwin L. Goldstein and Associates (eds), *Training and Development in Organizations*, Jossey-Bass, San Francisco.

Lepper, M. R., and Greene, D. (1978) *The Hidden Costs of Reward: New Perspectives on the Psychology of Human Motivation*, Erlbaum, Hillsdale, NJ.

Lepper, M. R., Greene, D. and Nisbett, R. E. (1973) 'Undermining Children's Intrinsic Interest with Extrinsic Reward: A Test of the "Overjustification" Hypothesis', *Journal of Personality and Social Psychology*, 28, 129–37.

Lieberman, D. A. (1990) *Learning: Behavior and Cognition*, Wadsworth, Belmont, CA.

Luthans, F. and Kreetner, R. (1975) *Organizational Behavior Modification*, Scott, Foresman, Glenview, Illinois.

McCarthy, T. E. and Stone, R. J. (1986) *Personnel Management in Australia*, John Wiley, Brisbane.

McIntyre, D. J., McLeod, G. R. and Griffiths, R. (1977) *Investigations with Microteaching*, Croom Helm, London.

MacMillan, D. L. (1973) *Behavior Modification in Education*, The Macmillan Company, New York.

Mann, N. R. (1989) *The Keys to Excellence: The Story of the Deming Philosophy*, Prestwick Books, Los Angeles.

Martin, G. and Pear, J. (1978) *Behavior Modification: What it is and How to Do It*, Prentice-Hall, Englewood Cliffs, NJ.

Maslow, A. H. (1970) *Motivation and Personality* (2nd edn), Harper & Row, New York.

Mawhinney, T. C. (1992) 'Total Quality Management and Organizational Behavior Management: An Integration for Continual Improvement', *Journal of Applied Behavior Analysis*, 25(3), 525–43.

Mehrabian, A. (1972) *Nonverbal Communication*, Aldine-Atherton, Chicago.

Minkin, N., Braukmann, C. J., Minkin, B. L., Timbers, G. D., Timbers, B. J., Fixsen, D. L., Phillips, E. L. and Wolf, M. M. (1976) 'The Social Validation and Training of Conversational Skills', *Journal of Applied Behavior Analysis*, 9, 127–39.

O'Leary, K. D. and O'Leary, S. G. (1972) *Classroom Management*, Pergamon, New York.

—— (1977) *Classroom Management* (2nd edn), Pergamon, New York.

Pearn, M., Roderick, C. and Mulrooney, C. (1995) *Learning Organizations in Practice*, McGraw-Hill, London.

Peters, T. (1987) *Thriving on Chaos*, Pan Books, London.

Psychology Today (1972) 'New Tool: Reinforcement for Good Work', *Psychology Today*, 5(11), 68–9.

Ramp, E. and Rhine, W. R. (1981) 'Behavior Analysis Model', in W. R. Rhine (ed.), *Making Schools More Effective: New Directions from Follow Through*, Academic Press, New York.

Redmon, W. K. (1992) 'Opportunities for Applied Behavior Analysis in the Total Quality Movement', *Journal of Applied Behavior Analysis*, 25(3), 545–50.

Reynolds, M. J., and Risley, T. R. (1968) 'The Role of Social and Material Reinforcers in Increasing Talking of a Disadvantaged Pre-School Child', *Journal of Applied Behavior Analysis*, 1, 253–62.

Rhine, W. R., Elardo, R. and Spencer, L. M. (1981) 'Improving Educational Environments: The Follow Through Approach', in W. R. Rhine (ed.), *Making Schools More Effective: New Directions from Follow Through*, Academic Press, New York.

Rogers, C. R. (1980) *A Way of Being*, Houghton Mifflin, Boston.

Rogers, E. M. and Agarwala-Rogers, R. (1976) *Communication in Organizations*, Free Press, New York.

Romanish, B. (1991) *Empowering Teachers: Restructuring Schools for the 21st Century*, University Press of America, Lanham, Maryland.

Rosenfeld, G. W. (1972), 'Some Effects of Reinforcement on Achievement and Behavior in a Regular Classroom', *Journal of Educational Psychology*, 63(3), 189–93.

Scheflen, A. E. and Scheflen, A. (1972) *Body Language and Social Order: Communication as Behavioral Control*, Prentice-Hall, Englewood Cliffs, NJ.

Schwartz, B. (1990) 'The Creation and Destruction of Value', *American Psychologist*, 45, 7–15.

Senge, P. M. (1992) *The Fifth Discipline*, Random House, Sydney.

Sims, H. P. (1977) 'The Leader as a Manager of Reinforcement Contingencies', in J. G. Hunt and L. L. Larson (eds), *Leadership: The Cutting Edge*, Southern Illinois University Press, Carbondale, Illinois.

—— and Szilagyi, A. D. (1975) 'Time Lags in Leader Reward Research', *Journal of Applied Psychology*, 64, 66–71.

Skinner, B. F. (1974) *About Behaviorism*, Vintage Books, New York.

Stolz, W. S. and Tannenbaum, P. H. (1963) 'Effects of Feedback on Oral Encoding Behavior', *Language and Speech*, 6, 218–28.

Sulzer, B. and Mayer, G. R. (1972) *Behavior Modification Procedures for School Personnel*, The Dryden Press, Hinsdale, Illinois.

Taylor, A., Rosegrant, T., Meyer, A. and Samples, B. T. (1986) *Communicating* (4th edn), Prentice-Hall, Englewood Cliffs, NJ.

Trower, P. (ed.), (1984) *Radical Approaches to Social Skills Training*, Croom Helm, London.

——, Bryant, B. and Argyle, M. (1978) *Social Skills and Mental Health*, Methuen, London.

Turney, C., Clift, J. C., Dunkin, M. J. and Traill, R. D. (1973) *Microteaching: Research, Theory and Practice*, Sydney University Press, Sydney.

Turney, C., Eltis, K. J., Hatton *et al.* (1983) *Sydney Micro Skills Redeveloped: Series 1 Handbook*, Sydney University Press, Sydney.

Verplanck, W. S. (1955) 'The Control of the Content of Conversations: Reinforcement of Statements of Opinions', *Journal of Abnormal Social Psychology*, 61, 668..

6 Reflecting

David A. Dickson

INTRODUCTION

Interpersonal communication has a fascinating dual status for those who study it. At the everyday level of leading ordinary lives as social beings, it is familiar, even mundane. As the subject of scientific study, it is often frustratingly complex and impenetrable. One of the commonly agreed features is that interpersonal communication is a transactional process that is multidimensional in nature – messages exchanged are seldom unitary or discrete (Wilmot, 1987; Burgoon, 1994). Attention was drawn by Watzlawick *et al.* (1967) to two separate but, nevertheless, interrelated levels at which this process operates. One has to do with substantive content, the other with relational matters which help determine how participants define their association in terms of, for instance, extent of affiliation, balance of power, and degree of intimacy and trust.

Content is probably the more immediately recognisable dimension of interpersonal communication, dealing as it does with the subject matter of talk – the topics of conversation. Through relational communication, interactors work at establishing where they stand with each other *vis-à-vis*, for instance, intimacy and liking. Dominance and control are also important aspects of relational communication that have to be dealt with and some sort of implicit or explicit working agreement reached. While the issue of who should control the conversation may be a topic for discussion, such matters are more often handled in indirect and subtle ways. It is in the manner in which interactors talk about what they talk about that relational work is carried on. Dominance and control may be manifested in a plethora of verbal, non-verbal and paralinguistic actions such as initiating topic changes, interrupting, maintaining eye contact, speaking loudly, etc., while the conversation is transacted.

Reflecting, as a technique associated with skilled interpersonal communication, can be located in such a conceptual frame. It is with both functional and structural aspects of this activity that the present chapter is concerned. The various functions of reflecting are outlined in a subsequent section and contrasting theoretical perspectives brought to bear upon it. A review of research into reflecting is also presented and conclusions drawn as to the interpersonal effects of this procedure. Let us continue, however, by giving some thought to styles of communication and the issue of 'directness'.

INTERACTIONAL STYLE AND DIRECTNESS

An important consideration in the exercise of control is that of interpersonal style, a construct which has been discussed extensively by Norton (1983) and DeVito (1993), among others. Style can be thought of as *how* what is done is done, with the characteristic manner in which someone handles an interactive episode. Interestingly, there is some evidence that students attribute distinct communicator styles to different occupational roles (Jablin and Krone, 1994). Communication stereotypes may exist, but not all who share an occupational role, of course, conduct themselves in exactly the same interpersonal manner. A broad stylistic feature of interaction would seem to be that of directness, and approaches which differ in this respect have been commented upon across a range of professional contexts including medicine (Street, 1992), teaching (Brown and Atkins, 1988), social work (Baldock and Prior, 1981), counselling and psychotherapy (Patterson, 1986), as well as interviewing (Stewart and Cash, 1991).

Directness involves the degree of explicit influence exercised by, for example, an interviewer and, correspondingly, the extent to which the interviewee is constrained in responding. At one extreme of this dimension, the interviewer following a direct style will uncompromisingly determine the form, content and pace of the transaction. At the other end of the continuum, the interviewer who favours an indirect approach will act essentially in response to the contributions of the interviewee, with the subjective concerns of the latter having the major influence on events during the encounter. As such, the interviewer will conversationally stay much more in the background, guiding and facilitating disclosure.

The types of specific utterance commonly associated with interviewing styles differing in this respect have been discussed by Benjamin (1987). Interviewers who follow a direct approach typically employ 'leads', while those whose style is less direct make greater use of 'responses'. Although both terms are difficult to define unambiguously, responding has to do with reacting to the thoughts and feelings of interviewees, with exploring their worlds and keeping them at the centre of things. On the other hand, the interviewer who leads tends to replace the interviewee on centre stage and become the dominant feature in the interaction. Benjamin (1987, p. 206) expressed it as follows:

> When I respond, I speak in terms of what the interviewee has expressed. I react to the ideas and feelings he has communicated to me with something of my own. When I lead, I take over. I express ideas and feelings to which I expect the interviewee to react. . . . When leading, I make use of my own life space; when responding, I tend more to utilise the life space of the interviewee. Interviewer responses keep the interviewee at the centre of things; leads make the interviewer central.

Reflections are a type of response in this sense. They involve the interviewer mirroring back to the interviewee what the interviewee has just said, as understood by the interviewer. Reflections can be contrasted with questions in this respect, which are a method of leading.

ISSUES OF DEFINITION

Reflecting, as a topic for deliberation and area of inquiry, is bedevilled by conceptual confusion, terminological inconsistency and definitional imprecision. An attempt is made here to disentangle the central themes. At a broad level, reflecting is operationally concerned in some way with presenting back to the other all or part of the message which has just been received. Commenting from a more profoundly functional point of view, Rogers (1951), who is commonly credited with coining the term, regarded it as a method of communicating an understanding of the interviewee's concerns and point of view, and of 'being with' that person. Attempts to introduce greater precision and, in particular, to specify how these effects can be achieved by the interviewer have, however, led to some of the difficulties mentioned above. (Causes of these incongruencies, traceable to the evolving theorisations of Rogers and colleagues are discussed in the following section, p. 165f.) These can be illustrated by considering the following definitions of the term: 'This [reflecting] is the act of merely repeating a word, pair of words or sentence exactly as it was said' (French, 1994, p. 188); and 'The distinguishing feature of [reflective skills] is the identification of clients' core messages and offering them back to them in your own words' (Culley, 1991, p. 4). According to the first definition, reflecting comprises mere repetition of the exact words used by the client in the preceding exchange. The second definition is at variance on two important accounts concerning both form and content of the expression, with reflection viewed as a rephrasing (rather than a simple repetition) of the core (rather than the total) message received.

Some have regarded reflecting as a unitary phenomenon (Benjamin, 1987), while others have conceived of it as a rubric subsuming a varying number of related processes (Brammer, 1993; Cournoyer, 1991). Among the latter, only limited consistency is evident in the discriminatory level achieved and the nomenclature employed. While the most common distinction would appear to be between reflection of feeling and paraphrasing (Ivey and Authier, 1978; Hargie *et al.*, 1994), reference can also be found to reflection of content (Nelson-Jones, 1988); reflecting experience (Brammer, 1993), content responses and affect responses (Danish and Hauer, 1973), restatement (Auerswald, 1974), and reflecting meaning (Ivey, 1988). In some cases, ostensibly different labels have essentially the same behavioural referent (for instance, paraphrasing, reflection of content and content responses), while in others the same label is used to denote processes which differ in important respects. In order fully to appreciate the issues involved and locate the sources of these confusions and inconsistencies, it is necessary to extend our discussion of communication and what it entails.

A common distinction is that between verbal and non-verbal communication. Laver and Hutcheson (1972) further differentiated between vocal and non-vocal aspects of the process. The latter relates to those methods of giving information which do not depend upon the vocal apparatus and includes, for example, facial expressions, posture, gestures and other body movements. Vocal communication incorporates all of the components of speech; not only the actual words used (verbal communication) but features of their delivery (the vocal element of non-verbal communication). These features encompass, for example, speech rate, volume, pitch and voice quality, and have been collectively referred to as extralinguistic or paralinguistic communication (Knapp and Hall, 1992). In the face-to-face situation, therefore, people make themselves known by three potential methods: first, and most obviously, by words used; second, via the paralinguistic accompaniment of language; and third, by means of various other bodily movements and states. (In the interests of clarity and convenience, 'non-verbal communication' will be restricted to the latter.)

Another common distinction with respect to content rather than mode of communication is that between the cognitive and the affective (Hargie *et al.*, 1994). The former has to do with the domain of the logical and rational, with facts and ideas which are mostly predicated on external reality (although they can be subjective) and lack emotional infusion. On the other hand, affect relates to emotional concerns, to feeling states and expressions of mood. In actual practice, of course, both types of communication coalesce. In addition, both can be carried verbally, non-verbally and paralinguistically, although it is generally more common for cognitive information to be conveyed verbally, emotional expression non-verbally and paralinguistically (Argyle, 1994). In addition to being *inferred* from such sources, emotional information can also be *implied* from what is said (e.g. 'I had waited all my life for that opportunity but when it finally came, I missed it!') as well as being *explicitly stated* in a declarative statement (e.g. 'I was bitterly disappointed!').

It may be useful to recap briefly at this point. The proposal is that communications may contain cognitive/factual material, affective/feeling information, or, indeed, as is more commonly the case, elements of both. Such content can be conveyed verbally (both explicitly and implicitly), paralinguistically, or non-verbally.

The cognitive-affective dimension would appear to be highly salient to this issue of reflecting, and is one factor at the centre of much of the inconsistency and confusion. A second concerns the extent of homomorphic correspondence between the reflection and the original message. This is, does the interviewer merely repeat verbatim what the interviewee has said, or reformulate it in the former's own words while retaining semantic integrity? (This dimension has more to do with the verbal than paralinguistic or non-verbal modes of delivery. It is possible, however, for the interviewer, when repeating, to echo, more or less accurately, the original paralinguistic accompaniment. Similarly, the interviewer can mirror a non-verbal gesture. While such paralinguistic and non-verbal features have been regarded as being an essential part of empathic communication, this has not usually been in the context of a simple verbal repetition and so will not be discussed further at this point.) Since the question of repetition-reformulation has been alluded to and since this issue is less convoluted than that of cognition-affect, it will be dealt with first.

Returning to the term 'reflecting', it is recalled that one example of a definition which suggests that reflections are essentially repetitions has already been provided (i.e. French, 1994). In a similar vein, Nicholson and Bayne (1984, p. 36) wrote that, when using this technique, 'The interviewer repeats a word or phrase which the client has used'. They contrasted reflections with paraphrases in this respect. For others, as will be shown shortly, the cognitive-affective dimension is of greater relevance in conceptualising paraphrases. Simple repetitions have alternatively been referred to as verbatim playbacks (Gilmore, 1973), reflections of content (Porter, 1950), but perhaps more frequently as restatements (Culley, 1991). In its most extreme form, according to Benjamin (1987), the restatement is an exact duplication of the original statement including the pronoun used, although more frequently this is changed and, indeed, the restatement may repeat in a more selective fashion.

Those who talk about restatements set them apart from reflections on the basis not only of form but also function. It is generally felt that restatements are of limited utility and have more to do with indicating attempts at rudimentary hearing than with understanding. Indeed, depending upon circumstances, they may convey incredulity, disapproval or sarcasm. Brammer *et al.* (1989, p. 110) commented that 'perhaps the most glaring reflection error of the novice counsellor is to express the reflection in words already used by the client'. Therefore, restraint has been recommended in their use.

Reflections are more commonly located at the reformulation end of the repetition–reformulation continuum and have been described as 'statements, in the interviewer's own words, which encapsulate and re-present the essence of the interviewee's previous message'

(Hargie *et al.*, 1994, p. 122). Comparable definitions in this respect have been provided by, among others, Nelson-Jones (1990) and Cormier and Cormier (1991).

Switching attention to matters of content, it has most commonly been regarded that reflections contain the essential core of the interviewee's previous communication. Thus, they may include both cognitive and affective material. It will be recalled that some who have conceived of reflections in this general way have typically made further distinctions between reflective statements which are restricted to feeling issues and those which are concerned with what is frequently called 'content' (e.g. Cormier and Cormier, 1991; Brammer, 1993), although it is generally accepted that the difference is more one of relative emphasis than mutual exclusion.

Reflective statements targeting the affective dimension of communication are known largely as reflections of feeling, those that focus upon factual content paraphrases. Reflecting feeling has been defined by Hargie *et al.* (1994, p. 133) as 'the process of feeding-back to the interviewee, in the interviewer's own words, the essence of the interviewee's previous statement, the emphasis being upon feelings expressed rather than cognitive content' (p. 104). Paraphrasing is defined similarly, although in this case the emphasis is placed 'upon factual material (e.g. thoughts, ideas, descriptions, etc.) rather than upon affect' (p. 129). In spite of this criterion, definitions of paraphrasing can be found which include both affect and cognition. According to French (1994), for example, paraphrasing 'involves the activity of putting the client's statement, thoughts or feelings into one's own words' (p. 189). Similar definitions have been offered by Gilmore (1973), among others.

In some of these cases, as previously mentioned, the repetition-reformulation dimension, rather than the cognitive-affective, would appear to be the major consideration, with para-phrases being contrasted with simple echoic repetitions. In other cases it would seem that a somewhat different and more subtle distinction is being exploited, although one which emerges only vaguely due to frequent lack of detail and clarity in the definitions provided. It would appear to involve primarily neither cognitive-affective content of interviewee message nor the extent of repetition-reformulation by the interviewer, but rather the mode of expression of the information divulged by the interviewee. In terms of the three modes of expression discussed earlier (verbal, paralinguistic and non-verbal), paraphrasing, according to those who have favoured this view, could be said to focus essentially upon the verbal statement and, since feelings can be related in this manner, encompass both cognition and affect.

It would seem, in this case, that it is very much the literal meaning of 'paraphrase' which is being operationalised. Thus, researchers such as Haase and DiMattia (1976) employed paraphrases to promote affective self-referenced statements among subjects. Paraphrases regarded in this manner are presumably contrasted with reflections as defined by Benjamin (1987, p. 215), for example, in the following way: 'Reflection consists of bringing to the surface and expressing in words those feelings and attitudes that lie behind the inter-viewee's words', or by Northouse and Northouse (1992, p. 175): 'the focus in reflection is on *how* something has been expressed, or the feeling dimension.' While paraphrases are restricted to what is actually said, reflections concentrate upon less obvious information frequently revealed in more subtle ways.

This confusion can, in large part, be traced back to the word 'content' which features in many definitions of paraphrasing and sets it apart from reflection of feeling. Ivey and Authier (1978), for instance, proposed that paraphrasing 'could be considered an attempt to feed back to the client the content of what he has just said, but in a restated form' (p. 83). However, 'content' has been used in slightly different ways, which have largely gone unnoticed, to refer to somewhat different aspects of the other's message, namely mode of communication (that is, verbal) and type of information conveyed in this manner (that is, cognitive). Note that the term is not used in a more global manner to describe *all* of the information communicated. The issue stated as unambiguously as possible would seem to be this: is 'content' taken to mean the verbal facet or, on the other hand, the non-affective component of the message? It is, of course, possible for the verbal to be affective. Since the word 'content' is commonly used in the literature as the antonym of 'feeling', one would suspect the latter.

Following this line of argument, paraphrases defined as involving content would emphasise the non-affective or factual (see the above definition by Hargie *et al.*, 1994), while reflections of feeling would deal with the feelings expressed both verbally and non-verbally. This is the stance taken by such as Cormier and Cormier (1991): 'The portion of the message that expressed information or describes a situation or event is referred to as the *content*, or the cognitive part, of the message. . . . Another portion of the message may reveal how the client feels about the content; expression of feeling or an emotional tone is referred to as the *affective* part of the message' (p. 92). The fact that 'content' concerns factual components and that reflections of feeling can draw upon affect, verbally stated, is underlined: 'Generally, the affect part of the verbal message is distinguished by the client's use of an affective or feeling word, such as *happy*, *angry* or *sad*. However, clients may also express their feelings in less obvious ways, particularly through various non-verbal behaviours' (p. 92).

Similar sentiments were manifested earlier by Barnabei *et al.* (1974), who defined a reflection of feeling as 'a restatement of what the client was saying in the counsellor's own words . . . used to reflect the feeling(s) the client was expressing, whether or not the feeling was directly expressed or only implied' (p. 356). By contrast, others would appear to equate 'content' solely with the verbal mode of communication. It is therefore permissible when paraphrasing to include both aspects of fact and feeling, as has already been mentioned. Unfortunately, the position is even less straightforward. Some seemingly straddle this particular divide. Ivey and Authier (1978), for example, wrote that 'responding to the feeling being expressed rather than attending solely to the content and decision issues is what is important in [reflection of feeling]. What the client is saying is the content portion of the message. One must also listen to how the client gives a message. It is this feeling portion of the communication to which you are to pay attention' (p. 539). Here, 'content' obviously refers to the verbal message, while the paralinguistic and non-verbal components are emphasised in relation to the communication of feeling states. Reflections of feeling utilise the latter, while paraphrases tap content. Thus, it could be assumed (and in accordance with the views of those already mentioned, e.g. Haase and DiMattia, 1976) that mode of expression was the defining characteristic and that paraphrases could mirror back facts and feelings *verbally* expressed. But in fact, Ivey and Authier (1978) stressed that paraphrases address the non-affective and, by so doing, invoke the cognitive-affective dimension as being of prime importance.

In concluding this section, it may be useful to re-present the three dimensions which seem to be conceptually central to the structural aspects of reflecting. Much of the inconsistency and ambiguity which exists in the literature stems from a lack of appreciation of or confusion among them. First, the cognitive-affective issue is concerned with the content of communication and the extent to which the reflective statement focuses upon facts, feelings or, indeed, both. The repetition–reformulation continuum addresses the extent to which the reflection recasts the original interviewee expression. The mode of communication of this message is the basis of the third dimension. (In actual practice this dimension is not entirely independent of the second, that is, opportunities for repetition decrease in conjunction with decreases in explicit verbal presentation.) Was the material transmitted verbally or by other and often less conspicuous means? Allied to this is the implication that information gleaned from paralinguistic and non-verbal features is typically less obvious and explicit than that which is verbally stated. (This, of course, is not invariably so.) The importance of the latter dimension should not be overlooked, however, especially in situations where the interviewee is striving to come to grips with a personal difficulty. Under these circumstances, a reflection which encapsulates an aspect of the problem of which the interviewee was but vaguely aware can be extremely beneficial (Egan, 1990).

The difficulty in producing a consensual definition of reflecting should be obvious from the foregoing discussion. Nevertheless, the following claims, although tentatively made, would appear warrantable. Reflections are statements which re-present the essence of the interviewee's previous message. They can incorporate cognitive and affective components and are expressed in the interviewer's own words. Reflections which concentrate more single-mindedly upon affective issues, whether or not these were *explicitly* shared by the interviewee in the original communication, have more frequently been labelled reflections of feeling. On the other hand, those which address the non-affective content of the utterance have been called, for the most part, reflections of content or paraphrases.

THEORETICAL PERSPECTIVES ON REFLECTING

At the theoretical level, the process of reflecting can be interpreted from at least three fundamentally different positions. These are humanistic psychology, behaviouristic psychology and pragmatics (a branch of linguistics). In keeping with the former it is, in part, the communication of those attitudes and conditions which promote psychological growth and maturity. To the behaviourist it is a means of influencing and modifying behaviour, verbal behaviour in particular. Finally, from the point of view of pragmatics, reflecting can be thought of as part of the elaborate business of managing talk in the course of interaction.

The humanistic approach

Carl Rogers is commonly credited with being one of the central figures of the humanistic movement in psychology and, in the helping context, the founder of person-centred counselling. A detailed consideration of his theoretical position lies far beyond the scope of this chapter. (For fuller details see Rogers, 1951, 1961, 1980; Thorne, 1992.) At a rudimentary level, however, an outline of his theory of human functioning can be provided, based upon several interrelated key concepts. These include the *organism*, *actualising tendency*, *phenomenological field*, *self*, *positive regard* and *incongruence*.

The *organism*, psychologically speaking, is at the centre of all experience and is a totally organised system comprising physical, cognitive, affective and behavioural facets of the individual. It is energised by a single and immensely powerful motivating force, the *actualising tendency*. This is a positive influence towards growth and development. Rogers (1951) wrote that 'The organism has one basic tendency and striving – to actualize, maintain, and enhance the experiencing organism' (p. 487).

Were this natural and constructive force permitted to operate unimpaired, the outcome would be a person in the ongoing process of becoming *self-actualised*. Such individuals show an openness to experience, self-trust, the adoption of an internal locus of evaluation and a willingness to continue the self-actualising process (Irving, 1995). They are not dependent on others as a source of evaluation but are confidently self-reliant in this respect. Few, unfortunately, live self-actualising lives. The personally experienced world of the individual is called the *phenomenological field* and consists of everything which is, at least potentially, available to awareness. Part of this totality relates to the self; the child develops a particular *self-concept*. This can be thought of as a view of self together with an evaluation of it. Significant others, such as parents, have a key role to play in this process due to the individual's need for *positive regard*. This need to gain the love, respect and esteem of others important to the person is deeply felt.

Such positive regard, however, is generally not provided unconditionally. Instead, certain conditions of worth are attached – the child knows that behaviour of a certain type must be displayed in order to win the approval of mother. Therefore, it becomes imperative for the child not only to behave in keeping with the actualising tendency but to ensure that conditions of worth are not violated. Such dual standards invariably lead to conflicts and attempted compromises. The outcome is incongruence; the self-concept becomes divorced from the actual experiences of the organism. Incongruence is associated with feelings of threat and anxiety and, consequently the falsification or, indeed, denial of experiences and the distortion of the self-concept. This is the antithesis of becoming self-actualised.

It will be realised from Rogers' theory of personality that the source of such problems is, to a great extent, the conditional nature of positive regard. This imposes a value system upon the individual which is at variance with that of the actualising tendency. In order to prevent this, conditions of worth should be removed from positive regard. The individual already subjected to incongruence can be encouraged to further growth and psychological maturity in this way within the context of a particular relationship with another. This other should manifest *congruence* and provide *unconditional positive regard*. Since no attempt to impose values or to be judgemental is made, threat is reduced, thus enabling the individual to explore feelings previously denied or distorted, and to assimilate them into the self-concept. Reflecting is one method of responding which, since it is centred within the interviewee's frame of reference, satisfies these requirements.

Reflecting is, however, more commonly associated with another characteristic of the effective relationship – accurate *empathic understanding*. In his earlier writings Rogers (1951) proposed that the empathic counsellor assumes, 'in so far as he is able, the internal frame of reference of the client, to perceive the world as the client sees it, to perceive the client himself as he is seen by himself, to lay aside all perceptions from the external frame of reference while doing so and to communicate something of this empathic understanding to the client' (p. 29). It was considered that accurate reflecting was the most effective means of communicating this understanding to the client although, as will be outlined, subsequent views on this issue changed somewhat.

Developments which have taken place in person-centred thinking have been charted by Gelso and Carter (1985). Three distinct phases in the ongoing evolutionary process labelled, chronologically, *non-directive*, *reflective* and *experiential* were identified, each characterised by a particular outlook on counsellor function and style. The non-directive counsellor strove to create a permissive, non-judgemental climate by unintrusively displaying acceptance. Clarification of client contributions in order gradually to promote increased insights was also provided. With the advent of the reflective era, greater stress was placed upon effecting a more integrated self-concept and putting the client more completely in touch with his or her phenomenological world. As far as technique is concerned, reflecting was employed extensively during both of these phases, but particularly in the latter. However, it would seem that subtle differences in use are detectable, which go some way to shedding light on the reasons for the various nuances of definition disentangled in the previous section. Thus, a gradual switch in emphasis took place from reflecting, largely at a fairly superficial level, the factual content of the client's verbalised message (and frequently doing so by simply repeating what was said) to dealing with the affective dimension through mirroring back, in fresh words, feelings expressed. Reflection of feeling became the most widely used technique.

Subsequently, Rogers (1975) utilised the concept of experiencing to account for what takes place during counselling and to provide an updated statement on the nature of empathy. Empathy became conceived of as a process of 'being sensitive, moment to moment, to the changing felt meanings which flow in this other person, to the fear, or rage ... or whatever, that he/she is experiencing' (p. 4). It requires a moving closer to clients by gaining a greater awareness of their presently experienced inner world of perceptions, thoughts and feelings and the personal meanings attached to these. It is this process and the corresponding attitude of the counsellor which are important, rather than the particular technique used. In marked contrast to earlier thinking, the supremacy of reflecting feeling as a means of interaction with the client is removed. Indeed, in rejecting the confusion of earlier definitions of empathy with the wooden application of technique, Rogers (1987, p. 39) wrote, 'I even wince at the term reflection of feeling'.

Reflecting is still a legitimate activity, nevertheless; but its effectiveness is dependent upon relating directly to clients' current experiencing and encouraging them to focus more intensely on and become more fully aware of it. It should also assist in the process of converting implicit (or unverbalised) meaning into a communicable form without misrepresentation. The effect is to promote the individual's experiential process and consequently produce change towards greater congruence. Since such responses must be directed at the felt meanings experienced by the client, there is no longer the stipulation that reflections must deal with only affective issues. Content in this sense becomes less important. The reflective statement may be cognitive, affective or perhaps more usefully both. Brammer (1993) introduced the variant 'reflecting experience' to describe this technique. A further development is a greater move away from the explicitly stated and obvious in the client's utterance to inchoate and vaguely expressed concerns. Egan (1990) proposed that at more advanced levels of empathic understanding the reflection should move beyond the familiar to point tentatively towards experiences only faintly hinted at and less clearly grasped by the client. Although possibilities of inaccuracy are increased, such reflections have the potential to move the client forward in personal experiencing and attain a greater level of realisation. Here again can be identified a further source of the conceptual confusion discussed previously.

A model of empathy as a multi-dimensional construct with cognitive, affective and behavioural aspects has been developed more recently by Irving (1995). As a piece of interpersonal behaviour, reflecting is only one of a number of possible ways of making clients aware of the fact that they are being empathically understood. It is one method, however, which is consistently mentioned when this behavioural dimension of the construct is discussed (Authier, 1986; Cormier and Cormier, 1991). Furthermore, analyses of Rogers in videotaped counselling sessions have confirmed that, in fact, he made extensive use of reflective skills (O'Farrell *et al.*, 1986).

Changes in person-centred thinking have taken place as the theory has evolved. As we have seen, much of the definitional confusion to do with the term 'reflecting' derives from this fact. Nevertheless, from the point of view of this branch of humanistic psychology, reflecting can be thought of as facilitative communication through the manifestation of unconditional positive regard and empathic understanding, leading the way to possibilities of personal growth and maturity through self-actualisation.

The behaviourist approach

Reflecting has also been interpreted and investigated in keeping with behaviourist principles. This theoretical outlook is in marked contrast to the basic assumptions promulgated by Rogers and his fellow humanists. Beginning with Watson (1913), behaviourists have traditionally regarded psychological inquiry as an extension of the natural sciences. While variants exist [see accounts of *methodological* and *radical* behaviourism by, for example, Baum (1994)], according to Day (1980) modern behaviourism has, at its core, four basic tenets. The first is a commitment to behaviour as an intrinsically worthy domain of scientific study. The second is a refutation of mentalism. In attempting to explain why people do the things they do, one should look not to the mentalistic world of inner thoughts, intentions and feelings, but to the objective world of physical reality; to their environment. Third, behaviourists eschew notions of free will, in favour of determinism, as a satisfactory basis for the scientific study of human action. Finally, there is an adherence to biological evolutionism. Stemming from Darwinian thinking on the continuity of species, human beings are not thought of as a species set apart from the rest of the animal world.

Behaviourists, therefore, have historically restricted psychology inquiry to behaviour, environmental happenings associated with it and the relationship between these two types of phenomena. Furthermore, events in the individual's environment are seen as belonging to the real world of objective reality rather than to some private phenomenological representation of it: they are of paramount importance in shaping what individuals do and what they become. The goal of psychology, it was held, is to describe, explain, predict and control behaviour by identifying the regularities which exist between it and features of the environment in which it is manifested.

The early theorists, including Pavlov and Watson, placed emphasis upon identifiable environmental stimuli serving to *elicit* particular responses from the organism according to predictable patterns. While some of these stimulus–response connections may be basic reflexes, others are learned. In either case, the individual was regarded as being essentially passive, with responses being triggered by stimuli in the form of environmental events.

Thorndike (1911) drew attention to the fact that the influence of the environment was not restricted to those features that precede and elicit action. The environmental consequences for the organism of those actions that are carried out have a considerable bearing upon what is done subsequently. These ideas, embodied in the Law of Effect, were extended more fully by Skinner (1938) in his work on operant conditioning. Skinner stressed the *operant* rather than the *respondent* nature of behaviour. Instead of merely responding to happenings, the organism was seen as spontaneously emitting behaviour which operated on the environment to effect consequences which, in some cases, led to an increased likelihood of similar behaviour being performed in the future under comparable sets of circumstances. Such consequences were termed *positive reinforcers* or *positive reinforcing stimuli*, and *operant conditioning* referred to the process whereby they acted to increase the frequency of occurrence of designated behaviour by being made contingent upon it. Reflecting has been conceived of and researched in terms of operant conditioning procedures (Dickson *et al.*, 1993).

Positive reinforcing stimuli can take a variety of different forms (see Chapter 5). *Primary reinforcers* include such things as food, drink, sex, etc., the reinforcing potential of which does not rely upon a process of prior learning. *Secondary* or *conditioned reinforcers*, on the other hand, come to be valued through prior association with primary reinforcers, money being an obvious example in contemporary society. Skinner (1953) also noted a group of conditioned reinforcers which are typically paired with several other reinforcing stimuli in a broad range of circumstances. These were labelled *generalised reinforcers*. The giving of one's attention to another is an example: 'The attention of people is reinforcing because it is a necessary condition for other reinforcements from them. In general, only people who are attending to us reinforce our behaviour. The attention of someone who is particularly likely to supply reinforcement – a parent, a teacher, or a loved one – is an especially good generalized reinforcer' (Skinner, 1953, p. 78).

The implication is that various verbal and non-verbal behaviours associated with attention-giving will have the ability to shape how others act in interpersonal situations, through making it more likely that certain ways of behaving will be favoured. Collectively, these reinforcers have been called *social* and have been isolated by, for instance, Sherman (1990) as one of several categories of conditioning event. Such rewards, according to Buss (1983), can be thought of in either *process* or *content* terms. The former are an inherent part of interpersonal contact and include, in order of increasing potency, the mere presence of others, attention from them and their conversational responsivity. An interesting observation, though, is that too much or too little of these activities can be aversive; it is only at some notional level of intermediacy that they become reinforcing. Correspondingly, Epling and Pierce (1988) commented that the attention given by a teacher to a pupil may well change from being reinforcing to being punishing as a function of the frequency of delivery.

Switching to the second element of Buss' bifurcation, the content of interaction can also have reinforcing ramifications. Here, Buss mentions acts such as showing deference, praising, extending sympathy and expressing affection. Unlike their process counterparts, these are held to operate along unipolar dimensions. In other words, there is a direct linear correlation between amount and reinforcing effect.

For some, reflecting acts as a social reinforcer due to the fact that it connotes attention, interest and acceptance, thereby acting selectively to increase verbal output of the type reflected. Powell (1968), for example, carried out an experiment which examined the effects of reinforcing subjects' self-referenced statements (statements about themselves) by means of reflections. The results showed that when, in an interview-type situation, the interviewer responded using this technique, the frequency of such statements increased significantly. In effect, subjects talked more about themselves! Other research, which is reviewed more fully in a later section of this chapter, has produced comparable findings (see p. 174f).

Some researchers, while remaining within an operant conditioning framework, see reflections working in a slightly different way. When a certain action only succeeds in eliciting reinforcement in the presence of particular accompanying stimuli, then that piece of behaviour is said to be under *stimulus control* and those stimuli have become *discriminative stimuli* in respect of it (Lieberman, 1990). Reflections may, therefore, function more as discriminative than reinforcing stimuli. Discriminative stimuli are part of the environmental context within which the organism responds. They signal that reinforcing stimuli are available and, as such, are present at the time of responding rather than afterwards (and differ from reinforcing stimuli in this respect). They cue the occasion for reinforcement but are not themselves reinforcing. By reflecting feeling, for example, the interviewer may actually be signalling to the interviewee that subsequent reinforcement is available for further affective responses (Merbaum, 1963; Kennedy *et al.*, 1971).

In the ongoing sequential stream of verbal interchange, the task of locating sources of influence is, however, fraught with difficulty. The listener's utterance can be thought of both as a response to the speaker's previous comment and as a stimulus for the next. While no attempt will be made to establish categorically the *modus operandi* of reflective statements in terms of either discriminative or reinforcing stimuli, there is some evidence tentatively favouring the latter explanation. In the study by Powell (1968) already cited, a difference in the reinforcing potential of interviewer utterances, including reflections, was found despite the fact that these were ostensibly equally intrusive and therefore, it could be argued, equally effective as discriminative stimuli. Similarly, Hoffnung (1969) found that rephrasing rather than merely restating interviewer responses led to a marked increase in affective self-reporting, despite the fact that both interjections would appear to be of equal discriminative value.

Pursuing a different line of argument, it could be reasoned that the non-contingent application of reflections (i.e. no systematic application of the technique following some targeted behaviour) would have a more detrimental effect on the modification of verbal behaviour if such interventions served as reinforcing rather than discriminative stimuli. Although the available evidence is meagre, partly due to lack of specificity by researchers in outlining experimental procedures, there would seem to be a trend confirming this proposition. It is of interest that in one of the few pieces of research which failed to report a conditioning capability, interviewer reflective statements were administered on a non-contingent or random basis (Barnabei *et al.*, 1974).

To summarise, reflecting is a method of influencing verbal behaviour by affecting the frequency of occurrence of particular types of response. This can be accounted for in terms of the behaviourist principles of operant conditioning. While the evidence is far from definitive, it would seem that such statements act as reinforcing stimuli and, by implication, are valued positively by interviewees.

The linguistic approach

A reflection, whatever else it may be, is a component of language and as such is subject to the sphere of influence of linguistics, particularly the branch called pragmatics.

Pragmatics has been defined by Mey (1993, p. 5) as 'the science of language . . . as it is used by real, live people, for their own purposes and within their limitations and affordances'. People normally succeed in understanding each other in ordinary conversation and manage their intercourse in a well-ordered fashion. But this can never be taken for granted. It occurs because participants, while conversing, are constantly working at making it happen that way. They anticipate possible confusions and misunderstandings and take steps to avoid them. When problems occur they are identified and repair strategies implemented. Stokes and Hewitt (1976) referred to these management procedures that keep conversation running smoothly as *aligning actions* and as specific examples, Nofsinger (1991) discussed *continuers* and *formulations*. From this background, reflections can be regarded as forming part of the complex and often subtle operation of organising and orchestrating conversation.

The process of formulating talk can be thought of as providing comment upon what has been said or what is taking place in the interaction. Garfinkel and Sacks (1970, p. 350) outlined it as follows: 'A member may treat some part of the conversation as an occasion to describe that conversation, to explain it, or characterize it, or explicate, or translate, or summarize, or furnish the gist of it, or take note of its accordance with rules, or remark on its departure from rules. That is to say, a member may use some part of the conversation as an occasion to formulate the conversation.'

Formulations, as discussed by McLaughlin (1984), serve to promote, transform, delete or indeed terminate talk. They may relate to something the person providing the formulation has contributed (A-issues or events), something the other participant has mentioned (B-issues or events) or, less frequently, both (AB-issues or events).

A further distinction is that between formulations of *gist* and *upshot* (Heritage and Watson, 1979). The former involves extracting and highlighting the central events and issues featured in the immediately preceding conversation. Formulations of upshot go beyond this frequently to draw conclusions based upon assumptions which may or may not meet with the agreement of the other partner. It would seem that from this standpoint reflections are essentially B-event or issue formulations of gist. It has been noted that formulations of this type are often tentative proposals and require a decision from the other interactor as to their acceptability. If the other is unwilling to agree to a particular representation of his or her position, one or more modifications are likely to be presented and worked through until agreement is forthcoming. The frequent association between a formulation of this type and confirmation by the other led Heritage and Watson (1979) to characterise them as adjacency pairs. It is of interest that those, such as Ivey (1988) and Cormier and Cormier (1991), who have discussed reflecting solely from the counselling/interviewing frame of reference, have stressed the necessity to be frequently tentative, and to give the interviewee the opportunity to agree or disagree with the reflection; they have also commented upon the tendency of the interviewee to express acceptance if it is, in fact, accurate.

According to the two theoretical interpretations previously considered, reflections promote more intense experiencing or reinforce continued discussion of a particular topic. In line with this effect, Nofsinger (1991) also discussed *continuers* as conversational alignment devices which mark a listener's intention to forgo making a substantive contribution to the conversation at that precise point. Following early work by Duncan and Fiske (1977) and Sacks *et al.* (1978) the mechanisms involved in conversational turn-taking have been extensively researched. *Back-channel* communication refers to listener contributions that sustain the listener role. They seem to signal that the listener is attentive, interested, even comprehending, and does not seek the floor at that point. The essential function of reflecting witnessed by the interviewing/counselling literature is presented precisely in these terms. It could be argued that reflections have an additional alignment role as continuers, promoting the continuity of the conversational status quo in respect of topic and speaker/listener arrangement.

One of the functions of formulations, though, would seem to be to engineer a change of topic or even the termination of conversation. It has been reported that conversational lapses are often immediately preceded by an utterance of this sort (McLaughlin and Cody, 1982). Likewise, from their detailed analysis of doctor–patient communication, Stiles and Putnam (1992) discovered that reflective statements by doctors often seemed conversationally to cut patients off, rather than encourage deeper exploration.

How can these seemingly contradictory findings be reconciled? One possible explanation has to do with the broader communicative context within which the reflective statement is delivered. The prosodic accompaniment of the verbal content of the reflection, for instance, may be crucially important. Variations in pitch can make a statement either interrogative or declarative (Knapp and Hall, 1992). Based upon the linguistic analysis of naturally occurring interactions, Schegloff and Sacks (1973) reported that words spoken with a downward intonation served to terminate topic discussion. Weiner and Goodenough (1977) conceived of reflections as repetition passes (that is, speech acts which serve to forgo the opportunity of making a substantive contribution to the continued exploration of the topic), which can be used in order to bring about a conversational change. However, it was emphasised that in order for reflections to function in this fashion, they had to be delivered with a downward rather than a sustained or rising vocal intonation. The corollary of this, it could be argued, is that when reflections are used to facilitate interviewee exploration, they should be spoken with a sustained or rising intonation pattern. Additional features of contemporaneous non-verbal behaviour may also be influential (see Nelson-Jones, 1990).

Three radically different views of reflecting have been outlined in this section. According to the person-centred humanist, reflections are a means of accepting the other without condition; of empathising with the other and facilitating that person in becoming more fully self-actualising. To the behaviourist, reflections act as social reinforcers to influence the verbal performance of the other by increasing the amount of preordained talk. Lastly, reflections have been depicted as techniques which are used in the organisation and management of conversation not only to maintain or change it, but also under certain circumstances to bring it to an end.

A FUNCTIONAL ANALYSIS OF REFLECTING

Functional aspects of reflecting have already been mentioned in this chapter, and particularly in the last section. Some of these have been elaborated upon to a greater extent than others. The present section, however, will concentrate more single-mindedly and in a pan-perspectives fashion upon the various potential effects attendant upon the proper use of this skill. Many are equally applicable to reflections generally, others are more specific to paraphrases or reflections of feeling. Those which are more specialised are identified as such.

One of the more basic functions of reflecting is to indicate to others that they are being fully attended to conversationally and that active listening is taking place (French, 1994). Unless this were so it would obviously be impossible for the core element of their previous communication to be accurately reproduced as the skill requires. The implication is that they are sufficiently valued and accepted for another to be interested in them, and prepared to become involved with them to this extent. It is, therefore, suggested that this technique forms the basis for the creation of a positive, facilitative relationship typified by openness, trust, respect and empathy. For this reason, Culley (1991, p. 41) described reflective techniques as 'the single most useful group of skills in the counsellor's skill repertoire'.

It is widely accepted that reflections are also frequently used in order to clarify. Mirroring back the core message contained in the interviewee's previous statement enables issues that are vague and confused to be thought through more clearly and objectively (Brammer, 1993). Since problems and concerns, especially of a personal nature, are things which are experienced, for the most part, at a 'gut' level rather than being intellectualised or even verbalised, it often proves difficult to find the words, and indeed thoughts, to express them unambiguously. By encapsulating and unobtrusively presenting the most salient features of what has just been said, the exigencies of clients' predicaments can be made more accessible to them. This is accomplished while maintaining their frame of reference, rather than that of the helper, at the centre of things (Hill, 1989). As put by Benjamin (1987, p. 218), 'When the therapist uses reflection, he responds not to his own inner frame of reference but solely to the feeling tone of the client'. Other clarifying techniques such as questioning tend to place the emphasis upon the interviewer.

In addition to acting as a means of enabling the interviewee to appreciate more clearly experienced concerns, reflecting assists the interviewer in obtaining a clearer realisation of the actualities of the case. As a continuation of this train of thought, the skill has been associated with the promotion of understanding. By reflecting, the interviewer not only conveys a desire to get to know, but, when accurate, also demonstrates to the interviewee the level of understanding accomplished, despite the fact that the original message may have been inchoate and vague. Dillon (1990, p. 186) argued that reflecting 'confirms the speaker in his effort to contribute. It helps him to express thoughts gradually more clearly and fully. It assures him of understanding'. Supported in this way, the latter is often motivated to continue to explore particular themes more deeply concentrating upon facts, feelings or both, depending upon the content of the reflective statement (Hartley, 1993). From the interviewer's point of view, confirmatory responses serve an important feedback function by indicating accurate understanding of the world of the client. In this sense, reflections can prove useful as a form of perception-check.

Commenting more particularly upon reflecting feeling states, Cormier and Cormier (1991) pointed out that, as a result, interviewees are influenced to devote greater attention to phenomena of this type. They can be assisted in becoming more completely aware of their feelings by being encouraged to explore and express them in this way. This can be difficult to accomplish and requires tact but is very worthwhile. Egan (1990) noted that, while some feelings are quite laudable and easily accepted, many others prompt defensive reactions and, consequently, are either consciously or subconsciously repressed and denied. As a result, people become estranged from these affective facets of their being. Through the reflection of feeling such individuals can be put more fully in touch with these realities. By using this technique the interviewer acknowledges the interviewee's right to feel this way and indicates that it is permissible for those feelings to be expressed and discussed. This frequently does not happen in everyday conversations, which typically dwell upon factual matters. Here, affective shifts can cause stress and embarrassment and tend to be actively avoided. This is especially so if the emotions disclosed are negative, currently experienced and about someone in the present company. In outlining the features of comforting communication, Albrecht *et al.* (1994, p. 437) mentioned that 'Messages that acknowledge, elaborate, and grant legitimacy to the feelings of a distressed other are perceived to be more sensitive and effective'.

The importance of assisting others, in a helping context, to 'own' their feelings has been mentioned by Brammer (1993), among others. Having acknowledged the existence of their feelings, interviewees must be brought to realise that ultimately they are the source, and encouraged to take responsibility for these affective states. By constantly using the pronoun 'you' when reflecting feeling, Brammer *et al.* (1989) suggested that this depersonalisation can be gradually overcome and the interviewee brought to appreciate the difference between what is felt, which can be controlled, and those events in the environment which have acted as a catalyst for these feelings but which may be beyond that person's sphere of influence.

Returning to a point already intimated, the helper should always be sensitive to the other's readiness to acknowledge and deal with affective states detected during their inter-action. Failure to do so in the medical interview, through indicating deeper levels of emotion than the patient is yet prepared to acknowledge, can damage the physician–patient relationship, according to Cohen-Cole (1991). A related point, as stressed by Lang and van der Molen (1990), is the importance of reflecting feelings at the level of intensity at which they were expressed, for the helper to be fully in touch with the client.

The frequent benefits to be derived from including affective and factual aspects of the interviewee's message in a single reflective statement have already been stated. Cournoyer (1991, p. 169) proposed the use of a format such as '"You feel —— because ——"; "You feel —— but/yet/however —— "', although this structure should not be permitted to become inflexible and habitual. However, by locating emotions in the context of associated thoughts, behaviours, ideas and happenings, an added dimension of understanding can be provided. Ivey (1988) referred to this process as 'reflecting meaning' and explained how, in this way, deeper meanings underlying expressed experiences can be located and sensitively surfaced.

Finally, the possibility of reflective statements being employed in order to regulate conversation by perhaps serving to engineer the termination of discussion, should not be overlooked. The various propositions outlined in this section differ considerably in terms of their epistemological basis. While many are, for the most part, theoretically derived or experientially grounded, others have emerged from systematic empirical inquiry. The final section of this chapter selectively reviews some of the research which has been conducted into reflecting.

A REVIEW OF RESEARCH ON REFLECTING

The lack of consistency in the operational definition of reflections and related terms has already been discussed at length. The work of categorising individual investigations and trying to abstract broad and consistent relationships between variables is consequently made that much more difficult. It may be useful to highlight the general definitions of *reflecting, reflections of feeling* and *paraphrasing* proposed earlier, since the present review is structured on this basis. Thus, reflections are considered as statements, in the interviewer's own words, which mirror back the essence of the interviewee's previous communication and may contain both affective and factual content. Utterances of this type, which concentrate upon affective issues, are called reflections of feeling; paraphrases, on the other hand, deal largely with the non-affective element of what is said. The reader is alerted to marked deviations from this convention. Further disparities in the research conducted relate to the theoretical basis of the inquiry, research design and procedures, number and type of subjects and dependent variables chosen for investigation.

Reflections

A number of empirical studies has compared the outcomes of an indirect, reflective style with a range of alternatives including an intrusive style (Ellison and Firestone, 1974), an evaluative style (Silver, 1970) and with both interrogative and predictive approaches (Turkat and Alpher, 1984). Most of this research has an interviewing or counselling orientation. In some cases, attitudes of both interviewees and external judges to interviewers manifesting contrasting styles have been sought. Silver (1970), for example, found that low-status interviewees felt much more comfortable with interviewers who displayed a reflective rather than a judgemental approach. Ellison and Firestone (1974) reported that subjects observing a reflective rather than an intrusive interviewer, who controlled the direction and pace of the interview in a particularly assertive manner, indicated a greater willingness to reveal highly intimate details. This interviewer was also perceived as passive, easy-going and non-assertive.

An interrogative approach in which further information was requested, and a predictive style which required the interviewer accurately to predict interviewees' reactions in situations yet to be discussed, were the alternatives to reflecting examined by Turkat and Alpher (1984). Although impressions were based upon written transcripts rather than actual interviews, those interviewers who used reflections were regarded as understanding their clients. Empathic understanding together with positive regard (two of the core conditions for effective counselling according to the client-centred school of thought) were related to the reflective style of interviewing in a study by Zimmer and Anderson (1968) which drew upon the opinions of external judges who viewed a videotaped counselling session. From the painstaking analysis of therapy sessions undertaken by Clare Hill and her colleagues (Hill *et al.*, 1988; Hill, 1989), not only was reflecting discovered to be one of the most common of the identified techniques utilised by therapists, but also clients reported that they found it one of the most helpful. They regarded it as providing support and seldom reacted negatively to its use. Such reflections assisted clients in becoming more deeply attuned to their emotional and personal experiences leading to more profound levels of exploration and greater insights into their circumstances and difficulties. One of the most marked outcomes was an association with significantly reduced levels of anxiety. (It should be noted that 'reflecting' in these studies was actually labelled 'paraphrasing'. Since the latter encompassed a range of different types of reflective statement, it will be included here.)

Other researchers, rather than focusing upon attitudes, have investigated the effects of reflecting upon the actual behaviour of the interviewee. Some form of interviewee self-disclosure has commonly been measured. Powell (1968), in a study already introduced, investigated the effects of reflections on subjects' positive and negative self-referent statements. 'Approval-supportive' and 'open disclosure' were the comparative experimental conditions. The former included interviewer statements supporting subjects' self-references while the latter referred to the provision of personal detail by the interviewer. Reflections were found to produce a significant increase in the number of negative, but not positive, self-references. Kennedy *et al.* (1971), while failing to make the distinction between positive and negative instances, similarly reported an increase in interviewee self-statements attributable to the use of this source.

Not all research, however, has attested to the efficacy of the technique of reflecting. According to Hill and Gormally (1977), this procedure was largely ineffective in increasing the use of affective self-referents by experimental subjects. However, not only was a non-contingent procedure of application employed in this study, but the rate of administration was low, thus militating against potential reinforcing influences.

When the effects of reflecting on the amount of subjects' self-disclosure and the quality provided were looked at, intimate detail was associated with this style of interviewing (Vondracek, 1969; Beharry, 1976). A similar result was reported by Mills (1983) in relation to rates, rather than quality, of self-disclosure. Feigenbaum (1977) produced an interesting finding concerning sex differences of subjects. While females disclosed more, and at more intimate levels, in response to reflections, male subjects scored significantly higher on both counts in response to interviewer self-disclosure.

In an investigation of marital therapists working with couples undergoing therapy, Cline *et al.* (1984) discovered that therapist reflectiveness was correlated positively with subsequent changes in positive social interaction for middle-class husbands but with negative changes for both lower-class husbands and wives. It was also positively related to changes in expression of personal feeling for middle-class husbands and wives. When assessed three months after the termination of therapy, a positive relationship emerged between therapist reflections and outcome measures of marital satisfaction, but for lower-class husbands only.

There seems to be little doubt now that there is a strong individual difference factor influencing reactions and outcomes to non-directive, reflective versus directive styles of engagement. In addition to demographic variables such as gender and class differences already mentioned, personality characteristics have also been researched. Some evidence, reviewed by Hill (1992), suggests that locus of control, cognitive complexity and reactance of clients may be important. Locus of control refers to a belief in personally significant events deriving from either internal or external sources, while reactance is a predisposition to perceive and respond to events as restrictions on personal autonomy and freedom. Cognitive complexity relates to the conceptual differentiation and sophistication with which individuals make sense of their circumstances. Hill (1992) came to the conclusion that those high on internality of control and cognitive complexity, but low on reactance were more suited to less directive interventions such as reflecting.

In sum, these findings would suggest that attitudes towards interviewers who use a reflective style are largely positive. At a more behavioural level, this technique would also seem capable of producing increases in both the amount and intimacy of information which interviewees reveal about themselves although it would not appear to be significantly more effective than alternative procedures such as interviewer self-disclosures or probes. In the actual therapeutic context there is some evidence linking reflecting with positive outcome measures for certain clients. However, the mediating effects of individual differences in demographic and personality factors should not be overlooked.

Reflections of feeling

The use of reflection of feeling has, for the most part, been based upon theory and practical experience rather than research findings. Again, studies which have featured this skill can be divided into two major categories: first, experiments, largely laboratory-based, designed to identify effects on subjects' verbal behaviour; second, those which have attempted to relate the use of the technique of interviewers to judgements, by either interviewees or observers, in terms of such attributes as empathy, warmth, respect, etc. In many instances, both types of dependent variable have featured in the same investigation.

A significant relationship between reflection of feeling and ratings of empathic under-standing emerged in a piece of research conducted by Uhlemann *et al.* (1976). These ratings were provided by external judges and were based upon both written responses and audio-recordings of actual interviews. Interviewers who reflected feelings not yet named by the interviewee were regarded by them as being more expert and trustworthy, according to Ehrlich *et al.* (1979). A similar procedure, labelled 'sensing unstated feelings' by Nagata *et al.* (1983), emerged as a significant predictor of counsellor effectiveness when assessed by surrogate clients following a counselling-type interview.

But not all findings have been positive. Highlen and Baccus (1977) failed to reveal any significant differences in clients' perceptions of counselling climate, counsellor comfort, or personal satisfaction between clients allocated to a reflection of feeling and to a probe treatment. Likewise, Gallagher and Hargie (1992) failed to report any significant relation-ships between ratings of counsellors' reflections, on the one hand, and, on the other, separate assessments by counsellors, clients and judges of empathy, genuineness and acceptance displayed towards clients. As acknowledged, the small sample size may have been a factor in the outcome of this investigation.

The effects of reflections of feeling on interviewees' affective self-reference statements have been explored by, for example, Merbaum (1963), Barnabei *et al.* (1974), Highlen and Baccus (1977) and Highlen and Nicholas (1978). With the exception of Barnabei *et al.* (1974), this skill was found to promote substantial increases in affective self-talk by subjects. Highlen and Nicholas (1978), however, combined reflections of feeling with interviewer self-referenced affect statements in such a way that it is impossible to attribute the outcome solely to the influence of the former. One possible explanation for the failure by Barnabei *et al.* (1974) to produce a positive finding could reside in the fact that reflections of feeling were administered in a random or non-contingent manner.

There is evidence, therefore, to suggest that reflecting feeling can contribute to positive interviewee perceptions and attitudes towards the interviewer, and is capable of influencing the extent to which interviewees reveal affective detail about themselves. Whether it is more effective in this respect than alternative procedures still has to be shown.

Paraphrases

Only a limited number of the research studies centred on reflecting in general have explored paraphrasing in particular. For the most part those that have, have been experimental in design, conducted in the laboratory and have sought to establish the effects of paraphrasing upon various measures of interviewees' verbal behaviour.

In some cases, though, paraphrases are defined in such a way as to include affective material (e.g. Hoffnung, 1969), while in others affective content is not explicitly excluded (e.g. Kennedy and Zimmer, 1968; Haase and DiMattia, 1976). These quirks should be kept in mind when interpreting the following findings. Kennedy and Zimmer (1968) reported an increase in subjects' self-referenced statements attributable to paraphrasing, while similar findings featuring self-referenced affective statements were noted by both Hoffnung (1969) and Haase and DiMattia (1976). According to Citkowitz (1975), on the other hand, this skill had only limited effect in this respect although there was a tendency for the association to be more pronounced when initial levels of self-referenced affect statements were relatively high. The subjects in this experiment were chronic schizophrenic inpatients and the data were collected during clinical-type interviews.

The distinction between the affective and the factual has been more explicitly acknowledged by others who have researched paraphrasing. Waskow (1962), for instance, investigated the outcome of selective interviewers responding on the factual and affective aspects of subjects' communication in a psychotherapy-type interview. It emerged that a significantly higher percentage of factual responses was given by those subjects who had their contributions paraphrased. Auerswald (1974) and Hill and Gormally (1977) produced more disappointing findings. In both cases, however, paraphrasing took place on an essentially random basis. Affective responses by subjects were also selected as the dependent variable.

The few studies which have considered the effects of this technique on attitudes towards the interviewer, rather than behavioural changes on the part of the interviewee, have reported largely favourable outcomes. A positive relationship was detailed by Dickson (1981) between the proportion of paraphrases to questions asked by employment advisory personnel and ratings of interviewer competence provided by independent, experienced judges. A comparable outcome emerged when client perceptions of interviewer effectiveness were examined by Nagata *et al.* (1983).

It would therefore seem that when paraphrases are used contingently and focus upon factual aspects of communication, interviewees' verbal performance can be modified accordingly. In addition, paraphrasing seems to promote favourable judgements of the interviewer by both interviewees and external judges. Counselling trainees have also indicated that this is one of the skills which they found most useful in their interviews (Spooner, 1976).

OVERVIEW

This chapter has been concerned at practical, theoretical and empirical levels with reflecting as an interactive technique. Having identified and attempted to disentangle a number of conceptual confusions, three contrasting theoretical perspectives on the process deriving from humanistic psychology, behavioural psychology and linguistics were presented. The various functional claims for the skill, based upon theoretical and experiential, as well as empirical considerations, were discussed. From the research reviewed it would seem that reflections, whether of fact, feeling or both, are perceived positively by both interviewees and external observers. There is also evidence that they can promote interviewee self-disclosure but that a range of psychological and demographic characteristics of the interviewee may mediate their effects.

Further research should concentrate on more naturalistic settings rather than the psychology laboratory. The possible effects of such interviewer and interviewee variables as sex, status, socio-economic class and ethnic background deserve further inquiry, as do situational factors including the nature of the encounter. The impact of the location of the reflection in the sequence of exchanges and the effects which paralinguistic and non-verbal accompaniments may have on the interviewee, merit closer examination.

REFERENCES

Albrecht, T. L., Burleson, B. and Goldsmith, D. (1994) 'Supportive Communication', in M. Knapp and G. Miller (eds), *Handbook of Interpersonal Communication*, Sage, Thousand Oaks.

Argyle, M. (1994) *The Psychology of Interpersonal Behaviour*, Penguin, Harmondsworth.

Auerswald, M. (1974) 'Differential Reinforcing Power of Restatement and Interpretation on Client Production of Affect', *Journal of Counselling Psychology*, 21, 9–14.

Authier, J. (1986) 'Showing Warmth and Empathy', in O. Hargie (ed.) *A Handbook of Communication Skills*, Croom Helm, London.

Baldock, J. and Prior, D. (1981) 'Social Workers Talking to Clients: a Study of Verbal Behaviour', *British Journal of Social Work*, 11, 19–38.

Barnabei, F., Cormier, W. and Nye, L. (1974) 'Determining the Effects of Three Counselling Verbal Responses on Client Verbal Behaviour', *Journal of Counselling Psychology*, 21, 355–9.

Baum, W. (1994) *Understanding Behaviourism: Science, Behaviour, and Culture*, HarperCollins, New York.

Beharry, E. (1976) 'The Effect of Interviewing Style Upon Self-Disclosure in a Dyadic Interaction', *Dissertation Abstracts International*, 36, 4677B.

Benjamin, A. (1987) *The Helping Interview: With Case Illustrations*, Boston, Houghton Mifflin.

Brammer, L. (1993) *The Helping Relationship: Process and Skills*, Prentice-Hall, Englewood Cliffs, NJ.

——, Shostrom, E. and Abrego, P. (1989) *Therapeutic Psychology: Fundamentals of Counselling and Psychotherapy*, Prentice-Hall, Englewood Cliffs, NJ.

Brown, G. and Atkins, M. (1988) *Effective Teaching in Higher Education*, Routledge, London.

Burgoon, J. (1994) 'Nonverbal Signals', in M. Knapp and G. Miller (eds), *Handbook of Interpersonal Communication*, Sage, Thousand Oaks.

Buss, A. (1983) 'Social Rewards and Personality', *Journal of Personality and Social Psychology*, 44, 533–63.

Citkowitz, R. (1975) 'The Effects of Three Interview Techniques – Paraphrasing, Modelling, and Cues – in Facilitating Self-referent Affect Statements in Chronic Schizophrenics', *Dissertation Abstracts International*, 36, 2462B.

Cline, V., Merjia, J., Coles, J. *et al.* (1984) 'The Relationship Between Therapist Behaviours and Outcome for Middle and Lower Class Couples in Marital Therapy', *Journal of Clinical Psychology*, 40, 691–704.

Cohen-Cole, S. (ed.) (1991) *The Medical Interview: The Three Function Approach*, Mosby Year Book, St Louis.

Cormier, W. and Cormier, L. (1991) *Interviewing Strategies for Helpers*, Brooks-Cole, Pacific Grove.

Cournoyer, B. (1991) *The Social Work Skills Workbook*, Wadsworth, Belmont, CA.

Culley, S. (1991) *Integrative Counselling Skills in Action*, Sage, London.

Danish, S. and Hauer, A. (1973) *Helping Skills: A Basic Training Program*, Behavioural Publications, New York.

Day, W. (1980) 'The Historical Antecedents of Modern Behaviourism', in R. Rieber and K. Salzinger (eds), *Psychology: Theoretical-Historical Perspectives*, Academic Press, New York.

DeVito, J. (1993) *Essentials of Human Communication*, HarperCollins, New York.

Dickson, D. (1981) 'Microcounselling: An Evaluative Study of a Programme', unpublished PhD thesis, Ulster Polytechnic, Jordanstown.

——, Saunders, C. and Stringer, M. (1993) *Rewarding People*, Routledge, London.

Dillon, J. (1990) *The Practice of Questioning*, Routledge, London.

Duncan, S. and Fiske, D. (1977) *Face-to-Face Interaction: Research, Methods and Theory*, Lawrence Erlbaum Associates, Hillsdale, NJ.

Egan, G. (1990) *The Skilled Helper*, Brooks-Cole, Pacific Grove, CA.

Ehrlich, R., D'Augelli, A. and Danish, S. (1979) 'Comparative Effectiveness of Six Counsellor Verbal Responses', *Journal of Counselling Psychology*, 26, 390–8.

Ellison, C. and Firestone, I. (1974) 'Development of Interpersonal Trust as a Function of Self-esteem, Target Status, and Target Style', *Journal of Personality and Social Psychology*, 29, 655–63.

Epling, W. and Pierce, W. (1988) 'Applied Behaviour Analysis: New Directions from the Laboratory', in G. Davey and C. Cullen (eds), *Human Operant Conditioning and Behaviour Modification*, John Wiley, Chichester.

Feigenbaum, W. (1977) 'Reciprocity in Self-disclosure within the Psychological Interview', *Psychological Reports*, 40, 15–26.

French, P. (1994) *Social Skills for Nursing Practice*, Chapman & Hall, London.

Gallagher, M. and Hargie, O. (1992) 'The Relationship Between Counsellor Interpersonal Skills and Core Conditions of Client-centred Counselling', *Counselling Psychology Quarterly*, 5, 3–16.

Garfinkel, H. and Sacks, H. (1970) 'On Formal Structures of Practical Actions', in J. McKinney and E. Tirayakian (eds), *Theoretical Sociology*, Appleton-Century-Crofts, New York.

Gelso, C. and Carter, J. (1985) 'The Relationship in Counselling and Psychotherapy: Components, Consequences and Theoretical Antecedents', *The Counselling Psychologist*, 13, 155–243.

Gilmore, S. (1973) *The Counsellor-in-Training*, Prentice-Hall, Englewood Cliffs, NJ.

Haase, R. and DiMattia. D. (1976) 'Spatial Environment and Verbal Conditioning in a Quasi-counselling Interview', *Journal of Counselling Psychology*, 23, 414–21.

Hargie, O., Saunders, C. and Dickson, D. (1994) *Social Skills in Interpersonal Communication*, Routledge, London.

Hartley, P. (1993) *Interpersonal Communication*, Routledge, London.

Heritage, J. and Watson, D. (1979) 'Formulations as Conversational Objectives', in G. Psathas (ed.), *Everyday Language: Studies in Ethnomethodology*, Irvington, New York.

Highlen, P. and Baccus, G. (1977) 'Effects of Reflection of Feeling and Probe on Client Self-referenced Affect', *Journal of Counselling Psychology*, 24, 140–3.

Highlen, P. and Nicholas, R. (1978) 'Effects of Locus of Control, Instructions, and Verbal Conditioning on Self-referenced Affect in a Counselling Interview', *Journal of Counselling Psychology*, 25, 177–83.

Hill, C. (1989) *Therapist Techniques and Client Outcomes*, Sage, Newbury Park.

—— (1992) 'Research on Therapist Techniques in Brief Individual Therapy: Implications for Practitioners', *The Counselling Psychologist*, 20, 689–711.

—— and Gormally, J. (1977) 'Effects of Reflection, Restatement, Probe and Non-verbal Behaviours on Client Affect', *Journal of Counselling Psychology*, 24, 92–7.

——, Helms, J., Tichenor, V. *et al.* (1988) 'Effects of Therapist Response Modes in Brief Psychotherapy', *Journal of Counselling Psychology*, 35, 222–33.

Hoffnung, R. (1969) 'Conditioning and Transfer of Affective Self-references in a Role-played Counselling Interview', *Journal of Consulting and Clinical Psychology*, 33, 527–31.

Irving, P. (1995) 'A Reconceptualisation of Rogerian Core Conditions of Facilitative Communication: Implications for Training', unpublished DPhil thesis, University of Ulster, Ulster.

Ivey, A. (1988) *Intentional Interviewing and Counselling: Facilitating Client Development*, Brooks-Cole, Pacific Grove.

—— and Authier, J. (1978) *Microcounselling, Innovations in Interviewing, Counselling, Psychotherapy, and Psychoeducation*, C. C. Thomas, Springfield.

Jablin, F. and Krone, K. (1994) 'Task/Work Perspectives: A Life-span Perspective', in M. Knapp and G. Miller (eds), *Handbook of Interpersonal Communication*, Sage, Thousand Oaks.

Kennedy, T. and Zimmer, J. (1968) 'Reinforcing Value of Five Stimulus Conditions in a Quasi-counselling Situation', *Journal of Counselling Psychology*, 15, 357–62.

Kennedy, T., Timmons, E. and Noblin, C. (1971) 'Non-verbal Maintenance of Conditioned Verbal Behaviour Following Interpretations, Reflections and Social Reinforcers', *Journal of Personality and Social Psychology*, 20, 112–17.

Knapp, M. and Hall, J. (1992) *Nonverbal Communication in Human Interaction*, Holt, Rinehart & Winston, Orlando.

Lang, G. and Van der Molen, H. (1990) *Personal Conversations: Roles and Skills for Counsellors*, Routledge, London.

Laver, J. and Hutcheson, S. (eds) (1972) *Communication in Face-to-Face Interaction*, Penguin, Harmondsworth.

Lieberman, D. (1990) *Learning: Behaviour and Cognition*, Wadsworth, Belmont.

McLaughlin, M. (1984) *Conversation: How Talk is Organised*, Sage, Beverly Hills.

—— and Cody, M. (1982) 'Awkward Silences: Behavioural Antecedents and Consequences of the Conversational Lapse', *Human Communication Research*, 8, 299–316.

Merbaum, M. (1963) 'The Conditioning of Affective Self-reference by Three Classes of Generalized Reinforcers', *Journal of Personality*, 31, 179–91.

Mey, J. (1993) *Pragmatics: An Introduction*, Basil Blackwell, Oxford.

Mills, M. (1983) 'Adolescents' Self-disclosure in Individual and Group Theme-centred Modelling, Reflecting, and Probing Interviews', *Psychological Reports*, 53, 691–701.

Nagata, D., Nay, W. and Seidman, E. (1983) 'Nonverbal and Verbal Content Behaviours in the Prediction of Interviewer Effectiveness', *Journal of Counselling Psychology*, 30, 85–6.

Nelson-Jones, R. (1988) *Practical Counselling and Helping Skills*, Cassell, London.

—— (1990) *Human Relationship Skills*, Cassell, London.

Nicholson, P. and Bayne, R. (1984) *Applied Psychology for Social Workers*, Macmillan, London.

Nofsinger, R. (1991) *Everyday Conversation*, Newbury Park, Sage.

Northouse, P. and Northouse, L. (1992) *Health Communication: Strategies for Health Professionals*, Appleton & Lange, Norwalk, CN.

Norton, R. (1983) *Communicator Style: Theory, Applications, and Measures*, Sage, Beverly Hills.

O'Farrell, M., Hill, C. and Patton, S. (1986) 'A Comparison of Two Cases of Counselling with the Same Counsellor', *Journal of Counselling and Development*, 6, 32–41.

Patterson, C. (1986) *Theories of Counselling and Psychotherapy*, Harper & Row, New York.

Porter, E. (1950) *An Introduction to Therapeutic Counselling*, Houghton Mifflin, Boston.

Powell, W. (1968) 'Differential Effectiveness of Interviewer Interventions in an Experimental Interview', *Journal of Consulting and Clinical Psychology*, 32, 210–15.

Rogers, C. (1951) *Client-centred Therapy*, Houghton Mifflin, Boston.

—— (1961) *On Becoming a Person: A Therapist 's View of Psychotherapy*, Houghton Mifflin, Boston.

—— (1975) 'Empathic: An Unappreciated Way of Being', *The Counselling Psychologist*, 5, 2–10.

—— (1980) *A Way of Being*, Houghton Mifflin, Boston.

—— (1987) 'Comments on the Issue of Equality in Psychotherapy', *Journal of Humanistic Psychology*, 27, 38–9.

Sacks, H., Schegloff, E. and Jefferson, G. (1978) 'A Simplest Systematics for the Organisation of Turn-taking for Conversation', in J. Schenkien (ed.), *Studies in the Organisation of Conversational Interaction*, Academic Press, New York.

Schegloff, E. and Sacks, H. (1973) 'Opening Up Closings', *Semiotica*, 8, 289–327.

Sherman, W. (1990) *Behaviour Modification*, Harper & Row, New York.

Silver, R. (1970) 'Effects of Subject Status and Interviewer Response Programme on Subject Self-disclosure in Standardised Interviews', Proceedings of the 78th Annual Convention, APA, 5, 539–40.

Skinner, B. F. (1938) *The Behaviour of Organisms*, Appleton-Century Crofts, New York.

—— (1953) *Science and Behaviour*, Collier Macmillan, London.

Spooner, S. (1976) 'An Investigation of the Maintenance of Specific Counselling Skills Over Time', *Dissertation Abstracts International*, February, 5840A.

Stewart, C. and Cash, W. (1991) *Interviewing: Principles and Practices*, W. C. Brown, Dubuque.

Stiles, W. and Putnam, S. (1992) 'Verbal Exchanges in Medical Interviews: Concepts and Measurement', *Social Science and Medicine*, 35, 347–55.

Stokes, R. and Hewitt, J. (1976) 'Aligning Actions', *American Sociological Review*, 41, 838–49.

Street, R. (1992) 'Communicative Styles and Adaptations in Physician–Parent Consultations', *Social Science and Medicine*, 34, 1155–63.

Thorndike, E. (1911) *Animal Intelligence*, Macmillan, New York.

Thorne, B. (1992) *Carl Rogers*, Sage, London.

Turkat, I. and Alpher, V. (1984) 'Prediction versus Reflection in Therapist Demonstrations of Understanding: Three Analogue Experiments', *British Journal of Medical Psychology*, 57, 235–40.

Uhlemann, M., Lea, G. and Stone, G. (1976) 'Effect of Instructions and Modelling on Trainees Low in Interpersonal Communication Skills', *Journal of Counselling Psychology*, 23, 509–13.

Vondracek, F. (1969) 'The Study of Self-disclosure in Experimental Interviews', *The Journal of Psychology*, 72, 55–9.

Waskow, I. (1962) 'Reinforcement in a Therapy-like Situation Through Selective Responding to Feelings or Content', *Journal of Consulting Psychology*, 26, 11–19.

Watson, J. (1913) 'Psychology as the Behaviourist Views It', *Psychological Review*, 20, 158–77.

Watzlawick, P., Beavin, J. and Jackson, D. (1967) *Pragmatics of Human Communication*, W. W. Norton, New York.

Weiner, S. and Goodenough, D. (1977) 'A Move Toward a Psychology of Conversation', in R. Freedle (ed.), *Discourse Production and Comprehension*, Ablex, Norwood, NJ.

Wilmot, W. (1987) *Dyadic Communication*, Random House, New York.

Zimmer, J. and Anderson. S. (1968) 'Dimensions of Positive Regard and Empathy', *Journal of Counselling Psychology*, 15, 417–26.

7 Explaining*

George Brown and Madeleine Atkins

INTRODUCTION

Explaining is a core skill of most professions. It is of obvious importance to teachers and lecturers but it is also of importance to medical practitioners, other health professionals, social workers, lawyers, architects and engineers. Together with questioning, it is the staple diet of everyday conversation: it challenges social realities and it is implicated in changes in people's behaviour.

Despite its ubiquity, it has, until recently, been relatively neglected in research in communication and social psychology. There are perhaps three reasons for the neglect. First, some members of professional groups such as counsellors, therapists, social workers and teachers of adults associate explaining with authoritarianism. In so doing they confuse authoritarianism and authority based on expert knowledge, and they assume that to explain is necessarily to coerce. Second, explaining is a taken-for-granted activity. We all spend a great deal of our time explaining in everyday life and in various professional contexts so we assume we know what an explanation involves, what the social act of explaining is and how to explain. Third, explaining, like so many taken-for-granted activities, is a deep concept. Explaining has interconnections with understanding, with language, with logic, with rhetoric, with critical theory and with culture. To embark upon the study of explaining requires one to reflect upon a wide range of epistemological, linguistic, social psychological and, perhaps, anthropological issues. Given that most researchers are experimentalists, topics in which conceptual issues loom large are likely to be neglected. Add to this the pressure faced by many academics in higher education to produce research publications quickly, and it is not surprising that research in such a messy but deep domain has tended to be neglected.

Fortunately, there are some signs that explaining is becoming recognised as an important topic. The psychology textbook by Banyard and Hayes (1994) contains a substantial section on communication and explanation, while Antakis (1994) has produced a cogent text on theories and methods of analysing everyday explanations and arguments. These texts are in part a manifestation of a shift of paradigm from the traditional laboratory-based approach in social psychology with its emphasis upon scientific method to a range of paradigms that encompass experimentation (Hewstone, 1989), accounts (Cody and McLaughlin, 1988), discourse analysis (Potter and Wetherell, 1994), the use of deconstructionism (Parker and Burman, 1993) and narrative (Gergen, 1988).

* We wish to thank Neville Hatton, Faculty of Education, University of Sydney, for his perceptive comments on the draft manuscript.

Given the importance and ubiquity of explaining, it seems to us useful to provide a wide variety of findings from different professional contexts. It also seems important not to shirk the deeper issues involved in studying explaining. Hence in this chapter we have developed a framework for examining the processes of explaining and their relationships to understanding. However, the philosophical arguments and issues underpinning the framework have had to be cropped brutally. Readers interested in an extended discussion of these issues are referred to Brown and Atkins (1986) and Antakis (1988). The framework itself, we hope, will be useful to anyone who wishes to explore explaining in his or her profession.

We then use the framework to consider the empirical research concerned with explaining in dyadic encounters such as the doctor–patient consultation, and explaining in a group context such as occurs in a lecture or class. However, this is not intended to be a litany of research findings on explaining, but rather a guide to the essential features of explaining in different contexts. The chapter ends with a discussion of the problems, issues and implications for providing and studying explanations.

A DEFINITION OF EXPLAINING

In modern English the term 'explain' has come to mean 'make known in detail' (*Oxford English Dictionary*). However, it is arguable whether providing more detail improves an explanation. Antakis (1988) offered the broad principle that explaining is 'Some stretch of talk hearable as being a resolution of some problematic state of affairs' (p. 4). This broad definition does not cover written explanations and it deliberately leaves open the question of intentions, meanings and interpretations of utterances. Its core is that there is a problem to be explained in terms of causes, reasons, excuses or justifications. The etymological root of explaining is from the Latin *explanare*, 'to make plain'. This root provides an inroad into the different approaches to the study of explaining that are discussed in a subsequent section of this chapter. Our own working definition of explaining (Brown and Atkins, 1986, p. 63) is: 'Explaining is an attempt to provide understanding of a problem to others.'

We developed this definition for pragmatic reasons. After much reading (e.g. Swift, 1961; Bellack *et al.*, 1966; Ennis, 1969; Smith and Meux, 1970; Martin, 1970; Taylor, 1970; Hyman, 1974; Turney *et al.,* 1983) and deliberation we decided upon a definition that would be helpful to professionals engaged in explaining and which would link transactions between explainers and explainees and the connections made in their heads. This definition has stood the test of time. Subsequent work on explaining (e.g. Antakis, 1988, 1994) provides interesting extensions and subtleties but, as yet, it has not demonstrated its usefulness to practitioners. The weight of our definition rests on the nature of understanding and we return to this topic after discussing various types of explaining and the task of explaining.

TYPES OF EXPLAINING

As hinted above, the literature abounds with typologies of explanations. We designed a robust, simple typology which would be relatively easy to use by researchers and practitioners. The typology consists of three main types of explanation: the interpretive, the descriptive and the reason-giving. They approximate to the questions 'What?' 'How?'

and 'Why?', although the precise form of words matter less than the intention of the question.

Interpretive explanations address the question 'What?' They interpret or clarify an issue or specify the central meaning of a term or statement. Examples are answers to the questions: What is a biome? What is enantriopy? What is a novel? What led Lord Jim to become the strange character he was? What uses do talons and curved beaks serve in birds of prey? What can unions do in an industrial dispute? What are the effects of a high inflation rate on currency?

Descriptive explanations address the question 'How?' These explanations describe processes, structure and procedures such as: How does a bicycle pump work? How is a sentence used in logic? How is sulphuric acid made? How do you make a light sponge cake? How can a perpendicular be constructed using only a compass and ruler? As animals, how do cats differ from dogs? How does the internal combustion engine work? How did colonial history lead to the Vietnamese war? How does the chairman lead a meeting?

Reason-giving explanations address the question 'Why?' They involve giving reasons based on principles or generalisations, motives, obligations or values. Included in reason-giving explanations are those based on causes, although some philosophers prefer to distinguish between causes and reasons. Examples of reason-giving explanations are answers to the questions: Why are some people cleverer than others? Why am I reading this book? Why do people pay income tax? Why is Shakespeare a greater writer than Harold Robbins? Why did this fuse blow? Why does the volume of a gas decrease as pressure increases? Why do certain mammals hibernate in winter? Why do heavy smokers have a greater risk of contracting cancer than non-smokers? Why is there more crime in inner city areas? Why do we say, 'he runs', but 'they run'? Why do we put a fork in the left hand?

Of course, a particular explanation may involve all three types of explanation. Thus, in explaining how a bill becomes a law one may want to describe the process, give reasons for it and perhaps define certain key terms.

THE TASKS OF EXPLAINING

The task of explaining is threefold: identifying and defining the problem, determining the process, clarifying and estimating the outcome.

The problem

First, the explainer has to identify and specify the problem that requires explanation. The problem may be posed initially by the explainer or by the explainee. The problem presented by a client (or by the explainer) may require clarification and refinement. It is well known by practitioners that the problem presented by a client is not necessarily *the* problem. One has to diagnose and communicate the problem in a way that is acceptable to the client. Herein lies the difficulty of ownership. If someone does not perceive or 'own' the problem, then the proposed solution may not be accepted and acted upon. Even if the problem is accepted, the solution proffered may not be acceptable. More subtly, the solution may be accepted but not acted upon. This observation is relevant to research using the health beliefs model (Janz and Becker, 1984). In teaching, a similar difficulty may arise. If pupils do not perceive the problem presented as one worthy of solution, then they may reject it and the process of acquiring the solution. Rhetoric, persuasion, principles of pedagogy and power all have a part to play in the acceptance of a problem and its solution.

Finally, the problem might helpfully be expressed in the form of a central question and that question may be then subdivided into a series of implicit questions or hidden variables. Thus, the question, 'How do local anaesthetics work?' contains the implicit questions 'What is a local anaesthetic?' and 'How are nerve impulses transmitted?' The patient question 'How can I reduce the pain in my shoulder?' may be diagnosed by a physiotherapist as supra-spinitis and a possible solution identified.

The process

Once the problem and its possible solution have been identified, the explainer has to present or elicit a series of linked statements, each of which is understood by the explainee and which together lead to a solution of the problem. These linked statements may be labelled 'keys' since they unlock understanding. Each of these keys will contain a key statement. A key statement may be a procedure, a generalisation, a principle, or even an appeal to an ideology or a set of personal values. The key may contain examples, illustrations, metaphors and perhaps qualifications to the main principle. When the problem to be explained is complex there might also be a summary of key statements during the explanation as well as a final summary.

The keys are the nub of explaining. But, as emphasised earlier, for an explanation to be understood, it follows that the explainer has to consider not only the problem to be explained but also the knowledge and characteristics of the explainees. What is appropriate as an explanation of the structure of DNA to postgraduate biochemists is unlikely to be appropriate as an explanation to first-year English literature students. There is no such thing as the 'good explanation'. What is good for one group may not be good for another. Its quality is contingent upon the degree of understanding it generates in the explainees. For different groups of explainees, the keys of the explanation and the explanation itself will be different – although the use of keys and other strategies may not be.

The essence of the problem is that understanding is a function of the existing cognitive structure of the explainee as well as of the new information being provided: hence the importance of similes, analogies and metaphors. These devices may, as understanding grows, be seen as crude, perhaps even as false, explanations. Hooks and balls may be a very crude analogy for explaining atoms and molecules but they may be a useful starting point for explaining molecular structure to young children. 'Rotting garden posts' may be an inadequate metaphor for describing the roots of a patient's teeth but the metaphor might be a useful device for justifying extraction.

The process of explaining is not just concerned with identifying problems and proffering solutions. Sometimes the task of the explainer is to explain the problem and sometimes to explain the connection between the problem and the solution. A problem, such as the relationship between truth and meanings, may not have any solution or it may have several unsatisfactory solutions but at least the problem may be understood. This point is emphasised since much high-level teaching and counselling is concerned not with explaining the solutions of problems but with explaining the nature of problems and exploring their possible solutions.

The outcome

The outcome hoped for when explaining is that the explainee understands. The explainer has to check that the explanation is understood. This task is akin to feedback, as discussed in the interpersonal interaction model presented in Chapter 2, and it is sometimes neglected by doctors, teachers and others. Understanding may be checked by a variety of methods. The most primitive method is to ask 'Do you understand?' The answer one usually gets is 'Yes'. The response is more a measure of superficial compliance than of understanding. Other methods are to invite the explainee to *recall* or *recite* the explanation, to *ask questions* of specific points in the explanation, to *apply* the explanation to another situation or related problem, to provide other *examples* of where the explanation might hold, or to *identify* similar sorts of explanations. All of these may be used to measure the success of an explanation – providing the procedures are appropriate and valid.

A check on understanding much favoured by health professionals is a change in behaviour. As a measure of explanatory power, it is weak. The explanation may be understood but it may not lead to action. The explanation may not be understood or imperfectly understood yet the patient does change behaviour. However, if the purpose of a particular explanation is to change behaviour, and understanding is a mere mediator, then changes in behaviour may be useful outcome measures. But one should bear in mind that such changes in behaviour are unlikely to be sustained unless they are integrated into the cognitive structure of the patient or client.

Summary

To sum up, explaining is an attempt to give understanding to another. It involves identifying the problem to be explained, a process of explaining which uses key statements and a check on understanding. However, it would be wrong to leave the nature of explaining without pointing out that explaining is only usually an intentional activity: one may intend to explain a particular problem but may end up explaining points that one did not intend to explain, and, alas, one may sometimes not explain what one intended to explain.

THE NATURE OF UNDERSTANDING

Given that explaining is an attempt to give understanding, it is necessary to explore the nature of understanding – otherwise one may be accused of explaining the known in terms of an unknown. Put simply, *understanding involves seeing connections which were hitherto not seen*. The connections might be between ideas, between facts or between ideas and facts.

This apparently simple definition has strong links with much of cognitive psychology. Dewey (1910) described five steps in arriving at understanding which began with 'felt' difficulty and proceeded to the search for corroborative evidence. His approach also describes neatly the process of explaining to oneself. Thyne (1966) emphasised the importance of recognising the appropriate cues in the information presented. Norman and Bobrow (1975), following the work of Piaget and Bruner, argued that the aim of cognitive processing is: 'to form a meaningful interpretation of the world. ... The problem of the perceptual processes is to determine the appropriate schemata and to match the present occurrence with the frame provided for them. If there are too many discrepancies then a new schemata must be selected or the current one must be reorganised' (p. 149).

Ausubel (1978) stressed that the most important single factor influencing learning is what the learner already knows. He highlighted the importance of anchoring ideas in the learner's cognitive structure, the use of advanced organisers and the learner's meaningful learning set. Pask's conversational theory of understanding (Pask, 1976) and research on how students learn (Entwistle, 1992) are built on the proposition that understanding is concerned with forming connections. Whereas research in the 1980s in psychology focused upon understanding in relation to problem-solving (Nickerson, 1985; Greeno and Riley, 1987), more recent work of Entwistle and his co-workers has focused upon how students deepen their understanding (Entwistle and Entwistle, 1992; Entwistle and Marton, 1994; Entwistle, 1996). Their work indicates that students experience a feeling of 'satisfaction' when they understand: they recognise coherence, connectedness and a 'provisional' wholeness. These feelings led them to express confidence about explaining what they had been studying. The qualitative work initiated by Entwistle has considerable implications for methods of learning and teaching in higher education. No comparable work has yet been attempted in the study of patients' understanding.

For an explanation to be understood, the explainee must recognise that there is a puzzle or problem to be explained. The explainee must also be able to identify the relevant cues in the explanation and these cues must match in some way those schemata of the explainees salient at the time the explanation is being attended to. This matching may lead to assimilation of the explanation into the existing cognitive structure or it may modify the existing cognitive structure. In both cases it produces new connections of concepts and/or facts. The degree of stability of those new connections depends in part upon the network of existing concepts and facts. The validity of the new connection, that is of the understanding, can only be tested by reference to corroborative evidence which may be from an external source or from other evidence and rules stored in the person's cognitive framework (see Chapters 1 and 2 for further discussion on cognition).

This brief exposition of understanding has obvious implications for providing explanations. The problem must be presented so as to be recognised as a problem, the cues given must take account of the existing cognitive structure of the explainees; they must be highlighted so they can readily be matched and, if possible, there should be a check on whether understanding has occurred.

PERSPECTIVES ON EXPLAINING AND UNDERSTANDING

Philosophical roots

The study of explaining has a long history. Aristotle provided a conceptually illuminating start to the study of explaining by distinguishing four causes: the material, the formal, the efficient and the final cause or purpose. The word 'cause' in Greek has a wider meaning than 'cause' in English. (In itself, this is a neat example of the problem of language and meaning in providing explanations.) Aristotle's work on rhetoric (translation by Freese, 1959) also laid the foundations for work by rhetoricians in the Middle Ages and subsequently. Cockroft and Cockroft (1992) use the Aristotelian concepts of *ethos* (personality and stance), *pathos* (emotional engagement) and *logos* (modelling and judging argument) as the organising

Table 7.1 The polar contrasts of scientific and personal understanding

Scientific understanding (erklärung)	Personal understanding (verstehen)
Experimentation	Other forms of research
Quantity	Quality
Measurement	Meaning
Reactions	Intentions
Outcomes, results	Processes
Repeated patterns and trends in phenomena	Relationships and distinctions between phenomena
Independent observer	Participant observer
Statistical prediction	'Clinical' prediction
Statistical generalisation	Generalisation based on cases

Based on Ricoeur, 1981

principles for their discussion of persuasive explanation and argument in speech and written texts. Atkinson (1984) in his analysis of persuasive explaining linked studies of classical rhetoric to the strategies used by twentieth-century politicians and dictators.

A framework

In modern German there are two major terms for understanding: *erklärung* and *verstehen*. The first may be described as scientific understanding and the second as personal understanding. This distinction provides a schema for classifying modes of understanding and explaining (Table 7.1).

The cluster of values associated with *erklärung* include the development of covering laws and models which enable explanations and predictions to be made. At the *erklärung* pole there is an underlying concern with quantitative measurement, with problems of measuring reliability and validity and with, as far as possible, identical repetition of experiments. Associated with the mode of scientific explanation is often an interest in the organic, in disease-centred models and in the search for mathematically based generalisations within a closed system of concepts.

In contrast, the pole of *verstehen* is concerned with personal understanding, with meanings rather than measurement, with intentions rather than directly observable actions. For example, from the *verstehen* standpoint a doctor–patient consultation is seen as a set of unique thought-related events, each of which is influenced by a particular cluster of conditions, including the doctor's history, the problem and the patient's history. Instead of searching for covering laws, one looks at how an individual doctor adduces the relevant hypotheses or explanatory principles – at how the doctor detects regularities, distinguishes differences and arrives at decisions. Associated with the mode of personal understanding is often an interest in the individual patient's conceptions of illness, in patient-centred models of management, and in a search for interpretations and meanings within the consultation.

The two poles – *erklärung* and *verstehen* – help to explain some tensions manifest within the study of communication and within social psychology. Furthermore, at an individual level, professionals may experience the conflicting pulls of scientific understanding and personal understanding in their daily work.

Finally, it is worth pointing out that the etymological root of explaining, *explanare*, 'to make plain', suggests two powerful metaphors: 'to strip bare' and 'to reveal'. These metaphors hint at different purposes of explaining. The first has connotations of getting down to the essentials. The second leans towards revelation, to revealing subtleties, intricacies and perhaps the uniqueness of an object, action, event, or occurrence. The first metaphor resonates with scientific approaches such as the development of attribution theory. This seeks to identify through statistical analysis the dimensions on which people provide explanations. These often are the dimensions of *internal/external*; *stable/unstable*; *controllable/uncontrollable*; *global/specific* (Hewstone, 1989). The second metaphor resonates with work in discourse analysis and hermeneutics (Potter and Wetherall, 1994). The review by Rae (1989) suggests that, although discourse methods are potentially useful, on balance, the work based on attributional coding and scientific methods is of more value to practitioners.

The covering law model

The core of scientific explanation is the triadic principle. There must be:

1 A generalisation or universal law
2 An evidential statement or observation that the situation being considered is an instance of that generalisation
3 A conclusion.

This covering law model has been variously known as the standard theory model or the regularity model. The model also appears in the guise of assertion, datum, warrant (grounds for belief) (Toulmin, 1958). The warrant, including its backing, is the generalisation or regularity principle. However, one should be wary of over-extending the model lest the explanation become vacuous. Appeals or universal laws such as 'God's will' or 'the firing of neurones' do not pick out the reasons for a particular action or event, so one needs to use the counter-factual model, sometimes known as the method of differences (White, 1990). In the counter-factual model one picks out the regularity which has most explanatory power in the given context. To answer the question, 'Why did the car ferry, the *Herald of Free Enterprise* sink so *quickly*?', one looks at the question, 'When does a car ferry sink *slowly*?', and looks for the regularity that accounts for the difference.

The covering law model focuses upon causes and reasons. Swift (1961), a determinist historian, was a strong advocate of this model. His not-so-hidden agenda was to move the study of history away from personal understanding towards scientific understanding and thereby increase the 'respectability' of historical research. The model was described by Taylor (1970) as 'especially elegant and clear'. Despite its clarity, it gave rise to considerable controversy amongst historians, philosophers and psychologists in the 1950s and 1960s (see Dray, 1957; Martin, 1970; Shotter, 1975).

Issues raised by the covering law model

At the heart of the controversy are three issues: first, whether all explanations must fit the covering law model; second, whether the explanation has to be understood before it can be regarded as an explanation; and third, what counts as 'understanding' an explanation.

The last of these questions has already been discussed in the section on the process of understanding (see p. 187f).

As Swift (1961) and subsequently Draper (1988) noted, some types of explaining do not require a covering law model. Not all 'How' questions or 'Because' explanations involve the covering law. However, the model can account for many explanations provided that the first statement of the model is not only universal laws and strong generalisations but also weak generalisations based on previous instances and appeals to values or accepted myths. This modification of the covering law model does then allow for the development of generalisations.

Kruglanski (1988) examined this theme in relation to the development of beliefs that are used by individuals to explain events. He argued that at some point an individual stops generating hypotheses and attains closure on a given belief. This frozen 'belief' then becomes the regularity principle of the covering law explanation. Without this modification one is left with the difficult problem of how to observe or arrive at a generalisation on which to build explanations and how an explanation becomes convincing to a recipient. The suggestion also has implications for the development and acceptance of 'practical' wisdom in a profession which may run alongside the evidence collected by research and, indeed, might be more influential than research findings *per se*. By extending the covering law to shared meanings, beliefs, values and ideologies, one is able to hold to the view that explanations should lead to understanding.

Even if the covering model holds, one still has to consider the truth of the explanation. Here one may wish to distinguish between the 'truth' and the phenomenological 'truth' or belief in the principle or regularity. We do not propose to enter that debate but it is worth pointing out that, for an explanation to be convincing, the universal principle has to be believed and thought relevant. An explanation might fit the covering law model but not be correct. The generalisation may not hold, the instance may not be an instance of the generalisation and, more subtly, the instance may fit more appropriately into another generalisation. To complicate matters further, an explanation may be incorrect yet believed, or may be correct but not believed. Examples of both complications abound in the history of medicine and science and in history itself.

Nor is it proposed to enter deeply into the question of validity. Every subject and every profession has its set of canons and shared beliefs, although many of these are changing rapidly. However, one can distinguish tests of validity that appeal to reasons, values and obligation and other tests that appeal to evidence. These may be described loosely as *rational* or *empirical*. The first task in determining validity is to decide whether the proposed explanation requires a rational test, an empirical test or both. For example, consider the question, 'Are there more grandfathers than fathers in the world?' At first sight this may appear to be an empirical question requiring a survey and population estimates. In fact, it is a conceptual matter requiring one to examine the definitions of fathers and grandfathers and the relations between the definitions. Clearly, there are more fathers in the world than grandfathers. The second step is to determine whether the explanation proffered fits either the rules of logic or the rules of evidence or testimony that are extant in the academic subject or profession.

Even if an explanation is valid, there remains the question of whether it is understood. The central issue here is whether it is possible to explain without giving understanding. Now certainly it is possible for a scientist or scholar to give an explanation that was not understood at that time, or, as was more frequently the case, the explanation may have been understood but was rejected by peers. Even in such extreme cases, one can assume that the scientists or scholars intended to give understanding to their audience. But is intention enough? On this issue there are various views.

Intention and outcome

As Martin (1970) pointed out, the process of explaining involves an explainer, a problem to be explained and a set of explainees. The explainer has to take account of the problem and of the existing knowledge, attitudes and skills of the explainees. The goal of explaining is to provide understanding to others. Martin's view stresses the importance of intentions. For her, explaining is essentially a task verb, like shooting or fishing (see Ryle, 1963). For Thyne (1966) – one of the few British authors to analyse explanatory teaching – explaining is an achievement verb, such that 'If the teacher really has explained something to his class, they will understand it, and if they do not understand it, despite his efforts, what purported to be an explanation was not an explanation after all' (p. 126).

Martin's work is part of a tradition concerned primarily with analysing intentions and processes of explaining (Bellack *et al.*, 1966; Ennis, 1969; Smith and Meux, 1970; Hyman, 1974; Turney *et al.*, 1983), whereas Thyne (1966) is almost a forerunner of the process-product researchers who explore relationships between the processes of teaching or communication and some external outcome such as student learning (Dunkin and Biddle, 1974; Dunkin, 1986) or patient compliance (Pendleton *et al.*, 1984; Ley and Llewelyn, 1995).

It seems to us that the intentional position is too weak and the outcome position too strong. We suggest that for the purposes of working with patients, clients and students, there must be an intention to explain and an attempt to use a non-relational or relational explanation. A full account of explaining as a process of communicating has to take account of the intentions of the explainer, the actual processes of explaining adopted and the subsequent changes in understanding of the explainee. This leads back to our working definition that: *Explaining is an attempt to provide understanding of a problem to others.*

It follows from this definition that explaining involves taking account of a problem in relation to a set of explainees. In other words, the explainer has to attempt to see the problem through the eyes of the explainees. Indeed, it could be argued that explaining is a supreme example of hermeneutics in action (Ricoeur, 1981). A identifies certain ideas which it is thought will assist B. A articulates the ideas: B receives and explores, perhaps with A, the articulations and constructs meanings from them which either fit B's existing framework of understanding, changes that framework, or are rejected.

This perspective on explaining can readily be understood within the interpersonal interaction model of skill as described in Chapter 2. It also provides, potentially, the connections between explaining, scientific understanding and personal understanding.

EXPLAINING AND TEACHING

Most research on explaining has been conducted in classrooms or lecture rooms or in doctor–patient consultations. It is only recently that studies of explaining in other professional contexts are beginning to emerge.

Table 7.2 Planning strategies and performance skills in explaining

---

Planning strategies
- Analyse topics into main parts, or 'keys'
- Establish links between parts
- Determine rules (if any) involved
- Specify kinds of explanation required
- Adapt plan according to learner characteristics

Key skills
Clarity and fluency
- through defining new terms
- through use of explicit language
- through avoiding vagueness
Emphasis and interest
- by variations in gestures
- by use of media and materials
- by use of voice and pauses
- by repetition, summarising, paraphrasing or verbal cueing
Using examples
- clear, appropriate and concrete in sufficient quantity
- positive and negative where applicable
Organisation
- logical and clear sequence pattern appropriate to task
- use of link words and phrases
Feedback
- opportunities for questions provided to test understanding of main ideas assessed
- expressions of attitudes and values sought

EXPLAINING IN THE CLASSROOM

Given that most teachers talk for two-thirds of the time in classrooms (Flanders, 1970) and two-thirds of their talk is lecturing, then explaining is clearly a common activity in the classroom. Estimates of the proportion of time spent on explaining by teachers vary between 10 to 30 per cent, according to the definition of explaining adopted (Dunkin and Biddle, 1974; Brophy and Good, 1986). Time spent on a task is but a crude measure of its importance. More important is the quality: the way the time is spent. As Gage *et al.* (1968, p. 3) wryly observed: 'Some people explain aptly, getting to the heart of the matter with just the right terminology, examples, and organization of ideas. Other explainers, on the contrary, get us and themselves all mixed up, use terms beyond our level of comprehension, draw inept analogies, and even employ concepts and principles that cannot be understood without an understanding of the very thing being explained.'

Reviews of the literature (Gage and Berliner, 1979; Turney *et al.*, 1983; Crowhurst, 1988; Wragg, 1993) reveal that good explanations are not only clearly structured, they are also interesting. However, clarity and interest are complex notions which involve, among other things, the use of structuring moves such as framing statements which delineate sections of the explanation, focal statements which highlight its essential features and the use of carefully chosen examples. While it is easy to offer the advice, 'Be clear and interesting', it is less easy to provide detailed guidelines which will help someone to provide clear, interesting explanations when teaching.

The main characteristics of explaining are summarised in Table 7.2. They have been identified in the literature, in discussions with teachers and from the studies of explaining which one of the authors and colleagues undertook at Nottingham and Exeter (e.g. Brown and Hatton, 1982; Brown and Armstrong, 1984; Wragg and Brown, 1993).

Views on explaining

Pupils' views on explaining appear to have been consistent over a period of at least fifty years. Studies show that the foremost reasons for liking a teacher are clear explanations of lessons, assignments and difficulties, helpfulness with school work and fairness (Wragg, 1984).

Preparation and planning

The maxim, 'Know your subject, know your students', appears to be borne out by the evidence on planning and preparation. Hiller (1971) showed that a teacher's prior level of knowledge is linked to clarity of explaining. In general, the teachers who were more knowledgeable made fewer vague statements and provided clearer explanations. The work of Calderhead (1996) indicates that successful teachers plan not by deducing methods from objectives, but by taking account of pupil understanding, other pupil characteristics and the resources available. Brown and Armstrong (1984) found that student teachers trained in methods of preparing, analysing and presenting explanations were significantly better than a comparable untrained group. The criteria were independent observers' ratings of the videotaped lessons and measures of pupil achievement and interest in the lesson. The study by Bennett and Carre (1993) highlighted a strong association between subject knowledge and teaching competence. However, knowledge of subject is a necessary but not sufficient condition of effective explaining. Some people are knowledgeable but remain poor explainers. In a recent experimental study, Wragg (1993) identified characteristics of explaining that produced high and low scores on specially designed pupil achievement tests. Both topics used in the study were familiar to the teachers. The high scorers matched closely the characteristics given in Table 7.2.

The studies and reviews by many authors provide suggestions on preparation and planning. For example, Brown and Hatton (1982) and Turney *et al.* (1983) provided guidelines on planning explanations. Wragg (1993) in his studies of subject knowledge and teaching offered some suggestions on preparation. Brown and Wragg (1993) in their text on questioning provided suggestions on preparation and planning including the use of mind-mapping to generate ideas and methods, the use of key questions as organising principles and a method of structuring different types of learning activities.

Processes and outcomes of explaining

Structure and presentation are the essential features of explaining. Of these, presentation techniques have been the subject of most studies and these have focused upon clarity, fluency, emphasis, interest and the use of examples and of summaries. Greater clarity, including the use of definitions, yields greater pupil or student achievement. Fluency, including the notions of emphasis, clear transitions, absence of vagueness, absence of false starts and of verbal tangles, have all been shown to be associated with effective presentation (Brophy and Good, 1986).

Studies of expressiveness (Rosenshine, 1972; Wragg, 1993) show that purposeful variations in voice, gesture, manner and use of teaching aids all contribute to the interest and effectiveness of an explanation. So, too, does the use of examples. Indeed, examples may promote both clarity and interest (Armento, 1977). However, examples *per se* are not sufficient. The number of examples provided is not a discrimination between effective and ineffective explanatory lessons (Gage, 1972). What may be more important is the pattern of examples and principles enunciated and elicited. Rosenshine (1972) claimed that the pattern of 'rule–example–rule' was more effective than rule–example or example–rule. This finding has not been borne out by other research (Shutes, 1969; Brown and Armstrong, 1984; Wragg, 1993). The Brown and Armstrong study suggests that the pattern of examples should be associated with both the type of explanation and the pupils' prior knowledge of the topic. Thus, in providing an interpretive explanation on an unfamiliar topic, examples should take primacy. In restructuring pupils' ideas, then, principles and generalisations should take primacy.

The use of summaries appears to be related to both ratings of clarity. As Turney *et al.* (1983, p. 3) noted, 'There is no doubt that teachers who pause to review prior material, who repeat main points in summary form and who repeat instructions slowly so that all can comprehend are favoured as clear teachers, and therefore competent explainers, by secondary pupils'.

In their study of explaining, in the classroom, Brown and Armstrong (1984) explored both presentational variables and structural features. The study revealed that better explanatory lessons had more keys and more types of keys. In other words, they varied the cognitive demands on the pupils and they used higher levels of cognitive demands. Better lessons also contained more framing statements, which delineate the beginning and ending of sub-topics, more focusing statements, which emphasise the key points, more relevant examples and better use of audio-visual aids and fewer unfinished summaries. However, the better lessons did contain more rhetorical questions. These were usually used as attention-gaining devices in the early stages of a new key.

Brown and Armstrong's qualitative analysis of the lessons showed that better lessons had a more meaningful structure to the pupils. For example, ten short lessons were taught by ten teachers on the topic 'What is an ecological succession?' This required an interpretive explanation of a topic which was completely new to the pupils. Thus, the teachers were faced with the problem of deciding how much it was necessary for the children to know in order to understand the process of ecological succession. The teachers of the low-scoring lessons assumed they had to explain differences between taxonomies and ecology, or between consumers and producers. The high-scoring lessons were the simple ones which described the process in words with which the children were familiar and to which they could relate. The low-scoring lessons introduced so many new ideas that the children became confused. This is illustrated in the examples given in the comparison of high- and low-scoring lessons in Table 7.3.

In a more recent study, Wragg (1993) developed a method of observing explanations in classrooms and related the scores obtained to pupil achievement and transcripts of the lesson. Two major styles and two minor styles of explaining were identified. The major styles involved drawing out the imaginative responses of pupils through open questions and encouraging longer responses. This was used most frequently in the English lessons. The second major style was used most frequently in science lessons in which teachers gave

Table 7.3 High- and low-scoring explanations

High-scoring	Low-scoring
Orientation	**Orientation**
Teacher – 'Well, first of all I wonder if you could tell me what this is.'	*Teacher* – 'I'm going to talk to you about ecological succession. It's not as difficult as it sounds.'
Pupil – 'A piece of concrete.'	
Teacher – 'Yes, it's a piece of concrete, a slab of concrete, out of my garden. Now, if I wanted to plant a tree or a shrub on here what would you say was missing?'	
Pupil – 'Soil.'	
Teacher – 'Yes, the soil. And today I want to start by talking about some plants that can grow straight on to a rock.'	
Keys	**Keys**
1 Which plants can grow straight on to rock?	1 In what two ways can we group organisms?
2 How do mosses replace lichens?	2 Which organisms are consumers?
3 Which plants replace mosses?	3 Which organisms are producers?
4 What is this process called?	4 What is it called when we group organisms that depend on each other together?
5 What other examples of ecological succession are there?	5 What do we call it when one community takes over from another?
	6 How does ecological succession take place on bare rock?

and elicited examples and provided summaries. The minor styles were variants on the major styles.

Wragg also demonstrated that a clue to the effectiveness of an explanation is often given by its opening. Consider the high-scoring lesson that follows:

Mrs Archer, the teacher, produced two large cases of insects.

T: Do you know what these are?

P1: Bees and wasps.

T: Yes. That's right. And what are these?

P2: Bluebottles.

T: Yes. Bluebottles, greenbottles. They're all flies . . . what about this beautiful creature?

P3: It's a dragonfly.

The teacher redirected and refocused and she recapped before coming to the key point:

T: All of these creatures are so different but (*emphasis, pause*) they do have one feature in common (*pause*). They all belong to the family called (*pause*) insects (*emphasis, pause*) insects.

The teacher also used examples and analogies such as 'The feelers are rather like radio aerials, they pick up all sorts of messages in the air around the insect'.

In contrast, a low-scoring lesson began with:

No visual aids were used by the teacher.

T: I'm going to give you the little word 'insect'. Immediately in your mind, there's a picture of something, I expect. There is in mine. What sort of picture have you got, Cassandra?

P: A spider.

T: OK. You think of a spider. You keep the spider there. Peter, what about you?

P: (No response)

T: When I say 'insect' what do you immediately think of – an insect?

P: A ladybird.

T: Yes, that's right.

P: A worm.

T: Yes. Anything else?

Wragg's work broke new ground in the study of explaining by identifying a form of imaginative explanation used predominantly in English. It also confirmed the important characteristics of effective explaining shown in Table 7.2.

Feedback and checking understanding

The studies of explaining in the classroom cited above have all been based upon measures of pupil achievement or reaction. They contained built-in checks on understanding and thereby provided measures of effective explaining.

In the hurly-burly of normal classroom life it is not always possible to conduct detailed evaluations of one's teaching or explanatory skills. None the less, it is worth noting that feedback and checks on understanding are important features of explaining. Without feedback, one is left only with one's intentions and hunches and these may not always be correct. For example, in a study of pupil learning in the primary school (Bennett *et al.*, 1984) it was shown that a group of infant teachers was not able readily to identify pupils' learning difficulties. Bright pupils' abilities were frequently under-estimated whereas those of less able pupils were frequently over-estimated. Most of the teachers focused upon assessing the final product of the children's work rather than checking the processes which the children used to arrive at their answers. Other studies showed that summarising, inviting questions and the use of recall questions at the close of a lesson leads to high achievement (Shutes, 1969; Tisher, 1970; Wragg, 1993). Tisher also illustrated how teachers tend not to correct wrong responses or explore reasons underlying answers. This evidence suggests that feedback and checks on understanding are necessary and that further studies of ways that teachers analyse and use responses from children to develop understanding are required.

Summary

Studies of explaining in the classroom indicate that clarity and interest are crucial but complex variables. These variables are valued by pupils and lead to better achievement. Preparation and planning are important aspects of training and using feedback to check understanding is an important, but relatively neglected, feature of explaining in the classroom.

EXPLAINING IN HIGHER EDUCATION

In higher education explaining occurs in lectures, small group teaching and laboratory work. Apart from the consultative study conducted by Saunders and Saunders (1993a), in which university lecturers analysed their own teaching in lectures, seminars and practicals, there appear to be no direct empirical studies of explaining in seminars or tutorials and virtually none in laboratories. Yet Daines (1985) reported that 'explaining clearly' is a much-valued characteristic of demonstrators.

Brown and Atkins (1988) and Brown (1993) have reviewed the research on effective lecturing, small group teaching and laboratory teaching. Most studies of explaining in higher education have been concerned with explaining in lectures or with brief, uninterrupted explanations. Indeed, lectures may be conceived of as a set of linked explanations (Brown, 1978) and brief uninterrupted explanations as microlectures which contain opening moves, a structure based on key points and a summary. A microlecture also provides a sample of verbal, extra-verbal and non-verbal behaviour of the presenter. The studies of explaining in higher education parallel those in classrooms. The same sets of variables are manifested and similar results obtained.

Views on explaining

Clarity of presentation and logical presentation are the most important features for students and the most frequently mentioned (Dunkin, 1986; Brown, 1987; Marsh, 1987). Students' main dissatisfaction with lecturers appears to be their inaudibility, incoherence, failure to pitch at an appropriate level, failure to emphasise main points, their being difficult to take notes from, displaying poor blackboard work and reading aloud from notes.

Lecturers' views on explaining are not dissimilar. In one study (Brown and Daines, 1981), lecturers were invited to rate a set of forty items for their value in explaining and their 'learnability' (whether lecturers could learn them). The most valued characteristics were clarity, interest, logical organisation and selection of appropriate content. The most learnable were use of diagrams, use of variety of materials, examples and selection of appropriate content. There were significant differences between the arts and science lecturers on seventeen of the items. Science lecturers valued logical and structural characteristics more highly than arts lecturers; science lecturers also considered that more features of explaining were learnable than did the arts lecturers.

In a study of styles of lecturing (Brown and Bakhtar, 1988), the five most common weaknesses reported by lecturers were: saying too much too quickly; assuming too much knowledge; forgetting to provide summaries; not indicating when making an aside (rather than a major point); and difficulty in timing length of lectures. Similar views to those described in this section are reported in other studies (Hildebrand, 1973; Kozma *et al.,* 1978; Saunders and Saunders, 1993b).

Planning and preparation

The planning and preparation of explanations and lectures are neglected research topics in higher education. While Bligh (1972), Beard and Hartley (1984), Brown (1978) and Brown and Atkins (1988) all suggest guidelines for preparing lectures, there are no studies extant of how lecturers actually prepare their lectures.

Table 7.4 Effective structuring moves in explaining

1 Signposts	*These are statements which indicate the structure and direction of an explanation:* (a) 'I want to deal briefly with lactation. First, I want to outline the composition of milk; second, its synthesis; third, to examine normal lactation curves.' (b) 'Most of you have heard the old wives' tale that eating carrots helps you to see in the dark. Is it true? Let's have a look at the basic biochemical processes involved.'
2 Frames	*These are statements which indicate the beginning and end of the sub-topic:* (a) 'So that ends my discussion of adrenaline. Let's look now at the role of glycogen.' *Framing statements are particularly important in complex explanations which may involve topics, sub-topics and even sub-topics of sub-topics.*
3 Foci	*These are statements and emphases which highlight the key points of an explanation:* (a) 'So the main point is . . .' (b) 'Now this is very important . . .' (c) 'But be careful. This interaction with penicillin occurs only while the cell walls are growing.'
4 Links	*These are words, phrases or statements which link one part of an explanation to another part, and the explanation to the explainees' experience:* (a) 'So you can see that reduction in blood sugar levels is detected indirectly in the adrenaline gland and directly in the pancreas. This leads to the release of two different hormones . . .'

Processes and outcomes of explaining

The process of explaining, as indicated earlier, has structural and presentational features. These types of feature fuse into one another. Thus, logical organisation – a structural feature – may also be considered as part of presentation. Enthusiasm, which is clearly a presentational variable, may be considered as a structural variable, if it includes the use of examples.

The sequence and organisation of explanations in lectures have not been studied in detail. Lecturers report that their most common method of organising lectures is the classical approach of subdividing topics and then subdividing sub-topics (Brown and Bakhtar, 1988). There appear to be no studies of the transcripts of lectures to identify pattern and sequence, although two early unpublished studies describe attempts to apply linguistic analyses to transcripts of lectures (Montgomery, 1976; Pirianen-Marsh, 1985). Brown (1980) analysed the structural moves in a series of transcripts of explanations and related these to ratings of clarity and interest. The structural moves which yielded high scores in clarity are shown in Table 7.4.

Expressiveness, which includes enthusiasm, friendliness, humour, dynamism and even charisma, has long been regarded as an essential ingredient of lecturing and explaining. The meta-analysis of twelve experimental studies of expressiveness conducted by Abrami *et al.* (1982) suggests that expressiveness is more likely to influence students' response to the lecturer and their attitude towards the subject than to produce marked changes in achievement. However, the studies reviewed were rather extreme in their use of expressiveness and variation in content. Furthermore, favourable changes in attitude to the subject may be important, long-term motivating characteristics.

Land (1985) summarised the main studies of clarity of explanations which were conducted in the USA during the 1970s and 1980s. Essentially, the results were that higher student achievement scores were obtained when explanations had fewer verbal mazes (false starts, redundant phrases, tangles of words) and greater use of specific emphasis and clear transitions from one sub-topic to another. The combination of the results described so far suggests that the ideal strategy for improving learning and generating interest is a blend of clarity and expressiveness.

This conclusion led to the development of a training programme for lecturers (Brown, 1982) which contained a series of activities concerned with preparation, planning and presentation. The training programme was evaluated using independent observers' ratings and analyses of transcripts of the pre-test and post-test microlectures. The independent observer ratings revealed that the openings of the explanations, and the structure, interest and use of audio-visual aids were significantly better at the end of the course. The transcript analyses revealed significant increases in the use of signposts, frames and links and fewer hesitations, stumbles and incomplete statements. The ratings and comments of the lecturers at the end of the course and six months later indicated it was highly valued, in particular the activities on preparing, presenting and analysing explanations.

Feedback and checks on understanding

Studies of explaining in higher education have been largely concerned with explaining as a lecture method. This mode of teaching has the disadvantage of not usually providing any checks on understanding during or soon after the lecture. Hence, some writers advocate the use of activities during lectures which require students to demonstrate their understanding (Brown and Atkins, 1988; Habeshaw, 1992). However, feedback signals may be used by lecturers to appraise the attending behaviour of students (Brown, 1978), and feedback signals from students may influence a lecturer's behaviour even though the latter is unaware of it. In one set of studies (Klein, 1971), the behaviour of the lecturer was manipulated by the simultaneous use of smiling, head nods, frowning and other signals by groups of students.

Summary

Studies of explaining in higher education have been confined largely to the lecture method. Students value clear, well-structured explanations and, to a lesser extent, interesting explanations. Training in explaining can improve the clarity, structure and interest of explanations. Explanations with these characteristics also yield higher measures of recall and understanding.

EXPLAINING IN THE HEALTH PROFESSIONS

It is sometimes forgotten that health professionals explain things not only to patients but also to other health professionals, managerial staff and students. For example, hospital-based doctors and general practitioners may teach students whilst the patient is present. These situations in which a doctor is explaining to a group have received scant attention although there are texts available for health professionals on teaching (e.g. Cox and Ewan,

1992), and a programme on presentation skills has been shown to be effective for this target group (Hargie and Morrow, 1995). The research on explaining in higher education is relevant here. There does appear to be a need to study the use of explaining at the bedside for this is a particularly delicate task which involves taking account of the patient as well as a set of students. Observations in various hospitals by one of the authors suggest that such explaining at the bedside is not always handled sensitively.

EXPLAINING IN THE MEDICAL CONSULTATION

The major studies of the consultation have been concerned with doctors and patients. Given that most GPs carry out about 10,000 consultations a year (Fry, 1992) it is clear that explaining and questioning are important skills for doctors – and patients. However, most studies of the doctor–patient consultation do not isolate the skill of explaining from the other skills involved in the consultation. But it is possible to identify features of the research on doctor–patient interactions which are relevant, if not crucial, to the processes of explaining to patients.

Patients' views and beliefs

Patients value in medical practitioners the characteristics of warmth, interest, concern and the ability to explain things in terms that they understand (Pendleton, 1983: Hall and Dornan, 1988). For the doctor to explain things clearly it may be necessary to understand the patient's perspective – in terms of anxieties, knowledge and beliefs about health. Robinson (1995, p. 129) argued in her review of patients' contribution to the consultation that 'the most important predictor of a positive outcome is that the doctor offers information and advice which fits easily in to the patients pre-consultation framework'.

This suggestion is of particular importance when a doctor is working with patients from relatively unfamiliar cultures and sub-cultures. Pendleton and Bochner (1980) stated that doctors offer fewer explanations to patients of social classes IV and V. Tuckett *et al.* (1985) found that a sample of general practitioners rarely discovered patients' beliefs about their problems and even more rarely presented explanations which took account of patients' beliefs. However, a study by Law and Britten (1995) indicated that female GPs are better than male GPs at eliciting and building explanations on patients' views and beliefs in their consultations with patients of either gender.

There do not appear to be, as yet, any substantial British studies of the beliefs and views of patients from different cultures, although this is clearly an important area for research and practice. Weston and Brown (1989) have discussed the evidence on patients' beliefs and pointed out the implications for management, compliance and outcomes, while Landrine and Klonoff (1992) argued that models in health psychology have neglected systems of belief and their impact upon compliance and other outcomes such as health behaviour.

Preparation and planning

Since Wakeford's survey of communication skills training in undergraduate medical schools in the UK (Wakeford, 1983), all medical schools now provide courses on communication as part of their newly defined curricula. There is clear evidence to demonstrate that communication skills can be taught effectively and are sustainable (Maguire, 1990; Dickson *et al.*, 1997).

Processes and outcomes of explaining

Doctors talk for about 60 per cent of the consultation of which about one-third is concerned with explaining. About half of patient talk is concerned with explaining (Stewart and Roter, 1989). Explanations by doctors occur, typically, towards the end of a consultation, whereas patients' explanations occur towards the beginning of a consultation (Byrne and Long, 1976). The quality of the doctor's explanation is therefore, in part, dependent upon the quality of the patient's explanation as well as the doctor's diagnostic skills. Hence the importance of research on patients' contribution to the consultation (Robinson, 1995).

Studies of processes have been tackled from the perspectives of discourse analysis (Skopek, 1979; Bergmann, 1992) and experimental studies based on interaction analysis (Roter, 1989; Henbest and Stewart, 1989; Meuwessen *et al.*, 1991). Explaining is regarded as one of the major types of utterances in discourse analysis. In these studies it leads to a consideration of problems of intentionality, shared meanings, credibility, acceptability and belief systems but not, as yet, of their relationships with outcomes. The interaction studies, like the studies of discourse analysis, tend to be fine-grained analyses which are useful to researchers but often too complex for training purposes.

Studies of processes *per se* may yield normative data but they do not reveal which strategies or methods of consulting are more likely to yield desired outcomes. Hence the importance of process-outcome studies. These are admirably reviewed by Pendleton (1983), Brownbridge (1987), Roter (1989) and Ley and Llewelyn (1995). Outcomes may be measured using such variables as patients' recall, understanding, changes in attitudes, beliefs, compliance and improvements in patient health. Each of these variables has been measured using a variety of methods; measures of outcome have been taken immediately after a consultation, soon afterwards and up to a year after a course of treatment. However, most of these studies have been concerned with immediate and short-term outcomes. This is largely because of the difficulty of attributing long-term outcomes solely to the consultation. The studies show that patients remember less than half of the doctor's explanations. Pendleton (1981) demonstrated that patients probably remember the important points, although the evidence of Tuckett *et al.* (1985) indicates that they may not understand what they recall.

Clear explanations are an important determinant of patient satisfaction with the consultation. The studies reviewed by Roter (1989) also demonstrate that patients' emotional satisfaction is related to their being given an opportunity to explain their condition, while patients' cognitive satisfaction is related to the clear explanation of the illness and its treatment by the doctor.

For many medical practitioners the most powerful test of a consultation is the compliance of the patients. Podell (1975) suggested a 'one-third rule' derived from his studies of hypertension. One-third of patients comply, one-third comply partially and one-third ignore advice and medication. Given that the cost of medication in General Practice in Britain is over £3 billion (Fry, 1992), it might also be useful to teach patients about health care and management without drugs. But, as Kafka's country doctor observed, 'To write prescriptions is easy, but to come to an understanding with people is hard' (quoted by Balint, 1970).

Ley and Llewellyn (1995) argued that compliance is a product of satisfaction which, in its turn, is a product of understanding and recall. However, the evidence they review shows well-defined links between recall, understanding and satisfaction but more tenuous links between satisfaction and compliance. Compliance is likely to be influenced by earlier experiences of compliance and non-compliance and the perceived cost/benefits of complying/non-complying. In addition to the variables in their model, one may have to take account of patients' 'locus of control', the causal attributions made by patients and their private theories of the problems that they present. Patients with an 'external' locus of control tend to be fatalistic and feel helpless; those with an 'internal' locus believe events are controllable to some extent through their own actions. Externals tend to be poorer compliers than internals, and internals who have a positive attitude to health are more likely to comply and attempt health-related actions (Strickland, 1978). Modifying patients' private theories and causal attributions through discussion and explanation, as well as treating their physical condition has been shown to contribute to long-term health (Law and Britten, 1995; Marteau, 1995).

However, modifying a patient's incorrect theory may not always be good for compliance. For example, a patient might 'explain' that exercise is necessary to avoid getting cancer (this explanation might be based on the facts that the same-sex parent never exercised and died of cancer). If the doctor corrected this belief by explaining successfully the probable cause of cancer, it could lead to the patient not complying with the regime of exercise.

The studies and reviews of processes and patient outcomes provide hints on how doctors might improve the quality of their explanations to patients. These include establishing rapport with patients, taking account of patients' existing knowledge, using simple direct speech, categorising clearly the different parts of the explanations and repeating the important points. The key features are summarised in Table 7.5. They should be interpreted in the context of adequate diagnosis and management. The measures are based on clinical tests, medical examinations and medical reports.

Table 7.5 Health improvement: processes and outcomes

Doctor	Patient	Outcome
Friendly, attentive, creates partnership with patient, encourages, is supportive, explains clearly	Tells own story clearly, is encouraged to ask questions, develops treatment with doctor and takes responsibility for own health tasks	Increases probability of positive health outcome
Cold, distant, non-attentive, frequently interrupts patient, asks quick-fire questions, gives several instructions, offers several pieces of advice	Passive, does not ask questions, unduly deferential, superficially agrees to comply	Decreases probability of positive health outcome

Feedback and checks on understanding

The process-outcome measures reviewed in the previous section highlight the importance of feedback and checks on understanding. There appears to be no direct study of feedback from patients or of checks on understanding *during* the consultation. However, it is clear that doctors interpret patients' non-verbal signals as well as their verbal behaviour (Friedman, 1982). Yet there is a tendency to reject or ignore such information once a diagnosis has been reached (Maguire and Rutter, 1976).

Summary

Studies of the consultation indicate that patients value warmth, care, concern and the ability to explain clearly. Patient recall and understanding are enhanced when doctors provide simple, clear and well-structured explanations. Improved recall and understanding lead to higher patient satisfaction and to higher patient compliance and contribute to health improvement.

EXPLAINING IN OTHER HEALTH CONTEXTS

Research on explaining in other health contexts follows a similar pattern to those of the medical consultation.

Dentistry

There appear to be no major reviews of dentist–patient interaction since Ayer and Corah (1984). Their review was concerned primarily with children's behavioural problems and the reduction of anxiety in patients. No survey of training in dentist–patient communication in the UK has been carried out but at least four of the eleven dental schools known to the authors do not provide any practical training in dentist–patient communication. However, explaining is clearly of importance to dentists. Jackson and Katz (1983) presented a list of communication skills – including explaining, listening and reducing anxiety – that they argued are necessary features of undergraduate courses. Furnham (1983) provided a strong justification for training in explaining and other social skills in terms of likely patient outcomes and job satisfaction. Corah (1984) and Gale *et al.* (1984) showed that inadequate explaining led to less anxiety reduction, less positive attitudes to dentistry and lower levels of satisfaction with dental care. Jepson (1986) reported that co-participation in which a dentist explains various options of treatment and their probable outcomes leads to higher levels of compliance. More recently, Hamilton *et al.* (1994) also illustrated how the sharing of information inhibited treatment anxiety in the patient and increased the perceived competence of the dentist.

The notion that the meetings between a dentist and a patient should be described as a consultation was first proposed by Pendlebury (1988). He outlined the purposes and skills involved in the consultation. These were, in part, based on his studies, as yet unpublished, of videotapes of final-year students, trainees and experienced dentists. These studies led to the development of a simple, robust rating system, ORDERED, to assess dental consultations. Training courses and workbooks on explaining and other skills have been developed by Brown and Pendlebury (1987, 1992) and these have been adapted and used by postgraduate dental tutors.

Pharmacy

Community pharmacists are often the last health professionals to see a patient before the latter embarks upon self-treatment. Thus, they have an important role in reinforcing and clarifying previously presented information, explaining and justifying procedures, offering suggestions, providing reassurance and responding to patients' questions (Hargie and Morrow, 1994). Indeed, surveys of the public have revealed a desire for community pharmacists to provide more information and advice (Morrow *et al.*, 1993). Hospital pharmacists communicate with a wide range of patients including the terminally ill, the elderly and stroke patients. Despite the importance of communication in their work it was not until 1981 that the Pharmacy Society of Great Britain (PSGB, 1984) recommended that communication be taught in undergraduate courses. Two years later Hargie and Morrow (1986) conducted a survey of UK schools of pharmacy. Only four out of fifteen provided more than twenty hours' training in communication skills. Subsequently, the same authors developed and tested a communication skills training package (Morrow and Hargie, 1987; Hargie and Morrow, 1989). This led them to conduct a more detailed field study based on videorecordings of actual pharmacist–patient interactions in which they identified eleven core communication skills (Hargie *et al.*, 1993). Explaining, questioning and building rapport were the most important and, of these, explaining was used most frequently. The authors concluded that 'explaining clearly lies at the heart of pharmacy practice' (p. 80).

Nursing

Project 2,000 has provided an impetus for training in explaining and other communication skills (CINE, 1986), and there has been a strong impetus within the nursing profession to advance the communicative skills of trainees (Dickson, 1995). However, studies of what nurses actually do, do not appear to be consonant with official wisdom or the wishes of patients or nurses. MacLeod Clark (1985), in her review of nurse–patient communication, found that nurses usually only talk to patients when performing some aspect of physical care and they avoided providing explanations on treatment or care. Maguire (1985), in his analysis of nurse–patient interactions, pointed to inadequate recognition of patients' problems, insufficient provision of information and inadequate reassurance and support. These findings suggest that the organisational context, role definitions and workloads of nurses inhibit the use of explanations. Our suspicion is that the increasing workloads on nurses over the past few years will weaken further their relationships with patients. Yet when nurses are given the opportunity and encouragement to provide explanations to patients the outcomes are good. For example, pre-operative information given to patients is related to lower levels of post-operative physiological anxiety, lower analgesic consumption, better sleep patterns and quicker return to normal appetite (Devine and Cook, 1983). But it is not always clear from these studies whether explaining led to understanding or whether explaining was merely a signal to patients that their nurses and doctors cared. But it is likely that the act of explaining dispelled anxiety, provided reassurance and, for some patients at least, provided deeper understanding.

Other health contexts

Most work on explaining and allied skills in the UK appears to have been conducted in the Social Skills Centre at the University of Ulster. Thus, Saunders and Caves (1986) carried out a detailed study in which they identified effective communication skills in speech therapist–client practice and, using a similar methodology, Adams *et al.* (1994) identified the communication skills required by physiotherapists, including explaining treatment procedures and their rationale. Crute (1986) and Gallagher (1987) provided detailed evidence on the effectiveness of training in explaining and other skills for health visitors and counsellors respectively, and Hargie *et al.* (1994) have described how such training has been employed with radiographers. Although social work is not, strictly speaking, part of health care it appears that their clients too appreciate the ability of a social worker to structure explanations, to specify tasks, to provide clear directions, to listen responsively and to express concern (Hudson, 1981; Dickson and Bamford, 1995). Clearly, explaining has its part to play in many professions. Hargie *et al.* (1994) provided a most useful summative text on social skills for the interpersonal professions, while Dickson *et al.* (1997) have published a text on communication skills training for trainers in the health professions.

OVERVIEW

This chapter has provided a conceptual framework for the exploration of explaining and brought together studies of explaining from a variety of professions. The framework provides a basis for analysing and providing explanations and their links with different forms of understanding. It is argued that the theoretical model outlined in Chapter 2 provides the connections between explaining, scientific and personal understanding. The evidence indicates that clear explanations are valued by students, patients and clients: that expressiveness is valued highly in teaching and friendliness in consultations. Clear explaining is related to improvements in all contexts and, less strongly, to patient or client compliance and health outcomes. The evidence on training indicates that professionals can be trained to be better explainers. The chapter has not analysed all aspects of explaining nor has it reviewed all the studies that are relevant to explaining – that would be a lifetime's work. However, the framework and findings are sufficiently robust to permit conjectures and suggestions for future research.

Explanatory teaching

This is sometimes characterised as active teacher–passive learner. Yet, just as the teacher is required to take actions to give explanations, so too must learners take actions to gain understanding. Hence the importance of studies of student understanding as well as those of teachers' thinking and explaining. The notion of active teacher–passive learner leads to the false belief that explaining is spoon-feeding. It is at least a tenable hypothesis that frequent exposure to explaining based upon problem identification, process and checks on understanding could encourage students to incorporate the model into their own thinking. Obviously, opportunities for students to analyse and use explanations are necessary for them to develop their explanatory prowess: explanatory teaching should not be the only method of teaching, but nor should it be rejected.

Explaining in the consultation

The medical consultation has an obvious power relationship so it may be thought inappropriate for all one-to-one situations. However, all consultant–client relationships have at least an implicit power relationship. Studies of language and power will unravel some of the complexities of explaining to singletons and groups. These are necessarily context-based. Some contexts, such as the court or probation office, have explicit rules but also implicit rules that are no less potent. Studies which tease out the implicit rules will, if suitably expressed, assist professionals and clients in the tasks of explaining.

Explaining, practice wisdom and training

Every profession has its practice wisdom and that practice wisdom is not independent of the profession's value systems. The work on reflective learning and craft knowledge (Hatton and Smith, 1995) and expert-novice studies (Genberg, 1992) are relevant here. Experimental studies derived from practice wisdom hypotheses should continue to be tested in the professions. Such studies might confirm much of practice wisdom: it would be odd if they did not. But the studies might also identify dissonances between official, including governmental, wisdom, practice wisdom and actual practice. Equally important are studies of what professionals actually do and matching findings to the practice wisdom and value systems of their professions. What, how and when a professional explains to students or clients is of particular importance for the design of training. The studies might also lead to a shift from descriptions of reality rooted in ideologies to descriptions of ideologies that are rooted in practice.

Explaining, process and outcome

There is an intriguing conceptual-empirical problem rooted in the findings of the effect of friendliness in consultations and expressiveness in explaining to groups. It may be that these are manifestations of a higher level construct such as empathy. Furthermore, effective explaining may operate on arousal and attitudes as well as cognitive structures. Thus, explaining is a not a purely cognitive act so much as a cogni-affective act which has links with influencing and persuasion.

The appraisal and measurement of outcomes is a vexing problem for all the professions. Most studies rely upon short-term measures. The constraints of time and budgets, ethical considerations and the lack of control of variables in professional contexts often prevent long-term studies being undertaken. There is no satisfactory answer to this problem. One may simply have to rely upon 'weak' generalisations and the covering law model referred to in this chapter. These remarks apply to studies of explaining and understanding. To measure the effectiveness of explaining one needs short-term measures of understanding to check that it has occurred and long-term measures to check that it has stabilised. But understanding may not be separated from other long-term measures such as changes in attitudes and health behaviours. Whilst the goal of explaining will always remain understanding, it may be that the goal of the professions is understanding that leads to action. It is hoped that this chapter will assist professionals in this task.

REFERENCES

Abrami, P. C., Leventhal, L. and Perry, R. P. (1982) 'Educational Seduction', *Review of Educational Research,* 52, 446–64.

Adams, N., Bell, J., Saunders, C. and Whittington, D. (1994) *Communication Skills in Physiotherapist–Patient Interactions*, University of Ulster, Jordanstown.

Antakis, C. (1988) (ed.) *Analysing Everyday Explanation: A Case Book of Methods*, Sage, London.

—— (1994) *Explaining and Arguing: The Social Organisation of Accounts*, Sage, London.

Aristotle (1959) *The 'Art' of Rhetoric*, translated and edited by J. H. Freese, Heinemann, London.

Armento, B.J. (1977) 'Teacher Behaviour Related to Student Achievement on a Social Science Concept Test', *Journal of Teacher Education*, 28, 46–52.

Atkinson, M. (1984) *Our Master's Voice*, Methuen, London.

Ausubel, D. (1978) *Educational Psychology: A Cognitive View*, Holt, Rinehart & Wiston, New York.

Ayer, W. and Corah, N. (1984) 'Behavioural Factors Influencing Dental Treatment', in L. Cohen and P. Bryant (eds), *Social Science and Dentistry: A Critical Bibliography*, Quintessence, London.

Balint, M. (1970) *Treatment or Diagnosis*, Tavistock Publications, London.

Banyard, P. and Hayes, N. (1994) *Psychology: Theory and Application*, Chapman & Hall, London.

Beard, R. and Hartley, J. (1984) *Teaching and Learning in Higher Education*, Harper & Row, London.

Bellack, A. A., Hyman, R. T., Smith F. L. *et al.* (1966) *The Language of the Classroom*, Teacher College Press, New York.

Bennett, N. and Carre, C. G. (1993) *Learning to Teach*, Routledge, London.

Bennett, N., Desforge, S. and Wilkinson, A. (1984) *The Quality of Pupil Learning*, Lawrence Erlbaum, London.

Bergmann, J. R. (1992) 'Veiled Moralities: Notes on Discretion in Psychiatry', in P. Drew and J. Heritage (eds), *Talk at Work: Interaction in Institutional Settings*, Cambridge University Press, Cambridge.

Bligh, D. (1972) *What's the Use of Lectures?*, Penguin, Harmondsworth.

Brophy, J. and Good, T. L. (1986) 'Teacher Behaviour and Student Achievement', in M. Wittrock (ed.), *Handbook of Research on Teaching*, Macmillan, New York.

Brown, G. A. (1978) *Lecturing and Explaining*, Methuen, London.

—— (1980) *Explaining: Studies from the Higher Education Context*, final report to the Social Science Research Council.

—— (1982) 'Two Days on Explaining and Lecturing', *Studies in Higher Education*, 2, 93–104.

—— (1987) 'Studies of Lecturing', in M. J. Dunkin (ed.), *International Encyclopaedia of Teacher Education*, Pergamon, Oxford.

—— (1993) 'Effective Teaching: Implications for Quality Assurance', in R. Ellis (ed.), *Quality Assurance in Teaching*, Open University Press, Milton Keynes.

—— and Armstrong, S. (1978) 'SAID: A System for Analysing Instructional Discourse'. in R.W. McAleese and D.R. Hamilton (eds), *Understanding Classroom Life*, NFER, Slough.

—— and Armstrong, S. (1984) 'On Explaining', in E. C. Wragg (ed.), *Classroom Teaching Skills*, Croom Helm, London.

—— and Atkins, M. (1986) 'Explaining in Professional Contexts', *Research Papers in Education*, 1, 60–86.

—— and Atkins, M. (1988) *Effective Teaching in Higher Education*, Methuen, London.

—— and Bakhtar, M. (1988) 'Styles of Lecturing: A Study and its Implications', *Research Papers in Education*, 3, 131–53.

—— and Daines, J. (1981) 'Can Explaining be Learnt? Some Lecturers' Views', *Higher Education*, 10, 575–80.

—— and Hatton, N. (1982) *Explaining and Explanations*, Macmillan, London.

—— and Pendlebury, M. (1987) *Using Video in Dental Training*, mimeograph, Postgraduate Dental Office, Queens Medical Centre, Nottingham.

—— (1992) *Talking with Patients*, mimeograph, Postgraduate Dental Office, Queens Medical Centre, Nottingham.

—— and Wragg, E. C. (1993) *Questioning*, Routledge, London.

Brownbridge, J. (1987) *Doctor–Patient Communication in the Consulting room: Use of Computers in General Practice*, unpublished PhD thesis, University of Sheffield, Sheffield.

Byrne, P. S. and Long, B. E. (1976) *Doctors Talking to Patients*, HMSO, London.

Calderhead, J. (1996) 'Teachers: Beliefs and Knowledge', in D. Berliner (ed.), *The Handbook of Educational Psychology*, Macmillan, New York.

CINE (1986) *Report on the Communication in Nursing Education Curriculum Development Project: (Phase One)*, Health Education Council, London.

Cockroft, R. and Cockroft, S. M. (1992) *Persuading People: An Introduction to Rhetoric*, Macmillan, London.

Cody, M. J. and McLaughlin, M. L. (1988) 'Accounts on Trial: Oral Arguments in Traffic Court', in C. Antakis (ed.), *Analysing Everyday Explanations: A Casebook of Methods*, Sage, London.

Corah, N. (1984) 'Reduction of Patient Stress and the Patient–Dentist Relationship', *New York State Dental Journal*, 30, 478–9.

Cox, K. and Ewan, C. (1992) (eds) *The Medical Teacher*, Churchill Livingstone, Edinburgh.

Crowhurst, S. J. (1988) *Explaining in the Primary Classroom*, unpublished PhD thesis, University of Exeter, Exeter.

Crute, V. (1986) *Microtraining in Health Visiting Education*, unpublished PhD thesis, University of Ulster, Jordanstown.

Daines, J. M. (1985) 'Self Assessment in a Laboratory Course on Dispensing', unpublished PhD thesis, University of Nottingham, Nottingham.

Devine, E. C. and Cook, T. D. (1983) 'A Meta-analysis of the Effects of Psycho-educational Intervention on Length of Post-surgical Hospital Stay', *Nursing Research*, 32, 267–74.

Dewey, J. (1910) *How We Think*, D. C. Heath, Boston.

Dickson, D. (1995) 'Communication and Interpersonal Skills', in D. Sines (ed.), *Community Health Care Nursing*, Blackwell Science, Oxford.

—— and Bamford, D. (1995) 'Improving the Interpersonal Skills of Social Work Students: The Problem of Transfer of Training and What to do About It', *British Journal of Social Work*, 25, 85–105.

——, Hargie, O. and Tittmar, H. (1977) 'The Use of Microcounselling in the Training of Employment Advisory Officers', *Vocational Aspects of Education*, 29, 45–7.

——, Hargie, O. and Morrow, N. (1997) *Communication Skills Training for Health Professionals* (2nd edn), Chapman & Hall, London.

Draper, S. (1988) 'What's Going on in Everyday Explanations?', in C. Antakis (ed.), *Analysing Everyday Explanation: A Case Book of Methods*, Sage, London.

Dray, W. (1957) *Laws and Explanation in History,* Oxford University Press, Oxford.

Dunkin, M. J. (1986) 'Research on Teaching in Higher Education', in M. Wittrock (ed.), *Handbook of Research on Teaching*, Macmillan, New York.

—— (ed.) (1987) *International Encyclopaedia of Teaching and Teacher Education*, Pergamon, Oxford.

—— and Biddle, B. J. (1974) *The Study of Teaching*, Holt, Rinehart & Winston, New York.

Ennis, R. H. (1969) *Logic in Teaching*, Prentice-Hall, New York.

Entwistle, A. and Entwistle, N. J. (1992) 'Experience of Understanding in Revising for Degree Examinations', *Learning and Instruction*, 2, 1–22.

Entwistle, N. J. (1992) *The Impact of Teaching on Learning Outcomes*, UCoS DA, Sheffield.

—— (1996) 'The Nature of Academic Understanding', in G. Kaufman, T. Helstrup and K. H. Tergen (eds), *Problem Solving and Cognitive Processes*, Fagbokforlaget, Bergen.

—— and Marton, F. (1994) 'Knowledge Objects: Understanding Constituted Through Intensive Academic Study', *British Journal of Educational Psychology*, 62, 161–78.

Flanders, N. A. (1970) *Analysing Teaching Behaviour*, Addison-Wesley, New York.

Friedman, H. S. (1982) 'Non-verbal Communication in Medical Interaction', in H. Friedman and M. Di Matteo (eds), *Interpersonal Issues in Health Care*, Academic Press, New York.

Fry, J. (1992) *General Practice: The Facts*, Radcliffe Medical Press, Oxford.

Furnham, A. (1983) 'Social Skills and Dentistry', *British Dental Journal*, 154, 404–8.

Gage, N. L. (1972) 'Explorations of the Teacher's Effectiveness in Lecturing', in I. Westbury and A. Bellack (eds), *Research into Classroom Processes*, Teachers College Press, New York.

—— and Berliner, D. C. (1979) *Educational Psychology* (2nd edn), Rand McNally, Chicago.

——, Belgard, M., Dell, D. *et al.* (1968) *Explanations of the Teacher's Effectiveness in Explaining*, Technical Report No. 4, Stanford University Center for R and D in Teaching, Stanford, CA.

Gale, E., Carlsson, S., Erikson, A. and Jontell, M. (1984) 'Effects of Dentists' Behavior on Patient Attitudes', *Journal of the American Dental Association*, 109, 444–6.

Gallagher, M. (1987) *The Microskills Approach to Counsellor Training*, unpublished PhD thesis, University of Ulster, Jordanstown.

Genberg, V. (1992) 'Patterns and Organising Perspectives: a View of Expertise', *Teaching and Teacher Education*, 8, 485–95.

Gergen, M. M. (1988) 'Narrative Structures in Social Explanations', in C. Antakis (ed.), *Analysing Everyday Explanations: A Casebook of Methods*, Sage, London.

Greeno, J. G. and Riley, M. S. (1987) 'Processes and Development of Understanding', in F. E. Wenert and R. H. Kleuwe (eds), *Metacognition, Motivation and Understanding*, Erlbaum, Hillsdale, NJ.

Habeshaw, T. (1992) *Teaching Larger Groups: Making the Best of a Bad Job*, Education and Technical Associates, Bristol.

Hall, J. and Dornan, H. C. (1988) 'What Patients Like About their Medical Care and How Often Are They Asked: A Meta-analysis of the Satisfaction Literature', *Social Science and Medicine*, 27, 935–9.

Hamilton, M. A., Rouse, R. A. and Rouse, J. (1994) 'Dentist Communication and Patient Utilization of Dental Services: Anxiety Inhibition and Competence Enhancement Effects', *Health Communication*, 6, 137–58.

Hargie, C., Dickson, D. and Tourish, D. (1994) 'Communicaton Skills Training and the Radiography Profession: A Paradigm for Training and Development', *Research in Radiography*, 3, 6–18.

Hargie, O. and Morrow, N. (1986) 'A Survey of Interpersonal Skills Teaching in Pharmacy Schools in the United Kingdom and Ireland', *American Journal of Pharmaceutical Education*, 50, 172–4.

—— (1989) 'The Effectiveness of Microtraining in Developing Pharmacists' Communication Skills: A Study of Personality and Attitudes', *Medical Teacher*, 11, 195–203.

—— (1994) 'Pharmacist–Patient Communication: The Interpersonal Dimensions of Practice', in G. Harding, S. Nettleton and K. Taylor (eds), *Social Pharmacy: Innovation and Change*, The Pharmaceutical Press, London.

—— (1995) 'Evaluation of a Presentation Skills Course for Pharmacists', *The International Journal of Pharmacy: Practice*, 3, 101–5.

Hargie, O., Morrow, N. C. and Woodman, C. (1993) *Looking into Community Pharmacy: Identifying Effective Communication Skills in Pharmacist–Patient Consultations*, University of Ulster Press, Jordanstown.

Hargie, O., Saunders, C. and Dickson, D. A. (1994) *Social Skills in Interpersonal Communication* (3rd edn), Routledge, London.

Hatton, N. and Smith, D. (1995) 'Reflection in Teacher Education: Towards Definition and Implementation', *Teaching and Teacher Education*, 11, 33–51.

Henbest, R. J. and Stewart, M. (1989) 'Patient-centredness in the Consultation', *Family Practice*, 6, 249–53.

Hewstone, E. (1989) *Causal Attribution from Cognitive Processes to Collective Beliefs*, Blackwell, Oxford.

Hildebrand, M. (1973) 'The Character and Skills of the Effective Professor', *Journal of Higher Education*, 44, 41–50.

Hiller, J. (1971) 'Verbal Response Indicators of Conceptual Vagueness', *American Educational Research Journal*, 6, 661–75.

Hudson, B. L. (1981) 'The Social Casework Interview', in M. Argyle (ed.), *Social Skills and Health*, Methuen, London.

Hyman, R. T. (1974) *Teaching: Vantage Points for Study*, Lippincott Press, New York.

Jackson, E. and Katz, J. (1983) 'Implementation of Interpersonal Skills in Dental Schools', *Journal of Dental Education*, 47, 66–71.

Janz, N. K. and Becker, M. H. (1984) 'The Health Belief Model a Decade Later', *Health Education Quarterly*, 11, 1–47.

Jepson, C. (1986) 'Some Behavioural Aspects of Dental Compliance', *Journal of Dental Practice Administration*, 3, 117–22.

Klein, S. S. (1971) 'Student Influence on Teacher Behavior', *American Educational Research Journal*, 8, 403–21.

Kozma, R. B., Belle, L. W. and Williams, G. W. (1978) *Instructional Techniques in Higher Education*, Educational Technology Publications, Englewood Cliffs, NJ.

Kruglanski, A. (1988) *Basic Processes in Social Cognition: A Theory of Lay Epistemology*, Plenum Press, New York.

Land, M. L. (1985) 'Vagueness and Clarity in the Classroom', in T. Husen and T. N. Postlethwaite (eds), *International Encyclopaedia of Education: Research Studies*, Pergamon, Oxford.

Landrine, H. and Klonoff, F. A. (1992) 'Culture and Health-related Schemas: A Review and Proposal for Interdisciplinary Integration', *Health Psychology*, 11, 267–78.

Law, S. A. T. and Britten, N. (1995) 'Factors that Influence the Patient Centredness of a Consultation', *British Journal of General Practice*, 520–4.

Ley, P. and Llewellyn, S. (1995) 'Improving Patients' Understanding, Recall and Satisfaction and Compliance', in A. Broome amd S. Llewelyn (eds), *Health Psychology*, Chapman & Hall, London.

MacLeod Clark, J. (1985) 'The Development of Research in Interpersonal Skills in Nursing', in C. Kagan (ed.), *Interpersonal Skills in Nursing: Research and Applications*, Croom Helm, London.

Maguire, P. (1985) 'Deficiencies in Key Interpersonal Skills', in C. Kagan (ed.), *Interpersonal Skills in Nursing: Research and Applications*, Croom Helm, London.

—— (1990) 'Can Communication Skills be Taught?', *British Journal of Hospital Medicine*, 43, 215–16.

—— and Rutter, D. R. (1976) 'History-taking for Medical Students: Deficiencies in Performance', *The Lancet*, 2, 556–8.

Marsh, H. W. (1987) 'Students' Evaluation of University Teaching', *International Journal of Educational Research*, 11, 255–378.

Marteau, T. M. (1995) 'Health Beliefs and Attributions', in A. Broome and S. Llewelyn (eds), *Health Psychology*, Chapman & Hall, London.

Martin, J. K. (1970) *Explaining, Understanding and Teaching*, McGraw-Hill, New York.

Meichenbaum, D. (1977) *Cognitive-behavior Modification*, Plenum Press, New York.

Meuwessen. J., Schaap, C. and Van der Staak, C. (1991) 'Verbal Analysis of Doctor–Patient Communication', *Social Science and Medicine*, 32, 1143–50.

Montgomery, J. (1976) 'The Lecture as Discourse', MPhil thesis, University of Aston, Birmingham.

Morrow, N. and Hargie, O. (1987) 'Effectiveness of a Communication Skills Course in Continuing Pharmaceutical Education in Northern Ireland: A Longitudinal Study', *American Journal of Pharmaceutical Education*, 51, 148–52.

Morrow, N., Hargie, O. and Woodman, C. (1993) 'Consumer Perceptions of and Attitudes to the Advice-giving Role of Community Pharmacists', *Pharmaceutical Journal*, 251, 25–7.

Nickerson, R. S. (1985) 'Understanding Understanding', *American Journal of Education*, 93, 201–39.

Norman, D. and Bobrow, D. (1975) 'Active Memory Processing Perception and Cognition', in C. N. Cofer (ed.), *The Structure of Human Memory*, W. H. Freeman, San Francisco.

Parker, I. and Burman, E. (1993) 'Against Discursive Imperialism, Empiricism and Constructionism: Thirty two Problems with Discourse Analysis', in E. Gurman and I. Parker (eds), *Discourse Analysis Research*, Routledge, London.

Pask, G. (1976) 'Styles and Strategies of Learning', *British Journal of Educational Psychology*, 46, 128–48.

Pendlebury, M. (1988) 'Let's Call it the "Dental" Consultation', *British Dental Journal*, 165, 276–77.

Pendleton, D. (1981) 'A Situational Analysis of General Practice Consultations', in M. Argyle, A. Furnham and J. Graham (eds), *Social Situations*, Cambridge University Press, Cambridge.

—— (1983) in D. Pendleton and J. Hasler (eds), *Doctor–Patient Communication*, Academic Press, London.

—— and Bochner, S. (1980) 'The Communication of Medical Information in General Practice Consultations as a Function of Social Class', *Social Science and Medicine*, 14, 669–73.

——, Schofield, T., Tate, P. and Havelock, P. (1984) *The Consultation: An Approach to Teaching and Learning*, Oxford University Press, Oxford.

Pirianen-Marsh, A. (1985) 'The Lecture as Discourse', PhD thesis, University of Oulu, Finland.

Podell, R. N. (1975) *Physician's Guide to Compliance in Hypertension*, Merck, Pennsylvania.

Potter, J. and Wetherell, M. (1994) *Discourse and Social Psychology: Beyond Attitiudes and Behaviour*, Sage, London.

PSGB (1984) 'First Report of the Working Party on Pharmaceutical Education and Training', *Pharmaceutical Journal*, 232, 495–505.

Rae, J. P. (1989) 'Explanations and Communication Constraints in Naturally Occurring Discourse', PhD thesis, University of Leeds, Leeds.

Ricoeur, P. (1981) *Hermeneutics and the Human Sciences*, Cambridge University Press, Cambridge.

Robinson, A. (1995) 'Patients' Contribution to the Consultation', in Broome, A. and Llewelyn, S. (eds), *Health Psychology*, Chapman & Hall, London.

Rosenshine, B. (1972) *Teaching Behaviours and Student Achievement*, IEA Studies No. I, National Foundation of Education Research.

Roter, D. (1989) 'Which Aspects of Communication have Strong Effects on Outcomes?', in M. Stewart and D. Roter (eds), *Communicating with Medical Patients*, Sage, London.

Ryle, G. (1963) *The Concept of Mind* (reprint), Penguin, Harmondsworth.

Saunders, C. and Caves, R. (1986) 'An Empirical Approach to the Identification of Communication Skills with Reference to Speech Therapy', *Journal of Further and Higher Education*, 10, 29–44.

Saunders, C. and Saunders, E. D. (1993a) *Expert Teachers' Perceptions of University Teaching: The Identification of Teaching Skills*, University of Ulster Press, Jordanstown.

—— (1993b) 'Expert Teachers' Perceptions of University Teaching: the Identification of Teaching Skills', in R. Ellis (ed.), *Quality Assurance for University Teaching*, Open University Press, Milton Keynes.

Shotter, J. (1975) *Images of Man in Psychological Research*, Methuen, London.

Shutes, R. (1969) 'Verbal Behaviours and Instructional Effectiveness', *Dissertation Abstracts International.*

Skopek, L. (1979) 'Doctor–Patient Conversations: A Way of Analysing its Linguistic Problems', *Semiotica*, 301–11.

Smith, B. O. and Meux, M. O. (1970) *A Study of the Logic of Teaching*, University of Illinois Press, Illinois.

Stewart, M. and Roter, D. (1989) (eds) *Community with Medical Patients,* Sage, London.

Strickland, B. (1978) 'Internal–External Expectancies and Health-related Behaviour', *Consulting Clinical Psychology*, 46, 1192–211.

Swift, L. F. (1961) 'Explanation', in R. H. Ennis and B. O. Smith (eds), *Language and Concepts in Education*, Rand McNally, Chicago.

Taylor, D. M. (1970) *Explanation and Meaning*, Cambridge University Press, Cambridge.

Thyne, J. M . (1966) *The Psychology of Learning and Techniques of Teaching*, University of London Press (2nd edn), London.

Tisher, R. P. (1970) 'The Nature of Verbal Discourse in Classrooms and Association Between Verbal Discourse and Pupil Understanding in Science', in W. J. Campbell (ed.), *Scholars in Context*, John Wiley, Sydney.

Toulmin, S. (1958) *The Uses of Argument*, Cambridge University Press, Cambridge.

Trower, P. (1981) 'Psychotherapy', in M. Argyle (ed.), *Social Skills and Health*, Methuen, London.

Tuckett, D.A., Boulton, M.G., Olson, C. S. *et al.* (1985) *Meetings Between Experts: A Study of Medical Consultations*, Tavistock, London.

Turney, C., Ellis, K. J. and Hatton, N. (1983) *Sydney Microskills Redeveloped, Vol.1*, University of Sydney, Sydney.

Wakeford, R. (1983) 'Communication Skills Training in United Kingdom Medical Schools', in D. Pendleton and J. Hasler, *Doctor–Patient Communication*, Academic Press, London.

Weston, W. W. and Brown, J. B. (1989) 'The Importance of Patients' Beliefs', in M. Stewart and D. Roter (eds), *Communicating with Medical Patients*, Sage, London.

White, P. A. (1990) 'Ideas about Causation in Philosophy and Psychology', *Psychological Bulletin*, 108, 3–18.

Wragg E. C. (ed.) (1984) *Classroom Teaching Skills*, Croom Helm, London.

—— (1993) *Primary Teaching Skills*, Routledge, London.

—— and Brown, G. A. (1993) *Explaining*, Routledge, London.

8 Self-disclosure

Charles H. Tardy and Kathryn Dindia

INTRODUCTION

Self-disclosure, the process whereby people verbally reveal themselves to others, constitutes an integral part of all relationships. As stated by Rubin, 'In every sort of interpersonal relationship, from business partnerships to love affairs, the exchange of self disclosure plays an important role' (1973, p. 168). People disclose to friends and spouses, to physicians and hairdressers, to solicitors and pub governors. The importance of self-disclosure for individuals and their relationships is not always apparent. Revelation of such mundane matters as the events of the day may be a cherished ritual in a marriage (Sigman, 1991; Vangelisti and Banski, 1993), while people sometimes confide personal problems to virtual strangers (Cowen, 1982).

The pervasiveness and importance of self-disclosure accounts for the intense interest in this phenomenon shown by social scientists. Literally thousands of quantitative studies have been conducted over a period extending forty years. The periodic publication of reviews of this literature has helped to provide coherence and to organise this body of knowledge. Both reviews of thematic issues (e.g. Dindia and Allen, 1992) as well as more comprehensive treatments (e.g. Derlega *et al.*, 1993) enable readers to cope with a mounting body of knowledge.

The present review offers a strategic perspective on the self-disclosure literature by highlighting the motivations and means by which people manage the disclosure of information in personal and work relationships. We review literature that describes the disclosure of personal information in friendships and romantic relationships as well as in relationships with supervisors, subordinates and co-workers. We focus on three facets of disclosure in these two contexts: the strategic use of disclosure, consequences of disclosures, and elicitation of disclosures.

SELF-DISCLOSURE IN PERSONAL RELATIONSHIPS

Self-disclosure and personal relationships are 'mutually transformative', meaning that self-disclosure changes the direction, definition and intensity of relationships, and the nature of the relationship changes the meaning or impact of self-disclosure (Derlega *et al.*, 1993). Revelations of information about the self serve important functions in the initiation, development, maintenance and termination of relationships. Self-disclosure has important relational consequences, including eliciting liking and reciprocal self-disclosure. Requests for disclosure are common when individuals want information about their partner, including details about the partner's sexual history in order to engage in safe sex.

Strategic disclosure of information

Self-disclosure performs important relational functions (Archer and Earle, 1983; Derlega and Grzelak, 1979). Revealing information about self can help people as they attempt to initiate and develop relationships with others. Some authors even suggest that self-disclosure may be a strategy by which people seek to obtain desirable responses from others (Schank and Abelson, 1977; Miller and Read, 1987; Baxter, 1987). On the other hand, self-disclosing some information creates problems for individuals and relationships. Telling others exactly how we feel can be cruel and destroy trust. Consequently, individuals must learn how to regulate or control their disclosures. Below we discuss both the role of self-disclosure in different stages of relationship development and the necessity of managing personal information by regulating self-disclosures (see Chapter 14 for a detailed discussion of relational communication).

Relationship initiation and development

Self-disclosure is used to initiate relationships. In initial interaction people reveal their names, home towns, hobbies, and so on. As stated by Derlega *et al.* (1993, pp. 1–2), 'it is hard to imagine how a relationship might get started without such self-disclosure'.

Self-disclosure in the initial phases of a relationship functions to promote liking (which we will discuss in more detail later) and to help people to get to know each other. Self-disclosure provides information that helps us to reduce uncertainty about the other person's attitudes, values, personality, and so on, thereby enabling the relationship to develop (Berger and Bradac, 1982). Similarly, through self-disclosure we acquire mutual knowledge, or knowledge that two people share, know they share and use in interacting with one another (Planalp and Garvin-Doxas, 1994).

Self-disclosure is also an important component in the development of a relationship, whereby: 'If you like this person, you will want to know more about him or her, and you will, in turn, be willing to share more information about yourself. You will begin to talk about attitudes, feelings, and personal experiences; in brief, you will begin to disclose more personal information. If your new friend likes you, he or she also will disclose personal information' (Derlega *et al.*, 1993, p. 2).

Research indicates that people strategically use self-disclosure to regulate the development of a relationship. In Miell and Duck's (1986) study of strategies individuals use to develop and restrict the development of friendships, subjects described how they got to know others and how they chose appropriate topics of conversation for interacting with someone they had just met and a close friend. They also indicated strategies they would use to restrict and intensify a relationship's development. Superficial self-disclosure, appropriate for conversing with a stranger, was also reported to restrict the development of a relationship. Similarly, intimate self-disclosure, appropriate for conversing with friends, was used to intensify a relationship. Thus, when individuals want to become friends, they talk like friends; when they want to remain distant, they continue to talk like strangers.

Similarly, in Tolhuizen's (1989) study of romantic relationships, seriously dating college students reported self-disclosing information about self (e.g. 'I told my partner a great deal about myself – more than I had told anyone before') as a strategy to intensify dating relationships. Another strategy was to disclose information about the relationship, feelings in the relationship, and what is desired for the future of the relationship (e.g. 'we sat down and discussed our relationship so far, how we felt about each other and what we wanted for the relationship'). Thus, disclosing information about yourself as well as your thoughts and feelings about the relationship are strategies to increase the intimacy of a relationship.

Relational maintenance

Self-disclosure is important for maintaining a relationship. Self-disclosure about the events of the day, referred to as 'catching up' or 'debriefing', is an important relationship maintenance strategy. All relationships involve periods when the partners are away from each other (e.g. while they are at work). One of the behaviours used by partners to maintain the continuity of their relationship across these periods of physical absence is catching up (Sigman, 1991). When couples are reunited at the end of the day they often talk about what happened during the day: how their day went, who they saw, what they did, etc. Research indicates that debriefing one another is a relationship maintenance strategy that is positively related to marital satisfaction (Vangelisti and Banski, 1993).

Self-disclosure of intimate information is also important for maintaining a relationship. Once partners feel they know each other, the exchange of objective or factual information about the self probably decreases (Fitzpatrick, 1987). As a relationship progresses the amount of subjective or emotional information that can be exchanged between partners increases; not only how the speaker feels about him or herself but also how the speaker feels about the partner and the relationship can be revealed. Thus, self-disclosure in ongoing relationships continues to include the disclosure of facts and feelings about the self, but it also includes feelings about the partner and the relationship. As stated by Fitzpatrick (1987, p. 40), 'Individuals in ongoing relationships may discuss their emotional reactions to one another, and these reactions may become a major part of the relationship'.

Research by Canary *et al.* (1993) indicates the prevalence of intimate disclosure as a relational maintenance strategy. People were asked how they maintained three different personal relationships over the course of the term. The most frequent relational maintenance strategy was intimate self-disclosure.

In the late 1960s to the early 1970s, openness was advocated and open communication was considered the essence of a good relationship. Jourard (1971, p. 46), as well as others, advocated full disclosure in relationships: 'the optimum . . . in any relationship between persons, is a relationship . . . where each partner discloses himself without reserve.' More recently, others (Bochner, 1982; Parks, 1982; Cline, 1982) have argued that moderate levels of self-disclosure lead to satisfaction in long-term relationships. Gilbert (1976) conducted a review of the research and found support for a curvilinear relationship between self-disclosure and satisfaction; moderate degrees of self-disclosure appeared to be most conducive to maintaining relationships over time.

An alternative conclusion is that openness is an effective communication strategy for some types of couples but not others. Fitzpatrick (1987) described three types of couples – traditionals, independents and separates – and argued that there are similarities within, and differences among, the types of couples in the degree to which they self-disclose and value self-disclosure in their marriages. Fitzpatrick argued that these couple types establish different norms about what is appropriate to reveal in their relationship and that these norms determine the relationship between communication and satisfaction. Fitzpatrick found that traditionals value self-disclosure in marriage and that they self-disclose to their spouses. However, their self-disclosure is limited to positive feelings and topics about the partner and the relationship. Independent couples value self-disclosure and disclose substantially more to their spouses than other types of couples and are willing to disclose both positive and negative feelings to one another. Separates do not value openness and self-disclosure in marriage and do not self-disclose to their spouses. Thus, self-disclosure is important to maintain a relationship but full disclosure should not be universally prescribed.

Relational de-escalation

Self-disclosure is also used to terminate relationships (Baxter, 1985, 1987). Although some relationships fade away without either party actively doing anything to actively and intentionally end the relationship, most relationship disengagements are accomplished through strategic communication by one or both relational partners.

Baxter (1987) argued that there are multiple stages to the dissolution of relationships and that self-disclosure is used differently in the stages. Baxter divides relationship disengagement into three stages: private decision-making, decision implementation, and public presentation. During private decision-making the individual contemplates existing dissatisfactions with the other partner and with the relationship, reaching the decision to end the relationship. Self-disclosure is strategically employed during this stage to acquire information about the partner's satisfaction with the relationship, to acquire information on the likelihood that the partner would be willing to repair the relationship and to acquire information from the social network regarding their perceptions of self, partner and the relationship. Relational disclosure, in which the discloser reveals personal feelings about the relationship, is a strategy used to induce reciprocal relational disclosure from the partner and from social network members. The likelihood of using this strategy is low but increases if alternative strategies have failed, the disengager lacks sufficient skill in enacting indirect information acquisition strategies, or the secondary goal of face-saving is relatively unimportant to the disengager.

During the decision implementation stage the disengager seeks to accomplish the dissolution of the relationship through actions directed at the partner. Withdrawal, including reduced self-disclosure, is the most common strategy and is used to indirectly terminate relationships (Baxter, 1985). Relational self-disclosure, in which a person directly presents the partner with personal feelings about the relationship ('I don't love you anymore') is used less frequently to terminate relationships.

At the public presentation stage the dissolution of the relationship becomes official to social network members. Here the goal of self-disclosure is to make public the dissolution of the relationship while simultaneously maintaining face with the social network. These goals require selective self-disclosure to others.

Relational dialectics/boundary management theory

One of the important principles of a strategic perspective on self-disclosure is that individuals usually have multiple goals in interaction and relationships. Sometimes the goals are compatible and the pursuit of one goal facilitates the accomplishment of the other. However, sometimes the goals are contradictory and the fulfilment of one goal conflicts with the fulfilment of the other (Schank and Abelson, 1977). For example, the goal of being open and honest with your partner may conflict with the goal of maintaining the relationship. Recent theories have attributed greater importance to the forces mitigating against self-disclosure in relationships.

Early theories on personal relationships, such as Altman and Taylor's Social Penetration Theory (Altman and Taylor, 1973; Taylor and Altman, 1987), argued that there is a linear relationship between self-disclosure and relationship development; self-disclosure gradually and incrementally increases as the relationship develops. Many scholars have rejected the idea that the development of relationships always follows a unidirectional and cumulative path, with ever-increasing openness of self-disclosure (Altman *et al.*, 1981). As argued by these authors, initial theory and research on self-disclosure was overly simplistic. Instead, more recent theories recognise the possibility that developing or continuing relationships might exhibit cycles of openness and closedness or that some relationships might not progress towards increased openness at all (Altman *et al.*, 1981). Although some relationships may generally proceed towards greater openness, they probably have cycles or phases of openness or closedness within this overall developmental pattern.

Recent scholarly literature views relationships as involving contradictory and opposing forces (Baxter, 1988; Baxter and Montgomery, in press; Montgomery, 1993). These theorists posit openness–closedness or expressiveness–protectiveness as a dialectical tension in relationships (Baxter, 1988; Rawlins, 1983). Individuals continually face the contradictory impulses to be open and expressive versus protective of self and/or of other. Self-disclosure is necessary to achieve intimacy and trust in a relationship but self-disclosure opens areas of vulnerability; to avoid hurting each other, people must undertake protective measures. Thus, the contradictory dilemma between being open and closed requires decisions to reveal or conceal personal information.

Rawlins (1983) identified two conversational dilemmas resulting from the contradictory impulses to be open and expressive and to be protective of self and/or of other. An individual confronts the contradictory dilemma of striving to be open or to protect self when deciding whether to self-disclose to the partner or restrict personal disclosure. Disclosing personal information to another makes one susceptible to being hurt by the other. The decision to self-disclose will be a function of at least two things: the individual's perceived need to be open about a given issue, and the individual's trust of the partner's discretion (the latter's abilities to keep a secret and exercise restraint regarding self's sensitivities). The decision to reveal or conceal involves assessing what will be gained or lost by either choice.

In deciding whether to disclose statements regarding partner (e.g. 'I don't like your haircut') an individual confronts the contradictory dilemma of protecting a partner versus striving to be open and honest. The decision to self-disclose or restrict disclosure of negative information will be a function of the self's perceived need to be honest about a given issue and the amount of restraint appropriate to the topic. An individual develops an awareness of topics which make the other vulnerable to hurt or anger. In particular, '*self must determine whether telling the truth is worth causing the other pain and breaching the other's trust in self's protective inclinations*' (Rawlins, 1983, p. 10, italics in original).

Individuals can respond to the dialectical tension of openness–closedness with a number of strategic responses. Baxter (1990) found that the most dominant strategy reported for the openness–closedness contradiction was segmentation, which involved a differentiation of the topic domains into those for which self-disclosure was appropriate and those regarded as 'taboo topics' (i.e. topics that are 'off limits' in a relationship). Baxter and Wilmot (1985) found the following 'taboo topics' in opposite-sex relationships: the state of the relationship, past relationships, other present relationships, relationship norms, conflict-inducing topics, and negatively valanced self-disclosures.

Similarly, privacy regulation is a strategic response to the dialectical nature of self-disclosure. Altman (1975) defined privacy as 'an interpersonal boundary process by which a person or group regulates interaction with others. By altering the degree of openness of the self to others, a hypothetical personal boundary is more or less receptive to social interaction with others' (p. 6). Similarly, Communication Boundary Management Theory (Petronio, 1988, 1991) argues that individuals manage their communication boundaries in balancing the need for disclosure with the need for privacy. The basic thesis of communication boundary management theory is that revealing private information is risky because one is potentially vulnerable when revealing aspects of the self. To manage disclosing private information, individuals erect a metaphoric boundary as a means of protection and to reduce the possibility of being rejected or getting hurt (Petronio, 1991). Thus, privacy regulation is a strategic response to the dialectical tension of the need to reveal and conceal. By regulating privacy we engage in a strategy designed to satisfy the oppositional forces of openness and closedness.

The dialectical perspective paints a more complex picture of the skills involved in competent self-disclosure. Competent self-disclosure is responsive to partners' needs for intimacy and privacy. Rawlins' (1983) analysis suggests that it may be just as important for an individual to develop skill at restrained remarks and selective disclosure of intimate information: 'An apt handling of the dialectic means that self limits self's own vulnerability and strives to protect other while still expressing thoughts and feelings' (Rawlins, 1983, p. 5). According to a dialectical perspective, 'we cannot mandate a specific style for relational interaction and scholars should be cautious in stressing open communication as the hallmark of intimacy' (Rawlins, 1983, p. 13).

Disclosure consequences

Self-revelations inevitably elicit reactions from recipients. They are rarely ignored or unrecognised. Some responses are highly predictable. Some are desired and some undesired, some positive and some negative. In this section, we discuss research on how people respond to the disclosures they receive from others.

Reciprocal disclosures

Perhaps the most enduring generalisation from the literature on this topic is that self-disclosure is reciprocal. The pioneering researcher, Sidney Jourard (1971, p. 66), noted: 'in ordinary social relationships, disclosure is a reciprocal phenomenon. Participants in dialogue disclose their thoughts, feelings, actions, etc., to the other and are disclosed to in return. I called this reciprocity the 'dyadic effect': disclosure begets disclosure.' A recent meta-analysis of over sixty studies (Dindia and Allen, 1995) found that self-disclosure is reciprocal, although the degree of matching depends on how reciprocity was measured.

Several theories explain reciprocity of self-disclosure, including trust-attraction, social exchange and modelling (Archer, 1979). The trust-attraction hypothesis assumes that disclosing intimate information to a recipient indicates that the other is liked and trusted and this leads the recipient to disclose, as a sign of liking and a willingness to trust the original discloser. The social exchange perspective suggests that receiving disclosure is a rewarding experience and that when we receive something of value, we feel obligated to return something of similar value (i.e. a similar disclosure). The modelling hypothesis posits that one person's self-disclosure serves as a model for the other person. If one person self-discloses and the other is unsure how to respond, the recipient will then reciprocate the first person's self-disclosure. In reviewing the research on the explanation for reciprocity of self-disclosure, Archer (1979) stated that the social exchange explanation has received the most support, although this support is indirect; that the modelling hypothesis has not been totally disconfirmed; and that the trust-attraction account has been virtually refuted. However, Archer goes on to say that any of the three could produce reciprocity under some circumstances and that all three may contribute to reciprocity in some combination in many settings. More recent theoretical explanations attribute reciprocity to more global constraints of conversational norms, i.e. rules that indicate the kinds of comments that would be appropriate given previous comments (Derlega *et al.*, 1993), such as the require-ment to make your message topically relevant to the previous statement (Cappella, 1981).

Reciprocity of self-disclosure is assumed to be a time-bound process in which people mutually regulate their self-disclosure to one another at some agreed-on pace. But little more is known about the temporal aspects of reciprocity. The rate at which it occurs, how it ebbs and flows, and factors that accelerate or retard reciprocity of exchange have not been discussed in detail. There is some reason to believe that immediate reciprocity declines as the relationship increases in intimacy and commitment (e.g. Altman, 1973).

Berg and Archer (1980) noted that a variety of responses to self-disclosure are appro-priate and that a common reaction to receiving intimate self-disclosure is to express concern or support, rather than to reciprocate self-disclosure. In their experimental study, Berg and Archer (1980) observed that the most favourable impressions were made by listeners who expressed concern for a discloser rather than listeners who responded with self-disclosures. Thus, it may be more important to respond to self-disclosure with interest and support, rather than to immediately reciprocate self-disclosure. You may always reciprocate self-disclosure at a later, more appropriate, time.

Self-disclosure and liking

Self-disclosure and liking are thought to be related in at least three ways: self-disclosure to another person causes the other person to like the discloser, liking another person causes an individual to self-disclose and individuals like another person as a result of having disclosed to him or her. A recent meta-analysis (Collins and Miller, 1994) of the research on self-disclosure and liking confirmed that we like people who self-disclose to us, we disclose more to people we like and we like others as a result of having disclosed to them (although the number of studies examining the latter effect is small and the finding should be interpreted with caution).

The effect of self-disclosure on a recipient's liking for the discloser has been of greatest theoretical interest; works examining this effect make up the bulk of the studies on self-disclosure and liking (Collins and Miller, 1994). This effect is typically referred to as the 'disclosure-liking hypothesis'. Although the research indicates that self-disclosure leads to liking, there are at least two qualifications to the disclosure-liking relationship. First, disclosure that violates normative expectations will not lead to liking. Low-intimacy, descriptive self-disclosures that reflect positively on the self are normative in initial interactions. Revealing information that deviates from this norm may produce negative evaluations (Bochner, 1982). Even in developed relationships, norms exist specifying appropriate and inappropriate topics for discussion (Baxter and Wilmot, 1985). Research also indicates that the disclosure of negatively valanced information does not lead to liking (Gilbert and Horenstein, 1975). As Bochner (1982, p. 120) stated, 'discriminating disclosers are more satisfied and more likely to remain attractive to their partners than are indiscriminating disclosers'. Second, people who disclose a lot to everyone are not liked more than low disclosers. Miller (1990) observed that sorority women who generally disclosed more to others were not more popular than other members. However, women who disclosed more to a particular partner than they generally disclosed to others were liked more by that partner.

People make attributions regarding another person's disclosure and the reasons or motivations we attribute to another person's self-disclosure are an important part of what the self-disclosure will mean to the relationship (Derlega *et al.*, 1993). People can attribute another person's self-disclosure to the person's disposition or personality ('he disclosed to me because he is an open person') or to their relationship ('he disclosed to me because he likes me or because we have an intimate relationship'). When we perceive another person's self-disclosure as personalistic (revealed only to the target) rather than non-personalistic (revealed to many people) it leads to increased liking (Berg and Derlega, 1987). Collins and Miller (1994) concluded from their meta-analysis of the research on self-disclosure and liking that the relationship between disclosure and liking is stronger if the recipient believes that the disclosure was only shared with the recipient. In sum, the relationship between liking and disclosure is not simple.

These results have important practical applications for the skill of self-disclosure. High disclosers are not liked more than low disclosers. Instead, disclosure leads to liking when the information is appropriate, i.e. not too intimate or too negative for the situation or the relationship, and when the recipient perceives the information is being selectively revealed.

Requests for disclosures

Strategies for eliciting self-disclosure

For a variety of reasons, people frequently desire personal information about others. Berger and Calabrese (1975) suggested that 'when strangers meet, their primary concern is one of uncertainty reduction' (1975, p. 100). To reduce that uncertainty, initial interactants engage in high levels of information-seeking. There are several strategies for acquiring information about a partner in interactions, the most obvious being to ask questions. However, because norms of social appropriateness restrict the use of information requests (Berger *et al.*, 1976; Berger, 1979), initial interactants are hypothesised to use less direct strategies as well. In particular, participants in initial interaction may use self-disclosure to acquire information about each other (Archer and Earle, 1983; Berger and Bradac, 1982). Because of the norm of reciprocity, self-disclosure is a 'potentially powerful way to induce the other to disclose similar information about himself' (Berger, 1979, p. 141). This is especially true in initial interaction, where the need to reciprocate self-disclosure immediately and on a tit-for-tat basis is strong.

Douglas (1990) found that self-disclosure occurred more frequently than asking questions during a 6-minute initial conversation between strangers: across the entire conversation 49 per cent of the utterances were coded as self-disclosures, whereas 18 per cent of the utterances were coded as questions. As the conversation continued, individuals' uncertainty level and question-asking decreased but their self-disclosure increased. Thus, disclosure appears to be a more appropriate strategy than asking questions for acquiring information in initial interaction.

Self-disclosure and safe sex

Although attaining information about past relationships, other present relationships, sexual habits and sexual experiences is necessary for making informed choices for sexual intimacy (Cline *et al.*, 1990), these topics are taboo in developing relationships (Baxter and Wilmot, 1985). Little is known about the extent to which people attempt to talk with their partners about AIDS prevention, either to know the partner or to obtain the partner's sexual history (Cline *et al.*, 1990). However, the few studies that have been conducted of college students (Bowen and Michal-Johnson, 1989; Chervin and Martinez, 1987; Cline *et al.*, 1992) indicate that only a minority talk about AIDS prevention (e.g. condom use, sexual history, monogamy) with a sexual partner.

Even less is known about how people go about talking about AIDS prevention. Edgar *et al.* (1992) examined the type of information-seeking strategies individuals use to reduce uncertainty about a potential partner prior to the first sexual encounter. The most frequently reported interaction strategy was question-asking: 39 per cent of the sample reported asking the partner directly about the partner's sexual history and health, etc. The second most common interaction strategy was unsolicited self-disclosure (17 per cent); the other person volunteered the information. Eight per cent of the participants reported that they introduced the topic into a conversation in hopes that the information would come out while they were talking. Five per cent of the sample reported reciprocal self-disclosure: 'I disclosed this information to him or her in hopes that she or he would reciprocate and disclose the same information to me.' This study indicates that although more direct methods of information-seeking (questions) may be used when soliciting information about something as important as AIDS prevention, less direct methods, such as requests for self-disclosure, unsolicited self-disclosure, bringing up the topic with the hopes that the other person will self-disclose and reciprocal self-disclosure, also function to provide information and reduce uncertainty about a potential sexual partner.

SELF-DISCLOSURE IN WORK ENVIRONMENTS

While considerable efforts have been expended assessing the role of self-disclosure in personal relationships, social scientists have not systematically examined the revelation of personal information in task or work relationships. This omission is unfortunate because work consumes a significant portion of most people's daily lives and talking about personal experiences at work is perhaps the most common activity among people in disparate occupations and professions. Moreover, a close examination of relevant organisational research indicates that self-disclosure plays an important role in the development and maintenance of relationships in the employment context (see Steele, 1975 for a practical discussion of these issues). Consequently, this half of the chapter reviews literature from diverse sources to identify the factors affecting the revelation of personal information and the consequences of self-disclosure in work organisations.

Strategic disclosure of information

Some self-disclosures may be revealed to further an individual's goals in an encounter with other people. These revelations may present a desired self-image or invoke a favourable response from the recipient (Archer and Earle, 1983; Derlega and Grzelak, 1979). Strategic disclosures may be made consciously and intentionally, following a careful consideration of the potential consequences of the revelation. Such mindful consideration of communicative behaviour appears most likely to occur when people cannot follow a preformulated interaction plan or script (Berger and Douglas, 1992) – i.e. when people encounter enigmatic episodes. However, self-disclosure might also be strategic when it is part of the script that people choose to implement in a social situation. Common to work organisations are several circumstances that are likely to evidence strategic disclosure: when bad news must be delivered to a superior, when support is being sought and when stigmatising information is revealed.

Revealing risky information

Employees should, and no doubt do, consider and weigh the consequences for the revelation of information that is risky, that is, will potentially produce adverse reactions from the receivers of the disclosure. Three distinct types of information may produce this risk and will be described below: negative job performance, personal problems and stigmas.

Bad news: upward distortion of performance-related information

Organisational researchers have long noted the problem of 'upward distortion', whereby negative information is withheld and only positive information is communicated up the organisational structure (for a discussion of the general bias against revealing negative information see Tesser and Rosen, 1975). Research consistently indicates that information will be distorted if it is unfavourable to the discloser (Dansereau and Markham, 1987). For example, the accountant doesn't want to tell the supervisor that inflation was not considered when estimating next year's expenses and the sales representative would not want the manager to know about the customer who took business to another company because of the rep's failure to return telephone calls. While troubling for the individual, such information is crucial for the effective functioning of organisations. Weick (1990) described one dramatic example in which job stress and organisational command structures contributed to pilots' and air traffic controllers' unwillingness to reveal their confusion or uncertainty, resulting in airliners crashing and killing hundreds of people. While few failures to disclose have such dramatic and costly consequences, the incident illustrates how important employee disclosures can be.

Few empirical investigations assess the factors that facilitate these revelations, though Steele (1975) recommended organisational development strategies for facilitating openness. Extant research consistently suggests that trust plays a decisive role in the disclosure of negative information. Fulk and Mani (1986) reported that employees are more likely to distort or withhold information from supervisors perceived to distort and withhold information. This conclusion supports the earlier findings of Mellinger (1956) that people are less likely to distort information communicated to people they trust. Consequently, supervisors who provide accurate information to subordinates should be more likely to receive negative disclosures than supervisors who provide distorted information. Likewise, Roberts and O'Reilly's (1974) frequently cited study indicated that perception of trust in a supervisor was negatively correlated with reports of withholding and distorting information. In general terms, then, trust plays an influential role in decisions affecting disclosure in the work environment just as it does outside of work (e.g. Larzelere and Huston, 1980).

Revelation of personal problems in support-seeking attempts

To gain assistance, emotional support or practical aid from others, people must reveal their problems (see review in Derlega *et al.*, 1993). Organisations can either encourage or discourage such revelations. In the last twenty years, many organisations have instituted procedures and programmes to foster employee disclosure of personal problems. People who seek this help must disclose events, incidents, issues from their lives that warrant change (see Sonnenstuhl *et al.*, 1988, for a discussion of differences among self-referrals and other referrals). Employee assistance programmes (EAPs) are seen by organisations as the preferred alternative for minimising the work place effects of employee problems, ranging from drug abuse to child care (e.g. Rosen, 1987; Soloman, 1992). Over the last two decades many organisations have instituted EAPs to help employees with any personal problems that interfere with job performance. For example, one report estimates there are more than 10,000 EAPs in the US and that more than three-quarters of Fortune 500 companies sponsor EAPs (Luthans and Walersee, 1990). Although reports of the success of these programmes abound, the empirical evidence is limited (Luthans and Walersee, 1990).

One review of the literature on this subject suggested that four steps are necessary to encourage self-referrals: eliminate stigma, assure anonymity, train employees and encourage employee self-analyses (Myers, 1984). The few quantitative studies of employee decisions to utilise EAPs indicate that employee confidence in the EAP was the most important attitudinal factor affecting propensity to use this service (Harris and Fennell, 1988; Milne *et al.*, 1994). Corporations are discouraged from giving these divisions names that accentuate negative connotations such as 'Drug Rehabilitation Programme'. This advice is particularly appropriate because only a small percentage of the problems dealt with by EAPs are drug- and alcohol-related (e.g. 'Success Story', 1991). Numerous authors note the importance of confidentiality (e.g. Feldman, 1991). However, the required secrecy that prevents peers from learning of the problems experienced by their co-workers also reduces the opportunity for peer support (e.g. Koch, 1990).

Revelation of stigmatising personal information

Examples of stigmatising information that are particularly salient in the work context include previously being fired from a job, disability, and ill health such as HIV infection or AIDS (Koch, 1990). Several authors suggest that persons with disabilities can lessen the uncertainties and tensions of their interactional partners by acknowledging their disability (e.g. Evans, 1976; Thompson, 1982). However, such disclosures may prove effective only if the disabled person reassures the other 'that a disabled person is not hypersensitive about the disability' (Coleman and DePaulo, 1991, p. 82).

Another type of information that is risky for employees to reveal, both to employers as well as to peers, is preference for alternative life-styles or non-heterosexual identities. Revealing a homosexual orientation may allow a person to 'be' himself or herself, remove the individual's fear of being 'outed', and/or relieve the person of feelings of shame, self-doubt, or hypocrisy. However, revealing an alternative life-style or sexual orientation has potential negative consequences: personal rejection, loss of job and disrupted relationships also can occur.

Schneider (1986) reported a study of factors that predict the revelation of lesbian identity to co-workers. She found that women working with adults, working in female-dominated settings and earning low incomes more frequently reported disclosing their sexual identity. Loss of prior job because of sexual identity discrimination mitigated against disclosure. These factors apparently affect the risk of negative consequences resulting from the disclosure. The process by which lesbians weigh these factors is described by Hitchcock and Wilson (1992).

Requests for disclosures

Sometimes individuals don't initiate disclosures but must respond to others' requests for information about self. Employment interviews routinely elicit disclosures from job applicants. Additionally, people are sometimes asked to make undesired disclosures.

Employment interviews

While performing numerous functions, the initial job interview primarily serves to provide the employer with information allowing the discrimination of applicants and to provide the interviewee with information concerning potential employment (see Chapter 15 for a full review of the employment interview). Although both the interviewer and interviewee roles require the selective revelation of information, the disclosures by the interviewee are much more likely to be personal than are the disclosures revealed by, and about, the employer. The standard script for employment interviews includes a section where questions are asked about the applicant's personal, educational and work history (Tullar, 1989). Additionally, some interview research (e.g. Janz, 1989) suggests that interviewers should rely less on speculative questions, such as, 'what would you do IF' (p.160) and more on questions requiring recollection of specific behaviours such as, 'what did you do WHEN' (p. 160). Interviews based on these questions have been shown to improve the selection decision process and result in hiring people who perform better on the job (Jablin and Krone, 1994). Additionally, a review of research on interviewing (Jablin and Miller, 1990) concluded that interviewees infrequently seek information about or opinions of interviewers. Thus, personal revelations by interviewees are an integral part of and may reasonably be said to be the primary focus of employment interviews.

What kind of disclosures do interviewees reveal? Given the importance of making a positive impression, it might be expected that the interviewee will reveal largely attributes and experiences that portray the speaker most favourably. As one guide suggests, interviewees 'try to demonstrate the characteristics of the interviewers' ideal employee through answers and references to their education and experience' (Stewart and Cash, 1988, p. 157). Research predictably indicates that interviewers rate more highly interviewees who present favourable information (Rowe, 1989), elaborate answers and talk fluently (Jablin, 1987). Gilmore and Ferris (1989, p. 200) stated: 'Most job seekers try to present their positive qualities in an interview, with self-enhancing statements intending to create a good impression. Statements that suggest positive qualities or traits, if credible, should positively influence the interviewer. This somewhat obvious ingratiation technique is employed frequently by applicants seeking to bolster their image in an interview.' Also, interviewers ask more questions designed to elicit positive information than ones to get negative information (Binning *et al.*, 1988; Sackett, 1982). Thus, the interview may be thought of as 'a search for confirmation of a positive hypothesis' (Rowe, 1989, p. 87).

The preference for positive disclosure should not result in a standardisation of interviews such that everyone professes honesty, dependability, helpfulness, etc. Rather, interviewees would be best advised to reveal experiences indicating personal traits consistent with job characteristics (Jackson *et al.*, 1980). For example, a person interviewing for a job as a counsellor might describe incidents of helping others while a candidate for a job writing advertising copy might disclose experiences that reveal independence and creativity.

Disclosures are, however, so commonly self-flattering that interviewers may discount as exaggeration some of the information revealed (Giacalone and Rosenfeld, 1986). One study suggested 25 per cent of interviewees falsified information (Kennan, 1980), while Barlund's polygraph study of 400 job applicants concluded that 20 per cent falsified or concealed information that might jeopardise their employment (cited in Ekman, 1992). Trinkaus' (1986) survey reported that most respondents would not disclose information that would potentially adversely and unfairly affect their employer's evaluation. Thus self-revelations may be viewed sceptically by interviewers. One professional publication even offered suggestions for detecting deception in employment interviews (Waltman and Golen, 1993). Interviewees can deflect such scepticism by providing supporting evidence, such as vitae, references, portfolios, etc., when appropriate. Interviewers might also take steps that will improve the accuracy or honesty of the disclosures made by interviewees. For example, explaining why information is being requested could increase the interviewee's willingness to reveal job-relevant information (Fletcher, 1992).

Ordinarily, people who reveal too much positive information may be perceived as bragging (Miller *et al.*, 1992) or overly aggressive (Dipboye and Wiley, 1977). However, interviewers expect a positive bias in information revealed and the general tendency of interviewees is to reveal only favourable information. Consequently, the thresholds will probably be very high for making these negative assessments and attributions. Also, aggressiveness may even be seen as a desirable trait in some occupations. Because the failure to reveal relevant qualifications or attributes may put the interviewee in a relatively unfavourable position relative to other interviewees and, since negative attributions are unlikely to be made because of the positive disclosures, people should reveal information in the employment interview that otherwise might appear self-serving.

Because of the bias towards positive information in the interview, negative information about the interviewee significantly and adversely affects interviewer perceptions and selection decisions (Rowe, 1989). These circumstances make it difficult for people to reveal past failures, shortcomings, or problems. For example, several studies suggest that voluntary disclosures about a disability may jeopardise an individual's prospects for being hired (Herold, 1995; Tagalakis *et al.*, 1988). However, a person who does not disclose this information in the employment interview may be subsequently perceived as devious or untruthful for withholding the information. These alternatives clearly present a dialectical dilemma. One strategy for managing this no-win situation is to reveal the negative after positive information has been disclosed (Tucker and Rowe, 1979).

Inappropriate requests for disclosure

Some requests for information may be uneventful, such as asking new employees about their education or previous work experience, but requests may also be problematic, such as asking a paraplegic about the cause of the disability (Braithwaite, 1991). Are you now, or have you ever been, a member of the Communist Party? Do you have children? How much did you pay for that necklace? Additionally, a person's unique circumstances may make innocuous questions problematic: for example, a person who has been paroled from prison may find it difficult to answer the question, 'What have you been doing for the last few years?' Workers undoubtedly encounter questions that ask them to make disclosures they would not voluntarily offer. Consideration of several issues influences people's responses to such questions.

There are legal limits on the right of employers to request personal information from employees. In many countries legislation now prohibits employers from giving preference in hiring, compensating or promoting individuals based on their sex, race, age, marital status, or disabilities, unless these characteristics are fundamental to the performance of the job. Information that can be used for illegal discrimination cannot be lawfully requested. For example, an employer could not ask a job applicant who would babysit his or her children while working (Stewart and Cash, 1988). However, interviewers may skirt the legal requirements using indirect tactics to acquire the desired information. For example, interviewers may provide interviewees with the opportunity to discuss the cause of their disabilities by asking general questions, such as 'tell me about yourself' or 'what were the significant events of your life?' (Hequet, 1993).

In either the case of the inappropriate, illegal explicit request or the case of the veiled request for self-disclosure, a person confronts the dilemma of being unhappily co-operative or combatively closed. Bavelas *et al.* (1990) showed how people use equivocal messages, (i.e. ones open to multiple interpretation) to extricate themselves in such situations. For example, a female asked if she had ever been treated for a mental illness might say, 'some people say that women aren't more depressed than men but women are more likely than men to seek help for their problems. I don't know which is correct but do know that it shouldn't matter.' Thus, responses other than denial of the request and open disclosure provide people with an alternative to the dilemma faced when receiving requests for inappropriate or unwanted disclosures.

Disclosure consequences

Self-disclosures produce a broad range of consequences for workers and their organisations. Some disclosures may foster positive reactions and others negative. In this section, we discuss disclosures that improve and debilitate work performance.

Positive consequences of disclosures

Use of disclosures to transmit organisational cultures

Part of becoming a productive employee involves acquiring the values of the organisation. This inculturation or socialisation process can involve self-disclosure in two ways. First, in many cases people develop an identity that includes their occupation, job, or company. People sometimes define themselves by what they do for a living or who they work for. Statements such as 'I work for Merril-Lynch' or 'I am a barrister with the Inns of Court' not only describe facts but can also reveal personal priorities, pride, or even at times embarrassment or shame. (For a formal discussion of the process of identification see Cheney, 1983.) Self-disclosures perform a role in the process by which people acquire these work identities. Disclosure of personal information will accompany the development of relationships between new and older or senior employees of a company. The sharing of personal history will allow people to establish commonalities and mutual bonds. Without developing a network of supportive peers, a person will remain or become an isolate and will be unlikely to develop a corporate identity.

Organisations also may have cultures that encourage distortion of feelings. Much research recently has focused on the ways that organisations control employees' emotions (e.g. Waldron, 1994). One work describing the culture of the employees of Disneyworld noted that employees 'may complain of being "too tired to smile" but at the same time may feel guilty for having uttered such a confession' (Van Maanen and Kunda, 1989, p. 69). Thus, the culture of the organisation may be a control system that encourages or discourages employee revelations in order to manage workers' emotions.

Van Maanen and Kunda (1989, p. 79) noted that personal disclosures can affect transmission of the organisation's culture. Their fieldnotes from an ethnographic study of an engineering company recount one example from an employee-orientation session:

> Toward the end of the session, the instructor gives a short, apparently impromptu speech of a personal, almost motherly sort: 'Be careful, keep a balance, don't overdo it, don't live off vending machines for a year. I've been there; I lived underground for a year, doing code. Balance your life. Don't say, "I'll work like crazy for four years then get married," Who will marry you? Don't let the company suck you dry. After nine or ten hours, your work isn't worth much anyway'.

That such strategic disclosures can increase not only credibility but also cohesiveness, task commitment and productivity has been demonstrated in an experimental study of small group interaction (Elias *et al.*, 1989).

Other people's disclosures can have positive consequences for the recipient's identification with and inculturation in the organisation. Bullis and Bach's (1989) study of the socialisation of graduate students indicated that socialising allowed 'students to talk about themselves, their interests, and their professors' (p. 282) and accounted for one of the largest changes in identification. Participating in these types of informal conversations increased students' identification with their new roles. Additionally, as established employees reveal stories of their work career, the new employee will learn not only the procedures and policies of the organisation but something of its values as well. Thus, disclosures by long-term employees will be personally and practically helpful to the new employee. Cheney's (1983) study of employees from a divisional office of a large industrial corporation revealed that employees in divisions that were relatively isolated (i.e. did not have frequent contact with other offices) had relatively lower levels of organisational identification (see also Eisenberg *et al.*, 1983). The opportunity to engage in disclosure, then, may facilitate the development of useful employee attitudes.

Reciprocal disclosures

As discussed above, research consistently demonstrates that self-disclosure is reciprocal in social relationships. A similar phenomenon also occurs in formal, task relationships. In work as well as social contexts, relationships in which mutual disclosure occurs evidence desirable characteristics or outcomes. Self-disclosure plays an important role in the development of superior–subordinate relationships. For example, a study by Waldron (1991) indicated that respondents who had better relationships with their supervisors reported more frequent personal contacts (e.g. 'Ask about his or her personal life', 'Share my future career plans with him or her') and direct negotiation of the relationship (e.g. 'Make it known when I am unhappy about something at work'; 'Speak up when I feel he or she has treated me unjustly') than workers who perceived their relationship with their supervisor to be lower in quality. Jablin (1987) suggested that new employees may disclose information to supervisors to elicit reciprocal disclosures that reveal the supervisor's expectations concerning the employee's work habits and values. Another study of new employees and transferees indicated that people who developed relationships characterised by mutual disclosure of ideas and feelings had clearer expectations and fewer uncertainties about their role in the organisation (Kramer, 1994).

Mutual disclosure can also have adverse consequences for the individual and the organisation. Bridge and Baxter (1992) noted that people who develop personal friendships with their work cohorts experience common problems or tensions. Likewise, the organisation can experience problems from mutually disclosive relationships such as cohesive work groups that develop norms and goals that are contrary to those of the employers or the organisation.

Innovations

Another important work-related behaviour, the discussion of new ideas, may be facilitated by self-disclosure. For people and organisations to change and improve their performances, people must identify and embrace innovations. Albrecht and Hall (1991) discovered that people are much more likely to talk about new ideas with co-workers with whom they have 'multiplex relations', that is, relationships based on multiple factors. Workers are more likely to talk about innovations with the people with whom they normally discuss other topics, such as their personal life, office politics, gossip, technical information, and so on. Being in relationships that are characterised by self-disclosure may allow people the confidence and freedom to talk about new ideas and issues that may be threatening, such as ways to solve problems that need correcting.

Negative consequences of disclosures

A wide range of negative reactions may also be generated by self-disclosures. Self-disclosures from employees are not always welcome or useful. People can be embarrassed, such as when profuse compliments about job performance are made to a modest person; puzzled, such as when a valued employee unexpectedly makes a resignation announcement; or, even angered, such as when a person falsely claims responsibility for work performed by another. The most widely investigated response is perhaps the perceptions of sexual harassment that follow some self-disclosures.

Self-disclosures that constitute sexual harassment

As numerous reports and court cases attest, self-disclosures from co-workers can be considered not only inappropriate but also illegal if they contribute to a hostile or threatening work environment (for a discussion of the legal issues see Paetzold and O'Leary-Kelly, 1993). Although offensive compliments are one of the least offensive, threatening and recognised forms of sexual harassment (Konrad and Gutek, 1986; Padgitt and Padgitt, 1986; Powell, 1986), they occur frequently and constitute a significant problem for many people. These same studies also indicate that women are more likely than men to see these behaviours as problematic. Additionally, Pryor and Day's (1988) experimental study noted that attributions of sexual harassment and negative intentions to a sexual compliment were greater when spoken by a superior than by a peer. Witteman suggested that the persistent sexual disclosures that are non-reciprocated and non-negotiated constitute a 'severe' form of sexual harassment (Witteman, 1993).

Disclosing incidents of sexual harassment

Women who have been harassed have to decide whether to disclose their problem to the offender and/or others. As Wood (1993) noted, even recounting the incidence of sexual harassment invokes 'a range of fierce emotions ... from shame and feeling wrong or stupid, to feeling violated, to guilt about allowing it to occur, to entrapment with no viable alternatives, to anger at being impotent to stop harassment' (p. 22). Consequently, sexual harassment necessarily involves subsequent considerations and enactments of self-disclosure.

Perhaps the most frequent recommendation is for the victim of sexual harassment to tell someone about the problem. Passively responding to the event legitimises and perpetuates the offense (Clair, 1993). Offensiveness of the harassment and perceived efficacy of reporting harassment influence victims' responses (Brooks and Perot, 1991). Options available to the victim include confronting the perpetrator, telling friends, or formal reporting to appropriate supervisory personnel.

Some organisations (e.g. American Association of University Women) recommend writing a letter to the offender describing how the statements made the victim feel. Bingham and Burleson (1989) concluded that attempting to change the harasser's behaviour while maintaining a cordial relationship with that person is required for the production of messages that others see as competent and effective. They point out (pp. 192–3) that telling an offender: 'We've got a great working relationship now, and I'd like us to work well together in the future. So I think it's important for us to talk this out. You're a smart and clear-thinking guy, and I consider you to be my friend as well as my boss. That's why I have to think you must be under a lot of unusual stress lately to have said something like this. I know what it's like to be under pressure. Too much stress can really make you crazy. You probably just need a break' is perceived by observers to be a much better response than: 'You are the most rude and disgusting man that I have ever met. You're nothing but a dirty old man. Where do you get off thinking you could force me to have an affair with you? You made me sick. I'm going to make sure you get kicked out on your ass for this – just you wait and see.'

Whether this strategy is effective or not, the victim of sexual harassment has the additional option of revealing the incident to friends, co-workers and management. Sharing reactions with others serves to document the occurrence of the offence, an important step if subsequent legal or other formal remedies are pursued. Additionally, disclosure to others enables a person to receive support from trusted friends, though undesired 'blame the victim' reactions may also be experienced.

All of these suggestions recognise the importance of actively rather than passively responding to the events. However, the research on the viability of disclosive and non-disclosive responses yields no clear recommendations (see also Bingham, 1991 and Clair *et al.*, 1993 for a comparison of alternative typologies of responses to sexual harassment). For example, on the basis of experience as a mediator, Gadlin (1991) suggested that mediation is an effective alternative for resolving allegations of sexual harassment and recommended that disputants enlist the help of a supporter throughout the process. Phillips and Jarboe (1993) advocated that women experiencing even severe forms of harassment should cope by subterfuge and manipulation rather than by revealing their true reactions, a conclusion strongly opposed by Kreps (1993). Bingham and Scherer (1993), in a study of university faculty and staff, noted that talking to the harasser in a non-confrontive style about the problem resulted in more favourable outcomes than did talking with friends. Yount's (1991) ethnographic study of women coal miners suggested that women's revelations of distress following incidents of sexual harassment resulted in perceptions of weakness and exacerbated their problems. Livingston's (1982) analysis of the American Merit System Protection Board data indicated that assertive reactions were perceived by the victim to be no more successful than non-assertive reactions to sexual harassment. No doubt many factors determine the response and its success to incidents of sexual harassment (Jones and Remland, 1992; Tempstra and Baker, 1989).

OVERVIEW

The research reviewed above clearly demonstrates that self-disclosure constitutes an important aspect of both personal and professional relationships. How we come to know others, get others to like us, learn our jobs, get along with spouses, select employees, get others to help us all depend, in part, on the selective revelation of personal information. Theorists who prescribe more, or less, self-disclosure oversimplify the complex and dialectical nature of human relationships. Individuals must weigh the potential rewards (personal, relational and professional) against the potential risks in making decisions regarding self-disclosure. In short, managing personal and professional relationships requires strategic self-disclosure.

REFERENCES

Albrecht, T. L. and Hall, B. (1991) 'Facilitating Talk About New Ideas: The Role of Personal Relationships in Organizational Innovation', *Communication Monographs*, 58, 273–88.

Altman, I. (1973) 'Reciprocity of Interpersonal Exchange', *Journal for the Theory of Social Behavior*, 3, 249–61.

—— (1975) *The Environment and Social Behavior: Privacy, Personal Space, Territory, and Crowding*, Wadsworth Publishing, Belmont, CA.

—— and Taylor, D. A. (1973) *Social Penetration: The Development of Interpersonal Relationships*, Holt, Rinehart & Winston, New York.

—— Vinsel, A. and Brown, B. H. (1981) 'Dialectic Conceptions in Social Psychology: An Application to Social Penetration and Privacy Regulation', in L. Berkowitz (ed.), *Advances in Experimental Social Psychology, Vol. 14*, Academic Press, New York, pp. 107–60.

Archer, R. L. (1979) 'Anatomical and Psychological Sex Differences', in G. J. Chelune and Associates (eds), *Self-disclosure: Origins, Patterns, and Implications of Openness in Interpersonal Relationships*, Jossey-Bass, San Francisco, pp. 80–109.

—— and Earle, W. B. (1983) 'The Interpersonal Orientations of Disclosure', in P. B. Paulus (ed.), *Basic Group Processes*, Springer-Verlag, New York, pp. 289–314.

Bavelas, J. B., Black, A., Chovil, N. and Mullett, J. (1990) *Equivocal Communication*, Sage, Newbury Park.

Baxter, L. A. (1985) 'Accomplishing Relationship Disengagement', in S. Duck and D. Perlman (eds), *Understanding Personal Relationships: An Interdisciplinary Approach*, Sage, London, pp. 243–65.

—— (1987) 'Self-disclosure and Relationship Disengagement', in V. J. Derlega and J. H. Berg (eds), *Self-disclosure: Theory, Research, and Therapy*, Plenum Press, New York, pp. 155–74.

—— (1988) 'A Dialectical Perspective on Communication Strategies in Relationship Development', in S. W. Duck (ed.), *A Handbook of Personal Relationships*, John Wiley, Chichester, pp. 257–73.

—— (1990) 'Dialectical Contradictions in Relationship Development', *Journal of Social and Personal Relationships*, 7, 69–88.

—— and Montgomery, B. M. (in press) 'Rethinking Communication in Personal Relationships from a Dialectical Perspective', in S. Duck (ed.), *Handbook of Personal Relationships* (2nd edn), John Wiley, Chichester.

—— and Wilmot, W. W. (1985) 'Taboo Topics in Close Relationships', *Journal of Social and Personal Relationships*, 2, 253–69.

Berg, J. H. and Archer, R. L. (1980) 'Disclosure or Concern: A Second Look at Liking for the Norm-breaker', *Journal of Personality*, 48, 245–57.

Berg, J. H. and Derlega, V. J. (1987) 'Themes in the Study of Self-disclosure', in V. J. Derlega and J. H. Berg (eds), *Self-disclosure: Theory, Research and Therapy*, Plenum Press, New York, pp. 1–8.

Berger, C. R. (1979) 'Beyond Initial Interaction: Uncertainty, Understanding, and the Development of Interpersonal Relationships', in H. Giles and R. St Clair (eds), *Language and Social Psychology*, Basil Blackwell, Oxford, pp. 122–44.

—— and Bradac, J. J. (1982) 'Language and Social Knowledge: Uncertainty in Interpersonal Relationships', Edward Arnold, London.

—— and Calabrese, R. J. (1975) 'Some Explorations in Initial Interaction and Beyond: Toward a Developmental Theory of Interpersonal Communication', *Human Communication Research*, 1, 99–112.

—— and Douglas, W. (1992) 'Thought and Talk: "Excuse Me, But Have I Been Talking to Myself?"', in F.E.X. Dance (ed.), *Human Communication Theory*, Harper & Row, New York, pp. 42–60.

——, Gardner, R. R., Parks, M. R., Schulman, L. and Miller, G. R. (1976) 'Interpersonal epistemology and interpersonal communication', in G. R. Miller (ed.), *Explorations in Interpersonal Communication*, Sage, Beverly Hills, pp. 149–71.

Bingham, S. G. (1991) 'Communication Strategies for Managing Sexual Harassment in Organizations', *Journal of Applied Communication Research*, 19, 88–115.

—— and Burleson, B. R. (1989) 'Multiple Effects of Messages with Multiple Goals: Some Perceived Outcomes of Responses to Sexual Harassment', *Human Communication Research*, 16, 184–216.

—— and Scherer, L. L. (1993) 'Factors Associated with Responses to Sexual Harassment and Satisfaction with Outcome', *Sex Roles*, 29, 239–69.

Binning, J. F., Goldstein, M. A., Garcia, M. F., Harding, J. L. and Scattaregia, J. H. (1988) 'Effects of Preinterview Impressions on Questioning Strategies in Same- and Opposite-sex Employment Interviews', *Journal of Applied Psychology*, 73, 30–7.

Bochner, A. P. (1982) 'On the Efficacy of Openness in Closed Relationships', in M. Burgoon (ed.), *Communication Yearbook 5*, Transaction Books, New Brunswick, NJ, pp. 109–42.

Bowen, S. P. and Michal-Johnson, P. (1989) 'The Crisis of Communicating in Relationships: Confronting the Threat of AIDS', *AIDS and Public Policy*, 4, 10–19.

Braithwaite, D. O. (1991) '"Just How Much Did that Wheelchair Cost?", Management of Privacy Boundaries by Persons with Disabilities', *Western Journal of Speech Communication*, 55, 254–74.

Bridge, K. and Baxter, L. A. (1992) 'Blended Relationships', *Western Journal of Speech Communication*, 56, 200–25.

Brooks, L. and Perot. A. R. (1991) 'Reporting Sexual Harassment: Exploring a Predictive Model', *Psychology of Women Quarterly*, 15, 31–47.

Bullis, C. and Bach, B. W. (1989) 'Socialization Turning Points: An Examination of Change in Organizational Identification', *Western Journal of Speech Communication*, 53, 273–93.

Canary, D. J., Stafford, L., Hause, K. S. and Wallace, L. A. (1993) 'An Inductive Analysis of Relational Maintenance Strategies: A Comparison Among Lovers, Relatives, Friends, and Others', *Communication Research Reports*, 10, 5–14.

Cappella, J. N. (1981) 'Mutual Influence in Expressive Behavior: Adult–Adult and Infant–Adult Dyadic Interaction', *Psychological Bulletin*, 89, 101–32.

Cheney, G. (1983) 'On the Various and Changing Meanings of Organizational Membership', *Communication Monographs*, 50, 352–62.

Chervin, D. D. and Martinez, A. M. (1987) *Survey on the Health of Stanford Students*, Colwell Student Health Center, Stanford, CA.

Clair, R. P. (1993) 'The Use of Framing Devices to Sequester Organizational Narratives', *Communication Monographs*, 60, 113–36.

——, McGoun, M. J. and Spirek, M. M. (1993) 'Sexual Harassment Responses of Working Women: An Assessment of Current Communication-oriented Typologies and Perceived Effectiveness of the Response', in G. L. Kreps (ed.), *Sexual Harassment: Communication Implications*, Hampton Press, Creskill, pp. 209–33.

Cline, R. J. (1982) *Revealing and Relating: A Review of Self-disclosure Theory and Research*, paper presented at the International Communication Association Convention, May.

——, Freeman, K. E. and Johnson, S. J. (1990) 'Talk Among Sexual Partners about AIDS: Factors Differentiating Those who Talk from Those who Do Not', *Communication Research*, 17, 792–808.

——, Johnson, S. J. and Freeman, K. E. (1992) 'Talk Among Sexual Partners About AIDS: Interpersonal Communication for Risk Reduction or Risk Enhancement?', *Health Communication*, 4, 39–56.

Coleman, L. M. and DePaulo, B. M. (1991) 'Uncovering the Human Spirit: Moving Beyond Disability and "Missed" Communications', in N. Coupland, H. Giles and J. M. Weimann (eds), *'Miscommunication' and Problematic Talk*, Sage, Newbury Park, pp. 61–84.

Collins, N. L. and Miller, L. C. (1994) 'The Disclosure-liking Link: From Meta-analysis Toward a Dynamic Reconceptualization', *Psychological Bulletin*, 116, 457–75.

Cowen, E. L. (1982) 'Help is Where You Find It', *American Psychologist*, 37, 385–95.

Dansereau, F. and Markham, S. E. (1987) 'Superior–Subordinate Communication: Multiple Levels of Analysis', in F. M. Jablin, L. L. Putnam, K. H. Roberts and L. W. Porter (eds), *Handbook of Organizational Communication: An Interdisciplinary Perspective*, Sage, Newbury Park, pp. 343–88.

Derlega, V. J. and Grzelak, J. (1979) 'Appropriateness of Self-disclosure', in G. J. Chelune (ed.), *Self-disclosure: Origins, Patterns, and Implications of Openness in Interpersonal Relationships*, Jossey-Bass, San Francisco, pp. 151–76.

Derlega, V. J., Metts, S., Petronio, S. and Margulis, S. T. (1993) *Self-disclosure*, Sage, Newbury Park.

Dindia, K. and Allen, M. (1992) 'Sex-differences in Self-disclosure: A Meta-analysis', *Psychological Bulletin*, 112, 106–24.

—— (1995) 'Reciprocity of Self-disclosure: A Meta-analysis', paper presented at the International Network on Personal Relationships conference, Williamsburg, PA, June.

Dipboye, R. L. and Wiley, J. W. (1977) 'Reactions of College Recruiters to Interviewee Sex and Self-presentation Style', *Journal of Vocational Behavior*, 10, 1–12.

Douglas, W. (1990) 'Uncertainty, Information-seeking, and Liking During Initial Interaction', *Western Journal of Speech Communication*, 54, 66–81.

Edgar, T., Freimuth, V. S., Hammond, S. L., McDonald, D. A. and Fink, E. L. (1992) Strategic Sexual Communication: Condom Use Resistance and Response, *Health Communication*, 4, 83–104.

Eisenberg, E. M., Monge, P. R. and Miller, K. I. (1983) 'Involvement in Communication Networks as a Predictor of Organizational Commitment', *Human Communication Research*, 10, 179–201.

Ekman, P. (1992) '*Telling Lies: Clues to Deceit in the Marketplace, Politics, and Marriage*, Norton, New York.

Elias, F. G., Johnson, M. E. and Fortman, J. B. (1989) 'Task-focused Self-disclosure: Effects on Group Cohesiveness, Commitment to Task, and Productivity', *Small Group Behavior*, 20, 87–96.

Evans, J. H. (1976) 'Changing Attitudes Toward Disabled Persons: An Experimental Study' *Rehabilitation Counseling Bulletin*, 19, 572–9.

Feldman, S. (1991) 'Trust Me', *Personnel*, 68, 7.

Fitzpatrick, M. A. (1987) 'Marriage and Verbal Intimacy', in V. J. Derlega and J. H. Berg (eds), *Self-disclosure: Theory, Research and Therapy*, Plenum Press, New York, pp. 131–54.

Fletcher, C. (1992) 'Ethical Issues in the Selection Interview', *Journal of Business Ethics*, 11, 361–7.

Fulk, J. and Mani, S. (1986) 'Distortion of Communication in Hierarchical Relationships', *Communication Yearbook, 9*, Sage, Beverly Hills, pp. 483–510.

Gadlin, H. (1991) 'Careful Maneuvers: Mediating Sexual Harassment', *Negotiation Journal*, 7, 139–53.

Giacalone, R. A. and Rosenfeld, P. (1986) 'Self-presentation and Self-promotion in an Organizational Setting', *Journal of Social Psychology*, 126, 321–6.

Gilbert, S. J. (1976) 'Self-disclosure, Intimacy, and Communication in Families', *Family Coordinator*, 25, 221–9.

—— and Horenstein, D. (1975) 'The Communication of Self-disclosure: Level versus Valence', *Human Communication Research*, 1, 316–22.

Gilmore, D. C. and Ferris, G. R. (1989) 'The Politics of the Employment Interview', in R. W. Eder and G. R. Ferris (eds), *The Employment Interview: Theory, Research, and Practice*, Sage, Newbury Park, pp. 233–45.

Harris, M. M. and Fennell, M. L. (1988) 'Perceptions of an Employee Assistance Program and Employees' Willingness to Participate', *Journal of Applied Behavioral Sciences*, 24, 423–38.

Hequet, M. (1993) 'The Intricacies of Interviewing', *Training*, 30(4), 31–6, April.

Herold, K. (1995) 'The Effects of Interviewees' Self-disclosure and Disability on Selected Perceptions and Attitudes of Interviewers', unpublished PhD thesis, University of Southern Mississippi, Hattiesburg, MS.

Hitchcock, J. M. and Wilson, H. S. (1992) 'Personal Risking', *Nursing Research*, 41, 178–83.

Jablin, F. M. (1987) 'Organizational, Entry, Assimilation, and Exit', in F. M. Jablin, L. L. Putnam, K. H. Roberts and L. W. Porter (eds), *Handbook of Organizational Communication: An Interdisciplinary Perspective*, Sage, Newbury Park, pp. 389–419.

—— and Krone, K. J. (1994) 'Task/Work Relationships: A Life-span Perspective', in M. L. Knapp and G. R. Miller (eds), *Handbook of Interpersonal Communication* (2nd edn), Sage, Newbury Park, pp. 621–75.

—— and Miller, V. D. (1990) 'Interviewer and Applicant Questioning Behavior in Employment Interviews', *Management Communication Quarterly*, 4, 51–86.

Jackson, N., Peacock, A. and Smith, J. P. (1980) 'Impressions of Personality in the Employment Interview', *Journal of Personality and Social Psychology*, 39, 294–307.

Janz, T. (1989) 'The Patterned Behavior Description Interview: The Best Prophet of the Future is the Past', in R. W. Eder and G. R, Ferris (eds), *The Employment Interview: Theory, Research, and Practice*, Sage, Newbury Park, pp. 158–68.

Jones, T. S. and Remland, M. S. (1992) 'Sources of Variability in Perceptions of and Responses to Sexual Harassment', *Sex Roles*, 27, 121–42.

Jourard, S. M. (1971) *The Transparent Self* (revised edn), Van Nostrand Reinhold, New York.

Kennan, A. (1980) 'Recruitment on Campus', *Personnel Management*, March, 43–6.

Koch, J. J. (1990) 'Employee Assistance: Wells' Fargo and IBM's HIV Policies Help Protect Employees' Rights', *Personnel Journal*, 69, April, 40–8.

Konrad, A. M. and Gutek, B. M. (1986) 'Impact of Work Experience on Attitudes Toward Sexual Harassment', *Administrative Science Quarterly*, 31, 422–38.

Kramer, M. W. (1994) 'Uncertainty Reduction During Job Transitions: An Exploratory Study of Communication Experiences of Newcomers and Transferees', *Management Communication Quarterly*, 7, 384–412.

Kreps, G. L. (1993) 'Providing a Sociocultural Evolutionary Approach to Preventing Sexual Harassment: Metacommunication and Cultural Adaptation', in G. L. Kreps (ed.), *Sexual Harassment: Communication Implications*, Hampton Press, Creskill, pp. 310–18.

Larzelere, R. E. and Huston, T. L. (1980) 'The Dyadic Trust Scale: Toward Understanding Interpersonal Trust in Close Relationships', *Journal of Marriage and the Family*, 42, 595–606.

Livingston, J. A. (1982) 'Responses to Sexual Harassment on the Job: Legal, Organizational and Individual Actions', *Journal of Social Issues*, 38, 5–22.

Luthans, F. and Walersee, R. (1990) 'What Do We Really Know About EAPs?', *Human Resource Management*, 28, 385–401.

Mellinger, G. D. (1956) 'Interpersonal Trust as a Factor in Communication', *Journal of Abnormal Social Psychology*, 52, 304–9.

Miell, D. E. and Duck, S. (1986) 'Strategies in Developing Friendships', in V. J. Derlega and B. A. Winstead, (eds), *Friends and Social Interaction*, Springer Verlag, New York, pp. 129–43.

Miller, L. C. (1990) 'Intimacy and Liking: Mutual Influence and the Role of Unique Relationships', *Journal of Personality and Social Psychology*, 59, 50–60.

—— and Read, S. J. (1987) 'Why am I Telling You This? Self-disclosure in a Goal-based Model of Personality', in V. J. Derlega and J. H. Berg (eds), *Self-disclosure: Theory, Research, and Therapy*, Plenum Press, New York, pp. 35–58.

——, Cooke, L. L., Tsant, J. and Morgan, F. (1992) 'Should I Brag?', *Human Communication Research*, 18, 364–99.

Milne, S. H., Blum, T. C. and Roman, P. M. (1994) 'Factors Influencing Employees' Propensity to Use an Employee Assistance Program', *Personnel Psychology*, 47, 123–45.

Montgomery, B. M. (1993) 'Relationship Maintenance versus Relationship Change: A Dialectical Dilemma', *Journal of Social and Personal Relationships*, 10, 205–24.

Myers, D. W. (1984) 'Establishing and Building Employee Assistance Programs', Quorum Books, Westport, CN.

Padgitt, S. C. and Padgitt, J. S. (1986) 'Cognitive Structure of Sexual Harassment: Implications of University Policy', *Journal of Student Personnel*, 27, 34–9.

Paetzold, R. L. and O'Leary-Kelly, A. M. (1993) 'Organizational Communication and the Legal Dimensions of Hostile Work Environment Sexual Harassment', in G. L. Kreps (ed.), *Sexual Harassment: Communication Implications*, Hampton Press, Creskill, pp. 63–80.

Parks, M. (1982) 'Ideology in Interpersonal Communication: Off the Couch and into the World', in M. Burgoon (ed.), *Communication Yearbook 5*, Transaction Books, New Brunswick, NJ, pp. 79–108.

Petronio, S. (1988) 'The Dissemination of Private Information: The Use of a Boundary Control System as an Alternative Perspective to the Study of Disclosures', paper presented at the Speech Communication Association Convention, New Orleans, November.

—— (1991) 'Communication Boundary Management: A Theoretical Model of Managing Disclosure of Private Information Between Marital Couples', *Communication Theory*, 1, 311–35.

Phillips, G. M. and Jarboe, S. (1993) 'Sycophancy and Servitude: Harassment and Rebellion', in G. L. Kreps (ed.), *Sexual Harassment: Communication Implications*, Hampton Press, Creskill, pp. 281–309.

Planalp, S. and Garvin-Doxas, K. (1994) 'Using Mutual Knowledge in Conversation: Friends as Experts in Each Other', in S. Duck (ed.), *Understanding Relationship Processes IV: The Dynamics of Relationship*, Guilford, NY, pp. 1–26.

Powell, G. N. (1986) 'Effects of Sex Role Identity and Sex on Definition of Sexual Harassment', *Sex Roles*, 14, 9–19.

Pryor, J. B. and Day, J. D. (1988) 'Interpretations of Sexual Harassment: An Attributional Analysis', *Sex Roles*, 18, 405–17.

Rawlins, W. (1983) 'Openness as Problematic in Ongoing Friendships: Two Conversational Dilemmas', *Communication Monographs*, 50, 1–13.

Roberts, K. R. and O'Reilly, D. A. (1974) 'Failures in Upward Communication in Organizations: Three Possible Culprits', *Academy of Management Journal*, 17, 205–15.

Rosen, T. H. (1987) 'Identification of Substance Abusers in the Workplace', *Public Personnel Management*, 16, 197–207.

Rowe, P. M. (1989) 'Unfavorable Information and Interview Decisions', in R. W. Eder and G. R. Ferris (eds), *The Employment Interview: Theory, Research, and Practice*, Sage, Newbury Park, pp. 77–89.

Rubin, Z. (1973) *Liking and Loving*, Holt, Rinehart & Winston, New York.

Sackett, P. R. (1982) 'The Interviewer as Hypothesis Tester: The Effects of Impressions of an Applicant on Interviewer Questioning Strategy', *Personnel Psychology*, 35, 789–804.

Schank, R. C. and Abelson, R. P. (1977) *Scripts, Plans, Goals, and Understanding*, Erlbaum, Hillsdale, NJ.

Schneider, B. E. (1986) 'Coming Out at Work: Bridging the Private/Public Gap', *Work and Occupations*, 13, 463–87.

Sigman, S. J. (1991) 'Handling the Discontinuous Aspects of Continuing Social Relationships: Toward Research on the Persistence of Social Forms', *Communication Theory*, 1, 106–27.

Soloman, C. M. (1992) 'Work/Family Ideas that Break Boundaries', *Personnel Journal*, 71, October, 112–17.

Sonnenstuhl, W. J., Staudenmeier, W. J. and Trice, H. M. (1988) 'Ideology and Referral Categories in Employee Assistance Program Research', *Journal of Applied Behavioral Science*, 24, 383–96.

Steele, F. (1975) *The Open Organization: The Impact of Secrecy and Disclosure on People and Organizations*, Addison-Wesley, Reading, MA.

Stewart, C.J. and Cash, W. B., Jr. (1988) *Interviewing: Principles and Practices*, W. C. Brown, Dubuque, IA.

'Success Story: Getting Substance Abusers into an EAP' (1991) *Personnel*, 68, 24.

Tagalakis, V., Amsel, R. and Fichten, C. S. (1988) 'Job Interviewing Strategies for People with a Visible Disability', *Journal of Applied Social Psychology*, 18, 520–32.

Taylor, D. A. and Altman, I. (1987) 'Communication in Interpersonal Relationships: Social Penetration Processes', in M. E. Roloff and G. R. Miller (eds), *Interpersonal processes: New Directions in Communication Research*, Sage, Newbury Park, pp. 257–77.

Tempstra, D. E. and Baker, D. D. (1989) 'Identification and Classification of Reactions to Sexual Harassment', *Journal of Organizational Behavior*, 10, 1–14.

Tesser, A. and Rosen, S. (1975) 'The Reluctance to Transmit Bad News', *Advances in Experimental Social Psychology*, 8, 193–232.

Thompson, T. L. (1982) 'Disclosure as a Disability-management Strategy: A Review and Conclusions', *Communication Quarterly*, 196–202.

Tolhuizen, J. H. (1989) 'Communication Strategies for Intensifying Dating Relationships: Identification, Use and Structure', *Journal of Social and Personal Relationships*, 6, 413–34.

Trinkaus, J. W. (1986) 'Disclosure of a Physical Disability: An Informal Look', *Perceptual and Motor Skills*, 62, 157–8.

Tucker, D. H. and Rowe, P. M. (1979) 'Relationship Between Expectancy, Causal Attribution and Final Hiring Decisions in the Employment Interview', *Journal of Applied Psychology*, 64, 27–34.

Tullar, W. L. (1989) 'The Employment Interview as a Cognitive Performing Script', in R. W. Eder and G. R. Ferris (eds), *The Employment Interview: Theory, Research, and Practice*, Sage, Newbury Park, 233–45.

Vangelisti, A. L. and Banski, M. A. (1993) 'Couples' Debriefing Conversations: the Impact of Gender, Occupation, and Demographic Characteristics', *Family Relations*, 42, 149–57.

Van Maanen, J. and Kunda, G. (1989) '"Real Feelings": Emotional Expression and Organizational Culture', *Research in Organizational Behavior*, 11, 43–104.

Waldron, B. (1991) 'Achieving Communication Goals in Superior–Subordinate Relationships', *Communication Monographs*, 58, 289–306.

Waldron, V. R. (1994) 'Once More, With Feeling: Reconsidering the Role of Emotion in Work', *Communication Yearbook*, 17, 388–416.

Waltman, J. L. and Golen, S. P. (1993) 'Detecting Deception During Interviews', *Internal Auditor*, 50(4), August, 61–3.

Weick, K. (1990) 'The Vulnerable System: An Analysis of the Tenerife Air Disaster', *Journal of Management*, 16, 571–93.

Witteman, H. (1993) 'The Interface Between Sexual Harassment and Organizational Romance', in G. L. Kreps (ed.), *Sexual Harassment: Communication Implications*, Hampton Press, Creskill, pp. 27–62.

Wood, J. T. (1993) 'Naming and Interpreting Sexual Harassment: A Conceptual Framework for Scholarship', in G. L. Kreps (ed.), *Sexual Harassment: Communication Implications*, Hampton Press, Creskill, pp. 9–26.

Yount, K. R. (1991) 'Ladies, Flirts, and Tomboys: Strategies for Managing Sexual Harassment in an Underground Coal Mine', *Journal of Contemporary Ethnography*, 19, 396–422.

9 The process of listening

Robert N. Bostrom

INTRODUCTION

Since communication researchers (like many other social scientists) are interested in a wide variety of phenomena, definitions require careful attention. Even the basic classification of behaviour as 'communicative' varies – for example, some researchers assume that unintentional non-verbal cues are communicative (Watzlawick *et al.*, 1967), while others, such as Motley (1992), assert that intentionality is a vital aspect of communicative activity. Other distinctions are made between mass and interpersonal, while some thinkers find this distinction to be largely one of academic politics (Reardon and Rogers, 1988).

A very fundamental distinction in research is made when researchers focus on mental activity rather than overt behaviour – often stressing 'meaning,' or cognitive events as opposed to overt activity. At the heart of such a distinction is our basic approach to communication itself – is it a process which is useful because it brings about alterations in activities, or is it useful because it brings about alterations in the way we think? An intermediate position is that communication is useful because it brings about alterations in our activities by means of altering the way that we think. The use of theoretical terms, such as 'information', 'schemas', 'attitudes' and 'messages', often seems to assume a reality residing in mental events, existing separately and apart from the responses from which they are derived.

Definitions and the assessment of listening have grown out of the cognitive tradition and have been importantly influenced by an assumption that listening and reading are simply different aspects of a single process – the acquisition and retention of information. If listening and reading produce the same outcomes, then it is easy to assume that they are similar (if not exactly the same) skills. Success or failure of listening activity can then be couched in cognitive (linguistic) terms. This assumption has been the dominant paradigm in listening and other communication research for the last fifty years. In other words, we have believed that linguistic events are central to the educational experience and that relational and affective issues are less important.

This paradigm is firmly rooted in Western philosophical thought. Thousands of years ago, when prehistoric people began to use tokens as an accounting system (Schmandt-Besserat, 1990), the possession of a clay token became the equivalent of possession of a jar of olive oil or some other agricultural product. By the time the Sumerians were writing on clay tablets, a full-blown symbol system existed in which words could take on great importance. The 'meaning' of these symbols seemed to possess an existence separate and apart from their users. Today, when we visit the British Museum and look at these clay tablets, we cannot help but be impressed with the relative permanence of written symbols that are 4,000 years old and whose users have long since turned to dust. The fact that the clay tablets have outlasted their authors seems to prove that the symbols are permanent (or 'real') and their readers and writers are less so. This assumption, of course, led to Plato's noumenalism and the subsequent development of philosophy (metaphysics).

The emphasis on symbols and the universal acceptance of philosophy has been the dominant paradigm in Western intellectual life ever since. It is interesting to note that in the last few years, critics of behaviourism have characterised their views as the 'new' paradigm, assuming that an emphasis on behaviour is the dominant paradigm in communication study. The assumption that behaviourism is dominant in communication research seems unlikely to many. The assumption that one is in the vanguard of a new paradigm has great appeal.

It is clear that philosophy has been intermingled with the study of language ever since its inception. We use language according to certain well-established principles, and even though a strong case can be made that this usage is 'hard-wired' or determined by the physiological nature of the human brain (Pinker, 1994), the principles seem to be inherently true – so much so that philosophers were led to contend that they indicate 'reality'. More recently 'social' reality is invoked as the aim of research in social interactions, especially communication. Language is primary in constructing this reality. The nature of language is so intermingled with the proofs of the reality hypotheses that it is impossible to approach them separately.

From the point of view of the cognitive/linguistic paradigm, communication (or symbolic behaviour) was an early evolutionary step in the development of human beings, which led to social behaviour and the beginning of civilization. This explanation asserts that human beings somehow acquired the ability to communicate and subsequently were able to engage in social behaviour. The depth of the commitment to this view is truly astonishing. It is just as easy to assume that social behaviour evolved first, and that this activity led to the use of symbols (Skinner, 1986). There is still a tendency among students of language to lean towards philosophical dualism and metaphysical assumptions.

This paradigm, then, tells us that to improve our abilities in communication, we should improve our facility with language. Words (cognitions) are generated, either from internal processing or received from others; and then behaviour follows the words. A popular example of this paradigm is 'symbolic interactionism' which takes as its basic assumption that our social life is constructed of words. Some organisational communication theorists (Eisenberg and Goodall, 1993) have taken the position that a symbolic interactionist perspective is the most productive way in which to study organisations, and they draw on symbolic interactionism as a basic conceptual framework for organisational study.

Symbolic interactionism begins with the assumption that all life is a search for meaning, which, according to symbolic interactionists, is found in the way that each of us interacts with other persons, our institutions and our culture. These interactions are *symbolic* in that they take place primarily through language and symbols. This is in contrast to the well-known 'hierarchy of needs', which proposes that 'self-actualisation' (meaningful) needs only are addressed when the more basic needs of food and shelter are satisfied (see Chapter 2). This approach relies both on interpretation and the acceptance of principles derived from linguistic frameworks. The recipe for social change, therefore, involves a change in the symbol system and behaviour is assumed to follow. Whether the changes are political, social, or organisational, the communicator must only 'manage meaning' to have significant effect. So, if we are to increase the numbers of women and minorities in our organisational systems, we should concentrate on building symbol systems that will facilitate changes in recruitment and promotional practices.

There is no doubt that changes in behaviour sometimes do follow changes in symbol systems. But at the same time, there is abundant evidence to indicate that changes in behaviour more often occur through coercion, social pressure, physiological and chemical changes, and sometimes random events. These changes, often termed 'mindless' ones, are then 'justified' by subsequent explanations by the participant. An individual who bows to social pressure in making a group decision then 'rationalises' the event by constructing evidence and logical processes. When this occurs, it is the case that language follows behaviour, rather than the other way around. There is abundant evidence in the research literature to support this notion. The manner in which attitudes follow behaviour has been well-demonstrated (Bem, 1965, 1967). This phenomenon (called 'self-persuasion' by Bem) is especially pronounced when behaviour is influenced by social phenomena, such as conformity (Griffin and Buehler, 1993). Communication aimed at behavioural changes has traditionally been termed persuasion (Miller, 1980; Bostrom, 1983) or influence, and while individuals certainly can make use of symbols as mediating phenomena, such use is definitely not essential (Miller and Burgoon, 1978; Bostrom, 1980).

Up to this point, communicative outcomes have been described as symbolic or behavioural. There are other communicative activities that may be as important, or even more important, than these. The development and maintenance of relationships may be far more important than any other aspect of our daily life. Concerns with relationships are clearly facilitated through interactive activity (Knapp *et al.*, 1994). We communicate in order to maintain and develop relationships with others, and the content of the interaction may only be secondary to the process. Whether we use terms like 'affinity-seeking' or 'homophily' (Rogers, 1962), interpersonal relationships are a fundamental human characteristic and are a significant outcome of communicative activity.

In summary, researchers in communication have placed an inordinate amount of emphasis on the linguistic, or cognitive aspects, of the communicative process. This focus on language led to ideas of 'reality' as dominant paradigms governing communicative activity. The rationale for this emphasis on language assumes that social change and behavioural alteration follow from changes in language and linguistic systems. The opposite view – that language follows behavioural change – is just as defensible but has not received as much attention. Recently, researchers in interpersonal communication have pointed out the importance of interactive behaviour, as well as the central role that relationships play in interpersonal communication (see Chapter 14). While these more recent trends would seem to lead to questioning the dominance of the language-centredness of traditional 'reality-based' research, we still see linguistic assumptions as pervasive ones. Since these assumptions have affected most thinking in communication, it is not surprising to see that this tradition has also affected examination of the process of listening.

RESEARCH IN LISTENING

Research in listening, like most communication research, has focused on symbolic, rather than behavioural or relational outcomes and, as a result, has had some of the same conceptual problems that have afflicted communication in general. Symbol-oriented definitions of information acquisition assume that, since reading, writing, listening and speaking are all communicative activities, they should share the same methods and outlook and aim for the same end product – the processing of information. Larger differentiation of communicative outcomes have not traditionally been a part of the research in listening. Instead, we have focused on the inherent differences *in persons*, looking to research to help us to understand why people differ in communicative skill.

Individuals vary widely in their ability to receive information that is presented symbolically, and the causes of this variation are poorly understood. Clearly, contexts and media affect the reception of messages. But individual differences are probably the most important source of variability in communication activities. The most logical explanation for differences in receiving ability would seem to be the possession of a generalised facility to manipulate and remember symbols. To this end, individual variations in reading, both in speed and comprehension, have been extensively studied. A 'general ability' explanation, however, is elusive. For example, reading and writing skills are not closely associated (Bracewell *et al.*, 1982). The lack of a strong association between reading and writing skills would lead us to expect that listening and speaking abilities would be similarly unrelated to reading skill. But these individual differences in listening ability, if any, have attracted much less attention. This seems anomalous, since listening is probably the most common communication activity.

In a much-cited study, Paul Rankin (1929) asked persons to report how much time they spent in various types of communication. They reported that they listened 45 per cent of the time, spoke 30 per cent of the time, read 16 per cent and wrote 9 per cent. In a more recent study, Klemmer and Snyder (1972) studied the communicative activity of technical persons. These persons spent 68 per cent of their day in communicative activity and, of that time, 62 per cent was 'talking face-to-face'. Klemmer and Snyder did not distinguish between speaking and listening, but it seems safe to assume that at least half of the face-to-face activity was listening. Brown (1982) estimated that executives in a modern corporation spend at least 60 per cent of their day listening. To say that listening is an essential communication skill is to risk restating the obvious.

Early attempts at measurement

Whether or not listening is a distinct skill – that is, different from reading and writing skills – is a different question. Academic interest in listening is a relatively recent phenomenon, probably beginning with discussions by Wesley Wiksell (1946) and Ralph Nichols (1947) appearing in the *Quarterly Journal of Speech*. Nichols' approach to studying listening was to assume that the methods used in studying reading could be used to examine listening. Nichols' dissertation (Nichols, 1948) attempted to discover what, if anything, could help us to predict good listening. In this pioneering study, Nichols adopted an information-based, cognitive definition of good listening. He constructed lectures with factual content in them, read them to respondents, and then measured subsequent retention in tests. Listening, in other words, was defined as what students do in a classroom.

Nichols examined the participants' retention and its relationship to many different factors, such as distance from the speaker, previous training in subject matter, hearing loss(!), size of family and parental occupation. He concluded that retention was related to intelligence, ability to discern organisational elements, size of vocabulary and very little else. In other words, he found that intelligent persons retained more information than did unintelligent ones, those who understood organisational principles also retained more and those with a large vocabulary retained more than those with a smaller vocabulary. Since Nichols' research, many investigators have used this criterion as a basis for an assessment of listening success. Studies of this type have been conducted by Thompson (1967), Hsia (1968), Beighley (1952, 1954), McClendon (1958), Rossiter (1972), Palamatier and McNinch (1972), Klinzing (1972), Buchli and Pearce (1974) and Beatty and Payne (1984).

Not long after Nichols' research was published, the factors relating to listening skill were used as the theoretical justification for a commercial test of listening skill (Brown and Carlsen, 1955). But instead of using the actual findings of the Nichols study, this test made use of subscales which measured vocabulary, recognition of transitions, ability to follow directions, immediate recall and the retention of facts from a lecture. With the exception of 'following directions', the subscales were all clearly language-related. Since Brown's principal training and expertise was reading, this bias was understandable. The Brown–Carlsen test has been used as a measure of listening ability as an independent variable by a few researchers (Ernest, 1968; Petrie and Carrell, 1976).

A similar listening test was published by the Educational Testing Service (1957); it also was a language-related, cognitive test (Dickens and Williams, 1964). At first, it was considered part of the STEP test group (Sequential Tests of Educational Progress), and then (after much revision) was incorporated into part of the communication skills assessment of the National Teacher Examination (NTE) (Educational Testing Service, 1984). The development of these tests and the research following from them seemed to demonstrate that persons do indeed vary in their ability to retain information from spoken messages and that often instructional efforts to improve this ability were successful. This research considered that listening took place if information from spoken discourse was retained. When a person scored better on a test of retention, that person was assumed to be a better listener. A person's listening ability was assumed to be a unique skill, that is, not related to other cognitive skills.

The assumption that the ability to listen was a separate and unitary skill was sharply attacked in the middle of the 1960s by Charles Kelly. He reasoned that if listening tests did indeed measure a separate ability, the Brown–Carlsen and STEP tests of listening would be more highly correlated with each other than they would with other measures of cognitive ability. He found that the tests of listening were not highly correlated with each other and, in fact, were more highly correlated with tests of intelligence. These data led Kelly, reasonably enough, to the conclusion that the ability that had previously been termed 'listening ability' was actually only an aspect of intelligence, and that the Brown–Carlsen and the STEP test were only different kinds of intelligence tests (Kelly, 1965, 1967). A clue to Kelly's findings was already present in Nichols' data: the single best predictor was cognitive ability – a correlation of 0.54 (Nichols, 1948). While intelligence is clearly not a unitary factor, defining listening as the 'remembering of facts' from a lecture is definitely isomorphic with at least one of them. Gardner (1983), in his theory of multiple intelligences, indicates that verbal processing is one of the many intelligences, and listening as defined as 'efficient word processing' would fit well into this definition. If we take Sternberg's (1985) definition of intelligence as the ability to manipulate the environment, then we probably would not see the same strong relationship exhibited by the Kelly and Nichols data.

The relationship of lecture-defined listening and intelligence is certainly not clear cut. Cognitive ability interacts with difficulty of material and rate of presentation in predicting retention (Sticht and Glassnap, 1972). Kelly's discovery that listening – as defined by the retention model – is probably not a separate and distinguishable mental ability complicates the problem. Almost everyone involved in the practical study of communication has had experience with persons who are obviously intelligent but could never be called good listeners.

Attitudes and listening

One method of reconciling Kelly's findings with everyday experience was to redefine listening so that it included something other than intelligence. Many invoked an attitude about listening to explain why some persons listen better than others. This attitude could also be termed a 'willingness to listen' – a basic interest in others' ideas. Often when we say that someone is a good listener we mean that they have a good attitude about the process, rather than a good retentive ability.

Carl Weaver was one of the first researchers to incorporate the attitudinal dimension into a formal definition of listening. He referred to research in perception showing that attitudinal predispositions affect both selection and perception of incoming stimuli. Listening was viewed by Weaver (1972, p. 12) as 'the selection and retention of aurally received data'. He discussed it in relation to selective exposure, an attitudinally and culturally determined activity. Weaver also included information-seeking as an important component.

Weaver's approach, while popular, still avoided the basic question of whether or not listening ability is a separate and distinct psychological characteristic. Normally, attitudes, even social attitudes, are not considered to be permanent traits or abilities. Kelly had pointed out that good listeners were intelligent, and now Weaver pointed out that good listeners were those who had respect and interest in others. 'Other orientation' was a popular theme in academic life in the early 1970s, and the humanistic psychology movement seemed to be in tune with concern for other people expressed in the goal of being good listeners. But more sceptical persons looked at listening as simply a redescription of other better known psychological processes, notably selective perception and intelligence.

Listening and memory

Cognitive researchers, in the meantime, have been carefully examining individuals' mental behaviour. One such cognitive process that would seem to be closely related to listening is memory. When one listens, one captures, however briefly, the message in memory. One of the most interesting results of memory research was the discovery that memory is of various types and is used in different ways. Some researchers, noting that the information in messages is almost always in the form of words, have called this process 'semantic memory'. Squire (1986), for example, has been careful to distinguish semantic memory from episodic memory. When we remember episodes, we remember what someone did, and when we remember words, we remember what they said. Semantic memory and episodic memory affect one another, even though one uses precepts and the other uses language (Chang, 1986). So memory research offered a distinct alternative to primarily symbolic approaches to listening.

Semantic memory is definitely related to the probabilistic nature of information. It has been studied from the point of view of 'category sizes' (Collins and Quillian, 1972), 'relatedness' (Kintsch, 1980) and 'familiarity' (McCloskey, 1980). And although Baddely and Dale (1968), Kintsch and Busche (1969) and Squire (1986) consider semantic memory to be part of long-term storage, Schulman (1972) has demonstrated that some semantic decoding does take place in shorter temporal situations. Further evidence is furnished by Pellegrino *et al.* (1975), who showed that short-term memory for words was different than it was for pictures. Monsell (1984), for example, speculated that it is the job of the 'input register' to hold the words or phonemes long enough for semantic encoding processes to be brought into play. If this is the case, then persons who cannot activate the input register would either encode immediately or lose everything. If they do the kind of grammatical processing suggested by Heen Wold's data (1978), material presented in a grammatically coherent structure would be easily processed, while material not having structure would be more difficult.

The standard description of how items are processed into long-term storage is highly linear (Loftus and Loftus, 1976). If this linear description is accurate, then a deficiency at one point of the process would clearly result in deficiencies at later temporal stages. A good way to identify such deficiencies would be to compare persons with different aptitudes at each stage in the process and see how the end product is affected. But the most important finding, and one that affects conceptions of listening most directly, is that memory has several stages, most probably best described as short-term, intermediate-term and long-term. The use of this memory model led to the hypothesis that verbal decoding can be divided into several components: short-term listening, short-term with rehearsal and lecture listening. When investigated, these three types (aspects) of listening were initially shown to differentiate among one another (Bostrom and Waldhart, 1980), and further, that short-term listening seemed to have little relationship to cognitive abilities, such as intelligence tests.

ALTERNATIVE APPROACHES TO LISTENING

If the linguistic/symbolic view is an acceptable one, and if listening is primarily a cognitive process, then the research reported above, including the memory-based models, would suffice for productive investigations into listening behaviour. The principal research tasks would be the development of reliable and valid tests of the process, and investigation into some of the varying relationships involved in the communicative process. However, many aspects of listening are not easily subsumed under a typical linguistic/symbolic framework. To begin with, the process of communication is a much more broadly defined activity than a linguistic/symbolic process alone. Defensible distinctions can be made among typical communicative functions such as relaying, stimulating, activating and linguistic functions (Bostrom, 1988a). On a more global level, communication often aims at both instrumental and relational goals.

The discovery that short-term listening (STL) was different from other aspects of listening and that individuals differ systematically in this ability was hardly earth-shaking. But what was more interesting was that the linear model proposed by Loftus and Loftus (1976) could not be maintained for listening because long-term retention did not depend on short-term retention (Bostrom and Bryant, 1980). Further, a curious finding appeared in a large-scale investigation of public speaking performance: good short-term listeners apparently performed better in oral presentations (Spitzberg and Hurt, 1983). In another interesting study of managerial effectiveness, it was demonstrated that STL was the best discriminator between good and poor branch managers in banks (Alexander *et al.*, 1992). Another even more interesting finding appeared in a long-term study of organisational success. Short-term listening was the best single predictor of upward mobility in the organisation (Sypher *et al.*, 1989). Bussey (1991) found that those respondents with good short-term skills asked more questions in an interview than those with poor short-term skills.

While the discovery that short-term listening skill is qualitatively different from long-term listening skill was an important step in separating listening research from the more traditional symbol-oriented frameworks, it did not go very far. More recently, Thomas and Levine (1994) raised some fundamental questions about the memory model of listening: (1) what is the relationship between the memory for symbols and the listening process, and (2) how can relational factors be introduced into the model? Thomas and Levine pointed out that there is no real basis for assuming a connection between short-term listening and interactive skill. While some of the studies cited above (Alexander *et al.*, 1992; Sypher *et al.*, 1989) demonstrate that some kind of relationship exists, there is no compelling theoretical or observational basis for such an assumption. Further, Thomas and Levine (1994, p. 106) contend that a conversation based on short-term memory alone would be 'nearly incoherent', and offer an alternate definition of listening that is primarily relational. In their study they examined relational cues – eye gaze, head nods, short backchat and long backchat. Short backchat consisted of utterances such as 'yes' or 'hmm' during speech, and long backchat was typically restatements of the speaker's utterances. Long backchat is identical to the 'statements and questions' aspect of the NTE listening test, but the other three are traditionally defined as non-verbal factors. Nods and gaze are clearly visual stimuli.

In short, while some research indicates that short-term listening ability (STL) is closely implicated in interpersonal activities, apparently much more than long-term skills (or ability), just how these abilities relate to one another is not known. These and other studies led to the conclusion that perhaps short-term listening was not a cognitive skill, but an interpersonal skill (Bostrom, 1990) and should not be confused with other forms of listening. 'Lecture' listening, on the other hand, seems to be very closely related to common definitions of intelligence (Bostrom and Waldhart, 1988). In other words, listening was originally modelled on memory models which contain a minimum of short- and long-term components. Dividing listening into those two kinds of abilities produced the serendipitous finding that short-term listening was apparently closely connected with interpersonal skills in a variety of settings.

But clearly no good theoretical explanation exists for this finding. On the other hand, several other aspects of listening are much more important in communication. Prominent among these is the expression and understanding of affective messages. Typically, this has been termed 'interpretive listening.'

Interpretive listening

Interpretive listening is identical to vocalic decoding. This is usually understood to mean the processing of emotional or affective content from a message, primarily from tone of voice, inflection and other variations of voice. Most persons feel that they are skilled in vocalic listening, but generally do poorly when called on to decode affect. For example, in one study using a standardised vocalic listening task, a very large sample of college students and adults only identified correct answers 55 per cent of the time (Bostrom, 1990). In other words, more than half of the time, people misinterpret vocalic signals. And while this kind of information access is universally considered to be of great importance, no one seems to have a clear idea as to how it should be improved. Individuals do vary in their 'affect orientation' (Booth-Butterfield and Booth-Butterfield, 1990).

Research indicates that improvements in interpretive listening can be accomplished with training procedures such as sensitivity training, role-playing and the like (Wolvin and Coakely, 1988). Interpreting the underlying affect implied in spoken messages may involve personal schemas (Fitch-Hauser, 1990), constructs, or 'cultural literacy' (Hirsch, 1987). These changes, however, are changes in attitude, awareness, or knowledge, not changes in basic ability. Changes in basic ability are much more difficult. A substantive body of research clearly indicates that interpretive listening is also strongly affected by an individual's ability to decode the non-verbal cues present in the exchange (Burgoon, 1994). Often when non-verbal signals contradict the verbal ones, individuals typically accept the non-verbal as a more valid expression of the true feelings of the interactant (Burgoon, 1994; Leathers, 1979). Most investigations of non-verbal cues centre on visual displays such as facial expression, posture and the like. Others have investigated vocalic messages, such as pitch, intonation and inflection. Visual cues have typically been shown to be of greater influence than the vocalic ones in most situations. However, some studies show that vocalic cues are of more use in detecting deception than visual ones (Littlepage and Pineault, 1981; Streeter *et al.*, 1977).

Recently, however, Keely-Dyreson *et al.* (1991) examined decoding differences in isolation. They compared the ability of respondents to decode visual cues with their ability to decode vocal cues, and found that visual cues were more accurately perceived than vocal ones. Some gender differences were also observed. In short, the division of messages into verbal and non-verbal categories may be too simple. Visual and vocal cues, both of which have been categorised as non-verbal messages, would seem to differ in important ways. Comparisons of decoding abilities are rare. What the relationships might be among visual/non-verbal decoding ability, vocal/non-verbal decoding ability and verbal decoding ability is not known.

In summary, decoding of non-verbal messages is an important aspect of all interactions, and this decoding usually involves visual and aural cues. Research indicates that visual cues are decoded with much greater accuracy and that the ability to decode vocalic messages is not nearly as good as most persons suppose. Lateral asymmetry of brain function may well be an unsuspected contributor to the lack of accuracy in vocalic decoding. Vocalic decoding is quite important because in mediated communications, such as the telephone, visual cues are not available. Other circumstances may preclude the inspection of facial expression and other body movements.

Schematic listening

Another way of examining the acquisition of information in spoken messages may involve the use of schemas (Fitch-Hauser, 1990). How would you interpret the following passage?

When the Kiwis took the field, they began their infamous Maori war dance. The Sydney team was forced to wait an inordinately long time for this dance to conclude, and at that time, were not mentally ready. As a consequence, and as a result of the emotionality of the ceremony, the Kiwis won easily.

If you didn't know that the event described was taking place in Australia, and involved Australian football, and that the Kiwis were distinctly the underdogs (and a host of other details), the passage would mean little to you. A good name for all the interlocking knowledge represented here would be an 'Australian football schema'.

Richard Mayer (1983) noted that schemas underlie almost all important cognitive activities and have been investigated using terms like 'frames' and 'scripts'. None the less, it is clear that quite often interpreting a prose passage is impossible without knowledge of the big picture in the situation. Hirsch (1987) extended the schema concept to general educational outcomes, calling for colleges and universities to teach a core of cultural knowledge that can serve as common schemas to assist in understanding one another.

Thain (1994) has used aspects of schema theory in formulating his definition of 'authentic' listening. He reasons that many aspects of listening skill are pure traits, such as memory and vocabulary, but an integrative act is vital to put the entire message into meaningful relationships. He presents an example of a situation in which decoding cannot take place without a larger understanding of the situation involved, similar to the Kiwi example above. Further evidence for the distinctiveness of schematic listening is furnished by the Educational Testing Service. Consider the following test item (presented on audiotape):

Man's voice: Well, what do you think is the most effective way of dealing with this matter?
Woman's voice: William has a great deal of respect for his parents. I suggest we set up a meeting with them.
Man's voice: I think William may feel threatened if we ask his parents to come in. I'd like to have the school staff try a bit longer before we call them.
Woman's voice: I think that we could involve them in such a way that William would not feel threatened.

Questioner: Why does the man hesitate to call William's parents?
    a. William could feel threatened if his parents were called.
    b. William is threatened by those who work with him at school.
    c. Children usually do not respect their parents.
    d. The man does not like to involve parents in school problems.

The correct answer is (a). Notice that the information given is provided in the man's second statement. However, the *implicit* information in the dialogue is clear: the two speakers were either teachers or school counsellors, and this type of conversation does not take place unless there is some kind of trouble. If you had absolutely no information about the school schema, you would not understand that. Your ability to respond correctly to questions like that would be determined by your knowledge of the schema, and not your ability to listen (what Thain called a 'pure trait'.) This item, together with other similar ones, is part of the forty-item listening portion of its National Teacher Examination. Other items reflect interest in short-term listening (short statements and answers), interpretive listening (the affective content of statements or dialogues) and lecture listening (responding to talks).

Table 9.1 Intercorrelations of various sections of the National Teacher Examination

Test Section		List A	List B	List C	Reading	Written task A	Written task B
1A	Statements and queries	1.00					
1B	Dialogue	0.56	1.00				
1C	Talks	0.59	0.48	1.00			
2	Reading	.72	0.58	0.68	1.00		
3A	Usage	0.63	0.49	0.58	0.71	1.00	
3B	Sentence comprehension	0.56	0.44	0.52	0.65	0.68	1.00
4	Essay	0.46	0.39	0.41	0.52	0.53	0.50

Table 9.2 Factors generated by intercorrelations of ETS 'communication skills' assessments

	I	II	III	IV	V
Statements and questions	0.27	0.85	0.23	0.24	0.17
Dialogue	0.20	0.24	0.19	0.91	0.14
Talks	0.26	0.25	0.89	0.18	0.15
Reading	0.45	0.52	0.44	0.27	0.22
Usage	0.68	0.39	0.26	0.17	0.25
Sentence comprehension	0.88	0.17	0.19	0.11	0.19
Essay	0.25	0.17	0.15	0.14	0.92

Table 9.1 presents the intercorrelations of the varying measures on the National Teacher Examination, including the results of an essay (writing) test, a reading test, a 'usage' test that measured grammatical choices and a sentence completion test of comprehension (Educational Testing Service, 1984). Unfortunately, a correlation table does not present a comprehensive view of the interrelationships in the data. To get a better idea of the relationships among these scales, factor analysis can be employed. Table 9.2 presents a simple factor analysis* of the variables in Table 9.1.

It is clear from Table 9.2 that the ETS data do conform to the tripartite model (Bostrom, 1990) very well. The 'Statements and Questions' measure, the 'Dialogue' task and the 'Talks' measure are clearly individual and distinct factors, as is the ETS 'Essay'. What exactly 'Reading' and 'Usage' are is not clear, but it seems that the original statements made in this paper about communication and language are borne out in this analysis. But most importantly, it is clear that the 'Dialogues' portion of the test is very distinct from the other subscales, and as the example of the test item above shows, the 'Dialogues' measure is dependent upon possession of a fairly well-articulated 'school' schema. In other words, the schematic aspects of the model are distinct (i.e. different) from the other skills involved.

As we review the history of listening research, we see that traditional studies of communication have centred on linguistic competence – understandably, since it has taken

---

* This is certainly not a sophisticated analysis. Principal components were used, rather than an oblique solution, and the five-factor solution is clearly arbitrary. None the less, it does illustrate some of the internal characteristics of these abilities.

place in the traditional learning paradigm in the Western world. The cognitive/linguistic approach has affected our basic orientation towards almost every effort in studying communicative competence. Unfortunately, sometimes it just isn't efficacious. Communication often needs to focus on behaviour, on relationships, and on affect. Traditional studies in listening assessment have not examined the overall communicative process, but have focused primarily on individual differences in the processing of orally presented symbols.

BROADER ASPECTS OF THE STUDY OF LISTENING

Clearly, it is time to take another look at the research in listening as a whole. Definitions of listening began with symbolic processing (synonymous with intelligence) and then were supplemented with other aspects, such as attitudes. Memory models were introduced, as well as an emphasis on schemas of various types. If we look carefully at all of the previous research in listening, we can see that the one common element in all of these different approaches has been information processing. This common thread is strong enough for us to say that the best definition of listening is the *acquisition, processing, and retention of information in the interpersonal context*. This is a much more inclusive definition, but has a number of advantages. One advantage of using this more inclusive model of listening is that visual stimuli are just as important as aural stimuli. The inclusion follows logically from integrating interpretive, relational and behavioural aspects of communication.

Some interesting research has been conducted on the comparison of audio and video modalities, much of which has important implications for the assessment of listening. In the next section, we will examine some of these.

Audio or video?

Comparisons of audio and video modalities are recent ones, and have only been made possible because modern technology has enabled researchers to control each artificially. In interpersonal situations, audio and video occur simultaneously. The introduction of electronic communication devices – the telephone, and then radio – separated video from audio. Television, of course, restored video, but in its own way. Commercial news broadcasts provided pictures of explosions and earthquakes while an announcer described the carnage but typically the audio and video *as presented by broadcasters* have little to do with one another. Some early research (Anderson, 1966, 1968) illustrates the way researchers thought at that time. Anderson compared the way that *adding* video could improve retention and effect. In effect, the audio contained *the message*. This way of thinking still persists, as we will see. Contrasts between audio and video are relatively new.

In other words, we see that the linguistic/symbolic bias in early research in telecommunication determined how investigations were conducted. We can also see this dominance in later research. Effectiveness has been defined as simple retention of news content (Gunter, 1987; Graber, 1988). Studies of violence and other antisocial effects have only been related to 'content', a global term which usually does not distinguish between modalities.

This is a truly odd assumption, given the universal assumption most theorists make about the preeminence of the video mode. The preoccupation with video by news directors is well known, at least in the US. Leslie Stahl, writing recently about her experience in

Table 9.3 Percentages of news headlines correctly recalled as a function of visual format and modality

Modality		Film	Stills	Newscaster	Mean
				Visual format	
	Audio-visual	90	54	29	51
Experiment 1	Audio only	44	41	50	45
	Mean	57	48	40	48
	Audio-visual	74	60	35	56
Experiment 2	Audio only	50	46	48	48
	Mean	62	53	42	52

the first Reagan campaign, reported that Michael Deaver, Reagan's media manager, was extremely co-operative in providing the candidate for video but kept absolute control of the video content. Ms Stahl reported that often she did a voice-over telling the world that Reagan's proposed economic policies were pure voodoo or that his proposed international policies would result in a Third World War, but the video always showed a smiling, genial, nice guy talking with Boy Scouts or homemakers. Stahl concluded that she had been 'had' by Deaver and the other Reagan managers, since, in her words, 'the video was always the more powerful of the messages'.

None the less, research seems to focus on propositional content of news programmes. This content is not always well remembered. For example, Stauffer *et al.* (1983) telephoned viewers immediately after they watched network news programmes and reported that the viewers contacted did not remember much news content. Of an average of 13.3 news items, only 2.3 were recalled (17.2 per cent). A cued group did better, but even this group never exceeded 25 per cent recall. Better educated persons did slightly better than the average, but the overall picture is a dismal one.

Barrie Gunter (1987) has conducted careful research in memory for news as a function of the modality of presentation. His research bears out much of the Stauffer *et al.* findings. Gunter points out that there are significant differences between modalities (audio plus video versus audio alone, and print). Gunter's research utilised illustrative tapes (one featured riots in the streets of Seoul), and his data show us that video added to audio improves the retention of headlines significantly. Table 9.3 presents some of these data (from Gunter, 1987, p. 235).

While the film and the still pictures improved the retention of headlines, adding video to the message when it consisted of a newscaster (a talking head) was quite the opposite. In these circumstances, the audio alone was superior. In other words, talking-head presentations are a poor way to utilise video. This finding has been repeated in other research (Searle and Bostrom, 1990).

Nevertheless, we can see that print is better than audio and audio-visual presentations. When Gunter examined these differences, he also found that gender plays a role. Table 9.4 (from Gunter, 1987, p. 225) presents these differences. Males in Gunter's studies remembered better almost universally. In a similar study, however, Searle and Bostrom (1990) found that females remembered more data from viewing a talking-head presentation than did males. Reports of gender differences of this type probably should not be taken seriously unless gender is defined psychologically rather than physiologically.

Table 9.4 Recall of news as a function of presentation modality

Presentation modality	Experiment 1			Experiment 2		
	Males	*Females*	*All*	*Males*	*Females*	*All*
Audio-visual	12.1	8.0	10.1	9.9	9.9	9.9
Audio only	10.4	7.1	8.8	13.1	11.6	12.4
Print	13.3	11.6	12.5	15.7	17.0	16.4
All modalities	11.9	8.9	10.5	12.9	12.8	12.9

Gunter generally explains the retention of information presented in the news as a function of the varying cognitive structures that may or may not affect processing the news. His assumption is that the cognitive structure for all processing is the same. Gunter reviews memory structures, such as semantic and episodic memory. He also reviews memory processes, such as encoding, arousal, selective attention, spacing, organising and retrieval. He applies all of these concepts (in a theoretic sense) to the manner in which television news is presented. Here is Gunter's (1987, p. 257) explanation for the way news is remembered:

> sentences that readily conjure up visual scenes in the minds of individuals can be assigned a context more easily than sentences that do not, leading to better memory performance. In other words, it may be easier to relate new sentence input whose content can also be 'pictured' to existing propositional knowledge structures in memory derived from other linguistic or picture inputs, providing an abundance of connections from permanent memory into the new information.

The preeminence of the linguistic/symbolic paradigm is evident in this explanation.

A true comparison of the differences between sound and sight as information inputs would occur only if the audio and video and video only presented *exactly the same material, or content*. Recently, Grimes (1991) conducted such a comparison. He compared attentional factors in what he called 'redundant', 'quasi-redundant' and 'non-redundant' video-audio comparisons. In the redundant condition, the video and audio exactly corresponded. Grimes prepared a videotape of a farmer drilling a hole in a tree to tap maple syrup, and added audio saying 'farmers drill holes in trees to tap maple syrup'. In the quasi-redundant condition the video was taken at a distance in which details were hard to make out, and in the non-redundant condition, the audio was the principal method of gaining information. Grimes examined the degree to which receivers attended to the message. Messages were inserted in the stimulus tape instructing watchers to press a lever. When the lever-pressing was delayed, Grimes reasoned that they were not paying attention as well as when the lever-pressing was instantaneous. The reaction times in these three conditions did not vary significantly.

Then Grimes examined recognition scores of information presented in newscasts to see if the degree of redundancy made a difference there. Video was only superior in a condition where no redundancy was present. Table 9.5 presents these scores.

Grimes' research has probably the best theoretical and methodological instances of the comparison of sound and sight and suggests that there is little difference in the modalities. Newhagen and Reeves (1992) provide an interesting analysis of the research on memory for television. They note that most of these studies rely on propositional memory – an obvious problem. Visual memory is tremendously difficult to measure, so Newhagen and

Table 9.5 Recognition scores

Redundancy	Visual	Audio
High	23.84	29.76
Medium	19.71	28.44
None	23.10	18.35

Reeves relied on a 'recognition' technique – i.e. asking 'Did you see this before?' These recognitions were inhibited by negative images preceding the stories or stimuli.

Further evidence for a hypothesis of no differences comes from research in deception. Bauchner *et al.* (1977) studied the ability of receivers to detect deception. Messages were presented by four different media: face-to-face, video, audio and printed transcript. No significant differences could be seen – judgemental accuracy was not more effective on any channel. So in two very careful studies of communication effectiveness, media effects seem to be exaggerated. In short, the way that commercial television operates probably has *created* the assumed superiority of the video modality rather than there being any innate superiority of one medium over another. Researchers have designed their studies to mirror what is practised, and the consequence is that the superiority is demonstrated by the research. This may well be an instance of what Melody and Mansell (1983) term 'administrative' research.

None the less, there is no question that future research in listening should expand to a search for explanations concerning the processing of information in general, not simply the oral channel. Interpersonal interactions do contain a strong visual component, and the visual component should be combined with what we know about non-verbal communication to add to our existing knowledge. But the audio-video contrasts should only be conducted in a framework of interpretive listening, not modelled after existing broadcasting practice.

Reading and listening

Few studies have been done comparing reading and listening as modalities for gaining information. Such studies would seem to be one of the most obvious kinds of comparisons, especially in educational research. But comparisons of reading and listening modalities are rare. Even in research reports which purport to examine the differences between reading and listening (Horowitz and Samuels, 1987), no instances of direct comparisons are reported. Comparisons of this kind are difficult to compare directly because of the problem in elapsed time. Reading can occur at roughly four or five times the rate of an audio or video signal. Announcers speak at a rate of between 100 and 125 words per minute. If you can process information at 500 words per minute and it is only coming to you at 150, there is a great gap here. This certainly explains why good short-term listeners who are also high sensation-seekers, do much more poorly on lecture listening than low sensation-seekers (Bostrom, 1990).

We do know that both reading and listening are affected by 'sensation-seeking' on the part of the receiver (Donohew *et al.,* 1984; Bostrom, 1990). The basic similarity in these two processes would seem to indicate that productive investigations should be a possibility in the future.

Listening and behaviour

Examining the behaviour involved in listening would seem to be a difficult task. Recall that Thomas and Levine (1994) examined immediate behavioural responses to listening – eye gaze, head nods, short backchat and long backchat, all of which are typically accepted indicators of attentional constancy. But other than attending to the speaker, what behavioural indications are there of listening? Simply acquiring and storing information do not suffice to bring about behavioural change. Smokers know that cigarettes affect their health, but continue to smoke. Drivers know that wearing seatbelts is a wise practice, but some are careless about the actual compliance. Steinhauer (1995) reports that knowledge about the nutritional value of foods had no appreciable effect on consumers' choices of foods. If we consider listening to be only an informational process, then little, if any, behavioural change will result. On the other hand, if individuals listen with an eye to changes in behaviour, then we would have to conclude that earlier models of listening might not be sufficient.

Information-seeking is a rather well-researched phenomenon in communication research. Examining the uses and gratifications individuals seek from television has been carefully explored (Palmgreen, 1984). If individuals seek information proactively in media consumption, why not in interpersonal interactions? Festinger (1957) outlined circumstances in which individuals sought information to reduce 'dissonance' created by buying decisions. The description by Reardon and Rogers (1988) of the interleaving of mass and interpersonal processes in a buying decision would seem to offer an excellent model for this kind of listening research.

Behavioural research in listening probably would depend heavily on the use of schemas as explanatory mechanisms. Recall that both Graber (1988) and Gunter (1987) depended heavily on this mechanism as an explanatory paradigm. But both of these researchers have missed some of the essential characteristics of schematic research, especially some of the implications for behavioural modifications. Thain (1994) proposed that the term 'authentic' listening be used to describe the broader aspects of the process, and Fitch-Hauser proposed an outline for looking at schemas in the listening process. The ETS National Teacher Examination provided some compelling data to convince us that schematic processes are different from the more specific skills. But behavioural change is a communicative effect that goes beyond simple retention effects, and may be a communicative outcome that is ultimately more important.

In a study of the impact of varying types of television programmes on children's attitudes about gender-oriented attitudes about work, the best format was found to be a mini-drama about a little girl who wanted to be a mechanic (Williams *et al.*, 1981). The key to its effectiveness was identification, a powerful force. These kinds of identification can be very destructive. Many persons (including former American Vice-President Quayle) believe that the dramatic programmes on television are affecting our culture in important ways.

The best explanation of this phenomenon is the development of an elaborate schema system and the attachment of propositional content to this system. Mary John Smith (1982) demonstrated how this effect seems to work. In a straightforward message, she told individuals that high-risk people made better firefighters or, in other words, a personality test with 'riskiness' as a personality trait would be a useful way to screen applicants for a fire department recruiting task. Then she asked these people either to (a) construct a short message supporting the belief, (b) construct a short message refuting the belief, (c) construct messages both pro and con arguments, or to (d) construct messages irrelevant to the schemata. Then she acknowledged to everyone that the message was false – no such research existed. Those who wrote arguments defending the belief stubbornly refused to change, even though they knew that the grounds for their belief were faked. Smith attributes the phenomenon to 'plugging in' the proposition to existing schemas, but an explanation that utilised scripts or semantic networks would be as defensible. Clearly, the event is related to connection-making of some type. Research in listening that explored such structures would be very productive.

PROBLEMS IN LISTENING RESEARCH

Certainly, two very important questions in communication research are 'How do people process information received from others?' and 'How can this processing be improved?' Common sense tells us that to claim that something has been improved we must be able to demonstrate that individuals are different in some fashion as a result of something that they had perceived. If we believe something can be improved the most logical way to demonstrate this is to measure its level prior to the improvement procedure hypothesised and then measure it after the procedure has been applied.

Unfortunately, self-report is not a highly reliable way to discover characteristics about an individual's behaviour. Questionnaires often probe respondents about their past, specifically getting to quantitative issues – 'During the past two weeks, on days when you drank alcohol, how many drinks did you have?'; 'In the past twelve months, how often did you go to your dentist?'; 'When did you last work at a full-time job?' – are all examples of these kinds of questions. These questions make an implicit demand to remember and enumerate specific autobiographical episodes. However, respondents frequently have trouble complying because of limits on their ability to recall. In these situations, respondents resort to inferences that use partial information from memory to construct a numeric answer.

Feinberg and Tanur (1989) have suggested reducing the error by placing embedded experiments in survey design, and this seems to be a promising method. This method randomly administers alternate questionnaires or other variations in procedure to subsets of the sample. Statistically, these subsets are partialled out as part of the error variance in the analysis of variance. Essentially, what results is an embedded randomised block design. Feinberg and Tanur demonstrated this technique by designing two sets of questionnaires, both of which contained items about abortion. In one questionnaire, the question context contained items generally relating to women's rights followed by questions about abortions. In a second questionnaire, the items related to medical practice and health issues followed by questions about abortion. The questionnaires produced dramatically different results (Feinberg and Tanur, 1989). Feinberg and Tanur explain their results by invoking schema theory.

The implications of these findings for listening research are clear – reliance on past events is probably poor practice. If responses can be designed to assess immediate responses, a greater degree of reliability can be produced. In another examination of questionnaire behaviour, Bradburn *et al.* (1987) have discovered strong evidence of schema theory in survey reports. Their respondents tended to group recalled happenings in terms of memory reconstructions, rather than in any straight linear form. They conclude that people will use any information they have available to generate any kind of reasonable answer. This is especially true when recalling events in their own lives. In other words, respondents may remember one or two pertinent facts and they produce an answer using some kind of inductive inference. Most of us are familiar with the telescoping phenomenon that occurs in surveys – we remember material as having occurred in smaller units of time. Since people recall events in terms of autobiographical events, surveys can and should be designed to trigger these events in the respondent's memory. For example, if asking a respondent about behaviour or reaction about the Chernobyl disaster, it would be useful to anchor the responses in terms of the respondents' own lives, such as tagging the response to events more familiar, such as graduations, marriages, etc.

Results from surveys certainly throw light on individual interpretation of activities, but listening research ought to aim at specific responses in which a clear indication of behaviour is present. This is especially important if the phenomena involved deal with situations that inhibit or facilitate recall and the accuracy of respondents' answers is at issue.

OVERVIEW: IMPLICATIONS FOR PRACTICE

In our organisational life, listening is most often invoked as an interpersonal skill and supervisors are clearly considered competent when they listen well. Individuals prize good listening in others even when they are unwilling to engage in it themselves. This well-known characteristic opens a manipulative channel that many have exploited. Supervisors may learn to offer the appearance of listening only to build a good attitude in a subordinate. When they proclaim 'I am a good listener', it is only an internal strategy to get others to go along. This strategy was utilised on a grand scale when a large American computer corporation adopted 'We listen better' as a theme for a series of television advertisements. The series was frankly copied from the Avis 'We try harder' slogans. In order to give the campaign credibility, the corporation decided to train its employees in listening, offering a series of seminars around the country. To everyone's surprise, the employees enjoyed the training and reported that learning about listening not only helped them in their organisational lives, but was instrumental in building better relationships at home! Training in listening, however inspired, is a worthwhile activity and, whether administered by experts or not, can convey some benefits.

The measurement approach to listening research should convince us all that individuals differ in their listening ability, and that these differences can make organisational co-ordination very difficult. Results from almost every aspect of listening measurement show that less than half of what is transmitted is retained, even within a few minutes. Undoubtedly, managers need to explore the information requirements of the organisation and examine the communicative tasks very closely. The first major task is to make sure communicative interactions have a clear, specific purpose. Consider the following communicative situations – all of which occur in daily life in organisations:

- A school board listening to a teacher advocating a new reading programme
- A social worker explaining the food stamp programme to a group of welfare mothers
- A group of new employees listening to a personnel supervisor explaining how to use the company's cash register system

- A soccer coach going over a new play with the team
- A lifeguard at a municipal pool explaining the rules to a newly formed swimming club
- An army officer giving instructions to a unit before a training exercise
- A student testifying before the city council concerning parking problems

All of these situations have several common elements. Each is an example of one individual presenting an extended message to a large group of other individuals. In addition, certain agreed-upon rules contribute to an element of formality in these occasions:

1 Some mutual goal or purpose is assumed, whether organisational or societal
2 Minimal structure and role expectations divide the group into one 'source' (speaker) and many 'receivers' (listeners)
3 The receivers assume that the source has some expertise
4 The receivers assume specific preparation on the part of the source
5 The receivers don't talk as much as the source

If all of these five requirements are met, then sensible inquiries can be made concerning differences in listening skills. If not, then problems in retention of messages may be lodged in one of the five characteristics above.

What does research tell us about improving our listening effectiveness? Actually, there is a good deal to be learned from the research efforts. First, we all vary in our ability to listen. This means that in a given situation, some receivers will retain only half as much as others do. This ability is uncorrelated with other cognitive skills, which means that even if you did well at school, you may be a poor listener. Probably the only way to ascertain an individual's skill-level is to use a standardised abilities test. Those who are poorer in this ability need to work harder in the process. Second, sensation-seeking contributes negatively to lecture listening. This means that if you are a high sensation-seeker (you enjoy auto racing, and downhill skiing) you will have difficulty concentrating during a lecture. Individuals can introduce self-interesting strategies during lectures to counteract these problems. Third, schematic listening is probably more important than most researchers thought. This means that individuals new to an organisation or a manufacturing system will have much more difficulty than those who have an extensive history in it. Managers need to be aware of these differences. Fourth, the organisation or system needs to be clear about what the goal of the communicative interaction can be. Cognitively oriented data can be reduced to writing or stored in a computer. Interpersonal interactions are probably better suited to relational matters and affective messages.

There is, sadly, an unfortunate tendency among managers or others in authority to assume that, if a communication is not efficacious, it is therefore the fault of the receivers. Many managers are notoriously poor transmitters, but since they enjoy organisational power, they are generally attended to. It is obviously true that individuals differ in receiving ability, but these differences are usually not ones that can be easily overcome with short courses or 'quick fix' programmes. A broader, more functional programme in listening research might help to find new applications.

REFERENCES

Alexander, E. R., Penley, L. E. and Jernigan, I. E. (1992) 'The Relationship of Basic Decoding Skills to Managerial Effectiveness', *Manangement Communication Quarterly*, 6, 58–73.

Anderson, J. (1966) 'Equivalence of Meaning Among Statements Present Through Various Media,' *Audiovisual Communication Review*, 14, 499–505.

—— (1968) 'More on the Equivalence of Statements Presented in Various Media,' *Audiovisual Communication Review*, 16, 25–32.

Baddely, A. and Dale, H. (1968) 'The Effect of Semantic Similarity on Retroactive Interference in Long- and Short-term Memory,' *Journal of Verbal Learning and Verbal Behavior*, 5, 471–20.

Bauchner, J. E., Brandt, D. R. and Miller, G. R. (1977) 'The Truth/Deception Attribution: Effects of Varying Levels of Informaiton Availability', in B. D. Rubin (ed.), *Communication Yearbook, Vol. 1*, 376–93, Transaction Books, New Brunswick, NJ.

Beatty, M. and Payne, S. (1984) 'Listening Comprehension as a Function of Cognitive Complexity', *Communication Monographs*, 51, 85–9.

Beighley, K. (1952) 'The Effect of Four Speech Variables on Listener Comprehension', *Speech Monographs*, 19, 249–58.

—— (1954) 'An Experimental Study of the Effect of Three Speech Variables on Listener Comprehension', *Speech Monographs*, 21, 248–53.

Bem, D. (1965) 'An Experimental Analysis of Self-persuasion', *Journal of Experimental Social Psychology*, 1, 199–218.

—— (1967) 'Self-perception: An Alternative Explanation of the Cognitive Dissonance Phenomenon', *Psychological Review*, 74, 183–200.

Booth-Butterfield, M. and Booth-Butterfield, S. (1990) 'Conceptualizing Affect as Information in Communication Production', *Human Communication Research*, 16, 451–76.

Bostrom, R. N. (1980) 'Altered Physiological States: The Central Nervous System and Persuasive Communications', in G. Miller and M. Roloff, *Persuasion: New Directions in Theory and Research*, Sage, Beverly Hills.

—— (1983) *Persuasion*, Englewood Cliffs, Prentice-Hall, NJ.

—— (1988a) *Communicating in Public*, Burgess, Minneapolis, Minnesota.

—— (1988b) 'Memory Models and the Measurement of Listening', *Communication Education*, 37, 1–18.

—— (1990) *Listening behavior: Measurement and Applications*, Guilford, New York.

—— and Bryant, C. (1980) 'Factors in the Retention of Information Presented Orally: the Role of Short-term Memory', *Western Speech Communication Journal*, 44, 137–45.

Bostrom, R. N. and Donohew, L. (1992) 'The Case for Empiricism: Clarifying Fundamental Issues in Communication Theory', *Communication Monographs*, 59, 109–128.

Bostrom, R. N. and Prather, M. E. (1992) 'Birth Order and Communicative Characteristics of Individuals', Paper presented at the International Communication Association Annual Meeting, Miami, FL, May.

Bostrom, R. N. and Waldhart, E. S. (1980) 'Components in Listening Behavior: The Role of Short-term Memory', *Human Communication Research*, 6, 211–27.

Bracewell, R. J., Fredericksen, C. H. and Fredericksen, J. D. (1982) 'Cognitive Processes in Composing and Comprehending Discourse', *Education Psychologies*, 17, 146–64.

Bradburn, N. M., Rips, L. J. and Shevell, S. K. (1987) 'Answering Autobiographical Questions: the Impact of Memory and Inference on Surveys', *Science*, 236, 157–61.

Brown, J. and Carlsen, R. (1955) 'Brown–Carlsen Listening Comprehension Test', Harcourt, Brace & World, New York.

Brown, L. (1982) *Communicating Facts and Ideas in Business*, Prentice-Hall, Englewood Cliffs, NJ.

Brown, M. H., Waldhart, E. S. and Bostrom R. N. (1990) 'Differences in Motivational Level in Listening Tasks', in R. Bostrom, *Listening Behavior: Measurement and Applications*, Guilford, New York, 144–51.

Buchli, V. and Pearce, W. (1974) 'Listening Behavior in Coorientational States', *Journal of Communication*, 24, 62–70.

Burgoon, J. (1994) 'Non-verbal Signals', in M. Knapp and G. Miller (eds), *Handbook of Interpersonal Communication* (2nd edn), Sage, Beverly Hills, pp. 344–93.

Burns, K. and Beier, E. (1973) 'Significance of Vocal and Visual Channels in the Decoding of Emotional Meaning', *Journal of Communication*, 23, 118–30.

Bussey, J. (1991) *Question Asking in an Interview and Varying Listening Skills*, paper presented at the annual meeting of the Southern Communication Association, Tampa, Florida, April.

Chang, T. (1986) 'Semantic Memory: Facts and Models', *Psychological Bulletin*, 99, 199–220.

Chesebro, J. (1984) 'The Media Reality: Epistemological Functions of Media in Cultural Systems', *Critical Studies in Mass Communication*, 1, 111–30.

Collins, A. and Quillian, M. (1972) 'Experiments on Semantic Memory and Language Comprehension', in L. Gregg, (ed.), *Cognition in Learning and Memory*, John Wiley, New York, pp. 117–37.

Dickens, M. and Williams, F. (1964) 'An Experimental Application of Cloze Procedure and Attitude Measures to Listening Comprehension', *Speech Monographs*, 31, 103–8.

Donohew, L., Nair, M. and Finn, S. (1984) 'Automaticity, Arousal, and Information Exposure', in R. Bostrom (ed.), *Communication Yearbook Eight*, Sage, Beverly Hills.

Educational Testing Service, (1957) *Sequential Tests of Educational Progress*, Educational Testing Service, Princeton, NJ.

—— (1984) 'Test Analysis: Core Battery', unpublished statistical report, Princeton, NJ, February.

Eisenberg, E. W. and Goodall, H. L., Jr., (1993) *Organizational Communication: Balancing Creativity and Constraint*, St Martin's Press, New York.

Ekman, P. and Friesen, W. (1969) 'Non-verbal Leakage and Clues to Deception', *Psychiatry*, 32, 88–106.

Ernest, C. (1968) 'Listening Comprehension as a Function of Type of Material and Rate of Presentation', *Speech Monographs*, 35, 154–6.

Ewen, S. (1983) 'The Implications of Empiricism', *Journal of Communication*, 33, 3, 219–25.

Feinberg, S. E. and Tanur, J. M. (1989) 'Combining Cognitive and Statistical Approaches to Survey Design', *Science*, 243, 1017–22.

Festinger, L. (1957) *A Theory of Cognitive Dissonance*, Harper & Row, New York.

Fitch-Hauser, M. (1990) 'Making Sense of Data: Constructs, Schemas, and Concepts', in R. Bostrom, *Listening Behavior: Measurement and Applications*, Guilford, New York, pp. 76–90.

Frandsen, K. (1963) 'Effects of Threat Appeals and Media of Transmission', *Speech Monographs*, 30, 101–4.

Gardner, H. (1983) *Frames of Mind: The Theory of Multiple Intelligence*, Basic Books, New York.

Graber, D. A. (1988) *Processing the News*, Longman, New York.

Griffin, D. and Buehler, R. (1993) 'Role of Construal Processes in Conformity and Dissent', *Journal of Personality and Social Psychology*, 65, 4, 657–69.

Grimes, T. (1991) 'Mild Auditory-visual Dissonance in Television News May Exceed Viewer Attentional Capacity', *Human Communication Research*, 18, 268–9.

Gunter, B. (1987) *Poor Reception: Misunderstanding and Forgetting Broadcast News*, Erlbaum, Hillsdale, NJ.

Heen Wold, A. (1978) *Decoding Oral Language*, Academic Press, London.

Hirsch, R. (1987) *Cultural Literacy*, Houghton-Mifflin, New York.

Horowitz, R. and Samuels, S. J. (1987) *Comprehending Oral and Written Language*, Academic Press, New York.

Hsia, H. (1968) 'Output, Error, Equivocation, and Recalled Information in Auditory, Visual, and Audiovisual Information Processing with Constant Noise', *Journal of Communication*, 18, 325–53.

Hubner, K. (1985) *Critique of Scientific Reason*, translated by P. Dixon and H. Dixon, University of Chicago Press, Chicago.

Huspek, M. (1991) 'Taking Aim at Habermas' Critical Theory: On the Road Toward a Critical Hermeneutics', *Communication Monographs*, 58, 225–33.

Keely-Dyreson, M., Burgoon, J. K. and Bailey, W. (1991) 'The Effects of Stress and Gender on Nonverbal Decoding Accuracy and Vocalic Channels', *Human Communication Research*, 17, 584–605.

Kelly, C. (1965) 'An Investigation of the Construct Validity of Two Commercially Published Listening Tests', *Speech Monographs*, 32, 139–43.

—— (1967) 'Listening: a Complex of Activities or a Unitary Skill?', *Speech Monographs*, 34, 455–66.

Kerlinger, F. (1986) *Foundations of Behavioral Research* (3rd edn), Holt, Rhinehart & Winston, New York.

King, P. E. and Behnke, R. R. (1989) 'The Effect of Compressed Speech on Comprehensive, Interpretive, and Short-term Listening', *Human Communication Research*, 15, 428–43.

Kintsch, W. (1980) 'Semantic Memory: A Tutorial', in R.S. Nickerson (ed.), *Attention and Performance VIII*, Erlbaum, Hillsdale, NJ, pp. 595–620.

—— and Busche, H. (1969) 'Homophones and Synonyms in Short-term Memory', *Journal of Experimental Psychology*, 80, 403–7.

Klemmer, E. and Snyder, F. (1972) 'Measurement of Time Spent Communicating', *Journal of Communication*, 22, 142–58.

Klinzing, D. (1972) 'Listening Comprehension of Pre-school Age Children as a Function of Rate of Presentation, Sex and Age', *Speech Teacher*, 21, 86–92.

Knapp, M. (1984) *Interpersonal Communication and Human Relationships*, Allyn & Bacon, Newbury Park, MA.

——, Miller, G. R. and Fudge, K. B. (1994) 'Basic Concepts in Interpersonal Communication', in M. L. Knapp and G. R. Miller (eds), *Handbook of Interpersonal Communication* (2nd edn), Sage, Newbury Park.

Knuf, J. (1993) '"Ritual" in Organizational Culture Theory: Some Theoretical Reflections and a Plea for Greater Terminological Rigor', in S. Deetz (ed.), *Communication Yearbook Sixteen*, Sage, Newbury Park, pp. 61–93.

Leathers, D. (1979) 'The Impact of Multichannel Message Inconsistency on Verbal and Non-verbal Decoding Behaviors', *Communication Monographs*, 46, 88–100.

Littlepage, G. E. and Pineault, M. A. (1981) 'Detection of Truthful and Deceptive Interpersonal Communications Across Information Transmission Modes', *The Journal of Social Psychology*, 114, 57–68.

Loftus, G. and Loftus, E. (1976) *Human Memory: the Processing of Information*, John Wiley, New York.

McClendon, P. (1958) 'An Experimental Study of the Relationship Between the Notetaking Practices and Listening Comprehension of College Freshmen During Expository Lectures', *Speech Monographs*, 25, 222–8.

McCloskey, M. (1980) 'The Stimulus Familiarity Problem in Semantic Memory Research', *Journal of Verbal Learning and Verbal Behavior*, 19, 485–502.

Mayer, R. (1983) *Thinking, Problem Solving, and Cognition*, Freeman, San Francisco.

Mehrabian, A. and Wiener, M. (1967) 'Decoding of Inconsistent Communications', *Journal of Personality and Social Psychology*, 6(1), 109–14.

Melody, W. H. and Mansell, R. E. (1983), 'On Critical and Administrative Research: A New Critical Analysis', *Journal of Communication*, 33(3), 103–16.

Miller, G. R. (1980) 'On Being Persuaded: Some Basic Distinctions', in G. R. Miller and M. E. Roloff (eds), *Persuasion: New Directions in Theory and Research*, Sage, Beverly Hills.

—— and Burgoon, M. (1978) 'Persuasion Research: Review and Commentary', in B. Rueben (ed.), *Communication Yearbook II*, Sage, Beverly Hills.

Miller, R. W. (1987) *Fact and Method*, Princeton University Press, Princeton, NJ.

Monsell, S. (1984) 'Components of Working Memory Underlying Verbal Skills: A "Distributed Capacities" View', in H. Bouma and D. G. Bowhuis (eds), *Attention and Performance, Vol. 10*, Erlbaum, Hillsdale, NJ.

Mosco, V. (1983) 'Critical Research and the Role of Labor', *Journal of Communication*, 33(3), 237–48.

Motley, M. T. (1992) 'Mindfulness in Solving Communicator's Dilemmas. Communication: Inherently Strategic and Primarily Automatic', *Communication Monographs*, 59, 306–14.

Myrdahl, G. (1967) *Objectivity in Social Research*, Random House, New York.

Newhagen, J. E. and Reeves, B. (1992) 'The Evenings's Bad News: The Effects of Compelling Negative Television News Images on Memory', *Journal of Communication*, 42(2), 25–41.

Nichols, R. (1947) 'Listening: Questions and Problems', *Quarterly Journal of Speech*, 33, 83–6.

—— (1948) 'Factors in Listening Comprehension', *Speech Monographs*, 15, 154–63.

Palamatier, R. and McNinch, G. (1972) 'Source of Gains in Listening Skill: Experimental or Pretest Experience', *Journal of Communication*, 22, 70–6.

Palmgreen, P. (1984) 'Uses and Gratifications: A Theoretical Perspective', in R. Bostrom (ed.), *Communication Yearbook Eight*, Sage, Beverly Hills, pp. 20–55.

Pellegrino, J., Siegel, A. and Dhawan, M. (1975) 'Short Term Retention for Pictures and Words: Evidence for Dual Coding Systems', *Journal of Experimental Psychology*, 104, 95–101.

Petrie, C. and Carrell, S. (1976) 'The Relationship of Motivation, Listening Capacity, Initial Information, and Verbal Organizational Ability to Lecture Comprehension and Retention', *Communication Monographs*, 43, 184–7.

Pinker, S. (1994) *The Language Instinct: How the Mind Creates Language*, William Morrow & Company, New York.

Pollock, D. and Cox, J. R. (1991) 'Historicizing "Reason": Critical Theory, Practice and Postmodernity', *Communication Monographs*, 58, 170–8.

Prather, M. E. (1991) 'Birth Order and Listening Ability', paper presented at the annual meeting of the Southern Speech Association, Tampa, FL, April.

Rankin, P. (1929) 'Listening Ability', *Proceedings of the Ohio State Educational Conference*, Ohio State University Press, Columbus.

Ray, E. B. and Bostrom R. N. (1990) 'Listening to Medical Messages: The Relationship of Physican Gender and Patient Gender to Long- and Short-term Recall', in R. Bostrom, *Listening Behavior: Measurement and Applications*, Guilford, New York, pp. 144–51.

Reardon, K. K. and Rogers, E. M. (1988) 'Interpersonal versus Mass Media Communication: A False Dichotomy', *Human Communication Research*, 15, 284–303.

Rogers, E. M. (1962) *Diffusion of Information*, Free Press, New York.

Rossiter, C. (1972) 'Sex of the Speaker, Sex of the Listener, and Listening Comprehension', *Journal of Communication*, 22, 64–69.

Schmandt-Besserat, D. (1990) 'Symbols in the Prehistoric Middle-East: Developmental Features Preceding Written Communication', in R. L. Enos (ed.), *Oral and Written Communication: Historical aspects*, Sage, Newbury Park, pp. 16–31.

Schulman, H. (1972) 'Semantic Confusion Errors in Short-term Memory', *Journal of Verbal Learning and Verbal Behavior*, 11, 221–7.

Searle, B. H. and Bostrom R. N. (1990) 'Encoding, Media, Affect and Gender', in R. Bostrom, *Listening Behavior: Measurement and Applications*, Guilford, New York, pp. 144–51.

Skinner, B. F. (1986), 'What is Wrong with Daily Life in the Western World?' *American Psychologist*, 41, 568–74.

Smith, M. J. (1982) 'Cognitive Schema Theory and the Perseverance and Attenuation of Unwarranted Empirical Beliefs', *Communication Monographs*, 42, 116–26.

Spitzberg, B. and Hurt, T. (1983) *Essays on Human Communication*, Ginn & Company, Lexington, MA, pp. 64–71.

Squire, L. (1986) 'Mechanisms of Memory', *Science*, 232, 1612–19.

Stauffer, J., Frost, R. and Rybolt, W. (1983) 'The Attention Factor in Recalling Network News', *Journal of Communication*, 33, 1, 29–37.

Steinhauer, J. (1995) 'Food Labels Don't Change Eating Habits', *New York Times*, 10 May 1995, B1.

Sternberg, R. (1985) 'Human Intelligence: The Model is the Message', *Science*, 230, 1111–18.

Sticht, T. and Glassnap, D. (1972) 'Effects of Speech Rate, Selection Difficulty, Association Strength, and Mental Aptitude on Learning by Listening', *Journal of Communication*, 22, 174–8.

Streeter, L.A., Krauss, R.M., Geller, V., Olson, C. and Apple, W. (1977) 'Pitch Changes During Attempted Deception', *Journal of Personality and Social Psychology*, 35, 5, 345–50.

Sypher, B. D., Bostrom, R. N. and Seibert, J. H. (1989) 'Listening, Communication Abilities, and Success at Work', *Journal of Business Communication*, 26, 293–303.

Thain, J. W. (1994) 'Improving the Measurement of Language Aptitude: The Potential of the L1 Measures', paper presented at the Language Aptitude Improvement Symposium, Washington, DC, September.

Thomas, L. T. and Levine, T. R. (1994) 'Disentangling Listening and Verbal Recall: Related but Separate Constructs?', *Human Communication Research*, 21, 103–27.

Thompson, E. (1967) 'Some Effects of Message Structure on Listener's Comprehension', *Speech Monographs*, 34, 51–7.

Watzlawick, P., Beavin, J. and Jackson, D. (1967) *Pragmatics of Human Communication*, Norton, New York.

Weaver, C. (1972) *Human Listening: Process and Behavior*, Bobbs-Merrill, Indianapolis.

Wiksell, W. (1946) 'The Problem of Listening', *Quarterly Journal of Speech*, 32, 505–8.

Williams, F., La Rose, R. and Frost, F. (1981) *Children, Television and Sex-role Stereotyping*, Prager, New York.

Wolvin, A. and Coakley, C. (1988) *Listening* (3rd edn), W. C. Brown, Dubuque.

10 Humour and laughter

Hugh C. Foot

Humour is appealing, infectious, recreational and delightful; one can usually go on and on with it.
Fry and Salameh, 1987, p. 216

INTRODUCTION

There can be few topics of research where psychologists feel greater pressure to justify their interest than in the field of humour. Its overtly frivolous nature militates against its acceptance as a serious subject of scientific inquiry and, for many, it would seem completely paradoxical to attempt to subject it to empirical scrutiny. There is, of course, also a prevailing view that just *because* humour is ephemeral, spontaneous, catching the mood of the moment, its very essence is stripped away or killed off as soon as we try to analyse it.

None the less, humour has become an established field of research with its own learned society (the International Society for Humor Studies) and its own journal (the *International Journal of Humor Research*) encouraging a substantial upswing in the volume of research on humour within the social and behavioural sciences in the last twenty years. Using counts from the entries in *Psychological Abstracts* Ruch (1993) has shown that in 1970 there were approximately twenty-five articles per year related to humour, rising to forty in 1980 and seventy-five by the end of the 1980s. For comparison purposes, in 1990 there were twice as many articles listed under depression and five times as many under anxiety. It is perhaps hardly surprising that states of negative affect with their associated clinical psychopathy should still attract so much more research attention.

One of the most marked trends of recent years is the way humour research has spilled over into other fields of psychology, like emotion, personality and motivation, and how it has been exploited and applied in practical domains, like the psychology of coping and stress, counselling, psychotherapy and health care.

To many, the idea of humour as a communicative or social skill is still relatively novel. We take it so much for granted that we have a sense of humour that we fail to consider any notion that it can, indeed should, be nurtured and cultivated. It was not without amusement that the national press in October 1995 carried the story of British Airways' 'discovery' that 'criticism softened by humour may be more effective than traditional forms of communication' (*The Guardian*, 12 October 1995). To implement this notion BA had appointed a 'Corporate Jester' to stalk executive offices and tell top managers where they are going wrong while putting a smile on their faces at the same time. First quarter profits were up by 57 per cent according to *The Guardian*, but the Confederation of British Industry remained sceptical!

Part of the apparent ludicrousness of this venture is the implication that humour can be marshalled and deployed to order, without immediately losing any of the positive impact that it may have had. It might work once but how can any beneficial effect possibly be sustained? There is a wide gulf in the potential effectiveness of humour which is spur of the moment, arising directly from the situation one is in, and humour that is rehearsed and carefully groomed to fit a particular occasion. Effective stage comedians always seem so fluent and effortless: their jokes are, of course, very well rehearsed, but it often comes as a surprise when we learn that, for many comedians, the off-stage banter with the audience and injections of apparently unintended humour are equally well-rehearsed and carefully inserted.

Perhaps this is why there is a degree of discomfort in considering humour as a skill: a skill by its very nature is practised and studied; humour is spontaneous, fleeting, situation-specific and so essentially frivolous and playful.

Much of the research on humour has occupied itself with explaining why we find jokes funny and why we are amused by certain episodes in real life. So the focus of attention has been primarily on the features or ingredients of the joke or episode which render it humorous. Rather less attention has been paid to the creation or production of humour, either in terms of the task facing the professional comedian in consciously constructing new jokes for a comedy show, or in terms of the ordinary man or woman deciding when or how to initiate humour in a social situation. Sometimes, we might argue, such a 'decision' to initiate humour is not under our conscious control; an amusing event occurs and quite spontaneously an apt comment or witticism 'pops out' which neatly captures the feeling of the moment. This is probably a naive view; with few exceptions we are in control of what we say and we do 'initiate' humour in order to achieve some interpersonal goal.

Essentially, the distinction we are drawing here is that between the 'decoding' of humour – understanding the meaning of a joke that we have just read or heard – and the 'encoding' of humour – understanding how and when we use humour to convey a message to others. To consider humour and laughter as social skills, therefore, is to be concerned with encoding characteristics, the reasons why we initiate humour. The bulk of this chapter is devoted to the social uses to which humour and laughter are put.

Before embarking upon this analysis, some of the main humour theories are briefly summarised.

THEORIES OF HUMOUR AND LAUGHTER

It is clear that there is no single theory of humour and researchers and theoreticians have traditionally been somewhat reluctant to define humour and laughter. Most have chosen to emphasise some particular elements, like incongruity or surprise, as necessary pre-requisites for a stimulus to appear humorous. It needs to be said that most of the theories address the question of humour appreciation and the outcome of our responses to humour rather than our motivation for encoding humour.

One of the problems is that humour is so multifaceted that it is simply not possible to develop a single broad theory that adequately accounts for all the main qualities of humour simultaneously. So one has to be content with a variety of different explanations which separately account for different aspects of humour.

As far as definitions are concerned, humour can be viewed as a stimulus, a response and a disposition. According to Chapman and Foot (1976, p. 3):

The Penguin English Dictionary allows all three possibilities: humour may refer to that which causes 'good tempered laughter' (stimulus); or 'cheerful and good-tempered amusement' (response); or 'the capacity for seeing the funny side of things' (disposition). While no-one would dispute that laughter is generally a response, it is just as much a response to non-humorous stimuli as it is to humorous stimuli. In fact, though not a humorous stimulus itself, laughter can act as a stimulus in inducing or augmenting laughter in other persons.

Historical conceptions of humour and laughter and problems of definition have been outlined in more detail in Goldstein and McGhee (1972), Chapman and Foot (1976) and McGhee (1979).

Incongruity and developmental theories of humour

These theories stress the absurd, the unexpected, the inappropriate or out-of-context events as the basis for humour. While these incongruities are necessary, they are not sufficient prerequisites for humour alone (McGhee, 1979). After all, incongruous events or state-ments can lead to curiosity or anxiety rather than to humour; so the perception of humour is dependent upon how the incongruity is understood in the context in which it occurs. Suls (1972) suggested that not only does an incongruity have to be perceived for humour to be experienced but it has to be resolved or explained. Rothbart (1976), on the other hand, proposed that the incongruity itself is sufficient to evoke humour as long as it is perceived in a joking or playful context.

This debate has proved exceptionally fertile ground for cognitive investigations. McGhee (1979) carried the debate forward by interpreting 'resolution' as the need to exercise 'cognitive mastery', without which the incongruity cannot be accepted and used in the humour context. He has proposed a developmental-stage approach which maps out the types of incongruity understood by children across the stages of their increasing cognitive development. For example, the child first recognises incongruity when making pretend actions with an absent object, based upon an internal image of that object. Then the child learns the fun of deliberately giving incongruous labels to objects: 'girls' may be called 'boys', 'cats' may be called 'dogs'. Later come more subtle forms of incongruity like endowing animals with human characteristics ('the dog is talking to me') and learning that words and phrases may have multiple meaning (puns and riddles).

Forabosco (1992, p. 60) has extended the cognitive model to show that mastery involves understanding the cognitive rule and identifying both aspects of congruity and incongruity with that rule: 'There is therefore a succession (diachronicity) of incongruity-congruence configurations that terminates in a contemporaneousness (synchronicity) of incongruity/ congruence. What is more, typical of the final act in the process is an attention-shift situation in which the subject passes from the perception of congruence to the perception of incongruity and, sometimes, vice versa, with several shifts.' Seen from this perspective both the perception of the incongruity and its resolution are essential components for the humour process.

Ruch and Hehl (1986) argued that we should not look for a general model of humour but rather just accept that there are at least two kinds of humour, one in which the solubility of the incongruity is important (e.g. congruous build-up to an unexpected and cognitively incongruent punch-line) and one in which the incongruity alone is sufficient (e.g. nonsense or absurd jokes). Research suggests that preference for these major dimen-sions of humour correlates with personality variables like conservation (Ruch, 1984).

Superiority and disparagement theories of humour

These theories have a long tradition going back at least three centuries to the work of the philosopher Thomas Hobbes. They are based upon the notion that humour stems from the observations of others' infirmities or failures. Hobbes spoke of 'sudden glory' as the passion which induces laughter at the afflictions of other people and it results from favourable comparison of ourselves with these others. So at one level, for example, we find it amusing when our companion slips on a banana skin; at another level we take delight in the downfall of our enemies. Zillmann (1983) and Zillmann and Cantor (1976) proposed a 'dispositional' view that humour appreciation varies inversely with the favourableness of the disposition towards the person or object being disparaged. In other words, the less friendly disposed we are towards someone, the more humorous we find jokes or stories in which that person is the butt or victim. The source of the disparagement is also important; we are highly amused when our friends humiliate our enemies but much less amused when our enemies get the upper hand over our friends. These ideas relate very much to jokes and humour involving social, national, ethnic and religious groupings, with which we personally identify.

What is interesting, as Ruch and Hehl (1986) pointed out, is that this model works well in predicting the behaviour of groups which are traditionally 'superior': for example, men appreciate jokes in which women are disparaged but show less appreciation for jokes in which a woman disparages a man. However, 'inferior' group members are no more amused at jokes which disparage a man than at jokes disparaging a member of their own sex. Indeed, sometimes the inferior groups laugh more at jokes putting down a member of their own group. Clearly, some moderating variables are at work here. From their factor analytic studies, Ruch and Hehl (1986) suggest that the personality dimensions of conservation and toughmindedness are conjointly associated with enjoyment of disparagement humour. This does not say much for the humour of men, who are more likely to score higher on these scales than women. Tough conservatives (chauvinistic, ethnocentric, authoritarian) will appreciate disparagement jokes directed at outside groups but tender-minded liberals will not. Authoritarians tend to be preoccupied with power relationships, the strengthening of in-group bonds, and feeling of superiority over the weak or out-group members (Adorno *et al.*, 1950). One might, however, question their sense of humour. Perhaps those who enjoy disparagement humour are singularly lacking in appreciation of other kinds of humour. We certainly might expect this if, as Allport (1954) claimed, a sense of humour and ability to laugh at oneself is a clear measure of self-insight.

Arousal theories of humour

A number of theories have been proposed which suggest that the most important qualities of humour operate at a physiological level. These theories assume that the initiation of humour brings about measurable arousal changes which directly influence the experience of amusement. Berlyne (1972) has linked humour with fluctuations in arousal in two ways: first, humour is associated with the reduction of high arousal and, second, it is associated with moderate increases in arousal followed by a sudden drop. This 'arousal boost-jag', as he terms it, accounts for the pleasure derived from many jokes. The build-up to the joke is moderately arousing in that it attracts attention (for example, the audience latches on to the fact that a joke is being told and becomes attentive). The joke may be additionally stimulating by virtue of having a sexual, aggressive or anxiety-arousing theme, or it may be intellectually arousing. The punch-line comes when the audience is suitably aroused and seeking a resolution to the joke; timing can be crucial here. The resolution produces a rapid dissipation of arousal frequently associated with laughter. The build-up and subsequent dissipation of arousal are rewarding and pleasurable, and produce the experience of amusement. An important aspect of Berlyne's position is his belief that there is a curvilinear relationship between arousal level and amount of pleasure experienced: that is, moderate levels of arousal are more enjoyable than either very low or very high levels.

Arousal theories of laughter also feature in explanations of certain kinds of non-humorous laughter. For example, *nervous laughter* occurs in states of tension after periods of shock and fright or when acutely embarrassed; more extreme *hysterical laughter* is conceived of as a psychogenic disorder (Pfeifer, 1994) and is often exhibited cyclically with weeping, possibly shouting, in an uncontrolled outburst after periods of intense stress or prolonged deprivation of some kind. Laughter through arousal can also be easily induced by tactile stimulation, normally *reflexive laughter*, rather than involving any cognitive process. Tickling is a more complicated kind of stimulus because the desired response may only be achieved when a mood of fun, compliance or self-abandonment is already operating. If unexpected, or in the wrong company or environment, tickling can be a very aversive stimulus and elicit an aggressive response.

Psychoanalytic theories of humour

Freud's (1905, 1928) view of the function of humour is akin to his view of dreaming, namely that they both serve to regulate sexual and aggressive desires. Humour is the outcome of repressed sexual and aggressive wishes which have been pushed into the unconscious due to society's prohibition of their expression. Wit and humour are not forbidden; indeed, they may be socially valued and therefore present an acceptable outlet for such repressed feelings. The process of repression, according to Freud, involves the use of 'psychic energy' which is saved once the joke has been emitted; thus repression is no longer necessary. The experience of humour and laughter flows directly from the saving of psychic energy whose repressive function is (momentarily) relaxed.

Freud's theory shares with arousal theory the basic view that humour serves a physical as well as a psychological function by manipulating arousal or the level of felt tension. The well-known criticism that psychoanalytic theory is rarely amenable to scientific investigation does not debase the insights and ideas which the theory has generated.

Another psychodynamic view has been expressed by Bokun (1986) who has linked humour with our over-serious construction of the world. This view stresses the need for humour as a means of offering us a more realistic vision of ourselves and the world around us, stripped of all our self-imposed fears, frustrations and suffering. Having a sense of humour, therefore, provides us with the ability to cope with the trials and tribulations of everyday life.

OUR SOCIAL EXPERIENCE OF HUMOUR AND LAUGHTER

As Norrick (1993, p. 1) put it, 'Everyday conversation thrives on wordplay, sarcasm, anecdotes, and jokes. Certainly these forms of humour enliven conversation, but they also help us break the ice, fill uncomfortable pauses, negotiate requests for favors and build group solidarity'.

Above all else, humour is an essentially shared experience. While on solitary occasions we may savour a joke or funny incident which we remember or may laugh privately at a funny sketch on television, our appreciation of humour is expressed much more expansively in company. In social situations there are few more useful social skills than humour and there are probably no contexts, however dire, in which humour is not a potentially appropriate response. Throughout history the more frequently remembered and oft-quoted last remarks of those waiting to be led to the gallows are their rueful witticisms about their fate, society, humankind, or life after death. There is humour in chronic sickness and adversity, humour about old age, adolescence and puberty, aggression and war, sex, love and marriage. The most formidable and powerful feature of humour as a source of social influence is its inherent ambiguity (Kane *et al.*, 1977). We can use humour to communicate a message that we mean; we can use it to communicate the opposite of what we mean. Because humour is playful and can be interpreted in several different ways at the same time, we can retract our message at any time, if it suits us. According to the reaction of our audience and the impression we wish to create, we can choose, through the use of humour, whether to claim or disclaim responsibility for our message or action.

The idea that humour can be interpreted in several different ways reflects our everyday experience of it; it has also been empirically supported. In a politically somewhat dated study by Suls and Miller (1976), a male speaker's joke about 'women-libbers' was interpreted entirely from the reaction of his audience. If the audience consisted of a group of liberated women who laughed at his joke, then the speaker was attributed with liberated views and as one who did not agree with the content of the joke. If the same group glared at him, he was seen as chauvinistic. Thus the response of the audience is taken as evidence of whether the speaker is merely teasing or in deadly earnest.

Hostile reactions to sarcastic humour can, of course, be readily countered by the source with the reply, 'Can't you take a joke?' Not only does the aggrieved party suffer from the affront to his or her own attitudes, knowledge or self-image provoked by the original joke but has made matters worse by virtue of appearing a humourless individual. The only satisfactory way of parrying humour of which one is the target may be to retaliate with humour, but too often the moment is past and the opportunity lost.

Although the mechanics of encoding humour are poorly understood, and there are wide individual differences, a variety of motives can be identified quite easily for our skilled use of humour and laughter. We shall now review what these motives are.

Humour as a search for information

Social probing

A common objective in social interaction, especially when striking up conversations with comparative strangers, is to discover what attitudes, motives and values the other individuals possess. Standards of propriety may prohibit us from directly asking their views on certain issues and, in any case, we may not initially want to engage in a detailed conversation about politics, religion or anything else which direct questioning may commit us to. Introducing a topic in a light-hearted way helps to probe indirectly the other interactant's general attitudes and values about an issue and to reveal 'touchy' subjects. We can take our cue in pursuing or changing the topic of conversation from the other person's response. Whether or not the humour is reciprocated may determine whether the discussion becomes more personal and intimate and whether the relationship moves forward.

Social acceptance

In addition to probing for information about others, we may also be interested in finding out how others respond to us. Telling jokes is a way not only of drawing attention to ourselves but of gauging others' acceptance of us and disposition towards us. It is their response to our humour which provides the social barometer by which we assess our popularity or lack of it. This constitutes a reason for encoding humour and is not to be confused with social laughter whose primary function is to win social approval.

Humour as a means of giving information

Self-disclosure

Humour may often be used as a vehicle for conveying to others our motives and intentions and it is especially useful when we wish to intimate feelings that we might not normally wish to reveal publicly: for example, fears about imminent hazards and anxieties about forthcoming ordeals. The use of humour can, of course, offset the embarrassment of revealing highly personal information (Bloch, 1987). Humour may also convey fairly explicit sexual interest in our companion in a light-hearted and socially acceptable way which is easily revoked or shrugged off if the message is not reciprocated. Of course, such 'humour' can become excessive and may reach the proportions of sexual harassment if carried too far.

Humour used as a tactic to disclose sexual interest was demonstrated in a study by Davis and Farina (1970). Male subjects were asked to rate the funniness of a series of sexual and aggressive jokes in front of either a rather plain female experimenter or in front of the same experimenter made up to be sexually attractive and provocative. The ratings were made privately on paper and pencil scales by half the subjects but reported orally to the experimenter by the other half. The sex jokes were rated as funniest by those subjects who made their ratings orally to the sexually attractive experimenter. Davis and Farina took this to indicate that the male subjects wanted the experimenter to know that they enjoyed sex and were sexually attracted to her. It could be argued further that self-disclosure is not an end in itself but a means of trying to elicit reciprocated feelings or interest by others, so it serves to obtain information as well as give it.

Self-presentation

Humour is an expression of character in times of adversity or stress. A humorous perspective on one's problems allows one to distance oneself from them, to take them less seriously, and thereby to experience them as less distressing or threatening. Martin (1989) has hypothesised that humour may reduce stress by means of several different processes, including appraisal-focused, emotion-focused and problem-focused coping. Lefcourt and Martin (1986) have demonstrated that sense of humour moderates on the relation between stressful life events and mood disturbance. Individuals with a low sense of humour typically experience greater upset (mood disturbance) during high levels of stress than individuals with a high sense of humour. Sense of humour is, therefore, related to more positive self-esteem and more realistic standards for evaluation of self-worth. Putting on a brave face and being 'seen to cope' also sustains the image of ourselves which we wish to maintain to the outside world.

Denial of serious intent

Kane *et al.* (1977, p. 14) referred to this function of humour as 'decommitment' whereby 'When a person faces failure, a false identity is about to be unmasked, an inappropriate behaviour is discovered or a lie uncovered, he or she may attempt to save the situation by indicating that the proposed or past action was not serious, but was instead meant as a joke'. Recourse to humour, then, is self-serving: a way of backing down without injury in the event of having our credibility or motives challenged. A serious confrontation or one in which our actions or intentions are likely to be maligned can be converted into jocular repartee by which we admit we were jesting all the time. Timing may be crucial here: the longer the delay between the initial action and the subsequent attempts to 'decommit' the source, the greater the suspicion that the action did have a serious intention behind it.

Unmasking hypocrisy

Another information-giving function of humour is when we use ridicule or sarcasm to show that we do not believe the ostensible motivation for someone's behaviour. Political cartoons are rife with examples of satirists' attempts to highlight what they believe to be the essential motivation for the actions or pronouncements of a prestigious political figure or the absurdity of professional pretensions, privileges of class or institutional rules. At an interpersonal level, our jest at the expense of other people may serve as a gentle hint that we do not accept the image of themselves that they are projecting; for example, the eager and over-earnest young trainee doctor presenting an identity as an experienced and competent expert on a medical symptom.

Humour in interpersonal control

Expression of liking and affiliation

Humour is valued as a social asset and, exercised judiciously, confers upon its encoder the animated interest and welcoming approval of others. Sharing humour fosters rapport and intimacy and promotes friendship by showing common sentiment and reducing tensions. As a basis for developing friendship and attraction, therefore, humour signals three affective ingredients about its encoder: first, as a jovial person who is rewarding and fun to be with; second, as a sensitive person who has a friendly interest and willingness to enter relationships with others; and third, as one who seeks, and probably wins, the social approval of others (or likes to be liked). Mettee *et al.* (1971) found that a job candidate giving a short lecture was rated as more likeable by an audience when he used humour.

Expression of dislike and hostility

We have already seen under the heading 'Unmasking hypocrisy' that humour can be used to inform others that we do not accept the image of themselves that they are trying to project. In a more general manner, humour is one way, possibly the only socially acceptable way, of expressing personal antagonism. We are inclined to enjoy cruel forms of humour, obtaining amusement from incompetence and deformity and from the oddities and incongruities of others' behaviour. On the one hand, we may not be able, on occasion, to conceal our amusement at the *faux pas* of our friends; our suppressed aggression leads us to savour their little defeats with gentle relish. On the other hand, against those we do not like, our ridicule and amusement at their undoing may be out of proportion to their defeat; we revel in their downfall out of the feeling of superiority that it gives.

Among social equals and friends, the use of reciprocal sarcasm and derision may constitute a normal and regular feature of their interactive style. Indeed, what may appear to an outsider as a hostile slanging match may be seen as playful bantering to the participants. Those with power and authority may avoid being cast as figures of fun to their face but may frequently be the butt of ribald laughter and ridicule behind their backs. In group situations an individual can be unjustly selected (scapegoated) as a target of repeated aggressive humour.

Controlling social interaction

Humour, like laughter, helps to maintain the flow of interaction in daily encounters, 'filling in pauses in our conversations and maintaining the interest and attention of our conversational partner' (Foot and Chapman, 1976, p. 188). In terms of sheer social expediency, therefore, the motive in encoding humour may be little more than to create and sustain a congenial atmosphere, as when breaking the ice at a party. Humour helps to regulate interactions and serves as a social mechanism to facilitate or inhibit the flow of conversation (LaGaipa, 1977). Hostile wit within a group, for example, may dampen the social interaction or the tempo of conversation because it threatens the cohesiveness of the group.

Humour also provides a smooth and acceptable means of changing the level or direction of a conversation. It provides spontaneous comic relief in the context of a turgid or boring conversation and draws attention away from a topic of conversation which one of the interactants does not wish to pursue. It also helps to indicate to others that they are taking things too seriously and need to look at their problems from a more detached or balanced perspective. As will be illustrated later, this is a particularly useful tactic in psychotherapy when the patient is over-anxious and completely bound up with personal problems.

Ingratiation

While humour can be used to win from others approval that is genuinely sought and valued for no other motive than friendship, it can also be employed to capture the approval of others from whom favours are sought or who happen to be in powerful positions. The humour may be self or other-enhancing or it may be self-disparaging as a tactic to express a submissive, dependent posture (Wilson, 1979). The risk with ingratiation humour is always that its insincerity will be revealed.

Humour as a device for group control

Intragroup control

Studies of group process and of emergent leadership have frequently revealed two types of process which need to be operative if a group is to be effective in its task (Bales, 1950, 1958). One process, unsurprisingly, relates to task-relevant variables such as ensuring that the group gathers relevant information, examines appropriate views and directs the group towards a solution. The second process is related to the maintenance of the cohesion and well-being of the group ('socio-emotional' process in Bales' terms). Sometimes these functions are channelled through one leader within the group, sometimes through two or more group members. Basically, if the group is to 'survive' intact as a group, it needs safe outlets by which to express its feelings, sustain its morale and deal with internal conflicts. Humour has an important role to play in this process. Yalom (1985) and Bloch and Crouch (1985) have identified humour as one important factor which gives group members a sense of belonging and acceptance and fosters caring and mutual support.

Building on the earlier work of Middleton and Moland (1959), Martineau (1972) provided a model of the intragroup processes that humour serves, based upon how the humour is judged by the members of the group. It is, of course, within such a group context that in-group jokes can thrive, often barely understood by others outside the group. As LaGaipa (1977, p. 421) says, 'Jocular gripes require some common experiences. Teasing requires knowledge about the butt of the joke and an acceptance and accurate perception of intent. Hostile wit is often not expressed unless the group has achieved a level of cohesiveness able to tolerate it. . . . Situational jokes are likely to reflect the dynamics underlying the social interactions at any given point in time'.

According to Martineau, when the humour is judged as esteeming the in-group, it functions to solidify the group. When it is judged as disparaging the in-group, it may still serve positively to solidify the group (for example, the football coach using sarcasm to motivate his players against imminent defeat) or to control group members who step out of line. But disparagement may also provoke demoralisation, conflict within the group and ultimately the disintegration of the group.

Intergroup control

Martineau's model also addresses itself to the effects of humour upon the in-group when that humour emanates from a member or members of an out-group. Zillmann and Cantor (1976) have stressed that hostile or derogatory jokes are least appreciated when they attack ourselves or group members whom we like or with whom we identify. And one reason for humorous disparagement in the first place is to bring about dissension in the out-group. An ethnic in-group, for example, will use anti-out-group humour not only to express hostility against that out-group, and in an attempt to undermine the morale of its members, but also to strengthen the morale and solidarity of its own members (Bourhis *et al.*, 1977).

Anti-out-group humour can, therefore, be a creative and effective way of asserting in-group pride and distinctiveness from a dominant out-group. But it cuts both ways because hostile humour directed at the in-group from an out-group may also tend to produce greater consensus and cohesion on the part of the in-group members as they close ranks to meet and challenge the implied threat to their position. Intergroup disparagement and hostile wit, therefore, serve only to increase the tension and conflict between the groups, and they are tactics used the world over in parliamentary wrangling, professional disputes, industrial strife and international gamesmanship.

Anxiety management

Saving face

Humour offers a path to control and restraint in more tense interpersonal encounters. An individual encodes humour, for example, to defuse a tense or hostile situation prevailing between two other interactants, thus enabling the contesting parties to back off from the confrontation without loss of face. At the very least, such humour may make it difficult for the parties to continue their altercation without incurring the wrath or scorn of other bystanders. The humour serves both as a corrective to restore the normal boundaries of social etiquette, and an admonition that the argument has gone quite far enough.

Coping with embarrassment

Humour is invoked as a control to restore composure and self-presentation on occasions when they are undermined by some sudden and perhaps unexpected event – for example, being caught out in a lie. More commonly, we are embarrassed by some little accident which spoils the image we wish to convey at that particular moment in time: the elegantly dressed lady at a formal dinner party tripping on the carpet as she is about to be presented to her fellow guests; the spilling of a drink down someone else's clothes; some clumsy or unscripted act by a well-known politician or television personality which becomes typical subject matter for satirical television programmes (e.g. *Spitting Image*). Joking is about the only way to save the situation, treating the event as a trivial one, merely an accident that could have happened to anyone.

Safety-valve for under- and over-arousal

Humour has already been suggested as a mechanism of social control in as much as it brings comic relief to a boring conversation or relieves the tedium of an uneventful activity like waiting for a bus or queuing for an exhibition. On the other side of the coin, humour can help to reduce unwanted and unpleasantly high levels of anxiety and stress. Laughter, according to Berlyne's (1969) arousal theory of humour, results from the tension-release that follows heightened arousal, albeit pleasant arousal, such as that created by the build-up of a joke before the punch-line. It may be that the impetus for encoding humour in times of anxiety stems from anticipation of the release of tension which dissipates pleasurably through laughter. Perhaps doctors and dentists could help to alleviate their patients' anxieties before the consultation by the liberal provision of humorous literature and cartoons in their waiting rooms! Some do, of course.

But solitary amusement may not be the answer here. In stressful situations, sharing humour with a fellow sufferer may be a more potent way of dissipating unwanted anxiety. The pleasurable experience of mutually appreciating a joke may establish rapport and reduce concern over one's own plight.

Humour may be experienced as a direct consequence of realising that one is safe after a threatening stimulus has been removed (Rothbart, 1973, 1976). Shurcliff (1968) varied the level of anxiety in three groups of college students. In the low anxiety group the students were told they would be asked to pick up a docile white rat and hold it for five seconds. In the moderate and high anxiety groups students were asked to take a blood sample from a white rat. In the moderate anxiety condition a small sample only was requested and the students were told it would be an easy task. In the high anxiety condition the students were asked to remove two cubic centimetres of blood from a rat that might be expected to bite through their glove. Having then discovered that the rat they were given was only a toy, the students were asked to rate how funny this trick upon them was. Of the three groups, students in the high anxiety condition found the trick most amusing. Shurcliff attributes this to their greater sense of sudden relief at realising that they were completely safe from a potentially harmful situation. He does not comment on their annoyance about the deception.

Humour as a means of changing and sustaining the status quo

Freedom from conventional thought

Writers and social commentators have waxed lyrical about the emancipating power of humour. Mindess' book, *Laughter and Liberation* (1971), outlines and illustrates all the many ways in which humour frees us from the shackles of our mundane daily lives. Humour is an escape; as Mindess put it, 'In the most fundamental sense, it [humour] offers us release from our stabilising systems, escape from our self-imposed prisons. Every instance of laughter is an instance of liberation from our controls' (p. 23).

It is also a frame of mind which transcends both reality and fantasy. It frees us from moral inhibitions, from the constraints of language, from rationality, from a sense of inferiority and feelings of inadequacy. It is a guilt-free release from frustration and aggression.

This perspective accords with Freud's (1905) view that humour and laughter occur when repressing energy, which normally keeps one's thoughts channelled in socially prescribed and rational directions, is momentarily freed from its static function of keeping something forbidden away from consciousness. A witticism starts with an aggressive tendency or intent which is repressed. The aggressive intentions are manipulated and disguised in the unconscious mind with 'playful pleasure repressed since childhood and waiting for a chance to be satisfied' (Grotjahn, 1957, p. 256). The thoughts emerge into consciousness when they are socially acceptable and the energy originally activated to keep the hostility under repression is freed. By this time the repressed energy is no longer needed and the shock of this freedom from repression spills out in pleasure and laughter.

Joking, therefore, may be seen as a revolt against the structure of society. It may not, in practical terms, bring about much change in the world, but it is enjoyable for its own sake in making the unthinkable thinkable.

The reinforcement of stereotypes

While this freedom of thought may be characteristic of the way humour is used to perceive and experience life, it is paradoxical but also true that, in its overt expression, humour serves to sustain and reinforce narrow-minded attitudes and blinkered vision within society. Wilson (1979) put his finger on the same point when he wrote that 'Joking is a powerful conservative. Its effects reinforce existing ideology, power, status, morality and values within a society' (p. 230). So much of the content of our humour concerns human weakness and foolishness that if we were freed from ignorance, inhibitions, fear and prejudice there would be little room left for humour: 'Though jokes feed on subversive thought, on deviations from the normal and expected, they reinforce established views of the world. Though their content appears to undermine norms, mores, established power and authority, jokes are potent in preserving that status quo' (Wilson, 1979, p. 228).

In the present author's view the power of humour in perpetuating myths and reinforcing stereotyped and traditional attitudes is greatly under-estimated. How else, except through humour, do we derive our stereotyped views about the Irish, the English, the Scots, the Welsh, the Latin-American temperament, Protestants, Jews and Catholics? Because the joke is a socially acceptable form, the message it conveys is extremely powerful and the recipient or target, however much offended, can scarcely denounce it without standing accused of the greatest crime of all – lacking a sense of humour. While real institutional changes have been taking place in the outside world through legal and social reform in relation to, say, homosexuality, equal pay and equal opportunities, the old attitudes about 'poofs' and 'women-libbers' still remain enshrined in jokes which can span a generation and are as popular as ever, although more usually disguised now under the veil of 'political correctness'.

We are undoubtedly caught in a cleft-stick. In an ironic way, as Husband (1977) pointed out in relation to racial humour in the mass media, such humour reinforces existing prejudice and yet its mere usage sustains the mythology of our national tolerance, since racial jokes are supposed to be characteristic of a tolerant society.

THE SOCIAL FUNCTIONS OF LAUGHTER

Although the foregoing section outlined different sources of motivation for encoding *humour*, it offers little guidance about the functions of *laughter* as social skill. The reasons for laughing may have nothing whatever to do with humour and it may occur in situations where nothing humorous has actually happened. Pfeifer (1994, p. 170) expresses this rather aptly: 'One of the interesting things about laughter is that it's a "middle range" behavior, in the sense that it falls between such physiologically determined behavior as blinking on the one hand and such culturally determined behavior as language on the other. We sometimes laugh at nothing, or else laugh at something, but for no particular reason. That's more or less at the level of what a dog does when it's barking?'

Of course, laughter itself may be a response to a situation in which a cognitive failure has occurred and where the individual is at a loss to know how to respond. This is not to deny that, on many occasions, humour and laughter may function as displays of the same social purpose: we may well be laughing as we encode humour.

McGhee (1977) drew particular attention to the problem of low intercorrelation between funniness ratings and laughter (or smiling) and suggested that researchers should use both measures as dependent variables in their studies. He also suggested that they report the correlation obtained between these measures to provide a database from which hypotheses can be made concerning factors which will influence the relationship between expressive and intellectual measures of appreciation. Ruch (1990) has proposed that exhilaration is a consistent emotion elicited by humour and that this accounts for the behavioural, physiological and experiential changes typically occurring in response to some non-humorous (e.g. tickling) as well as humorous stimuli. Ruch (1995) has also shown that correlation size may be a methodological artefact: for example, within-subject designs tend to yield higher correlations than between-subject designs.

To understand laughter, one must inquire into the situational context from which it emerges. In her book *Laughter: A Socio-scientific Analysis*, Hertzler (1970) made the useful point about the function of laughter in society that it is an economical aid ('almost a gift') in getting things done. It is a quick, spontaneous reaction to the immediate situation which, often because it is not subject to the normal controls of deliberate speech, gives away directly the perpetrator's thoughts, feelings or desires: 'A good laugh may contribute more than vocal or written admonitions or commands; it may be easier, cheaper, and more successful than laws and ordinances, police and supervisors, hierarchical chains of command, or other regulative and operative personnel and organisational machinery' (Hertzler, 1970, p. 86).

This is not to signify that laughter is not regulated by conscious control. There would be little point considering it as a social skill if it were entirely outside one's control. As in the case of most other habitual behaviours, we have each developed our own particular style of expressing ourselves: for some individuals laughter is free-flowing and virtually automatic, for others it is a scarce commodity, reserved for a more limited range of social occasions.

Attempts to distinguish between different functions of laughter based upon the physical characteristics of laughs (for example, their intensity or amplitude) have generally failed, although small effects from measures of laughter duration have sometimes been reported. For example, LaGaipa (1977) found that hostile wit directed towards an out-group generated longer laughter than either teasing or 'jocular gripes', whereas laughter lasted longer when teasing an in-group member than when teasing an out-group member.

Within everyday language, one talks about laughs as being 'hollow', 'forced', 'mocking', 'bubbling', and so on, as if they possessed characteristic attributes which were uniquely disparate. There is also a rich vocabulary by which to denote types of laughter – giggle, titter, chortle, chuckle, guffaw, cackle, roar, crow, snigger, jeer – which also give substance to the view that there are many types of laughter which qualitatively differ from each other. No one would deny this. What humour researchers have failed to show is any systematic correlation between particular types of social situations and particular types of laughter. So when an individual displays incompetence in front of others, audience reaction is just as likely to consist of raucous guffaws as a quiet chuckle or a restrained snigger. The interpretation of what the laugh means, therefore, comes from the participants' understanding of the social situation they are in and not from any inherent characteristics of the laugh itself.

The functions and purposes of laughter have been reviewed at length by Gruner (1978) and by Hertzler (1970). Giles and Oxford (1970), Foot and Chapman (1976) and Pfeifer (1994) have summarised these functions. For the purposes of this social skills analysis it is important to recognise that laughter is wholly a social phenomenon. As Hertzler (1970) pointed out, it is 'social in its origin, in its processual occurrence, in its functions, and in its effects' (p. 28). Let us briefly outline these functions here.

Humorous laughter

Following Giles and Oxford's (1970) analysis, humorous laughter may be regarded as an overt expression of rebellion to social pressures, codes and institutions. Continually conforming to such social constraints places an insufferable limitation on individual freedom, which causes an accumulation of frustration, which, in turn, is perfectly displaced through humorous laughter. Such laughter is, of course, very responsive to social facilitation effects, and the frequency and amplitude of its emission is governed by the responsiveness of those around us (Chapman, 1973, 1974, 1975; Chapman and Chapman, 1974; Chapman and Wright, 1976). The more responsive they are, the more we reciprocate. So our primary purpose in engaging in humorous laughter may typically be to convey the message to others that we also find social conventions funny and that we also are continually frustrated by social pressures and social niceties by which our lives are largely controlled.

Social laughter

Social laughter serves the primary purpose of expressing friendship and liking, of gaining social approval and of bolstering group cohesiveness. This function of laughter for integrating ourselves within a particular group does not depend upon the individual having experienced anything amusing, and, far from expressing rebellion against social pressures, it can be viewed as an act of social conformity, fulfilling normative group expectations. It is more intended to convey an image of good-natured 'sociability'. Possibly as much as humour, social laughter is used for controlling conversations and 'oiling the wheels' of social interaction. An obvious form that social laughter takes is polite laughter when we laugh at what others have said, not because we find it funny but out of consideration for them or in order to make them feel that we are attentive to them or appreciate them. We laugh at our own boss' feeble jokes because it might be undiplomatic not to do so.

Ignorance laughter

A third type of laughter is ignorance laughter which implies both the presence of humour stimuli and the presence of others. Typically, we recognise that a joke has been told but wish to conceal our ignorance or inability to comprehend it. So we laugh along with everyone else in the group in order not to be left out or not to look stupid. This is also a version of imitative or feigned laughter as described by Pfeifer (1994).

Evasion laughter

In an important way, laughter, like humour, may serve as an emotional mask behind which to hide our true feelings. If a friend or acquaintance of ours is being attacked or ridiculed by others behind his or her back, we have a choice to defend our friend or, out of expediency, go through the motions of joining in the ridicule in order not to appear different. Laughter gives the impression of sharing in the prevailing feeling of the group. Embarrassment laughter is another example of masking our feelings and stalling for time. We laugh because we are not quite sure what the other person's comments to us mean, or whether his or her intentions towards us are amicable or hostile.

We use laughter, therefore, in ambiguous encounters as a means of deflecting potential animosity directed at us and to earn a little more time to decide how we are going to respond. The very act of laughing may cause us to tilt our head back, avert our gaze and thereby relieve our embarrassment by momentarily detaching ourselves from the interaction. Chapman (1975) has argued that children break off interactions in this way to draw attention away from themselves when the interaction is too intense.

Apologetic laughter

Related to embarrassment laughter and laughter designed to mask our feelings, is apologetic or defensive laughter. This may precede an action on our part, the outcome of which we are uncertain about. We sometimes say, 'I've never done this before' or 'I can't guarantee what's going to happen' when we embark upon a novel task. Laughter may either accompany or substitute for the oral statement and its meaning is clear. We are paving the way for possible failure or for making ourselves look foolish and thereby preparing the audience to believe that we are not taking the situation too seriously ourselves. We may also preface the telling of bad news with laughter, perhaps partly in an attempt to soften the blow and partly by way of apologising for being the one to announce it. Defensive laughter also occurs retrospectively, as when we wish to excuse our lack of action or indecision with respect to some earlier event.

Anxiety laughter

Tension in social encounters stems from anxiety as well as from embarrassment, and anxiety laughter is a manifestation of tension-release to a specific anxiety-provoking situation. Such laughter may be provoked directly by the feeling of relief when a period of acute tension comes to an end. To cite an extreme example, the hostages from a hijacked aircraft may, when suddenly freed, break down in laughter (often alternating with weeping) bordering on the hysterical at the sheer relief that they are safe and the crisis has passed. Rothbart (1976) has noted the close relation between laughter and fear in young children and has argued that laughter comes as a consequence of the child realising that he or she is safe again, the moment the fear or distress is over.

Various theories of laughter have taken the view that laughter serves as a 'safety-valve' against excessive social arousal (see Berlyne, 1969; Chapman, 1975; Godkewitsch, 1976) and that it is a way of dissipating unwanted high arousal. In reflecting 'felt tension', therefore, it assists in the regulation of intimacy development.

Derision laughter

Derision laughter (also referred to as sinister, sarcastic, mocking or acerbic laughter) is another category of laughter which is obviously an alternative, or an additive, to the encoding of hostile humour in situations where one wishes to express superiority over another individual. It is particularly prevalent among children whose laughter may be deliberately cruel or mocking, for example, in the face of another child's physical or mental deformity or stupidity. But as McGhee (1979) noted, children under the age of 7 have great difficulty in taking the perspective of another person and therefore they are largely unaware of other children's feelings. Consequently, their laughter cannot be evaluated as hostile in intent as it may appear to adults. As children grow older, they can begin to understand what the victim must feel, so they begin to inhibit this kind of laughter, especially if the victim is present. Adults use derision laughter as a weapon in more subtle, psychological ways and less for deriding the physical abnormalities of their victims (for which they cannot be blamed) and more for ridiculing the odd behaviours, mannerisms, attitudes or incompetence of their victims (for which they can more readily be blamed).

Derision laughter is also used as a form of refusal or exclusion, particularly when aimed at an individual by the members of a group and at that individual's expense. Such laughter may draw attention to some characteristics of the individual (voice, accent, manner of dress, age, size) which sets the person apart from the rest of the group and it may be based upon the group's desire to exclude that person from joining in their activities.

Joyous laughter

One final category of laughter might be described as joyous laughter which is a pure expression of excitement or *joie de vivre* (Foot and Chapman, 1976). This is a spontaneous reaction to pleasurable and exhilarating activities and is often an expression of mastery, like riding a horse without a saddle, climbing a difficult mountain, experiencing a fairground roller-coaster. Joyous laughter is of less interest in the present context because it is largely non-functional, at least as far as its impact on others is concerned.

APPLICATIONS OF HUMOUR TO MENTAL HEALTH AND THERAPY

Humour and laughter have been hailed as good for the body and good for the mind, and according to Keith-Spiegel (1972), the body benefits because they 'restore homeostasis, stabilise blood pressure, oxygenate the blood, massage the vital organs, stimulate circulation, facilitate digestion, relax the system and produce a feeling of well-being' (p. 5). Goldstein (1987) in reviewing the evidence points to the inevitable conclusion that most studies on the arousal and tension-reducing properties of laughter are short-term experimental studies. Studies that examine the long-term consequences of laughter are almost non-existent (Mantell and Goldstein, 1985). Popular books on humour, however, clearly imply that it unquestionably leads to a healthy and prolonged life. Norman Cousins (1979) has documented his relief and 'cure' (through laughing at *Candid Camera* episodes) from a painful rheumatic inflammation of the vertebrae. Yet to associate humour and laughter with longevity is hardly compatible with the clear evidence that professional comedians and comic writers do not live longer than anyone else. As Goldstein (1987) put it: 'the quality of life is surely enhanced by a sense of humour and not necessarily its duration' (p. 13). It should, however, be noted that laughter is not totally unconnected with the life-threatening states. Fry (1979) has suggested that laughter is actively related to the reduction of stress and hypertension which can lead to risk of heart attack, especially in those who smoke, are overweight, lack exercise or have tension-related conditions. Mantell and Goldstein (1985) suggest that 'Type B' personalities displace anger, anxiety and aggression through humour, while 'Type A' personalities are more at risk to heart attacks because of the seriousness and impatience (and therefore lack of humour) which they typically display.

In the realm of mental health, there has been a burgeoning of interest in the harnessing of humour for therapeutic (as well as entertaining) purposes. This is perhaps not surprising. Millions of pounds are spent each year by the mass media in the provision of comedy shows and on the assumption that their value lies in their therapeutic potential (McGhee, 1979). Few would dispute that humour provides an acceptable outlet for sexual and aggressive energy; without some such form of substitute expression, sexual and aggressive impulses would either be bottled up or spill over in (sexually) aggressive behaviour. This cathartic function, therefore, pleads the case that humour promotes healthy adjustment, and that those possessing a sense of humour will enjoy good mental health.

What evidence is there, though, that a sense of humour is associated with good mental health? Little actual research has been undertaken on this question, but there are a few studies which support the view that humour does reflect good adjustment. O'Connell (1976) found appreciation of humour to be a relatively stable personality trait and positively associated with maturity. O'Connell (1968a, 1968b) also found that individuals who appreciate humour have a more constructive and creative orientation to life, with little preoccupation or anxiety about death and dying. Greenwald (1977) echoed the view that humour is one of the few ways by which we can deal with the knowledge that we all have to die sometime, which is why there are so many jokes about death. Conversely, individuals who lead a more repressed life-style tend to be 'more limited in their reactions to humour' (O'Connell and Cowgill, 1970). Teenage children who are judged by their teachers to be more poorly adjusted tend to show a predilection for aggressive and non-social forms of humour (Nicholson, 1973).

While the positive connection between sense of humour and good adjustment has been demonstrated, there is little evidence to link lack of humour appreciation with poor adjustment or mental ill-health. Ecker *et al.* (1973) found that clients from clinical populations fail to see the humour in jokes that are closely related to their area of conflict, but this is not to say that they fail to appreciate other kinds of humour. Derks *et al.* (1975) were unable to pinpoint any particular differences in the kinds of humour appreciated by samples of neurotic, schizophrenic and normal individuals. Thus, as a diagnostic tool for aiding in the discrimination of different types of mental disorders, humour may not be very helpful, with the possible exception of acute depression. McGhee (1979) argued that depth of depression is reliably mirrored by the absence of laughter and joking, and that an increasing level of humour by the client is a good index of day-to-day progress towards recovery.

It is, therefore, more on the basis of experience than research that professional helpers have begun to see humour as something to be cultivated and strategically deployed rather than ignored or used purely incidentally. Most therapists accept that humour is an index of self-knowledge, a prerequisite for personal exploration (Bloch, 1987).

Let us be quite clear what kind of humour we are talking about in relation to therapy. Clearly, it is not the intrusion of jokes nor any direct attempt to make the patient or client laugh. Mindess (1971) endeavours to define it as conveying an 'inner condition, a stance, a point of view, or in the largest sense an attitude to life' (p. 214). As a therapeutic tool it must be flexible, unconventional and playful, the kind of humour which erupts as a spontaneous reaction to the patient's account of his tale of sorrow or state of mind. Killinger (1987) describes humour in therapy as an interactive personal experience that occurs between client and therapist. Its potential lies in its usefulness as a tool to enable people to view their problems from a new perspective. It serves to broaden clients' self-awareness by improving their ability to take stock of themselves and others more objectively and to develop fuller affective reactions (Rosenheim, 1974).

This broadening of perspective, from which clients begin to see the irony or absurdity of their own predicament, must none the less be facilitated cautiously and sensitively. Kubie (1971) has warned that humour introduced by the therapist too soon can be destructive if the therapist is assumed to be laughing at, rather than with, the client.

Humour in therapy

Therapeutic contexts vary, of course, and recent literature on therapy methodology gives examples of therapists' experience of using humour in individual contexts, in group therapy and in family therapy.

Individual therapy

Killinger (1987) believes fundamentally in the creative, but spontaneous, development of humour to capture and crystallise the essence or meaning within the immediate client–therapist interchange. Her clinical approach emphasises gentleness and therapeutic sensitivity to a client's needs. Killinger (1987, p. 31) believes that this sensitivity can be best achieved through 'verbal picture painting or framing an image' which is designed to open the client's eyes while at the same time maintaining some 'psychic distance':

> In the process of active listening and attempting to understand what clients are thinking or saying about themselves, the therapist can focus the intervention at a significant point by creating a humorous word picture to frame the essence of the client's dynamics. The humorous interpretation hopefully serves to shift clients from a fixed view of themselves or their situation while simultaneously reinforcing the *now* by expanding on what clients are saying about themselves. By focusing the subject matter of the humor onto objects, people or situations slightly removed from the client this change of focus can be achieved without being 'too close' and raising undue anxiety in the client.

The humorous intervention may be a simple metaphor or consist of a short story and may draw upon any one or a combination of humour techniques, such as exaggeration, incongruity, superiority, surprise. Particular care has to be taken to ensure that these interventions do not appear contrived and do not strike 'too close to home'.

It is, of course, particularly satisfactory if the client generates and initiates the humour. Then the therapist's role is merely one of reinforcing the humour by appreciating it. However, the therapist may have to activate the humour in indirect ways, as by setting an example. The main consideration is that the humour used by the therapist should not overwhelm or threaten the client, but should make the client aware of the therapist's understanding of the former's feelings (Grossman, 1977).

Group therapy

Most long-established groups (like therapy groups) whose members develop a sense of belonging and loyalty create what Yalom (1985) called a 'social microcosm' – shared experiencing of a broad array of emotions. Inevitably, humour appears to be an intrinsic feature of the therapy group and, far from repressing it, the main concern is how it can be optimally built into a group's culture without making it too contrived.

Bloch (1987) has considered the various advantages and disadvantages of using humour in long-term group therapy. In particular, he has stressed the desirability of adopting an interactional model in which change stems mainly from the relationship between members rather than from the relationship between each client and the therapist. Thus it is important that humour revolves around or emanates from the clients' relationships with each other rather than with the therapist. Bloch has identified ten ways in which humour can be therapeutically useful. Three of these are classified as therapist-related uses, four as client-related and three as group-related.

Therapist-related uses include *modelling* – good-natured expressions of attitude or behaviour which help to dislodge obstacles to a client's more spontaneous self-expression; *transparency* – self-disclosure by the therapist which shows a willingness to laugh at him- or herself; *interpretation* – helping clients, through humour, to examine themselves in a different way.

Client-related uses include several techniques for facilitating clients to perceive the light-hearted nature of some experiences which arise during discussion among group members. These involve helping clients to put their experiences into a proper *sense of proportion*, to *overcome earnestness*, to *promote social skills* (by forging social relationships) and provide opportunities for *catharsis and self-disclosure*.

Group-related uses include *cohesiveness* – the use of humour within the group to foster cordiality and friendliness; *insight into group dynamics* – helping group members to appreciate the relevance of processes like undue dependency on the therapist, avoidance of distressing topics; *reduction of tension* – the use of humour to handle conflict and embarrassment.

Family therapy

According to Madanes (1987), a therapist can follow one of two broad approaches in using humour to change the 'drama of a family': one is based on the use of language to redefine situations; the other relies on organising actions that change a course of events and modify sequences of interaction.

In relation to language, the art of the therapist is much the same as we have just been discussing (i.e. to facilitate the family members' reinterpretation of the meaning of their behaviour towards each other). Often humorous interventions do not appear humorous to the family members at the time; only in retrospect do they appear so. The therapist can sometimes revisit with the family events which happened earlier in the therapy and help them, through humour, to penetrate the family system, to loosen their grasp of cyclical dysfunctional patterns of family behaviour and to reorganise the tasks which alter the interactions among family members.

In relation to action, the use of comic or slapstick routines may be helpful in situations where the behaviour of one family member irritates another. Madanes' device here is to have the behaviour deliberately practised by the perpetrator but responded to in an exaggeratedly affectionate way by the individual who is irritated (e.g. a sulky pout of the lips or angry finger-stabbing). This draws attention to the behaviour in a non-threatening way which can release amusement by both family members in the exchange.

In all humour there may be an element of defiance of authority – of rules, or socially accepted norms. Defiance can be used in ways that are not only humorous but therapeutic as antagonism is changed into playful challenge.

Most therapists would agree that if humour is to be used in therapy it must be used sensitively and caringly, in a way which indicates that the therapist values and respects the client and is concerned about his or her well-being. Many warn against the sudden and unguarded insertion of humour into therapy and view its introduction as a delicately judged business. This view of the psychological fragility of clients, however, has been questioned. Farrelly and Matthews (1981) and Farrelly and Lynch (1987) describe the technique of provocative therapy in which humour is explicitly used as a means of challenging the clients' pathology and provoking them into a strong emotional reaction designed to make them relinquish their self-defeating behaviours.

APPLICATIONS OF HUMOUR TO OTHER PROFESSIONAL CONTEXTS

While there has been a recent explosion of interest in the therapeutic use of humour, its commercial and educational value has continued to receive remarkably little research attention. This is not to say that humour is not widely used in fields such as advertising, political propaganda and teaching, but rather that little empirical evaluation of its effectiveness has been undertaken. Judging by the steadily increasing use of humour in television advertising, however, faith in its effectiveness may seem beyond challenge and one might be forgiven for thinking that an attitude prevails that research is just not necessary. Let us consider briefly the little research there is on the persuasive power of humour.

As Gruner (1976) argued, there are several theoretical reasons why the addition of humour to a message might be expected to enhance the persuasiveness of that message. These may be summed up as follows: (1) Appropriate humour may make the audience more favourably disposed towards the source of the message: for example, the teacher, the advertiser, the public speaker. If the source is more favourably perceived, then the credibility and the persuasiveness of that source are likely to be increased; (2) Appropriate humour is entertaining and may make the message more interesting and therefore more actively attended to by its audience. If the message is attended to more closely its persuasive power should be increased; (3) Appropriate humour may serve as additional supporting material for a position or idea which the source wishes the audience to accept, and may therefore boost the persuasiveness of the message; (4) Appropriate humour may make a persuasive message more memorable and therefore render it more effective over a longer period of time; (5) Appropriate humour may distract the audience from concocting counter-arguments to the message and therefore increase the persuasiveness of the message. There is another argument, too, that humour relaxes the audience which might make it more receptive to the message (Hegarty, 1976).

Empirical research which has addressed these questions has generally found little evidence to support the idea that humour enhances the persuasiveness of a message. In probably the earliest controlled study on the effect of humour in persuasive messages, Lull (1940) used serious and humorous versions of the same speeches either in favour of or against 'state medicine'. The speeches were presented live to audiences whose previous attitudes towards the issue had been measured. After hearing one of the speeches the audience's attitudes were retested and ratings were obtained of the perceived 'interestingness', 'humour' and 'convincingness' of the speaker. The amount of audience laughter was also measured during the speech presentations. Clearly, the funniness of the humorous speeches was perceived; audience members laughed considerably during the presentation of these speeches and they rated them as humorous. The serious speeches elicited no laughter at all and were not rated as humorous. However, there were no differences whatsoever between the humorous and serious speeches in their rated interestingness and convincingness, nor in the amount of actual attitude change they elicited.

Later studies by Kilpela (1961), Youngman (1966), Brandes (1970), Gruner and Lampton (1972) and Kennedy (1972) confirmed that humour added to a speech or sermon has no effect upon the persuasiveness of the message. However much the humour may be appreciated and anticipated by the audience, it does not seem to matter whether the humour is appropriate or inappropriate to the content of the speech nor what form the humour takes: jokes, puns or sarcasm.

Whatever the effect of the use of humour and satire upon the persuasiveness of a message, there is no doubt that they enhance the image of the source. People still flock to hear entertaining speakers or preachers who pepper their speeches and sermons with jokes and witticisms. So, not only do people enjoy humour but they react more favourably towards the speaker who provides it. Nevertheless, the kind of humour used is important to judgements of the speaker. Goodchilds (1959) has suggested that 'sarcastic wits' are seen as influential but not popular, while 'clowning wits' are seen as popular but not influential. It has also been suggested that speakers who use too much humour make a poor impression by virtue of being judged as 'frustrated comedians' (Taylor, 1974). So the judicious use of the right kind of humour is inevitably related to the speaker's credibility.

One would also imagine that liking would be closely associated with perceived credibility or authoritativeness: the more popular a speaker is, the more the message would be likely to be evaluated as authoritative. This appears to be the case for dull, uninteresting speeches. Gruner (1970) found that dull but humorous speakers were evaluated as more authoritative than dull and non-humorous speakers. However, interesting speakers were judged as equally authoritative whether they were humorous or non-humorous: the intrinsic interest of the speech presumably made the use of humour redundant.

Turning from these general considerations, humour is now briefly considered in some specific applied contexts.

Humour and teaching

Humour in the classroom can clearly make lessons more enjoyable. *Sesame Street* is an obvious example of an educational television programme designed to present teaching in an atmosphere of fun by use of the 'Muppets' as well as to inject humour into specific lessons to be taught. The question is, does humour actually help children to learn? Unfortunately, the evidence is equivocal; studies showing that humour does not aid memory outnumber the studies that show a positive or negative effect.

Clearly, humour may distract from the lesson in the sense that it draws the child's attention towards the joke and away from the message, but if the humour is related to and integrated directly with the items to be learned, it may assist the learning of those items (Chapman and Crompton, 1978). Davies and Apter (1980) argue that the type of humour, length of the joke, temporal position of the insertion of the humour and the method of presentation may all contribute to the humour's effectiveness; the type of lesson or material to be learned may also be crucial. So there are no easy answers. The case for humour as a means of aiding subsequent recall is not yet proven, but this is no reason why teachers should abandon it as a means of maintaining their pupils' attention (see also Brown and Bryant, 1983). There is very little evidence supporting the view that it could be detrimental, and some evidence suggests that it makes individuals more creative by improving their flexibility of thinking (Isen *et al.*, 1987).

It is also worth noting, first, that much of the research has involved students rather than children and, second, that the materials which have typically been used in research are relatively novel or of high intrinsic interest value. As has already been seen, the use of humour with less interesting material serves to increase the perceived authoritativeness of the source and it may, therefore, be a relatively useful adjunct to a boring lesson or with uninteresting material to be memorised.

Humour, advertising and political propaganda

Welford (1971) simulated a radio debate between two (anonymous) political candidates in which one candidate was heard to refute the speech of the other, either in a completely serious vein or in a humorous vein where each issue addressed was accompanied by a joke. When the audience's attitudes towards the content of the serious and humorous refutational speeches were compared, there were virtually no differences except on two of the issues; in both cases the serious version of the speeches led to more favourable attitudes on the part of the audience members.

Memorability for humorous and non-humorous printed advertising was tested by Perreault (1972) who found no difference between them as far as audience recall was concerned. This is perhaps not surprising; one might expect humour to work more effectively through radio or television than through the medium of print, where it is difficult to do justice to everyone's tastes. There is no doubt that humour is remarkably popular in television advertising and there is no doubt that it can be successful in selling products.

According to Gruner (1974), significant increases in sales of cigarettes, soft drinks, food, cosmetics, airlines and other 'products' have been found in the US when advertisers have turned from serious to humorous advertising. However, it appears that very little field research has been conducted to demonstrate the power of humour in influencing potential customers' choice of one product over another. The laboratory research has tended to test the influence of humour with more sophisticated social messages and, in consequence, has failed to find an effect.

Advertisers and political actors may at least derive some satisfaction from knowing that little research has ever shown that humour actually detracts from the persuasiveness of a message, that is, as long as the humour is appropriate to the audience and does not make the source of the message appear too clownish.

OVERVIEW

For whatever purposes we use humour in our daily lives, it is above all else a coping mechanism: it buffers us against stress and against the criticisms of others; it enables us to maintain and possibly enhance our own self-concept and preserve our self-esteem

(Martin *et al.* 1993). The evidence we have surveyed in this chapter demonstrates just how goal-directed humour is and how it comes to be involved in a broad range of human activities and functioning. Not only does humour appear to be an effective means of mitigating stress, but it also appears to be associated with a greater enjoyment of positive life experiences and a more positive orientation towards self (Martin *et al.*, 1993). Patently, humour is a subtle and complex skill and some individuals are more proficient in its use than others. The origins and development of the skill are poorly understood and little is known about why some adults and children become particularly versed and adept at using it to express themselves. As a social skill, however, humour is an ability and everyone has the capacity for developing it. As Fry (1994, p. 112) expressed it:

> The sense of humor of each person is slightly different from everyone else's sense of humor. A sense of humor is a kind of psychological fingerprint, distinctive for each person. There are broad overlaps of humor appreciation among groups – family, community, regional, national, cultural. There is humor which has universal appeal, humor recognised as humor and enjoyed throughout the world. But each person develops a sense of humor which is slightly different from that of each other person.

There seems little danger that the intrinsic pleasure of humour will be destroyed by our serious attempts to comprehend and exploit it.

REFERENCES

Adorno, T. W., Frenkel-Brunswick, E., Levinson, D. J. and Sanford, R. N. (1950) *The Authoritarian Personality*, Harper & Row, New York.
Allport, G. W. (1954) *The Nature of Prejudice*, Addison-Wesley, London.
Bales, R. F. (1950) *Interaction Process Analysis: A Method for the Study of Small Groups*, Addison-Wesley, Reading, MA.
—— (1958) 'Task Roles and Social Roles in Problem-solving Groups', in E. Maccoby, T. Newcomb and E. Hartley (eds), *Readings in Social Psychology* (3rd edn), Holt, Rinehart & Winston, New York.
Berlyne, D. E. (1969) 'Laughter, Humor and Play', in G. Lindzey and E. Aronson (eds), *Handbook of Social Psychology, Vol 3*, (2nd edn), Addison-Wesley, Reading, MA.
—— (1972) 'Humour and Its Kin', in J. H.Goldstein and P. E. McGhee (eds), *The Psychology of Humour*, Academic Press, New York.
Bloch, S. (1987) 'Humour in Group Therapy' in W. F. Fry and W. A. Salameh (eds), *Handbook of Humour and Psychotherapy*, Professional Resource Exchange, Sarasota, Florida.
—— and Crouch, E. (1985) *Therapeutic Factors in Group Psychotherapy*, Oxford University Press, Oxford.
Bokun, B. (1986) *Humour Therapy*, Vita Books, London.
Bourhis, R. Y., Gadfield, N. J., Giles H. and Tajfel, H. (1977) 'Context and Ethnic Humour in Intergroup Relations', in A. J. Chapman and H. C. Foot (eds), *It's a Funny Thing, Humour*, Pergamon, Oxford.
Brandes, P. D. (1970) 'The Persuasiveness of Varying Types of Humor', paper presented at the Speech Communication Association Convention, New Orleans in *SCA Abstracts*, 12–13.
Brown, D. and Bryant, J. (1983) 'Humor in the Mass Media', in P. McGhee and J. Goldstein (eds), *Handbook of Humor Research, Volume II: Applied Studies*, Springer, New York.
Chapman, A. J. (1973) 'Social Facilitation of Laughter in Children', *Journal of Experimental Social Psychology*, 9, 528–41.
—— (1974) 'An Experimental Study of Social Facilitated "Humorous Laughter"', *Psychological Reports*, 35, 727–34.
—— (1975) 'Humorous Laughter in Children', *Journal of Personality and Social Psychology*, 31, 42–9.
—— and Chapman, W. A. (1974) 'Responsiveness to Humor: Its Dependency Upon a Companion's Humorous Smiling and Laughter', *Journal of Psychology*, 88, 245–52.
Chapman, A.J. and Crompton, P. (1978) 'Humorous Presentations of Material and Presentations of

Humorous Material: A Review of the Humour and Memory Literature and Two Experimental Studies', in M. M. Gruneberg, P. E. Morris and R. N. Sykes (eds), *Practical Aspects of Memory*, Academic Press, London.

Chapman, A. J. and Foot, H. C. (eds) (1976) *Humour and Laughter: Theory, Research and Applications*, John Wiley, Chichester.

Chapman, A. J. and Wright, D. S. (1976) 'Social Enhancement of Laughter: An Experimental Analysis of Some Companion Variables', *Journal of Experimental Child Psychology*, 21, 201–18.

Cousins, N. (1979) *Anatomy of an Illness as Perceived by the Patient*, Norton, New York.

Davies, A. P. and Apter, M. J. (1980) 'Humour and its Effects on Learning in Children', in P. E. McGhee and A. J. Chapman (eds), *Children's Humour*, John Wiley, Chichester.

Davis, J. M. and Farina, A. (1970) 'Humour Appreciation as Social Communication', *Journal of Personality and Social Psychology*, 15, 175–8.

Derks, P. L., Leichtman, H. M. and Carroll, P. J. (1975) 'Production and Judgement of "Humour", by Schizophrenics and College Students', *Bulletin of the Psychonomic Society*, 6, 300–2.

Ecker, J., Levine, J. and Zigler, E. (1973) 'Impaired Sex-role Identification in Schizophrenia Expressed in the Comprehension of Humour Stimuli', *Journal of Personality*, 83, 67–77.

Farrelly, F. and Lynch, M. (1987) 'Humour in Provocative Therapy', in W. F. Fry and W. A. Salameh (eds), *Handbook of Humour and Psychotherapy*, Professional Resource Exchange, Sarasota, Florida.

Farrelly, F. and Matthews, S. (1981) 'Provocative Therapy', in R. Corsini (ed.), *Handbook of Innovative Psychotherapies*, John Wiley, New York.

Foot, H. C. and Chapman, A. J. (1976) 'The Social Responsiveness of Young Children in Humorous Situations', in A. J. Chapman and H. C. Foot (eds), *Humour and Laughter: Theory, Research and Applications*, John Wiley Chichester.

Forabosco, G. (1992) 'Cognitive Aspects of the Humor Process: the Concept of Incongruity', *Humor: International Journal of Humor Research*, 5, 45–68.

Freud, S. (1905) 'Wit and its Relationship to the Unconscious', in A. Brill (ed.), *Basic Writings of Sigmund Freud*, Modern Library, New York, pp. 633–803.

—— (1928) 'Humour' in *Collected Papers, Vol. V*, Hogarth, London, pp. 215–21.

Fry, W. F. (1979) 'Humor and the Cardiovascular System', in H. Mindess and J. Turek (eds), *The Study of Humor: Proceedings of the Second International Humor Conference*, Antioch College, Los Angeles.

—— (1994) 'The Biology of Humor'. *Humor: International Journal of Humor Research*, 7, 111–26.

—— and Salameh, W. A. (1987) *Handbook of Humor and Psychotherapy*, Professional Resource Exchange, Sarasota, Florida.

Giles, H. and Oxford, G. S. (1970) 'Towards a Multi-dimensional Theory of Laughter Causation and its Social Implications', *Bulletin of the British Psychological Society*, 23, 97–105.

Godkewitsch, M. (1976) 'Physiological and Verbal Indices of Arousal in Rated Humour', in A. J. Chapman and H. C. Foot (eds), *Humour and Laughter: Theory, Research and Applications*, John Wiley, Chichester.

Goldstein, J. H. (1987) 'Therapeutic Effects of Laughter', in W. F. Fry and W. Salameh (eds), *Handbook of Humor and Psychotherapy*, Professional Resource Exchange, Sarasota, Florida.

—— and McGhee, P. E. (eds) (1972) *The Psychology of Humor*, Academic Press, New York.

Goodchilds, J. D. (1959) 'Effects of Being Witty on Position in the Social Structure of a Small Group', *Sociometry*, 22, 261–72.

Greenwald, H. (1977) 'Humour in Psychotherapy', in A. J. Chapman and H. C. Foot (eds), *It's A Funny Thing, Humour*, Pergamon, Oxford.

Grossman, S. A. (1977) 'The Use of Jokes in Psychotherapy', in A. J. Chapman and H. C. Foot (eds), *It's a Funny Thing, Humour*, Pergamon, Oxford.

Grotjahn, M. (1957) *Beyond Laughter: Humor and the Subconscious*, McGraw-Hill, New York.

Gruner, C. R. (1970) 'The Effects on Speaker Ethos and Audience Information Gain of Humor in Dull and Interesting Speeches', *Central States Speech Journal*, 21, 160–6.

—— (1974) 'Dogmatism: A Factor in the Understanding and Appreciation of Editorial Satire?', paper presented at the SCA Convention, Chicago.

—— (1976) 'Wit and Humour in Mass Communication', in A. J. Chapman and H. C. Foot (eds), *Humour and Laughter: Theory, Research and Application*, John Wiley, Chichester.

—— (1978) *Understanding Laughter: The Workings of Wit and Humour*, Nelson-Hall, Chicago.

—— and Lampton, W. E. (1972) 'Effects of Including Humorous Material in a Persuasive Sermon', *Southern Speech Communication Journal*, 38, 188–96.

Hegarty, E. J. (1976) *Humor and Eloquence in Public Speaking*, Parker, West Nyack, New York.

Hertzler, J. O. (1970) *Laughter: A Socio-scientific Analysis*, Exposition, New York.

Husband, C. (1977) 'The Mass Media and the Functions of Ethnic Humour in a Racist Society', in A. J. Chapman and H. C. Foot (eds), *It's a Funny Thing, Humour*, Pergamon, Oxford.

Isen, A. M., Daubman, K. A. and Nowicki, G. P. (1987) 'Positive Affect Facilitates Creative Problem Solving', *Journal of Personality and Social Psychology*, 52, 1122–31.

Kane, T. R., Suls, J. M. and Tedeschi, J. (1977) 'Humour as a Tool of Social Interaction', in A. J. Chapman and H. C. Foot (eds), *It's a Funny Thing, Humour*, Pergamon, Oxford.

Keith-Spiegel, P. (1972) 'Early Conceptions of Humour: Varieties and Issues', in J. H. Goldstein and P. E. McGhee (eds), *The Psychology of Humor*, Academic Press, New York.

Kennedy, A. J. (1972) 'An Experimental Study of the Effects of Humorous Message Content upon Ethos and Persuasiveness', unpublished PhD thesis, University of Michigan, Michigan.

Killinger, B. (1987) 'Humor in Psychotherapy: A Shift to a New Perspective', in W. F. Fry and W. A. Salameh (eds), *Handbook of Humor and Psychotherapy*, Professional Resource Exchange, Sarasota.

Kilpela, D. E. (1961) 'An Experimental Study of the Effect of Humor on Persuasion', unpublished MSc thesis, Wayne State University, Detroit.

Kubie, L. S. (1971) 'The Destructive Potential of Humor in Psychotherapy', *American Journal of Psychiatry*, 127, 861–86.

LaGaipa, J. J. (1977) 'The Effects of Humour on the Flow of Social Conversation', in A. J. Chapman and H. C. Foot (eds), *It's a Funny Thing, Humour*, Pergamon, Oxford.

Lefcourt, H. M. and Martin, R. A. (1986) *Humor and Life Stress: Antidote to Adversity*, Springer, New York.

Lull, P. E. (1940) 'The Effects of Humor in Persuasive Speeches', *Speech Monographs*, 7, 26–40.

McGhee, P. E. (1977) 'Children's Humor: a Review of Current Research Trends', in A. J. Chapman and H. C. Foot (eds), *It's a Funny Thing, Humour*, Pergamon, Oxford.

—— (1979) *Humor: its Origin and Development*, Freeman, San Francisco.

Madanes, C. (1987) 'Humor in Strategic Family Therapy', in W. F. Fry and W. A. Salameh (eds), *Handbook of Humor and Psychotherapy*, Professional Resource Exchange, Sarasota, Florida.

Mantell, M. and Goldstein, J. H. (1985) 'Humour and the Coronary-prone Behaviour Pattern', paper presented at the fifth international conference on Humour, Cork, Ireland.

Martin, R. A. (1989) 'Humor and the Mastery of Living: Using Humor to Cope With the Daily Stresses of Growing Up', in P. E. McGhee (ed.), *Humor and Children's Development: A Guide to Practical Applications*, Haworth Press, New York.

—— Kuiper, N. A., Olinger, L. J. and Dance, K. A. (1993) 'Humor, Coping with Stress, Self-concept and Psychological Well-being', *Humor: International Journal of Humor Research*, 6, 89–104.

Martineau, W. H. (1972) 'A Model of the Social Functions of Humor', in J. H. Goldstein and P. E. McGhee (eds), *The Psychology of Humor*, Academic Press, New York.

Mettee, D. R., Hrelec, E. S. and Wilkens, P. C. (1971) 'Humor as an Interpersonal Asset and Liability', *Journal of Social Psychology*, 85, 51–64.

Middleton, R. and Moland, J. (1959) 'Humor in Negro and White Subcultures: A Study of Jokes Among University Students', *American Sociological Review*, 24, 61–9.

Mindess, H. (1971) *Laughter and Liberation*, Nash, Los Angeles.

—— (1976) 'The Use and Abuse of Humour in Psychotherapy', in A. J. Chapman and H. C. Foot (eds), *Humour and Laughter: Theory, Research and Applications*, John Wiley, Chichester.

Nicholson, W. S. (1973) 'Relation Between Measures of Mental Health and a Cartoon Measure of Humor in Fifth Grade Children', unpublished PhD thesis, University of Maryland, CA.

Norrick, N. R. (1993) *Conversational Joking: Humor in Everyday Life*, Indiana University Press, Bloomington, Indiana.

O'Connell, W.E. (1968a) 'Organic and Schizophrenic Differences in Wit and Humor Appreciation', *Diseases of the Nervous System*, 29, 276–81.

—— (1968b) 'Humor and Death', *Psychological Reports*, 22, 391–402.

—— (1976) 'The Adaptive Functions of Wit and Humor', *Journal of Abnormal and Social Psychology*, 61, 263–70.

—— and Cowgill, S. (1970) 'Wit, Humor and Defensiveness', *Newsletter for Research in Psychology*, 12, 32–3.

Perreault, R.M. (1972) 'A Study of the Effects of Humor in Advertising As Can Be Measured By Product Recall Tests', unpublished MSc thesis, University of Georgia, Georgia.

Pfeifer, K. (1994) 'Laughter and Pleasure', *Humour: International Journal of Humor Research*, 7, 157–72.

Rosenheim, E. (1974) 'Humor in Psychotherapy: An Interactive Experience', *American Journal of Psychotherapy*, 28, 584–91.

Rothbart, M. K. (1973) 'Laughter in Young Children', *Psychological Bulletin*, 80, 247–56.

—— (1976) 'Incongruity, Problem-solving and Laughter', in A. J. Chapman and H. C. Foot (eds), *Humour and Laughter: Theory, Research and Applications*, John Wiley, Chichester.

Ruch, W. (1984) 'Conservatism and the Appreciation of Humor', *Zeitschrift fur Differentielle und Diagnostische Psychologie*, 5, 221–45.

—— (1990) *The Emotion of Exhilaration*, unpublished habilitation thesis, University of Dusseldorf, Dusseldorf.

—— (1993) 'Introduction: Current Issues in Psychological Humor Research', *Humor: International Journal of Humor Research*, 6, 1–7.

—— (1995) 'Will the Real Relationship Between Facial Expression and Affective Experience Please Stand Up: The Case of Exhilaration', *Cognition and Emotion*, 9, 33–58.

—— and Hehl, F.-J. (1986) 'Conservation as a Predictor of Responses to Humour – II: The Location of Sense of Humour in a Comprehensive Attitude Space', *Personality and Individual Differences*, 7, 861–74.

Shurcliff, A. (1968) 'Judged Humor, Arousal, and the Relief Theory', *Journal of Personality and Social Psychology*, 8, 360–3.

Suls, J. J. (1972) 'A Two-stage Model for the Appreciation of Jokes and Cartoons: An Information-processing Analysis', in J. H. Goldstein and P. E. McGhee (eds), *The Psychology of Humor*, Academic Press, New York.

Suls, J. M. and Miller, R. L. (1976) 'Humor as an Attributional Index', cited by T.R. Kane, J. Suls and J. Tedeschi, in A. J. Chapman and H. C. Foot (eds), *It's a Funny Thing, Humour*, Pergamon, Oxford.

Taylor, P. H. (1974) 'An Experimental Study of Humor and Ethos', *Southern Speech Communication Journal*, 39, 359–66.

Welford, T. W. (1971) 'An Experimental Study of the Effectiveness of Humor Used as a Refutational Device', unpublished PhD thesis, Louisiana State University, Louisiana.

Wilson, C. P. (1979) *Jokes: Form, Content, Use and Function*, Academic Press, London.

Yalom, I. D. (1985) *The Theory and Practice of Group Psychotherapy*, Basic Books, New York.

Youngman, R. C. (1966) 'An Experimental Investigation of the Effects of Germane Humor Versus Non-germane Humor in an Informative Communication', unpublished MSc thesis, Ohio University, Ohio.

Zillman, D. (1983) 'Disparagement Humor', in P. E. McGhee and J. H. Goldstein (eds), *Handbook of Humor Research, Volume I: Basic Issues*, Springer, New York.

—— and Cantor, J. R. (1976) 'A Dispositional Theory of Humour and Mirth', in A. J. Chapman and H. C. Foot (eds), *Humour and Laughter: Theory, Research and Applications*, John Wiley, Chichester.

Part III
Specialised contexts

11 Asserting and confronting

Richard F. Rakos

If not I for myself, who then?
And being for myself, what am I?
And if not now, when?
                    Rabbi Hillel

These words by the ancient Sage Hillel, though discussing knowledge and meritorious behaviour in general (Goldin, 1957), also speak to the three critical issues intrinsic to the effective
use of assertion in contemporary interpersonal interactions: the right to express the assertive
response, the social responsibilities attached to assertive expression, and the decision
actually to engage in such expression. The plethora of research over the past twenty-five
years has confirmed the wisdom of Hillel's philosophy: his words not only stand the test of
time but also the shift in *Weltanschauung* from Judaic monotheism to secular humanism.

Assertion as a social skill rose to prominence in the mid-1970s as both a pop psychology
fad and as a legitimate clinical focus of behaviour therapy (Rakos, 1991). In the past few
years, the popular and professional obsession with assertion has receded, and with it the
view of assertiveness as the panacea for much, if not all, human unhappiness. Clinicians
today recognise that assertion is a complex social skill embedded in a social context, and
that the acquisition of assertive skills may contribute powerfully but incompletely to the
remediation of ineffective interpersonal functioning.

The emergence of assertion as a desirable ability was linked to the guiding philosophies
and cultural changes that characterised the US, and to a lesser extent other Western indus-
trialised nations, in the late 1960s and early 1970s (Rakos, 1991). *Rationality* is an effective
and therefore highly valued attribute in a scientific and technological society. *Social and
political activism*, by challenging the legitimacy of traditional institutional authority and
structure, provided the cultural impetus for the advent of a skill that promoted personal
empowerment. *Ethical relativism*, and the rejection of absolute standards of morality, paved
the way for behavioural styles that might prompt social disapproval. Finally, *pragmatism*
continued to be a hallmark of American philosophy (cf. Dewey, 1957), in which outcome
takes precedence over ideology. Today, these four philosophical tenets remain at the heart
of assertion, which now emerges as a potent behavioural *option* for coping with, and
adjusting to, the rapidly changing postmodern technological environment. However, as we
shall see, the ability to perform assertively does not imply that such a response is always
the preferred option; in many cases, in fact, it is not. The purpose of this chapter, therefore, is succinctly to summarise the current understanding of the conditions under which
assertive behaviour in conflict situations is both appropriate and effective.

DEFINING ASSERTIVE BEHAVIOUR

The first widely promoted definitions of assertion were fairly general ones emphasising the individual's right to express personal desires while simultaneously respecting the rights of the other person (e.g. Alberti and Emmons, 1970; Lange and Jakubowski, 1976). They were developed by clinicians from the pioneering formulations introduced by Salter (1949) and Wolpe (1969), and specified components (be direct, use a firm but respectful tone, maintain eye contact) derived from face or content validity. However, researchers found such conceptualisations unhelpful for guiding systematic theoretical and empirical inquiry because content will vary with situational, individual and cultural factors. This led Rich and Schroeder (1976, p. 1082) to propose a functional, contentless operant definition: '[Assertive behaviour is] the skill to seek, maintain, or enhance reinforcement in an inter-personal situation through the expression of feelings or wants when such expression risks loss of reinforcement or even punishment . . . the degree of assertiveness may be measured by the effectiveness of an individual's response in producing, maintaining, or enhancing reinforcement.'

This definition is particularly useful in concisely highlighting the several essential features of assertion (Rakos, 1991). First, assertion is a *learned skill*, not a 'trait' that a person 'has' or 'lacks'. The performance of the skill, as with any skill, varies as a function of the situation and the person–situation interaction. Second, assertion occurs only in an *inter-personal* context. Third, it is an *expressive* skill, involving verbal and non-verbal compo-nents. Fourth, assertion always entails *risk* – either that the recipient will react negatively to, or fail to comply with, the assertion. Finally, the extent of assertiveness is determined by *outcome*, which has frequently been considered to be the 'ultimate criterion for evalu-ating performance' (McFall, 1982, p. 17).

However, assertion must be measured by more than a simple *outcome criterion* . Because assertion by definition involves risk, it follows that even technically proficient behaviour may fail to produce reinforcement in any given instance. This *technical criterion* is not readily appreciated by the many people who judge assertiveness solely through outcome, without consideration of response quality. Additionally, assertion may achieve its imme-diate goals but significantly injure the relationship. Such a response 'works' only in a limited way; the 'net' effect of a presumably 'self-enhancing' skill (Masters *et al.*, 1987) must be determined by a *cost-benefit criterion*. Finally, behaviour must have social validity – legitimacy through social acceptability (Kazdin, 1977; Wolf, 1978). Since unskilled behaviour can still produce reinforcement, a *cultural criterion* that judges social appro-priateness is often necessary. Thus, the immediate impact of the response is but one limited way to measure assertiveness; in fact, in training regimens technical expertise, net benefit and cultural appropriateness are stressed far more than actual outcome (cf. Heimberg and Etkin, 1983). Indeed, when numerous instances of assertion are aggregated, attention to the technical, cost-benefit and cultural criteria will facilitate self-enhancing yet socially responsible behaviour.

The reintroduction of criteria such as technical expertise and cultural appropriateness necessitates abandonment of a purely functional definition: some content is necessary. Unfortunately, consensus has been elusive. St Lawrence (1987), for example, identified more than twenty distinctly different definitions of assertion in use in research and training. Thus, a discussion of ways to approach the concept of assertion is essential.

CLARIFICATION OF THE ASSERTION CONCEPT

Response classes of assertion

Assertive behaviour is a situation-specific, learned skill comprising a number of partially independent response classes. The specific response classes that have emerged depend to some degree on the methodology employed, but an extensive review of the literature (Schroeder *et al.*, 1983) distilled the data into seven categories that appear to have the necessary breadth, flexibility and utility. Four 'positive' response classes include admitting personal short-comings (self-disclosure), giving and receiving compliments, initiating and maintaining interactions and expressing positive feelings. Three 'negative' or 'conflict' response classes include expressing unpopular or different opinions, requesting behaviour changes by other people and refusing unreasonable requests.

Recently, several writers have distinguished assertive response classes in terms of the asserter's initiative. Trower (1995) identified active assertive skills (self-disclosure, asking favours, disagreeing, expressing negative and positive feelings) and reactive assertive skills (refusing requests, responding to disagreement, responding to negative and positive feelings). Similarly, Gambrill (1995) classified negative assertion as a response to another's initiative (refusing unwanted and tempting requests, responding to criticism) or as an initiative response (requesting a behaviour change, disagreeing, apologising, ending interactions). She categorised positive assertion as an initiative response (asking favours, complimenting others). From this perspective, responding to compliments and to expressions of positive feelings would be positive assertions in response to another's initiative.

The conflict response classes have received the bulk of the research and clinical attention, probably due to social and historical factors (such as the dominance of male values) rather than to scientific or clinical ones. While the focus here will remain on conflict assertion, it is important to recognise that assertiveness encompasses interpersonal expressiveness in both positive and negative contexts (Gambrill, 1995; Rakos, 1991).

Distinguishing assertion from aggression

Assertion typically has been conceptualised as the mid-point on the continuum between non-assertive (passive) and aggressive behaviour. While research has generally supported this approach (Galassi *et al.*, 1981), recent data suggest that socially appropriate assertion may include limited elements of aggressive and submissive behaviour (Wilson and Gallois, 1993). Further, though a single conceptual continuum highlights the appropriateness of assertiveness training for aggressive as well as timid individuals, it fails to offer a clear differentiation between socially appropriate conflict assertive behaviour and inappropriate aggressive behaviour. This is a critical distinction since lay persons often fail to distinguish the two styles of responding, describe assertion as pushy, rude and insensitive and label conflict assertion as aggression (cf. Rakos, 1991). Such confusion compromises the social acceptability and attractiveness of assertive response alternatives.

Most attempts to distinguish between assertion and aggression have involved the notion of social acceptability. Both Alberti and Emmons (1995) and Lange and Jakubowski (1976) argue that appropriate conflict assertion, unlike aggression, respects the other person's rights and dignity through the use of non-hostile verbal content and vocal attributes. Assertion is expected to produce stronger relationships and minimal negative emotions, whereas aggression is predicted to result in a strained emotionally charged relationship. Hollandsworth (1977) criticised these formulations' failure to establish objective criteria; he proposed instead that aggressive responses were defined by their use of coercive content (verbal disparagement, name-calling and verbal threat of punishment). Alberti (1977) responded that the distinction cannot rest on content alone, but must also acknowledge intentions, consequences and context. Rakos (1979) contended that Hollandsworth failed to recognise that after repeated non-compliance to an assertion it may be appropriate to 'escalate' (Masters *et al.*, 1987) the assertion to include reasonable threats (e.g. initiation of legal action, appeal to higher authority, refusal to co-operate further, withdrawal of resources).

Pure functional definitions, such as Rich and Schroeder's (1976), also are unable to distinguish between the two behavioural styles. Such definitions lack any content, and thereby fail to incorporate critical context such as social values, behavioural goals and cultural expectations. For instance, Wilson and Gallois (1993) demonstrated that most people endorse 'the general goals of avoiding conflict and not straining the relationship' (p. 99). However, Rakos (1979) suggested that the functional definition can serve as the basis from which other functionally related behaviours with specified but general content can be identified. Assertion, which is generally viewed as a discrete behaviour and a personal right, should instead be considered as a chain of overt and covert responses encompassing rights (actually, *rights behaviours*) and their functionally related antecedent and consequent responsibilities (*obligation behaviours*). Verbalisation of the rights behaviour alone, without the attendant social obligations, is *expressive behaviour*, and by itself, aggressive. Conflict assertion, in contrast, requires the emission of specific categories of socially responsible behaviour.

Antecedent obligations (emitted prior to expressive behaviour):

- Engaging in sufficient overt and covert behaviour to determine the rights of *all* participants;
- Developing a verbal and non-verbal response repertoire that is intended to influence the other person's offending behaviour but not the self-evaluation of personal 'worth';
- Considering the potential negative consequences the other person may experience as a function of expressive behaviour.

Subsequent obligations (emitted after expressive behaviour):

- Providing a brief, honest, but non-apologetic explanation for the expressive behaviour;
- Providing clarifying or alternative interpretations of the expressive behaviour and empathic communications concerning its implications, in an attempt to minimise any hurt, anger, or unhappiness experienced by the other person as a consequence of the expressive behaviour;
- Protecting the other person's rights if that person is unable to do so;
- Seeking a mutually acceptable compromise when legitimate rights of both parties exist and are in conflict.

The antecedent obligations, according to Rakos, are necessary prerequisites to expressive behaviour in all conflict situations, but the subsequent ones are essential elements of assertion only when the relationship is a continuing one. The subsequent obligations serve as relationship-enhancing behaviours and are therefore pragmatic – and particularly relevant to the goals women emphasise in conflict resolution: relationship development and interpersonal sensitivity (Wilson and Gallois, 1993). As will be discussed shortly, the obligation components improve the social reaction to conflict assertion and thereby increase both the net benefits and the social validity of the response. While they can be emitted as part of an assertion to a stranger with whom no further contact is anticipated, they are unnecessary (there is no relationship to enhance) and potentially problematic (they extend the conflictual interaction and increase the content that is open for discussion). Furthermore, when the legitimate rights of strangers conflict, the nature of the situation usually precludes a search for a mutually acceptable compromise. Empirical support for this recommendation is provided by Heisler and McCormack (1982), who found that an empathic statement improved the social reaction of an assertion to a familiar person but had little effect when directed towards a stranger.

The conceptualisation of assertion as a behaviour chain rather than as a discrete response provides a way to distinguish assertion from aggression. Assertion is characterised by the emission of the appropriate obligation behaviours as well as the expressive ones, whereas aggressive behaviour involves only the expression of rights. Expressing rights alone violates the general norm of conflict minimisation and employs dominance and power to achieve an outcome (Wilson and Gallois, 1993). It is not surprising, therefore, that in conflict situations persons exhibiting the dominating, hostile Type A behaviour pattern are less likely than Type Bs to include obligation components within assertive responses (Bruch *et al.*, 1991). Thus simply saying to your supervisor, 'Janice, I'm sorry, I can't work late tonight' – which is assertive according to Hollandsworth (1977) and, if it 'works', Rich and Schroeder (1976) – would be classified by the chain definition as an expressive response, and by itself, aggressive. In a continuing relationship with a supervisor, the antecedent and subsequent responsibilities also define assertive behaviour.

When assertion is conceptualised as a chain of responses rather than as a discrete action, the context in which the conflict occurs assumes importance. Thus, the chain perspective is contextualistic: it specifies components that are general and flexible in content, so that variability due to situational, social and cultural norms and values can be accommodated. The components themselves have little meaning apart from the chain. Nevertheless, sufficient specificity is included so that competent emission of the individual components can be reliably trained and then effectively generalised to the natural environment (Rakos and Schroeder, 1979).

THE SKILL OF CONFLICT ASSERTION

Conflict assertion competencies characterise psychologically adaptive, 'healthy' individuals (see Rakos, 1991, for an extensive review). Research in clinical, school and work contexts compellingly indicates that the ability to perform assertively facilitates personal growth and satisfactions, particularly, but by no means exclusively, in cultural contexts dominated by secular Western norms and values. But exactly what is appropriate assertion that contributes so strongly to positive psychological adaptation? The public (overt) response elements are now recognised as important but limited components of effective assertion. Furthermore, the overt behaviours identified as components of assertion are not absolutes: there is rarely, if ever, one and only one correct way to resolve a particular conflict.

Effective assertion requires the ability to emit flexible responses that are sensitive to unique circumstances. Notions of 'flexibility' and 'sensitivity' suggest that covert behaviours are integrally involved in the selection of the overt responses, and the idea of selection implies that overt responses will vary across situations. Therefore, the research can only provide general guidelines for the development of a diverse overt and covert response repertoire that can then be adapted to the specific interpersonal context.

Overt behavioural components of conflict assertion

The overt response elements can be categorised as follows:

- Content: the verbal behaviour of the asserter, or what the person *says* to the other person(s);
- Paralinguistic elements: the vocal characteristics of the verbal behaviour, or how the asserter *sounds*;
- Non-verbal behaviours: the body movements and facial expression that accompany the verbal behaviour, or how the asserter *appears*;
- Social interaction skills: the timing, initiation, persistence and stimulus control skills that enhance the impact of the verbal behaviour, or how the asserter behaves in the *process* of the interaction.

Content

The verbal content of conflict assertion can be divided into two general categories corresponding to the chain conceptualisation presented above: expression of rights and the emission of elaborations (the functionally related obligations that address the context in which the expressive behaviour is performed).

Expression of rights

The expression of rights is the core of any assertion, its *raison d'être*. The specific content will vary not only with the context but also as a function of the response class, and will always include a statement of desire, affect, or opinion (Kolotkin *et al.*, 1984; Romano and Bellack, 1980). For example:

Refusal 'No thank you, I am not interested.'
Behaviour change request 'I feel that I am doing all of the housework.' (Statement of opinion or affect.) 'I would like us to renegotiate our agreement.' (Request for new behaviour.)
Expression of unpopular or different opinion 'I don't see a problem with our household responsibilities.'

These rights statements exemplify several important topographical features of skilled responding. First, they utilise 'I-statements' in which the speaker assumes responsibility for feelings, rather than 'you-statements' that attribute responsibility for personal feelings to the other person (Lange and Jakubowski, 1976; Winship and Kelly, 1976). For example, 'You make me angry when you don't do your share of the housework' is a very different communication from 'I am angry because I feel you don't do your share of the housework'. Note also that the 'I-statement' offers a perception that is legitimate but open to disconfirmation, while the 'you-statement' presents a statement of fact that must be denied. Thus it is not surprising that 'I-statements' are strongly related to judgements of overall assertion, while 'you-statements' are associated with aggression (Kolotkin *et al.*, 1984). However, 'I-statements' do not characterise ordinary conversation and may be difficult for many individuals to adopt (Gervasio, 1987). It is likely that 'I-statements' will be most useful in specific situations, as when the recipient of an assertion is likely to be very sensitive to blame or when there is an ongoing emotionally charged dispute.

Expressions of rights are also direct, specific and respectful. A *direct* statement contains a clear, honest and succinct message that describes the relevant feelings, desires, perceptions, or opinions. However, brevity should not violate conversational rules; compound sentences joined by 'and' or 'but' should be employed (cf. Gervasio and Crawford, 1989). Additionally, an introductory 'orienting statement' that signals the topic to be discussed is usually appropriate (e.g. 'I have some concerns about the plans we made . . .': Kolotkin *et al.*, 1984). Explanations or apologies are not included in the rights statement as they obscure the focus of concern and dilute the impact of the assertion; they may, however, be appropriate elaborations that are emitted later (see below, p. 296f.). A *specific* statement delineates the central issue clearly and avoids generalisations. 'I have concerns about how we divide the housework' is much more specific than 'I have concerns about how we divide our responsibilities'. The latter statement introduces a myriad of other issues (child care, financial matters, etc.) that can only confuse the discussion, dilute the focus, increase perceived demands and impede problem-solving. A *respectful* expression adheres to norms of politeness and avoids labelling, blaming, demeaning, attacking, or making motivational assumptions about the other person.

Thus, a direct, specific and respectful behaviour change request simply describes the offending behaviour and then politely asks for a behaviour change. The expression of an unpopular opinion is similarly constructed: 'I feel Issue 1 fails to recognise the real needs of the schools' is quite different from 'Anyone who supports Issue 1 is deceiving himself and rationalising'. The latter generalises ('anyone'), labels ('deceiving himself') and makes motivational assumptions ('rationalising'). Refusal of unreasonable requests also incorporates these three features: 'No thank you, I am not interested' is all that is necessary in terms of expression of rights. Conflict assertions that lack directness are likely to be seen as non-assertive, those lacking respect as aggressive, and those lacking both as passive-aggressive, while lack of specificity may characterise all three alternatives to assertion.

Several comments regarding the content of behaviour change requests and refusals are necessary. Behaviour change requests are conceptualised as containing a statement of feeling and a specific request for altered behaviour. While the specific request component is judged to be part of an assertive response by trained judges, lay persons evaluate it as bordering on aggressiveness and of little functional value (Mullinix and Galassi, 1981). This suggests that the specific request statement may be most appropriate and useful when a desired response to the conflict statement alone is not forthcoming (escalation and persistence are discussed below). Finally, the stereotypical 'no' is indeed an important element of refusals. However, its direct verbalisation may be socially awkward and breach conversational conventions (cf. Gambrill, 1995; Gervasio, 1987), as when a spouse responds to a partner, 'No, I don't want to see that movie. Let's choose one we both want to see.' An alternative approach is to embed the refusal within the elaboration components: 'Dear, I know I will really dislike that movie. Let's find one that we will both enjoy.'

A conflict assertion that only expresses a right has been termed a 'standard assertion'. Research has consistently demonstrated that such communications are judged (1) to be equally potent to, and somewhat more desirable than, aggressive behaviour and (2) to be distinctly less likeable, but more socially competent than, non-assertive behaviour (see Rakos, 1991, for an extensive review of this literature). Further, standard assertion is judged to be less likeable and more unpleasant than ordinary non-conflict conversation (Wildman and Clementz, 1986) and the expression of positive feelings (commendatory assertion: Cook and St Lawrence, 1990). However, a few studies suggest that situational variables may moderate the social reaction: standard assertion was a more highly valued conflict resolution style than non-assertion for competitive (Levin and Gross, 1987) and socially skilled (Frisch and Froberg, 1987) persons, and by persons working in corporations (Solomon *et al.*, 1982) and psychiatric hospitals (Dura and Beck, 1986). Overall, however, the standard assertion is likely to introduce an identifiable risk of social disapproval – including being labelled as aggressive behaviour.

Expression of elaborations

Experienced clinicians have always recognised that the standard assertion (expressing a right) does not address the social context, cultural norms, or growth potential of a continuing relationship. Researchers did not investigate the elaboration components until the late 1970s. Woolfolk and Dever (1979) found that a short explanation and an acknowledgement of the other person's feelings enhanced the evaluation of the assertion without detracting from its potency. Additional studies appeared shortly after, suggesting that other elaborations also improved the social reaction to assertion while maintaining its efficacy, including compromises and alternatives, reasons, praise and apologies (Pitcher and Meikle, 1980; Romano and Bellack, 1980; Twentyman *et al.*, 1981). These elaborations are strikingly similar to the 'obligations' Rakos (1979) initially proposed as a means to distinguish assertion from aggression.

Subsequent research confirmed that the elaboration verbalisations are key elements for minimising a negative social reaction to conflict assertion. Assertions that include explanations, acknowledgements of feelings, compromises and praise have been termed 'empathic assertions' (Rakos, 1986) and are judged to be as potent as, but more likeable and appropriate than, standard assertions. Empathic assertions provoke less anger than, but are as effective as, aggressive responses. They are comparable to non-assertions in terms of likeability, but more efficacious. Finally, they are as pleasant as neutral non-conflict conversation (see Rakos, 1991, for a comprehensive review).

Therefore, the interpersonally potent yet socially acceptable empathic assertion, comprised of elaborations that can be easily operationalised and reliably assessed (Bruch *et al.*, 1981), as well as successfully trained (Rakos and Schroeder, 1979), has emerged as the generally preferred training goal, particularly when maintenance or enhancement of a continuing relationship is important. The specific elaboration components can be categorised as follows:

1 A short, truthful, non-defensive explanation for the expression of rights;

2 A statement conveying understanding of the effects of the expression of rights on the other person;

3 Praise or another positive comment directed towards the other person;

4 A short apology that is directed towards the inconvenience or disappointment that will result from the expression of rights (e.g. 'I am sorry you will have to miss the concert'), rather than an apology that refers to the necessity for the expression of rights (e.g. 'I am sorry I have to say no');

5 An attempt to achieve a mutually acceptable compromise when legitimate rights conflict, recognising that such a solution may not always be possible. (The determination of legitimate rights involves covert response components to be discussed below, p. 304f.).

It is worth noting that these obligation behaviours are likely to be more consistent with women's approach towards and expectations for conflict resolution than with those of men (Wilson and Gallois, 1993).

Paralinguistic and non-verbal components

The paralinguistic and non-verbal features of a verbalisation are critical components of effective communication (see Chapter 3), social skill (see Chapter 1) and assertion (Gambrill, 1995). In fact, women identify the self-management of these components, such that emotional control and conscious non-stereotypical presentation are achieved, as among their high priority goals in confrontations (Wilson and Gallois, 1993). Not surprisingly, these non-content skills have been the focus of a great deal of research, which is summarised below.

Paralinguistic characteristics

The features commanding the greatest attention are voice volume, firmness and intonation and response latency, duration and fluency. An extensive review of the numerous research studies can be found in Rakos (1991).

Latency

The observation that non-assertive people seem to hesitate before responding suggested that a short response latency is an important component of assertion. However, the research has failed to confirm this hypothesis; the contradictory data suggest that a variety of situational variables are influential, including sex of the participants and type of assertion. For example, latency is greater in conflict situations than in positive ones, with conflict assertions to males producing the longest latency (Pitcher and Meikle, 1980). The speed with which a person responds will be related to ability to process the situational information and determine the desired and appropriate response (see below, p. 309f.). Clinically, it appears that a short latency is less important for effective conflict resolution than is the avoidance of a very long latency. If the desired response is difficult to determine or not in the current behavioural repertoire, then the appropriate assertion, with modest delay, would be to request additional time to reformulate a reply or to arrange a specific time for further discussion.

Response duration

Originally, a short duration was assumed to be characteristic of assertion, since non-assertive persons tend to produce long explanations, excuses, lies and apologies. However, because appropriate assertion involves verbalising elaborations as well as expressing rights, the duration of an assertion may be longer than other responses (Gervasio, 1987), especially when (as is the case for latency) the assertion involves conflict and is directed towards a male (e.g. Pitcher and Meikle, 1980). The assertion must be sufficiently long to communicate effectively in a given context; mere verbiage in and of itself is neither assertive nor unassertive. In fact, Heimberg *et al.* (1979) found a curvilinear relationship between assertiveness and duration: moderately assertive individuals exhibited much shorter duration than either highly assertive or non-assertive persons. However, excessive verbalisation increases the chances for confusion, diversion and irrelevancy. Therefore, the guideline here is similar to that for latency: response duration must be flexible to meet the demands of unique circumstances.

Response fluency

Fluency is considered to be an important paralinguistic feature of assertion, yet it has been poorly investigated. In fact, the few studies to address the issue directly find a very weak relationship (e.g. Kolotkin *et al.*, 1984). However, hesitant, choppy speech is associated with anxiety (Linehan and Walker, 1983), which is presumed to be detrimental to, and perhaps even incompatible with, effective assertion (Wolpe, 1990). Thus, common sense suggests fluency will contribute to the judgement of skill. Interestingly, speech *rate* has not attracted the attention of researchers or clinicians. It, too, makes intuitive sense: non-anxious, assertive individuals would be expected to adjust their rate of talking to reflect the particular environmental context.

Voice volume

The data on loudness, in contrast to the previous characteristics, are fairly consistent: effective conflict assertion is characterised by an appropriate, moderate volume that is louder than the speech produced in ordinary conversation (e.g. Rose and Tryon, 1979) and by non-assertive persons (e.g. Eisler *et al.*, 1973).

Intonation (inflection)

Lay people consider intonation to be one of the most important features of effective assertion (Romano and Bellack, 1980), but, like response duration, both highly assertive and non-assertive people evidence greater inflection than moderately assertive individuals (Heimberg *et al.*, 1979). Inflection is therefore an important attribute of assertion, but not a distinguishing characteristic. As with many of the other paralinguistic components, intermediate levels of intonation are judged to be most appropriate (Rose and Tryon, 1979).

Firmness (affect)

High levels of firmness are strongly correlated with judgements of assertion (Bordewick and Bornstein, 1980; Kolotkin *et al.*, 1984) and may even contribute more than actual content (Kirschner and Galassi, 1983). Assertive psychiatric patients manifest greater affect than non-assertive ones (Eisler *et al.*, 1973), particularly in conflict situations (Eisler *et al.*, 1975). With the exception of a study by Bourque and Ladouceur (1979), the data suggest that the absence of vocal firmness is likely to detract from the impact of a conflict assertion, and that the development of an appropriately firm 'tone' should be a high training priority.

Summary of paralinguistic qualities

Firmness, intermediate levels of volume and intonation, and moderate response latency and duration appear to characterise effective conflict assertion. Intuitively, a fluent response and a moderate speech rate make sense but lack, at present, empirical support. Firmness, latency and duration have shown a particular sensitivity to situational variables: they are likely to increase in conflict interactions and when directed towards a male. In general, appropriate conflict assertion requires flexible paralinguistic abilities that are sensitive to changing environmental conditions.

Non-verbal characteristics

Motoric behaviours convey a great deal of information in an assertive interaction (McFall *et al.*, 1982) as they do in interpersonal communication in general (see Chapter 3). Research has examined the contribution eye contact, facial expression, gestures and global 'body language' make towards effective conflict assertion.

Eye contact

Western culture regards eye contact as an important aspect of interpersonal communication (Kleinke, 1986) and social skill (Trower, 1980). Predictably, it emerges as an important component of conflict assertion (Rakos, 1991). The duration of eye contact is longer in conflict situations than in positive ones (Eisler *et al.*, 1975). However, the actual amount of eye contact is not a clear distinguishing feature of assertion: skilled and unskilled persons do not consistently differ in its duration (Bourque and Ladouceur, 1979; Heimberg *et al.*, 1979). The topography of eye contact, rather than simple duration, may be the critical feature: it must be emitted flexibly and perhaps somewhat intermittently (as opposed to a fixed stare), especially since it is engaged in by the listener and not by the speaker in general social conversation between Caucasians (LaFrance and Mayo, 1976).

Facial expression

Deception and anxiety are both betrayed by a variety of facial movements and expressions (Ekman, 1992). Thus, it is not surprising that judgements of assertion, a presumably honest and non-anxious communication, are strongly influenced by overall facial expression (Romano and Bellack, 1980) as well as by specific mouth, eyebrow and forehead cues (McFall *et al.*, 1982). Uncontrolled fidgety mouth movements, wrinkled forehead and animated, constantly moving eyebrows communicate unassertiveness. These cues convey more information when the speaker is male but are more influential in evaluating female asserters (McFall *et al.*, 1982). While McFall *et al.* did not detect differences in the way males and females used these cues, Romano and Bellack (1980) found that '(M)ales and females differed substantially in the number, pattern and valence of the cues used . . . female judges seemed to be sensitive to and made use of more behavioral cues' (p. 488). In particular, they noted that smiles, which in general contribute minimally to perceptions of assertiveness (Kolotkin *et al.*, 1984), strongly detracted from women's – but not from men's – evaluations of female asserters.

Facial expression, then, is an important component of assertion, especially for women. Females may be more astute than men at discriminating these cues in others, but as asserters they emit them in more subtle ways that nevertheless strongly impact on the perception of their assertion. Their concern with controlling their emotional personas (Wilson and Gallois, 1993) appears warranted. Males may require focused training in attending to and interpreting facial cues, particularly when emitted by women. Females should recognise that other women may react negatively to smiles during an assertion, but that males may be unaffected by that response.

Gestures

Socially competent persons increase their use of gestures in conflict situations (Trower, 1980). They also use their arms and hands differently from less skilled individuals – arm movements that are smooth and steady while speaking and inconspicuous while listening are the greatest non-verbal contributors to judgements of male assertion (McFall *et al.*, 1982). Such movements are also highly influential in the perception of female assertion, especially when rated by males: physical gestures enhance the evaluation while extraneous and restrained movements are viewed negatively (Romano and Bellack, 1980). Arm and hand gestures may be most important when the conflict interaction involves opposite sexed participants (Rose and Tryon, 1979). Clearly, an appropriate repertoire of gestures will enhance the effectiveness of conflict assertion.

Body language

Experts discount the importance of body language (Kolotkin *et al.*, 1984) but lay people consider it significant (Romano and Bellack, 1980). Head, neck, shoulder and torso positions that are upright, exhibit minimal extraneous movement, squarely face the other person, and involve purposive movement while speaking yet remain quiet while listening are linked with assertive behaviour. Non-assertiveness is associated with excessive nodding and head tilting, stooped, hunched, or shrugging shoulders, and squirming, rotating, or rocking torsos; these cues are more influential in the evaluation of male asserters, but overall are the least important non-verbal responses (McFall *et al.*, 1982; Romano and Bellack, 1980). Finally, while meaningful posture shifts are appropriate (Trower, 1980), actually approaching the other person while asserting is perceived by lay people as aggressive (Rose and Tryon, 1979). These data suggest that body language contributes modestly to perceptions of assertion, and is more important for males.

Summary of non-verbal responses

Eye contact, facial expression, gestures and, to a lesser extent, body language, all influence evaluations of conflict assertion. Facial expression for female asserters and gestures for male asserters may be especially important variables. Overall, steady but not rigid eye contact, a calm, sincere, serious facial expression, flexible use of arm and hand gestures, and a relaxed, involved body posture characterise behaviour judged to be assertive. Body movements should be fluid and purposeful when speaking but quiet and inconspicuous when listening.

Process (interactive) skills

The overt skill components are emitted within an ongoing social interaction. Their impact, therefore, depends on competence in the process skills of response timing, initiation and persistence, and stimulus control.

Response timing

Socially unskilled persons fail to time their statements and gestures adequately (Fischetti *et al.*, 1977; Peterson *et al.*, 1981) and respond inappropriately to situational cues (Fischetti *et al.*, 1984). Trower (1980), for example, found that skilled individuals spoke more than unskilled persons, and did so at socially appropriate moments. The importance of skilled timing has been acknowledged more in the general social skill training field than in the assertiveness literature. Nevertheless, the effectiveness of an assertion will be related to the appropriateness with which it is introduced into the conflict interaction. It is essential that individuals discriminate the verbal, non-verbal and situational cues that indicate the appropriateness of a response. When these stimuli fail to provide clear guidelines, other communication skills may be required (e.g. questioning, paraphrasing, reflecting, self-disclosing, explaining, or reinforcing, as detailed in other chapters of this volume).

Initiation and persistence

The decision to emit an assertive response in a particular situation involves covert responses to be discussed shortly. On occasion, passivity or compliance may be preferred options, as when the realistic risk of assertion is excessive or the offending person's situation invites extraordinary 'understanding' (cf. Rakos, 1991). However, when assertion is the selected option, the initial verbalisation should be the *minimal effective response* (MER), defined as 'behavior that would ordinarily accomplish the client's goal with a minimum of effort and of apparent negative emotion (and a very small likelihood of negative consequences)' (Masters *et al.*, 1987, p. 106). The MER operationalises the ubiquitous goal of minimising conflict and relationship strain (cf. Wilson and Gallois, 1993). If the MER proves ineffective, and the decision is made to persist, *escalation* is appropriate. This may involve increasing the intensity of paralinguistic qualities (voice volume, intonation, affect, response duration) and/or expanding the use of non-verbal behaviours such as gestures and body language. Typically, the verbal content will be modified in some manner. For example, in continuing relationships, further explanation may be provided, empathy increased, or additional potential compromises suggested. Aversive consequences may be identified or the specific behaviour change request added if the statement of the problem alone fails to alter the offender's behaviour. Determination of the MER is critical because an escalated response emitted as an initial assertion (a common error by novices) will be likely to be evaluated as inappropriate and aggressive, which may result in negative consequences for the asserter and reinforce beliefs that such behaviour is indeed risky. For a simple example, imagine that a cosmetic salesperson in a department store approaches you with a product you do not want and does not respect your lack of interest. Appropriate assertion might involve the following:

MER: 'No, I am not interested. Good day.'

Escalation 1: 'No, I told you: I am not interested.'

Escalation 2: 'I am *not* interested.' (Louder volume, firmer affect and intonation)

Escalation 3: 'I told you three times I am not interested. If you do not stop bothering me, I will contact your supervisor and register a formal complaint against you.' (Volume, affect, intonation maintained or increased slightly from previous response, and aversive contingency specified; gestures may increase.)

Effective persistence requires that the asserter maintain the conflict focus and resist manipulations. In non-continuing relationships, the asserter must basically provide a repetitive response that avoids the introduction of new material. If the cosmetic salesperson persists, and begins to describe the 'free' travel bag, umbrella and perfume that accompany a purchase, and that can be given as extra 'gifts' or used for oneself, the appropriate assertive response remains: 'No, thank you, I am not interested.' This avoids the manipulative ploy of discussing gifts or uses of products; such a shift in focus allows the interaction to continue and may soon force the asserter into explaining gift-giving or cosmetic usage, neither of which is the issue. Maintaining the assertive focus in such a situation usually means simple repetition without qualification. If one says, 'I am not interested at this time', one may be asked why not 'now', and then 'when', and if 'cost' is the problem there is a smaller size, and if no person is available to receive the 'gift' now, it will be good to have a gift available when that person surely comes upon the scene.

Maintaining the focus is particularly difficult when a valued continuing relationship is involved and when the asserter is starting to behave less submissively and thereby no longer meeting the expectations of others. Expectations that are unfulfilled are likely to arouse one or more negative feelings, such as hurt, anger, rejection, depression, or vengeance. Therefore, persistence by the novice asserter in ongoing relationships is a greater challenge than for experienced asserters who have taught their social environment to expect self-enhancing behaviour. Escalation must be highly skilful to maintain the focus while simultaneously addressing the issues that impact on the long-term integrity of the relationship. The escalations must embed repetitions in diverse syntactic surface structures (Gervasio, 1987) and in layers of elaborations. For example, suppose a father whose grown daughter comes to his house for dinner every Sunday now learns that she won't be coming this week:

MER: 'Dad, I won't be coming to dinner this Sunday. I've made plans to see some friends – we're going to a party. I hope you won't be too disappointed. I'll see you again next Sunday as usual.' (This MER expresses the unpopular communication along with an explanation, attention to feelings, and a potential mutually acceptable compromise.)

Father: 'But I look forward to your visits so much. I don't get out often any more, and your company is so special. Couldn't you meet your friends after dinner?' (Father at this point is responding with an appropriate assertion of his own – a request for a behaviour change – and includes an explanation and potential compromise.)

Escalation 1: 'Dad, if I come to dinner, I'll miss a good deal of the party. I know how much you enjoy my visits, but this is an exception. It's a special party that I really want to attend. I know you'll miss me, but it's only one week.' (Repeated expression of the unpopular content, with additional explanation and empathy, all offered with a changed surface structure.)

Father: 'Then go with your friends to your party! I'll be all right. I'm sorry they are more important to you. One day you'll see how important it is that your kids care, and show that they care!'

Here we are dealing with one of the most complex of continuing relationships, that of an adult child with a parent. The daughter initiates assertive behaviour, resulting in the father experiencing an unexpected loss of reinforcement and the feelings of hurt and anger that frequently accompany aversive consequences. Protecting the relationship and maintaining the focus in this situation involve an increased attention to underlying feelings, repetition and possible expansion of the explanation, and a wider search for a mutually acceptable compromise. The focus will be maintained best if the asserter can manage the exceptionally difficult task of addressing these verbalisations to the *existence* of the feelings rather than to the *content* of the feelings.

Escalation 2: 'Dad, I can see how angry and disappointed you are that I will not be coming for dinner this Sunday. I know how important our dinners together are to you, but as I said, I very much want to go to this party. There will be a lot of new people there, and I've been feeling a bit isolated lately. I hope you understand my feelings. I'm thinking about how to solve this problem, and I know I'm free Wednesday evening – I can stop by for a few hours after work instead of waiting until next Sunday. How does that sound?'

This escalated response repeats the assertion, attends to the feelings the father is experiencing, expands the explanation, offers a new compromise and changes the surface structure. It does not lose the focus by becoming defensive through a debate on the extent of 'caring' for father or the relative 'importance' of different relationships. Caring, if present, can be demonstrated through the compromise. Sometimes, however, the interaction will continue and the content of the feelings will have to be addressed more directly, resulting in an increased probability of losing the assertive focus.

Escalation 3: 'Dad, I really do understand how much you look forward to our Sunday dinners and the time we spend together. I enjoy our dinners too, but sometimes other important engagements occur on Sundays. I feel very close to you, and care about you very much. My missing dinner this week has nothing to do with how I feel about you. I wish you saw this as I do, but all I can do is try to explain my point to you. Anyway, as I said, I am free Wednesday evening. I'd like to stop by then – would you like me to?'

Escalation in continuing relationships will always involve expanded content (and hence response duration), but louder volume, greater firmness and inflection, or increased use of non-verbal cues will depend on the context. If the other person continues to experience negative feelings as a consequence of the assertion, and the relationship is a valued one, a new assertion directed at the unresolved conflict may be necessary, either immediately or at a later, planned time. Persistence should be conceptualised as the behaviours required to solve the problem as best as possible. As the interaction continues, issues may shift, and further escalation may become counter-productive. A new, legitimate issue usually indicates the need for a new MER rather than endless escalation:

MER: 'Dad, I want to talk to you about our phone conversation last week. You sounded quite hurt and angry, and seemed to feel that if I cared about you I would always make the Sunday dinner. I would like to talk about that because I think I need some flexibility in my plans.' (This MER includes an orienting verbalisation and the conflict statement component of a behaviour change request.)

Persistence increases the chances for a desired outcome but cannot guarantee it, since assertion is, by definition, risky. The car mechanic may not reduce unwarranted charges regardless of the extent of escalation. An assertion specifying a future contingency ('you will hear from my attorney') may not be very satisfying. Even when a desired outcome is achieved in a continuing relationship, the possibility of arousing negative feelings introduces additional risks. Skilful use of the covert components of assertion (see below, p. 304f.) is necessary to assess the situation accurately, avoid rationalisations that justify passivity and decide, first, whether to assert and, second, the extent of escalation that is desirable given the importance of the conflict at issue, the nature of the relationship, and the realistic probability of potential positive and negative outcomes. The acquisition of assertive skills expands the individual's behavioural freedom and therefore the option of asserting. But there is no mandate always to assert oneself or continue the escalation process.

Stimulus control skills

Antecedent and consequent stimulus control skills facilitate effective, socially acceptable assertion by altering the context in which the assertion is emitted. Antecedent stimulus control refers to arranging the environment prior to asserting so that the likelihood of a favourable outcome is maximised. These skills are assertive behaviours themselves: requests to move to a private room prior to a confrontation, requests for a delay prior to making a decision (which provides time to identify and rehearse appropriate responses), or inquiries to the other person regarding convenient times to set aside for the discussion of concerns. They may also involve self-management skills that inhibit assertion because the context is judged to be inappropriate or counter-productive. Conflicts that are discussed in private, at the right time, without time pressures, and with prior deliberation are more likely to be resolved with mutual satisfaction. Consequent stimulus control refers to reinforcing the other person (see Chapter 5) for listening to and/or complying with the assertion. Providing contingent verbal reinforcement for desired behaviour in response to the assertion is likely to encourage similar behaviour in the future and may also minimise negative perceptions of the conflict interaction (Levin and Gross, 1984; St Lawrence *et al.*, 1985).

Covert behavioural components of conflict assertion

Cognitive skills are central elements in contemporary conceptualisations of social skill (see Chapter 1). They permit the individual to categorise and manipulate information and are thereby essential for conscious self-regulation of behaviour, which involves self-monitoring, self-evaluation and self-reinforcement (Kanfer and Schefft, 1988). For example, socially skilled and unskilled persons differ in the standards they employ to evaluate their actions. Skilled persons utilise objective criteria based on situational and interpersonal cues that generate social roles, norms and rules, as well as empirically grounded expectations generated by personal experience. Unskilled individuals, on the other hand, rely on subjective standards that focus on idiosyncratic, non-empirical beliefs, perceptions and expectations (Trower, 1982). An illustration of this is provided by Hung *et al.* (1980), who found that non-assertive persons performed more assertively after exposure to a severely passive model than to a moderately or minimally submissive model, presumably because their subjective performance standards were modified.

The ability to use empirically based, objective criteria requires conceptual complexity (CC; Schroeder *et al.*, 1967), which permits the individual to: (1) make increasingly precise discriminations among situational cues, allowing consideration of broader and more varied viewpoints; (2) increase the use of internally but rationally developed standards for problem-solving; and (3) integrate more information and increase tolerance for conflict. The importance of CC for assertive performance is clear (Bruch *et al.*, 1981): assertive individuals demonstrate greater CC than non-assertive persons and, further, high CC people, compared to low CC ones, manifest a better knowledge of assertive content, superior delivery skills and more effective use of adaptive cognitions. Further, high CC individuals behave more assertively and emit more elaborative statements in conflicts involving continuing relationships. Such situations demand the greatest ability to utilise multiple perspectives and internal rational standards, so that flexible, relationship-enhancing behaviours can contribute to an effective yet socially acceptable assertion. Conflicts involving non-continuing relationships require less CC since social norms provide fairly straightforward behavioural guidelines.

The specific cognitive abilities necessary to produce a sophisticated, rational, empirical analysis of and response to a conflict include knowledge, self-statements, expectancies, philosophical beliefs, problem-solving skills, social perception skills and self-monitoring skills.

Knowledge

Non-assertive as well as assertive individuals can accurately categorise passive, assertive and aggressive responses (Alden and Cappe, 1981; Bordewick and Bornstein, 1980). Thus, the behavioural styles can be discriminated regardless of level of assertiveness. However, the extent to which non-assertive people have acquired the recall knowledge necessary to produce an assertive response is less clear. The majority of studies find that non-assertive individuals can describe or role-play appropriate assertive responses (see Rakos, 1991, for summary), suggesting that the observed discrepancy is due to other covert variables. These data reflect clinical observations that while some non-assertive individuals lack relevant *response content knowledge*, many others possess the information yet are still unable to perform assertively.

A second category of essential knowledge concerns the social rules, norms and expectations that are likely to operate in particular contexts or circumstances, so that an array of appropriate response options can be generated (Wilson and Gallois, 1993). Unskilled persons, as noted above, are likely to lack accurate *social cue knowledge* (Trower, 1982).

Self-statements

Meichenbaum *et al.* (1981) emphasised that a 'negative internal dialogue' is a class of cognitions that interferes with competent social responding. Negative self-statements are exemplified by 'I will be embarrassed if I speak up' or 'He won't like me unless I agree'. Positive versions might be 'My opinions are valuable' and 'I have the right to express myself'. The data are clear (cf. Rakos, 1991): assertive persons emit approximately twice as many positive as negative self-statements when confronted with social conflict, while non-assertive individuals emit approximately equal numbers of each. Further, the 'mix' of positive and negative self-statements may be as important as the absolute frequency of each (Blankenberg and Heimberg, 1984). For example, assertive persons often use negative self-statements as cues to verbalise positive coping ones (Bruch, 1981).

Wine (1981) noted that the masculine perspective is adopted when self-statements associated with non-assertion are labelled 'negative' or 'dysfunctional'. Such self-verbalisations typically focus on the needs of others and fear of rejection, stem from the 'feminine' emphasis on relationships (Gilligan, 1982; Wilson and Gallois, 1993), and are conciliatory, nurturant and affiliative. Because the situation determines the utility of any particular self-statement, Rakos (1991) suggested that using descriptive labels (autonomous or affiliative) rather than functional ones might eliminate the underlying sexism.

In summary, the research strongly identifies autonomous self-statements as important and perhaps essential components of effective conflict assertion. In fact, direct training in autonomous self-instruction, apart from any other intervention, has resulted in significant gains in assertiveness (e.g. Craighead, 1979).

Expectancies

An expectancy is a cognitive behaviour that makes a specific prediction about performance in a particular situation. *Outcome expectancies* predict the probability that specific consequences will be produced by a particular response. Assertive and non-assertive persons expect standard assertion, and to a lesser extent empathic assertion, to have greater negative long-term effects on a relationship than non-assertion (Zollo *et al.*, 1985). However, assertive individuals expect conflict assertion to produce more positive short-term consequences and fewer negative ones than do non-assertive persons (see Rakos, 1991, for summary). Non-assertive and assertive persons do not differ in their identification of the *possible* consequences but in the *probability* that the potential outcomes will actually occur.

Further, the possible outcomes are evaluated differently: assertive individuals perceive the potential positive consequences of assertion as more desirable and the potential negative ones as more unpalatable (Blankenberg and Heimberg, 1984; Kuperminc and Heimberg, 1983). Non-assertive persons may rationalise to reduce the perceived demand for engaging in a conflict interaction.

Self-efficacy expectations refer to a belief in personal ability to emit a specific response in a particular circumstance (Bandura, 1977). Assertive individuals evidence much stronger self-efficacy in conflict situations than do non-assertive persons. Finally, when the other person behaves in a highly unreasonable manner, assertive individuals demonstrate greater *situational efficacy expectancies*, which describe the confidence a person has that he or she can generate any successful response to deal with a specific situation (Chiauzzi and Heimberg, 1986). Thus, assertive persons approach conflict situations with an adaptive appraisal of the context and a realistic self-confidence in their ability to emit appropriate behaviours.

Philosophical beliefs

Ellis' (1962; Ellis and Grieger, 1977) identification of at least a dozen 'irrational' beliefs as the core of psychological maladjustment has stimulated research into their role in non-assertive behaviour. Six of them seem most directly related to assertion: demands for perfection in self and others in important situations; blaming self or others for fallible behaviour; demands for universal and unwavering approval from significant others; defining personal rights and self-worth by external achievement in subjectively important areas; catastrophising, or exaggerating the meaning of an undesired outcome; and viewing passivity as preferable to active intervention, in the belief that things will 'work out' eventually without 'rocking the boat'. These irrational thoughts are generally produced only in response to subjectively important issues: the person fails to accept that events in the world occur without regard to the personal value ascribed to a particular situation. Thus, a person may very rationally tolerate incompetence in a meaningless hobby (e.g. failure to perform well in a volleyball game), yet react with extraordinary emotion to an objectively similar event of subjective import (e.g. failure to get a role in a community play).

Underlying all irrational thinking is a basic logical error: things, people, or events *should* be a certain way. Ellis argues that the use of 'should' elevates desires into demands and prevents rational analysis of the situation. Unmet demands lead to upset, which does not facilitate effective problem-solving. If, on the other hand, unfulfilled desires were viewed as unfortunate events that one wished were otherwise ('it would be better if . . .' rather than 'it should not have happened . . .'), the person will exhibit concern that can contribute to resolution of the problem.

Ellis' theory has been investigated in terms of assertive skills (see Rakos, 1991, for a review). Non-assertive persons endorse more irrational ideas than do assertive individuals. In conflict situations, non-assertive people entertain the possibility of many more negative 'overwhelming consequences' than positive ones, while assertive persons consider similar frequencies of each. As with self-statements, the 'mix' of extreme outcome expectancies may be more important than their intensity or frequency. Thus, rational alternatives to the irrational beliefs are likely to facilitate assertive responding.

The typical non-assertive person might engage in the following thought process: 'I must assert myself without any mistakes or the assertion will fail [self-perfection], the other person will think I'm a jerk or will be hurt or angry [universal approval], and that would be absolutely terrible [catastrophising]. It would be my fault [self-blame] and confirm that I am no good [self-denigration]. It will work out better if I let it pass and see what happens [inaction].' These belief statements might be prefaced by additional irrational ideas: 'I don't have the right to infringe or make demands on this other person [self-denigration]' and/or 'I should not even have to deal with this situation because the other person should not be acting this way [other-perfection/other-blame].'

Rational alternatives to irrational beliefs can be taught fairly directly. The initial step requires the identification of the specific irrational thought(s) produced in the particular context. Non-assertive people frequently are so practised in irrational thinking that they do not actually verbalise them, but behave 'as if' they did. Following specification of the actual or implicit thought, the individual is taught to challenge it and actively substitute a rational alternative, first in safe and structured rehearsal and later in the actual situation. The general content of the rational alternatives would include the following.

Acceptance of imperfection I am human and the world is very complicated; therefore I will make mistakes even when the situation is important to me and I very much want to behave competently. The importance of an issue to me does not increase its objective status: there is no reason I should behave competently simply because it is important to me that I do so, although it would be nice if I were able to respond competently. The other person is also human, lives in the same complex world, and will also make mistakes in situations that are important to me. There is no reason that others should act in a desirable fashion, just because it is important to me, although it would be nice if they were able to do so. (These thoughts avoid self- or other-blaming and accept the inevitable frailty and imperfection of the human condition.)

Acceptance of disapproval There is no way I can always satisfy everyone who is important to me, even if I always place their needs ahead of my own, because the world is too complicated and its operation too capricious. It would be nice if I could please everyone, but I must recognise that there is no reason why I should do so. (These beliefs recognise that some rejection or disapproval from others is unavoidable.)

Non-catastrophising Negative outcomes are unfortunate, inconvenient, unpleasant, perhaps even bad – but not terrible, horrible, awful, or unbearable. I will try to resolve the problem when possible and adapt to the situation when change is not feasible. I must do this even when the undesired outcome involves a personally important issue, because the world does not know or care what is important to me. Things are as they should be, and demanding that they should be different ignores the complexity of the world – though it would be nice if they indeed were different. (These cognitions clarify the nature of the world and foster a realistic understanding and acceptance of one's place in it.)

Action Since the world is not oriented towards fulfilling my desires, active attempts to influence it will increase the probability that my wishes will be achieved. Without action on my part, it is unlikely that events in the complex world will fortuitously meet my desires. (These thoughts promote personal responsibility for change, though they do not demand that such efforts be successful.)

Self-worth I am worthy, and have the same basic human rights as anyone else, regardless of how much or how little I or others have achieved. I have the basic right to assert myself, if I so choose, in an effort to influence the situation and maximise my rewards. (These ideas accept one's basic, unconditional self-worth and human rights.)

The direct modification of irrational thinking has been an important component of assertiveness training programmes since the early 1970s (Rich and Schroeder, 1976). 'Rational relabelling' or 'cognitive restructuring' improves conflict assertive performance,

but contributes only minimally to a training package that emphasises overt skill competence (see Rakos, 1991, for a review). This supports Bandura's (1978) contention that
though performance may be cognitively mediated, those cognitions are most efficaciously
changed when the behaviours upon which they are based are first changed. It is also
possible that rational relabelling procedures may prove to be more important in promoting
generalisation of assertive responses to novel people and situations (Scott *et al.*, 1983)
than in facilitating initial acquisition of the response.

Social perception skills

Accurate perception and empathic role-taking are two distinct cognitive skills involved in
interpersonal perception (Argyle *et al.*, 1981). Accurate perception has been investigated
more thoroughly and the evidence, with one exception (Robinson and Calhoun, 1984),
strongly suggests that non-assertive individuals are deficient in this skill. They are less
sensitive to external cues (Trower, 1980), misjudge the amount of anger communicated by
assertive and aggressive responses (Morrison and Bellack, 1981), and place exaggerated
emphasis on the status of the other person and the extent of social norm transgression
when analysing conflict situations (Rudy *et al.*, 1982). A realistic assessment of social norms
provides an important guideline for judging behaviour; for example, the reasonableness
of a request influences compliance and emotional responses to the asserter (Epstein, 1980).
However, non-assertive persons perceive 'reasonableness', and therefore social norms and
the legitimate rights of the other person, differently from assertive individuals, especially
when requests are consensually evaluated to be of low or moderate legitimacy.

Conflict situations of moderate legitimacy pose a particular challenge to accurate perception: assertive as well as non-assertive persons produce more thoughts but fewer objective
ones (Chiauzzi and Heimberg, 1983) and report a decreased intention to assert and weakened specific self-efficacy beliefs (Chiauzzi and Heimberg, 1986). The legitimate rights of
all participants are most difficult to determine in ambiguous contexts, requiring refined
conceptual skills that can assess situational considerations, make appropriate reasonableness determinations and synthesise the resulting increase in positive and negative thoughts
into adaptive, accurate discriminations. Distorted judgements of circumstances, particularly
those of questionable legitimacy and hence most appropriate for assertion, may be a prime
contributor to a decision to behave non-assertively.

A second important perceptual skill is the ability to understand the viewpoint of the
other person, termed role-taking or metaperception (see Chapter 1). It provides the basis
for determining the impact of an assertion on the recipient (an antecedent obligation) and
it is the foundation upon which the asserter will develop an empathic statement (a subsequent obligation). The superior social evaluation of the empathic assertion relative to the
standard one highlights the importance of this skill in conflict resolution. The perceptual
skill involves discrimination of the cues that indicate an empathic response will facilitate
the interaction. For example, Fischetti *et al.* (1984) found that heterosocially skilled and
unskilled persons differed in their ability to recognise when a vocal or gestural response
from them would help a speaker continue to talk. The ability to discriminate such
cues may explain why skilled and unskilled persons differ in the timing or placement of
vocalisations and gestures, but not in the frequency (Fischetti *et al.*, 1977; Peterson *et al.*,
1981).

Interpersonal problem-solving skills

The systematic problem-solving skills necessary for social competence are deficient in a variety of clinical populations (Schroeder and Rakos, 1983). The problem-solving sequence involves problem recognition, problem definition and formulation, generation of potential response alternatives, decision-making (assessment of alternatives in terms of likely outcomes) and solution implementation and evaluation (D'Zurilla and Nezu, 1982). Chiauzzi and Heimberg (1986) investigated these abilities as they relate to assertion and found that non-assertive persons manifested deficits in problem recognition and assessment (a social perception skill) and in their ability to select an appropriate response. No inadequacies were observed in their capacity to generate response alternatives, either in terms of number or quality. However, therapist-generated alternatives produce higher outcome expectancies than client-generated ones (Arisohn *et al.*, 1988), suggesting that unskilled individuals lack confidence in their own alternatives. Robinson and Calhoun (1984) also found a situational effect: more complex and assertive alternatives were produced in response to an angry male as compared to a pleasant male. Finally, Deluty (1981, 1985) found that assertive, aggressive and submissive children generated equal numbers of alternatives in conflict situations, but that the assertive children's possibilities included assertive options to a proportionately greater extent.

Problem-solving skills assume a critical role in assertion when it is conceptualised as a sequence of overt and covert responses. Indeed, the antecedent obligations described earlier are involved in problem definition and assessment (determining the rights of all participants and whether assertion is the preferred option). In fact, problem-solving skills may provide a way for conceptual complexity to be operationalised and trained.

Self-monitoring skills

Responsible assertion is based on an accurate perception that the situation appropriately calls for such action; in other words, an assertion situation must be distinguished from other social ones and acquire the properties of a discriminative stimulus. This learned cue, which will prompt the early behaviours in the assertion chain (the antecedent obligations), will be comprised of the person's own reactions. Thus, the assertive individual must learn to attend to personal behaviours and discriminate those reactions that indicate assertion should be considered.

The self-monitored discriminative stimuli can be behaviours, emotions, or cognitions (Rakos and Schroeder, 1980). Behavioural cues include coping strategies that are indirect, hostile, or avoidant (e.g. hinting at desires, using fake excuses or excessive apologies, engaging in withdrawal, aggression, passive-aggression, or submission). Emotional cues include frustration, resentment, shame, guilt, anger, depression and upset. Cognitive cues are present when the person engages in excessive ruminations and self-statements that blame or denigrate the self and others, rationalise the unimportance of the concern and are generally affiliative ('negative') or irrational. When these behavioural, emotional and cognitive reactions are produced in response to a social conflict, they should serve as cues to initiate the antecedent obligations of assertion: in fact, these will usually be the primary stimuli available for identifying potential assertion situations.

THE SOCIAL VALIDITY OF CONFLICT ASSERTION

Technical proficiency, cultural appropriateness, immediate outcome and overall net cost-benefit were discussed earlier as four distinct and partially independent measurements of the assertive response. For instance, a skilled assertion that meets social and cultural norms may still fail to produce desired short-term outcomes or enhance the long-term stability of a relationship. But because the functional value of an assertion will provide the tangible benefits, the social reaction to assertion assumes critical importance.

General findings

The social validity of standard assertion (expression of the assertive right without elaboration) was discussed earlier. Briefly, it is generally judged to be more socially competent, but less likeable, than non-assertive behaviour, and to be at least as potent as, and more favourably evaluated than, aggressive behaviour. Empathic assertions, which express rights and elaborations, are judged more favourably than standard assertions and comparable to non-assertion. The elaborations, moreover, do not detract from the potency of the response. Contextual variables, as well as response topography, influence the social reaction to assertion. The evaluation is less positive when the assertion requires a significant sacrifice on the part of the recipient or is in response to a relatively reasonable request (Epstein, 1980; McCampbell and Ruback, 1985). Adults judge assertion to be most appropriate when directed towards strangers rather than towards friends or intimates (Linehan and Siefert, 1983), but college students perceive it to be the preferred option for resolving conflicts with friends and relatives (Heisler and McCormack, 1982).

These studies demonstrate that conflict assertion, either empathic or standard, is judged by observers to be socially appropriate and competent, if not always exceptionally likeable. However, the person whose reaction is most important is the real-life recipient, not an observer. Although an observer may appreciate the abstract value of an assertion, the natural social environment may react differently. In fact, two studies that assessed the evaluations of actual recipients of assertion delivered by confederates in staged encounters suggest that non-assertive behaviour is judged to be more likeable than standard assertion or empathic assertion (Gormally, 1982; Delamater and McNamara, 1991). Thus, assertion may be valued as an abstract concept more than as a concrete skill. On the other hand, *in vivo* and abstract comparisons of standard assertion and aggression suggest that the superior observer evaluation of assertion is magnified in the *in vivo* situation (Christoff and Edelstein, 1981; McCampbell and Ruback, 1985).

The social acceptance of a standard assertion can be increased by use of the empathic assertion's elaborations, as noted above, and also by more extensive interaction with the asserter that includes experience with non-conflict as well as conflict behaviours, as will occur in most continuing relationships. Thus, individuals who emit standard assertion and commendatory assertions (such as requests or offers for help, giving compliments, offering thanks), general conversational comments, or task-oriented interactions are viewed as more likeable and competent than persons exhibiting standard assertion alone (see Rakos, 1991, for review). In a naturalistic investigation, Kern and Paquette (1992) found that college students' evaluations of their room-mates' likeability and social competence were significantly correlated with the room-mates' level of conflict assertion ability. Thus, empathic elaborations and contextual experience can moderate the evaluation of assertion. As noted earlier, concerns regarding social evaluation are most relevant in continuing relationships, while instrumental utility is usually the primary consideration in transient interactions.

Gender

Conflict assertion has been viewed by women as a powerful means through which legitimately to challenge pervasive societal sexism (see Gambrill, 1995; Rakos, 1991; Wilson and Gallois, 1993, for extensive discussions).† But because of that sexism, women writers have strongly contended that behaving assertively entails significantly greater risks for females than for males (e.g. Fodor, 1980; Gervasio and Crawford, 1989; Kahn, 1981; MacDonald, 1982). Intuitively and perhaps experientially, such a stance seemed justified: assertion has not been a component of stereotypical views of healthy (Broverman *et al.*, 1970) or appropriate (Broverman *et al.*, 1972) female behaviour. However, the data – which include over thirty studies – do not support such a generalised assumption. In fact, the research fails to isolate any systematic gender biases in the evaluation of either standard or empathic assertion or the various conflict response classes. Further, the sex role orientation of the judge is unrelated to the social evaluation of assertion by women.

Despite the research, the experience of women should not be dismissed; rather, a more vigorous search for situational variables that affect the evaluation of female assertion should be undertaken. Several possibilities present themselves. Wilson and Gallois (1993) determined that the *social rules* governing conflict assertion by women – but not by men – emphasise obligation behaviours and even submission. Such rules may account for Zollo *et al.*'s (1985) finding that female judges expected empathic assertion (defined so as to exclude submission) to produce greater immediate positive consequences as well as greater long-term negative consequences than did males. The specific circumstance may be critical as well. For example, the social role of the person may impact on the social rules that are operative. Several studies suggest that when pragmatism is important and general competence required, such as in business, corporate, or legal contexts conflict assertion by women is judged no differently from similar behaviour by males, and more positively than non-assertion (Gallois *et al.*, 1992; Mullinix and Galassi, 1981; Sigal *et al.*, 1985; Solomon *et al.*, 1982). In such contexts, the professional role demands may be more powerful than the sex role stereotypes. But when emotional considerations are primary, the risk may be greater for females: when confronting a citizen, an assertive female police officer is judged more critically than an assertive male officer (Sterling and Owen, 1982).

The perception of appropriate social roles will change as society evolves, sometimes as a result of the dissemination of research data (Gergen, 1973). Both men and women who have adopted a non-traditional view of women's role in society value standard and empathic assertion by women, while men and women adhering to conservative views of women's role in society devalue female assertion (Kern *et al.*, 1985). Clearly, the risk to a female asserter is embedded in the context, including the recipient: she must be taught to discriminate between the expectations that are operating in the situation so that the social response can be accurately predicted and an informed decision made (see Gallois, 1994).

---

† Some feminists contend that the assertion construct is 'androcentric' (Cameron, 1994) and blames women rather than challenging societal prejudice (Crawford, 1995). Crawford's criticisms, however, lack persuasive force due to her selective discussion of the immense literature.

Response classes

The studies assessing the perception of various response classes of standard assertion have produced conflicting data. Schroeder and his colleagues (Hull and Schroeder, 1979; Schroeder *et al.*, 1983) determined that expressing unpopular opinions involved the greatest amount of assertiveness, behaviour change requests next and refusals the least. Behaviour change requests were perceived to be most socially acceptable and expressing unpopular opinions the least appropriate. Lewis and Gallois (1984), on the other hand, obtained contradictory results: behaviour change requests (conflict statement only) were judged most assertive but least socially desirable, while expressing unpopular opinions was perceived most favourably. Further, expressions of different opinions by friends were more positively evaluated than such behaviour by strangers or refusals by friends. Refusals by strangers were judged more positively than refusals by friends or the conflict statement component of a behaviour change request. Finally, Crawford (1988) found no differences in the reactions to the expression of negative feelings, positive self-presentation and the setting of limits. However, these three response categories appeared to be variations of behaviour change requests rather than representatives of distinct response classes.

The conflicting data obtained by Schroeder and Lewis and Gallois may be due to cultural differences between the US and Australia or to several methodological differences, such as varying response topographies and specification of degree of familiarity of friends. Further, these investigations evaluated standard assertion only. Friends, as part of an ongoing relationship, may very well accept a difference of opinion without explanation, compromise, or empathy, but are likely to expect those elaborations to accompany a refusal of a request. These data, then, are consistent with the emphasis on employing empathic assertion for resolving conflicts in continuing relationships.

Level of assertiveness

Socially competent persons judge assertive responses to be more likeable, effective and appropriate than aggressive and non-assertive ones (e.g. Frisch and Froberg, 1987). Because non-assertive persons expect more negative outcomes from assertion, it is not surprising that many studies find that their perception of such behaviour is relatively unfavourable (see Rakos, 1991, for review). However, when non-assertive persons have the opportunity to evaluate a spectrum of behaviour that is broader than a single standard assertive inter-action, their evaluation of the asserter is similar to that of assertive persons (Alden and Cappe, 1981; Delamater and McNamara, 1991; Kern and Paquette, 1992; Levin and Gross, 1984; Wojnilower and Gross, 1984). Non-assertive persons, with their lower level of concep-tual complexity, may moderate their judgements of conflict assertion only when it is portrayed concretely and in concert with other responses that have greater social accept-ability.

Racial and cultural values

The values that legitimise assertion are grounded in American democracy: individual activism, pragmatism, rationality and ethical relativism. These values are most consistent with those of the Caucasian middle class (and some argue, of males only, e.g. Wine, 1981).

Thus, the specific behaviours and attitudes fostered by this ideology will not be congruent with the cultural assumptions of all societies or ethnic groups (Furnham, 1979; Rakos, 1991). In American society, the issue of race must be considered directly. A system of cultural values that originated in Africa and the legacy of brutal discrimination (e.g. inter-racial distrust and discomfort, the development of distinct communication and linguistic patterns) raise questions about the social acceptability of assertion by African Americans. In fact, the more recent research suggests that there are important differences in the way African Americans and whites react to conflict assertion. In general, African Americans perceive assertive behaviour by an African American as more aggressive than similar behaviour emitted by a white person, and seem to value aggressive and standard assertive behaviour more, and empathic assertion less, than do whites (see Rakos, 1991, for summary).

When the race of all participants in an assertive interaction is examined, different conclusions emerge. Hrop and Rakos (1985) compared the reactions of African American and white observers to standard and empathic assertion emitted in white–white, white–black, black–white and black–black male dyads. White observers were influenced by race of asserter but not by race of recipient. They felt more intimidated by either style of assertion by an African American than by a white. Further, they judged the empathic assertion more positively than the standard assertion when the asserter was white but not when he was African American. These data suggest that the elaboration statements are appropriate training goals for whites asserting to whites, but that for blacks asserting to whites, training goals might place greater emphasis on strategies to foster awareness of, and then to decrease, whites' discomfort with black assertiveness. African American judges had relatively unfavourable perceptions of both styles of assertion when performed by a white as compared to a black, judging the behaviour to be more aggressive. In addition, African Americans were influenced by both the race of asserter and recipient. They perceived empathic assertion by whites to blacks as less positive than standard assertion in the same context, but reversed their judgement for black-to-black interactions, in which the elaborative verbalisations significantly enhanced the evaluation of assertion. Therefore, different training goals for assertion to African Americans may be indicated: standard assertion for white asserters, empathic assertion for black asserters.

Generalisations about the appropriateness of assertive response styles for members of diverse cultural and ethnic groups must be made cautiously. There are no studies that directly assess the perception of assertion as a function of ethnic or religious group membership. However, sensitivity to cultural values that are more communitarian and tradition-bound than mainstream American ones can form the basis of successful intervention with a wide array of ethnic groups (cf. Fodor, 1992; Wood and Mallinckrodt, 1990).

OVERVIEW

Assertion is a situation-specific social skill that has been touted in the pop psychology literature as a panacea for all social frustrations, but has also been rejected by many researchers as a concept that has outlived its usefulness. Despite these polarised judgements, assertion and its accompanying training procedures have settled into a comfortable role within mainstream behaviour therapy. Beyond this, it is essential explicitly to recognise that conflict assertion – unlike any other social skill – embodies an egalitarian social philosophy that encourages responsible individual action for the purpose of challenging the legitimacy of barriers – be they interpersonal, societal, cultural, legal, or whatever – that prevent fair and equitable sharing of power and resources. Human nature being what it is, conflict assertion is a concept, and skill, that will remain relevant for all who seek to redress social inequity.

REFERENCES

Alberti, R. E. (1977) 'Comments on Differentiating Assertion from Aggression: Some Behavioral Guidelines', *Behavior Therapy*, 8, 353–4.

—— and Emmons, M. L. (1970) *Your Perfect Right: A Guide to Assertive Behavior*, Impact, San Luis Obispo.

—— (1986) *The Professional Edition of 'Your Perfect Right': A Manual for Assertiveness Trainers*, Impact, San Luis Obispo.

—— (1995) *Your Perfect Right: A Guide for Assertive Living* (7th edn), Impact, San Luis Obispo.

Alden, L. and Cappe, R. (1981) 'Non-assertiveness: Skill Deficit or Selective Self-evaluation?', *Behavior Therapy*, 12, 107–15.

Argyle, M., Furnham, A. and Graham, J. (1981) *Social Situations*, Cambridge University Press, Cambridge.

Arisohn, B., Bruch, M. A. and Heimberg, R. G. (1988) 'Influence of Assessment Methods on Self-efficacy and Outcome Expectancy Ratings of Assertive Behavior', *Journal of Counseling Psychology*, 35, 336–41.

Bandura, A. (1977) 'Self-efficacy: Toward a Unifying Theory of Behavior Change', *Psychology Review*, 84, 191–215.

—— (1978) 'The Self-system in Reciprocal Determinism', *American Psychologist*, 33, 344–58.

Blankenberg, R. W. and Heimberg, R. G. (1984) 'Assertive Refusal, Perceived Consequences, and Reasonableness of Request', paper presented at the annual convention of the Association for Advancement of Behavior Therapy, Philadelphia, PA, November.

Bordewick, M. C. and Bornstein, P. H. (1980) 'Examination of Multiple Cognitive Response Dimensions Among Differentially Assertive Individuals', *Behavior Therapy*, 11, 440–48.

Bourque, P. and Ladouceur, R. (1979) 'Self-report and Behavioral Measures in the Assessment of Assertive Behavior', *Journal of Behavior Therapy and Experimental Psychiatry*, 10, 287–92.

Broverman, I. K., Broverman, D. M., Clarkson, F. E., Rosenkrantz, P. G. and Vogal, S. R. (1970) 'Sex-role Stereotypes and Clinical Judgments of Mental Health', *Journal of Consulting and Clinical Psychology*, 34, 1–7.

Broverman, I. K., Vogal, R. S., Broverman, D. M., Clarkson, F. E. and Rosenkrantz, P. S. (1972) 'Sex-role Stereotypes: A Current Appraisal', *Journal of Social Issues*, 28, 59–78.

Bruch, M. A. (1981) 'A Task Analysis of Assertive Behavior Revisited: Application and Extension', *Behavior Therapy*, 12, 217–30.

——, Heisler, B. D. and Conroy, C. G. (1981) 'Effects of Conceptual Complexity on Assertive Behavior', *Journal of Counseling Psychology*, 28, 377–85.

Bruch, M.A., McCann, M. and Harvey, C. (1991) 'Type A Behavior and Processing of Social Conflict Information', *Journal of Research in Personality*, 25, 434–44.

Cameron D. (1994) 'Verbal Hygiene for Women: Linguistics Misapplied?', *Applied Linguistics*, 15, 382–98.

Chiauzzi, E. and Heimberg, R. G. (1983) 'The Effects of Subjects' Level of Assertiveness, Sex, and Legitimacy of Request on Assertion-relevant Cognitions: An Analysis by Post Performance Videotape Reconstruction', *Cognitive Therapy and Research*, 7, 555–64.

—— (1986) 'Legitimacy of Request and Social Problem-solving: A Study of Assertive and Non-assertive Subjects', *Behavior Modification*, 10, 3–18.

Christoff, K. A. and Edelstein, B. A. (1981) 'Functional Aspects of Assertive and Aggressive Behavior: Laboratory and *in vivo* Observations', paper presented at the annual meeting of the Association for Advancement of Behavior Therapy, Toronto, Canada, November.

Cook, D. J. and St Lawrence, J. S. (1990) 'Variations in Presentational Format: Effect on Inter-personal Evaluations of Assertive and Unassertive Behavior', *Behavior Modification*, 14, 21–36.

Craighead, L. W. (1979) 'Self-instructional Training for Assertive-refusal Behavior', *Behavior Therapy*, 10, 529–42.

Crawford, M. (1988) 'Gender, Age, and the Social Evaluation of Assertion', *Behavior Modification*, 12, 549–64.

—— (1995) *Talking Difference: On Gender and Language*, Sage, London.

Delamater, R. J. and NcNamara, J. R. (1991) 'Perceptions of Assertiveness by Women Involved in a Conflict Situation', *Behavior Modification*, 15, 173–93.

Deluty, R. H. (1981) 'Alternative-thinking, Ability of Aggressive, Assertive, and Submissive Children', *Cognitive Therapy and Research*, 5, 309–12.

—— (1985) 'Cognitive Mediation of Aggressive, Assertive, and Submissive Behavior in Children', *International Journal of Behavior Development*, 8, 355–69.

Dewey, J. (1957) *Reconstruction in Philosophy*, Beacon Press, Boston.

Dura, J. R. and Beck, S. (1986) 'Psychiatric Aides' Perceptions of a Patient's Assertive Behavior' *Behavior Modification,* 10, 301–14.

D'Zurilla, T. J. and Nezu, A. (1982) 'Social Problem Solving in Adults', in P. Kendall (ed.), *Advances in Cognitive-Behavioral Research and Therapy, (Vol. 1)*, Academic Press, New York.

Eisler, R. M., Miller, P. M. and Hersen, M. (1973) 'Components of Assertive Behavior', *Journal of Clinical Psychology*, 29, 295–99.

Eisler, R. M., Hersen, M., Miller, P. M. and Blanchard, E. (1975) 'Situational Determinants of Assertive Behavior', *Journal of Consulting and Clinical Psychology*, 43, 330–40.

Ekman, P. (1992) *Telling Lies: Clues to Deceit in the Marketplace, Politics, and Marriage*, Norton, New York.

Ellis, A. (1962) *Reason and Emotion in Psychotherapy*, Lyle Stuart, New York.

—— and Grieger, R. (1977) *Handbook of Rational-emotive Therapy*, Springer, New York.

Epstein, N. (1980) 'The Social Consequences of Assertion, Aggression, Passive Aggression and Submission: Situational and Dispositional Determinants, *Behavior Therapy*, 11, 662–9.

Fischetti, M., Curran, J. P. and Wessberg, H. W. (1977) 'Sense of Timing: A Skill Deficit in Heterosexual-socially Anxious Males', *Behavior Modification*, 1, 179–94.

Fischetti, M., Peterson, J. L., Curran, J. P., Alkire, M., Perrewe, P. and Arland, S. (1984) 'Social Cue Discrimination versus Motor Skill: A Missing Distinction in Social Skill Assessment', *Behavioral Assessment*, 6, 27–32.

Fodor, I. G. (1980) 'The Treatment of Communication Problems with Assertiveness Training', in A. Goldstein and E. B. Foa (eds), *Handbook of Behavioral Interventions: A Clinical Guide*, John Wiley, New York, pp. 501–603.

—— (ed.) (1992) *Adolescent Assertiveness and Social Skills Training: A Clinical Handbook*, Springer, New York.

Frisch, M. B. and Froberg, W. (1987) 'Social Validation of Assertion Strategies for Handling Aggressive Criticism: Evidence for Consistency across Situations', *Behavior Therapy*, 18, 181–91.

Furnham, A. (1979) 'Assertiveness in Three Cultures: Multidimensionality and Cultural Differences', *Journal of Clinical Psychology*, 35, 522–7.

Galassi, J. P., Galassi, M. D. and Vedder, M. J. (1981) 'Perspectives on Assertion as a Social Skills Model', in J. Wine, and M. Smye, (eds), *Social Competence*, Guilford Press, New York, pp. 287–345.

Gallois, C. (1994) 'Group Membership, Social Rules, and Power: A Social-Psychological Perspective on Emotional Communications', *Journal of Pragmatics,* 22, 301–24.

——, Callan, V. J. and McKenzie Palmer, J.-A. (1992) 'The Influence of Applicant Communication Style and Interviewer Characteristics on Hiring Decisions', *Journal of Applied Social Psychology*, 22, 1041–60.

Gambrill, E. (1995) 'Assertion Skills Training', in W. O'Donohue and L. Krasner (eds), *Handbook of Psychological Skills Training: Clinical Techniques and Applications*, Allyn & Bacon, Boston, pp. 81–117.

Gergen, K. J. (1973) 'Social Psychology as History', *Journal of Personality and Social Psychology*, 26, 309–20.

Gervasio, A. H. (1987) 'Assertiveness Techniques as Speech Acts', *Clinical Psychology Review*, 7, 105–19.

—— and Crawford, M. (1989) 'Social Evaluations of Assertiveness: A Critique and Speech Act Reformulation', *Psychology of Women Quarterly*, 13, 1–25.

Gilligan, C. (1982) *In a Different Voice*, Harvard University Press, Cambridge, MA.

Goldin, J. (1957) *The Living Talmud*, Mentor, New York.

Gormally, J. (1982) 'Evaluation of Assertiveness: Effects of Gender, Involvement and Level of Assertiveness', *Behavior Therapy*, 13, 219–25.

Heimberg, R. G. and Etkin, D. (1983) 'Response Quality and Outcome Effectiveness as a Factor in Students' and Counselors' Judgements of Assertiveness', *British Journal of Cognitive Psychotherapy*, 1, 59–68.

Heimberg, R. G., Harrison, D. F., Goldberg, L. S., DesMarais, S. and Blue, S. (1979) 'The Relationship of Self-report and Behavioral Assertion in an Offender Population'. *Journal of Behavior Therapy and Experimental Psychiatry*, 10, 283–6.

Heisler, G. H. and McCormack, J. (1982) 'Situational and Personality Influences on the Reception of Provocative Responses', *Behavior Therapy*, 13, 743–50.

Hollandsworth, J. G. (1977) 'Differentiating Assertion and Aggression: Some Behavioral Guidelines', *Behavior Therapy*, 9, 640–6.

Hrop, S. and Rakos, R. F. (1985) 'The Influence of Race in the Social Evaluation of Assertion in Conflict Situations', *Behavior Therapy*, 16, 478–93.

Hull, D. B. and Schroeder, H. E. (1979) 'Some Interpersonal Effects of Assertion, Nonassertion, and Aggression', *Behavior Therapy*, 10, 20–9.

Hung, J. H., Rosenthal, T. L. and Kelley, J. E. (1980) 'Social Comparison Standards Spur Immediate Assertion: "So you Think you're Submissive?"', *Cognitive Therapy and Research*, 4, 223–34.

Kahn, S. E. (1981) 'Issues in the Assessment and Training of Assertiveness with Women', in J. D. Wine and M. S. Smye (eds), *Social Competence*, Guilford Press, New York, pp. 346–67.

Kanfer, F. H. and Schefft, B. K. (1988) *Guiding the Process of Therapeutic Change*, Research Press, Champaign, IL.

Kazdin, A. E. (1977) 'Assessing the Clinical or Applied Importance of Behavior Change through Social Validation', *Behavior Modification*, 1, 427–52.

Kern, J. M. and Paquette, R. J. (1992) 'Reactions to Assertion in "Controlled" Naturalistic Relationships', *Behavior Modification*, 16, 372–86.

Kern, J. M., Cavell, T. A. and Beck, B. (1985) 'Predicting Differential Reactions to Males' versus Females' Assertions, Empathic Assertions, and Nonassertions', *Behavior Therapy*, 16, 63–75.

Kirschner, S. M. and Galassi, J. P. (1983) 'Person, Situational, and Interactional Influences on Assertive Behavior', *Journal of Counseling Psychology*, 30, 355–60.

Kleinke, C. L. (1986) 'Gaze and Eye Contact: A Research Review', *Psychological Bulletin*, 100, 78–100.

Kolotkin, R. A., Wielkiewicz, R. M., Judd, B. and Weiser, S. (1984) 'Behavioral Components of Assertion: Comparison of Univariate and Multivariate Assessment Strategies', *Behavioral Assessment*, 6, 61–78.

Kuperminc, M. and Heimberg, R. G. (1983) 'Consequence Probability and Utility as Factors in the Decision to Behave Assertively', *Behavior Therapy*, 14, 637–46.

LaFrance, M. and Mayo, C. (1976) 'Racial Differences in Gaze Behavior during Conversations: Two Systematic Observational Studies', *Journal of Personality and Social Psychology*, 33, 547–52.

Lange, A. J. and Jakubowski, P. (1976) *Responsible Assertive Behavior*, Research Press, Champaign, IL.

Levin, R. B. and Gross, A. M. (1984) 'Reactions to Assertive versus Nonassertive Behavior: Females in Commendatory and Refusal Situations', *Behavior Modification*, 8, 581–92.

—— (1987) 'Assertiveness Style: Effects on Perceptions of Assertive Behavior', *Behavior Modification*, 11, 229–40.

Lewis, P. N. and Gallois, C. (1984) 'Disagreements, Refusals, or Negative Feelings: Perception of Negatively Assertive Messages from Friends and Strangers', *Behavior Therapy*, 15, 353–68.

Linehan, M. M. and Seifert, R. F. (1983) 'Sex and Contextual Differences in the Appropriateness of Assertive Behavior', *Psychology of Women Quarterly*, 8, 79–88.

Linehan, M. M. and Walker, R. O. (1983) 'The Components of Assertion: Factor Analysis of a Multimethod Assessment Battery', *British Journal of Clinical Psychology*, 22, 277–81.

McCampbell, E. and Ruback, R. B. (1985) 'Social Consequences of Apologetic, Assertive, and Aggressive Requests', *Journal of Counseling Psychology*, 32, 68–73.

MacDonald, M. L. (1982) 'Assertion Training for Women', in J. P. Curran and P. M. Monti (eds), *Social Skill Training: A Practical Guide for Assessment and Treatment*, Guilford Press, New York, 253–79.

McFall, M. E., Winnett, R. L., Bordwick, M. C. and Bornstein, P. H. (1982) 'Nonverbal Components in the Communication of Assertiveness', *Behavior Modification*, 6, 121–40.

McFall, R. (1982) 'A Review and Reformulation of the Concept of Social Skills', *Behavioral Assessment*, 4, 1–33.

Masters, J. C., Burish, T. G., Hollon, S. D. and Rimm, D. C. (1987) *Behavior Therapy: Techniques and Empirical Findings* (3rd edn), Harcourt Brace Jovanovich, New York.

Meichenbaum, D., Butler, L. and Gruson, L. (1981) 'Toward a Conceptual Model of Social Competence', in J. Wine and M. Smye (eds), *Social Competence*, Guilford Press, New York, pp.36–60.

Morrison, R. L. and Bellack, A. E. (1981) 'The Role of Social Perception in Social Skill', *Behavior Therapy*, 12, 69–79.

Mullinix, S. B. and Galassi, J. P. (1981) 'Deriving the Content of Social Skills Training with a Verbal Response Components Approach', *Behavioral Assessment*, 3, 55–66.

Peterson, J. L., Fischetti, M., Curran, J. P. and Arland, S. (1981) 'Sense of Timing: A Skill Defect in Heterosocially Anxious Women', *Behavior Therapy*, 12, 195–201.

Pitcher, S. W. and Meikle, S. (1980) 'The Topography of Assertive Behavior in Positive and Negative Situations', *Behavior Therapy*, 11, 532–47.

Rakos, R. F. (1979) 'Content Consideration in the Distinction between Assertive and Aggressive Behavior', *Psychological Reports*, 44, 767–73.

—— (1986) 'Asserting and confronting', in O. Hargie (ed.), *A Handbook of Communication Skills*, Croom Helm, London, pp. 407–40.

—— (1991) *Assertive Behavior: Theory, Research, and Training*, Routledge, London.

—— and Schroeder, H. E. (1979) 'Development and Empirical Evaluation of a Self-administered Assertiveness Training Program', *Journal of Consulting and Clinical Psychology*, 47, 991–3.

—— (1980) *Self-administered Assertiveness Training*, BMA Audio Cassettes, New York.

Rich, A. and Schroeder, H. E. (1976) 'Research Issues in Assertiveness Training', *Psychological Bulletin*, 83, 1084–96.

Robinson, W. L. and Calhoun, K. S. (1984) 'Assertiveness and Cognitive Processing in Interpersonal Situations', *Journal of Behavioral Assessment*, 6, 81–96.

Romano, J. M. and Bellack, A. S. (1980) 'Social Validation of a Component Model of Assertive Behavior', *Journal of Consulting and Clinical Psychology*, 4, 478–90.

Rose, Y. J. and Tryon, W. W. (1979) 'Judgements of Assertive Behavior as a Function of Speech Loudness, Latency, Content, Gestures, Inflection and Sex', *Behavior Modification*, 3, 112–23.

Rudy, T. E., Merluzzi, T. V. and Henahan P. T. (1982) 'Construal of Complex Assertion Situations: A Multidimensional Analysis', *Journal of Consulting and Clinical Psychology*, 50, 125–37.

St Lawrence, J. S. (1987) 'Assessment of Assertion', in M. Hersen, R. M. Eisler and P. M. Miller (eds), *Progress in Behavior Modification, Vol. 21*, Sage, Newbury Park, CA, pp. 152–90.

——, Hansen, D. J., Cutts, T. F., Tisdelle, D.A. and Irish, J. D. (1985) 'Situational Context: Effects on Perceptions of Assertive and Unassertive Behavior', *Behavior Therapy*, 16, 51–62.

Salter, A. (1949) *Conditioned Reflex Therapy*, Farrar, Straus & Giroux, New York.

Schroeder, H. E. and Rakos, R. F. (1983) 'The Identification and Assessment of Social Skills', in R. Ellis and D. Whitington (eds), *New Directions in Social Skill Training*, Croom Helm, London, 117–88.

Schroeder, H. E., Driver, M. and Streufer, S. (1967) *Human Information Processing*, Holt, Rinehart & Winston, New York.

Schroeder, H. E., Rakos, R. F. and Moe, J. (1983) 'The Social Perception of Assertive Behavior as a Function of Response Class and Gender', *Behavior Therapy*, 14, 534–44.

Scott, R. R., Himadi, W. and Keane, T. M. (1983) 'A Review of Generalization in Social Skills Training: Suggestions for Future Research', in M. Hersen, R. Eisler, and P. M. Miller (eds), *Progress in Behavior Modification. Vol. 15*, Academic Press, New York, pp. 113–72.

Sigal, J., Braden-Maguire, J., Hayden, M. and Mosley, N. (1985) 'The Effect of Presentation Style and Sex of Lawyer on Jury Decision-making Behavior', *Psychology: A Quarterly Journal of Human Behavior*, 22, 13–19.

Solomon, L. J., Brehony, K. A., Rothblum, E. D. and Kelly, J. A. (1982) 'Corporate Managers' Reaction to Assertive Social Skills Exhibited by Males and Females', *Journal of Organizational Behavior Management*, 4, 49–63.

Sterling, B. S. and Owen, J. W. (1982) 'Perceptions of Demanding versus Reasoning Male and Female Police Officers', *Personality and Social Psychology Bulletin*, 8, 336–40.

Trower, P. (1980) 'Situational Analysis of the Components and Processes of Behavior of Socially Skilled and Unskilled Patients', *Journal of Consulting and Clinical Psychology*, 48, 327–39.

—— (1982) 'Toward a Generative Model of Social Skills: A Critique and Syntheses', in J. Curran and P. Monti (eds), *Social Skills Training: A Practical Handbook for Assessment and Treatment*, Guilford Press, New York, pp. 399–427.

—— (1995) 'Adult Social Skills: State of the Art and Future Directions', in W. O'Donohue and L. Krasner (eds), *Handbook of Psychological Skills Training: Clinical Techniques and Applications*, Allyn & Bacon, Boston, pp. 54–80.

Twentyman, C. T., Zimering, R. T. and Kovaleski, M. E. (1981) 'Three Studies Investigating the Efficacy of Assertion Training Techniques', *Behavioral Counseling Quarterly*, 1, 302–16.

Wildman, B. G. and Clementz, B. (1986) 'Assertive, Empathic Assertive, and Conversational Behavior: Perception of Likeability, Effectiveness, and Sex Role', *Behavior Modification*, 10, 315–32.

Wilson, K. and Gallois, C. (1993) *Assertion and its Social Context*, Pergamon, Oxford.

Wine, J. D. (1981) 'From Defect to Competence Models', in J. D. Wine and M. D. Smye (eds), *Social Competence*, Guilford Press, New York, pp. 3–35.

Winship, B. J. and Kelly, J. D. (1976) 'A Verbal Response Model of Assertiveness', *Journal of Counseling Psychology*, 23, 215–20.

Wojnilower, D. A. and Gross, A. M. (1984) 'Assertive Behavior and Likeability in Elementary School Boys', *Child and Family Behavior Therapy*, 6, 57–70.

Wolf, M. M. (1978) 'Social Validity: The Case for Subjective Measurement or How Applied Behavior Analysis is Finding Its Heart', *Journal of Applied Behavior Analysis*, 11, 203–14.

Wolpe, J. (1969) *The Practice of Behavior Therapy*, Pergamon, Oxford.

—— (1990) *The Practice of Behavior Therapy* (4th edn), Pergamon, New York.

Wood, P. S. and Mallinckrodt, B. (1990) 'Culturally Sensitive Assertiveness Training for Ethnic Minority Clients', *Professional Psychology: Research and Practice*, 21, 5–11.

Woolfolk, R. L. and Dever, S. (1979) 'Perceptions of Assertion: An Empirical Analysis', *Behavior Therapy*, 10, 404–11.

Zollo, L. J., Heimberg, R. G. and Becker, R. E. (1985) 'Evaluations and Consequences of Assertive Behavior', *Journal of Behavior Therapy and Experimental Psychiatry*, 16, 295–301.

12 Interacting in task groups

Arjaan P. Wit and Henk A. M. Wilke

INTRODUCTION

There are several related reasons for group members to communicate with one another when they are working on a common task. Imagine a number of students and faculty members, who have volunteered to form a committee to formulate proposals to update the current curriculum. Before they can plan any specific actions, they have first to arrive at a shared understanding of the task of the committee. Once they learn that they differ among themselves in their interpretation of the group task, as is often the case in ambiguous task environments, the divergence in cognitions may be resolved by mutually exchanging interpretations. In the first part of this chapter we will see how communication and its resultant conformity pressures affect the process of *cognitive tuning* (i.e. attempts to arrive at a commonly shared task representation).

A given group task cannot be performed unless the members of the group arrive at some sort of agreement about the division of the work that has to be done. Group members may realise that their common and private interests coincide with respect to successful task completion, but that there is also a temptation for any of them to act merely in their own private interest by, for example, leaving unpleasant work to fellow group members. The second part of this chapter elaborates on the role of communication in the process of *tuning of interests* (i.e. attempts to deal with the potential conflict between common and private interests).

Cognitive tuning and tuning of interests may be considered as two basic processes in groups (Wilke and Meertens, 1994). In both tuning processes, communicating group members exert strong normative pressure on one another to consider the cognitions and interests that they have in common. Although essential for successful completion of the group task, strong normative pressures to arrive at a common task representation may have its drawbacks when it comes to innovative and divergent thinking. We will discuss some preventive measures that have been developed to weaken dysfunctional conformity pressures.

In contrast, in the process of tuning of interests, normative pressures on group members to consider their common interests cannot be strong enough. As we will see at the end of this chapter, groups often need to take additional measures to strengthen normative pressures to counteract group members' temptation to take advantage of their fellow group members' co-operative efforts.

COGNITIVE TUNING

Newly formed groups, or existing groups faced with a new problem, can only come up with solutions after a common representation of the task is achieved. We will discuss three basic modalities of cognitive tuning towards a commonly shared frame of reference (Moscovici, 1985), namely normalisation, conformity and innovation. *Normalisation* occurs when there is no *a priori* socially endorsed interpretation of the task stimuli. When the task is very ambiguous and fluid, group members mutually and gradually converge on a common frame of reference, which serves from then on as the group norm. *Conformity* assumes prior normalisation: the majority of the group tries to maintain a socially anchored group norm by putting pressure on deviating individuals to conform. Deviates are induced to go along, otherwise they risk being rejected by the group. *Innovation* may be the result of an explicit cognitive conflict, created when a persisting minority of deviates tries to introduce a new frame of reference. Innovation occurs when the cognitive conflict is resolved through the movement of members of the majority towards the position of the minority.

As can be seen from their respective definitions, these three modalities of cognitive tuning embody increasing levels of cognitive conflict. The next three sections will describe a few classic studies on the role of communication in group members' attempts to form, maintain and change their common frame of reference, respectively. To illustrate some implications of the research findings, we will refer to our hypothetical educational committee.

Normalisation

When there is no *a priori* socially endorsed interpretation of the group task, the question is: How will group members arrive at such a common frame of reference? For example, although all of the members of the educational committee may share the conviction that the current curriculum needs an update, their participation in the committee may initially feel like a leap in the dark to (some of) them.

In a very literal sense, darkness has been employed by Sherif (1936) in a classic series of experiments on the formation of a commonly shared task representation in a very ambiguous task environment. Sherif made use of the autokinetic phenomenon, a compelling optical illusion occurring when a person stares at a tiny light bulb, that is presented in an otherwise completely darkened room. Even though the light is in fact stationary, after watching it for a minute or two, it appears to move (due to unconscious eye movements and neural processes in the eyes of the perceiver). To maximise the illusion, the room has to be pitch dark and subjects have to be unfamiliar with the room's size so that they lack any physical standard against which to compare the position of the dot of light. Their task was to estimate the apparent distance that the light moved from its origin after each of a number of exposures.

Sherif's first series of studies investigated the formation of a personal frame of reference. Subjects were run in isolation and there was no opportunity to communicate. It appeared that a subject's initial responses varied widely from one exposure to the next, but with repeated exposure to the illusion, a subject's responses gradually converged on a single value. This single value eventually arrived at differed widely across subjects, suggesting that each built up a stable personal frame of reference (or personal norm) to judge subsequent task stimuli.

Sherif's second series of studies investigated what happens if inexperienced subjects are placed together in the pitch dark room and are allowed to communicate with one another. It appeared that, as in the first series of studies, subjects' individual responses showed a pattern of extreme initial variability. However, as a result of their communication, subjects' responses soon converged on a single group value. Mutual adjustment between group members' estimates resulted in a common group value. These group values differed widely across groups, suggesting that each of the groups developed its own frame of reference (or local group norm). The question arises why members of some groups converged on a high, while members of other groups converged on a low, group estimate. To address the role of the content of the communication, in some studies Sherif paid experimental confederates, acting as if they were regular fellow group members, to offer extremely high (or low) estimates. In response to these extreme judgements given by the confederates, naive subjects drastically increased (or decreased) their estimates. In subsequent studies (e.g. MacNeil and Sherif, 1976), it was observed that, once such a group norm had been established, it acquired a life of its own. When the experimenter removed the confederates from the group after a number of trials and replaced them by new naive subjects, the artificially high or low group estimates still continued to affect the group's judgements in subsequent trials.

In the above studies, the naive inexperienced subjects felt so unsure about the correctness of their own responses that the cognitive conflict about the correctness of the responses resided merely within themselves. In the absence of any communication with fellow subjects in the first series of studies, the cognitive conflict had to be resolved by the individual subject alone. In the second series of studies, the possibility to communicate with fellow group members helped subjects to resolve their internal cognitive conflict. Subjects were so uncertain about their own responses that the discrepancy between the estimates of the various group members did not pose a cognitive conflict to them. As a result, they gave much weight to the estimates expressed by their fellow group members.

In a subsequent series of studies a much stronger cognitive conflict was experienced by the subjects, not merely at an intrapersonal level (as in the above-mentioned studies), but now also at an interpersonal level. It appeared that subjects, who had first been exposed to a number of trials on an individual basis (in isolation) before they were placed in the group, were less willing to adjust their own estimates to those of their fellow group members, which were now seen as highly discrepant from their own estimates. Many of the subjects stuck to their personal norm, that they had developed in isolation before they entered the group. As a result, the progress of cognitive tuning towards a socially shared norm (i.e. a single group value) took much more time and was far less complete than when no personal norm had been previously established.

The strongest cognitive conflict was felt by subjects in yet another series of studies. After having naive inexperienced subjects respond to repeated trials of the autokinetic effect in separate groups (so that a socially anchored local group norm had been developed within each separate group), Sherif took individuals from these separate groups and created new groups for a next series of exposures. Unlike completely inexperienced subjects, who had already built up a personal norm in isolation before they entered the group, these subjects were least easily influenced by their fellow members of the newly created group. To a large extent they persisted in the norm which they had developed in their previous group.

Taken together, Sherif's studies suggest that once task ambiguity has been cognitively resolved by the formation of an internalised frame of reference, group members attach less weight to new perspectives, which may then be seen as discrepant from one's own frame of reference. With respect to our example of the educational committee, these results imply that the communicative process of cognitive tuning towards a commonly shared frame of reference very much depends on group members' previous experiences. If (some of the) members enter the committee with a well-developed frame of reference about their common task, which may differ widely from one member to another due to previous normalisation in other social settings (such as student meetings or faculty meetings), the formation of a common frame of reference will not be easily achieved. This is very likely to happen, since one usually does not recruit inexperienced naive candidates to participate in advisory committees. When (some) members stick to their previously developed, socially anchored frame of reference, the committee has to find ways to resolve the cognitive conflict between the group members before task solutions can be efficiently implemented.

Under these conditions of prior normalisation, the question arises as to whether an individual group member, who is being faced with a number of fellow group members advocating a discrepant perspective that does not seem correct, will go along or stick to the previously developed, socially anchored frame of reference. The following two sections address situations in which such an individual group member is being faced with a discrepant majority or with a discrepant minority, respectively.

Conformity pressures from a majority

How will individual group members respond when they learn that their own frame of reference, that has been established by previous experience, differs from the one held by the majority of the fellow members of their present group?

The classic experimental paradigm for studying this issue was developed by Asch (1952), who asked small groups of subjects to make a series of relatively simple judgements. Their task was to state publicly, and in the same fixed order, which of three comparison lines matched a fourth 'target' line in length. The correct answer was obvious: when making these simple judgements in isolation, few subjects made mistakes. In the typical group experiment, only one of the group members present was a naive subject, who responded next to last in the row after hearing the responses of the preceding group members, who (unknown to the naive subject) were all confederates of the experimenter. The group judged a series of stimulus sets and on many of these (the so-called 'critical' trials) the confederates had been instructed to agree on a clearly incorrect response. By having the confederates advocate a clearly incorrect response, Asch assessed an individual group member's willingness to conform to a majority when the individual could be completely certain of being right and of the majority being wrong. Being faced with a unanimous majority who offered an obviously incorrect answer created a strong intra- and inter-personal cognitive conflict for the naive subject, who became puzzled about the discrepancy between personal judgement and the unanimous judgement of all of the fellow group members. The dilemma was whether to comply with the unanimous majority of the present group or to stick to one's own internalised frame of reference. It appeared that only 25 per cent of the naive subjects showed no conformity at all, remaining independent of the social pressure from the majority throughout the session. Only a few subjects conformed on all critical trials to the blatantly incorrect judgements of the majority. However, 33 per cent of all subjects conformed on more than half of the critical trials.

What can be learned from these results? On the one hand, Asch's results demonstrate the potential of majority influence. One out of every three naive subjects solved the cognitive conflict by adjusting their own response to the incorrect responses of the majority on many (but not all) of the critical trials. On the other hand, the same results demonstrate that conformity in a group is not easily achieved when group members are strongly convinced that they themselves are right and that the majority of their fellow group members are wrong. At least one out of every four naive subjects remained completely independent from the majority pressure, whereas two-thirds of all naive subjects remained independent on more than half of the critical trials. Note that such a reluctance to conform to the judgements of fellow members of one's present group was also observed in Sherif's subjects, who had previously developed a socially anchored frame of reference before they entered their present group.

The case of one (naive subject) against all other group members (confederates) is a special case, however. Whereas lone individuals will have a hard time resisting the pressure of the majority, since their view can be dismissed by fellow group members as a personal idiosyncrasy, the presence of some fellow dissenters may cast more doubt on the majority's view. In related studies, Asch (1955) instructed one of the confederates to agree with the naive subject on some of the critical trials, and in these cases when the naive subject was not alone in disagreeing with the clearly incorrect majority, conformity rates were much lower. In yet another variation, Asch arranged for one confederate to disagree with the majority, but also to disagree with the (correct) answer of the naive subject. It appeared that even the presence of such a fellow deviate, who did not agree with the subject, made it easier for a naive subject to express personal opinions during the group discussion and to withstand pressures from the majority. Apparently, the cognitive conflict of being faced with a unanimous majority is more intense (and, as a result, elicits more conformity) than the cognitive conflict of being faced with a non-unanimous majority.

Subsequent research by Asch revealed that naive subjects were less willing to go along with the majority when they were not required to state their judgements publicly, but were allowed to state their judgements privately in writing. This suggests that conformity does not necessarily reflect subjects' true opinions. This suggestion is corroborated by other findings. In private post-experimental interviews (away from the group), many subjects, who had publicly agreed with their fellow group members in the group session, pointed out that they did not believe that the others were correct, but that they themselves did not want to appear different from their fellow group members. Their anxiety about appearing different was not unrealistic. In a reversal of the above described studies, Asch (1952) replaced the confederates with naive subjects, so that there was a majority of naive subjects facing one incorrect confederate. Under these conditions, the naive subjects expressed strong confidence in the correctness of their own responses and exposed the persisting deviate to amusement and scorn.

The hypothesised relationship between non-conformity and rejection by one's fellow group members has been confirmed by Schachter (1951), who showed that throughout group discussions, communication directed towards disagreeing group members tends to increase over time in order to put pressure on these deviants to conform to the majority. Later on in the discussion, the amount of communication towards deviants decreases, either because initial deviants yield to the majority pressure, or because the majority gives up trying to persuade a persisting deviant. In the latter case, the deviant is literally excommunicated.

Reviewing the above and many other studies (that used a large variety of tasks, ranging from perceptual tasks to attitude tasks), Wheeler (1991) concluded that pressures to communicate in a group increase when the issue has more relevance for the group and when group members feel the need to maintain a congenial group atmosphere. Furthermore, pressures to communicate to a specific group member are stronger when the perceived likelihood that communication will change that particular group member in the desired direction is greater. Pressures to communicate with an unyielding deviate will eventually diminish. Applied to the process of cognitive tuning in the educational committee, these studies suggest that its members may feel compelled to conform to the norms of the majority of their present group (i.e. the committee). Learning that a majority of the committee has reached agreement about a particular representation of the common task, that differs from one's own representation, may lead one to doubt whether personal task representation is valid and whether one will be liked as a group member. With increasing cohesion or when the topic of discussion has more relevance for the committee, it will be harder for one deviating group member to withstand the majority's conformity pressures. Resistance to majority pressure is more likely, however, when there is still another group member advocating a perspective that differs from the one held by the majority. Whereas a single dissenter's arguments can be dismissed as personal idiosyncrasies, more than one dissenter in the group may cast doubt on the majority's perspective. In the next section we will elaborate on the potential innovative impact of such a few determined dissenters.

Innovative pressures from a minority

Members of a minority, who challenge the prevailing group norm by maintaining their own discrepant views in a consistent and confident way, may not only successfully withstand conformity pressures of the majority, but may also have innovative impact on the group. Consistency in the responses of the minority in the face of majority opposition (and sometimes even ridicule) may be considered by the members of the majority as a sign of certainty and commitment to a coherent idea and thereby focus their attention on the minority's line of reasoning. Herein lies the potential of minority influence. It can purposely create cognitive conflict and cast doubt and uncertainty about the prevailing group norm, exploiting most group members' dislike of cognitive conflict and their need for uniformity. When the cognitive conflict cannot be resolved by mutual convergence (as in Sherif's autokinetic effect studies), it may be solved either by excommunication of the discrepant minority (as in Asch's and Schachter's studies) or by a shift of the majority in the direction of the minority.

Effective minority influence was demonstrated in a series of ingenious studies by Moscovici *et al.* (1969). Groups of six individuals were shown a series of blue slides which varied in brightness. Their task was to judge the colour of the slides and to announce their judgement aloud. When the group consisted of six naive subjects, 99 per cent of all subjects labelled the slides as blue. By planting two confederates in the six-person groups to advocate an unusual response (i.e. by labelling the blue slides as green), Moscovici and his co-workers were able to assess naive subjects' willingness to go along with a discrepant minority. (Note that it was unlikely that the unusual responses by the minority would be dismissed as blatantly incorrect, as had been the case in Asch's studies, since the colour perception task faced subjects with more ambiguity about the correct response than Asch's line matching tasks.) The results showed that when the judgements of the two confederates were consistent, both over time and across themselves, the four naive subjects described the slide more often as green (8 per cent of all responses given by the naive subjects were green) than when the judgements of the two confederates were inconsistent (i.e. sometimes labelling the slides as blue, sometimes as green – resulting in only 1 per cent of all responses being green). Thus, it appears that a consistent minority may exert innovative influence, whereas an inconsistent minority may have virtually no impact on the group.

Although naive subjects were even more likely to agree publicly with the unusual colour judgements when these were made by a majority (four confederates labelling the slides as green) than when these were made by a consistent minority (two confederates labelling the slides as green), their private beliefs were influenced more by minority influence than by majority influence. From private interviews (away from the group) after the group sessions, it appeared that subjects who had followed the minority's suggestion that the slides were green had a stronger belief that the slides were green than subjects who had yielded to a majority labelling the slides as green. These results were conceptually replicated with various other tasks (e.g. discussion tasks: Maass and Clark, 1984). It appeared that naive subjects' private beliefs were more affected by minority influence than by majority influence. When naive subjects could express their opinion at the end of the discussion in private, they more often tended to agree with the minority, whereas they tended to agree more often with the majority if they had to express their opinions in the presence of the fellow group members.

Taken together, majority influence appears to be particularly effective in eliciting public compliance, whereas group members' private beliefs are more strongly affected by minority influence. Applied to the educational committee, these results suggest that if a small subgroup within the committee demonstrates a consistent and confident behavioural style in expressing a discrepant perspective, this minority creates a cognitive conflict in the group and may be able to introduce a new frame of reference. The innovative impact of the minority on other group members' opinions may not be visible right away, however. Minority influence may not immediately come to the surface during plenary committee meetings, but only in the absence of the majority of the committee members: for example, during private discussions between single members before or after a plenary meeting. In order to enhance its innovative impact on the committee, a minority should encourage individuals, who have been privately persuaded by the minority's arguments, to support publicly the new frame of reference. To increase the size of the minority (and thereby its impact), members of the minority may, for instance, persuade individual converts that some fellow committee members have also privately expressed their support for the minority position, making it less threatening for individual converts publicly to adhere to the minority position during a next plenary committee meeting.

Informational versus normative pressures

The preceding section has dealt with cognitive tuning processes in groups, in which there exists either a broad range of perspectives held by the various group members, or in which there is a majority or minority favouring one particular perspective. The three associated modalities of cognitive tuning (i.e. normalisation, conformity and innovation, respectively), can be described in terms of two basic social pressures in groups: informational pressure and normative pressure (Deutsch and Gerard, 1955).

Informational pressure is based on group members' tendency to rely upon fellow group members' definitions of reality. Group members who are primarily interested in determining what is an appropriate frame of reference in an ambiguous task environment will be eager to communicate about their own and fellow group members' understanding of the task. Communication may induce group members to converge on a common frame of reference or social norm. This process of normalisation has been observed in Sherif's groups of inexperienced subjects, who were literally in the dark and lacked any standard against which to compare the position of the dot of light. Internalisation of such a socially anchored norm may result in individual group members attaching less weight to new, discrepant perspectives, but it does not immunise them.

When being faced with a majority holding a discrepant perspective, individual group members may yield to *normative* pressures (i.e. the implicit power of a majority to reward conforming group members and reject persisting deviates). A comparison between Asch's and Sherif's research findings suggests, however, that conformity in the interest of being liked as a group member has less powerful ramifications than conformity that results from viewing fellow group members for the purpose of gaining information about a proper representation of the task environment. Many of Asch's subjects, who were completely certain that their own frame of reference was right and that the fellow group members were wrong (no informational social pressure), publicly conformed to the local majority norm because they were reluctant to be seen as different. Their compliance persisted only as long as normative pressures were felt: once outside the group, they were more likely to express their private beliefs. By contrast, local group norms that had been established through communication between inexperienced, naive subjects in Sherif's studies (on the basis of their informational needs to determine an appropriate representation of a very ambiguous task) acquired a life of their own and tended to persist even in the absence of the fellow group members with whom the norm had previously been developed.

Not only a majority, but also a consistent minority may induce individual group members to shift their opinion in the direction of the minority. Particularly when the task environment leaves some room for different interpretations (cf. Moscovici *et al.*, 1969), a minority's discrepant perspective cannot be easily dismissed as blatantly incorrect. Since they lack a numerical advantage and their positions are often quite unpopular, minorities cannot exert normative pressure on individual group members. By intentionally raising doubt about the validity of the prevailing opinion of the majority, minorities may instead set the stage for *informational* social influence. To be effective, arguments supporting the minority position must be well articulated by its members. In addition, it can be observed that minorities often evoke elaborate discussions that are less likely to be initiated by members supporting the majority opinion. When the contents of their persuasive arguments become clear, minorities may induce a real change in group members' private beliefs.

Following this line of reasoning, Nemeth (1992) argued that majority influence may induce a fixation in thought because it focuses group members mainly on the normative requirement to reduce any discrepancy between their own opinion and the opinion held by the majority. The fear of being rejected by the majority of one's group may impede creative and divergent thinking. Given a minority's lack of normative pressure, minority influence mainly relies on informational pressure. The cognitive conflict evoked by a persistent minority is likely to promote careful consideration of the reasons for the apparent discrepancy, laying the ground for innovative and divergent thinking. Nemeth and Kwan (1987) indeed demonstrated that group members not only expressed more, but also more divergent and original, ideas in response to a discrepant minority than group members who were exposed to a discrepant majority. Thus, a dissenting minority appears to stimulate creativity and openness in the exchange of information rather than adaptation and fixation.

Although normative and informational pressures can be distinguished conceptually, these two types of pressure are strongly related. Normative pressures can inhibit informational social influence by determining what information gets exchanged in a task group. During discussions, group members may be so concerned with receiving social approval from their peers rather than with careful evaluation of the available information, that some information never gets expressed. As a result, they tend to discuss information that they assume they share in common and often fail to mention distinguishing bits of information that are known only to single individuals within the group (Stasser and Titus, 1985) or information that might contradict an emerging group consensus. In its most extreme form, normative pressures may lead to 'groupthink' (i.e. a process of premature concurrence seeking that can be observed in highly cohesive task groups). Such a failure to take relevant alternative perspectives into account may result in serious policy disasters (Janis, 1972).

Given the importance of open-mindedness to alternative perspectives and approaches at various stages of task completion, task groups should find ways to row against the current of normative pressures. The following section will elaborate on some formal procedures that have been developed to push group members past the bounds of restrictive thinking along the lines of the prevailing local group norm.

Overcoming dysfunctional normative pressures

How can premature concurrence seeking, that may result in biased information exchange within the group, be avoided? One way to stimulate group members to generate divergent ideas about a certain issue might be the method of *brainstorming* (Osborn, 1957). Here, group members receive instructions from a formally installed group facilitator, who introduces several rules to encourage group members to express as many ideas as possible within a certain time interval. Group members should not screen their own ideas. They are encouraged to 'piggyback' on ideas from their fellow group members in order to generate even more ideas. One person records all the expressed ideas to be presented and placed before the group as rapidly as possible, without discussion, clarification or comment. Evaluation of one's own and others' ideas has to be postponed.

In a review of many studies, McGrath (1984) concluded that, in spite of the popularity of the interactive brainstorming procedure and common beliefs about its efficacy, there was little empirical evidence to show that groups following this procedure generate more ideas of superior quality than individuals working separately. On the contrary, separate individuals may produce more and better ideas than the same individuals acting as members of an interactive brainstorming group (see also Diehl and Stroebe, 1987; Paulus *et al.*, 1995). One of the reasons why brainstorming groups may not always produce many creative ideas seems to be that group members, despite the instruction not to evaluate one another's contributions, fear negative evaluations from their fellow group members. Groups that use the conventional interactive brainstorming techniques tend to pursue a limited train of thought because normative conformity pressures are still too strong to express freely one's idiosyncratic ideas. Furthermore, it has been demonstrated that members of a conventional interactive brainstorming group tend to converge on similar amounts of idea expressions. This convergence appears to be biased in the direction of the least productive group members (Paulus and Dzindolet, 1993). The social influence opportunities of real group interaction leads to a mutual matching process that normalises a low performance level. How can these drawbacks be prevented?

In order to overcome these dysfunctional normative pressures, a modification of the face-to-face brainstorming method has been developed. The so-called *Nominal Group Technique* (NGT) involves a process with two formally distinct stages (Delbecq *et al.*, 1975). In the first, or elicitation stage, individual group members work separately, generating alternative perspectives on the task at hand. In order to minimise normative pressures, group members are not required to express their ideas aloud in the presence of the fellow group members, but to write their ideas down (cf. Asch's research findings, suggesting that normative conformity pressures can be weakened when group members are not required to express their opinions publicly, but are allowed to state them privately in writing). The second, or evaluation, stage involves the collective listing and evaluation of the perspectives that have been generated during the first stage. In an impressive series of studies (e.g. Van de Ven and Delbecq, 1974), comparing NGT with conventional inter-active brainstorming techniques, NGT was found to produce superior results. This suggests that interaction and communication between members of brainstorming groups may be most useful if individual group members have first generated ideas separately for a period of time and thereafter get additional social stimulation of others' ideas.

Some groups may use yet another formalised procedure to stimulate an unbiased discussion about alternative perspectives. In order to promote the examination of both supporting and detracting evidence, a group may decide to install a 'devil's advocate', that is, a group member who has been assigned the role of presenting any information that may lead to the disqualification of the prevailing frame of reference (Herbert and Estes, 1977). Unlike the lone dissenter in Asch's studies, this dissenting group member's popularity in the group is not harmed since the individual is formally installed to play that role. Moreover, the role may be shifted regularly from one group member to another. The cognitive conflict created by having one specific group member disagree consistently with one's fellow group members sets the stage for informational social influence, as in the case of minority influence. Severe cognitive stress should be avoided, however, by instructing the 'devil's advocate' carefully to present arguments in a low-key, non-threatening manner.

Yet another procedure to inhibit dysfunctional normative conformity pressures may be to arrange for members of the task group to meet in *separate sub-groups*, which will each develop its own frame of reference (Wheeler and Janis, 1980). The presence of these two sub-groups in a subsequent combined meeting may elicit discussion and critical examination of the reasons for the differences between the perspectives that have been developed within each of the sub-groups. If the sub-groups eventually come to agree in their cognitions, which may not be easily achieved (cf. Sherif's findings, suggesting less convergence to a common group opinion in the case of prior normalisation), it is less likely that the combined group will overlook or ignore any important considerations. The common frame of reference on which they may eventually come to agree may then be adopted with more confidence than if only a single group had worked on it.

Although normative conformity pressures can be dysfunctional and can produce even erroneous group judgements (cf. Asch's findings and Janis' studies on 'groupthink'), one should not lose sight of the fact that normative pressures ensure mutual social control. Mutual control becomes increasingly important the more group members are motivated to act in their own way. As long as they are merely concerned with the process of tuning their cognitions, group members' motivation to act in their own way may be relatively weak: they may publicly conform to the local group norm, despite keeping strong private reservations about its correctness. But, in other stages of task completion, group members may become increasingly concerned with their private positions and interests. When the division of labour becomes an issue, for instance, the costs of acquiescing with the group (i.e. living up to the normative expectation to contribute as much as one can to promote group success) may be more tangible than the costs of conformity in the process of cognitive tuning. To save themselves personal costs of contributing, some of the group members may yield to the temptation to leave unpleasant work to fellow members. As we will see in the next section, the tuning of interests requires strong normative pressures.

TUNING OF INTERESTS

Once a common cognitive frame of reference has been developed, group members have to arrive at some sort of agreement about the division of labour actually to complete the group task. The division of labour may give rise to a conflict between group members' common and private interests. Groups have to ensure that group members' common and private interests are properly tuned because an unrestrained pursuit of private interests will cause the whole group to fail or fall apart. Communication plays a crucial role in this process of tuning conflicting interests.

Entwining of common and private interests

Since a group member's outcomes depend not only on personal performance, but also on the performance of fellow group members, members of task groups are mutually inter-dependent. Two basic types of interdependence can be distinguished: promotive and contrient interdependence (Deutsch, 1949).

To the extent that one group member's successful performance directly promotes the success of fellow group members, group members are *promotively interdependent*. As far as their private interests coincide, group members will be motivated to co-operate (i.e. serve their common interest). Co-operation requires co-ordinated action. For example, it is in the common interest of all members of the educational committee that each of them submits proposals to change the curriculum before a certain deadline, so that all individual proposals can be assembled and sent to all the members of the committee before the next meeting. Group members' private interests coincide, since it is in nobody's private interest to be late in submitting proposals. Co-ordination requires clear communication (e.g. about submission deadlines) to structure the interaction process in such a way that group members optimally combine their contributions. If the group falls short in optimally combining its members' contributions, the group suffers from so-called 'co-ordination losses' (Steiner, 1972). In the next sub-section we will elaborate on this type of loss.

By contrast, group members are *contriently interdependent* to the extent that a gain by one group member entails a loss by other group members. Usually, the distribution of positive or negative outcomes among the group members increases the salience of this type of interdependence. For example, when a group has to elect a chairperson, one group member can only achieve personal success at the expense of other group members. Since only one of them can be installed, the election may create a competitive atmosphere between members of the committee. To give another example of conflicting interests in the division of outcomes: it may be in the students' best interest to increase the number of seminars and tutorials in the curriculum, whereas faculty members of the committee may advocate student self-tuition in order to decrease their own teaching load. Students can only achieve success if the faculty members give in. Opposing group members (or parties) will not be motivated to communicate in order to co-ordinate their actions. If problems arising from pure contrient interdependence remain unsolved, however, the resulting competition within the group may form a serious threat to group productivity.

The above-described dichotomy is an oversimplification, however, since pure promotive and pure contrient interdependence are rare. The mixture of both types of interdependence in almost any task group evokes a motivation to co-operate (group success can only be achieved by co-operating *with* fellow group members) as well as a motivation to act in a self-interested way (what is to be gained by one group member in the division of positive or negative outcomes can often only be obtained *at the expense of* fellow group members). Even when the motivation to act in a self-interested way seems to prevail, as in the election of a chairperson or in the final phrasing of the committee's recommendations, opposing parties may eventually resume their communication out of concern for their common interest, which to some extent is ever present; in an attempt to resolve the conflict of interests between the parties, they may start negotiating and bargaining (see Chapter 13). The present chapter focuses on mixed motive task situations, in which the motivation to co-operate may prevail. These situations still face group members with a choice between serving their common or their private interests. Even under predominantly co-operative circumstances, group members' self-interest may lead them consciously or subconsciously to reduce their personal contributions to the group, taking advantage of fellow group members' co-operative efforts to achieve group success. Such reduced contributions constitute a second type of productivity losses, namely 'motivation losses' (Steiner, 1972; Kerr, 1983). Before we elaborate on group members' communicative attempts to overcome motivation losses, we will first address the issue of co-ordination losses.

Co-ordination losses

To the extent that group members experience promotive interdependence, they are eager to contribute to their common interest since there is no incentive for any of them to refrain from contributing. Co-operation requires good co-ordination (i.e. structuring the interaction process in such a way that group members optimally combine their efforts). Co-ordination losses occur when the group falls short in optimally combining its members' efforts. The achievement of co-ordinated action is usually a problem to the extent that the behavioural requirements are not immediately clear to all group members.

Some tasks require simultaneity in group members' efforts. Simultaneity is required, for instance, in the sequence of activities during task completion. Research by Tschan (1995) shows that groups, whose members are properly tuned to focus simultaneously on one and the same part of the task, perform better than groups whose members' contributions are less well tuned in time. Communication may help to concentrate the attention of the group members on one of the aspects of the task, to make sure that everyone is aware of what has been achieved so far and to ensure that people will make further contributions that are compatible (see also Harper and Askling, 1980). Successful task groups, relative to those that fail, boast a larger proportion of participants who actively stimulate task-relevant communication by focusing their own and fellow members' attention on one and the same part of the task at hand (e.g. the submittance of individual proposals, the evaluation of these proposals, reaching agreement upon one particular course of action, and its subsequent implementation and evaluation).

This does not mean that the completion of a group task will always benefit from simultaneity in group members' contributions. In interactive brainstorming groups, for example, it would be unproductive if all participants were to express their ideas aloud at the same time. While one group member speaks, other group members have to keep silent. Group members have to wait for others to express their own ideas. This type of co-ordination loss, which is called 'production blocking' (Diehl and Stroebe, 1987) may hinder group members in presenting or even remembering their own ideas. One way to overcome the problem of production blocking in the generation of ideas is the nominal group technique discussed earlier. Another alternative is computer-based brainstorming, in which individuals are exposed to ideas from others on their computer screen as they generate their own ideas. As in the NGT, the lack of face-to-face interaction may limit production blocking, which may be particularly important in task groups with more than ten members (Valacich *et al.*, 1994).

In summary, clearly communicated co-ordination rules are essential for preventing co-ordination losses in task groups. Unfortunately, group members rarely show much interest in planning the co-ordination process. Yet, controlling the process by communicating about how to sequence group members' contributions properly has positive effects on group productivity (Hackman *et al.*, 1976).

Motivation losses

Even if task groups are so well organised that virtually all losses due to faulty co-ordination are eliminated, group productivity might still decrease due to motivation losses. Motivation losses occur because task groups are seldom characterised by pure promotive inter-dependence, but almost always involve a mixture of promotive and contrient interdependence. Group members are motivated to contribute as much as they can in order to achieve group success, but at the same time they may lose their motivation to contribute fully out of concern for their private interests (Kerr, 1983; Baron *et al.*, 1992). The mixture of common and private interests sets the scene for motivation losses, reflecting the tendency (conscious or subconscious) to decrease one's personal share in the collective burden by letting one's fellow group members do the work. Motivation losses are more likely if group members can take advantage of circumstances, in which their own contribution to the group product is hardly identifiable (e.g. in large groups), while they still share in the collective benefits of group success. When motivation losses are more or less unconscious, the decrease of individual contributions to the group is termed 'social loafing'. Group members who intentionally let others do the work are called 'free riders'. A very likely reaction in response to the (assumed) presence of free riders in the group is to reduce one's own efforts, too, rather than to take the risk of being exploited. This latter type of motivation loss is due to the fear of being the 'sucker'.

The scientific study on this type of productivity losses started with studies by Ringelmann in 1913 (see Kravitz and Martin, 1986), who had young men pull a rope, either alone or in groups of varying size. Subjects working alone pulled with an average force of 63 kgs, subjects working in dyads pulled with a force of 118 kgs (i.e. an average of 59 kgs per person), subjects working in triads pulled with a force of 106 kgs (i.e. an average of 53 kgs per person), while eight-person groups pulled with an average of 31 kgs per person. Thus, the average individual performance decreased with increasing group size.

To estimate the relative impact of motivation losses in the total productivity loss, Ingham *et al.* (1974) employed an experimental method that eliminated all co-ordination losses (i.e. productivity losses due to faulty co-ordination, such as a lack of simultaneity of the muscular contractions of the individuals). Ingham *et al.* blindfolded the rope-pulling subject and contrived that the subject was ahead of any other subjects on the rope, closest to the gauge which measured performance. In fact, there were no other people pulling on the rope. In this way, Ingham *et al.* assessed the performance of individual naive subjects who believed they were part of a group. It appeared that, as the apparent group size increased, the individual performance of the naive subject declined, suggesting that group members are less motivated to do their ultimate best when the size of their (imagined) group increases. Latané *et al.* (1979) found the same pattern of results in a cheering task. Naive subjects were made to believe that they were cheering as part of a group. They were wearing headphones so that they would not be distracted by the cheers of the 'other subjects'. In fact, they were the only one cheering. Again, it appeared that individual performance declined with apparent group size. Subsequent research has shown that motivation losses also occur in cognitive and perceptual group tasks (Petty *et al.*, 1980; Jackson and Williams, 1985).

Normative pressures to prevent motivation losses

Communication may help to overcome motivation losses in mixed motive situations if it sets the stage for normative social pressure on group members to contribute their fair share (or even, as much as they can). Communicating simply to get better acquainted with one's fellow group members is not sufficient, however (Dawes *et al.*, 1977). What might be relevant topics to discuss?

Communication may in the first place facilitate group members' understanding of the extent to which they are promotively interdependent. When their attention becomes focused on their common interests, group members may come to agree with one another that mutual co-operation is preferable to mutual non-co-operation. Thus communication may help them to agree on mutual co-operation as a shared goal. However, it is rather risky to co-operate unless members can count on their fellow group members to co-operate. If others cannot be trusted, those who co-operate run the risk of being the sucker. Therefore, the second important function of communication in mixed motive task situations is to reduce group members' uncertainty about fellow group members' willingness actually to contribute.

Mutually agreed upon co-operative goals and mutual trust are the two key concepts in Pruitt and Kimmels' goal-expectation theory (1977) about the evolution of co-operation in mixed motive situations. Group members who share a co-operative goal *and* expect fellow group members to co-operate, may eventually come to evaluate their own and others' performances in terms of accomplishment of their common goals. As such, communication may establish a co-operative group norm.

Two norms are of particular importance, namely the commitment norm and the norm of equity or reciprocity. The *commitment* norm prescribes that group members should actually carry out those actions which they have publicly promised to perform. Effective interaction in groups would be impossible without such a norm. Unless others can be expected to keep their commitments, mistrust and mutual exploitation are likely to occur. Communication between group members may present an opportunity to establish mutual commitment to co-operate, as a binding social contract. It appears that promises to co-operate are usually kept, even when the subsequent behaviour will be anonymous and contrary to group members' immediate private interests (Orbell *et al.*, 1988).

The *equity norm* prescribes that the rewards of group performance are distributed in proportion to group members' individual contributions. When all group members have an equal share in the collective outcomes of group success, as is often the case in task groups that provide a common good, the equity norm prescribes that all of them should exert equal amounts of effort. The equity norm may both encourage and discourage co-operation in task groups, however. When a group member learns that fellow group members are exerting considerable effort, a failure to work as hard as they violates the equity norm; a reason to co-operate would then be that free riding would violate the equity norm. However, if the same group member learns that fellow group members are free riding upon the former's co-operative effort, the most likely response would then be simply to cease co-operating. Few group members will endure the inequitable 'sucker' role in their task group.

A co-operation-inducing strategy, based upon the equity norm, may be to start co-operating and just keep co-operating as long as fellow group members co-operate; when-ever fellow group members act unco-operatively, also refrain from co-operation. This so called 'tit-for-tat' strategy (Axelrod, 1984) establishes the norm of reciprocity, which is an excellent way of tuning common and private interests in small groups. If group members discover that fellow group members' co-operation is contingent on their own co-operation, it becomes clear to them that they can influence one another and that free riding is very unlikely since fellow group members will immediately refrain from co-operating as soon as they themselves stop co-operating. Group members who employ the 'tit-for-tat' strategy communicate that they are willing to co-operate as long as fellow group members do the same. This strategy is a much better way of interest tuning than unconditional co-operation, which would make the co-operators very vulnerable to being exploited by free riders, whose unco-operative behaviour is then reinforced.

Building on research findings that normative pressures to conform to local group norms are stronger in cohesive groups (Wheeler, 1991), it can be expected that the above-discussed norms have more impact when the salience of a common group membership is high. Communication in groups appears to enhance feelings of being a part of the group and creates a sense of group identity or group cohesion (Orbell *et al.*, 1988). Research by Bonachich (1976) has shown that the content of communication among group members in mixed motive task situations indeed tends to focus on the normative requirement of co-operation towards group success and on how angry the group will be towards group members who do not take their fair share of the collective burden. Furthermore, it has also been demonstrated (Brewer and Kramer, 1986) that the more group members feel part of their group, the less strongly they distinguish between their common and private interests. Members who strongly identify with their own group appear to be even more likely to perceive their fellow group members in generally favourable terms, particularly as being trustworthy and co-operative (Brewer, 1981). Such favourable attributions may pave the way for trust in the co-operative intentions of fellow group members, even in the absence of explicit information about the extent to which they actually co-operate. Together, all these potential beneficial effects of task-relevant communication in groups make co-operation more likely.

Additional measures to strengthen normative pressures

In spite of these normative pressures promoting co-operation, a task group remains vulnerable to motivation losses of (some of) its group members. A first reason may be the size of the group. If only one of the group members refrains from co-operating, this non-co-operation may elicit non-co-operative responses by fellow group members, who may feel justified to do so on the basis on the equity/reciprocity norm. Reciprocal co-operation is not easily established in task groups with more than two members. Many studies suggest that co-operation declines as groups become larger (e.g. Fox and Guyer, 1977). Other factors inhibiting the evolution of co-operation in large task groups may be the perceived efficacy of one's own contribution, the extent to which one's own contribution is identifiable and the extent to which one feels responsible for the achievement of the common interest.

A second reason for task groups' vulnerability to motivation losses is that the beneficial effects of enhanced group identification on individuals' willingness to conform to co-operative group norms may be weakened by subordinate group boundaries that give rise to conflicting loyalties (Kramer and Brewer, 1984). For example, members of our educational committee may refrain from taking their fair share of the work that has to be done by the committee because they may be more concerned with work that has to be done on behalf of their own particular sub-group (students or staff).

Therefore, communicative attempts to promote co-operation have often to be combined with additional measures. If co-operative behaviour is the result of normative pressures to serve the common interest, one would expect that co-operation can be further promoted by enhancing the salience of co-operative norms and/or increasing the severity of social sanctions for non-co-operation. Several lines of research confirm this assumption.

Enforcement of any social norm requires the ability to monitor inputs and outcomes, so that norm violations can be detected and that the social sanctions to punish norm violation will be salient to the group members. Social loafing (more or less unconsciously hiding in the crowd) and free riding (its deliberate pendant, when one expects that fellow group members will do the necessary work) are less likely to occur when identification and evaluation of one's own contribution are more likely. Group members appear to be very sensitive to the risk of being detected as an under-performing group member (Harkins and Jackson, 1985). As a result, groups achieve higher levels of co-operation when group members have to make their contributions publicly than they do when their acts remain unidentifiable (cf. Asch's findings, suggesting that subjects are more likely to comply with the local group norms when they have to state their opinions publicly than when they are allowed to express their opinions in the absence of any social control by their fellow group members). Increased identifiability of individual contributions in task groups by record-keeping, for instance, allows group members to check whether each of them has done a fair share of the work that is necessary to complete the group task successfully. As such, record-keeping may serve some of the same purposes as communication, namely to promote feelings of social control that encourage group members to conform to co-operative norms.

Once group members' (non-)contributions are made identifiable, a group may decide further to increase social control over its members by the use of explicit supplementary pay-offs or costs, such as promises to reward co-operators or threats to punish non-co-operators. Komorita and Barth (1985) have shown that co-operation is promoted when group members believe that fellow group members are able to punish non-co-operative behaviour and/or reward co-operative behaviour. Rewarding co-operation seems to yield more beneficial effects than punishing non-co-operative behaviour, although rewards may arouse reactance and prove even counter-effective if the rewards are perceived by the group members as an attempt to bribe them (Wit and Wilke, 1990).

When the above interventions do not suffice to ensure satisfactory levels of co-operation, a group may eventually come to the conclusion that it is preferable completely to restrain group members' decisional freedom. Rutte and Wilke (1984) demonstrated that group members who learn that the group falls short in the realisation of its common goals and that its members differ considerably in their individual contributions are quite willing to hand their decisional freedom over to one of the (co-operative) group members, who will have the exclusive authority to make decisions on behalf of all group members.

OVERVIEW

Communication in a task group allows its members to exert strong normative pressure on one another to consider the cognitions and interests that they have in common. In the process of cognitive tuning, normative pressure is a double-sided sword, however. On the one hand, normative pressure leads group members to converge on a common task representation, which may be beneficial to achieve group success; on the other, normative pressure may make the group members so concerned with receiving social approval from their peers that idiosyncratic and innovative perspectives that might contradict the emerging group consensus never get expressed. Since premature concurrence-seeking constitutes a serious threat to group success, some formalised procedures have been developed (like the nominal group technique or installing a devil's advocate) to regulate the communication process in such a way that it becomes less likely that important alternative perspectives are overlooked or ignored.

In contrast, when group members are tuning their interests, normative pressure to ensure that individuals give priority to common interests over private interests cannot be strong enough. The normative expectation that all group members should contribute their fair share to achieve group success may promote co-operation, but may at the same time increase the temptation (for some group members) to free ride upon others' co-operative efforts. To prevent the resulting productivity losses, task groups often need to take additional measures by increasing both the likelihood and the severity of social sanctions for non-co-operation. Overcoming productivity losses is a continuous concern for task groups: even if group members realise that time and energy must be devoted to find effective solutions to these threats to their common interest, many of them may prefer not to become involved in the activities necessary actually to implement these solutions, and thus leave the work to (one or some of the) co-operative fellow group members.

REFERENCES

Asch, S. E. (1952) *Social Psychology*, Prentice Hall, Englewood Cliffs, NJ.
—— (1955) 'Opinions and Social Pressures', *Scientific American*, 193, 31–5.
Axelrod, R. (1984) *The Evolution of Cooperation*, Basic Books, New York.
Baron, R. S., Kerr, N. L. and Miller, N. (1992) *Group Process, Group Decision, Group Action*, Open University Press, Milton Keynes.
Bonachich. P. (1976) 'Secrecy and Solidarity', *Sociometry*, 39, 200–8.
Brewer, M. B. (1981) 'Ethnocentrism and its Role in Interpersonal Trust', in M. Brewer and B. Collins (eds), *Scientific Inquiry and the Social Sciences*, Jossey-Bass, San Francisco.
—— and Kramer, R. M. (1986) 'Choice Behavior in Social Dilemmas: Effects of Social Identity, Group Size, and Decision Framing', *Journal of Personality and Social Psychology*, 50, 543–9.
Dawes, R. M., McTavish, J. and Shaklee, H. (1977) 'Behavior, Communication, and Assumptions about other People's Behavior in a Commons Dilemma Situation', *Journal of Personality and Social Psychology*, 35, 1–11.
Delbecq, A. L., Van de Ven, A. H. and Gustafson, D. H. (1975) *Group Techniques for Program Planning*, Scott, Foresman, Glenview, IL.
Deutsch, M. (1949) 'A Theory of Cooperation and Competition', *Human Relations*, 2, 129–52.
—— and Gerard, H. B. (1955) 'A Study on Normative and Informational Social Influence upon Individual Judgement', *Journal of Abnormal and Social Psychology*, 51, 629–36.
Diehl, M. and Stroebe, W. (1987) 'Productivity Losses in Brainstorming Groups: Towards the Solution of a Riddle', *Journal of Personality and Social Psychology*, 53, 497–509.
Fox, J. and Guyer, M. (1977) 'Group Size and Others' Strategy in an N-person Game', *Journal of Conflict Resolution*, 21, 323–38.
Hackman, R. J., Brousseau, K. R. and Weiss, J. A. (1976) 'The Interaction of Task Design and Group Performance Strategies in Determining Group Effectiveness', *Organizational Behavior and Human Performance*, 16, 350–65.
Harkins, S. and Jackson, J. (1985) 'The Role of Evaluation in Eliminating Social Loafing', *Personality and Social Psychology Bulletin*, 11, 457–65.
Harper, N. L. and Askling, L. R. (1980) 'Group Communication and Quality of Task Solution in a Media Production Organization', *Communication Monographs*, 47, 77–100.
Herbert, T. T. and Estes, R. W. (1977) 'Improving Executive Decisions by Formalizing Dissent: The Corporate Devil's Advocate', *Academy of Management Review*, 2, 662–7.
Ingham, A. G., Levinger, G., Graves, J. and Peckham, V. (1974) 'The Ringelmann Effect, Studies on Group Size and Group Performance', *Journal of Experimental Social Psychology*, 10, 371–84.
Jackson, J. M. and Williams, K. D. (1985) 'Social Loafing on Difficult Tasks', *Journal of Personality and Social Psychology*, 49, 937–42.
Janis, I. L. (1972) *Victims of Group Think*, Houghton Mifflin, Boston.
Kerr, N. L. (1983) 'Motivation Losses in Task-performing Groups: A Social Dilemma Analysis', *Journal of Personality and Social Psychology*, 45, 819–28.
Komorita, S. S. and Barth, J. M. (1985) 'Components of Reward in Social Dilemmas', *Journal of Personality and Social Psychology*, 48, 364–73.
Kramer, R. M. and Brewer, M. B. (1984) 'Effects of Group Identity on Resource Use in a Simulated Commons Dilemma', *Journal of Personality and Social Psychology*, 46, 1044–57.
Kravitz, D. A. and Martin, B. (1986) 'Ringelmann Rediscovered: The Original Article', *Journal of Personality and Social Psychology*, 50, 936–41.

Latané, B., Williams, K. and Harkins, S. (1979) 'Many Hands Make Light the Work: The Causes and Consequences of Social Loafing', *Journal of Personality and Social Psychology*, 37, 822–32.

Maass A. and Clark, R. D. (1984) 'Hidden Impact of Minorities: Fifteen Years of Minority Influence Research', *Psychological Bulletin*, 95, 428–50.

MacNeil, M. K. and Sherif, M. (1976) 'Norm Change Over Subject Generations as a Function of Arbitrariness of Prescribed Norm', *Journal of Personality and Social Psychology*, 34, 762–73.

McGrath, J. E. (1984) *Groups: Interaction and Performance*, Prentice-Hall, Englewood Cliffs, NJ.

Moscovici, S. E. (1985) 'Social Influence and Conformity', in G. Lindzey and E. Aronson (eds), *The Handbook of Social Psychology. Vol. 2*, (3rd edn), Random House, New York.

——, Lage, E. and Naffrechoux, M. (1969) 'Influence of a Consistent Minority on the Responses of a Majority in a Color Perception Task', *Sociometry*, 32, 365–80.

Nemeth, C. J. (1992) 'Minority Dissent as a Stimulant to Group Performance', in S. Worchel, W. Wood and J. A. Simpson (eds), *Group Processes and Productivity*, Sage, Newbury Park.

—— and Kwan, J. L. (1987) 'Minority Influence, Divergent Thinking and Detection of Correct Solutions', *Journal of Applied Social Psychology*, 17, 786–97.

Orbell, J., Dawes, R. and Van der Kragt, A. (1988) 'Explaining Discussion Induced Cooperation', *Journal of Personality and Social Psychology*, 54, 811–19.

Osborn, A. F. (1957) *Applied Imagination*, Scribner's, New York.

Paulus, P. B. and Dzindolet, M. T. (1993) 'Social Influence Processes in Group Brainstorming', *Journal of Personality and Social Psychology*, 64, 575–86.

Paulus, P. B., Larey, T. S. and Ortega, A. H. (1995) 'Performance and Perceptions of Brainstormers in an Organizational Setting', *Basic and Applied Social Psychology*, 17, 249–65.

Petty, R., Harkins, S. and Williams, K. (1980) 'The Effects of Diffusion of Cognitive Effort on Attitudes: An Information Processing View', *Journal of Personality and Social Psychology*, 38, 81–92.

Pruitt, D. G. and Kimmel, M. J. (1977) 'Twenty Years of Experimental Gaming: Critique, Synthesis, and Suggestions for the Future', *Annual Review of Psychology*, 28, 363–92.

Rutte, C. G. and Wilke, H. A. M. (1984) 'Social Dilemmas and Leadership', *European Journal of Social Psychology*, 14, 105–21.

Schachter, S. (1951) 'Deviation, Rejection and Communication', *Journal of Abnormal and Social Psychology*, 46, 190–207.

Sherif, M. (1936) *The Psychology of Social Norms*, Harper & Row, New York.

Stasser, G. and Titus, W. (1985) 'Pooling of Unshared Information in Group Decision Making: Biased Information Sampling During Group Discussion', *Journal of Personality and Social Psychology*, 48, 1467–78.

Steiner, I. D. (1972) *Group Process and Productivity*, Academic Press, New York.

Tschan, F. (1995) 'Communication Enhances Small Group Performance if it Conforms to Task Requirements: The Concept of Ideal Communication Cycles', *Basic and Applied Social Psychology*, 17, 371–93. .

Valacich, J. S., Dennis, A. R. and Connolly, T. (1994) 'Idea Generation in Computer-based Groups: A New Ending to an Old Story', *Organizational Behavior and Human Decision Processes*, 57, 448–76.

Van de Ven, A. H. and Delbecq, A. L. (1974) 'The Effectiveness of Nominal, Delphi and Interacting Group Decision-making Processes', *Academy of Management Journal*, 17, 605–21.

Wheeler, D. D. and Janis, I. L. (1980) *A Practical Guide for Making Decisions*, Free Press, New York.

Wheeler, L. (1991) 'A Brief History of Social Comparison Theory', in J. Suls and T. A. Wills (eds), *Social Comparison: Contemporary Theory and Research*, Erlbaum, Hillsdale, NJ.

Wilke, H. A. M. and Meertens, R. (1994) *Group Performance*, Routledge, London.

Wit, A. P. and Wilke, H. A. M. (1990) 'The Presentation of Rewards and Punishments in a Simulated Social Dilemma', *Social Behaviour*, 5, 231–45.

13 Negotiating and bargaining

Ian E. Morley

INTRODUCTION

The purpose of this chapter is to review theories which examine psychological aspects of negotiation, in an attempt to say what, of practical value, has been learned about the skills of negotiation. There are five main kinds of model: synthetic models; behavioural models of strategies and tactics in negotiation; information processing models; models of the personal characteristics of effective negotiators; and discursive models which focus on the social construction of cognition and action. I shall consider each in turn.

SYNTHETIC MODELS OF NEGOTIATION

Synthetic models of negotiation are formal models which use simple and elegant notations to describe the process of negotiation in very general terms (Lockhart, 1979). They are used to spell out the consequences of certain basic processes. It is then an empirical question whether such general models are useful in guiding our understanding of any particular case.

The key assumption is that the most important thing to say is that negotiation is an exercise in bargaining. There are at least two kinds of model: utility theories (which form part of micro-economic theory) and models of strategic interaction (which form part of the theory of games).

Utility models

Utility models begin by describing a bargaining problem in which there are two parties – A, a contractor, and B, a client. It is assumed that A and B have wants which conflict to a greater or lesser extent, and that bargaining is a process of deciding on an allocation of goods. The process is one in which A and B exchange bids, where each bid is a proposal to allocate some goods to A and others to B. It is assumed that A and B will each estimate the various costs and benefits each will expect if the other agreed with the proposal on the table. It is also assumed that each will estimate the costs and benefits they would each face in the event of a failure to agree. An agreement is reached when the process of bid and counter-bid converges on to a proposal both A and B find acceptable and both think is the best they could have obtained in the circumstances.

Such models capture the idea that each proposal has a net worth (expected utility) for each of the bargainers, so that the process of bargaining may be described as an allocation

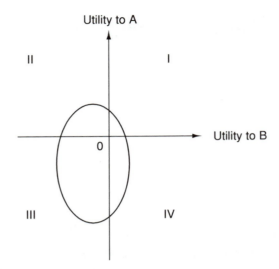

Figure 13.1 The space of possible bids

of utility between A and B. Formally, the space of possible bids may be represented in terms of the four quadrants shown in Figure 13.1. Quadrant I contains all those agreements which are positively valued by both A and B, and has therefore received the most attention. However, the extension of the space into quadrants II, III and IV represents the fact that there may be outcomes A or B wishes to avoid (because they may each harm the other in the event of no agreement). It is not too difficult to see that any movement in a direction from top left to bottom right may be regarded as movement along a line of conflict. Similarly, any movement in a direction from bottom left to top right may be regarded as movement along a line of common interest. Consequently, utility models capture the idea that conflicting interests always occur in the context of common interests.

Some writers focus on the first quadrant of Figure 13.1 and translate talk about utilities into talk about aspiration zones, contract zones and settlement ranges. For example, Walton and McKersie (1965) argued that A and B each form an aspiration zone with a target and a resistance point. The target is determined by their highest estimate of what is needed; by their most optimistic estimates of what is possible; and by their most favourable estimates of their bargaining skill. The resistance point (sometimes called the *minimum necessary share*) is determined by their lowest estimate of what is needed; by their most pessimistic assumptions about what is possible; and by their least favourable estimates of their bargaining skill. The four points may be plotted on a single line, known as the conflict line. The distance between A's resistance point and B's resistance point is known as the *settlement range*. When these points are compatible there is a contract zone or positive settlement range (because both prefer some agreement to their best alternative to a negotiated agreement). When these points are incompatible there is a negative settlement range, and agreement will be impossible until either A or B or both change their minimum terms. Analyses of this kind have been used to gain insight into historical cases. To take one example, it has been shown that the Berlin Wall was built because it was the only option preferred to no agreement by both Soviet and Western negotiators (Snyder and Diesing, 1977).

Although there is a common statement of the bargaining problem there are many different solutions.

- Some describe constraints proposals must satisfy if they are to be turned into outcomes which are fair, acceptable, optimum, etc. Such constraints are known as arbitration schemes (see Nash, 1950; Braithwaite, 1955);
- Some locate the main impetus for concession-making in estimates of the risks of disagreement, but give different treatments of the nature of those risks (Coddington, 1968; Lockhart, 1979; Bacharach and Lawler, 1981);
- Some view the process of bargaining as a learning process in which various expectations are revised (Coddington, 1968).

Each of the three kinds of models identified above points to different kinds of skill.

- The focus on arbitration schemes has prepared the way for a consideration of principled bargaining (e.g. Fisher and Ury, 1983).
- The focus on perception of risk has prepared the way for a more general consideration of negotiators' reputations for resolve (Snyder and Diesing, 1977).
- The focus on learning has prepared the way for more detailed explorations of how negotiators define issues, interpret feedback and revise expectations (Lockhart, 1979).

In addition, some of the models imply typologies of conflict tactics which have proved useful in studies of industrial and international negotiations (Walton and McKersie, 1965; Snyder and Diesing, 1977; Lockhart, 1979).

Models of strategic interaction

Models of strategic interaction are models of games of strategy which were developed in the context of work on the theory of games (Weintraub, 1992). This was an ambitious theory which attempted to define rational action in contexts where the outcomes for each person depended partly on their own actions and partly on the actions of others (Morgenstern, 1949).

Negotiation is seen as a game in which the parties, A and B, make separate strategic choices to make concessions or to maintain their current level of demand. The former is usually described as the C strategy; the latter as the D strategy. The outcome of the game depends on the combination of the choices made by A and B. Thus, A's pay-offs depend on B's choices and B's pay-offs depend on A's choices. The generalised form of the game is shown in Figure 13.2.

The letters, R, S, T, and P stand for 'reward', 'sucker', 'temptation' and 'punishment'. They are used to refer to the pay-offs which accrue to A (the left member of each pair) and to B (the right member of each pair). Thus, when A chooses C and B chooses D, A receives S and B receives T: and so on.

Different values of R, S, T and P define different games. The two best-known games are the Prisoner's Dilemma Game and Chicken (Poundstone, 1992). In Prisoner's Dilemma pay-offs are ordered so that $T > R > P > S$. In Chicken the order is $T > R > S > P$. In both games, pay-offs satisfy the additional constraint that $2R > S + T$. It has been suggested that the strategic choice between problem-solving (C) and contending (D) has the structure of Prisoner's Dilemma and that the choice between conceding (C) and

Player B

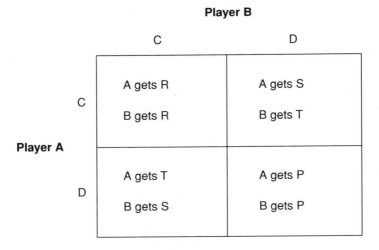

Figure 13.2 Two-person two-choice matrix game

maintaining demand (D) has the structure of Chicken (Snyder and Diesing, 1977; Pruitt and Carnevale, 1993).

Evaluation

It is clear that synthetic models treat only some aspects of negotiation. Bargaining is described in terms of a small number of processes, capable of mathematical treatment. Other activities are either ignored or somehow interpreted in terms of the variables included in the model. Such drastic simplification is not without value. It helps us to realise that negotiation begins when someone sees change, or the possibility of change, in the status quo: and it helps us to realise that different people might look at the status quo in very different ways.

Once negotiation begins it is important to realise that the process is one which engages mixed motives. The description of lines of conflict and lines of common interest given above has encouraged some writers to draw a distinction between distributive bargaining and integrative bargaining (Walton and McKersie, 1965; Raiffa, 1982). In the two-person case, distributive bargaining is competitive bargaining in which A and B struggle to get as much as they can of a good that they each desire. Integrative bargaining is collaborative bargaining in which A and B actively search for new agreements from which each will gain.

Because distributive bargaining is competitive and integrative bargaining is collaborative negotiators face certain strategic dilemmas. Typically, distributive bargaining is bargaining in which negotiators struggle to exploit asymmetries in power. However, to the extent that they misrepresent their own positions they make it difficult to explore ways in which the requirements of the parties might be reconciled. Such dilemmas may be particularly acute when negotiations are complex (Raiffa, 1982). Raiffa's own solution is to advise negotiators to keep secret their minimum necessary terms, but otherwise to behave openly and honestly.

Synthetic models have performed a major service by identifying negotiators' dilemmas in the choice of strategy and tactics. The most valuable treatment remains that of Walton and McKersie (1965), partly because it includes the value of the relationship between the negotiators as something to be included in any cost-benefit analysis (also see Polzer *et al.*, 1995).

Nevertheless, synthetic models of this kind have very important weaknesses. The way they simplify the bargaining problem is too drastic. Consequently, they provide inadequate models of people, parties, processes and contexts:

- They provide inadequate models of people because they take the character of the conflict for granted (Lockhart, 1979; Morley *et al.*, 1988);
- They provide inadequate models of parties because parties are usually loose coalitions in which bargaining within sides is at least as important as bargaining between sides (Snyder and Diesing, 1977; Morley, 1992);
- They provide inadequate models of processes because they neglect the ways in which parties identify issues, develop solutions, choose between alternatives and implement policies (Morley *et al.*, 1988; Hosking and Morley, 1991);
- They provide inadequate models of contexts because they abstract away from the historical relationship between the sides. They neglect the fact that agreements have to be justified as rules which make sense, because they link what is happening now to what has happened in the past, and to what needs to happen in the future (Morley, 1992).

In short, such models are individualistic.

Nevertheless, strategic models have formed one important input into a more general study of conflict spirals. For example, it has been suggested that yielding to punitive tactics may result in a loss of face, and that attempts to save face are often obstacles to serious negotiation (Bacharach and Lawler, 1981). This may help to explain why many skilled negotiators are wary of making explicit threats (Iklé, 1964; Rackham and Carlisle, 1978). It may also help to explain why skilled negotiators have to learn not to treat attacks on party positions as if they were attacks on people (Fisher and Ury, 1983).

BEHAVIOURAL STUDIES OF STRATEGIES AND TACTICS IN NEGOTIATION

Broadly speaking, there have been two rather different kinds of attempt to find empirical instantiations of synthetic models. On the one hand, there have been attempts to classify the activities observed in real-life negotiations in terms of the tactical and strategic manoeuvres which form part of the synthetic models. On the other hand, there have been attempts to predict the outcomes of experimental negotiations by examining the process of negotiation and its preconditions, background factors and concurrent conditions. The first kind of activity has been something of a minority pursuit, with most attention paid to the work of Walton and McKersie (1965) and Snyder and Diesing (1977). The second kind of activity includes most, though not all, of the experimental studies of negotiation extant in the literature. The reader will find useful reviews of this material in Rubin and Brown, 1975; Druckman, 1977; Morley and Stephenson, 1977; Pruitt, 1981; Pruitt and Carnevale, 1993; and Kramer and Messick, 1995.

The various experimental tasks which have been used include matrix games (such as Prisoner's Dilemma and Chicken); distribution games, in which participants negotiate the division of a quantified scarce resource; games of economic exchange, in which participants take the roles of buyers and sellers; role-playing debates, in which participants learn the details of a particular dispute and then negotiate as if they were representing a party in that dispute; and substitute debates, in which an encounter which occurs in laboratory conditions is substituted for one which might have occurred elsewhere. It is still the case that the vast majority of experimental research has used matrix games or tasks in which negotiation is limited to little more than the exchange of bids.

The use of matrix games

There is a very large literature which examines repeated play in matrix games such as Prisoner's Dilemma and Chicken (excellently reviewed by Colman, 1982). One concern has been to explore the ways in which the strategy choices change, assuming that these changes simulate certain aspects of the process of real-life negotiations.

First, early research suggested that what happened depended on the fine details of play, so that outcomes could not be predicted in advance. It became clear that people who wanted to be co-operative in such games were often forced to compete when they met a competitive opponent. It was also suggested that those with a global disposition to be competitive had little insight into the effects their actions have on others (Kelly and Stahelski, 1970). This suggestion remains controversial (Colman, 1982). There is evidence that professional negotiators develop preferences for co-operative or competitive stances which reflect their personalities (Williams, 1993) as well as their beliefs about the social world (George, 1969; Snyder and Diesing, 1977; Lockhart, 1979). However, it seems likely that each type of person may make unfounded assumptions about the other when they meet in mixed pairs (Williams, 1993). One clear implication is that skilled negotiators need to consider the effects which their own actions may have on the actions of others.

Second, Axelrod (1984) has shown that certain general strategies – notably 'tit-for-tat' – seem fairly successful in a variety of contexts. This may be because people who adopt this strategy project an image of negotiators who are firm but fair (Pruitt and Carnevale, 1993).

Third, games with the same logical form may be presented to people in different ways, by 'decomposing' or 'separating' the matrix, leading to quite different outcomes (Hamburger, 1979; Colman, 1982). It may be thought that the results obtained from decomposed Prisoner's Dilemma games presage findings which suggest the importance of cognitive factors such as frames (Bazerman and Carroll, 1987).

The process of bid and counter-bid

Since the pioneering work of Siegel and Fouraker (1960) there have been many attempts to predict, and thereby explain, the process of bid and counter-bid. Much of the literature has been organised around five strategic options: concession-making; contending (competitive bargaining); problem-solving (co-operative bargaining); inaction; and withdrawal.

The most popular experimental task simulates a situation of bilateral monopoly in which there is integrative potential because there is more than one issue. Sometimes buyer A and seller B have to agree on the price-quantity combination at which a particular product will be traded. Sometimes there are several products, for which A and B agree a price for each, regardless of quantity. Sometimes there is a single product, but A and B agree prices for linked elements such as delivery time, discounts and finance. Typically, the buyer and seller have complete information about their own profits but none about those of their opponent.

Two features of the profit tables are important. First, A and B are able to offer a variety of possible contracts at a given level of profit. Two contracts which are of equal (or near equal) value to A may differ considerably in their value to B, and vice versa. Second, the profit tables contain some agreements which are Pareto optimal in the sense that they maximise the joint gain available to the participants. The most important finding from this research is that A and B often fail to find agreements which are referred to as Pareto optimal (Pruitt, 1981; Pruitt and Carnevale, 1993). This means that there is some other agreement which would give either A or B or both significant gains, at little or no cost to the other.

According to Pruitt and his associates, the main predictor of agreements which are Pareto optimal is that A and B each adopt a problem-solving strategy. One obvious possibility is that this will occur when A and B each exhibit high concern for their own outcomes and high concern for the other's outcomes. The model which specifies the factors which lead to this combination of motives is known as the dual concern model (Carnevale and Keenan, 1992). It has been used to integrate findings which deal with negotiators' assigned goals; with their relationship to their constituents; with the possibility of future interaction; and with the effects of mood. Some of the most important findings are that: factors which encourage systematic trial and error increase maximum joint profit (Pruitt, 1981; Carnevale and Isen, 1986); attempts to avoid conflict make this sort of trial and error less likely (Fry *et al.*, 1983); negotiators who have to please powerful constituents and who also have to please their opponents are more likely to adopt a problem-solving approach (Ben-Yoav and Pruitt, 1984a, 1984b).

This last point needs to be considered with care. In some cases, negotiators may only be free to adopt a problem-solving approach when they have first established an image of intransigence in competitive bargaining (Douglas, 1962; Snyder and Diesing, 1977). The dual concern model is not a complete model of problem-solving in bargaining.

Recent work has shown some of the ways in which bargaining is influenced by cognitive and social factors (Pruitt and Carnevale, 1993; Kramer and Messick, 1995). Much of the research is reminiscent of early work linking the study of bargaining to the study of relations between groups (see Morley and Stephenson, 1977). It has confirmed that negotiators often perceive conflict where none exists, so that agreements reached are not Pareto optimal. Attempts have also been made to relate cognitive aspects of negotiation to formal theories of decision-making. One such theory, called *prospect theory*, suggests that people are more concerned to minimise loss than maximise gain (Tversky and Kahneman, 1981). It leads to the prediction, confirmed by Bazerman *et al.* (1985), that negotiators are more likely to find integrative agreements when profit tables are framed in terms of gains rather than losses.

The social factors studied have included social norms and group processes. Consideration of the effects of social norms has led to a critique of Fisher and Ury's (1983) account of principled negotiation. Fisher and Ury urge negotiators to insist from the beginning that any agreements be based on norms of fairness. They also urge them to seek objective evidence to show that their claims are consistent with those norms. Whilst some see principled negotiation as part of a problem-solving strategy which offers an opportunity to make mutual gains, others see it as limited to special cases. The reader will find a useful summary of this debate in Johnson (1993) and Pruitt and Carnevale (1993).

The emphasis on group process has had two important effects. First, it has forced a recognition (long overdue) that differences within parties are just as important as differences between parties; that negotiations cycle through internal (within party) and external (between party) stages; and that internal negotiations may affect external negotiations, and vice versa. Second, it has led to a consideration of the effects of social decision schemes and issue agendas in multi-person negotiations. The main findings have been that majority rules and sequential agendas lead to compromise rather than integrative agreements (Thompson *et al.*, 1988; Mannix *et al.*, 1989; Bazerman *et al.*, 1990).

Evaluation

It would be naive to suppose that negotiators do not struggle to get their own way. Much can be learned by classifying communication into defensive strategies, offensive strategies and integrative strategies (Putnam and Jones, 1982). It would also be naive to suppose that the struggle does not involve strategic dilemmas of one kind or another. The major contribution of empirical research on the process of bid and counter-bid has been to show that negotiators often fail to reach agreements which are Pareto optimal because they fail to realise the effects of their own actions on the strategy of the other person, or because they do not grasp the underlying logical form of the problem. Nevertheless, attempts to extend this kind of model have only just begun to grapple with the complexities of real-life tasks, and have only just begun to locate them in the context of the social and historical relationship between the parties. For a more radical critique the reader is referred to Greenhalgh and Chapman (1995).

INFORMATION PROCESSING MODELS

So far, negotiation has been treated as an exercise in bargaining, dominated by strategic or tactical concerns. These concerns have come to the fore partly because most research has been laboratory research, utilising simple negotiation tasks. However, those tasks which use role-playing games, or those which bring real-life disputes into the laboratory (see Morley and Stephenson, 1977), introduce some of the complexities found in actual cases (see Warr, 1973; Chalmers, 1974; Snyder and Diesing, 1977; Friedman and Meredeen, 1980; Meredeen, 1988; Morley, 1992).

Complexity may be created because negotiators have to process a great deal of information or because negotiators have to make decisions under uncertainty (Winham, 1977; Midgaard and Underdal, 1977; Morley, 1982). This makes it difficult for negotiators to understand the issues and to establish that the policies they propose are practical ways of handling them. They may also find that their capacities to process information are insufficient to cope with the demands of the task. In such cases it seems likely that questions of strategy – how to outwit an opponent – will be subordinated to questions of structure – how to find a definition of the problem that compels assent (Winham, 1977; Winham and Bovis, 1978).

Making sense of change

To make sense of change, negotiators must organise a collective process in which they identify issues, develop solutions, choose between alternatives and implement policies (Hosking and Morley, 1991). There is evidence that more-skilled and less-skilled negotiators structure these processes in different ways.

Let us suppose that some change in existing circumstances has created a situation in which A must confront B. A and B must plan suitable responses. Furthermore, they must plan those responses in contexts which are ambiguous and cannot be completely described. This means that negotiators interpret changes in the status quo in terms of more or less well-organised systems of attitudes, values and beliefs, and pass on those interpretations to others, in summary form (George, 1969; Holsti, 1970; Jervis, 1970, 1976; Marengo, 1979). Such construct systems allow negotiators to identify threats and opportunities and to work out what to do about them (Hosking and Morley, 1991).

What is important is that, through the experience of negotiation, skilled negotiators have been able to build up more or less systematically organised knowledge of the negotiation task and how to work in it. This means that they have schooled and highly specific ways of perceiving and are able to see relatively quickly what other people may never see at all. Thus, the skilled negotiator is a skilled perceiver.

There are good reasons to believe that learning about the world requires people to use organised systems of belief to anticipate the future and to explain the past. However, if they are not to see only what they expect to see they must also be sensitive to new information. There is a dialectical contradiction between these two requirements (Neisser, 1976) which means that some negotiators find it extremely difficult to learn from the process of negotiation (Snyder and Diesing, 1977). Early research located the problems in the structure of the belief systems (Holsti, 1970; Jervis, 1970). Later research has implicated a wide range of cognitive, social and contextual factors (Hosking and Morley, 1991; Kramer and Messick, 1995).

According to Snyder and Diesing (1977), negotiators will always disagree about how to describe events, and how they contributed to the development of social settings (also see Friedman and Meredeen, 1980). They will maintain general images of their opponents which are not likely to change. However, a combination of cognitive, social and contextual conditions combine to produce two kinds of activity, which Snyder and Diesing have articulated in terms of a 'rational bargaining module' and an 'irrational bargaining module'.

Two features of the rational bargaining module are important in the present context. First, Snyder and Diesing found that rational bargainers had low confidence in their initial diagnoses of what had happened, and why. They used the process of bargaining to test hypotheses: to root out ideas which were plausible, but false or incomplete. Second, they initiated an active search for information to find out which aspects of others' positions were flexible, and to what extent. (Presumably using both verbal and non-verbal cues. See Walton and McKersie, 1965; Miron and Goldstein, 1979.)

Matching capacities to demands

Much of the early work in cognitive psychology was intended to establish which features of our cognitive systems limited our ability to process information. One clear implication of this work is that effective performers find ways of working that allow them to match their intellectual capacities to the information-processing demands of the task (Welford, 1980). A second implication is that those who are effective performers in social domains recognise the processing problems faced by other people. As a result, they use a variety of techniques designed to reduce ambiguity, clarify communications and slow things down.

Methods of behaviour analysis have been used to identify some of the ways in which effective negotiators tailor their performances to help their opponents to deal with the information-processing demands of the negotiation task (e.g. Rackham and Carlisle, 1978). Effective negotiators recognise that social actions are inherently ambiguous. Consequently, unless special care is taken, it is all too easy for people to see only what they want to see. So, effective negotiators take pains to label their actions, making frequent use of verbal forms such as, 'May I ask you a *question*?', 'If I could make a *suggestion . . .*', and so on. They are significantly more likely than average negotiators to *test understandings* often by *summarising* what has been said.

Much of the work which has contributed to the Harvard Program on Negotiation fits within the framework of matching capacities to demands (see Fisher and Ury, 1983; Fisher and Brown, 1988; Hall, 1993). This is one reason why those within the programme have often emphasised that the cheapest concession which can be made is to show that you are actively listening to what is being said. There are actually two sides to this. First, it is important to be able to see the negotiation as others see it because, if you want to influence them, it is important to see the appeal *for them* of *their* point of view. Second, it is important to communicate that understanding to members of the other side. Otherwise, when you try to say something they will not be listening. They will, instead, be using their limited processing capacity to complete a different task. To be specific, they will be considering how to rephrase their argument so that this time you will understand it. For similar reasons, a good rule seems to be: 'Present your proposals as solutions to problems. State the problem before you give your answer.' If you begin with your own proposal you may find that the other side will stop paying attention. They will not be listening to what you have to say. Instead, they will devote their mental resources to the task of working out their own responses (Fisher and Ury, 1983).

Evaluation

Information-processing approaches give negotiators the respect they are due as intelligent social actors. They force us to consider aspects of complexity in negotiation which other theories ignore. They show that skilled negotiators are skilled perceivers. Negotiators have well-organised and well-schooled systems of evaluative beliefs which allow them quickly to see what less skilled negotiators may never see at all. They avoid the problem that they may see only what they expect to see by making active attempts to root out ideas which are plausible, but false or incomplete. Studies which have compared the performance of effective and less effective negotiators, using techniques of behaviour analysis, are consistent with Welford's theory that skill is the use of effective strategies which match the capacities of performers to the demands of their task (see Chapters 1 and 2). The best of the 'how to negotiate' texts include practical advice which follows from the application of information-processing perspectives.

THE CHARACTERISTICS OF EFFECTIVE NEGOTIATORS

It is commonplace to find that those who write about the psychology of negotiation include checklists of negotiation skills. Much of the literature is anecdotal, but some is based on questionnaire studies asking experienced negotiators to identify the personal characteristics which make negotiators effective.

Studies of this kind need to be interpreted with care. Some do little more than reflect some of the central characteristics of the negotiation task (Morley, 1981). It is also likely that characteristics deemed unimportant in one context may be deemed important in others (Karrass, 1970; Raiffa, 1982). But the most important limitation is that almost none of the studies simultaneously consider the characteristics of average or effective negotiators.

One important exception is Williams (1993). His sample is limited to legal attorneys, but is important for several reasons. First, he used Q-sort – a statistical technique designed to identify behaviour highly characteristic of a person – to identify a number of distinct approaches to negotiation, each producing some effective, some average and some ineffective negotiators. The main contrast was between co-operative and competitive approaches. The main objectives of the co-operative negotiators were to act ethically, to get the best settlement for their client and to get a fair settlement. The main objectives of the competitive negotiators were to get the best settlement for their clients, to make a profit for themselves and to outdo or outwit their opponents. Second, It was possible within these sub-groups to identify the personal characteristics associated with effective, average and ineffective negotiators. Third, Williams was able persuasively to suggest that the two kinds of negotiators do not understand one another because they have quite different ideologies. One is problem-solving; the other is aggressive.

Williams' studies showed that effective legal negotiators had some traits in common, regardless of their preference for a co-operative or competitive stance. They were prepared on the facts, prepared on the law and self-controlled (also see Karrass, 1970; Raiffa, 1982). They observed the manners of the Bar, took satisfaction in using legal skills and were effective trial attorneys. In contrast, there were no such personal characteristics shared by ineffective negotiators, regardless of stance.

The co-operative negotiators had some traits in common, regardless of their level of effectiveness. They were all seen as trustworthy, ethical, fair, courteous, personable, tactful and sincere. The effective negotiators within the co-operative group were seen as fair minded, with realistic opening positions. They did not use threats, were willing to share information, and actively explored their opponents' positions. In contrast, ineffective negotiators within the co-operative group were seen as trustful, gentle, obliging, patient, forgiving, intelligent, dignified and self-controlled.

In some ways, the contrast between effective and ineffective negotiators is even more marked when negotiators are competitive. The effective negotiators were dominant, forceful and attacking. Their strategy was simple: to push their opponents as far as they would go. To do this they were willing to stretch the facts, take unrealistic opening positions and withhold information. The effective negotiators were seen as irritating, argumentative, quarrelsome, aggressive, rigid, egotistical, headstrong, arrogant, intolerant and hostile. They had not learned to cope with the negative side of efficiency (see Morley, 1981).

According to Williams, the combination of co-operator and competitor causes the majority of the psychological problems in negotiation. This is too strong a claim, but there is little doubt that each may misinterpret the intentions and actions of the other.

Williams has shown that both strategies can be effective. He argues that skilled negotiators should be able to use both. This is important if negotiations cycle through competitive and collaborative stages, and if the difference between the stages is more marked in those negotiations which end in success (see Stephenson, 1981). It seems likely that ineffective negotiators will find it extremely difficult to switch from one stance to the other as the situation demands.

Evaluation

Questionnaire studies of the personal characteristics of effective negotiators have to be treated with care (Morley, 1981). Nevertheless, studies such as those of Raiffa (1982) and Williams (1993) suggest that there is much more to negotiation than a process of bid and counter-bid. The top five characteristics reported by Raiffa (1982) were, in order of importance: preparation and planning skill; knowledge of the relevant subject matter; ability to think quickly and clearly despite pressure and uncertainty; ability to express thoughts verbally; and listening skill. Williams' evidence suggests that there is no one ideal negotiation style, but that skilled negotiators need to be able to switch from a competitive to co-operative stance as the situation demands. Williams' work has also helped to increase our understanding of the dynamics which occur when someone with a co-operative stance negotiates against someone with a competitive stance.

DISCURSIVE MODELS

It has been argued that, as negotiations become more complex, there needs to be a shift from a concern with strategy and tactics to a concern with messages and meanings (Putnam, 1985); a shift from talk about manipulation to talk about what makes sense in particular historical contexts (Hosking and Morley, 1991).

Negotiation is used to manage change. It is a process in which people meet to define the terms of their relationship, or that of reference groups they represent. They are concerned to establish whether certain changes are possible and, if so, at what cost. The outcome of their deliberations is a set of rules, defining the terms on which the persons, or parties, will do business in the future. This is why negotiators have been described as writing social history (Morley, 1986; Morley *et al.*, 1988).

The writing part of the metaphor is used to remind us that negotiations are conducted in the context of existing rules, and that the effect of an agreement is to change those rules. The social part of the metaphor is used to make the point that, in formal negotiation, the changes have to be explained to other people and accepted by them. This is why one of the major tasks of negotiation is to find a formula, linking what is happening now to what has happened in the past and to what will happen in the future (Zartman, 1977). The formula provides a rationale showing that people have developed lines of action which make sense in particular social and historical contexts (Harré, 1979; Morley, 1992). Without such a rationale negotiation is likely to be prolonged, or to break down. Unless the rationale is accepted by those not at the negotiation table the rules will be broken when attempts are made to put the agreements into effect.

The language-action approach which is set out below considers negotiation as a form of reflective social action which functions to create social settings (Sarason, 1972; Tsoukas, 1994). It is an attempt to contribute to the emerging body of work in discursive psychology (e.g. Harré and Gillett, 1994; Harré and Stearns, 1995) which examines the social construction of cognition. It is called discursive psychology because it suggests that cognitions are constructed in conversations guided by the interpretive schemes of particular social groups (Hosking and Morley, 1991).

One way of introducing discursive psychology is to begin with three axioms: the ambiguity axiom, the reference group action, and the incompleteness axiom (Morley and Ormerod, 1966). The ambiguity axiom states that social actions are inherently ambiguous and require interpretation (see Bennett and Feldman, 1981). The reference group axiom states that such interpretation is partisan and made from a particular point of view, according to the interpretive practices of particular social groups (Hosking and Morley, 1991). The incompleteness axiom states that interpretations are always passed on to others in summary form (Dunsire, 1978).

Taken together, these axioms imply that negotiators face two main kinds of problem. The first is cognitive. Negotiators have to describe change, or the possibility of change, and reach a working consensus, within each party, that the changes are changes of a certain kind. The second is political. Negotiators with different levels of investment in the issues, with different sources of power and with different levels of skill have to forge commitments based on those descriptions, and show that they make sense. This means that negotiators will attempt to find arguments which make sense of what they are doing and disseminate them to others. It is no accident that successful teams send more information to members of their reference groups, and take greater pains to put that information in an appropriate context (Winham and Bovis, 1978).

This kind of analysis raises two further considerations. First, internal negotiations (within groups) involve the same kinds of process as external negotiations (between groups). Second, negotiation is a form of joint decision-making. What is negotiated is the identification of issues, the development of solutions, the choice between alternatives and the implementation of policies. Morley has argued that the organisation of such internal and external negotiations depends upon the knowledge and experience of the negotiators on the skills with which they build social networks and on the skills of those who lead the negotiation teams (Morley, 1981, 1986, 1992).

The central idea is that skilful negotiators are better able to organise the process of negotiation to deal with the cognitive and political aspects of their decision-making task. It is also argued that the cognitive and political aspects of the negotiation task lead to dilemmas in internal and external negotiations. Furthermore, the way in which the dilemmas are handled will have a major impact on the process of negotiation and on the ways in which agreements are shaped. Each of these elements will be considered in turn.

The knowledge base

Some aspects of this knowledge base have been discussed previously (p. 346–8). Other important aspects of the knowledge base may be described as technical information and political information.

The importance of technical information is rarely discussed in texts dealing with psychological aspects of negotiation. One exception is Marsh (1974), who treated the topic at some length in his discussion of leadership in contract negotiations. In his view, team leaders should not be selected because they are the technical expert on a problem, since professional expertise is not enough. It is also important that they are suitable for the negotiation in question, having an understanding of both the process of negotiation and the dynamics of power in use in a particular social setting (see Morgan, 1986).

Negotiators need to obtain at least two kinds of political information. The first is information about existing stakes in the issues. The second is information about the needs of others who may be affected by the current negotiation, but who are not directly engaged in it. Without such information any attempt at change is unlikely to succeed.

Building social networks

Kanter (1984) has argued that the basic commodities of organisational power are the abilities to build relationships based on the exchange of information, resources and support. This implies that those negotiators who put more effort into building relationships with other people are more likely to be successful, although much of the literature emphasises the size of the network rather than the quality of relationships with focal persons (Hosking and Morley, 1991).

There are two aspects to this. It is important to be in contact with a sufficient number of people to triangulate the different points of view of those people close to the action because this is how to gain authentic information. At the same time, one reason why some people are more influential than others is that they are linked into networks of relationships through which arguments may be tested or promoted (Huff, 1984; Batstone *et al.*, 1978). Thus, networking serves two functions: that of collecting organisational intelligence and that of building commitments to particular lines of action.

Negotiators may sometimes develop close bargaining relationships with members of opposing teams (Brown, 1973; Batstone *et al.*, 1977; Batstone, 1979). There is an exchange of information which gives participants increased understanding of what is happening, what is likely to happen, and why. It is this understanding which makes them credible as negotiators. It means that agreements reached are more likely to stick because they are realistic politically, or otherwise make sense. There may also be an exchange of support in the sense that each helps the other to work out how goals can be achieved and legitimised in terms of previous agreements, or rules of custom and practice.

The skills of leadership

Case studies show that many problems arise when teams lack an experienced leader, able to cope with the cognitive and political aspects of the negotiation task (Hosking and Morley, 1991). Negotiation, whether internal or external, needs to be properly organised. Leaders have a clear responsibility to organise a process in which participants build shared interpretations of what is going on (and why) and of what can be negotiated (and how, and when) (Morley, 1992).

Cognitive and political aspects of the negotiation task

Processes which are cognitive help negotiators to organise their intellectual activity and think clearly about the issues. Processes which are political function to manage differences between the parties. Morley (1986) has suggested that skilful negotiators remove unnecessary cognitive obstacles to agreement and thus make negotiation no harder than it need be. In some cases, the solution is to slow things down. In other cases, it is to locate events explicitly in the context of what has gone before. At the same time, skilful negotiators are not afraid to disagree. There is evidence that less skilful negotiators are more concerned to reach an agreement – any agreement – than to reach the right agreement (Rackham and Carlisle, 1978). Effective negotiators realise that premature agreement may mean that the issues have not been properly understood (Drucker, 1970). In addition, a long period of struggle may be necessary before negotiators look beyond ready-made solutions and find those which are Pareto optimal (Douglas, 1962; Morley and Stephenson, 1977; Pruitt, 1981).

It is important, however, that cognitive and political concerns are integrated so that tactics are seen to follow naturally from the bargaining process as it unfolds (Brandt, 1972). It is possible, for example, to slow negotiation down to the point where one is seen not to be negotiating at all (Warr, 1973). This may lead to a hardening of attitudes and a breakdown of negotiation. For further discussion the reader is referred to Hosking and Morley (1991) and Morley (1992).

Dilemmas in the process of negotiation

Dilemmas arise when negotiators search for acceptable ways of handling issues. The first to be identified were dilemmas to do with strategy and tactics (Walton and McKersie, 1965; Pruitt, 1971). Later, it became clear that there were many other dilemmas concerned with negotiation as a form of joint decision-making (Warr, 1973; Morley, 1992). Warr has identified two dilemmas which are central in the process of internal negotiation. The first raises issues of the most appropriate social decision scheme, given a distribution of opinion within the group: unanimity is hard to achieve, but majority rule is not without problems (Bazerman *et al.*, 1990). The second, whether to adopt a leader or delegate role, sets the need for strong leadership against the need for members to participate in decision-making (Hartley *et al.*, 1983).

Friend and Hickling (1987) have provided an elegant and informative treatment of dilemmas in decision-making (which they describe as judgements of balance in strategic choice). Given that negotiation is a form of joint decision-making, negotiators may be seen to make judgements of the following kinds: the treatment of scope may be more focused or more synoptic; the treatment of complexity may be more simplifying or more elaborating; the treatment of conflict may be more reactive or more interactive; the treatment of uncertainty may be more reducing or more accommodating; and the treatment of progress may be more exploratory or more decisive. A careful reading of case studies of negotiation will reveal examples of each kind of dilemma and illustrate some of the ways in which they shaped the process and outcomes concerned (see, for example, Elcock, 1972; Warr, 1973; Morley, 1982, 1992; Hosking and Morley, 1991; Meredeen, 1988).

One example, taken from Morley (1992), may illustrate the power of the analysis. It concerns the treatment of progress. The dilemma arises because internal and external negotiations may be seen as the planning and action stages of a single process (Marsh, 1974; Morley, 1982). The balance of strategic judgement is between: (1) a view of an ideal planning process as one in which people become increasingly committed to plans as they narrow the options from broad lines of development to specific proposals (see Levin, 1976); and (2) a recognition that it may be costly to delay too long because it may allow other people to articulate their own definitions of the situation and seek support for partisan positions, perhaps narrowly defined (see Huff, 1984). There is a clear example of a failure to make a balanced strategic judgement of this kind in the pay and productivity negotiations described by Warr (1973).

Evaluation

Pruitt and Carnevale (1993) have been generous enough to suggest that the language-action perspective may eventually lead to a fundamental shift in the way we think about negotiation. Certainly, it draws attention to aspects of negotiation which are not given sufficient attention in other models. One aspect concerns the shift from talk about strategy and tactics to talk about messages and meanings; a second aspect concerns the metaphor that negotiators write social history; a third aspect concerns the axioms which underlie a discursive psychology; a fourth aspect concerns negotiation considered as a form of joint decision-making. In this enterprise considerable attention is paid to the kind of knowledge negotiators need; to the activities of networking; and to the skills of leadership. Overall, the effect is to insist that studies of the skills of negotiation need to locate negotiation in its socio-historical context.

OVERVIEW

Each of the models set out above has its strengths and weaknesses, and has direct implications for the study of negotiation skill. Two general messages stand out. The first is that negotiation is a struggle. Skilled negotiators are not afraid to disagree: they are interested in reaching the right agreement, rather than any agreement. At the same time, skilful negotiators remove unnecessary obstacles to agreement by slowing things down, or by taking care to locate events in the context of what has gone before. They know when to compromise and when to stand firm. They recognise that some kinds of compromise are worse than useless in the long run. Agreements reached must be compatible with each side's power in use. They will not be viable otherwise, and may therefore do little except generate misunderstanding and ill will (Morris, 1973).

An adequate social psychological account of the skills of negotiation requires four main components: a model of the negotiators; a model of the parties to the negotiation; a model of the process of negotiation; and a model of the larger social context. The research and theory summarised in this chapter shows what progress has been made on each of these endeavours. The discursive approach is clearly the most general, and seems most likely to provide a general framework which will build on what has gone before.

REFERENCES

Axelrod, R. (1984) *The Evolution of Cooperation*, Basic Books, New York.

Bacharach, S. B. and Lawler, E. J. (1981) *Bargaining: Power, Tactics, and Outcomes*, Jossey-Bass, San Francisco.

Bartlett, F. C. (1932) *Remembering: A Study in Experimental and Social Psychology*, Cambridge University Press, Cambridge.

Batstone, E. (1979) 'The Organization of Conflict', in G. M. Stephenson and C. J. Brotherton (eds), *Industrial Relations: A Social Psychological Approach*, John Wiley, Chichester.

——, Boraston, I. and Frenkel, S. (1977) *Shop Stewards in Action*, Basil Blackwell, Oxford.

—— (1978) *The Social Organization of Strikes*, Blackwell, Oxford.

Bazerman, M. H. and Carroll, J. S. (1987) 'Negotiator Cognition', in B. M. Staw and L. L. Cummings (eds), *Research in Organizational Behaviour, Vol. 9*, JAI Press, Greenwich, CT.

Bazerman, M. H., Magliozzi, T. and Neale, M. A. (1985) 'Integrative Bargaining in a Competitive Market', *Organizational Behavior and Human Decision Processes*, 35, 294–313.

Bazerman, M. H., Mannix, E. A., Sondak, H. and Thompson, L. (1990) 'Negotiator Behavior and Decision Processes in Dyads, Groups, and Markets', in J. S. Carroll (ed.), *Applied Social Psychology in Organizational Settings*, Lawrence Erlbaum Associates, Hillsdale, NJ.

Bennett, W. L. and Feldman, M. S. (1981) *Reconstructing Reality in the Courtroom*, Tavistock, London.

Ben-Yoav, O. and Pruitt, D. G. (1984a) 'Accountability to Constituents: A Two-edged Sword', *Organizational Behavior and Human Performance*, 34, 283–95.

—— (1984b) 'Resistance to Yielding and the Expectation of Cooperative Future Interaction in Negotiation', *Journal of Experimental Social Psychology*, 34, 323–35.

Braithwaite, R. B. (1955) *Theory of Games as a Tool for the Moral Philosopher*, Cambridge University Press, Cambridge.

Brandt, F. S. (1972) *The Process of Negotiation: Strategy and Tactics in Industrial Relations*, Industrial and Commercial Techniques, London.

Brown, W. (1973) *Piecework Bargaining*, Heinemann, London.

Carnevale, P. J. and Isen, A. M. (1986) 'The Influence of Positive Affect and Visual Access on the Discovery of Integrative Solutions in Bilateral Negotiation', *Organizational Behavior and Human Decision Processes*, 37, 1–13.

Carnevale, P. J. and Keenan, P. A. (1992) 'The Resolution of Conflict: Negotiation and Third Party Intervention', in J. Hartley and G. M. Stephenson (eds), *Employment Relations: The Psychology of Influence and Control at Work*, Basil Blackwell, Oxford.

Chalmers, W. E. (1974) *Racial Negotiations: Potentials and Limitations*, Institute of Labor and Industrial Relations, The University of Michigan – Wayne State University, Ann Arbor.

Chamberlain, N. W. and Kuhn, J. W. (1986) *Collective Bargaining* (3rd edn), McGraw-Hill, New York.

Coddington, A. (1968) *Theories of the Bargaining Process*, London, George Allen & Unwin Ltd.

Colman, A. (1982) *Game Theory and Experimental Games: The Study of Strategic Interaction*, Pergamon Press, Oxford.

Davey, H. W. (1972) *Contemporary Collective Bargaining* (3rd edn), Prentice-Hall, Englewood Cliffs, NJ.

Douglas, A. (1962) *Industrial Peacemaking*, Columbia University Press, New York.

Drucker, P. (1970) *The Effective Executive*, Pan Business Management, London.

Druckman, D. (ed.)(1977) *Negotiations: Social Psychological Perspectives*, Sage, Beverly Hills.

Dunsire, A. (1978) *The Execution Process Volume 1: Implementation in a Bureaucracy*, Martin Robertson, London.

Elcock, H. (1972) *Portrait of a Decision: The Council of Four and the Treaty of Versailles*, Methuen, London.

Fisher, R. and Brown, S. (1988) *Getting Together: Building a Relationship that Gets to YES*, Houghton Mifflin, Boston.

Fisher, R. and Ury, W. (1983) *Getting To YES: Negotiating Agreement Without Giving In*, Houghton Mifflin, Boston.

Friedman, H. and Meredeen, S. (1980) *The Dynamics of Industrial Conflict*, Croom Helm, London.

Friend, J. K. and Hickling, A. (1987) *Planning Under Pressure: The Strategic Choice Approach*, Pergamon Press, Oxford.

Fry, W. R., Firestone, I. J. and Williams, D. L. (1983) 'Negotiation Process and Outcome of Stranger Dyads and Dating Couples: Do Lovers Lose?', *Basic and Applied Psychology*, 4, 1–16.

George, A. L. (1969) 'The Operational Code: A Neglected Approach to the Study of Political Leaders and Decision-making', *International Studies Quarterly*, 13, 190–222.

Greenhalgh, L. and Chapman, D. I. (1995) 'Joint Decision Making: the Inseparability of Relationships and Negotiation', in R. M. Kramer and D. M. Messick (eds), *Negotiation as a Social Process*, Sage, Thousand Oaks.

Hall, L. (ed.)(1993) *Negotiation: Strategies for Mutual Gain: The Basic Seminar of the Harvard Program on Negotiation*, Sage, Newbury Park.

Hamburger, H. (1979) *Games as Models of Social Phenomena*, W.H. Freeman and Co, San Francisco.

Harré, R. M. (1979) *Social Being: A Theory for Social Psychology*, Blackwell, Oxford.

—— and Gillett, G. (1994) *The Discursive Mind*, Sage, Thousand Oaks.

Harré, R. M. and Stearns, P. (eds)(1995) *Discursive Psychology in Practice*, Sage, London.

Hartley, J., Kelly, J. and Nicholson, N. (1983) *Steel Strike*, Batsford, London.

Holsti, O. (1970) 'The "Operational Code" Approach to the Study of Political Leaders. John Foster Dulles: Philosophical and Instrumental Beliefs', *Canadian Journal of Political Science*, 3, 123–57.

Hosking, D.-M. and Morley, I. E. (1991) *A Social Psychology of Organizing: People, Processes, and Contexts*, Harvester Wheatsheaf, London.

Huff, A. S. (1984) 'Situation Interpretation, Leader Behaviour, and Effectiveness', in J. G. Hunt, D.-M. Hosking, C. A. Schriesheim and R. Stewart (eds), *Leaders and Managers: International Perspectives on Managerial Behaviour and Leadership*, Pergamon Press, Oxford.

Iklé, F. C. (1964) *How Nations Negotiate*, Praeger, New York.

Jervis, R. (1970) *The Logic of Images in International Relations*, Princeton University Press, Princeton.

—— (1976) *Perception and Misperception in International Politics*, Princeton University Press, Princeton.

Johnson, R. A. (1993) *Negotiation Basics: Concepts, Skills, and Exercises*, Sage, Newbury Park.

Kanter, R. M. (1984) *The Change Masters: Corporate Entrepreneurs at Work*, George Allen & Unwin, London.

Karrass, C. L. (1970) *The Negotiating Game*, Thomas Y. Crowell Company, New York.

Kelly, H. H. and Stahelski, A. (1970) 'Social Interaction Basis of Cooperators' and Competitors' Beliefs About Others', *Journal of Personality and Social Psychology*, 16, 190–7.

Kochan, T. A. (1980) *Collective Bargaining and Industrial Relations: From Theory to Practice*, Irwin, Homewood, Illinois.

Kramer, R. M. and Messick, D. M. (eds)(1995) *Negotiation as a Social Process*, Sage, Thousand Oaks.

Levin, P. H. (1976) *Government and the Planning Process*, George Allen & Unwin, London.

Lockhart, C. (1979) *Bargaining in International Conflicts*, Columbia University Press, New York.

Mannix, E. A., Thompson, L. L. and Bazerman, M. H. (1989) 'Negotiation in Small Groups', *Journal of Applied Psychology*, 74, 508–17.

Marengo, F. D. (1979) *The Code of British Trade Union Behaviour*, Saxon House, London.

Marsh, P. D. V. (1974) *Contract Negotiation Handbook*, Gower Press, Epping.

Meredeen, S. (1988) *Managing Industrial Conflict: Seven Major Disputes*, Hutchinson, London.

Midgaard, K. and Underdal, A. (1977) 'Multiparty Conferences', in D. Druckman (ed.), *Negotiations: Social-Psychological Perspectives*, Sage, Beverly Hills.

Miller, D. T. and Holmes, J. G. (1975) 'The Role of Situational Restrictiveness on Self-fulfilling Prophecies: A Theoretical and Empirical Extension of Kelley and Stahelski's Triangle Hypothesis', *Journal of Personality and Social Psychology*, 31, 661–73.

Miron, M. S. and Goldstein, A. P. (1979) *Hostage*, Pergamon Press, Oxford.

Morgan, G. (1986) *Images of Organization*, Sage, Beverly Hills.

Morgenstern, O. (1949) 'The Theory of Games', *Scientific American*, May, 86–9.

Morley, I. E. (1981) 'Negotiation and Bargaining', in M. Argyle (ed.), *Social Skills and Work*, Methuen, London.

—— (1982) 'Preparation for Negotiation: Conflict, Commitment, and Choice', in H. Brandstätter, J. H. Davis and G. Stocker-Kreichgauer (eds), *Group Decision Making*, Academic Press, New York.

—— (1986) 'Negotiating and Bargaining', in O. Hargie (ed.), *A Handbook of Communication Skills*, Croom Helm, London.

—— (1992) 'Intra-organizational Bargaining', in J. Hartley and G. M. Stephenson (eds), *Employment Relations: The Psychology of Influence and Control at Work*, Basil Blackwell, Oxford.

—— and Ormerod, R. (1996) 'A Language-action Approach to Operational Research', *Journal of the Operational Research Society*, 47, 731–40.

Morley, I. E. and Stephenson, G. M. (1977) *The Social Psychology of Bargaining*, George Allen & Unwin, London.

Morley, I. E., Webb, J. and Stephenson, G. M. (1988) 'Bargaining and Arbitration in the Resolution of Conflict', in W. Stroebe, A. W. Kruglanski, D. Bar-Tal and M. Hewstone (eds), *The Social Psychology of Intergroup Conflict*, Springer-Verlag, Berlin.

Morris, E. (1973) *Blockade: Berlin and the Cold War*, Hamish Hamilton, London.

Nash, J. F. (1950) 'The Bargaining Problem', *Econometrica*, 18, 155–62.

Neisser, U. (1976) *Cognition and Reality: Principles and Implications of Cognitive Psychology*, Freeman, San Francisco.

Polzer, J. T., Mannix, E. E. and Neale, M. A. (1995) 'Multiparty Negotiation in its Social Context', in R. M. Kramer and D. M. Messick (eds), *Negotiation as a Social Process*, Sage, Thousand Oaks.

Poundstone, W. (1992) *Prisoner's Dilemma*, Doubleday, New York.

Pruitt, D. G. (1971) 'Indirect Communication and the Search for Agreement in Negotiation', *Journal of Applied Social Psychology*, 1, 205–39.

—— (1981) *Negotiation Behavior*, Academic Press, New York.

—— and Carnevale, P. J. (1993) *Negotiation in Social Conflict*, Open University Press, Milton Keynes.

Putnam, L. L. (1985) 'Collective Bargaining as Organizational Communication', in P.K. Tomkins and R. McPhee (eds), *Organizational Communication: Traditional Themes and New Directions*, Sage, Beverly Hills.

—— and Geist, P. (1985) 'Argument in Bargaining: An Analysis of the Reasoning Process', *The Southern Speech Communication Journal*, 50, 225–45.

Putnam, L. L. and Jones, T. S. (1982) 'Reciprocity in Negotiations: An Analysis of Bargaining Interaction', *Communication Monographs*, 49, 171–91.

Rackham, N. and Carlisle, J. (1978) 'The Effective Negotiator – Part 1. The Behaviour of Successful Negotiators', *Journal of European Industrial Training*, 2(6), 6–10.

Raiffa, H. (1982) *The Art and Science of Negotiation*, Harvard University Press, Cambridge, MA.

Rubin, J. Z. and Brown, B. (1975) *The Social Psychology of Bargaining and Negotiations*, Academic Press, New York.

Sarason, S. B. (1972) *The Creation of Social Settings and Future Societies*, Jossey-Bass, San Francisco.

Siegel, S. and Fouraker, L. E. (1960) *Bargaining and Group Decision Making*, McGraw-Hill, New York.

Snyder, G. H. and Diesing, P. (1977) *Conflict Among Nations: Bargaining, Decision Making, and System Structure in International Crises*, Princeton University Press, Princeton, NJ.

Stephenson, G. M. (1981) 'Intergroup Bargaining and Negotiation', in J. C. Turner and H. Giles (eds), *Intergroup Behaviour*, Basil Blackwell, Oxford.

Thompson, L. L., Mannix, E. A. and Bazerman, M. H. (1988) 'Group Negotiation: Effects of Decision Rule, Agenda, and Aspiration', *Journal of Personality and Social Psychology*, 54, 86–9.

Tsoukas, H. (1994) 'Introduction: from Social Engineering to Reflective Action in Organizational Behaviour', in H. Tsoukas (ed.) *New Thinking in Organizational Behaviour*, Butterworth-Heinemann, Oxford.

Tversky, A. and Kahneman, D. (1981) 'The Framing of Decisions and the Rationality of Choice', *Science*, 211, 453–8.

Walton, R. E. and McKersie, R. B. (1965) *A Behavioral Theory of Labor Negotiations: An Analysis of a Social Interaction System*, McGraw-Hill, New York.

Warr, P. B. (1973) *Psychology and Collective Bargaining*, Hutchinson, London.

Weintraub, E. R. (ed.)(1992) *Toward a History of Game Theory*, Duke University Press, Durham.

Welford, A. T. (1980) 'The Concept of Social Skill and its Application to Social Performance', in W. T. Singleton, P. Spurgeon and R. Stammers (eds), *The Analysis of Social Skill*, Plenum Press, London.

Williams, G. R. (1993). 'Style and Effectiveness in Negotiation', in L. Hall (ed.), *Negotiation: Strategies for Mutual Gain: The Basic Seminar of the Harvard Program on Negotiation*, Sage, Newbury Park.

Winham, G. R. (1977) 'Complexity in International Negotiation', in D. Druckman (ed.), *Negotiations: Social-Psychological Perspectives*, Sage, Beverly Hills.

—— and Bovis, H. E. (1978) 'Agreement and Breakdown in Negotiation: Report on a State Department Training Simulation', *Journal of Peace Research*, 15, 285–303.

Zartman, I. W. (1977) 'Negotiation as a Joint Decision-making Process', in I. W. Zartman (ed.), *The Negotiation Process: Theories and Applications*, Sage, Beverly Hills.

14 Relational communication

Colin T. C. Hargie and Dennis Tourish

INTRODUCTION

The central role of relationships in our lives is becoming increasingly, and sometimes surprisingly, apparent. Relationships help to define our sense of who and what we are, and in so doing intrude into every aspect of what makes us both fully individuated and intensely social beings. Thus, the presence of close confidants helps to ward off depression (Brown and Harris, 1978), a variety of clinical problems (O'Connor and Brown, 1984) and physical ailments (Reis, 1984). Being married, for men, has been correlated with lower levels of suicide and better health (Kurdek, 1991). The availability of social support in the form of relationships has also been associated with general mental health (Wethington and Kessler, 1986), good immune function (Jemmott and Magliore, 1988) and reduced mortality rates (Blazer, 1982). Longitudinal studies support the notion that patterns of communication experienced between infants and parents have a profound impact on the later development of adult personality and behaviour (Shaver and Hazan, 1994). Freedman (1978) found that when people were asked what made them most happy close relationships came ahead of work, leisure, money or even health.

There is also growing evidence to suggest that the importance of relationships in the work context have often been under-estimated. One review (Argyle, 1987) suggested that the quality of relationships at work is the single biggest determinant of job satisfaction, outstripping security of employment, pay and the intrinsic value we attach to the task itself. From a different perspective, Hutton (1995) argued that a failure to promote positive relationships within the work place, founded on mutual trust, is a key factor in the systemic weakness of the British economy! It is little wonder that when relationships go wrong they have an extraordinary power to stimulate depression, low self-regard and a feeling of incompetence in other areas of our lives. Likewise, not disclosing to others when we have experienced traumatic events has been associated with increased physical illness and mental distress (Pennebaker *et al.*, 1988). Therefore, it can be concluded that overall levels of physical and emotional health are correlated with membership of various social networks (Duck, 1992) and it is important to develop a wide repertoire of communication skills to enhance our effectiveness in such contexts.

Accordingly, this chapter explores the communication issues which arise during the initiation, maintenance and dissolution of relationships, since these are built, consolidated and ended through communication. Given the central importance of relationships in the building of human identity, we will also examine the role of relational communication in self-concept formation and our attempts to reduce uncertainty in our dealings with others, the implications this raises for various strategies we deploy in impression management, the rules and scripts which underpin much relational communication and how principles of supportive communication underlie the main phases of relationship development.

INTERPERSONAL PERCEPTION AND IMPRESSION MANAGEMENT

A key reason for the overwhelming significance which we attach to all kinds of relationships is that our sense of self-esteem is intertwined with the feedback and rewards which people exchange in the process of developing their relationships. How does this work?

As discussed in Chapter 2, people are fundamentally concerned with how we project ourselves to others, and we develop interaction goals which help to determine how this process of impression management is conducted (Jones, 1990). These goals embody and express the different roles we play (parent, teacher, daughter, political representative, etc.), our aspirations for the varied contexts in which these roles are actualised and the unique human contexts in which they occur. With the exception of purely ritualistic interactions (during which, for example, we might ask a fellow diner to pass the salt), different interaction goals mean that we will emphasise/de-emphasise varied facets of our character, social skills and motivational orientations. Thus, how we present ourselves (through self-disclosure) is largely determined by the goals we set ourselves for our dealings with others (Derlega *et al.*, 1993), while these goals tend to emerge from the underlying human desire to be seen by others in a favourable manner and to avoid being seen negatively (Rosenfeld *et al.*, 1995).

These goals also influence our perceptions of other people (see Chapter 2). We selectively discriminate between different stimuli and pay more attention to those behaviours other people employ which most suggest that they are capable of helping us to achieve our interaction goals. For example, we may be most concerned when interacting with others about their wealth in the world. Accordingly, we will pay most attention to what they do and say which gives us this information, and we will be inclined to judge them on the basis of the information we receive which pertains to this issue.

In turn, we will also be attempting to understand the interaction goals of the other person. We will be attributing agency and intent to what they do – often misunderstanding both (Sutherland, 1992). This is a prime source of stereotyping and the formation of functional/dysfunctional expectations concerning our respective roles (Leyens *et al.*, 1994). So, if we judge that a selection interviewer values a consistent career track record, we are more likely to downplay incidences of erratic employment behaviours on our part and put great stress on the unbending path which we have followed to this employing organisation.

This means that much of relational communication can be conceptualised as an attempt to manage reputation and make sense of the behaviour and personality of others. Our attempts to do so, while frequently leading us to erroneous attributions of intent (Pettigrew, 1979), constitute a driving force in human relationships and underlie many of the communicative activities in which we engage.

Underpinning such attributional drives is the desire to find sources of social support. This can be defined as the sense we have that if a need arises there will be someone within the family or extended circle of friends and acquaintances who will be willing and capable of giving it (Cutrona *et al.*, 1990). This support may be instrumental, in that it may consist of activities or assistance which directly facilitate problem-solving. It may also be emotional, and include expressions of support, caring and the validating of the other's self-esteem. Such positive feedback is central to the construction of a healthy self-concept and clearly presumes the existence of rewarding social relationships. Although it has been suggested that the mere presence of social relationships is supportive (Cobb, 1976), it is also useful to consider what behaviours are commonly construed as social support. In general, it is recognised that supportive communication involves: focusing on problems rather than attacking someone's personality; providing specific feedback about detailed behaviours which people can change rather than making hostile judgements; listening attentively; validating rather than invalidating the people concerned; and ensuring that there is a strong consistency and connection rather than disconjunction between the messages which we transmit (Whetten and Cameron, 1991). This acknowledges the fact that not all relationships or interactions are helpful to people and some may, in fact, be destructive and harmful (Rook, 1984). Many people exhibit a poor propensity to comfort or support others when they are experiencing distress, despite the fact that such communicative behaviours impact significantly on the other person and are widely appreciated (Burleson, 1990).

REDUCTION OF UNCERTAINTY

Relationships depend, to some considerable extent, on the existence of persistent assumptions about others, which we seek to confirm during our dealings with them. In addition, the existence of supportive relationships (as characterised above) contributes to a feeling of belonging to important social networks, on which we rely in order to feel secure. We become disoriented if these suppositions are unsettled by inexplicable behaviour – for example, competing relationships or hobbies which leave less time for interaction, changes in values, the betrayal of confidences and acts of deception (Planalp *et al.*, 1988). As highlighted in Chapter 2, it has been proposed that a key communicative objective throughout all the various phases of relationships is uncertainty reduction – what has become known as uncertainty reduction theory (URT) (Berger, 1988).

URT recognises that everyone can behave in inconsistent or inexplicable ways. However, during our interactions with others we are motivated by predictive and explanatory needs – we need to predict what is most likely to happen next and to explain why this is the case. Thus, a subordinate who knows that appraisal by a manager is imminent, when confronted by a sudden summons to the manager's office, may predict that the reason for the summons is the appraisal, but that the explanation for the manager's tone of voice is that the appraisal is going to be negative. This judgement will influence the selection of strategies for self-presentation during what follows.

The reduction of uncertainty has been explicitly linked to the building of trust between interactors – what has been defined as 'the confident expectation that a partner is intrinsically motivated to take one's own best interests into account when acting – even when incentives might tempt him or her to do otherwise.' (Boon, 1994, p. 88). To some extent, we judge whether this expectation is fulfilled by the quantity and quality of communication we receive from, and extend to, others. For example, research by Tourish and Hargie (1996) and Hargie and Tourish (1996), examining communicative relationships in the work environment, suggests a positive correlation between the amount of communication people engage in and the development of interpersonal trust. Those within the work place with whom a greater amount of interaction was carried on received more positive trust evaluations than those with whom contact was less frequent and who were perceived to be more organisationally remote. It has also been found that in the work environment people place greater trust in communication which they receive from those above them if it comes through informal rather than formal communication channels (Johnson *et al.*, 1994), although it has also been noted that managers have a marked propensity to rely on formal methods of approach (Jablin, 1987).

An understanding of this process is fundamental to a great deal of interaction. Police interrogators may seek to increase uncertainty on the part of suspects by implying that they know a great deal more than they are disclosing, thus disorientating the suspect and ensuring that the latter's communication competencies and self-presentation strategies are undermined. By the same token, an increase in communication may sometimes create more uncertainty than it does when it diminishes. For example, a couple may meet to finalise the dissolution of their marriage, but then spend some time reviewing the earlier happier stage of the relationship. This could introduce an element of unhelpful ambiguity into their decision to separate. Thus, it is the quality of communication rather than its sheer quantity that can be said to reduce uncertainty and so solidify the emergent relationship. A partial exception to this, it has been argued, occurs in romantic relationships. Livingstone (1980) highlighted the importance of strong emotions in such relationships, which are partly caused by the disruption of expected action sequences and of existing life patterns. Clearly, as the relationship progresses it becomes more predictable and explicable, thereby reducing the scope for behavioural disruptions and so – the argument goes – their power to arouse strong emotions. This may be one reason why people sometimes initiate affairs: their effect is to arouse the strong emotions which may have eased with the consolidation of the primary relationship.

The formation of stereotypical judgements about others is particularly common in the initial stages of a relationship, when we form our impressions based on what we know of the other person's physical characteristics and social group (Blieszner and Adams, 1992). As a result, initial interaction rituals tend to involve exchanges of non-evaluative, demographic information relating to home towns, occupation and family characteristics, which gradually reduce initial stereotype formation and so contribute to uncertainty reduction. Berger and Kellerman (1983) identified three main categories of behaviour which can be used to gather information during interactions and so reduce uncertainty: question asking, disclosure and relaxation of the target.

INGRATIATION

If uncertainty reduction is a prime focus in relational communication, it has also been widely noted that this is accompanied by a fundamental desire to be liked. This desire is expressed in a series of self-presentation behaviours which include ingratiation, intimidation, exemplification (the holding of oneself as in some way a desirable associate) and supplication (Jones and Pittman, 1982). Jones (1964, 1990) has argued that ingratiation is the most ubiquitous of these behaviours, and it is therefore on this which the present discussion concentrates.

Ingratiation has been defined as 'a class of strategic behaviours illicitly designed to influence a particular other person concerning the attractiveness of one's personal qualities'

(Jones, 1964, p. 11). It is not suggested that the participants are consciously aware of deploying strategies to be liked: rather, the suggestion is that ingratiation subverts exchange theory assumptions of relationships and amounts to an attempt to secure a positive attitude on the part of the other person in excess of what we on our part have done to deserve their esteem. However, as Burgoon *et al.* (1994) point out, it is crucial for the success of this approach that what we do is not recognised as ingratiation by the other party! The behaviours that have been noted to be effective include, unsurprisingly, showing an interest in the other person, facilitating them in speaking about what is on their mind, and using positive non-verbals such as smiles and eye contact (Jones, 1964).

However, the effectiveness of these strategies is somewhat militated by issues of status. Burgoon and Hale (1987) offered a typology of themes which serve as an indicator of relational status. These include: submission–dominance (control); formality–informality; task–social; arousal; composure; intimacy; and trust. Along the control continuum, communication exchange signifies the pattern of superiority and subordination. The degree of formality or informality expected and indicated in early relational communication is critical for success in the initial stages of relationship development. This may be related to the extent to which the emphasis of the relationship is on the task or is more socially oriented. It may well be that communication needs to be managed so that both aspects of the relationship are successfully addressed. Effective communication strategies, both verbal and non-verbal, have to be utilised to 'arouse' the participants to respond appropriately and so activate the relationship at the outset and as the relationship progresses. The degree of composure, or self-control, manifested by participants in relational interaction is also verbally and non-verbally indicated by their communicative exchanges indicating, for example, enthusiasm, excitement, boredom, worry, or anxiety which is then interpreted and responded to by the other. The level of intimacy experienced within a relationship is revealed through the type of communicative messages exchanged. These differ, for example, in the amount of affection or hostility conveyed; the degree to which inclusion or exclusion is signalled; and the intensity of involvement indicated. Trust as a dimension of intimacy in relationships can be regarded as a measure of the extent to which participants communicate self-disclosures which are unique to the recipient and which have a minimal chance of being signalled to others.

In terms of ingratiation, research suggests that high status people can influence others without overt attempts to gain influence, and that such attempts are more likely to be successful than those attempted by people of lower status. At the same time, people of lower status have a low level of trust towards those of higher status and so may distrust some of the communication which emanates from them (Collins and Guetskow, 1964). Thus, behaviours designed 'to get the other person to like me' can be more open and straightforward when they emanate from a higher status person to a lower status person rather than vice versa. Jones (1990) explained such results in terms of what have been called incentive values. These refer to the importance we attach to getting others to like us, which is greatly influenced by the extent of our dependence on the other person. Our assessment of this dependence influences the perceived credibility of their communications towards us. So, lower status people are apt to assume that the higher status person does not need their approval, and this therefore increases the subjective probability that their compliments are sincerely meant and accurate. Such compliments are therefore regarded as more credible. In contrast, flattery from a lower status individual to a higher status person (e.g. a subordinate at work to the boss) has a high incentive value (i.e. it is assumed that the person stands to gain materially from being liked) and what is said therefore is more likely to score low in subjective probability.

For these reasons it is imperative to find other means of boosting one's credibility. Recurrent themes in the literature suggest that lower status individuals can achieve this by disagreeing on trivial issues (therefore ensuring that their agreement on important issues carries more credibility), or by showing low confidence when one disagrees but showing high confidence when one agrees. The suggestion is that constant, and therefore indiscriminate, agreement with others produces low source credibility and reduced esteem.

Likewise, attempts by higher status individuals to secure positive feedback on performance from those below them while actively avoiding negative feedback, although an understandable human characteristic, has been correlated with poor regard on the part of others. On the other hand, actively seeking negative feedback has been observed to result in increased positive attitudes (Ashford and Tsui, 1991).

INTERPERSONAL BEHAVIOURS IN RELATIONAL COMMUNICATION

So far, it has been pointed out that much of our communication with others is an attempt to manage the impression we are making, with a view to being liked and securing the positive feedback on our own behaviours which we seek. However, the very act of relating to others in this way impacts on our core self-image, on which we rely to make sense of the world. Our reliance on feedback from others to construct our own identity has indeed been a long-standing strand of psychology research – at the turn of the century Cooley (1902) coined the expression 'the reflected or looking glass self' to characterise what is involved. This sought to explain our view of ourselves as the product of our interactions with others; in particular, the feedback (direct and indirect) that we receive from them about ourselves.

More recent research suggests that it would be erroneous to attribute complete causal power to such factors. For example, Felson (1985) established that already existing self-appraisals have a powerful impact on reflected appraisals, by themselves shaping both the behaviour of others and influencing how we interpret their behaviour. In turn, the accuracy of reflected appraisals is distorted by the fact that our relationships with people are often hedged about with tact, discretion and deference (McCall and Simmons, 1978), leading to self-concepts that may be idealised, erroneous, or distinctly odd. Thus, the role of impression management and reflected appraisals on self-concept formation and relational communication is many-faceted, multi-directional and difficult to pin down in a simple causal model. It remains clear, however, that how we interact with others directly influences our self-concept, which in turn influences how we communicate with others, how they communicate with us and how the self-images of all parties concerned are constructed. This could be defined as an interactional view of the self, which conflicts at various points with the highly individualistic culture in which many of us now live.

Writing of Western society, Sampson (1989, p. 5) pointed out that 'the ideology of autonomy and individuality remains carved deeply in the subjective consciousness of the culture'. In other words, the outward expression of what is perceived to be one's own unique personality, and the realisation of glorious fantasies, is exalted as the goal of self-development, with the consequence that we often exaggerate our own responsibility for dilemmas and problems in our life and downplay the significance of the social, emotional and relational environment within which we act. However, the feedback that we give and receive from others helps to define our own sense of who and what we are, so that how we communicate and exchange impressions becomes a dynamic reconstruction of the self (Wilmot, 1995). As Gergen (1991, p. 178) expressed it, 'without others there is no self'. Thus, our self-concept is formed and re-formed through communication with others: we are crucially dependent on the quality of our relationships to help define the essence of what and who we are.

In a sense, relational communication is the interaction of people's self-concepts, in search of acceptance, reward and validation. Sharing information about the self then becomes a cornerstone of the initiation, development and termination of relationships, through the self-disclosure of pertinent information about the self. Self-disclosure is discussed in depth in Chapter 8. Discussion here will be restricted to some of the implications of self-disclosure research for the development of relationships.

It has been noted that, as relationships become more intimate, people generally exchange more information about themselves on a personal level (Altman and Taylor, 1973), while what has been described as a norm of reciprocity means that we assume the level of disclosure we engage in will be matched by the other (Derlega *et al.*, 1993). This extends and deepens the relationship. In terms of the discussion above, however, it is also clear that a major function of self-disclosure is the obtaining of support and confirmation of an individual's sense of self-worth. These are major goals of relationship formation and to which self-disclosure particularly contributes. Others cannot provide us with feedback (i.e. reflected appraisals) in the absence of information from us about ourselves. By giving information we facilitate feedback, and therefore strive to find our self-concept and self-perception validated. We are acutely sensitive to the success of these ventures, correctly perceiving that a high cost may be attached to non-reciprocation or negative disclosures about ourselves. Thus, if our disclosure is reacted to positively we see it as successful and, if we think that we are being seen by others as we see ourselves, then it is said to be validating (Derlega, 1984). Problems exist with negative feedback, since most of us think we score more highly on socially desirable traits than we actually do and are convinced that our opinions on almost everything (particularly on ourselves) are more correct than they really are (Sutherland, 1992). In addition, if we persist in what are perceived to be excessive or indiscriminate disclosures about intimate issues it does not lead to increased liking by other people (Miller, 1990). Therefore, the need for validation is deeply rooted, but depends on our willingness to engage in self-disclosure, with all the attendant risks that this implies.

However, not everyone establishes mutually rewarding personal relationships. To some extent, this reflects poor communication skills. There is some evidence to suggest that individuals who are less socially successful than others do not follow strategies that enable them to self-disclose adequately (Thorne, 1987; Langston and Cantor, 1989). In addition, when people do not have a clear sense of their own self-concept they may not be capable of constructive disclosures or of understanding, accepting and internalising feedback from others (Scheier and Carver, 1981; Schlenker, 1984).

DIMENSIONS OF CONTROL IN RELATIONAL COMMUNICATION

In relational communication, situational control of the interaction is an important issue. Communication patterns develop which establish rules of control affecting all the behaviour of participants (Burgoon *et al.*, 1994). Communication exchanges signal, both verbally and non-verbally, the amount of status and power that each partner holds along a dominant–submissive continuum of relational control, indicating the degree of equality or inequality within the relationship. Communication strategies adopted and messages exchanged can send clear signals as to how it is intended that each participant should relate during social encounters.

A three-dimensional model of interpersonal control within relationships highlights the differing communicative patterns of relational interaction regarding three types of relationships: complementary, symmetrical and parallel (Burgoon *et al.*, 1994). Complementary relationships are characterised by a situation in which one partner is in a dominant position, and has control of the relationship and communicative exchanges, while the other person is submissive, playing a subordinate role. Relational communication here indicates the degree to which the partners are either controlling or being controlled and the communication strategies employed. By contrast, a symmetrical relationship is established on a more equal basis. The differences between the participants are minimised to the extent that both feel they have an equal say in relational definition and in its control. Patterns of communication are therefore more competitive, and are marked by highly charged communicative exchanges as each vies for control of the interaction. Communication tends to be focused on defining status in such a situation. Within parallel relationships there is a cross-over of the other two types, where each person is able to have some areas of control. Consequently, participants may at one time play a more 'dominant' type of role and at another be in a more 'subordinate' role. On other occasions, there may be a more egalitarian approach where there is a greater recognition that each partner has a right to share in the direction and to exercise control. In these parallel relationships, there is a more flexible approach to communication exchange, displayed in a greater interchangeability of patterns of communication control between the participants.

Control becomes a particularly piquant issue in superior–subordinate relationships. As discussed earlier, such dichotomies of power and status often confound attempts at communication between the people concerned. The main defining features of the relationship between subordinate and superior, and the source of this tension, is that it is characterised by a continuum of submissiveness and dominance in terms of the degree to which one participant exercises power and control relative to their partner's experience of weakness in being dominated (Richmond *et al.*, 1991). One important role of non-verbal communication is in defining the status and power of individuals, for example, in the work place. Within hierarchical organisations that status is often clearly demarcated so as to enable members of different 'rank' to communicate appropriately with one another. A variety of status symbols is employed to communicate the nature of the status hierarchy; for example, job title, size and location of office and its furnishings, size and type of car. Superior and subordinate positions within a relationship are also delineated and communicated through non-verbal messages such as appearance, body language and paralanguage, together with the use of time, environment and space.

RELATIONAL COMMUNICATION RULES, SCRIPTS AND CO-REGULATION

These issues of control point to the fact that relationships are realised through communication between people, in which the underlying assumptions which guide the relationship are sometimes made explicit but more often simply enacted in practice. Key features of relationships, which must be taken into account in any analysis of the communicative dimensions, include: *Goals*, or *sources of satisfaction* where people must receive enough from the relationship to justify the effort involved, or to repay the investment they make in time, emotion and commitment; *Repertoire* referring to the behaviours and activities which are regarded as acceptable in the relationship (e.g. the physical touch which is accepted in romantic relationships is precluded in work relationships, and people who fail to distinguish between the appropriateness and situation-specific nature of their behaviours will endanger the relationship, and much more besides); and *Roles* where each person has a specific role to play in the relationship. For example, it is anticipated that parents will have more of a role in determining boundaries on their children's behaviour than children will in shaping the behaviour of their parents. In terms of communication, we need to consider how these roles are conveyed between each party.

So far, our discussion of relational communication has implied a series of exchanges between interactors designed to achieve predictable outcomes, operating within constraints of what is and is not generally acceptable, and building consistently on the common folklore of experience on relationships that we all possess. Implicit in this approach is the recognition that much relational communication is governed by rules, which can be defined as 'behaviour that most people, such as most members of a group, neighbourhood or subculture, think or believe should be performed or should not be performed' (Argyle and Henderson, 1985, p. 63). Rules, then, codify the normal standards of behaviour which people find acceptable, and from which we are reluctant to accept digressions. There are clearly areas of communication skill where such norms have been identified – for example, self-disclosure (Hargie *et al.*, 1994) – while such professional contexts as interviewing also carry a great deal of mutual expectations about roles and acceptable modes of behaviour (Millar *et al.*, 1992). It could be posited that the learning of these rules (and the modifications imposed on them by social context) constitutes a major part of our attempts to reduce uncertainty during interactions with others. Clearly, also, familiarity with the given rules of a particular social context (e.g. within the boundaries of marriage) is useful in the selection of particular communication strategies for the resolution of relationship differences and the strengthening of the underlying relationship.

The evidence suggests that all relationships are governed by generally agreed and strongly endorsed sets of rules. As Argyle and Henderson (1985) put it, 'Social relationships are in some respects like games. Both are miniature social systems, producing co-operative behaviour which leads to the attainment of goals, by play within the rules' (p. 36). They identified rules on which there is common agreement and which generally prevail across relationship typologies as including: not disclosing confidences; respecting privacy; refraining from public criticism; and repaying debts and favours. Generally speaking, people attach a high degree of importance to maintaining these rules, although the precise weight varies according to the rule. For example, when people have been asked to identify those rule breaks that contributed to the termination of past friendships, being jealous or critical of other relationships attracts a far higher score than not giving enough emotional support; not keeping confidences is more important than not standing up for someone in their absence; and criticising in public is more vital than not volunteering help in time of need. Effective relational communication implies familiarity with these rules and a high commitment to their maintenance alongside a low incidence of divergence.

Given this, there is clearly a correlation between relationship breakdown and the increased propensity of people to break basic relationship rules. Argyle and Henderson (1985) pointed out that marriage attracts more rules than any other relationship, and includes prohibitions against unfaithfulness and not keeping the partner informed of one's personal schedule. Clearly, as the relationship moves towards termination more of these rules are likely to be broken and become part of the spiral of decline which leads to divorce. Marital therapy, therefore, can usefully look at the detailed behaviours the spouses are employing in their interactions, point towards areas where greater agreement on rules is required and facilitate the warring partners to ascribe to this.

However helpful the underlying concept of rules has proved to be, it fails to answer all human contingencies. Fogel (1993) is particularly critical of attempts to compress all relational communication into a rule-bound framework, pointing out that a typical inter-action such as a game of draughts between an adult and a child, involves the rules of the game itself, the relationship between the players, the banter between them, friendly advice from one to the other, one-upmanship and rules for handling all the emotions that arise during it. Clearly, much of this activity is regulated – we could hypothesise, for example, that a general rule in such an encounter is that the child would be permitted to win most of the games. On the other hand, there is a great deal of innovative activity in which various rules break down, or the interactors reach a position (such as a childish tantrum at losing, for which neither side is prepared) when access to a set of rules is unavailable. Thus, although rules exist, they do not cover all contingencies and they rarely have the prescriptive force that one finds in law.

For these reasons, Fogel (1993) argued that human communication in the context of relationships is best viewed as a system of co-regulation: that is to say, the co-ordination involved in the interaction is continuously modified by the changing actions of each partner. This view places more weight on the innovative individual roles of each side rather than a body of commonly agreed rules, which are subject to innovation precisely because so much human communication is a rule-breaking activity. Rules are located within broadly agreed social frames which define the situation, the expectations of the interactors, the behavioural norms which are acceptable and are not acceptable, and within which the interactors are free to improvise or even (at the risk of changing the relationship) to leave behind. Thus, a parent who will never let a child win at a game of draughts could be said to be moving beyond the social frame we expect in those situations, is disregarding the rules completely, and will run the risk of seriously endangering the co-regulational base for interaction between the two parties. In short, the child might become reluctant ever to play draughts or other games with the parent again!

Complicating matters still further, and making us marvel at the capacity of human beings to absorb so much knowledge unconsciously, there are different types of rules. The most fundamental would appear to be *rewardingness*. Exchange theory postulates that the exchange of rewards, so that we perceive a greater benefit to ourselves from being in the relationship than outside, is the key to human relationships (Thibaut and Kelley, 1959; Kelley and Thibaut, 1978). The fundamental premise is that we seek to maximise the rewards that we obtain while attempting to minimise the costs during our interactions with others. People who are perceived as rewarding in a number of ways are generally viewed as more attractive than those who are not (Foa and Foa, 1975), while it is also clear that being associated with a rewarding event may be enough to increase an individual's attractiveness. As Dickson *et al.* (1993) pointed out, this often means that we are judged not on the basis of our actions but on the basis of the emotionally arousing context in which they occur. The behaviours that are generally viewed as rewarding are discussed in detail by Dickson *et al.*, and reprised in Chapter 5. Exchange theory, despite its value, does not apply to all relationship categories nor does it neatly characterise all communication episodes. For example, it is known that when relationships are at an early stage and when they are starting to deteriorate people tend to think of reward much more than at other stages (Murstein *et al.*, 1977).

However, most of our time is not spent developing or ending relationships – it is spent on sustaining them (Duck, 1988). In addition, many people choose to remain in highly destructive relationships for long periods of time, when costs clearly outweigh any potential benefits. As Wilmot (1995) argued, this tendency to over-emphasise the issue of rewards is rooted in a view of relationships as something external to the individual concerned, whose real self-concept and personal identity exist independently of the dialectical dynamics of the relationship itself. Gilbert (1991) also pointed out that it can sometimes appear to suggest that all individuals are intrinsically locked into conflict, by implying that a desire for self-aggrandisement is the motor force behind all interactional behaviour. While such a depressing view of relationships is not supported by the evidence, it is not surprising to find that when people identify what they prize in relationships, what constitutes in essence the rule-based foundations of their commitment to the relationships, issues like providing help to friends feature high.

It has also been suggested that another useful template to assist in the conceptualisation of relationships is that of scripts. For example, partners may attempt to achieve relational co-ordination by following the existing cultural norms governing that particular relationship (e.g. beginning and developing a romantic relationship). In doing so, they employ appropriate and acceptable communication scripts and embrace the interactive behavioural role patterns that are already well established within society. The norm of reciprocity, alluded to earlier, is one example of a cultural norm which can form the basis of such a communication script. This requires that in an emerging relationship each partner's revelations should match the other's level of intimacy. These scripts and role patterns are acquired from a variety of cultural sources such as the family, ethnic group, neighbourhood, social networks, churches and the media, which act directly or more indirectly as agencies of socialisation in providing models to follow. Plainly, the notion of script as opposed to rule accommodates more innovation on the part of the participants in the relationship, and it is this which constitutes its strength.

Relational partners do not always conform to the dominant normative communication scripts which attempt to prescribe patterns of behaviour for their particular relationship. Instead, there is a wide latitude within society for individuals to develop standards for relational communication that vary markedly from the cultural norm. Hence partners can actively negotiate their own sense of relationship and create their own world of meanings. Through their everyday interaction the couple may develop their own beliefs about and behavioural standards for relating satisfactorily. Consequently, there is greater opportunity for individuals to generate novel ways of relating by creating their own unique way of interacting and their own interpretation of communicative events. They develop communication patterns that are especially suited to their particular relationship. Over time their communicational behaviour acts to establish and sustain an identity to the couples' unique relationship, both to themselves and to the outside world. In this way, partners construct what has been referred to as their own relational culture (Woods, 1982). As Montgomery (1994, p. 73) pointed out, a relational culture emerges when the participants develop 'unique ways of engaging, interpreting, and evaluating communication behaviour that represent and reinforce the special identity of the couple in comparison with others'.

Much of the research on these issues focuses on romantic couple relationships and it is not always clear to what extent such findings can be replicated in other relational contexts. Nevertheless, with that qualification in mind, it has been found (Krueger, 1983; Jacobson, 1984) that satisfied couples as opposed to dissatisfied couples tend to:

- Reward each other at equal rates;
- Blame and threaten less;
- Emphasise the importance of the relationship when they disagree;
- Resolve conflict more effectively;
- Confirm each other;
- Use more positive statements in response to the other;
- Reciprocate pleasing behaviours;
- Perceive their partners more accurately;
- Agree more on the status of their relationship;
- Disclose more to one another.

Many of the these behaviours have also been identified as positive factors in general conflict mediation (Hocker and Wilmot, 1994) and they are likely to have a general utility in promoting effective relational communication. It has also been noted that the list cited above relies heavily on disclosure (Wilmot, 1995), which in turn has been positively linked to liking and loving romantic partners (Sprecher, 1987), levels of marital satisfaction (Rosenfeld and Bowen, 1991) and friendship satisfaction (Jones, 1991). Therefore, again it would seem that self-disclosure is crucial in developing the skills vital to the initiation and maintenance of effective relationships.

In general, it is possible to view social skills as the means we use to adhere to rules, or, in breaking them, to do so in a manner which has a better chance of being accepted by the other person, if we want the relationship to survive. These skills must be employed throughout the whole process of relationship development since circumstances constantly change, which means that the identities of interactors change, creating new challenges and thus the need to become familiar with new rules. Clearly, it is the failure of partners sometimes to acknowledge this, or the changes which have occurred in others, which contributes to relationship breakdown.

THE ROLE OF COMMUNICATION IN RELATIONSHIP FORMATION AND DISSOLUTION

It has been suggested that, in terms of relational development, communication serves two crucial functions: one is *instrumental* and the other is *substantive*. First, communication acts instrumentally as a vehicle by which participants relate and in doing so provides the means whereby relationships are formed and sustained. In this way, communication acts as 'the glue of social bonds' (Montgomery, 1994, p. 69).

Second, communication functions to provide the meanings which are generated in the interactions of participants within relationships. These meanings which are associated with the participants' verbal and non-verbal communicative exchanges help to differentiate and define various relationship events which occur (such as discussions, agreements, disagreements). Relationships are embedded in communication behaviours and in their interpreted meanings. It is through such communication over a wide range of relational events that partners gain a sense of the nature and quality of their relationship. Hence, relationships are created, sustained, enhanced and, in some instances, repaired, by the interactions of the participants and by the meanings that are generated in that process.

In order to interact together as partners, two participants must achieve an appropriate degree of meaningful relational co-ordination of their activities. It is through interpersonal communication that this is successfully brought about. As result of interaction partners discover and acquire normative patterns for interacting, develop their own unique relational culture and communicate their partnership to other people.

THE ROLE OF COMMUNICATION IN RELATIONSHIP FORMATION

Relationships are constructed by individuals through communication over time. Indeed, for most people, communication takes place within the context of ongoing relationships. As Fogel (1993) has illustrated, it is within the context of relationships that individuals develop and grow. There is a close association between good communication and relational satisfaction. The relational aspects of communicative efforts are as crucial to effective communication as is the content of the message itself; a sharp dichotomy does not exist since the message communicated tends also to transmit relational cues (Burgoon *et al.*, 1994).

However, contrasting models of relationship formation have been suggested. Two of the most important are the *stage model*, which is often contrasted with the *continuous process model*. The most salient features of these are discussed below.

The stage model

This treats the development of relationships as progressing through a number of distinct phases or stages. One of the most influential typologies of relational development has been the social penetration model propounded by Altman and Taylor (1973). This outlines the processes by which participants come to share more and more aspects of themselves through interpersonal communication as their relationship develops. The phrase 'social penetration' highlights how both verbally and non-verbally the relational partners progress from relatively cautious, superficial communication exchanges to a limited range of topics in the early encounters, towards increasingly more spontaneous, expansive and intimate interactions as the relationship becomes more established. The model specifies a gradual, sequential development towards intimacy, which is reflected in the participants' communicative behaviours. The focus of this model is on relationship development and growth. A number of phases of development are postulated: orientation; exploratory affective exchange; affective exchange; and stable exchange. The model suggests that relationships develop more deeply as they progressively move through this series of phases, with each new phase building on its predecessor.

In the initial phase of *orientation* individuals are cautious. They reveal little of their 'selves', and topics of communication are restricted to the impersonal exchange of super-ficial messages. The participants will tend to communicate largely in restrained, polite conventional ways (Montgomery, 1994). As the relationship develops to the *exploratory* phase it becomes more relaxed, casual and friendly. The communication exchanges begin to show greater spontaneity, with the participants starting to reveal those aspects of their personality which they have previously guarded. The public topics of communication begin to widen and more intimate areas of conversation are initiated.

The third stage of this model of development, *affective exchange*, is characterised by romantic relationships and close friendships. The relationship is increasingly holistic with participants discovering a great deal about each other through their communication exchanges. Previous barriers are broken down. Communication involves much more disclo-sure of personal information and feelings. In the final stage of *stable exchange*, Altman and Taylor (1973) suggest that the partners know each other so well that their developing relationship is now characterised by continuous openness. They come to share intimately a social world of common meanings in which they can confidently interpret and predict the feelings and likely behaviour of each other.

The work of Altman and Taylor has been extended by a number of researchers who have refined the model of how communication functions in developing relationships (e.g. Baxter, 1987; Duck, 1991). One finding is that direct, open and disclosing communication does not take place all that frequently in emerging relationships, but instead tends to occur on special occasions that are 'embedded within a dominant pattern of indirectness' (Montgomery, 1994, p. 71.). At the outset of a relationship partners tend not to reveal their interest in the other overtly but do so by employing more indirect and subtle commu-nication strategies. These include highlighting shared interests, which creates the basis for further and deeper relationship involvement. It appears that this tentativeness around expressing a direct interest in the relationship tends to persist. Research by Baxter and Wilmot (1984) suggests that close partners themselves are more likely to rely on indirect methods secretly to test the other's commitment, rather than talking openly and directly about the state of the relationship.

Knapp and Vangelisti (1992) also offered a model of relationship growth through stage development which utilises different communication strategies and activities. Five stages are identified: initiating; experimenting; intensifying; integrating; and bonding.

1 *Initiating*. Communication at this stage is characterised by a focus on conventional modes of interaction, with an emphasis on small talk during the participants' opening lines and reactions to each other;

2 *Experimenting*. Small talk is used to extend the scope of communicative exchanges. This widens the scope and depth of topics that might be now discussed. It also provides a relatively safe means for reducing relational uncertainty by affording a procedure whereby participants can go on to find out more about each other;

3 *Intensifying*. Here the partners continue the process of revealing personal aspects of themselves, by communicating information that calls for a reciprocal response. This may

be imperceptible, to the extent that the participants are not necessarily aware of their deepening relationship. At this level communication is more informal and personally focused towards the other;

4   *Integrating.* Integration occurs when participants achieve a sense of relational coupling. This will also receive public recognition from others who begin to treat them as a unit. Communication will reflect a shared social world and increased joint decision-making;

5   *Bonding.* This represents the final significant stage of relational growth and development where it is now decided that the relationship should be publicly communicated formally to the outside world, for example, through ceremony and ritual as in a wedding service.

The continuous process model

One criticism of the stage perspective is that it treats relationship development as an invariant sequence of discretely different stages, suggesting that the development of a relationship can be regarded as following 'discretely different time periods in such a way that the characteristics of the relationship at prior time periods are necessary precursors to the current and future characteristics' with each stage containing the 'seeds of the next' (Fogel, 1993, p. 85). One problem with a discrete stage model is the assumption that participants can on their own evaluate the costs/benefits of moving on to the next level of intimacy as if they were aware of what was ahead and could therefore act independently of the other in making that decision. The danger with such a model is that what starts out as a descriptive metaphor becomes reified into a deterministic mechanism which assumes linear inevitability, taking insufficient account of discontinuities and disconjunctions in relational development. The view that relationships are composed of single, discrete interactions has been challenged by Duck (1991), who argued that they are much more than merely sequences of behaviours or cumulative individual acts. Relationships occur in a context of 'ongoingness' and are created and sustained by the meanings attributed by the participants to such interactive sequences and behaviours.

While Duck (1991) described relationships as moving through stages of increased intimacy, such a view can be regarded as in keeping with a continuous process model of relationship formation, emerging through the communicative behaviours of mutual interaction. Interactors do not in the early phase of their relationship start out talking about intimacy right away, but rather as they become increasingly more intimate the partners turn their conversations 'towards the topic of intimacy itself' (Fogel, 1993, p. 88). Discussion of mutual commitments leads to socially co-regulated joint decision-making rather than a purely individualistic one based on personal calculation of costs and benefits. At the same time the partners increasingly become aware of the 'concreteness' of their relationship through engaging in greater communication about their shared experiences and a corresponding reduction in the emphasis on individual past. Underpinning the continuous process model of relationship development is the view that new consensual frames emerge through a continuously changing and co-regulating dynamic. These consensual frames are the increasingly shared worldviews of the relational partners through which they interpret their social realities and together make sense of their common experiences. In so doing a historical perspective is established through which each new encounter generates additional information which is then incorporated as part of the ongoing consensual frame that the participants share.

RELATIONALLY CONSTRICTING COMMUNICATION

Relationships also change, and often terminate. Much of the research discussed so far in this chapter has focused on the earlier phases of initiation and maintenance. It is also important to examine the particular issues raised by relationships in decline and, in particular, how conflict tends to be managed.

It is, however, perfectly clear that dysfunctional communication causes relational damage at all stages of the process. Damaging communication patterns leading to tension in a relationship may be expressed in either (1) an over-emphasis on the self at the expense of the other partner and the relationship or, conversely, (2), an over-emphasis on the other and the relationship at a cost to the self (Wilmot, 1995). In the first case this may be due either to an inability to relate effectively to others or relating effectively but in doing so to misuse them. An over-emphasis on the self finds an expression in a variety of forms such as a communication skills deficit, deceptive behaviours, relational rule-breaking and domination. In the second, too little self-assertion or being relationally overly involved leads to relationship constriction. An over-dependence on the other partner robs the relationship of its spark and vitality and so imperils the health of the relationship. Similarly, those who are overly enmeshed in a relationship (such as carers, or partners of addicts) may experience the severe role overload associated with carrying excessive relational burdens. This may lead to co-dependency through being tied to a relationship where everything revolves around the partner and her or his condition.

In unsatisfactory, constricting relationships negative changes in communicative behaviour manifest themselves in a variety of forms including cross-complaining; put-downs; insults; giving more weight to negative rather than positive communication; and the attribution of blame to the other person, alongside increasing levels of uncertainty (Wilmot, 1995). Relational dissolution can be regarded as a particularly severe form of relational constriction. Dissolution, however, should not be merely assumed to be a straightforward, linear stage deterioration moving to an inevitable collapse. While in the end a final break-up is the outcome, the process of dissolution may be uneven, with the levels of intimacy between partners fluctuating, as they oscillate between coming closer together and moving further, and irrevocably, apart.

RELATIONAL DISSOLUTION

Relational deterioration and decay occurs for a variety of reasons. Breakdown and collapse often happen in spite of the best efforts of the partners to make it work. They may dissolve slowly through a 'gradual passing away' in which intimacy is imperceptibly eroded to the point where the relationship can no longer be sustained, or by a more rapid collapse through 'sudden death'. In the latter case the relationship is abruptly ended unilaterally by one or other partner, or by a mutual decision of the partners involved (Davis, 1973). Two contrasting approaches have been taken to the conceptualisation of relational disengagement. Broadly speaking, they see disengagement as an event, on the one hand, and as a process, on the other.

The first perspective treats the phenomenon of dissolution as a single event in time characterised by issues surrounding two key dimensions: (1) precursors of the relational failure, and (2) the outcomes in terms of the consequences of such a failure.

By contrast, the process model offers a complementary perspective on relational decay which queries the dynamics of deteriorating relationships. Baxter (1985) identified the key issues as whether disengaging relationships pass through various discernible phases, and how the relational partners achieve their uncoupling. An early attempt to provide a conceptual framework for this process (Duck, 1982) posited the existence of different but related phases in dissolution. Of the various attempts to expand our understanding of this process made since then, we will here examine the work of Knapp and Vangelisti (1992). Disintegrating relations are seen to be characterised by five stages with each having unique interactional properties. These are differentiating; circumscribing; stagnating; avoiding; and, finally, terminating.

Differentiating

This occurs in the early phase of relational uncoupling where partners who are coming apart begin to communicate in ways that show emerging differences in interests and outlook. A greater stress on individualisation occurs and shared action diminishes. A shift in communication emphasis takes place, from a focus on joint resolution of differences to a unilateral demand for personal satisfaction of issues. The resulting arguments and conflict become a test of the willingness of the other to put up with a situation which may represent a threat to the survival of the relationship itself. Differentiation does not necessarily lead to the disintegration of the relationship. It may instead lead to the re-establishment of the relationship on a different footing

Circumscribing

The process of circumscribing leads to an escalation in restrictive communication. At this stage communication becomes increasingly curtailed and relational partners avoid discussing sensitive topics that are the source of unresolved tensions and conflict. As further unresolved issues emerge, efforts to communicate about these may all but have ceased. Such an unwillingness to communicate typifies the collapsing state of the relationship where to open discussion may run the risk of having to face up to a whole range of unresolved issues. Any consequent attempt to communicate about a problem is likely to be unsuccessful and risk ending in frustration, as the other partner will tend to close down the discussion. Communication will be kept at a superficial level, and in the 'public' rather than in the 'private' domain. Communication messages now indicate the emergence of new rules of restrictive relational communication superseding the previous more open approach to dealing with problems which was the mark of the earlier phase of the relationship.

Stagnation

Here, the status of the relationship is 'put on hold'. Discussion of the state of the relationship is taboo. This phase is characterised by a very low level of communicative exchange. Verbal communication is at a stalemate, due to previous failures. These have so contaminated expectations that very little effort is made to attempt communication. Each partner feels they know the other's predictable response, and so important issues are not discussed. A painful silence becomes the norm. What communication does take place has become highly formalised in carefully thought out and worded exchanges. By contrast, negative emotional messages (e.g. of mistrust and anger) are non-verbally communicated. For most, this is generally too painful a state of affairs to endure for any length of time and so it tends to be a relatively brief period in the overall disintegration process.

Avoidance

A wide range of avoiding tactics is adopted at this point to enable the participants to escape the kind of pressure and problems generated in the earlier circumscribing and stagnating phases. The aim of communication during this time is to obviate the physical necessity for any direct face-to-face confrontation and interaction.

Termination

At this point one or more of the partners will make it clear that the relationship is now finished. Some indication will also be given as to the future status of any interaction between the participants.

One criticism of such models of relationship development and decay is that they tend to suggest an oversimplified, one-way, linear and mechanistic stage perspective that ignores and masks 'the ongoing dynamism inherent in most relationships' (Wilmot, 1995, p. 55). They presume that relationships develop incrementally or dissolve in a much more systematic and ordered manner than may be the case in reality. Fogel (1993, p. 86) underlined the danger of the notion of 'stage' which 'is created purely as a descriptive metaphor' being reified 'into a determinism of inevitable secession'.

From an alternative perspective, the 'plateau/change' model offers a contrasting view of the nature of relational development and decay. In this account, relational change is characterised in both satisfying and dissatisfying relationships by periods of stability punctuated by key 'turning points' leading to rapid, qualitative change rather than a slow, steady, incremental transition. Here, relationships are seen to be internally oscillating in a state of change, continually expanding or contracting while appearing to be stable. A relationship is regarded as being able to absorb many changes until some unfolding event acts as a turning point which pushes it to a new level to the extent even of changing the relational definition. As Duck (1988, p. 49) noted, 'We rise from plateau to plateau rather than up a continuously rising gradient of intimacy'.

An alternative perspective on relational change is that of communication spirals. This approach to relational development focuses on the fluctuating nature of relational change over time. Wilmot (1995, p. 72) in identifying three types of communicative spirals – generative, degenerative and oscillating – pointed out that 'When people's behaviours interlock such that each one's behaviour and view of the other are intensified, they are in a spiral'. These communication spirals are seen as pervasive in human relationships regardless of whether they have a positive or negative trajectory. At any point in the relationship such a spiral is influencing its development in a generative or degenerative manner. Relationships are dynamic over time, oscillating through spiralling phases of change. The rate, direction and extent of this change is variable as it is influenced by the communicative behaviours of the participants involved.

In spiralling relationships, the communicative behaviours have a direct impact on participants, amplifying one another. As they pick up momentum they feed back each on the other creating an accelerating relational dynamism of change. This pattern is likely to continue until checked by some significant action taken by the participants. Spirals, however, are subject to possible change. The rate of change may be accelerated or slowed down, or, indeed, even reversed by the communicative stratagems of those involved. Within relationships, communication spirals may be characterised by symmetrical or complementary moves (Bateson, 1979). Where the communication is symmetrical the participants are engaging reciprocally in 'more of the same', matching each other's communicative moves. By contrast, in complementary communicative spirals 'more of the same' on the part of one is matched by 'more of the opposite' by the other partner.

In attempting to halt the negative cycle of degenerative spiralling it is argued that changes in communicative patterns will have the effect of altering the spiral. Since the communicative patterns of the participants are interlocked, persisting with the change will bring rewards, even if the attempts are at first met with suspicion. Indeed, Wilmot and Stevens (1994) found that persistence was one of the key factors in bringing about a change in relationships. Communicating a reaffirmation of relational goals by the partners can also act as a counter to continuing on a degenerative communication spiral by emphasising a commitment to sustaining the relationship itself and concentrating on remedial action to repair the damage that has been done.

COMMUNICATION STRATEGIES IN RELATIONSHIP DISENGAGEMENT

As explained above, the process of relation disengagement is complex and multifaceted and, therefore, cannot be treated merely as a single, sequential pattern (Baxter, 1985). Since communication plays a central role when such relationships are in decay, it is not surprising that a number of disengagement communication models and strategies has been postulated.

For example, Baxter (1987) identified a variety of individual communication strategies which were grouped along three dimensions: direct to indirect; other-orientation to self-orientation; unilateral to bilateral. Direct communicative strategies are those whereby the wish to terminate the relationship is explicitly stated to the other. Indirect strategies, on the other hand, are employed where the aim is to bring the relationship to an end without openly indicating that intention. Other-orientation focuses on face-work by adopting those communicative strategies which seek to prevent embarrassment to, or manipulation of, the other person (Brown and Levinson, 1987; Goffman, 1967). By contrast, communicative strategies which are self-oriented employ expedient tactics in pursuit of self-interest at the other's expense. The unilateral-bilateral dimension highlights the degree to which communication strategies reflect whether the desire to make the break is a one-sided or a joint endeavour.

The three dimensions discussed above embrace six clusters of communication strategies: indirect-unilateral; indirect-bilateral; direct-unilateral; direct-bilateral; self-orientation; and other-orientation.

In unilateral moves to withdraw from a relationship three basic strategies may be utilised: *withdrawal, cost escalation* and *pseudo de-escalation*. Withdrawal is where one partner employs avoidance tactics in order to reduce the frequency and/or intimacy of contact with the other. Cost escalation is used to bring an end to the relationship indirectly without having to explicitly communicate to the other that it is over by indulging in behaviour which raises the relational cost to the other of continuing. Pseudo-de-escalation occurs indirectly in that the person's wish to terminate is not explicitly stated to the other but is masked by an assertion of a desire to change the essential nature of the relationship itself.

Two types of indirect action can be utilised in a bilateral dissolution: (1) pseudo-de-escalation and (2) fading away. With pseudo-de-escalation there is a shared mutual deception in that the partners maintain a fiction of continuing the relationship while knowingly intending to end their contact. In fading away there is an implicit assumption that the relationship has come to an end without a formal declaration.

In the situation of unilateral disengagement directness may take two forms: (1) state of the relationship talk and (2) *fait accompli*. The former involves communicating one's views on the 'health' of the relationship, while the latter may be no more than a blunt message of intent.

In a bilateral desire to terminate the relationship, directness can be manifested in two communicative strategies: (1) attributional conflict and (2) a negotiated farewell. In the first example, conflict centres not on whether the relationship should finish but on such things as why this is necessary and who is to blame. A negotiated farewell, by contrast, displays little in the way of hostility but focuses rather on communication which explicitly brings the relationship formally to an end.

Terminating a relationship could be considered to be among one of the most face-threatening situations a person might encounter when their sense of worth and self-esteem is severely threatened. While the person on the receiving end experiences 'positive face threat', the partner who initiates the break may also experience a 'negative' form of face threat. It is often the case, therefore, that both partners to the disengagement need and want to save face. As a consequence, the initiator may seek to balance a wish to end the relationship with a desire to preserve both personal and the other's face. In deciding to bring a relationship to an end participants may therefore adopt communication strategies in which they try to balance a desire to terminate with this wish to preserve their own and their partner's face.

A model of disengagement based on 'politeness' has been developed in an attempt to understand why certain communication strategies are chosen in dissolving a relationship which is perceived as unsatisfactory (Cupach and Metts, 1994). The model of politeness and disengagement centres on three aspects: (1) the seriousness of the 'offence' of disengaging; (2) the types of communicative interaction; and (3) the degree of politeness of the interaction and the message communicated. The model asserts that as the level of seriosity of break-up increases, the greater will be the emphasis placed on support for the person affected, thereby increasing the likelihood of 'politeness' in disengaging. A range of different communication strategies are depicted in the model, deployed according to the degree of severity (from low to high level) in which the offence of breaking up is regarded. These cluster around two major strategies: (1) off-record and (2) on-record.

Off-record strategies are associated with low politeness and are used where there is a low level perception of seriosity. They include tactics such as withdrawal, manipulation, cost escalation, behavioural de-escalation and drifting apart. There are several types of on-record strategies, some of which are less polite than others. Bald strategies such as *fait accompli*, justification and negative identity management reflect little commitment to, or respect for, the relationship and are very low in politeness because there is no attempt to save either person's face. Going on-record with redressive action indicates that termination is regarded as a more serious offence. This can take the form of: attributional conflict, relational talk, or unilateral face-work.

RELATIONAL CONFLICT

There has been a great deal of research in interpersonal communication into the skills which we use to enhance our standing in the eyes of others, and in the initiation and maintenance of relationships. Effective communication has been summarised as that which is clear, consistent, direct, supportive, focused and reciprocal (Sillars and Weisberg, 1987). The skills discussed throughout this volume are aimed at enhancing effectiveness in these important areas: however, many of them can also be applied to the more upsetting issues of managing both conflict and the ending of relationships. Interpersonal conflict is a major problem for which most of us seem completely unprepared.

Conflict can be defined as: 'A situation in which interdependent people express (manifest or latent) differences in satisfying their individual needs and interests, and they experience interference from each other in accomplishing these goals' (Donohue and Kolt, 1992, p. 4). This suggests that some form of conflict may be inherent to all phases of relationship development, in personal, work, romantic, leisure and other contexts. Interdependency does not imply absolute commonality of interest or background: the existence of different self-concepts and motivational orientations serves to spark feelings of dissonance in terms of achieving goals, and hence a conflict over which goals to adopt, and possibly how to secure them. As individuals develop, they may become less prepared to interact on the basis of old role expectations, and this reluctance to conform to such standards is often a cause of anger and conflict (Fisher *et al.*, 1989). Thus, Thomas (1983, p. 891) defined conflict as 'the process which begins when one party perceives that the other has frustrated, or is about to frustrate, some concern of his'.

Donohue and Kolt (1992) suggested that there are different 'levels' of conflict and tension, from the absence of conflict through to latent conflict in which one person senses the existence of an unresolved difference, through to the opening up of the issues, the emergence of a dispute about how to resolve difficulties and the seeking of whatever outside help may facilitate a resolution. This may lead to either 'flight', in which the parties remain bitterly opposed and seek to destroy the bargaining position of the other, or intractability, in which the entire conflict becomes over-emotionalised, leading to over-commitment to mutually opposed positions and a refusal to engage in the process of conflict resolution. As discussed earlier, when relationships approach dissolution the partners may resort to such tactics as avoidance: communication with the other person ceases (Banks *et al.*, 1987), so becoming a form of conflict in its own right.

Various interpersonal behaviours are associated with these stages. Patterson (1976) developed a 'coercion hypothesis', which postulates that coercion becomes a dominant means of resolving conflict because people reinforce coercive messages and fail to reinforce more positive methods of conflict resolution. Behaviours that fall into this category include yielding to repeated tantrums, capitulating to aggression at work, yielding to violence in the home, reciprocating negative messages and failing to reciprocate positive messages. Thus it has been found that incompatible couples are more likely than compatible couples to follow complaints with counter-complaints or defensive comments (Ting-Toomey, 1983). The assumptions here are guided by principles derived from social learning theory (Bandura, 1986) and which have been summarised as suggesting that we watch what others do, note what happens to them because of their actions, evaluate whether we should act in the same manner and decide whether replicating their behaviours is worth the effort (Dickson *et al.*, 1993). In short, we have a tendency to imitate the behaviour of others, particularly if we perceive it as having been successful in reaching important goals. As social exchange theorists would put it, we consider whether the benefits outweigh the costs. It can, indeed, often appear that aggressive behaviour 'succeeds', although we would approach any view of success in this context with great caution, and it thus becomes integrated as a dynamic into the relationship concerned.

Donohue and Kolt (1992) suggest that destructive conflicts are characterised by a tendency to focus critically on the other person's needs, by attacking their personal rights, emphasising personalities rather than behaviours, by trying to save one's own face rather than that of others and by promoting a desire for revenge rather than conflict resolution. This leads to extended cycles of escalation or avoidance, rather than a confronting of the central problems in the relationship. Thus the literature is replete with behaviour modification suggestions to avoid these pitfalls. For example, marital therapists would suggest that we avoid making statements to partners such as 'You never show me any respect', but instead identify specific, measurable and alterable behaviours such as 'I feel rejected when you slam the door in my face'. The notion is that a listener is more responsive to the identification of behaviours which they can change, rather than the application of labels which threaten their face needs and attack their central assumptions of personal dignity and self-worth.

Donohue and Kolt (1992) summarise the main positive approaches to conflict resolution as resting on the twin pillars of demonstrating empathy/reflecting, to create an unthreatened focus on problem-solving. This could be manifest in the following approach:

- Receive the other's comments, without interrupting or allowing oneself to become defensive;
- Repeat the person's comments as objectively as possible;
- Request the other person's proposed way of dealing with the problem;
- Review the options and decide on the best approach.

The use of this approach, in general, may offer some way of averting needlessly destructive conflicts and enable people to manage the difficult task of relationship disengagement without causing unnecessary suffering to themselves and to others.

OVERVIEW

This chapter has sought to explore pertinent communication issues during the initiation, maintenance and dissolution of relationships. Relationships remain crucial to our sense of well-being. Whatever the constraints, we will always seek the warm embrace of extended social networks, in which we can seek to realise essential aspects of our own personality. It has been argued throughout that effectiveness in relational communication depends on the utilisation of a wide range of supportive communication behaviours at all stages of the relationship cycle. The evidence reviewed here suggests that, even in the terminal stage of a relationship, such behaviours remain a useful alternative to destructive conflicts and offer some means of safeguarding the essential face needs of all parties concerned. The study of relational communication, therefore, offers exciting opportunities for the effective management of relationships in personal, work and wider social contexts.

REFERENCES

Altman, I. and Taylor, D. A. (1973) *Social Penetration: The Development of Interpersonal Relationships*, Holt, Rinehart & Winston, New York.

Argyle, M. (1987) *The Psychology of Happiness*, Routledge, London.

—— and Henderson, M. (1985) *The Anatomy of Relationships*, Heinemann, London.

Ashford, S. and Tsui, A. (1991) 'Self-regulation for Managerial Effectiveness: The Role of Active Feedback Setting', *Academy of Management Journal*, 34(2), 251–80.

Bandura, A. (1986) *Social Foundations of Thought and Action: A Social Cognitive Theory*, Prentice-Hall, Englewood Cliffs, NJ.

Banks, S. P., Altendorf, D. M., Greene, J. O. and Cody, M. J. (1987) 'An Examination of Relationship Disengagement: Perceptions, Breakup Strategies and Outcomes', *Western Journal of Speech Communication*, 51, 19–41.

Bateson, G. (1979) *Mind and Nature: A Necessary Unity*, Bantam Books, New York.

Baxter, L. A. (1985) 'Accomplishing Relationship Disengagement', in S. Duck and D. Perlman (eds), *Understanding Personal Relationships: An Interdisciplinary Approach*, Sage, London.

—— (1987) 'Cognition and Communication in the Relationship Process', in R. Burnett, P. McGhee and D. Clarke (eds), *Accounting for Relationships: Explanation, Representation and Knowledge*, Methuen, London.

—— and Wilmot, W. W. (1984) 'Secret Tests: Social Strategies for Acquiring Information About the State of the Relationship', *Human Communication Research*, 11, 171–201.

Berger, C. (1988) 'Uncertainty and Information Exchange in Developing Relationships', in S. Duck (ed.), *Handbook of Personal Relationships: Theory, Research and Interventions*, John Wiley, New York.

—— and Kellerman, K. (1983) 'To Ask or Not to Ask: Is That a Question', in R. N. Bostrom (ed.), *Communication Yearbook 7*, Sage, Newbury Park, pp. 342–68.

Blazer, D. G. (1982) 'Social Support and Mortality in an Elderly Community Population', *American Journal of Epidemiology*, 115, 685–94.

Blieszner, R. and Adams, R. (1992) *Adult Friendship*, Sage, London.

Boon, S. (1994) 'Dispelling Doubt and Uncertainty: Trust in Romantic Relationships', in S. Duck, *Dynamics of Relationships*, Sage, London.

Brown, G. and Harris, T. (1978) *Social Origins of Depression: A Study of Psychiatric Disorder in Women*, London, Tavistock.

Brown, P. and Levinson, S. (1987) *Politeness: Some Universals in Language Usage*, Cambridge University Press, Cambridge.

Burgoon, J. and Hale, J. L. (1987) 'Validation and Measurement of the Fundamental Themes of Relational Communication', *Communication Monographs*, 55, 58–9.

Burgoon, M., Hunsaker, F. and Dawson, E. (1994) *Human Communication* (3rd edn), Sage, London.

Burleson, B. R. (1990) 'Comforting as Social Support: Relational Consequences of Supporting Behaviours', in S. Duck (ed.), *Personal Relationships and Social Support*, Sage, London.

Cobb, S. (1976) 'Social Support as a Moderator of Life Stress', *Psychosomatic Medicine*, 38, 300–14.

Collins, B. E. and Guetzkow, H. (1964) *A Social Psychology of Group Processes for Decision Making*, John Wiley, New York.

Cooley, C. H. (1902) *Human Nature and the Social Order*, Scribner, New York.

Cupach, W. and Metts, S. (1994) *Facework*, London, Sage.

Cutrona, C., Suhr, J. and MacFarlane, R. (1990) 'Interpersonal Transactions and the Psychological Sense of Support', in S. Duck and R. Silver (eds), *Personal Relationships and Social Support*, Sage, London.

Davis, M. S. (1973) *Intimate Relations*, Free Press, New York.

Derlega, V. J. (1984) 'Self Disclosure and Intimate Relationships', in V. J. Derlega (ed.), *Communication, Intimacy and Close Relationships*, Academic Press, New York.

——, Metts, S., Petronio, S. and Margulis, S. (1993) *Self Disclosure*, Sage, London.

Dickson, D., Saunders, C. and Stringer, M. (1993) *Rewarding People: The Skill of Responding Positively*, Routledge, London.

Donohue, W. and Kolt, R. (1992) *Managing Interpersonal Conflict*, Sage, London.

Duck, S. W. (1982) 'A Topology of Relationship Disengagement and Dissolution', in S. W. Duck (ed.), *Personal Relationships. Vol. IV: Dissolving Personal Relationships*, Academic Press, New York.

—— (1988) *Relating to Others*, Open University, Milton Keynes.

—— (1991) *Understanding Relationships*, Guilford Press, New York.

—— (1992) *Human Relationships* (2nd edn), Sage, London.

Felson, R. (1985) 'Reflected Appraisal and the Development of Self', *Social Psychology Quarterly*, 48, 71–8.

Fisher, C. B., Reid, J. D. and Melendez, M. (1989) 'Conflict in Families and Friendships of Later Life', *Family Relations*, 38, 83–9.

Foa, U. and Foa, E. (1975) *Resource Theory of Social Exchange*, General Learning Press, Morrison, NJ.

Fogel, A. (1993) *Developing Through Relationships*, Harvester Wheatsheaf, London.

Freedman, J. (1978) *Happy People*, Harcourt Brace Jovanovich, New York.

Gergen, K. (1991) *The Saturated Self: Dilemmas of Identity in Contemporary Life*, Basic Books, New York.

Gilbert, P. (1991) *Human Relationships*, Basil Blackwell, Oxford.

Goffman, E. (1967) *Interaction Ritual: Essays on Face-to-Face Behaviour*, Pantheon, New York.

Hargie, O. and Tourish, D. (1996) 'Auditing Communication Practices to Improve the Management of Human Resources: An Inter-Organisational Study', *Health Services Management Research*.

Hargie, O., Saunders, C. and Dickson, D. (1994) *Social Skills in Interpersonal Communication* (3rd edn), Routledge, London.

Hocker, J. L. and Wilmot, W. W. (1994) *Interpersonal Conflict* (4th edn), W. C. Brown, Dubuque.

Hutton, W. (1995) *The State We're In*, Jonathan Cape, London.

Jablin, F. (1987) 'Formal Organization Structure', in F. Jablin, L. Putnam, K. Roberts and L. Porter, (eds), *Handbook of Organizational Communication*, Sage, Newbury Park.

Jacobson, N. S. (1984) 'A Component Analysis of Behavioral Marital Therapy: The Relative Effectiveness of Behavior Change and Communication/Problem Solving Training', *Journal of Consulting and Clinical Psychology*, 52, 295–305.

Jemmott, J. B. and Magliore, K. (1988) 'Academic Stress, Social Support and Secretory Immunoglobin', *Journal of Personality and Social Psychology*, 55, 803–10.

Johnson, J., Donohue, W., Atkin, C. and Johnson, S. (1994) 'Differences Between Formal and Informal Communication Channels', *Journal of Business Communication*, 31(2), 111–22.

Jones, D. C. (1991) 'Friendship Satisfaction and Gender: An Examination of Sex Differences in Contributions to Friendship Satisfaction', *Journal of Social and Personal Relationships*, 8, 167–85.

Jones, E. (1964) *Ingratiation*, Appleton-Century Crofts, New York.

—— (1990) *Interpersonal Perception*, Freeman, New York.

—— and Pittman, T. S. (1982) 'Towards a General Theory of Strategic Self Presentation', in J. Suls, (ed.), *Psychological Perspectives on the Self. Vol. 1*, Erlbaum, Hillsdale, N.J.

Kelley, H. H. and Thibaut, J. W. (1978) *Interpersonal Relations; A Theory of Interdependence*, John Wiley, New York.

Knapp, M. L. and Vangelisti, A. (1992) *Interpersonal Communication and Human Relationships*, Allyn & Bacon, Boston.

Krueger, D. L. (1983) 'Pragmatics of Dyadic Decision Making: A Sequential Analysis of Communication Patterns', *Western Journal of Speech Communication*, 47, 99–117.

Kurdek, L. A. (1991) 'Marital Stability and Changes in Marital Quality in Newly Wed Couples: A Test of the Contextual Model', *Journal of Social and Personal Relationships*, 9, 125–42.

Langston, C. A. and Cantor, N. (1989) 'Social Anxiety and Social Constraint: When Making Friends is Hard', *Journal of Personality and Social Psychology*, 56, 649–61.

Leyens, J. P., Yzerbyt, V. and Schadron, G. (1994) *Stereotypes and Social Cognition*, Sage, London.

Livingstone. K. (1980) 'Love as a Process of Reducing Uncertainty – Cognitive Theory', in K. S. Pop (ed.), *On Love and Loving*, Jossey-Bass, San Francisco.

McCall, G. J. and Simmons. J. L. (1978) *Identities and Interactions* (2nd edn), Free Press, New York.

Millar, R., Crute, V. and Hargie, O. (1992) *Professional Interviewing*, Routledge, London.

Miller, L. C. (1990) 'Intimacy and Liking: Mutual Influence and the Role of Unique Relationships', *Journal of Personality and Social Psychology*, 59, 50–60.

Montgomery, B. M. (1994) 'Communicating in Close Relationships', in A. L.Weber and J. H. Harvey (eds), *Perspectives On Close Relationships*, Allyn & Bacon, Boston.

Murstein, B. I., MacDonald, M. G. and Cerreto, M. (1977) 'A Theory and Investigation of the Effects of Exchange Orientation on Marriage and Friendship', *Journal of Marriage and the Family*, 39, 543–8.

O'Connor, P. and Brown, G. W. (1984) 'Supportive Relationships: Fact or Fancy?', *Journal of Social and Personal Relationships*, 1, 159–76.

Patterson, G. (1976) 'The Aggressive Child: Victim and Architect of a Coercive System', in E. Mash, L. Hamerlynck and L. Handy (eds), *Behavior Modification and Families*, Brunner/Mazel, New York.

Pennebaker, J. W., Colder, M. and Sharp, L. K. (1988) 'Accelerating the Coping Process', *Journal of Personality and Social Psychology*, 58, 528–37.

Pettigrew, T. F. (1979) 'The Ultimate Attribution Error: Extending Allport's Cognitive Analysis of Prejudice', *Personality and Social Psychology Bulletin*, 5, 461–76.

Planalp, S., Rutherford, D. and Honeycutt, J. M. (1988) 'Events that Increase Uncertainty in Personal Relationships 11', *Human Communication Research*, 14, 516–47.

Reis, H. T. (1984) 'Social Interaction and Well Being', in S. Duck (ed.), *Personal Relationships 5: Repairing Personal Relationships*, Academic Press, London and New York.

Richmond, V., McCroskey, J. and Payne, S. (1991) *Nonverbal Behavior in Interpersonal Relations* (2nd edn), Prentice-Hall, Englewood Cliffs, NJ.

Rook, K. S. (1984) 'The Negative Side of Social Interaction: Impact on Psychological Well Being', *Journal of Personality and Social Psychology*, 46, 1097–1108.

Rosenfeld, L. B. and Bowen, G. L. (1991) 'Marital Disclosure and Marital Satisfaction: Direct-effect versus Interaction Effects Models', *Western Journal of Communication*, 55, 69–84.

Rosenfeld, P., Giacalone, R. and Riordan, C. (1995) 'Impression Management', in N. Nicholson (ed.), *Blackwell Dictionary of Organizational Behavior*, Basil Blackwell, Oxford.

Sampson, E. E. (1989) 'The Deconstruction of the Self', in J. Shotter and K. J. Gergen (eds), *Texts of Identity*, Sage, London, 1–19.

Scheier, M. F. and Carver, C. S. (1981) 'Private and Public Aspects of Self', in L. Wheeler (ed.), *Review of Personality and Social Psychology*, Sage, Beverly Hills.

Schlenker, B. R. (1984) 'Identities, Identifications, and Relationships', in V. J. Derlega (ed.), *Communication, Intimacy and Close Relationships*, Academic Press, New York.

Shaver, P. and Hazan, C. (1994) 'Attachment', in A. Weber and J. Harvey (eds), *Perspectives on Close Relationships*, Allyn & Bacon, London.

Sillars, A. and Weisberg, J. (1987) 'Conflict as a Social Skill', in M. Roloff and G. Miller (eds), *Interpersonal Processes: New Directions in Communication Research*, Sage, London.

Sprecher, S. (1987) 'The Effects of Self Disclosure Given and Received on Affection for an Intimate Partner and Stability of the Relationship', *Journal of Social and Personal Relationships*, 4, 115–27.

Sutherland, S. (1992) *Irrationality*, Constable, London.

Thibaut, J. W. and Kelley, H. H. (1959) *The Social Psychology of Groups*, John Wiley, New York.

Thomas, K. (1983) 'Conflict and its Management', in M. Dunnette (ed.), *Handbook of Industrial and Organizational Psychology*, John Wiley, New York.

Thorne, A. (1987) 'The Press of Personality: a Study of Conversations Between Introverts and Extroverts', *Journal of Personality and Social Psychology*, 53, 718–26.

Ting-Toomey, S. (1983) 'An Analysis of Verbal Communication Patterns in High and Low Marital Adjustment Groups', *Human Communication Research*, 9, 306–19.

Tourish, D. and Hargie, O. (1996) 'Communication Audits and the Management of Change: A Case Study from an NHS Unit of Management', *Health Services Management Research*, 9, 125–35.

Wethington, E. and Kessler, R. C. (1986) 'Perceived Support, Received Support, and Adjustment to Stressful Life Events', *Journal of Health and Social Behavior*, 27, 78–89.

Whetten, D. and Cameron, K. (1991) *Developing Management Skills* (2nd edn), HarperCollins, London.

Wilmot, W. (1995) *Relational Communication*, McGraw-Hill, London.

—— and Stevens, D. C. (1994) 'Relationship Rejuvenation: Arresting Decline in Personal Relationships', in R. Colville (ed.), *Communication and Structure*, Ablex, New York.

Woods, J. (1982) 'Communication and Relational Culture: Bases for the Study of Human Relationships', *Communication Quarterly*, 30, 75–83.

Part IV
Interviewing contexts

15 The selection interview

Rob Millar and Mary Gallagher

INTRODUCTION

Despite considerable criticism over the past half-century, the use of the interview as a central element in the employment selection process remains popular (Harris, 1989; Lowry, 1994; McDaniel *et al.*, 1994; Smith and George, 1992). Reviews of such practices have confirmed the extensive inclusion of interviews for all types of applicant in a number of countries (Robertson and Makin, 1986; Shackleton and Newell, 1991; Taylor *et al.*, 1993). Given that effective selection is vital for the fitness of an organisation (Smith and Robertson, 1993) and the common usage of the interview method, it seems imperative that effective selection interviewing develops from a base of sound understanding and competent deployment of strategies and skills.

Before embarking on our exploration it will be helpful to set out briefly what is meant by the term 'selection interview'. At a general level, after reviewing a number of definitions, Millar *et al.* (1992, p. 3) proposed that an interview is 'A face-to-face dyadic interaction in which one individual plays the role of interviewer and the other takes on the role of interviewee, and both of these roles carry clear expectations concerning behavioural and attitudinal approach. The interview is requested by one of the participants for a specific purpose and both participants are willing contributors'.

As in many social interactions, participants hold expectations of acceptable behaviours likely to be encountered whether playing the role of interviewer or interviewee (Herriot, 1981). Furthermore, behaviours deployed by interview participants operate in a reciprocal fashion whereby what interviewers do has a direct impact on the subsequent behaviour of interviewees. The response of the latter, in turn, acts as one determinant of the interviewer's next action (Dipboye, 1992; Millar *et al.*, 1992).

Ultimately, the social processes which operate throughout the interview contribute to the purpose for which the interview has been convened. With respect to selection interviews the purpose may be described as gathering information on applicants and evaluating it against the demands of specific jobs with a view to making hiring decisions. For example, McDaniel *et al.* (1994, p. 599) defined the selection interview as 'a selection procedure designed to predict future job performance on the basis of applicants' oral responses to oral enquiries'. In similar fashion, a slightly more comprehensive definition was provided by Wiesner and Cronshaw (1988, p. 276): 'The employment interview is an interpersonal interaction of limited duration between one or more interviewers and a job-seeker for the purpose of identifying interviewee knowledge, skills, abilities and behaviours that may be predictive of success in subsequent employment.'

The main features of these definitions emphasise the social nature of the interview, specify the participants and the main organisational goal of predicting job performance and indicate the nature of the information required from interviewees. Implicit within these definitions, and a possible reason for their popularity, is the belief that employers have to meet potential employees face-to-face and that this meeting will enable them to make valid assessments of their suitability for the position (Smith and George, 1992) and the organisation (Herriot, 1989).

As Smith and Robertson (1993) pointed out, whilst the major purpose of any selection interview is to identify the most suitable candidate for a particular job, there are other purposes which selection interviews may serve. Of some relevance in this context are the informational and recruitment functions whereby interviewers seek to communicate accurate job-relevant information and to encourage sought-after applicants to join the organisation (Rynes and Barber, 1990). Herriot (1989) emphasised the latter function as becoming increasingly important in the ever-changing job market where at times a supply shortage can move employers from selection to seduction.

Interviewing, as a means of carrying out recruitment and selection functions, is essentially different from other main techniques primarily because of the substantial dependence on interpersonal communication skills. It follows that the selection interview, being viewed as a particular type of social interaction, may be better understood through the application of social interaction models (e.g. Millar *et al.*, 1992), social process models (e.g. Dipboye, 1992), or in terms of key interpersonal skills (Hargie *et al.*, 1994) relevant to the selection interview context. Of course, interpersonal skills and strategies contribute to goal attainment of interviewers *and* applicants who are engaged in a reciprocal social relationship and hence each perspective warrants consideration.

THE INTERVIEWER'S PERSPECTIVE

In terms of the definitions previously cited, interviewers, by way of social interaction, attempt to achieve their identified goals; that is, to make successful predictions of job/organisation suitability across a range of applicants. It is incumbent upon interviewers to make considered choices pertaining to the type of interview to be employed and the use of appropriate interpersonal skills, which together contribute to the success of the selection interview.

Interview structure

One of the major dimensions along which interviews can be differentiated relates to their degree of structure. Millar *et al.* (1992, p. 111) suggested that the main structuring criteria 'relate to the degree of interviewer flexibility with respect to the content of the interview, what is included, how it is sampled, in what sequence and how much freedom is offered to interviewees with respect to their answers (i.e. open ended or multiple choice formats)'. Herriot (1989) identified two major forms of selection interview, the first being a dynamic unstructured approach where the interviewer has an agenda to cover but will do so dependent on the interviewee's responses. Thus, the sequence of topics and the specific questions are not pre-planned and in part are controlled by the applicant. In contrast, the second form of interview is structured, being composed of a set of questions which are derived from a job analysis and which are presented to all applicants concerning their past, present or future behaviour.

Unstructured interviews

The totally unstructured interview format, whilst appropriate for some interpersonal encounters such as counselling, is increasingly being viewed as inappropriate for use in the selection context (Millar *et al.*, 1992). The inconsistent use of questions about topics which may not be relevant conspire to reduce both reliability and validity of the procedure. Assessments made by unstructured techniques are more likely to relate to general personality traits which encourages interviewers to make questionable inferences between such traits and job performance (Keenan, 1989). Moreover, interviewers may reach different conclusions based on similar applicant responses (Latham *et al.*, 1980). Indeed, Herriot (1985, p. 35) advocated that 'What needs to be avoided is the use of the interview as a quasi-personality test with interview behaviour being used as evidence of personal characteristics'.

A major consequence of using unstructured interview formats, which may help to explain their poor assessment qualities, is the increased likelihood of introducing errors commonly encountered in any social interaction. Stevens (1981) identified six main types of selection errors. (1) *Halo effect* where interviewers tend to rate applicants highly on every dimension because they scored highly on one – for example, Athey and Hautaluoma (1994) found evidence of a general halo effect for most highly educated applicants. (2) *Central tendency* where interviewers rate all applicants as average and fail to use the whole of the scale. (3) *Leniency* where interviewers rate all applicants favourably, again failing to discriminate effectively. Baron (1993) has shown that interviewers in positive mood rate ambiguously qualified applicants more positively and better qualified than interviewers who are more negative. (4) *Strictness* where interviewers rate all applicants unfavourably. For example, Furnham and Burbeck (1989) found that the greater the interviewer's job or interviewing experience the stricter were their ratings of candidates. (5) *Contrast effect* where the rating of applicants is influenced by how they compare to a previous applicant. (6) *Stereotyping* where interviewers rely on initial impressions or schemas, set about confirming these impressions and subsequently rate on this basis.

Although research has suggested that all these human errors contribute to poor selection decisions, a considerable amount of research effort has been expended in elucidating the important role played by initial impressions formed by interviewers of applicants. Dipboye (1992, p. 120) summarised the evidence in favour of a confirmatory model for the role played by initial impressions: 'Interviewers are more than passive observers simply taking in data and turning out judgements. Interviewers are active agents whose prior impressions can lead them in the direction of shaping the events that occur in the interview. Several decades of research have shown that the search for and processing of information on applicants can be influenced to an inordinate degree by the data encountered in the initial phases of the interview.' Most interviews begin with an examination of applications, references and any other relevant documentation and interviewers during this phase form initial impressions of applicants. Macan and Dipboye (1994) found that these impressions, formed from pre-interview information, influenced the subsequent interpretation of actual applicant behaviour in the selection interview.

Further support for the effects of pre-interview information comes from a recent field study by Dougherty *et al.* (1994) who investigated the concept of expectancy confirmation thought to operate in selection interviews. In their study of semi-structured interviews they found that positive first impressions were followed by more positive regard, job information and selling the company, less information-gathering and more establishment of rapport by the interviewer coupled with more confident and effective behaviours on the part of the applicant. Dougherty *et al.* (1994) viewed these findings as supporting the operation of a self-fulfilling prophecy process and commend to interviewers the need to employ highly structured interviews in order to reduce the influence of confirmatory biases.

Orpen (1984) carried out a large field study of the selection of life insurance salespeople and found that actual and, more importantly, perceived similarity of the interviewer and applicant were strongly related to candidate attractiveness and to recruitment decisions. In an experimental study, Gilmore *et al.* (1986) found that attractive applicants were perceived more favourably in terms of personality, expected job performance and were more likely to be recruited. In a field study of graduate selection interviews, Anderson and Shackleton (1990) identified perceived similarity as one construct that exerted an influence on impression formation which, in turn, was strongly related to outcome decisions. The idea that interviewers show tendencies to select people similar to themselves was explained by Herriot (1989) in terms of organisational identity and culture or person-organisation 'fit' (Billsberry, 1995).

Several studies have tried to identify ways in which interviewers process information and reach selection decisions (e.g. Anderson, 1991). It is clear that the perceptual and cognitive tasks facing interviewers are immense given the relatively short amount of time available for the collection of relevant information on applicants. Under such circumstances the need to employ 'short cuts' becomes necessary if overload is to be avoided. However, in addition to limited information being available, the price to be paid may be a considerable distortion of applicant information and possibly discriminatory practice (Millar *et al.*, 1992). For example, where information is not only limited but is not job-related, the likelihood of biases occurring on the basis of gender (Kacmar *et al.*, 1994; White and White, 1994) or disability (Marchioro and Bartels, 1994) is high.

An influential means of taking short cuts for interviewers is to label or categorise applicants based on one or two pertinent characteristics. As Kacmar *et al.* (1994, p. 812) stated, 'if a decision maker in an employment interview situation has limited access to other job-relevant information, he or she may assign the candidate to a category consistent with race or gender stereotypes using automatic perceptual processing'. Alternatively, interviewers may operate by comparing applicants with an ideal or prototypical candidate. Anderson and Shackleton (1990) studied over 300 graduate selection interviews and found that recruiters saw the ideal candidate as being interesting, relaxed, strong, successful in life, active, mature, enthusiastic, sensitive, pleasant, honest and dominant. Their findings suggested that regardless of occupation, interviewers recruit a prototypical graduate personality rather than for occupation-specific personality stereotypes. Thus, in the typical, time-pressured selection context, interviewer information-processing may be guided by the employment of prototypes made up of features such as physical characteristics, traits and behaviours which can be associated with a notional ideal employee. The idea that interviewers then compare applicants to these ideal features in order to evaluate them has received some support from exploratory experimental studies (Perry, 1994; Van Vianen and Willemsen, 1992). Van Vianen and Willemsen (1992) compared interviewers' identification of the ideal candidate's personality with their assessments of the personalities of accepted and rejected candidates and found that those accepted fitted the ideal description more than those rejected.

Investigations into the social processes involved in selection interviews have therefore revealed its apparent vulnerability to errors in perceptual, information and decision-making processes. As a result of these findings more recent research has focused on reducing these 'human' errors by developing alternative approaches to the unstructured interview. The direction of these developments has been towards the introduction of increasing amounts of structure, and to varying degrees the reduction of human discretion in the process.

Structured interviews

The development of the structured selection interview represents attempts to design an interview in such a way as to reduce the possible influence of individual biases and errors on interviewer decisions. These attempts appear to be generating increasing support for the interview as a valid selection tool (Lowry, 1994). While early research reviews and meta-analyses suggested that the interview had little reliability or validity as a selection method, it has been noted that the widespread differences between interviews and their generally unstructured and unstandardised nature contributed substantially to these disappointing conclusions (Smith and George, 1992). More recent reviews by Wright *et al.* (1989) and Wiesner and Cronshaw (1988) and results from Motowildo *et al.* (1992) have reported significant increases in both reliability and validity of more highly structured approaches.

Structuring may take a number of forms. However, the main approaches currently documented have been derived from one main approach – the situational interview of Latham *et al.* (1980). They based the interview on a series of questions derived from an analysis of critical incidents which differentiated between effective and ineffective job performance. The main features of the situational interview have been summarised by Latham (1989, p. 179) where 'the questions are based on a job analysis and hence are job-related, the questions are sufficiently abstruse that applicants cannot determine the desired answer, and hence must state their true intentions, the interviewers have a scoring guide for each item, and the predictors and the criteria are similar so that one is using "apples to predict apples rather than oranges"'.

The underlying assumption of this approach to interviewing is that intentions are closely related to actual behaviour. Furthermore, the nature of the questions reduces opportunities for applicants to engage in impression management by selecting desired responses. Latham *et al.* (1980) carried out a series of studies using the situational interview and found high inter-interviewer reliability. Moreover, there was a high correlation between interviewer ratings and supervisors' ratings of subsequent job performance. Latham (1989) cited internal reliability co-efficients ranging from 0.61 to 0.78, inter-observer co-efficients of 0.76 to 0.96 and predictive validity values of 0.14 to 0.45 for situational interviews.

Although alternative methods of structuring the selection interview have been documented (Campion *et al.*, 1988; Feild and Gatewood, 1989; Janz, 1982, 1989; Motowildo *et al.*, 1992), they are simply derivatives of the original situational interview outlined above. Janz's (1989) patterned behaviour description interview was based on the premise that future behaviour is best predicted by past behaviour rather than on stated intentions.

Moreover, it focused on the elicitation of information about how applicants performed in previous work-related contexts. However, as with the situational interview the content is derived from job analyses. Interestingly, an investigation into graduate recruitment interviews found that interviewers typically spent little time discussing candidates' past achievements and behaviours compared to the time allocated to the organisation and their reasons for applying (Keenan and Wedderburn, 1980).

Structured approaches were developed primarily to reduce subjectivity and inconsistency, to increase reliability and validity and to guard against infringing legal guidelines pertaining to fair employment practice. The development of structured approaches comprises six main steps which contribute to increased effectiveness (Campion *et al.*, 1988). First, the interview content is based on a thorough analysis of the job in question such that all derived questions are job-related. Basing questions on job analysis substantially reduces the potential for questions unrelated to the job which, in turn, may introduce unwanted error into the interview process (Wright *et al.*, 1989). Second, all derived questions are asked of all applicants without exception and, generally speaking, no prompting or follow-up questions are permitted. Third, the rating scales constructed to 'score' the applicants' responses should be anchored scales with the anchor points identified through discussion with personnel and job experts. Fourth, in a further attempt to reduce interviewer bias it is recommended that an interview panel be comprised of at least three individuals all of whom should be familiar with the job and the structured interviewing process. However, whilst Roth and Campion (1992) found panel interviews to be valid predictors of job performance, Wiesner and Cronshaw (1988) found them to be no more valid than individual interviewers. Fifth, all candidates should experience the same process and panel members should not discuss questions, answers or candidates between interviews. Finally, special attention should be given to ensuring that the process is as job-related as possible, that each candidate is treated fairly and that adequate documentation is maintained. (A highly structured procedure was employed by Campion *et al.* (1988) in selection interviews for jobs in a pulp and paper mill whereupon reliability ($r = 0.88$) and validity ($r = 0.56$) co-efficients were reported which compared favourably with figures typically quoted for employment tests. The authors did note that the procedure may require modifications for different level jobs, such as management, where probing and follow-up questioning might be beneficial.)

Recent meta-analytic studies have offered further support for the superior technical qualities of structured interview methods. Wiesner and Cronshaw (1988) concluded that structured interviews were significantly more valid than unstructured interviews and that validity was also associated with the use of formal job-analytic information in developing interview questions. Similarly, Wright *et al.* (1989) concluded from their meta-analytic study that the structured approach demonstrated superior predictive validity. A more recent meta-analytic study by McDaniel *et al.* (1994) revealed that, in addition to confirming the positive effects of structuring interviews, the situational approach had higher validity than a general job-related approach and, furthermore, that both approaches were significantly more valid than the less structured (and possibly less job-related) psychological interview.

Although, as indicated above, structured approaches have demonstrated superior levels of reliability and validity with respect to selection decisions, there are some disadvantages associated with the use of highly structured interviews. Whilst cutting down on human errors, structuring reduces the opportunities to follow up and probe candidates' responses and hence introduces considerable inflexibility (Dougherty *et al.*, 1994). Millar *et al.* (1992) also sounded a note of caution against which improvements in technical characteristics might be judged. The heavy focus on the task of assessing job suitability by adherence to a highly rigid standardised procedure with which many applicants will be unfamiliar and indeed may not recognise as 'an interview' (or as a particularly social encounter) may evoke negative affect in candidates. As Goodale (1989, p. 320) observed, 'highly structured interviews can appear to the applicant a bit like an interrogation, and may place too much emphasis on the *selection* objective at the expense of the *attraction* objective'.

The use of situational-type interviews may present particular difficulties for applicants who, in order to reduce their pre-interview anxiety, prepare for the encounter on the assumption that it will take a more unstructured format moving through a series of traditional stages (Tullar, 1989). Given the prevalent preference for recruiters to base applicant evaluation on 'intuition', 'feelings', 'experience' or 'body language' (Taylor *et al.*, 1993), the use of structured interviews may also create difficulties for these types of interviewers. They may not, according to Daniel and Valencia (1991, p. 131), wish to be viewed as 'a robot, an impersonal unfeeling scientific instrument'.

In summary, the evidence suggests that interviewers should consider their tactics carefully. Adherence to guidelines which impose structure on and ensure job-relevant content of the interview process will enhance the predictive power of the selection interview. However, in the process of striving for enhanced technical qualities, highly structured interviews may reduce the social acceptability or face validity for many candidates. It is to this social dimension that we now turn our attention and examine the contribution of interviewer interpersonal skills to the conduct of selection interviews.

Interviewer interpersonal skills

As indicated in the introduction, the range of interpersonal communication skills available to selection interviewers is well documented in not only this volume, but also Hargie *et al.* (1994) and Millar *et al.* (1992). The extent to which interviewers open the interview effectively, collect their information through adequate questioning technique, demonstrate active listening to the responses, reward applicants for their participation and close the interview competently all contribute to meeting interview objectives for both the interviewer and the interviewee. However, prior to commenting on interview skills the reader is reminded of the cautionary observation made by Dipboye (1992) that much of the conventional wisdom and copious advice offered to prospective selection interviewers tends to be rooted in common sense and much of it still awaits empirical validation.

Opening the interview

In order to meet the joint demands of creating a non-threatening atmosphere and keeping interviewer behaviour constant across interviews (Lowry, 1994), emphasis might be placed on two types of opening, detailed by Saunders (1986). Factual opening – where the nature, purpose and format of the interview are specified – provides the opportunity to structure the interview for all participants. Social opening, on the other hand, focuses more on establishing rapport and the climate of the forthcoming interview. In this way, it exerts considerable influence on applicants' emotional state. Although non-task comments may help to reduce anxiety levels of nervous applicants, it is equally possible that the use of social chit-chat may introduce unwanted variations into the procedures and elicit non-job-related material which then contributes to judgement errors (Campion *et al.*, 1988). With respect to selection interviewing, there is little evidence to support the positive effects of social banter and, in fact, Stewart and Cash (1974) suggested it may even increase anxiety as applicants simply have to wait longer for the inevitable (i.e. tough, task-related interview questions). The elicitation of information by *ad hoc* dialogue may also increase the risks of illegal and discriminatory practices occurring (Dipboye, 1992). However, despite the misgivings of some authors, specific interview guides do recommend that interviewers begin by talking about something they have in common with candidates (Hackney and Kleiner, 1994).

Questioning

Ultimately the main function of the selection interview is to predict job performance, based on the collection of relevant job-related information preferably derived from systematic job analyses (Smith and George, 1992). Structured interviews are comprised of a series of pre-planned job-related questions, primarily open in format and which have preferred codable responses (Wright *et al.*, 1989). All applicants are presented with the same specific questions in the same sequence where the content of questions, according to Wright *et al.* (1989), may pertain to: (1) a description of work situations followed by 'What would you do?' or 'What did you do?' type inquiries; (2) extent of job knowledge; (3) samples or simulations of the actual job; and (4) worker requirements, such as their willingness to perform certain tasks under certain working conditions (e.g. shift work). Recent models of the selection interview have placed great emphasis on the use of specific job-related questions (Taylor, 1993). Jablin and Miller (1990) concluded their review of questioning in the selection interview by recommending the use of pre-planned, open, job-related questions in order to guard against bias and subsequent inaccurate decisions. That interviewers have some facility for following up and probing applicant responses (e.g. 'Could you give me an example of what you mean?') has been supported. Motowildo *et al.* (1992) found that interviewers who were more adept at asking questions gained significantly more relevant information about applicants which contributed to more accurate judgements. Effective questioning skills related to asking for relevant information for clarification, for probing past experiences (situations, behaviours and outcomes), restating responses accurately and requesting examples of behaviour (Motowildo *et al.*, 1992). With respect to question content, Goodale (1989) cautioned against the use of 'traditional' interview questions (e.g. 'What are your strengths/weaknesses?', or 'Where do you want to be in five years' time?') which, due to their predictability, simply elicit prepared, rehearsed answers.

Finally, there are occasions where interviews can deteriorate into interrogations where closed question after closed question is fired at applicants. Not only does this approach fail to gather sufficiently comprehensive information but also the interviewer is required to work extremely hard thinking up large numbers of questions. In circumstances where applicants tend to contribute less to the interaction than is warranted, Quay (1994) provided some useful advice. Although working in the field of management consultancy the suggestions of Quay (1994) appeared readily transferable to the selection context. He suggested that rather than asking more and more questions the interviewer considers the use of 'command statements' coupled with what Hargie *et al.* (1994) called open questions (e.g. 'Let's talk about', 'Tell me about', 'Let's explore the reasons for . . .', or 'I'd be interested in your ideas about . . .'). The onus is placed firmly on the interviewee rather than the interviewer.

Non-verbal behaviour

As outlined earlier, interviewer non-verbal behaviour can influence interview climate from the outset but it can also affect the achievement of additional goals of selection interviews, such as persuasion or attraction. For example, an experimental study by Goltz and Giannantonio (1995) found that students, having viewed a videotape of a friendly interviewer (non-verbally speaking) and an unfriendly interviewer, with the verbal content held constant, made more positive inferences regarding the organisation and were more likely to be attracted to the job in the former condition. Alderfer and McCord (1970), in a study of graduate selection interviews, found that positive evaluation of the interview and a higher probability of job acceptance were related to interviewer cues of interest and concern. Similar findings were reported by Young and Heneman III (1986) where reactions of administrators and teachers to the selection process were more positive when interviewers were perceived by applicants to project personal warmth.

Listening

As Dipboye (1992) noted, interviewees should be given the opportunity and encouraged to do most of the talking if the immediate purpose of the interviewer is to gather sufficient relevant information from each applicant. Stevens (1981) supported this by suggesting that interviewers should be wary of a tendency to talk too much themselves! According to Shaffer *et al.* (1990), some individuals were very effective at encouraging others to self-disclose information possibly because they actively communicated personal interest and attention.

Lowry (1994) viewed checking the accuracy of interviewees' responses as crucial to effective selection interviewing, a task which could be achieved only by active and accurate listening. It seems preferable to conduct interviews in the absence of any interruptions and to take notes as both conditions contribute to enhanced accuracy of reported information (Schuh, 1978).

Closing interviews

The nature of selection interviews, where decisions have not yet been formally taken about the suitability of the candidate for the job, requires a cautious closure. It would seem important that this phase of the interview acknowledges the effort invested and participation by the interviewee in the interview yet this must be achieved in a 'neutral' way so as not to raise expectations (Dipboye, 1992). Conventional practice typically allows applicants the opportunity to ask questions at this stage, although highly structured approaches recommend that this be carried out in a separate interview with a personnel representative to ensure that only job-related information is considered for the purposes of reaching a selection decision (Campion *et al.*, 1988). In somewhat less structured methods, applicant questions may be regarded as an important source of information. For example, Burns and Morehead (1991) suggested that selection of school personnel should include assessment of the types of questions asked (and not asked) by candidates in the interview.

In summary, the role of selection interviewers requires them to assume substantial responsibility for convening and conducting the interview. Therefore, it is vital that they are knowledgeable of interview tactics and skilled in the utilisation of interpersonal communication skills. Effective interviewers need to focus attention on both the technical qualities of their procedures and on the social context in which candidate selection takes place. The extent to which objectives are attained is not simply a function of interviewer competence but will also be influenced by the effectiveness by which applicants play out their role.

THE APPLICANTS' PERSPECTIVE

It is generally assumed that an interview for a job will be viewed by applicants as one of the most important events in their lives. That applicants for such openings desire success tends to be taken for granted by the providers. Under such circumstances applicants can be expected to interact with interviewers in ways designed to create the best possible impression of their qualifications. So, how do applicants create a 'good' impression in the selection interview?

Playing the game

A number of researchers have conceptualised the selection interview as comprising a relatively narrow set of rules and roles (Herriot, 1981, 1989; Sarangi, 1994). Sarangi (1994, p. 168) considered the selection interview as what Levinson called an 'activity type' and defined it as 'a fuzzy category whose focal members are goal-defined, socially constituted, bounded, event with constraints on participants, setting and so on, but above all on the kinds of allowable contributions'. For applicants to create a favourable impression it will be important that they are knowledgeable about the norms, behavioural expectations and limitations associated with their role as players in the interview game. The notion of guiding structures has been explicated by Tullar (1989) who suggested that applicants can prepare for an interview by adherence to a 'cognitive performing script'. This script indicates what might be appropriate behaviour to deploy within each of the major scenes which together constitute the selection interview. Such scripts implicitly set out behaviour which would be deemed inappropriate and ineffective for goal attainment.

So, applicants entering the selection interview do so knowing that there are a number of rules governing their actions and that breaking the rules or acting out-of-role may carry severe consequences for their future careers. Millar *et al.* (1992) noted that individuals who acted in a manner which did not conform to the expected norms tended to be attributed more negative labels (such as unco-operative, difficult, unhelpful). Herriot (1981) observed that similar behaviour was interpreted as indicative of a 'bad applicant'. Interviewers, it appears, are more impressed by applicants who behave according to the rules of the selection interview 'game' (or follow their script) despite the possibility that such attributions may lead to erroneous conclusions pertaining to applicant characteristics (Herriot, 1989; Millar *et al.*, 1992).

The assumption that applicants are aware of the rules and their role behaviours may be justified at a general level but there may be substantial differences of opinion concerning what is acceptable and what is not within and between cultures. The potential for miscommunication and misunderstanding may be considerable (Furnborough *et al.*, 1982; Sarangi, 1994). If such out-of-role and unexpected behaviour is regarded as intentional and subsequently attributed to the stable internal traits of the applicant, the outcome is likely to be negative for the applicant in the selection context. Miscommunication of this type has been illustrated by Sarangi (1994, p. 165) where 'it is characteristic for Asian speakers to begin a response in a general way since a more direct answer is considered by them to be rather impolite . . . the British interviewer preferring a "direct and relevant" answer and the Asian interviewee opting for an "indirect and polite" response'. From the interviewer's perspective applicants who fail to behave in accordance with expected norms of communication are likely to be designated as 'poor' applicants and as a consequence rejected.

Furthermore, the selection interview has been described as comprising a sequence of stages (Lopez, 1975) or scenes (Tullar, 1989). Lopez (1975) suggested a four-stage process commencing with establishing rapport, followed by getting and then giving information and concluding with closure. In a similar fashion, Tullar (1989) outlined the major 'scenes' of the selection interview as pre-interview preparation, greeting and small talk, interviewer questioning, applicant inquiries and interviewer wrap-up. It is important that applicants are aware of such structures and that they have knowledge of appropriate behaviours within each of the main stages – that is, that they are aware of the cognitive performing script for applicants. Thus, it is crucial that applicants realise the potential impact of their behaviours during the early scenes where rapport is being established and initial impressions formed.

Awareness of question types and what would comprise a preferred answer, cues of turn-taking, expectations of the content agenda and taking the opportunity to assume control of the interview by asking questions when allowed all contribute to the smooth flow of communication throughout the selection interview. However, not all interviews demonstrate these qualities and difficulties may be particularly evident in inter-cultural encounters.

Sarangi (1994) presented an important analysis of the selection interview and indicated a number of points of potential breakdown in communication between British interviewers and Asian interviewees. For example, interviewers posed questions to which they expected, what Sarangi (1994) termed, 'preferred' answers. So, in response to the highly expected question 'Why have you applied for this position?', candidates were expected to communicate evidence of high motivation and enthusiasm for the particular opening, even if the level communicated is somewhat exaggerated. This posed considerable problems for candidates who regarded the preferred response as insincere, untruthful and therefore unacceptable (Furnborough *et al.*, 1982). In addition, the fact that they had applied for and were attending an interview was regarded as sufficient evidence of their interest and motivation, making the need for a 'doctored' answer quite unnecessary. But this is not playing the interview game and may be viewed by interviewers as dispreferred or doubtful behaviour, rather than simply different behaviour.

Towards the end of many selection interviews candidates are offered the opportunity to ask questions of the interviewer, to take control. Many applicants would expect such an offer, for as Tullar (1989, p. 242) stated, 'applicants have been taught that it is important to ask informed questions about the organization. Most applicants understand that taking control and asking some intelligent sounding questions is not optional'. This would concur with traditional advice dispensed to prospective candidates even if it means writing down some questions in case of a failing memory. Culturally different applicants may, however, be completely taken by surprise by any offer made by an interviewer to assume, even for a short period, control of the interview (Sarangi, 1994). Their cultural experience suggests that as the lower status participant in a highly structured encounter they have no 'speaker rights' and therefore have no right to ask questions of the interviewer. From the British interviewer's perspective, a decline to assume control constitutes a dispreferred response and conveys a passive and negative impression. Indeed, ending an interview in such a manner contravenes traditional advice, illustrated by Grier and Trenta (1992), who suggested ending on 'a strong note' by being positive, enthusiastic, confident, energetic and dependable.

Effective interviewee behaviour

A considerable amount of research has been documented concerning effective interviewee behaviour during selection interviews. Much of this work, summarised in recent texts on selection in general (e.g. Smith and Robertson, 1993), and selection interviews in particular (e.g. Dipboye, 1992), suggests some consistency in reported findings. First, it should be emphasised that what applicants say and how they say it in interviews constitutes a major set of determinants of interviewers' final impressions. In fact, Dipboye (1992, p. 90) tentatively proposed that the applicant's communication behaviour during the interview was 'perhaps the most salient determinant' of impressions formed by the interviewer.

Non-verbal communication

The influence of applicant non-verbal communication has been identified by a number of researchers. In a rare and early field study, Forbes and Jackson (1980) found that interviewers were more impressed by applicants who displayed more head movement (e.g. nodding), direct eye contact and smiling. In a more recent field study, Anderson and Shackleton (1990) investigated the influence of candidate non-verbal behaviour on interviewers' impressions in graduate selection interviews. Based on their finding that impressions formed by interviewers of applicant personality were substantially based on applicant facial non-verbal behaviours, they concluded that 'It seems that interviewees would be well advised to maintain high levels of eye contact with the interviewer and to display frequent positive facial expressions so as to maximize their chances of success' (p. 74).

These findings were supportive of conclusions presented by Young and Beier (1977) where eye contact, smiling and movements of the head accounted for most of the variance in interviewer ratings of applicant suitability. Anderson (1991) also reported that candidates' facial expressions and eye contact affected recruiters' ratings of character, motivation and competence. Again, advice to prospective applicants suggests, particularly at the beginning and end of the interview, making direct eye contact with the interviewer, smiling and offering a firm handshake (Grier and Trenta, 1992).

Many of the differences between successful and unsuccessful interviewees, identified by Einhorn (1981), pertained to non-verbal components of communication. Successful candidates tended to communicate more positively or more enthusiastically by modulating their speech rate, tone and pitch, by projecting a more human and less statuesque image (e.g. smiling, nodding, gesturing) and by displaying overall attentive behaviour (e.g. posture, eye contact and gaze).

Verbal communication

There are, of course, strong expectations held by both participants that applicants will be required to talk and self-disclose relevant material in the interview. Work completed by Shaffer *et al.* (1990) indicated that interviewees (and interviewers) may display signs of what were termed 'high openers'. These were people adept at inducing others to self-disclose and so contributed significantly to more harmonious interactions. Of relevance to this context Shaffer *et al.* (1990, p. 520) concluded that 'anyone whose life outcomes are likely to depend on information he or she provides in an interview (e.g. job applicants, medical patients, legal clients) would be well advised to cultivate the social/conversational skills that high openers display'. Failure to self-disclose as expected may be taken as non-compliance to role expectations and result in somewhat negative personal attributions (Millar *et al.*, 1992). The significance of verbal material has been indicated by Hollandsworth *et al.* (1979) who found 'appropriateness of verbal content' and 'fluency of verbal communication' to be the two most important variables with respect to post-interview decisions. The importance of speaking fluently was also identified by Einhorn (1981) where unsuccessful interviewees were characterised by hesitant and ponderous verbal responses. More recently the positive influence of fluent speech punctuated by lower frequencies of speech disturbances has been documented (Ferwerda, 1995).

A further factor related to the verbal content of interviewee speech concerned what Dipboye (1992) called 'powerfulness of speech'. Drawing on the work of Einhorn (1981) and Bradac and Mulac (1984), he suggested that the most powerful and effective messages were perceived as comprising powerful and polite language – rather than saying, 'I might', effective interviewees would say, 'I would'. Messages containing words called intensifiers were rated as next most effective: these words enhanced the affective components of messages; for example, instead of 'I liked', and 'It was challenging', interviewees would say, 'I really liked', and 'It was extremely challenging'. Consistent with previous findings, the hesitation message type was perceived as the least powerful and most ineffective (Bradac and Mulac, 1984).

The importance of considering both of the main channels of communication in attempting to develop an understanding of social interaction is crucial (Keenan, 1989). For example, Rasmussen (1984) investigated the interaction of verbal and non-verbal behaviour in selection interviews and found that suitability ratings were influenced by positive non-verbal behaviours only when the verbal content was impressive. Where it was not positive, non-verbal behaviours resulted in lower ratings.

In addition, Dipboye (1992) cited research which examined the influence of applicant response latencies to interviewer questions. The influence on the credibility of applicant responses depended on both the length of the pause and on the content of the dialogue. Longer latency times tended to increase the credibility of the applicant's information where the content was self-detrimental (for example, do you believe in taking drugs, have you a criminal record?). However, where the response was self-serving, longer applicant pauses tended to decrease the credibility of the verbal content. In summary, Dipboye (1992, p. 106) stated that 'the applicant's interview performance consists not only of the content of statements made during the interview (linguistic behavior) but also the applicant's "style" of response as defined by the verbal and non-verbal behavior accompanying these statements (nonlinguistic behavior)'.

As with much social behaviour, it is the integration of all message components that ultimately influences the intensity and clarity of the impression made on another – in this case, the interviewer. Accordingly, interviewers appear to be influenced by the applicant's overall social performance and form a global impression of applicant suitability (Charisiou *et al.*, 1989; Dipboye, 1992; Roth and Campion, 1992). Indeed, Dipboye (1992) went further by concluding that these highly subjective global impressions were more influential than objective data on final selection decisions. This conclusion was supported by findings of a survey of recruiters by Ugbah and Evuleocha (1992) which indicated that the relative importance of applicant oral communication during the interview had a much greater effect than their written credentials on selection decisions.

Therefore, the overall impression created by the applicant by way of social interaction with the interviewer during the interview is of immense importance. As a consequence, awareness and deployment of appropriate impression management strategies may form an important element of interview preparation by applicants (and interviewers).

Impression management in the selection interview

Drawing on social psychological theory, Kacmar and Carlson (1994, p. 688) stated that impression management has been defined as 'the conscious or unconscious attempt to construct and portray a particular image by controlling the information available to others (i.e. targets) so that they will view the actor as he or she intended'. Given the importance of the interview as a potential gateway to a whole life career it is not surprising that applicants make tremendous efforts to persuade interviewers that they are the best persons to fill their vacancies. However, in attempting to achieve this goal applicants face a difficult decision as to which particular communication tactic will lead to goal achievement – that is, creating the most favourable impression (Gallois *et al.*, 1992). Applicants must decide what image they wish to convey and what specific behaviours would convey the desired impression; then they must be able to do so in a manner that appears to be genuine, spontaneous and unrehearsed so that it is believable from the interviewer's perspective. Furthermore, applicants should be able to defend the projected image against attempts that may threaten it as contained in material presented by the interviewer in the interview (Dipboye, 1992). As indicated by social interaction models (Hargie and Marshall, 1986), the effectiveness of attempts to exert social influence are dependent on influencing agents being sensitive to the cues inherent in the social situation. In this way, applicants in the interview context can engage in what Herriot (1981) called 'anxious scanning' to monitor the effects of their attempts at projecting a desired image and, as a consequence, can make necessary corrections to maximise goal attainment (Dipboye, 1992; Gilmore and Ferris,

1989). Furthermore, the accuracy with which interviewees evaluate their own interview behaviours is crucial. Tourish and Hargie (1995) found that interviewees were prone to making poor self-evaluations of most aspects of their interview performance. Indeed, such evaluations were predominantly worse than those proffered by their interviewers. Interviewees also presented other candidates as being superior to themselves.

In general, there appear to be two main categories of self-presentation behaviours which have been referred to as *assertive* and *defensive* (Kacmar *et al.*, 1992). Liden and Parsons (1986) adopted the terms 'offensive' and 'defensive' psychological sets to reflect a similar dichotomy. Relating specifically to the selection interview context, Kacmar *et al.* (1992) proposed tactics that either focused the interview conversation on the interviewee (referred to as *self-focused*) or which focused attention on the interviewer (referred to as *other-focused*). The advantage of adopting the former tactics is that applicants can focus the direction of their interviews' content on areas which will allow them to excel, hence creating as positive an impression as possible.

Assertive, offensive or many self-focused tactics are utilised by applicants actively to enhance their image in the eyes of an interviewer. Gilmore and Ferris (1989) and Kacmar *et al.* (1992) suggested a number of tactics such as taking an exaggerated personal responsibility for positive life experiences and achievements (called *entitlements*), making efforts to enhance the value and significance of an event to enhance its importance (called *enhancements*) and engaging in self-promotion of one's individual qualities. These impression-management tactics are methods by which applicants 'sell themselves' to interviewers by embellishing their qualifications and minimising their weaknesses.

Defensive impression-management tactics have also been documented (Dipboye, 1992; Gilmore and Ferris, 1989). These subtle forms of influence include trying to flatter the interviewer (for example, by saying, 'That's another excellent question'), appearing to have beliefs, attitudes and opinions similar to those espoused by the interviewer and through appealing to the interviewer's compassion (termed 'feigned helplessness'). In addition, where interviewees find themselves or their image under threat from the interviewer, they may engage in other defensive tactics which include making excuses, offering justifications or making apologies, in order to maintain a positive image (Gilmore and Ferris, 1989).

The evidence is indicative of the relative superiority of more assertive, self-focused impression-management tactics as means of achieving positive self-images in the selection interview. According to Gallois *et al.* (1992) interviewers definitely favoured applicants (male and female) who employed an assertive communication style over those who were either aggressive or passive (that is, non-assertive). Similar findings were reported by Kacmar *et al.* (1992) where applicants who employed self-focused tactics were more highly rated and were more likely to be offered jobs. These findings are consistent with evidence presented by Tullar (1989), Fletcher (1990) and as summarised by Dipboye (1992). The lack of significant gender differences in impression-management tactics was supported in a questionnaire study by DuBrin (1994) although Kacmar and Carlson (1994, p. 690) suggested gender differences tended in the direction such that 'When women use self-focused tactics they may be more subtle than men who use this tactic. On the other hand, women may be more comfortable than men using other-focused tactics because these tactics allow them to take a less dominant stand'.

Not surprisingly, candidates who employ assertive impression-management tactics tend to be attributed positive internal traits, such as being self-confident, approachable, mature, flexible and competent (Gallois *et al.*, 1992; Kacmar *et al.*, 1992). The converse circumstances were noted by Gallois *et al.* (1992, p. 1056) where 'nonassertive candidates were judged to be lacking in confidence and incompetent in their social interactions. Aggressive candidates were also described as incompetent but were seen as overconfident, unapproachable, inflexible, and self-interested'.

It is noteworthy that interviewers were not only able to distinguish between assertive and passive applicants but clearly differentiated between assertive and aggressive candidates. So, creating the desired impression in an interview is fraught with risk. Assertive tactics may be perceived as aggressive by interviewers, the consequences of which have been alluded to. There is a fine line between appearing confident and being perceived as arrogant. Indeed, the potential for misrepresentation by applicants of previous experiences and achievements by embellishing is often counteracted by interviewers seeking to verify such claims through the soliciting of additional and independent information (Gilmore and Ferris, 1989). However, as Knouse (1994) indicated, candidates who engage in embellishing tactics may be relatively unaware of utilising such methods and therefore may not be deliberately misleading interviewers.

Certain impression-management tactics carry particular risks for applicants. Other-focused tactics such as ingratiation (through flattery) may produce an entirely contrary impression if the interviewer views the influence attempts as being insincere or explicitly manipulative (Gilmore and Ferris, 1989). Similarly, attempts to appeal to the interviewer's compassion may readily lead to attributions of weakness and dependence in the applicant. The justifications and accounts proffered for past failures or conditions may exert a considerable influence on the impression conveyed to an interviewer. For example, Gilmore and Ferris (1989, p. 199) noted that 'Using poor health, alcoholism, or mental illness as a justification for one's poor performance may maintain some degree of self-esteem, but does not enhance one's chances for employment'.

In terms of managing impressions, there is one further strategy that warrants attention. Where applicants possess information that may be potentially damaging to their chances of securing employment they could manipulate their impression by simply withholding the information. This may be especially tempting where the topic is not raised by the interviewer, either because it had not been thought of or because raising it would have contravened the law. Although there are differences of opinion pertaining to this issue, Einhorn (1991) offered a sound discussion and questioned the need to volunteer negative information that had no bearing on the applicant's ability to perform the job. Einhorn (1981, p. 51) did, however, suggest that 'Applicants certainly do not want to raise objections that the interviewer has not thought of, but in cases where almost any interviewer, given the facts, would have a particular concern, applicants should raise and answer the objection even if the interviewer does not raise the issue directly'. In taking such advice applicants need to give some attention to *how* they respond to the potential predicament in which they may find themselves once they have chosen to volunteer the material. Again, Einhorn (1991) offered a number of strategies for overcoming potential objections, all of which are founded on the cultivation of a strong self-belief and a positive self-image. Emanating from this foundation applicants can focus their attention on (1) what can be changed, (2) their abilities rather than their disabilities, (3) insights and learning from past experiences, and (4) positive strengths learned from problems encountered. In discussing the effects of a disability, Dipboye (1992, p. 115) observed that 'As important as a disability might be in influencing judgments of an applicant's qualifications, how the applicants deal with the disability during the interview may be more important ... frank discussion of a disability during the interview can lead to more positive impressions than nondisclosure'.

There may be an important role here for attributions of cause and personal responsibility as mediators of trait ascriptions. For example, where the disability is seen as being under the control of the applicant more negative attributions to the person may follow (Dipboye, 1992). As Einhorn (1991) stated, applicants who attribute blame for their predicaments to others tend to be described in more negative terms and as lacking maturity. Therefore, explanations offered by applicants for past events, especially self-damaging events, may serve as powerful evidence from which interviewers make influential internal attributions used to predict future work behaviour (Herriot, 1989; Silvester and Chapman, 1995).

A final caution requires attention and relates to applicants who 'go too far' in their strenuous efforts to create a good impression. As with much social behaviour 'more of' may not necessarily be best and this seems to apply to impression management behaviour. This effect, termed by Baron (1989) as the 'too much of a good thing' effect, operates to reduce the credibility of the projected image, possibly by overloading the interviewer, and leads to lower evaluations.

Reference to social interaction models (see Chapter 2) draws attention to the importance of a range of personal and situational factors which affect social behaviour. The employment of impression-management behaviours by applicants is influenced by a range of personal determinants such as self-esteem (Liden and Parsons, 1986), self-evaluation (Tourish and Hargie, 1995), extroversion (Fletcher, 1987), gender (DuBrin, 1994; Kacmar and Carlson, 1994) and cultural background (Sarangi, 1994). The extent to which assertive-type tactics are deployed by applicants is not simply dependent on applicants' knowledge of such strategies but is influenced by the interview climate, compatibility with their personality types and/or on the moral and cultural acceptability of the tactics required. For example, Furnborough *et al.* (1982, p. 255) stated that 'The interviewer, according to British norms, expects the applicant to show his best side and underplay his weak points. This is often explicitly described as "selling oneself", a concept which many Muslims ... find difficult to understand and morally repugnant'. Kacmar *et al.* (1992) noted that the consequences for applicants who, for whatever reason, do not play the expected game of impression management may be lower ratings and probable rejection.

THE INTERACTION BETWEEN INTERVIEWER AND APPLICANT

Although this chapter has considered each participant separately, it is important to recognise that the outcomes of the selection interview are significantly influenced by the emerging interaction between the participants. For example, applicants of lower self-esteem may be unable to deploy effective self-focused impression-management tactics due to an intimidating and controlling interviewer. Similarly, Liden *et al.* (1993) demonstrated the 'devastating' effect that a cold interviewer (in terms of their non-verbal behaviour) had on the performance (verbal and non-verbal) of low self-esteem candidates. Keenan (1976) found that interviewees who were interviewed by more approving interviewers were judged as more friendly, relaxed, talkative, successful and less ill at ease than when interviewed by more disapproving interviewers. Evidence summarised by Dipboye (1992, p. 95) indicated that 'the interview is a relationship characterized by mutual causality. The behaviour observed in the interview is not just the result of the interviewer's traits and behavior or the applicant's traits and behavior, but it emerges from the interaction of interviewer and applicant'.

Dipboye (1992) further emphasised the importance of applicants accommodating interviewers' behaviours by showing symmetry on the affiliation dimension and by responding in a compensatory way on the control dimension. In interviews that seem to 'go well' applicants attempt to mirror the interviewers' sociability and concurrently compensate for control dictated by the interviewer with appropriately passive behaviour – fighting for control of the interview may not be the most advantageous tactic!

APPLICANTS' REACTIONS TO THE SELECTION PROCESS

It is only in the recent past that the significance of applicants' reactions to the selection procedures has been acknowledged. Smither *et al.* (1993) noted that such reactions were of some practical importance because they impacted on the attraction of suitable applicants, contributed to the likelihood of litigation and influenced the validity of the selection procedures themselves. Recent research has suggested that, contrary to the traditional view that assessment of individuals is 'psychologically neutral' (Smith and Robertson, 1993, p. 275), the contribution of the interviewer to the selection process may exert an influence on the reaction of applicants to the organisation (Powell, 1991; Ralston *et al.*, 1993; Robertson and Smith, 1989; Young and Heneman III, 1986). Furthermore, applicants' reactions are in part based on their subjective perceptions of the qualities of interviewers as representatives of organisations, and not on any objective reality.

These subjective perceptions made by applicants of interviewers may result in the formation of more favourable impressions of interviewers themselves (Fletcher, 1989; Harn and Thornton III, 1985; Jablin and Miller, 1990; Ralston *et al.*, 1993), job vacancies (Goltz and Giannantonio, 1995; Powell, 1991), the fairness of the interview procedures (Smither *et al.*, 1993) and an increased likelihood of positive post-interview decisions (Harn and Thornton III, 1985; Harris and Fink, 1987; Powell, 1991). Reference was made earlier to the study by Goltz and Giannantonio (1995) where students who viewed the friendly interviewer made significantly more positive inferences regarding the organisation and were more likely to be attracted to the job than students who viewed the less friendly one. In contrast, Rynes and Barber (1990) concluded that improving the performance of organisational representatives as a means of increasing job acceptance rates finds little support in the literature. Likewise, Keenan (1989) on reviewing the evidence, stressed the additional influence of information on job attributes provided by a credible source which can be more dominant than interviewer style. None the less, where procedures are perceived to have low face validity and constitute unfair procedures, applicants, feeling more aggrieved, are more likely to consider taking legal action to salvage some justice (Smither *et al.*, 1993).

ETHICAL ISSUES

Finally, comment should be included on the very important area of ethics as it relates to selection interviewing. Somewhat different approaches have been taken in dealing with ethical issues. For example, Smith and Robertson (1993) presented a consideration of such issues by structuring the discussion around five general principles, transferred in large part from the caring and helping setting. The five principles which served to safeguard the welfare of 'clients' related to: (1) positive self-regard, whereby applicants on leaving the interview should not be in any way psychologically damaged by the experience; (2) informed consent, whereby applicants are fully aware of the procedures and their role therein before consenting to participate; (3) competence, which requires interviewers to operate to a high standard within their context and not beyond; (4) confidentiality, whereby interviewers treat all personal information such that it cannot be misused or used to the detriment of the applicant; and (5) client welfare, which 'involves a civilised and fair way of relating to clients' (Smith and Robertson, 1993, p. 12). These five principles subsume those cited by Fletcher (1992) as relating to whether actions are effective or purposeful (utilitarianism), fair and equitable (justice) and protective of the individual's rights.

In a wide-ranging account, Fletcher (1992) related questions of ethics to a number of interview themes. For example, the principle of utilitarianism raises important questions pertaining to interview preparation by applicants. It is important that applicants, when attending for interview, perform to their maximum and give a good account of themselves – here interview preparation and coaching may prove beneficial. However, Fletcher (1992, p. 362) went on to state that 'It is one thing to provide training and guidance to interviewees in how to present the talents and other attributes they possess as effectively as possible, but quite another to coach them in strategic impression management tactics that are deliberately intended to lead to favourable assessments irrespective of their actual merits. There is also the question of whether preparing candidates for deceitful impression management violates the rights of the interviewer'.

Second, the issues of openness, self-disclosure and invasion of privacy constitute important sources of ethical questions. A major function of interviewers is to collect as much relevant applicant information as possible prior to making selection decisions. However, what comprises relevant and non-discriminatory information must be carefully considered by all selection interviewers lest they infringe not only the individual rights of applicants but the law. According to Poteet (1984) and Wilson (1991), the use of illegal questioning still persists and indeed may be widespread with the most common topic areas being criminal record, age and disabilities. Less common areas were related to marital/family status, religion, sex, national origin and race. Wilson (1991) also noted that many candidates were unaware that certain questions were illegal and generally acceded to the interviewers' requests for information. If applicants perceive such questions as relevant and where they receive a favourable interview outcome, the request for such information is less likely to be regarded as an invasion of privacy (Fletcher, 1992). Where applicants are unhappy about the use of certain illegal and potentially discriminatory questions, Wilson (1991, p. 45) set out a number of possible applicant strategies, all but one of which sought to do 'the least damage to the interviewee's candidacy'. The choice of strategy depends on the perceived use of the information, the importance of revealing the information to the interviewer, and the desire to secure the job, and ranges from terminating the interview or making a direct refusal to expressing concern about the question and then responding to the question itself.

The extent to which applicants assert themselves in selection interviews may also be crucially dependent on the power relationships in the situation. Generally speaking, the distribution of power in selection interviews is not equal, with the greater power residing with the interviewer. As Fletcher (1992) noted, 'Inevitably, where there is power there lies the potential for its abuse and hence for unethical behaviour that violates the rights of the individual'. Interviewers who, inadvertently or not, treat applicants in ways that would be detrimental to their performance by inducing states of discomfort, lowered self-esteem, stress or anger are behaving in an unethical fashion. This, ultimately, will prove to be counter-productive in the sense that applicants will be unable to display their potential qualities, will be unimpressed with the organisation's representative and may be less likely to accept offers of employment.

OVERVIEW

This chapter presented research pertaining to the selection interview as a specific example of a complex social interaction governed by a number of rules and regulations by which participants are expected to conform. The focus of the material initially dealt with the selection interview from the interviewer's perspective, setting out the issues relating to the various strategies and skills found to be relevant for improved practice. This was followed by a similar focus on the role played by the applicant in the selection interview and emphasised the interaction of participants in the outcome of the process. Finally, a brief consideration was given to selected ethical issues as they related to the selection interview context.

REFERENCES

Alderfer, C. P. and McCord, C.G. (1970) 'Personal and Situational Factors in the Recruitment Interview', *Journal of Applied Psychology*, 54, 377–85.

Anderson, N. R. (1991) 'Decision Making in the Graduate Selection Interview: An Experimental Investigation', *Human Relations*, 44, 403–17.

—— and Shackleton, V. (1990) 'Decision Making in the Graduate Selection Interview: A Field Study', *Journal of Occupational Psychology*, 63, 63–76.

Athey, T. R. and Hautaluoma, J. E. (1994) 'Effects of Applicant Overeducation, Job Status, and Job Gender Stereotype on Employment Decisions', *The Journal of Social Psychology*, 134, 439–52.

Baron, R. A. (1989) 'Impression Management by Applicants During Employment Interviews: The "Too Much of a Good Thing" Effect', In R. W. Eder and G. R. Ferris (eds), *The Employment Interview: Theory, Research and Practice*, Sage, Newbury Park, pp. 204–15.

—— (1993) 'Interviewers' Moods and Evaluations of Job Applicants: The Role of Applicant Qualifications', *Journal of Applied Social Psychology*, 23, 253–71.

Billsberry, J. (1995) 'The Fit Selection Model: An Innovative Model of Selection that Incorporates Person-organisation Fit and Person-job Fit Considerations', *Proceedings of the Occupational Psychology Conference*, British Psychological Society, Leicester, pp 169–74.

Bradac, J. J. and Mulac, A. (1984) 'A Molecular View of Powerful and Powerless Speech Styles: Attributional Consequences of Specific Language Features and Communicator Intentions', *Communication Monographs*, 51, 307–19.

Burns, C. L. and Moorehead, M. A. (1991) 'Interviews – A Candidate's Questions Can Be Enlightening', *American Secondary Education*, 20, 25–7.

Campion, M. A., Pursell, E. D. and Brown, B. K. (1988) 'Structured Interviewing: Raising the Psychometric Properties of the Employment Interview', *Personnel Psychology*, 41, 25–42.

Charisiou, J., Jackson, H. J., Boyle, G. J., Burgess, P. M., Minas, I. H. and Joshua, S. D. (1989) 'Which Employment Interview Skills Best Predict the Employability of Schizophrenic Patients?', *Psychological Reports*, 64, 683–94.

Clark, C. (1994) 'Number and Gender in Selection Interviews: Effects on Outcomes and Candidates' Views', *Social Work Education*, 13, 24–38.

Daniel, C. and Valencia, S. (1991) 'Structured Interviewing Simplified', *Public Personnel Management*, 20, 127–34.

Dipboye, R. L. (1992) *Selection Interviews: Process Perspectives*, South-Western Publishing Co, Cincinnati, Ohio.

Dougherty, T. W., Turban, D. B. and Callender, J. C. (1994) 'Confirming First Impressions in the Employment Interview: A Field Study of Interviewer Behavior', *Journal of Applied Psychology*, 79, 659–65.

DuBrin, A. J. (1994) 'Sex Differences in the Use and Effectiveness of Tactics of Impression Management', *Psychological Reports*, 74, 531–44.

Eder, R. W. and Ferris, G. R. (eds) (1989) *The Employment Interview: Theory, Research and Practice*, Sage, Newbury Park.

Einhorn, L. J. (1981) 'Investigations of Successful Communicative Behaviors', *Communication Education*, 30, 217–28.

—— (1991) 'Effective Strategies for Overcoming Objections in an Employment Interview', *Bulletin of the Association for Business Communication*, 54, 50–4.

Feild, H. S. and Gatewood, R. D. (1989) 'Development of a Selection Interview: A Job Content Strategy', in R. W. Eder and G. R. Ferris (eds), *The Employment Interview: Theory, Research and Practice*, Sage, Newbury Park, pp. 145–57.

Ferwerda, M. (1995) 'Sex and Race Differences in Applicants' Nonverbal Behaviour and Attitudes in Selection Interviews', *Proceedings of the Occupational Psychology Conference*, British Psychological Society, Leicester, pp. 79–82.

Fletcher, C. (1987) 'Candidate Personality as an Influence on Selection Interview Assessments', *Applied Psychology: An International Review*, 36, 157–62.

—— (1989) 'Impression Management in the Selection Interview', in R. A. Giacalone and P. Rosenfield (eds), *Impression Management in the Organization*, Lawrence Erlbaum Associates, Hillsdale, NJ.

—— (1990) 'The Relationships Between Candidate Personality, Self-Presentation Strategies, and Interviewer Assessments in Selection Interviews: An Empirical Study', *Human Relations*, 43, 739–49.

—— (1992) 'Ethical Issues in The Selection Interview', *Journal of Business Ethics*, 11, 361–7.

Forbes, R. J. and Jackson, P. R. (1980) 'Non-verbal Behaviour and the Outcome of Selection Interviews', *Journal of Occupational Psychology*, 53, 65–72.

Furnborough, P., Jupp, T., Munns, R. and Roberts, C. (1982) 'Language, Disadvantage and Discrimination: Breaking the Cycle of Majority Group Perception', *Journal of Multilingual and Multicultural Development*, 3, 247–66.

Furnham, A. and Burbeck, E. (1989) 'Employment Interview Outcomes as a Function of Interviewers' Experience', *Perceptual and Motor Skills*, 69, 395–402.

Gallois, C., Callan, V. J. and McKenzie-Palmer, J. A. (1992) 'The Influence of Applicant Communication Style and Interviewer Characteristics on Hiring Decisions', *Journal of Applied Social Psychology*, 22, 1041–60.

Gilmore, D. C. and Ferris, G. R. (1989) 'The Effects of Applicant Impression Management Tactics on Interviewer Judgments', *Journal of Management*, 15, 557–64.

Gilmore D. C., Beehr, T. A. and Love, K. G. (1986) 'Effects of Applicant Sex, Applicant Physical Attractiveness, Type of Rater and Type of Job on Interview Decision', *Journal of Occupational Psychology*, 59, 103–9.

Goltz, S. M. and Giannantonio, C. M. (1995) 'Recruiter Friendliness and Attraction to the Job: The Mediating Role of Inferences about the Organization', *Journal of Vocational Behavior*, 46, 109–18.

Goodale, J. G. (1989) 'Effective Employment Interviewing', in R. W. Eder and G. R. Ferris (eds), *The Employment Interview: Theory, Research and Practice*, Sage, Newbury Park, pp.307–23.

Grier, T. B. and Trenta, L. (1992) 'Landing The Big One', *The Executive Educator*, 14, 20–2.

Hackney, M. and Kleiner, B. H. (1994) 'Conducting an Effective Selection Interview', *Work Study*, 43, 8–13.

Hargie, O. and Marshall, P. (1986) 'Interpersonal Communication: A Theoretical Framework', in O. Hargie (ed.), *A Handbook of Communication Skills* (1st edn), Routledge, London.

Hargie, O., Saunders, C. and Dickson, D. (1994) *Social Skills in Interpersonal Communication* (3rd edn). Routledge, London.

Harn, T. J. and Thornton III, G. C. (1985) 'Recruiter Counselling Behaviours and Applicant Impressions', *Journal of Occupational Psychology*, 58, 57–66.

Harris, M. M. (1989) 'Reconsidering the Employment Interview: A Review of Recent Literature and Suggestions for Future Research', *Personnel Psychology*, 42, 691–726.

—— and Fink, L. S. (1987) 'A Field Study of Applicant Reactions to Employment Opportunities: Does the Recruiter Make a Difference? *Personnel Psychology*, 40, 765–84.

Herriot, P. (1981) 'Towards an Attributional Theory of the Selection Interview', *Journal of Occupational Psychology*, 54, 165–73.

—— (1985) 'Give and Take in Graduate Selection', *Personnel Management*, May, 33–5.

—— (1989) 'Selection as a Social Process', in M. Smith and I. T Robertson (eds), *Advances in Selection and Assessment*. John Wiley, Chichester, pp. 171–87.

Hollandsworth, J. G., Kazelskis, R., Stevens, J. and Dressel, M. E. (1979) 'Relative Contributions of Verbal Communication to Employment Decisions in the Job Interview Setting', *Personnel Psychology*, 32, 359–67.

Jablin, F. M. and Miller, V. D. (1990) 'Interviewer and Applicant Questioning Behavior in Employment Interviews', *Management Communication Quarterly*, 4, 51–86.

Janz, T. (1982) 'Initial Comparison of Patterned Behavior Description Interviews Versus Unstructured Interviews', *Journal of Applied Psychology*, 67, 577–80.

—— (1989) 'The Patterned Behavior Description Interview: The Best Prophet of the Future Is the Past', in R. W. Eder and G. R. Ferris (eds), *The Employment Interview: Theory, Research and Practice*, Sage, Newbury Park, pp. 158–168.

Kacmar, K. M. and Carlson, D. S. (1994) 'Using Impression Management in Women's Job Search Processes', *American Behavioral Scientist*, 37, 682–96.

Kacmar, K. M., Delery, J. E. and Ferris, G. R. (1992) 'Differential Effectiveness of Applicant Impression Management Tactics on Employment Interview Decisions', *Journal of Applied Social Psychology*, 22, 1250–72.

Kacmar, K. M., Wayne, S. J. and Himes Ratcliff, S. (1994) 'An Examination of Automatic vs. Controlled Information Processing in the Employment Interview: The Case of Minority Applicants', *Sex Roles*, 30, 809–28.

Keenan, A. (1976) 'Effects of Non-verbal Behaviour of Interviewers on Candidates' Performance', *Journal of Occupational Psychology*, 49, 171–6.

—— (1989) 'Selection Interviewing', *International Review of Industrial and Organizational Psychology*, 4, 1–25.

—— and Wedderburn, A. A. I. (1980) 'Putting the Boot on the Other Foot: Candidates' Descriptions of Interviewers', *Journal of Occupational Psychology*, 53, 81–9.

Knouse, S. B. (1994) 'Impressions of the Resume: the Effects of Applicant Education, Experience and Impression Management', *Journal of Business and Psychology*, 9, 33–45.

Latham, G. P. (1989) 'The Reliability, Validity, and Practicality of the Situational Interview', in R. W. Eder and G. R. Ferris (eds), *The Employment Interview: Theory, Research and Practice*, Sage, Newbury Park, pp. 169–82.

——, Saari, L. M., Pursell, E. D. and Campion, M. A. (1980) 'The Situational Interview', *Journal of Applied Psychology*, 65, 422–7.

Liden, R. C. and Parsons, C. K. (1986) 'A Field Study of Job Applicant Interview Perceptions, Alternative Opportunities and Demographic Characteristics', *Personnel Psychology*, 39, 109–22.

Liden, R. C., Martin, C. L. and Parsons, C. K. (1993) 'Interviewer and Applicant Behaviors in Employment Interviews', *Academy of Management Journal*, 36, 372–86.

Lopez, F. M. (1975) '*Personnel Interviewing: Theory and Practice* (2nd edn), McGraw-Hill, New York.

Lowry, P. E. (1994) 'The Structured Interview: An Alternative To The Assessement Center?', *Public Personnel Management*, 23, 201–15.

Macan, T. H. and Dipboye, R. L. (1994) 'The Effects of the Application on Processing of Information From the Employment Interview', *Journal of Applied Social Psychology*, 24, 1291–1314.

McDaniel, M. A., Whetzel, D. L., Schmidt, F. L. and Maurer, S. D. (1994) 'The Validity of Employment Interviews: A Comprehensive Review and Meta-Analysis', *Journal of Applied Psychology*, 79, 599–616.

Marchioro, C. A. and Bartels, L. K. (1994) 'Perceptions of a Job Interviewee with a Disability', *Journal of Social Behavior and Personality*, 9, 383–92.

Millar, R., Crute, V. and Hargie, O. (1992) *Professional Interviewing*. Routledge, London.

Motowildo, S. J., Carter, G. W., Dunnette, M. D., Tippins, N., Werner, S., Burnett, J. R. and Vaughan, M.J. (1992) 'Studies of the Structured Behavioral Interview', *Journal of Applied Psychology*, 77, 571–87.

Orpen, G. (1984) 'Attitude Similarity, Attraction, and Decision-Making In the Employment Interview', *The Journal of Psychology*, 117, 111–20.

Perry, E. (1994) 'A Prototype Matching Approach to Understanding the Role of Applicant Gender and Age in the Evaluation of Job Applicants', *Journal of Applied Social Psychology*, 24, 1433–73.

Poteet, G. W. (1984) 'The Employment Interview. Avoiding Discriminatory Questioning', *The Journal of Nursing Administration*, 14, 38–42.

Powell, G. N. (1991) 'Applicant Reactions to The Initial Employment Interview: Exploring Theoretical and Methodological Issues', *Personnel Psychology*, 44, 67–83.

Quay, J. (1994) 'Training the Interviewee', *Journal of Management Consulting*, 8, 51–2.

Ralston, S. M., Redmond, M. V. and Pickett, T. A. (1993) 'An Exploratory Study of Recruiters' Self-ratings of Interpersonal Communication and Applicants' Decisions about Employment', *Perceptual and Motor Skills*, 77, 135–42.

Rasmussen, K. G. (1984) 'Nonverbal Behavior, Verbal Behavior, Resume Credentials, and Selection Interview Outcomes', *Journal of Applied Psychology*, 69, 551–6.

Robertson, I. T. and Makin, P. J. (1986) 'Management Selection in Britain: A Survey and Critique', *Journal of Occupational Psychology*, 59, 45–57.

Robertson, I. T. and Smith, M. (1989) 'Personnel Selection Methods', in M. Smith and I. Robertson (eds), *Advances in Selection and Assessment*. John Wiley, Chichester, pp. 89–112.

Roth, P. L. and Campion, J. E. (1992) 'An Analysis of The Predictive Power of the Panel Interview and Pre-employment Tests', *Journal of Occupational and Organizational Psychology*, 65, 51–60.

Rynes, S. L. and Barber, A. E. (1990) 'Applicant Attraction Strategies: An Organizational Perspective', *Academy of Management Review*, 15, 286–310.

Sarangi, S. (1994) 'Accounting for Mismatches in Intercultural Selection Interviews', *Multilingua*, 13, 163–94.

Saunders, C. (1986) 'Opening and Closing', in O. Hargie (ed.), *A Handbook of Communication Skills* (1st edn). Routledge, London, pp. 175–200.

Schuh, A. J. (1978) 'Effects of an Early Interruption and Note Taking on Listening Accuracy and Decision Making in the Interview', *Bulletin of the Psychonomic Society*, 12, 242–4.

Shackleton, V. J. and Newell, S. (1991) 'A Comparative Survey of Methods Used in Top British and French Companies', *Journal of Occupational Psychology*, 64, 23–36.

Shaffer, D. R., Ruammke, C. and Pegalis, L. J. (1990) 'The "Opener": Highly Skilled as Interviewer or Interviewee', *Personality and Social Psychology Bulletin*, 16, 511–20.

Silvester, J. and Chapman, A. J. (1995) 'An Attributional Model of Unfair Discrimination in the Selection Interview', *Proceedings of the Occupational Psychology Conference*, British Psychological Society, Leicester, pp. 145–50.

Smith, M. and George, D. (1992) 'Selection Methods', *International Review of Industrial and Organizational Psychology*, 7, 55–97.

Smith, M. and Robertson, I. T. (eds) (1989) *Advances in Selection and Assessment*, John Wiley, Chichester.

—— (1993) *The Theory and Practice of Systematic Personnel Selection* (2nd edn), Macmillan, London.

Smither, J. W., Reilly, R. R., Millsap, R. E., Pearlman, K. and Stoffey, R. W. (1993) 'Applicant Reactions to Selection Procedures', *Personnel Psychology*, 46, 49–76.

Stevens, G. E. (1981) 'Taking the Chance Out of Selection Interviewing', *Journal of College Placement*, 49, 44–8.

Stewart, C. J. and Cash, W. B. (1974) *Interviewing: Principles and Practices*, W. C. Brown, Dubuque.

Taylor, C. (1993) 'How to Make the Right Choice: a New Model for the Selection Interview', *Journal of Advanced Nursing*, 18, 312–20.

Taylor, P., Mills, A. and O'Driscoll, M. (1993) 'Personnel Selection Methods Used by New Zealand Organisations and Personnel Consulting Firms', *New Zealand Journal of Psychology*, 22, 19–31.

Tourish, D. and Hargie, C. (1995) 'Student Selection Interview Performance: Candidate, Peer Group and Skilled Interviewer Perceptions of Effectiveness', *Research in Education*, 53, 31–40.

Tullar, W. L. (1989) 'The Employment Interview as a Cognitive Performing Script', in R. W. Eder and G. R. Ferris (eds), *The Employment Interview: Theory, Research and Practice*, Sage, Newbury Park, pp. 233–45.

Ugbah, S. D. and Evuleocha, S. U. (1992) 'The Importance of Written, Verbal, and Nonverbal Communication Factors in Employment Interview Decisions', *Journal of Employment Counseling*, 29, 128–37.

Van Vianen, A. E. M. and Willemsen, T. M. (1992) 'The Employment Interview: The Role of Sex Stereotypes in the Evaluation of Male and Female Job Applicants in the Netherlands', *Journal of Applied Social Psychology*, 22, 471–91.

White, G. B. and White, M. J. (1994) 'Overvaluation and Undervaluation of Women Job Applicants: How General are the Vagaries of Sex Bias?', *Journal of Business and Psychology*, 9, 59–68.

Wiesner, W. H. and Cronshaw, S. F. (1988) 'A Meta-analytic Investigation of the Impact of Interview Format and Degree of Structure on the Validity of the Employment Interview', *Journal of Occupational Psychology*, 61, 275–90.

Wilson, G. L. (1991) 'Preparing Students for Responding to Illegal Selection Interview Questions', *Bulletin of the Association for Business Communication*, 54, 44–9.

Wright, P. M., Lichtenfels, P. A. and Pursell, E. D. (1989) 'The Structured Interview: Additional Studies and a Meta-analysis', *Journal of Occupational Psychology*, 62, 191–9.

Young, D. M. and Beier, E. G. (1977) 'The Role of Applicant Nonverbal Communication in the Employment Interview', *Journal of Employment Counseling*, 14, 154–165.

Young, I. P. and Heneman III, H. G. (1986) 'Predictors of Interviewee Reactions to the Selection Interview', *Journal of Research and Development in Education*, 19, 29–36.

16 The helping interview: a cognitive-developmental approach

Sandra A. Rigazio-DiGilio and Allen E. Ivey

INTRODUCTION

Helping people to talk about their thoughts, feelings and behaviours in relation to important issues and to develop the knowledge and skills necessary to work through these issues is a natural part of everyday life. Whether we are called upon to listen empathically to a friend who has lost a loved one or to assist our young nephew to understand his maths lessons, we are often engaged in helping relationships. The skills we use to handle these interactions (e.g. effective listening, conflict management, multiple-perspective taking, problem-solving) are developed and reinforced over our lifetimes. Although some of us are well-endowed with such attributes, we may not be consistent in how we apply these skills and we may not always attend successfully to the reactions triggered in those we are attempting to help.

Everyone can benefit from obtaining a familiarity with the knowledge and practice of counselling skills. In this chapter we systemically apply a specific set of communication skills that can be used in the service of helping others. Our particular focus is on how to integrate communication theory, psychological research and developmental perspectives to construct a cognitive-developmental model of helping that can be used in the immediacy of any interview. This model helps us to access the cognitive, emotional and behavioural aspects of an individual's world, and to expand options for more adaptive functioning in these three areas.

At some time in their lives, most people will find themselves engaged in a helping encounter. It is our belief that knowledge about communication and developmental theories and approaches can assist professionals to make helping interviews more client-centred.* Specifically, the model presented in this chapter provides ways for eliciting and organising the information individuals share with you when they seek help. By learning how to understand the unique ways these individuals perceive and work through their issues, you can develop helping strategies that are in tune with how they already operate in their lives. In this way, you are helping by entering their world and assisting them to expand their cognitive, affective and behavioural options for change. This is in contrast to the types of helping models that tend to impose a particular way of thinking, feeling and acting on clients seeking help.

The skills presented here are drawn from developmental counselling and therapy (DCT), an alternative model of helping that integrates traditional counselling theories and

* The term 'client' will be used throughout this chapter to refer to the person seeking assistance.

approaches and presents new concepts for impactful interviewing and counselling practice.†
What is presented are basic developmental skills which can be effectively integrated into
practice whether in the helping field, the business field, or a service-related occupation.

DEVELOPMENTAL COUNSELLING AND THERAPY

Developmental counselling and therapy (Ivey, 1986, 1991), along with its extension to
partners and families (systemic cognitive-developmental therapy – SCDT) (Kunkler and
Rigazio-DiGilio, 1994; Rigazio-DiGilio, 1993, in press; Rigazio-DiGilio and Ivey, 1991,
1993) and to larger social and organisational groups (DCT/SCDT) (Ivey, 1991; Rigazio-
DiGilio, 1994a, 1994b), offers a conceptually coherent developmental framework that is
easily learned and directly applicable to interviewing, counselling and therapy (Borders,
1994). DCT provides highly specific, yet flexible assessment and helping strategies that
assist helpers to understand how clients make sense of their world and the issues
that prompt them to seek help.

DCT as a helping model and a classification system

DCT represents an *alternative approach* to the helping relationship that is holistic and
non-pathological. DCT combines the descriptive and analytic power of developmental
constructs with the interactive precision of skilful interpersonal communication theory.
Additionally, the model offers a larger, *integrative classification system* that can be used
to organise familiar counselling and interviewing approaches within a developmental
framework. As such, DCT provides ways to: (1) use specific types of questioning strategies
and attending skills that help the interviewer to understand the unique ways clients make
sense of and work on their issues; and (2) organise helping interventions from various
counselling models that are tailored to the developmental and cultural needs of these
clients, assisting them to obtain wider perspectives on their issues and broader alternatives for change.

The philosophical foundation underlying DCT

DCT is based on a synthesis of neo-Platonic philosophies, developmental theories (cf.
Gilligan, 1982; Hill and Rodgers, 1964; Kegan, 1982; Piaget, 1954) and constructivist
thought (Kelly, 1955; Vygotsky, 1986; Watzlawick, 1984). This synthesis allows for a reinterpretation of how people construct their worldviews over time and in relation to the
environments within which they interact.

The theoretical assumptions underlying DCT

The *primary theoretical assumption* underlying DCT suggests that development is a spherical and recursive process. As such, DCT rejects the traditional notion that development

---

† Further information regarding DCT as a model of helping and as a comprehensive framework for organising
the multitude of theories and approaches at our disposal can be found in the writings of Ivey (1986, 1991); Ivey
and Gonçalves (1988); Ivey *et al.* (1989); Rigazio-DiGilio (1994a), and Rigazio-DiGilio and Ivey (1991, 1993).

represents linear and hierarchical movement towards increasing levels of cognitive complexity. Rather, maturity is equated with cognitive, affective and behavioural flexibility. Within this holistic perspective DCT metaphorically transforms Piaget's idea that individuals sequentially move through stage-specific, cognitive-developmental levels over their lifespan. DCT instead proposes that human growth and adaptation require a more fluid and repetitive movement within and between the various cognitive-developmental levels as individuals are faced with new developmental or situational tasks. The DCT translation from linear to spherical development is epitomised by the use of the term 'orientation', rather than 'level', to express the idea that individuals repeatedly move through various cognitive-developmental orientations as they try to make sense of their experience, construct meaning and operate in their worlds. The four orientations identified by DCT are *sensorimotor* (experiencing), *concrete* (doing), *formal* (reflecting) and *dialectic/systemic* (analysing).

A *second theoretical assumption* undergirding DCT suggests that development is a *co-constructive* phenomenon. Within this postmodern perspective, human development occurs as a function of a dialectic relationship among individuals, relationships and wider environments. In other words, development and adaptation are considered to occur within a person–environment dialectic transaction. Within this view individuals, partners, families, social organisations, employers, supervisors, co-workers, teachers and counsellors interact within a collective environment. As such, any portion of the environment can influence, or be influenced by, any other part.

The conceptual implications embedded in the constructs of *orientations* and *co-constructivism* provide the framework for the application of developmental and communication theories to the helping interview. Again, these ideas provide a framework that interviewers can use to: (1) ask specific questioning strategies that elicit a client's cognitive-developmental orientation within the natural language of the helping relationship; and (2) plan various helping strategies that are tailored to facilitate client growth within and between different cognitive-developmental orientations. As indicated in Box 16.1 there is research evidence to support these conceptual elements of DCT.

Identifying congnitive-development orientations

DCT posits that, while individuals may use a variety of cognitive-developmental orientations or vantage points to interpret and act in their world, most rely significantly on one or two orientations. An individual's *predominant orientation* is the major frame through which he or she experiences, interprets and interacts within the world. Research conducted to test this primary hypothesis confirms that, by attending to clients' natural language during the helping interview, their predominant cognitive-developmental orientation can be identified with a high degree of reliability (Rigazio-DiGilio and Ivey, 1990). The predominant orientation provides interviewers with clues as to how clients organise their world and their life tasks, as well as to how they think, feel and act in relation to themselves, other people and various situations.

The first step in a successful interview is for the helping interviewer to apply effective communication skills to determine the predominant cognitive-developmental orientation of the client. Knowing this orientation empowers the interviewer to employ expressive communication skills that mirror the linguistic and cognitive frames of reference used by

---

Box 16.1   Research supporting DCT constructs and assumptions

Research has been conducted to determine if the cognitive-developmental orientations upon which DCT is based can be reliably identified in the natural language of the interview. Additionally, the predictive validity of the DCT questioning strategies has been investigated, as well as the claim that cognitive flexibility – using several orientations to understand and act in the world – is a healthy response to growth and adaptation. Two of these studies relate to the work discussed in this chapter.

1 Rigazio-DiGilio and Ivey (1990) determined that independent raters could indeed classify the predominant cognitive-developmental orientations used by inpatient depressed clients as they explained the issues that promoted treatment. These raters could identify a client's primary orientation with a high degree of reliability (0.98; kappa = 0.87). Additionally, this same investigation determined that questions designed to elicit explorations within particular cognitive-developmental orientations actually did elicit such explorations. In effect, both short- and long-term depressives responded to questions consistent with the theory (98 per cent of all responses).

2 Heesacker *et al.* (in press) conducted a factor analytic study of DCT constructs with 1,700 subjects. The factor structure for the four cognitive-developmental orientations was substantiated. Further, it was found that subjects who were able to access resources within several of the cognitive-developmental orientations showed more positive indicators of physical and emotional health than individuals who primarily functioned within one orientation.

---

the client. The idea of matching our language style to that of the client is important. For example, clients who talk in concrete specifics and tell linear stories may have trouble understanding the formal abstractions often associated with interviewing and counselling. The concrete client may have difficulty seeing repeating patterns of behaviour and reflecting on the role of self or the similarities across situations. Therefore, if interviewers can identify their clients' constructions and match their own language style to these constructions, they will have maximum opportunity to join with their clients and to help them to learn expanded or alternative ways of thinking, feeling and behaving.

The four major cognitive-developmental orientations considered by DCT are briefly defined below, along with a corresponding illustration. Additionally, Box 16.2 presents an in-depth description of each orientation.

The sensorimotor/elemental orientation

Clients relying on this orientation tend not to separate cognition and emotion. They are able to experience the 'here and now' directly and immediately. You may find them a bit random in their presentation of issues and concerns. They are often able to experience situations and feelings deeply and at times may be overcome by emotion.

Example client statement (dealing with death and dying)

(In tears and overwhelmed.) 'I'm so confused. It was AIDS. I feel lonely and lost. I don't know what to do now.'

The concrete/situational orientation

These clients are good storytellers. They can tell you in detail what happened to them and who said what to whom. Many clients within this orientation will want to tell you detailed stories about their lives.

Example client statement

'My partner died last week of AIDS. The funeral was held last Friday at Jones Funeral Home over in the south end of town. There were over a hundred people there. I was glad so many people came.'

The formal/reflective orientation

These clients usually prefer to talk in abstractions and think about or reflect on what happened to them. Often, they will avoid concrete storytelling and direct sensorimotor experiencing. They are likely to be good at defining repeating patterns in themselves and others. They are good at analysis and examination of self, especially on an intellectual level.

Example client statement

'My partner and I had a perfect relationship. We had learned how to live with AIDS and still enjoy one another. I am the type of person who cares a lot for the one I am with. Generally speaking, I was able to deal positively with this whole situation.'

The dialectic/systemic orientation

Like formal clients, these clients are good at analysis. In addition, they are interested in contextual issues, such as how the wider environment affects their sense of themselves. Women who seek to discover how their personal issues relate to sexism, and minority groups who wish to explore issues of systemic discrimination, are using a dialectic/systemic orientation to understand and operate within their world. You will also find that clients who focus on multiple perspectives of themselves and the world tend towards this orientation.

Example client statement

'My partner's death can be seen from several perspectives. First, I hurt a lot, but, on the other hand, the last several months were so awful that I'm glad the pain is over – we were able to part in dignity and love. I was both shocked and not surprised at all by my family's reaction to this time of crisis. Some of my aunts and uncles seemed to be afraid of me. I understand that our culture does not openly embrace homosexuality, but I cannot condone their behaviour at all. Aren't they aware of the messages they're sending to my younger cousins?'

Box 16.2   The four cognitive-developmental orientations

When clients can work within several orientations, then they can access the resources inherent in each to assist them to experience, understand and act in their world. When clients rely on one orientation at the expense of all others, then they can be constrained within the limits of that orientation. Clients who haphazardly fluctuate among the orientations appear also to be constrained by ineffective processing. Each orientation is described, along with corresponding types of affect, cognitions and behaviours.

The sensorimotor/elemental orientation

Affect   Clients who work within this orientation are dominated by sensory stimuli and affect, seeing minimal distinction between sensory input, cognitions and emotions. Emotions are sensory-based and reactive. These clients can easily experience the immediacy of their emotions in the here and now.
Cognition   These clients show minimal capacity to coordinate sensory-based data into an organised understanding or Gestalt. They offer interpretations that, no matter how sophisticated, are illusionary or irrational.
Behaviour   Behaviourally, these clients are unable to take effective action based on their beliefs or experiences.

The concrete/situational orientation

Affect   Clients working within this orientation can name and describe emotions within themselves and others from one perspective, and with minimal differentiation. They express emotions outwardly and are unlikely to recognise obvious emotions in others unless clearly made available to them, verbally and non-verbally.
Cognition   These clients focus primarily on a factual description of the details evident in a situation – only seeing these details from their own perspective. There is minimal emphasis on evaluation or analysis. These clients can demonstrate if/then linear thinking, emphasising causality and predictability from a single perspective.
Behaviour   These clients are able to control and describe broad-based, undifferentiated, outwardly focused affect. They are able to find ways to act predictably in their worlds.

The formal/reflective orientation

Affect   Clients who primarily operate within this orientation demonstrate an awareness of the complexity of their feelings and are able to separate self from feelings to reflect on their emotions. They can analyse patterns of feelings. However, they have difficulty experiencing their emotions directly.
Cognition   These clients can describe repeating patterns of affect, thoughts and behaviours in themselves, in others and across situations. They can engage in an analysis of the self and the situations they are involved in. However, they have difficulty seeing the constraints in these patterns.
Behaviour   These clients are able to generalise their behaviours to adapt to novel situations. However, they have difficultly determining new behaviours, outside of their own patterns.

The dialectic/systemic orientation

Affect   Clients who primarily use this orientation can offer a wide range of emotions and can recognise that their emotions can change in relation to their context. These clients, however, have difficultly experiencing their emotions directly, in the immediacy of the here and now.

Cognition   These clients can operate on systems of knowledge and can reflect on how they arrive at their ways of thinking. They are aware that their evolving cognitions are co-constructed over time and in response to differing contexts. They also can challenge their own assumptions and integrations. At times, because they see flaws in virtually all reasoning processes, they involve themselves in deconstructions and reconstructions, without being able to stay within a predictable frame of reference for any period of time.
Behaviour   These clients can interact in their environment, accessing resources and influences within many contextual realms. Those who depend on this orientation, at the expense of using others, may become lost in their thought process, and find it difficult to interact predictably.

No matter what the issue – coping with AIDS, depression, performance anxiety, vocational decisions, poverty, or anything else, no two clients will talk about their concerns in the same way. We have to assess how our clients are predominantly processing their experience and to match their language with appropriate cognitive, emotional and behavioural questions, strategies and tasks. The objective is to help them to explore their issues *where they are*. For example, when with clients experiencing emotional catharsis, it is best to support them within the sensorimotor orientation. If a client needs to tell a concrete story, listen and paraphrase instead of interpreting the deeper meaning. If a father needs assistance structuring his life after a crisis (e.g. caring for a child disabled in a car accident), assist him to set up a predictable environment so that he can manage day to day before you facilitate his emotional release.

Implicit in DCT is the ability of helping interviewers to use a full repertoire of familiar communication strategies corresponding to each of the four cognitive-developmental orientations so that they can: (1) demonstrate empathy and make a strong connection with clients within their predominant orientation; (2) assist them to expand the resources available within their predominant orientation; and (3) introduce them to resources available within other, less utilised orientations, helping them master these alternative resources.

Generally, clients ask for assistance when they are depending on resources within their predominant orientation that are not 'in tune' with developmental or environmental demands. Once you join with them in their primary orientation, you can assist them to expand their use of the resources within it. For example, a client may know how to use problem-solving skills (concrete) to deal with a simple demand, but may be unable to access a more comprehensive problem-solving repertoire for more complicated demands. Assisting such a client to expand the use of problem-solving skills would promote an expanded use of familiar resources.

It is also the case that once clients fully explore their issues from the vantage point of their predominant orientation, they may want you to help them to explore their issues from the various frames of reference that are associated with these orientations which they access less frequently. For example, a battered woman may need to tell you several stories of what has happened (concrete), and also may need assistance to reorganise her life away from the batterer (concrete). Once the stories are told and a safe environment is established, she may want help in exploring the deep emotions associated with her experiences (sensorimotor). She may also benefit from a dialogue in which she can analyse the ways the wider environment assists or ignores the problems of the battered woman and how it either succeeded or failed to attend to her needs and her continued safety (dialectic/systemic). Finally, it may be appropriate to work with her regarding how the trauma experience relates to her own self-concept and self-esteem (formal).

Note in the preceding paragraph that a comprehensive treatment programme may require you to be able to work with clients within all orientations. There is no 'higher' form of cognition or emotion in the DCT model. The primary goal is to expand the depth and breadth of understanding within each of the cognitive-developmental orientations.

Facilitating cognitive, emotional and behavioural development

DCT identifies two directions which development can follow – horizontal and vertical. *Horizontal development* occurs when we encourage a client to experience life in more depth within one of the four orientations. For example, clients often need to grieve their losses emotionally, whether it is a failed examination, the loss of a job, or a divorce. Emotional grieving can occur within all four orientations, but may be experienced most fully at the sensorimotor orientation. Horizontal development within the sensorimotor orientation can be facilitated by using skilful communication tools carefully to phrase questions and statements within that orientation, thereby assuring learning within a safe helping environment.

Vertical development occurs when clients shift their orientation. For example, you may work with clients who are very effective at discussing issues within the formal or dialectic/systemic orientations. You may note, however, that their very abstract discussions are sometimes used to protect themselves from sensorimotor experiencing or from taking concrete action to change their circumstances. Your task as a helper may be to encourage and linguistically support these clients to move vertically by phrasing questions and comments that help them to consider their issues from more concrete or sensorimotor vantage points.

Many clients come for help during times of developmental transition – points at which they must separate from old ways and move on to the new. These include many of life's milestones – a birth of a child, high school and college graduation, the first job, a big promotion, the loss of a job, establishing or dissolving a relationship, the death of loved ones, reaching a particular age, retiring or facing death or illness. As these changes happen, the individual may need counselling and help to cope with new ways of living.

The use of DCT questioning strategies

DCT offers a set of systemic questioning strategies that are used to: (1) access and assess a client's predominant cognitive-developmental orientation; (2) access and assess a client's ability to move within and between the other three orientations; and (3) promote horizontal and vertical development. These questioning strategies are presented in Box 16.3.

Box 16.3   The DCT questioning sequence (abbreviated)*

1 Opening presentation of issue

(a) Could you tell me what you would like to focus on today?
(b) Could you tell me what occurs to you when you focus on the issues that prompted you to seek assistance?

Goal   Obtain the client's story. Identify the cognitive-developmental orientation predominantly used by the client.

Techniques   Use encouraging statements, paraphrasing and reflection of feeling to bring out data, but try to impact the client's story minimally. Get the story as he or she constructs it. Summarise key facts and feelings about what the client has said before moving on.

2 Sensorimotor/elemental orientation

(a) Could you think of one visual image that occurs for you when you think of the issue that prompted you to seek help?
(b) What are you seeing? Hearing? Feeling? It will be helpful to locate the feeling in your body.

Goal   Elicit one example and then ask what is being seen/heard/felt. Aim for here-and-now experiencing. Accept randomness.

Techniques   Summarise at the end of the segment. You may want to ask 'What one thing stands out for you from this?'

3 Concrete/situational orientation

(a) Could you give me a specific example of the situation/issue/problem?
(b) Can you describe your feelings in the situation?

Goal   Obtain a linear description of the event. Look for if/then, causal reasoning.

Techniques   Ask 'What did he or she do? Say? What happened before? What happened next? What happened after?' Possibly pose the question 'If he or she did X, then what happened?' Summarise before moving on.

4 Formal/reflective orientation

(a) Does this happen in other situations? Is this a pattern for you?
(b) Do you feel that way in other situations? Are those feelings a pattern for you?

Goal   Talk about repeating patterns and situations and/or talk about self.

Techniques   Ask 'What were you saying to yourself when that happened? Have you felt like that in other situations?' Again, reflect feelings and paraphrase as appropriate. Summarise key facts and feelings carefully before moving on.

5 Dialectic/systemic orientation

(a) How do you put together/organise all that you told me? What one thing stands out for you most?
(b) How many different ways could you describe your feelings and how they change?

Goals　To obtain an integrated summary of what has been said. To enable the client to see how reality is co-constructed versus developed from a single view. To obtain different perspectives on the same situation and be aware that each is just one perspective. To note flaws in the present construction, co-construction, or perspective, and move to action.

Techniques　As we move towards more complex reasoning, several options are open. Before using any of these, summarise what the client has been saying over the entire series of questions.

Integration　How do you put together/organise all that you told me? What one thing stands out for you most?

Co-construction　What rule were you (they) operating under? Where did that rule come from? How might someone else (perhaps another family member) describe the situation? (Feelings can be examined using the same types of questions.)

Multiple perspectives　How could we describe this from the point of view of some other person or using another theoretical framework or language system? How else might we put it together using another framework?

Deconstruction and action　Can you see some flaws in the reasoning or in the patterns of feelings above? How might you change the rules? Given these possibilities, what action might you take?

* This Box is modified from *Developmental Strategies for Helpers* (Ivey, 1991), and is used here with the author's permission.

Example interview*

The following is an illustrative interview designed to show how the DCT framework, along with the use of *basic attending skills* (Ivey, 1991) (e.g. paraphrasing, reflection of feelings, summation), can facilitate client growth and understanding. A mother comes for help because she is having many fights with her teenaged daughter who is about to leave home and enter college. This is a common occurrence in many Western cultures – often daughters and mothers work out their need to separate by fighting rather than expressing the sadness of loss. The following actual session is abbreviated for clarity. Identifying data have been disguised to ensure confidentiality.

Interviewer:　Lisa, what would you like to talk about today?
The interviewer poses an open-ended question to determine the primary cognitive-developmental orientation being used by the client to understand the issue promoting treatment.
Lisa:　My daughter, Christine, and I have been having an immense number of fights lately. We always seem to argue and I find myself becoming really upset. It's her final year in school and she will be leaving home soon. I wanted us to separate smoothly and to remain close to each other.
Lisa presents her issues within the formal orientation. She talks about patterns between herself and her daughter. She reflects on herself and her own feelings.
Interviewer:　So you have been fighting a lot and you feel angry at yourself. What you really want is to remain close. What is the pattern you see emerging that is troubling you?

* The interview maintains a copyright (1991) with Allen E. Ivey and Mary Bradford Ivey, and is used here with their permission.

The interviewer reflects Lisa's feelings, paraphrases and follows with a question posed within the formal orientation to join with her.

Lisa: Ever since last summer we just seem to be on two different tracks. Before then, we have really been able to talk about anything and even enjoyed lots of things in common. Now it's just bicker, bicker, bicker.

Interviewer: You are noticing a big shift in the way you and Christine relate. Can you give me some specific examples of the type of arguments you are having with one another?

The interviewer is moving Lisa from a formal perspective to a concrete orientation in order to examine the details of the situation.

Lisa: Sure, just last week we really had a big argument. She was going to the college admissions office and came down dressed up in jeans and a T-shirt. She looked awful.

Interviewer: She was in jeans and you didn't like it.

Interviewer paraphrases Lisa's comments within the concrete orientation.

Lisa: Right. Then I said to her, 'You can't go to an admissions interview dressed like that. You look terrible.' I guess I was too critical. Then she said that she was tired of me telling her what to do all the time. So we argued a bit and I felt terrible.

Lisa offers the concrete, descriptive details of the fight. The statement, 'I guess I was too critical' is an indication that Lisa has shifted the concrete conversation to a formal self-reflection. Most clients will discuss their issues from multiple cognitive-developmental orientations, although usually one orientation will be primary.

Interviewer: You felt terrible because of the argument?

Interviewer reflects Lisa's feeling, expanding the story horizontally by remaining within the concrete orientation. The question mark at the end indicates a raised tone of voice and an implied perception check.

Lisa: Yes, but then she went upstairs and changed. She looked a lot better. But as she walked out, her eyes were flashing and angry.

Interviewer: Is that the type of thing that happens a lot? Is that typical of the pattern you spoke about before?

These are formal operational questions and, if successful, will lead Lisa to talk about the difficulty she is experiencing within the formal orientation. The movement back to formal, after gathering some concrete details, will help make the pattern analysis more meaningful.

Lisa: Yes, exactly. We have been having these little tiffs for about a year now. I just know that the situation makes me feel terrible and I can see that Christine feels badly as well. We have always been so close until this last year. Now she makes me so angry that sometimes I just want her to go and leave.

Although Lisa notes her angry feelings she is not directly experiencing the emotion at this time. Instead, she is commenting on the change in her relationship with Christine, so her comments are actually at a formal (examining) orientation.

Interviewer: I can sense your frustration and hurt. You want something to be different. Do you want to try an exercise in imagery and see what happens? These types of exercises have been helpful before in understanding complex situations.

The interviewer provides a summation, followed by a closed-ended question with information. DCT seeks to have the client join in the process of deciding which intervention to use in the session in the belief that clients should have as much say as possible in the path of their own interview.

Lisa: OK, let's try one of these exercises again.

Interviewer: Lisa, I'd like you to sit back and relax (*pauses while Lisa closes her eyes*). Now, you said you were feeling hurt by your constant fights with Christine. Could you focus on that feeling of hurt? (*Pause.*) Can you locate that hurt in your body in some specific place? (Lisa points to her heart.)

Now, Lisa, start with that feeling in your body and let your mind wander to whatever comes. (*Pause.*) Can you get an image in your mind? What are you seeing?

The interviewer is using a basic sensorimotor imaging exercise which we have found is useful in helping clients discover their deeper feelings. As such techniques are often surprisingly powerful, use these carefully and with a full sense of ethics.

Lisa: I am seeing Christine when she was two (*tears*) and remembering (*pause*) what she was like when she was an infant (*more tears*).

Interviewer: You seem to be feeling that sensation very deeply right now. What else are you aware of?

The interviewer reflects Lisa's feelings and provides an open invitation for Lisa to go where she needs to.

Lisa: I really do care for her a lot – in fact so very much. I think maybe she cares for me too in much the same way. Could it be that we care so much that it's hard for us to separate?

Lisa moves away from the sensorimotor experience to formal reflection. With some clients it may be important to help them stay focused within the sensorimotor orientation, but Lisa seems to have got a new insight which may be helpful for her to process within her primary formal orientation. Having returned to sensorimotor experience, she recalls and relearns how important the relationship between herself and Christine is. With that awareness, she may be ready to take new action and find new behaviours that will better serve her and her daughter.

Interviewer: So, you feel that your caring for one another shows itself in the arguments you are having?

The interviewer reflects Lisa's meaning. Lisa is finding that deeper meanings and feelings underlie the surface of the fights she is having with her daughter. The discussion has moved further into the more abstract formal orientation.

Lisa: I guess so. It seems strange to fight when one is close, but I guess that happens.

Interviewer: Let's go a bit further. Could you tell me a bit about what happened for you when you were Christine's age and you left home for college?

The interviewer introduces an open-ended question to examine possible parallels between the two situations. At one level this is concrete, as the interviewer is asking for specifics, but at another level it is formal and possibly even dialectic/systemic as here she is searching for patterns of patterns and possible intergenerational family issues.

Lisa: Well, it was different for me. My mom and I were close, but not so close as Christine and I. I guess being a single parent makes the two of us even closer.

Lisa responds within the formal orientation, noting the differences in meaning between the two situations. Comparisons and contrasts between situations are usually associated with formal reasoning. In addition, Lisa brings up the issue of single parenthood.

Interviewer: So, the two situations are different. You feel closer to Christine than perhaps you did to your own mother. Could you go a bit farther with that?

The interviewer reflects Lisa's meaning with an invitation to expand her analysis via an open-ended question.

Lisa: One thing occurs to me. My mom always said, 'Healthy birds fly away'. I wonder if I've been hanging on too much and maybe I'm more of the problem than I thought I was.

Lisa is now beginning to draw on strengths from within her intergenerational family history. This represents a transition point between the formal and dialectic/systemic orientations.

Interviewer: So, in your family of origin, health is represented by the saying, 'Healthy birds fly away'. What meaning do you make of that? How do family factors relate to what's going on between you and Christine?

The focus has changed from the individual to the family, an indicator of a shift to dialectic/systemic questioning.

Lisa: I've got it. Christine and I really bonded after the divorce. Sometimes I depended on her too much. But, as mom said, it is the healthy ones who are able to leave home. I should be glad for my successes and maybe let go more easily.

Lisa is thinking now using a dialectic/systemic frame of reference. She is beginning to see how the concrete difficulties she is experiencing with her daughter were influenced by the family's developmental history – the divorce. Simultaneously, she is discovering how learnings from her family of origin may be of help to her and her daughter during their own separation process.

Interviewer: That is great. It sounds like the situation is making more sense to you now. And, perhaps you can draw on the strengths of your mom's legacy to move nearer to beginning the steps towards resolution with your daughter.

Comments on the interview: The importance and power of the sensorimotor/elemental and dialectic/systemic orientations

The above excerpt illustrates several issues. Let us consider two of these and the implications from a communication perspective.

Images and sensorimotor experiencing

First, you may have noted that imaging was particularly important in discovering the deeper emotions underlying the issues between Lisa and her daughter. Imaging, particularly when based on bodily sensations, can be particularly powerful, thus emphasising the influential role of non-verbal communication in the interview process. Often clients will be rapidly moved to tears or other deep emotions. This type of work should not be done with a client unless the client knows beforehand what to expect. In the example above, note that Lisa had already gone through a similar process before.

DCT stresses the importance of egalitarian relationships in the interview. If the interviewer had simply started the sensorimotor imagery exercise without preparation and consent, it might have been equally powerful and yet potentially more threatening and mysterious to the client. DCT emphasises the importance of sharing in advance what is to happen with clients rather than surprising them. We argue strongly against using powerful techniques unless the client is fully informed. We have found the client's direct involvement in the selection and application of techniques has a positive effect on the quantity and quality of self-disclosure, motivation and commitment during the interview process.

Box 16.4   Options for dealing with sensorimotor affect*

1   Observe non-verbal processes

Breathing directly reflects emotional content. Rapid or frozen breathing signals contact with intense emotion. Other cues include facial flushing, pupil contraction/dilation and body tension.

2   Pace clients and lead them to more expression of affect

Many people get right to the edge of a feeling, and then back away with a joke, a change of subject, or an intellectual analysis. In such instances, you could:
(a) Say the person looks like he or she was close to *something important*. 'Would you like to go back and try again?'
(b) Discuss some positive aspect of the situation. This could free them to face the negative. Anchoring a positive emotion in the body can be a useful resource for clients which you can use from time to time. You as the helper also represent a positive asset yourself.
(c) Use here and now sensorimotor techniques and questioning strategies. Using the present tense (e.g. 'What are you seeing/hearing/feeling?') is particularly helpful. Gestalt exercises are also useful, or other such interventions that help clients become more aware of body feeling. Use the word 'do' if you find yourself uncomfortable with emotion (e.g. 'What do you feel?' or 'What did you feel then?'). Such questions begin to move clients away from the intensity of here and now experiencing.

3   Be prepared to deal with tears, rage, despair, joy, or exhilaration

Your own comfort with emotional expression will affect how clients face emotion when in a helping relationship. If you are not comfortable with a particular emotion – yours or your client's – your client will likely avoid this emotion or you may handle it less effectively than other emotions.
A balance of being very present, being aware of your own breathing, providing culturally appropriate and supportive eye contact and still allowing room to sob, yell, or shake is important.
Keep emotional expression within a fixed time. Ten minutes is a long time when you are crying, and helping the person to reorient is important.

* This Box is adapted from a presentation by Leslie Brain at the University of Massachusetts in 1988.

If sensorimotor work of this type is new to you, practise it first with an informed volunteer and utilise it in your work only with appropriate supervision. Even after sufficient practice you must be prepared to deal with the intensity of the emotions that these types of techniques can trigger in a client. Imagine that, even with informed consent, you and/or the client begin to feel uncomfortable with the depth of emotion expressed. What do you need to do? First, you need to validate whatever experience the client shares with you, for each person experiences deep emotion in a different way. Several additional options for dealing with deep sensorimotor affect are presented in Box 16.4. These ideas can assist you both to help clients express more emotion and to help them cope with more emotion than either you or they feel able to at the moment.

The dialectic/systemic orientation

Most helping interviews operate within the concrete and formal orientations. DCT argues that these orientations are important, but that the field needs more emphasis on the deeper feelings associated with sensory experience and the complex issues which arise when we view life from the perspectives provided by dialectic/systemic emotion and reasoning. The dialectic/systemic orientation was only beginning to be explored in the interview example. Lisa starts to realise that the context of her daughter leaving and the history of her divorce are important parts of the concrete, specific fights she and her daughter have been experiencing. This is perhaps, at best, a beginning. Among the many systemic issues which may relate to mother–daughter relationships and single parent families are gender roles, the impact of cultural expectations, economic issues and broader social support questions such as the extended family and community.

A conceptual model for matching and expanding client orientation

A helping interviewer must be able to establish an environment that first responds to a client's primary orientation and then helps this person to explore issues from other orientations. In this way, the interviewer must be able to engage in a co-constructive process – developing helping environments, with clients, that are 'in tune' with the cognitive-developmental orientation being explored. DCT posits four basic styles, each one corresponding to one of the four orientations. These are illustrated in Figure 16.1 and further explained below.

Style 1: Environmental structuring for the sensorimotor/elemental orientation

The interviewer/counsellor directs the session, using communication skills extensively. Examples of clients who predominantly rely on this orientation are individuals seen in inpatient psychiatric settings, correctional settings and traditional one-to-one instructional or teaching settings. It is also true, however, that many other clients will often work within the sensorimotor orientation, for it is here that deeper emotional experience may be reached.

There is a number of environmental-structuring therapies and techniques that are highly useful to clients needing to explore or master resources within this orientation. Directive psychiatry and counselling are characteristic. In these cases, the helping interviewer 'takes over' for the client and makes necessary decisions. In cases of trauma such as rape or child abuse, the interviewer has the responsibility of taking action to help the individual. When helping children and families in crisis, the interviewer may be required to take such direct action. With clients who have less severe problems, directive techniques such as relaxation training, structuring an environment for behaviour (for example, working with a hyperactive child), and body-oriented therapies, such as dance and movement therapy may be appropriate.

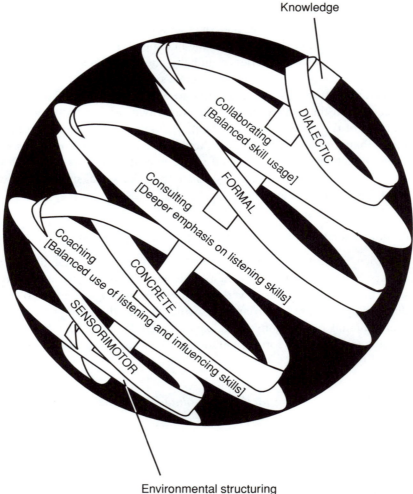

Figure 16.1 The developmental sphere*

Appropriate theories and applications

Style 1   Behaviour modification, relaxation training
Style 2   Assertiveness training, decisional counselling,
           reality therapy, rational-emotive therapy
Style 3   Person-centred therapy, logotherapy,
           psychodynamic therapy
Style 4   Feminist therapy, intercultural counselling,
           systematic therapies

Figure 16.1 The developmental sphere*

* The developmental sphere was drawn by Lois T. Grady and is adapted here with her permission.

Style 2: Coaching for the concrete/situational orientation

To create this environment, the interviewer balances attending and influencing skills and works with the client in a participative manner. The interviewer knows things that the client does not and is willing to share them. Examples are vocational decision-making around a specific issue, assertiveness training, many behavioural techniques, and reality therapy. Here, the helper takes the present developmental capabilities of the client and helps the client enhance, expand and practise these.

Style 3: Client-directed consulting for formal/reflective orientation

To create this environment, the helper supports the client's reflective search primarily through the use of attending skills and posing reflective questions. Non-directive and modern Rogerian counselling styles typify this approach. Within the formal orientation, techniques of Frankl's logotherapy, psychoanalytic methods and the narrative models of therapy may be used. Interpretations and reframes which help the client to examine patterns of self and situations also are germane within this orientation.

Style 4: Mutual collaboration for dialectic/systemic orientation

Here, the helper promotes self-starters to develop their own goals and methods. Feminist counselling, multicultural counselling and systemic counselling are prime examples of the type of helping offered within this orientation. For example, the feminist therapist's emphasis on working with the client as a co-equal typifies this mutual, collaborative style of helping. At times a therapist using a feminist approach may provide strong direction (Style 1), assertiveness training (Style 2), or listening (Style 3); but ultimately the goal is a co-constructed view of the world in which client and therapist learn together.

The sphere illustrated in Figure 16.1 indicates the need to match a helper's style with a client's predominant cognitive-developmental orientation in order to understand and discuss the primary issues at hand. Some clients will be well grounded in the perceptual frames and methods of interpretation which their preferred orientation provides. Some of these people may be so comfortable with only using the resources of one orientation that they may have significant difficulty shifting to a new perspective within an alternative orientation (rigid movement within and among cognitive-developmental orientations). Conversely, some clients are not well grounded in any of the four orientations and use resources associated with all four orientations but in a rather haphazard manner (diffuse or chaotic movement within and among cognitive-developmental orientations). Finally, there are those clients who will have a strong mastery of the perceptual and communication skills found within each orientation and are cognisant of how and why they choose a particular strategy to interpret events (flexible movement within and among cognitive-developmental orientations). This kind of client typifies the goal of DCT – to knowingly access a variety of perspectives in order to experience, interpret, discuss and act on their issues. It is because of the variety of client styles and the stated goal of DCT that the helper must be comfortable operating within all four of the orientations.

While the three types of client described above (i.e. rigid, diffuse, flexible) are common, most do not simply operate within one orientation. An example of a client operating within multiple orientations may illustrate the complexity of many clients. An older woman entering the job market for the first time may be operating within a confused sensorimotor orientation vocationally, and may not have even the most elementary job-seeking skills. At the same time, she may have had a wide range of experience in volunteer work and might be a successful parent and 'counsellor' to her children and to the neighbourhood families. In these areas of her life, she may be thinking within a formal or even dialectic/systemic frame of reference. She may need concrete skills training as she practises for job interviews and prepares her résumé.

Thus, in a single interview it may be necessary to move through several different interviewing/counselling styles, depending on the issue being discussed. In relation to this woman, for the purposes of her vocational issues, it may be best to begin by using a structured style, to assist her in navigating through unfamiliar territory. It may also be necessary, however, to assist her in formal reflection in order to facilitate her understanding of the job or career choices she wishes to pursue. It may also be necessary to assist her with the concrete skills of job searching and interviewing. As this client develops more confidence, knowledge and experience, successful counselling may help her to examine her vocational identity from other orientations. She may need to look at herself and her patterns of experience (formal) and then analyse possible job discrimination for older women (dialectic/systemic). It might well also be helpful to enable her to explore emotional experience within the sensorimotor orientation.

A note about helper flexibility

You will find that you can change your counselling style as your clients grow. The cycle suggested here starts by attending to where the client is developmentally, then moves to consolidate the psychological and interpersonal resources available within the client's predominant orientation before shifting to an alternative perspective. Again, the ultimate DCT goal is to help clients effectively access resources from within several of the orientations so that they develop a multitude of resources that they can later access along their developmental journey.

Many helpers, however, try to 'hang on' to an old style that worked with the client, and fail flexibly to alter the helping environment as the client moves and grows. If you find, through observation and other types of client feedback, that your interviewing style is no longer working as it did before, shift your style to meet the new developmental needs of your client. Remember: interviewing and counselling are for the client, not for the helper. Quality use of communication skills and developmental theory can provide clients with an optimum range of helping environments that change in conjunction with their growth.

Using DCT within a multicultural perspective

Where does the socio-cultural context end and the individual begin? This question is at the heart of the multiculturalism controversy evident in the literature on helping and interviewing. In the past, it was assumed that a helper, regardless of ethnic background, gender, sexual orientation and economic class, was objective and minimally biased. Helping was viewed as a neutral interaction and helpers were trained to discount their cultural preconceptions and to attend to the mastery of counselling theory and practice. Unfortunately, this emphasis on the 'technical' aspects of the helping profession minimised the human/cultural aspects of our work. At best, it produced well-intentioned professionals who accepted that they were probably ineffective when working with clients of differing cultural backgrounds. At worst, it continued a type of cultural imperialism that further led to the alienation of many diverse client populations (Rigazio-DiGilio and Ivey, 1995).

Many recent models of helping are based on the knowledge that counselling is an inter-cultural exchange process (Pedersen, 1994; Sue, 1981). These models place the technical skills of helping (i.e. communication skills, empathy skills, awareness of the knowledge base) in a subordinate position to understanding the importance of the socio-cultural forces operating on the interview process. Implicit in this awareness is the need to recognise how our own cultural backgrounds enter the helping relationship and interact, with all biases intact, with the cultural backgrounds of our clients.

DCT posits that all counselling takes place in a cultural context. Our model of helping values the *client's own language*, including all the culturally bound assumptions, frames of reference and unique perspectives which clients use to make meaning of their world. Conversely, our own helping language is extremely important. By posing questions and comments at specific orientations we can help clients to examine issues from multiple perspectives while still maintaining a firm sense of self, rather than pushing clients into orientations that they are not developmentally ready to enter. As we are given verbal and non-verbal cues that clients are experiencing difficulty within an orientation, the developmentally appropriate response is to return to an orientation with which they are more comfortable.

DCT questioning strategies and sensitivity to the natural language clients use to process and communicate their feelings, thoughts and interaction intentionally stress the importance of cultural heritage and the role it plays in a client's construction of the world. By allowing cultural influences to be accepted and used as elements of the interview process, DCT helps to make meaning of the individual's family, community, socio-cultural and political context. Helping individuals learn to perceive social, political and economic contradictions and to take action against the oppressive elements of reality should be one of our primary goals as helpers (Rigazio-DiGilio, 1994b).

OVERVIEW

The effectiveness of the DCT model of helping is based on the careful application of a wide range of communication skills. By integrating developmental theory with interviewing skills, counsellors can fine tune treatment plans that address the natural changes clients experience over the course of their development and during the counselling relationship. Developmental skills can be an important and useful addition to your practice as a helper. It does little good to speak of complex and abstract ideas with a client working through a divorce who is tearful and confused and needs sensorimotor direction and support and, later, concrete problem-solving skills.

At the heart of the ideas presented here is the importance of noting where your client 'is at'. How are they thinking and feeling and how are they making sense of the world? Your ability to note whether your client is presenting within the sensorimotor, concrete, formal and/or dialectic/systemic orientations will enable you to match your style and language to the client's idiosyncratic needs.

The DCT questioning strategies presented here can enable you to help clients to expand their thinking and emotion within each orientation or move to another orientation for further growth. The developmental framework reminds us that different clients need to work within different orientations throughout the course of an interview process and that the most helpful interventions will be geared to an orientation the client is comfortable working within. If your first counselling style does not work, shift your style to another orientation that is aligned to the client's mode of making sense of and operating in the world.

Finally, DCT provides a helping model that recognises the importance of cultural influences operating within the interview and seeks to maximise the value of these influences. The linguistic processes and multicultural sensitivity of DCT allow clients to explore their issues through their natural language and to maximise the cognitive, affective and behavioural resources each cognitive-developmental orientation has to offer. This is the ultimate goal of DCT – to empower clients to be able eventually to help themselves.

REFERENCES

Borders, L. D. (1994) 'Potential for *DCT/SCDT* in Addressing Two Elusive Themes of Mental Health Counselling', *Journal of Mental Health Counselling*, 16, 75–8.

Gilligan, C. (1982) *In a Different Voice*, Harvard University Press, Cambridge, MA.

Heesacker, M., Rigazio-DiGilio, S. and Prichard, S. (in press) *A Paper and Pencil Measure for DCT's Cognitive-Developmental Orientations*

Hill, R. and Rodgers, R. H. (1964) 'The Developmental Approach', in H. Christensen (ed.), *Handbook of Marriage and Family Therapy* Rand McNally, Chicago, pp. 171–209.

Ivey, A. (1986) *Developmental Therapy: Theory into Practice*, Jossey-Bass, San Francisco.

—— (1991) *Developmental Strategies for Helpers*, Microtraining, North Amherst, MA.

—— and Gonçalves, O. F. (1988) 'Developmental Therapy: Integrating Developmental Processes into Clinical Practice', *Journal of Counselling and Development*, 66, 406–13.

—— and Ivey, M. B. (1989) 'Developmental Therapy: Theory and Practice', in O. F. Gonçalves (ed.), *Advances in the Cognitive Therapies: The Constructive-Developmental Approach*, APPORT, Porto, pp. 91–110.

Kegan (1982) *The Evolving Self*, Harvard University Press, Cambridge, MA.

Kelly, G. (1955) *The Psychology of Personal Construct*, Vol I. Norton, New York.

Kunkler, K. P. and Rigazio-DiGilio, S. A. (1994) 'Systemic Cognitive-developmental Therapy: Organizing Structured Activities to Facilitate Family Development', *Simulation and Gaming: An International Journal of Theory, Design, and Research*, 25, 75–87.

Pedersen, P. B. (1994) 'Multiculturalism as a Fourth Force in Counselling', *Journal of Counselling and Development*, 70.

Piaget, J. (1954) *The Language and Thought of the Child*, New America Library, New York.

Rigazio-DiGilio, S. A. (1993) 'Family Counseling and Therapy: Theoretical Foundations and Issues of Practice', in A. Ivey, M. Ivey and L. Simek-Morgan, *Counselling and Psychotherapy: A Multicultural perspective*, (3rd edn), Allyn & Bacon, Needham Heights, MA. pp. 333–58.

—— (1994a) 'A Co-constructive Developmental Approach to Ecosystemic Treatment', *Journal of Mental Health Counselling*, 16, 43–74.

—— (1994b) 'Beyond Paradigms: The Multiple Implications of a Co-constructive-developmental Model', *Journal of Mental Health Counselling*, 16, 205–11.

—— (in press) 'Systemic Cognitive-developmental Therapy: A Counselling Model and an Integrative Classification System for Working with Partners and Families, *International Journal for the Advancement of Counselling*.

—— and Ivey, A. E. (1990) 'Developmental Therapy and Depressive Disorders: Measuring Cognitive Levels through Patient Natural Language', *Professional Psychology: Research and Practice*, 21, 470–5.

—— (1991) 'Developmental Counselling and Therapy: A Framework for Individual and Family Treatment', *Counselling and Human Development*, 24, 1–20.

—— (1993) 'Systemic Cognitive-developmental Therapy: An Integrative Framework', *The Family Journal: Counselling and Therapy for Couples and Families*, 1, 208–19.

—— (1995) 'Individual and Family Issues in Intercultural Counselling and Therapy: A Culturally-centered Perspective', *Canadian Journal of Counselling*, 29, 244–61.

Rigazio-DiGilio, S. A., Gonçalves, O. and Ivey, A. E. (1994) 'Developmental Counselling and Therapy: A Model for Individual and Family Treatment, in D. Capuzzi and D. Gross (eds), *Counselling and Psychotherapy: Theories and Interventions*, Macmillan/Merill, Columbus, pp. 471–513.

Sue, D. W. (1981) *Counseling the Culturally Different: Theory and Practice*, Basic Books, New York.

Vygotsky, L. (1986) *Thought and Language*, MIT Press, Cambridge, MA.

Watzlawick, P. (ed.) (1984) *The Invented Reality*, Norton, New York.

17 The appraisal interview and the performance evaluation interview*

Henk T. Van der Molen and Frits Kluytmans

INTRODUCTION

One of the key activities for personnel officers and managers is employee assessment. Assessment is not a goal in and of itself. Depending on its specific purpose, assessment can fall into one of three categories: assessment of achievements, assessment of performance and assessment of potential. Each requires a different approach. If they are not kept sufficiently distinct, ambiguities can quickly arise. That is why clarity concerning both the purpose of the assessment and the most suitable approach is a prerequisite.

This chapter looks at the appraisal interview and the performance evaluation interview. The first section discusses the main points of difference between these two types of assessment. There are a number of factors which ensure that both the appraisal and performance evaluation interview run smoothly. These general requirements will be discussed in the second section. The third section will subsequently discuss the appraisal interview and the fourth section, the performance evaluation interview. In order to discuss specific communication skills in this type of interview, we present a practical example in this section. The final section contains a brief summary of this chapter.

THE DIFFERENCE BETWEEN AN APPRAISAL INTERVIEW AND A PERFORMANCE EVALUATION INTERVIEW

The purpose of assessment

Employee assessment can serve many purposes. These purposes can be roughly divided into three main categories: (1) to put into words the views underlying certain decisions in the field of personnel management (including those affecting pay); (2) to encourage and improve the employee's performance in the work situation; (3) to determine further growth opportunities for the employee (Hoogstad and Weststeijn, 1993).

When the purpose is to arrive at personnel decisions such as those involving employee transfers, firing or pay issues, the term we use here is 'appraisal' or 'appraisal interview'. When referring to the second purpose (i.e. improving the employee's performance), we will use the term 'performance evaluation' or 'performance evaluation interview'. Finally,

* The authors want to express gratitude to Dr Wim Westera for his contribution to the practical example and to Cecilia Willems for the translation of the text.

when the aim is to determine the employee's further growth opportunities, we use the term 'assessment of potential'. The latter form of assessment will not be discussed here, since the specific know-how and skills required to determine where an employee's opportunities lie are beyond the scope of this chapter.

Differences between appraisal and performance evaluation interviews

Appraisal and performance evaluation interviews differ not only in their purpose. The object of the assessment, the temporal perspective and the relationship between the assessor and the employee being assessed are also different.

Object of the assessment

An appraisal interview and a performance evaluation interview differ in terms of their object (what precisely is being assessed?). The emphasis in an appraisal interview is on the employee's performance during the past period. The purpose is to arrive at certain conclusions and/or decisions concerning this performance. For example, one conclusion may be that the employee is due for a pay rise or extra bonus, should undertake further training, or, in the most extreme instance, should be dismissed for severe incompetence or negligence.

The point of a performance evaluation interview is to discuss the performance of the employee during a specific period of time and the co-operative relationship between employee and superior or colleagues. The goal is to try to improve that performance and that relationship in the (near) future by means of analysis and evaluation. The agenda for the performance evaluation interview covers much more, then, than the agenda for the appraisal interview. Any and all features of the job or working conditions which could stand improvement must be discussed: job content, working habits, supplementary training courses, but also things that the employee is not directly responsible for, such as the physical working environment, colleagues' performance and the performance of the superior with whom the interview is taking place.

Temporal perspective

The differences in purposes and goals mean that the two types of interview also differ in terms of their temporal perspective. The appraisal interview focuses much more on the recent past and on the employee's performance during a specific period of time. The analysis and evaluation in a performance evaluation interview are geared towards the near future. The point is to improve the employee's future performance.

Relationship between employee and superior/colleagues

The balance of power between employee and superior during an appraisal interview is much more lopsided than in a performance evaluation interview. The discussion and the decision-making are unilateral. The superior gives a personal opinion of the employee's performance. The employee may take heed of this opinion and respond to it, but what this person says will have little impact on the final outcome.

In a performance evaluation interview, it is not the superior's opinion, but rather the goal of improving the employee's performance and the relationship between the employee and the superior, or between the employee and colleagues or customers, that are the focus of attention. The discussion and decision-making are therefore more bilateral. Formal differences in power must be set aside for the time being. The employee is actively involved in searching for further opportunities for improvement. Specifically, the ability to accept a proposed solution plays a major role in determining the ultimate impact of the interview.

PREPARING THE INTERVIEW

Both the appraisal and performance evaluation interview can be a stressful experience for the employee. The consequences of the first are frequently immediate; for example the appraisal may determine whether or not the employee is given a permanent contract, a pay rise or a promotion. While the second type of interview has no real tangible consequences, it is frequently where employees hear what others think of their performance. That can be an emotional experience for many people, both in a positive and in a negative sense. In both cases, then, the manager should be well prepared (King, 1984). Not only is this the employee's right, but it also adds to the quality of the interview.

Preparing the topic

To begin, the superior should prepare the topic of the interview carefully. Before the interview takes place, the superior should consider the period under review closely. How has the employee performed? How well does this person work as part of a team? Has the employee achieved the goals set at the time of appointment or during the previous interview? Have both parties lived up to their agreements? If this is the first performance evaluation interview that the superior has had with this particular employee, it might be useful to take the employee's job description as the starting point. If this is a follow-up interview, then the superior should read through an earlier assessment or the report covering the previous performance evaluation interview.

Time and place

Second, the superior should set aside enough time for the interview and conduct it in an appropriate place. Appointments should be made well in advance, the interview should take place in a quiet spot and there should be no annoying interruptions. The ideal situation would be to reserve a separate room suitable for conducting a personal conversation, with no incoming calls or passers-by to interrupt the discussion.

THE APPRAISAL INTERVIEW

Main goal

The emphasis during an appraisal interview is to assess the employee's performance. Based on that appraisal, the superior should be able to arrive at various decisions – for example, whether the employee merits a bonus, should be transferred or fired, or whether other measures should be taken. Given their far-reaching consequences, it is important for managers to exercise great care in reaching an assessment. Before concentrating on the appraisal interview itself, let us turn to a few aspects which may influence a superior's appraisal.

How does a superior arrive at an appraisal?

In most cases, superiors use a particular *appraisal system*: a set of procedures, rules and regulations specifying how to reach an appraisal. There are many different systems in use in companies (see Kirkpatrick, 1986). Among these systems are the objective measurement of results, rating scales and the 'open essay' method.

With respect to assessment of performance, the *objective measurement* of results is preferable, especially if the employee's work consists of simple tasks, for example, entering data, typing texts or carving stone. In many cases, however, more subjective criteria also play a role in performance. Some examples are the quality of the product, how well the employee takes care of tools and instruments, the relationships with colleagues, and so on. When such aspects are to be included in the appraisal, managers generally make use of rating scales which allow them to assess performance according to a number of relevant characteristics. Unfortunately, in practice such characteristics are often open to interpretation. Qualities such as independence, willingness to co-operate, verbal and written skills can be interpreted in many different ways and are therefore open to discussion. That is less true for *anchored rating scales*, which describe what is meant by good and poor performance in terms of concrete behaviour.

In the *open essay method*, the superior is completely free to choose the language with which to assess a subordinate's work. While this system does make it possible to discuss every characteristic that the manager considers relevant, it is also more susceptible to subjectivity and, consequently, to endless and irritating discussions.

It is therefore recommended that the manager assess the employee's performance as objectively as possible and describe it in terms of concrete behaviour. One way to ensure that subjectivity is kept to a minimum is, for example, to have two (independent) superiors fill in the rating scales.

Factors that may influence or disrupt an appraisal interview

Regardless of the nature of the appraisal system, there are a number of processes that come into play when we appraise someone else's behaviour which can have a very negative effect on that appraisal. We will discuss the most important of these below.

The assessor

Every assessment is subjective to some degree. Everyone has prejudices, is selective and individualistic in their observations, making it almost impossible to arrive at an unbiased, objective view of reality. Such subjectivity increases when:

- The supervisor relies on the subordinates, in the sense that the recognition and personal income gained depend on the way the department performs. In that case, the supervisor will tend to be more helpful and less critical towards subordinates whose performance is mediocre or poor than if these aspects did not depend on them;

- The employee being assessed does not consider the assessor an expert. Conversely, subordinates are more likely to accept the appraisal of a superior whom they consider an expert;
- The superior is in a bad mood. To some extent, mood determines the nature of the incidents that attract the superior's attention.

Leaning towards the middle

To avoid getting into heated discussions with subordinates, assessors tend to choose the 'middle of the road' when using scales (Roe and Daniëls, 1984). For example, if the assessor uses a five-point scale, where (1) is 'poor in every respect' and (5) 'excellent', the inclination will be towards central tendency by choosing (3) 'satisfactory'. Very seldom will the extremes (1) or (5) be selected, reducing the five-point scale to only three points. It is possible to counteract this movement towards the middle by using a four- or a six-point scale.

Attribution

When assessing performance, superiors look not only at an employee's performance, but also at the causes behind that performance. The process of ascribing performance to certain factors is known as attribution. Assessors are more likely to attribute poor performance to the personality of the subordinate (motivation, commitment or qualities), whereas the subordinate is more likely to attribute any personal failure to environmental factors (see Chapter 2). The same effect can be seen in cases of satisfactory performance, but then in reverse. In addition to appraising an employee's performance, the assessor must back up these views by investigating, as thoroughly as possible, whether the employee can be held responsible for that performance.

Cognitive mechanisms

There are a number of cognitive mechanisms that play a significant role in assessing employees. The most important of these are:

- *The recency effect.* Events which took place only a short time ago will have a bigger impact than events that occurred longer ago (Millar *et al.*, 1992). Thorough preparation and taking continuous notes on results can reduce the effect of this mechanism.
- *The 10 per cent/90 per cent effect* means that 90 per cent of the interview time is taken up discussing the 10 per cent of the job in which the employee performed poorly. Western culture is probably somewhat to blame for this effect; the reasoning is that a person who delivers an excellent performance doesn't need to be patted on the back for it, since it might give the person a sense of inflated self-worth. However, as in the case of raising children, rewards and compliments can be a highly effective way of stimulating employees (Likert, 1961; Trower and Van der Molen, 1995).
- *The halo effect and the horn effect.* These two effects are closely allied with the mechanism described above. One positive or negative aspect of the person's work overshadows

everything else. When that aspect is positive, it is termed the halo effect; when it is negative, it is known as the horn effect.

Specifying goals and feedback

Employees are more inclined to accept their superior's appraisal of them when it is couched in specific terms: the manager is seen as more of an expert who understands the details of the job. Vague goals make it difficult to provide specific feedback, and vague feedback linked to specific goals will have no effect whatsoever. It is therefore important to formulate both the employee's goals and the feedback in as specific terms as possible.

How to prevent errors of judgement

The errors of judgement summarised above are difficult to avoid. Managers, after all, are only human. Still, there are a number of steps that they can take to reduce the risk of falling into one of these judgement traps.

Be aware of the mistakes

First of all, it is important for the superior to be on guard for errors of judgement, never losing sight of them when appraising a subordinate.

Objectify performance

In the second place, the chance of making a mistake is reduced when the superior looks at the employee's performance objectively. We stated earlier that this is by no means a simple task, but we do not wish to imply that every attempt to do so will end in failure. For example, superiors can attempt to express the employee's performance (i.e. the quality thereof) in concrete products and behaviour. These products and behaviours should be monitored as closely as possible over a longer period of time. In deciding on an appraisal system, anchored rating scales are to be preferred above more global scales or the open essay method.

Multiple assessors

Third, it is easier to arrive at a reliable appraisal when more than one assessor is involved. That considerably reduces the risk of a unilateral, subjective appraisal. Of course, the other assessors must also be familiar with the employee's performance.

The interview model

The interview itself is entirely geared to the appraisal and the superior's justification of this appraisal. Pinder (1986) describes three methods of conducting appraisal interviews: *inform and sell*, *inform and listen* and the *problem-solving* method. He concludes that the latter method is the most effective one because it encourages the interviewee to engage in problem-solving, is less problem-centred and encourages growth and development. In our view, however, this approach leads to confusion between the appraisal interview and the performance evaluation interview. In the latter, the problem-solving approach is appropriate, whereas in the former the point is to arrive at a judgement. We believe, hence, that the 'inform and listen' approach is clearer for both parties. A concrete description of this approach is given below.

Starting the interview

The superior should begin the interview by stating the goal of the interview as concretely as possible: whether or not the subordinate will receive a pay rise, a permanent employment contract, etc. The superior then indicates which criteria were used to arrive at the appraisal. Ideally, of course, these criteria should be made known ahead of time. The superior then outlines what the structure of the interview will be and how long it will last.

Making the appraisal known

The superior then tells the employee, as briefly as possible, the general appraisal and explains the assessment criteria used to arrive at this judgement. Two scenarios are possible at this point:

- The overall appraisal is a positive one. In that event, the superior would do well to begin by mentioning the criteria on which the employee performed satisfactorily. The employee is then given the opportunity to respond. Next, the superior discusses the criteria on which the appraisal was less than satisfactory. Skill at giving criticism plays an important role here. The employee is once again given the opportunity to respond. The superior listens, paraphrases, reflects and summarises, but continues to assert a personal appraisal;
- The overall appraisal is a negative one. In this event, as in the previous case, it is important that the superior lets the employee know immediately what the assessment is, and then employs reflections to allow the employee to express initial emotional reactions. Once the employee appears to have recovered enough to absorb further information, the superior can go through the various assessment criteria to back up this judgement. Once again, the superior should listen to the employee's responses, paraphrase, reflect and summarise, but continue to assert the arguments underlying the judgement.

Rounding off the interview

Once all of the criteria have been discussed, the superior summarises the conversation by repeating the general appraisal and the consequences of this appraisal in the light of the goals stated at the beginning of the interview. In the case of a negative appraisal, it may be necessary to make an appointment for a follow-up interview to discuss any further repercussions. Appraisal interviews can have a demotivating impact on the employee (especially when they are negative), and they may also affect the relationship between superior and subordinate negatively. That is why they should be undertaken with the utmost care. Appraisal interviews are not very suitable tools for guiding and improving an employee's performance and motivating them to do better. Those goals are better achieved by the performance evaluation interview.

THE PERFORMANCE EVALUATION INTERVIEW

Emans *et al.* (1995) have described the development of the performance evaluation interview in historical terms. They situate it within the evolution of ideas concerning effective leadership. Whereas it was once thought that sound leadership meant taking up an authoritarian position, nowadays effective leaders are expected to consider their employees' opinions and therefore involve them more closely, not only in arranging their own work, but also in taking decisions important to the company as a whole. McGregor (1957) was one of the first to point out that the traditional approach to assessment stemming from authoritarian attitudes only generates resistance, both on the part of the superior and on the part of the employees. The outlines of today's performance evaluation interview are already visible in the solution that he proposed. He argued that the traditional appraisal interview should be modified by putting more emphasis on the employee's share of the responsibility and the possibility of analysing and solving problems *together*.

If conducted systematically and correctly, the performance evaluation interview can be one of the most important conversations that a superior has with a subordinate. Because it focuses on improving the employee's work, it can lead to better performance and to a higher level of motivation. It can also improve the relationship between superior and employee.

The main focus of this type of interview is to solve any problems in the employee's work, and to discuss openly the relationship between superior and subordinate or between the subordinate and colleagues. Because the subordinate is the one who will have to put the solutions into practice, it is important to involve him or her closely in coming up with such solutions. The chance of achieving and effectuating a solution increases when the employee takes a leading role. Maier's formula (1963) is important in this respect: $E = Q \times A$ (i.e. the Effect of a solution depends on the Quality and the Acceptance of the solution).

Effective interviewing also depends upon three important facets, namely: (1) situating the performance evaluation interview; (2) conditions and preparation; and (3) interview phases. These three aspects will now be discussed.

Situating the performance evaluation interview: part of the planning cycle

Superiors can do better justice to the performance evaluation interview when they make it part of a planning cycle. They can do this, first of all, by drafting a plan of the activities to be performed for a specific period of time based on an analysis of their subordinate's job. The subordinate implements this plan and after some time has passed (usually six to twelve months), performance and output are evaluated. By emphasising the tasks, activities and concrete products which have been determined in consultation, the superior has already avoided focusing too much on the employee's personal characteristics. It is also important that the superior learns to compliment subordinates and offer them support whenever necessary. In that sense, it is essential for the success of the interview that the superior should take steps and follow up on any agreements made.

Conditions and preparation

Unambiguous goal

One important condition is that the goal of the performance evaluation interview is unambiguous. In other words, the focus should be on improving the employee's work and the relationship with the superior or with colleagues or customers, and that focus should not be extended to include a whole range of personnel measures as in the case of the appraisal interview. Combining these goals is doomed to failure. For that reason, in many organisations the system of performance evaluation interviews is kept strictly separate from the appraisal cycle: performance evaluation interviews are held one to two times a year, whereas the appraisal interviews are scheduled once every other year. Sometimes appraisal interviews only take place when there is a concrete reason to schedule them: for example, when an employee is moving from a fixed-term to a permanent employment contract.

Willingness to improve

A second condition is that the superior and the subordinate have a fairly good relationship and that the employee is willing to improve wherever possible. Likewise, the superior must be capable of taking steps to help the employee improve.

Preparation

Before embarking on a performance evaluation interview, the parties involved must prepare themselves. Both the superior and the subordinate should reflect on the topics to be discussed during the interview. The superior should also be aware of the errors of judgement mentioned above, since the possibility cannot be ruled out that the same errors will be repeated in evaluating the employee's performance.

Interview phases

A performance evaluation interview is divided into four phases (Gramsbergen-Hoogland and Van der Molen, 1992; Kikoski and Litterer, 1983): (1) starting the interview; (2) drafting the agenda; (3) discussing the various agenda items; (4) rounding off the interview.

We will illustrate this type of interview in practice with an example from a telecommunications organisation (see Box 17.1). First, in order to sketch the background, we provide a more detailed description of the actual situation. Then, we present a general description of the phases of the interview, followed by part of the concrete performance evaluation interview. We also discuss relevant skills, when used in the separate phases, in more detail.

Box 17.1 Sketching the interview

The interview situation

The interview is conducted in a telecommunications company and concerns the customer service centre, where people call to report problems with telephone lines. Using a question-and-answer procedure, the customer service employees should be able to find out what is causing the problem: is the customer using the equipment incorrectly, is the equipment malfunctioning, is there a defect in the infrastructure (cables, switchboards)? If it appears from the procedure that the customer is not to blame for the problem, the employees make an appointment with the person on the computer or refer the customer to another department for further analysis. The customer service department has a staff of twelve, all of them part-time employees. Working hours are from 8.00 a.m. to 2.00 p.m. and from 2.00 p.m. to 8.00 p.m. Supervising the twelve employees is the team supervisor Judy Daniels. The department itself is managed by the head of emergency services, Harry Jensen. Harry has scheduled a performance evaluation interview with one of the customer service employees, Barbara Petersen.

Prior history/reason for the interview

Barbara has been employed in the department for a year-and-a-half and was hired because of her experience and excellent references as a switchboard operator for a mail-order company. Most of her colleagues have been working in the department much longer than she has, and have had to deal with a sea-change in company culture after a reorganisation. Excellent service, a focus on the customer and efficiency have become the new priorities. The new climate has led to a considerable increase in pressure. In addition, the company now makes use of a larger variety of increasingly complicated equipment, so that the question-and-answer procedure must meet higher and higher demands. The change in company culture is not complete.

Interviewer and interviewee

Harry Jensen (50) is aware of the crucial position that his department has within the organisation. Complaints must be handled flexibly, quickly and efficiently. He expects his employees to provide good service to their customers, to be friendly and to act immediately and effectively to solve customer problems. Harry is friendly and self-assured. He gives his subordinates the space they need, and is interested in them. He is also always ready to listen to their comments.

Barbara Petersen (35) joined the staff about eighteen months ago when sickness absenteeism rose after the reorganisation. She was set to work in the customer service department without any real training and appeared able to hold her own from the beginning. Her production (= number of complaints dealt with) is relatively high, and she gets somewhat irritated at the 'old guard'; in her opinion they still have too much of a 'civil-service mentality' and are inefficient in their work. She feels they should model themselves after her, and would like her boss to crack the whip a bit more. She works part time and is the mother of three children.

Harry and Barbara's goals

The performance evaluation interview takes place once a year. This is Barbara's first interview since she joined the team. Her boss tries to stick to the interview model throughout. He would like to do as much as possible in co-operation with her to solve any bottlenecks. He himself would like to cover two areas.

- He wants to show his appreciation for her general performance.
- He has been told by the team supervisor that customers regularly complain about the way Barbara treats them. The team supervisor has noticed this herself, and Barbara's colleagues have also discussed it on occasion. Harry believes that it is extremely important to treat customers with respect.

Barbara would also like to discuss two points:

- She wants to propose changing her working schedule. She works the afternoon shift (2.00 p.m. to 8.00 p.m.), but now that her children are getting older she is finding this shift increasingly difficult to manage. Her husband is also on a different schedule now, making child care a real problem. She would like to move over to the day shift, when her children are at school. The working hours are based largely on 'ancient privileges', but because her production is so high, she feels that she has the right to speak her mind and expects that she can push for a change.
- When she started the job, she expressed the desire to see more variety in her work. At the time Harry said he would get back to her on that, but he never did and that bothers her.

Starting the interview: the purpose and how long the interview will last

After some brief social comments, the superior starts off by indicating what the purpose of the interview is, emphasising that the point is not to judge the employee's performance but to improve the latter's work and the level of co-operation between employee and superior and/or colleagues or customers. The superior then sketches how the interview will proceed and indicates how long it will last.

1   *Harry*: Hello Barbara, take a seat. So, has it been busy this morning?
    Barbara: Not too bad. Yesterday it was an absolute zoo. Now we have three unoccupied lines, so we can handle that.
2   *Harry*: Well, enjoy it while it lasts!
    Barbara: (*Smiles, nods.*)
3   *Harry*: Before we begin, I want to explain that the purpose of our interview is to see how you're doing in your job, review any problems you might be encountering and what we can do about them. I've set aside about 45 minutes in all for our talk. I think that should be enough, don't you?
    Barbara: As far as I'm concerned, yes.

Drafting the agenda

The interview begins when the superior and subordinate sum up the various points they wish to discuss and draft an agenda covering these items. Ideally, both parties should have noted the topics down on paper ahead of time; when that happens, the interview can begin by taking stock of the different items and explaining them briefly. Points of discussion should be indicated by a key word and explained briefly when necessary. Neither party should launch into a long and detailed explanation of the various items.

In *determining the sequence* of the various points of discussion, it is important for a variety of reasons to give the points raised by the employee priority over those raised by the superior (as in interventions (4)–(9)). First of all, the employee is likely to want to discuss problems that are truly crucial, and will be highly motivated to solve these problems. Second, this approach will encourage employees to discuss other problems as well. They will subsequently be more open to the points raised by the superior.

4 *Harry*: Let's start by looking at the issues you wanted to discuss. Have you thought about the points you'd like to raise?

   Barbara: Yes, I have two things. The first is that I'd like to transfer to the morning shift . . .

5 *Harry*: (*Nods.*) So you want to talk about changing your working schedule (*makes a note of this topic*).

   Barbara: Yes. I've been saddled with the kids since Theo got another job. If I could switch to the morning shift, that would make a big difference to me.

6 *Harry*: I understand. And your second point?

   Barbara: (*Hesitates slightly.*) Well . . . uh . . .

7 *Harry*: (*In a friendly voice.*) Well?

   Barbara: Well, I'm about ready to do something more than just answer the phones all day long.

8 *Harry*: (*Realising that she has raised a pertinent topic, which he was afraid she would do.*) You mean you're beginning to find the work a little tedious.

   Barbara: (*Slightly irritated.*) A little . . .? I'm beginning to find it *very* tedious!

9 *Harry*: OK, I'll make a note of 'tedium of work'. Is that all right?

   Barbara: Yes, that's all right.

10 *Harry*: Fine, that's that. I also have two points I'd like to discuss. The first concerns your general performance. I have just a few comments to make about that. The second is that we've received a number of complaints from customers who feel that you haven't treated them properly.

   Barbara: (*Interrupts him.*) What!? Aren't I doing a good job then?

11 *Harry*: (*Continues calmly.*) No, I didn't say that. But I have received the odd complaint from people who feel that they've been treated rather brusquely.

   Barbara: Well gee! I think that's putting it rather extremely. (*Reflecting.*) It does happen sometimes that I have to cut short a conversation – I don't have all the time in the world, naturally . . . but I never realised that there were so many complaints.

12 *Harry*: Now I didn't say that there were so many . . . it isn't that bad, you know.

   Barbara: (*Somewhat ruffled.*) Yes, but give me an example.

13 *Harry*: I understand that you want to discuss this immediately, but I think it would be a better idea to go through all the points we've listed one by one.

   Barbara: (*Reluctant, coming to her senses.*) Well, all right.

14 *Harry*: OK, let's see what we've got here. Your wish to transfer to the morning shift and second, the monotony of your work. I myself had one point about your work and the point about the complaints. Which topic would you like to start with?

   Barbara: Well, I'm very curious to see what your general comments are on my work. So let's start with that.

15 *Harry*: And then?

   Barbara: Well, I'm getting pretty fed up with my job, so I'd like to discuss the tedium factor next. After that I don't care.

16 *Harry*: Okay, then let's begin with my general comment, and then move on to the tedium of your job. We'll then discuss the schedule change and then the complaints. Is that all right with you?

    Barbara: (*Nods.*) Just fine.

It is worthy of note that Harry briefly paraphrases Barbara in interventions (5) and (9) in order to structure the agenda. After he introduces a point of criticism in intervention (10), Barbara immediately wants to discuss it. In intervention (13) Harry uses the skill of regulation to finish drawing up the agenda first. He summarises the points of discussion in intervention (14) and asks Barbara what her order of preference is. By so doing, Barbara is made to feel that she is also responsible for the performance evaluation interview.

Discussing the various agenda items

As mentioned above, the first step is to go through the points in the order preferred by the employee. After posing a general opening question – for example, 'You wanted to talk about the monotony of your work? Can you tell me precisely what the problem is?' – the superior should put listening skills to work: asking open questions, paraphrasing, reflecting and summarising. Once the problem is sufficiently clear, the two parties should look for a solution together. It is very important to time the transition to this problem-solving phase precisely; there is a danger that the employee will merely touch on a problem and immediately want to look for a solution. First, however, the superior should obtain a very clear idea of what the problem is. This is called the 'phase of problem clarification'. The parties then give their opinion of the topic under discussion and reach a decision on it. The process of decision-making must subsequently be formulated in concrete terms by determining 'who, what, where, when and how' action is to be taken.

17 *Harry*: Well, to begin, my general comment is that I am extremely satisfied with the way you tackle your job.

    Barbara: Well that's nice to hear.

18 *Harry*: Yes, you've adapted rapidly to the new environment and your work pace certainly merits a compliment.

    Barbara: (*Somewhat shy and embarrassed.*) Gee! Thanks a lot ... but I ... I didn't find it too hard.

19 *Harry*: No really, I take my hat off. I think it's important to let you know what a great job you're doing.

    Barbara: Well, I'm really pleased to hear that.

20 *Harry*: So my advice is: just keep doing whatever you're doing. Insofar as there is any criticism of your work, you should remember to see it in this light.

    Barbara: (*Nods.*) Uh-huh.

Before discussing any problems with the employee's performance, the superior should begin by providing positive feedback. It should be noted that Harry starts the discussion of his own points in intervention (17) with *general positive feedback*. In intervention (18) he makes this general feedback more concrete. As often happens when employees – and people in general – receive positive feedback, Barbara's reaction is characterised by modesty and the tendency to minimise the praise. However, Harry insists on his reinforcement (intervention (19)). If the general evaluation is positive, as in this example, it is also important to let the employee know that eventual points of criticism should be placed against this background of positive evaluation (intervention (20)). Demonstrating appreciation for the good aspects of the employee's work will have a positive impact on the latter's motivation and willingness to listen. Of course, the general positive feedback should not be given when the superior has an abundance of criticisms.

21 *Harry*: OK, we've covered the first item. Now the following: you wanted to talk about the tediousness of your work.

   Barbara: (*Whining a bit.*) Yes, I really find it a problem. I've been working here for eighteen months now, and when I came I said right off that I wanted more variety in the job.

22 *Harry*: Uh-huh.

   Barbara: Well, that hasn't changed.

23 *Harry*: Yes, I understand, and you asked me then if we couldn't have you do something else once in a while.

   Barbara: But you never got back to me on that . . .

24 *Harry*: (*Reflecting.*) So if I understand you correctly, you're saying that I didn't keep my promise to you . . .

   Barbara: In a manner of speaking, yes. At least, you never brought it up again.

25 *Harry*: Well, I think you're probably right. I just didn't give it another thought. I'm very sorry. Maybe it's because I was under the impression that you enjoyed your job.

   Barbara: That's true, but you said you would get back to me about it in a few months . . . and you just didn't do that.

26 *Harry*: Again, I apologise. I simply forgot. I hope you haven't been walking around for months brooding about this! Wondering 'Where the heck is he?'

   Barbara: No, not at all. But it's not easy to just walk over and knock on the boss' door.

27 *Harry*: Well, as far as I'm concerned you're very welcome to do so! If something is bothering you, don't think twice, just come and tell me. That's a lot better than stewing about it. Anyway, it's my fault, I simply forgot. The question now is, what should we do about it? Do you have any suggestions?

   Barbara: Not really . . . except that I wouldn't mind filling in for one of the secretaries once in a while. I think that would be enjoyable.

Handling complaints

During the discussion of the first agenda item, Barbara already indicates that she is critical of Harry. It is important that Harry is open to her criticism (intervention (24)) and does not react defensively, but agrees with her. We also see that he apologises to her in intervention (25); in intervention (27) he indicates that he would appreciate it if Barbara could let him know right away when something is bothering her. He also asks her whether she has any ideas herself about making her job less monotonous. He is sticking very close to a participation model in this fashion (Lang *et al.*, 1990).

   The following general comments concern how to handle criticism. The employee may see the interview as an opportunity to voice complaints about the organisation and the way it is run. Such complaints can be divided into two categories:

- *Complaints that the superior can do something about* (for example, supplies from another department, draughtiness in the work place, etc.). The employee will have more faith in the superior if the latter takes action within a few days; that gives the employee the feeling that opinions count and that complaints are being heard. It will also motivate the employee during subsequent interviews;
- *Complaints about company policy* (for example, the pay scales, punching in, etc.). In this case, the danger is that the superior will feel called upon to defend the company. Such defensive behaviour is not wise. Again, it is better for the superior to indicate what he or she does and does not agree with, and to come to an understanding about what can or cannot be done.

The employee may also be critical of the superior. The latter's response to such criticism calls for special skills. Criticism should never be taken personally, but should be seen as an important contribution that can clarify a difficult situation. That is why it is very important to listen closely to another's criticism. Once the superior believes that the employee's critique is fully understood (and has checked this out by paraphrasing it), there are two options open. First, the superior may agree with the subordinate's criticism. If so, the superior should admit as much and agree to work on changing. Second, the superior may disagree with the criticism. In that case, the superior should paraphrase what the subordinate has said and then state a personal opinion. Both parties can then try to reach an agreement, perhaps in the form of a compromise (Gramsbergen-Hoogland and Van der Molen, 1992).

The interview between Harry and Barbara continues in the following vein.

28 *Harry*: Yes, I can imagine. (*Considers*.) But there's two problems. First, you know that you have to have certain certificates to do secretarial work. And second, we'd have to check with the head of the secretarial pool first.
  Barbara: Yes, that's clear.
29 *Harry*: So I guess the certificates aren't a problem?
  Barbara: I have a typing certificate and I also worked for a few years as a secretary.
30 *Harry*: Of course (he remembers). Another thing: when it gets really busy here, it would be hard to spare you.
  Barbara: I realise that, but maybe I could simply swap with someone once in a while?
31 *Harry*: That would be fine, in that case we wouldn't be understaffed. I think the next step is for me to talk to Susan as soon as I can.
  Barbara: Great!
32 *Harry*: Now, let's just round off this discussion by going over our agreements. First, I should learn to stick to my promises (*laughs*) and you should simply come and see me next time something like this comes up. As for the real issue: I'll have a word with Susan about the possibility of your swapping places with someone once in a while. OK?
  Barbara: OK!

In this part of the interview, Harry is trying to reach a concrete agreement on the issue under discussion. He does this at intervention (32) with an accurate, agreed, summary.

33 *Harry*: Now shall we move on to the second agenda item?
  Barbara: Fine with me.

34 *Harry*: OK. The change in your home situation means you'd like to transfer to the morning shift ...

Barbara: Yes, absolutely. I run around like an idiot trying to organise everything right now. It would be a lot easier if I could transfer to mornings because the children are in school then.

35 *Harry*: And your husband has a new job, you said?

Barbara: Yes, he can't be there in the afternoon anymore to look after the kids, so we've had to come up with another solution ...

36 *Harry*: I see, so he used to watch the children but isn't able to anymore.

Barbara: No. He's gone all day now, so that's become impossible ... I've arranged something with our next-door neighbours, but that's just temporary. And the kids don't have a good time either.

37 *Harry*: I understand your dilemma. I wonder whether you've thought about other solutions. Because I'm afraid that it will be pretty hard for us to change your schedule.

Barbara: We thought about taking a babysitter, but neither of us really likes the idea ... I think five days a week is way too much. I'd much prefer that one of us pick up the children from school.

38 *Harry*: I understand why you'd prefer that. Well, to get back to the schedule, the problem is that during the reorganisation we all committed ourselves to certain agreements. Of course, you had no way of knowing what the future had in store for you, but we specifically asked you then whether you would agree to work afternoons.

Barbara: (*Slightly upset.*) Yes but that was eighteen months ago! If I'd known then what I know now!

39 *Harry*: No, of course you had no way of knowing. I think you should try to switch schedules with someone. Have you talked to anyone about that yet?

Barbara: Sure, but it didn't get me anywhere. Margaret said she would think about it, but only for one day a week. And she wasn't even sure. Anne said she would be willing to swap once in a while, but not permanently. Otherwise ... otherwise nobody was interested as far as I know.

40 *Harry*: (*Thinking along with her.*) Well, this is a difficult dilemma. I can't force Karen or Liz to work afternoons because you're having child care troubles. I hope you understand that.

Barbara: (*Upset.*) Of course I do, but ... listen, I've come to you with a serious problem, but you just don't want to do anything about it! I'll ask around myself. But you're the one who's supposed to take care of the schedules!

41 *Harry*: (*Very calmly.*) I understand how annoying this is for you. And you're right in saying that the schedules are my job. But I don't think you can say that I simply don't wish to deal with this problem. Of course I do, but you must understand that I have to consider the clear-cut agreements we made about scheduling. I can't just go against them.

Barbara: (*Angry.*) Well I don't believe in hanging on to old agreements like they were some kind of national treasure. That means we can never change anything!

42 *Harry*: It isn't easy, as you've noticed. I mean: what precisely do you think I should do?

Barbara: Well they might respond differently to you than they did to me ...

43 *Harry*: I seriously doubt whether that would make any difference . . . (*pause*) . . . I'm more than willing to ask around, but I refuse to put anyone under pressure. I am committed to the earlier agreements.

   Barbara: Yes, but that doesn't solve my problem!

44 *Harry*: (*Silence.*) I'm not sure that there's anything we can do about that. (*Silence.*) It might be interesting to note that in about six months' time we'll probably be staying open until 10 p.m.

   Barbara: Really?

45 *Harry*: That probably won't make much difference to you since you want to go to the morning shift, but the schedules will probably change a little then anyway. Perhaps there'll be more chance of switching then.

   Barbara: That's still a long way off . . .

46 *Harry*: Yes, but I'm afraid you'll have to come up with something else for the time being. And even so, I can't make any promises.

   Barbara: (*Disappointed.*) So for now there's just no chance . . .

47 *Harry*: No, just a second. Your scheduling problem is clear to me, it's just that I don't have a cut-and-dried solution at the moment. Let's agree that I'll approach some of your colleagues, not to ask them if they want to switch with you, but to see how they feel about a schedule change in general. And we should keep a close eye on what will happen to the schedules if we decide to stay open until 10 p.m.

   Barbara: Well, all right.

As may become clear from this segment of the interview, superiors do not always have to agree with their subordinate's ideas about possible solutions. They should be able to express their own opinion clearly. Before doing so, they would do well to indicate which points they do agree with first. But they also have to be aware of the possibilities and impossibilities in their organisation. In this example, after clarifying the problem (interventions (33)–(36)) Harry has to make it clear that an immediate change in the work schedule is not possible (interventions (37)–(39)). This is a bit of bad news for Barbara and her reaction is rather upset (40). Harry reacts calmly to her anger with a reflection of feeling and an explanation why he is not able to fulfil Barbara's wish immediately (intervention (41)). Afterwards he reacts in an assertive manner (e.g. interventions (41), (43) and (47)).

Points of discussion on the superior's side

In a performance evaluation interview superiors almost always have points of criticism, which they want to pass to their employees. To ensure that such criticism has the desired effect, the superior would do well to formulate it in terms of concrete behaviour (what precisely is the point?), to describe this behaviour in very specific terms, and to finish off by asking the employee to alter that behaviour. The employee then has the opportunity to respond, and together superior and subordinate can try to find a solution that satisfies them both. That solution should be stated as concretely as possible in the form of an agreement.

In this performance evaluation interview Harry has one main point of criticism: the way Barbara deals with the complaints of customers.

48 *Harry*: Now for the final point, dealing with customers.

Barbara: Yes, the complaints ... I just don't understand that.

49 *Harry*: Let's take a look at the situation first. The reason I want to discuss this point is because Judy filed a report in which she states that she's regularly received complaints about you.

Barbara: But what kind of complaints? Give me an example!

50 *Harry*: I've got a few letters here. ... Here's a random sample. A woman who writes 'She said: "Get lost, I don't have time for this!"' I must say I find that shocking.

Barbara: (*Cowed, shocked.*) Gosh, I ... I think ... Did I really say that?

51 *Harry*: You seem surprised.

Barbara: I can hardly imagine myself saying that.

52 *Harry*: But that's what this customer claims.

Barbara: Well then, I just don't remember, but I suppose it's true ...

53 *Harry*: And what do you think about it yourself?

Barbara: Well, if it's true, then ... well, I must have been pretty irritated...

54 *Harry*: I understand where that might be the case, but there are a few other examples ...

Barbara: Say, I don't like hearing all this.

55 *Harry*: You seem surprised that you evidently lose your temper sometimes.

Barbara: Yes, well I do get irritated once in a while. Some of the people you have to deal with. ... But I always thought that I was pretty polite.

56 *Harry*: What do you mean by 'pretty polite'?

Barbara: Well, we often get people who just drone on and on complaining, and then we have to cut off the conversation abruptly. Sometimes they launch into their whole life story. ... What else are we supposed to do in that case?

57 *Harry*: I understand, but I still think you have to treat the customers politely, regardless.

Barbara: But what am I supposed to do? Chatter away to them the way Anne or Liz do? If that's the case, then you'd better arrange for extra staff.

58 *Harry*: That's one of the difficulties of the job, isn't it: you have to deal with complaints as quickly as possible and still remain friendly and polite to the customers.

Barbara: And that's what I try to do! But when I see that we have a bunch of people on hold, I try to work a little faster. And then maybe I do cut off a conversation too abruptly. I suppose that's true ...

59 *Harry*: So the more people you have on hold, the shorter you try to keep the calls.

Barbara: Yes, and I get really pissed off that the 'old guard' simply ignore what's happening. That makes me feel even more pressurised.

60 *Harry*: You have the feeling that the others just keep taking their sweet time.

Barbara: Yes. You should do something about that.

61 *Harry*: Well, I agree with you that some of your colleagues could work a little faster now and again. But I don't think it's their fault that complaints are coming in about you.

Barbara: I'm not saying that. But the two things are related.

62 *Harry*: I think you should remember that I'll be having this kind of interview with your colleagues as well, and that I'll be discussing things like putting people on hold, work pace, and so on. Our discussion is about you and the problem that you're some-times – how should I put it – rather 'short' with the customers. The question is, what can we do about that?

Barbara: (*Considers.*) Well ... Maybe I can try to watch my words a little more.

63 *Harry*: I think that's a good solution. What do you think about taking a course in complaints handling? Where you learn how to bring a conversation to a speedy end without hurting someone's feelings?

Barbara: I don't think that will be necessary. I took a course like that at my last job. No, I really don't think that would do much good.

64 *Harry*: So, as far as you're concerned it isn't necessary ... (*Decides.*) OK, but can we agree that you'll try to be more careful from now on?

Barbara: Yes, I'll try.

65 *Harry*: Good. I think we've covered everything now.

In this portion of the interview, Harry acts assertively in criticising Barbara and backing up his critique by giving her concrete examples (intervention (50)). He responds to Barbara's initial shock by reflecting her feelings (interventions (51) and (55)). He then attempts to describe precisely what happened when complaints were not dealt with correctly (intervention (56)). By showing that he understands Barbara's side of the story, he helps to foster a sense of co-operation in working towards improving her professional behaviour (interventions (58)–(65)). He also avoids falling into the trap of blaming the problem on her colleagues (intervention (62)).

Rounding off the interview

When all agenda items have been discussed in this fashion, the interview can be rounded off by summarising the decisions that have been reached (intervention (66)). The most useful approach is for the superior to write down the problems discussed as well as the possible solutions mentioned. Such a list can be helpful when the parties begin to summarise and draw conclusions. It can also help to ground the conversation and keep it as concrete as possible. A written summary also serves to remind both parties of what has been agreed and can be a solid basis for a follow-up interview.

66 *Harry*: Let's just review what we've been talking about. In general I'm very happy with your work. As far as the tediousness of your job goes, I'll talk to Susan as soon as possible to see whether you can't swap places with someone there once in a while. I'll get back to you on that as soon as I can. Changing your schedule will be difficult. I'll raise the subject with a few of the others, and we'll keep an eye on what happens to the scheduling if we decide to stay open longer. On the topic of the complaints: you promised to be more careful from now on. Is that correct?

Barbara: Yes, that seems fine.

67 *Harry*: I'll write up a summary, and you'll get a copy.

Barbara: OK.

It will be clear that an interview conducted in this manner is by no means a voluntary affair. If the employee expresses legitimate desires prompted by a discussion of problems, the superior must get to work (for example, by ensuring material support). The superior must do more than simply listen; if it is left at that, the employee will be much less willing to engage in similar discussions in the future. Listening, then, must be followed by action!

OVERVIEW

There can be many reasons for wanting to assess an employee's performance. The discussion in this chapter was restricted to assessments associated with personnel decisions and assessments aimed at improving an employee's work and the relationship between the employee and the superior and/or colleagues. In the case of the former, the focus is on the superior's assessment or appraisal of the employee. That is why it is important to do everything possible beforehand to ensure that the superior arrives at a well-founded judgement. Once that has happened, this judgement can be conveyed to the employee during an appraisal interview.

To open up a discussion of problems in the employee's performance and the co-operative relationship between employee and superior, the performance evaluation interview, if properly conducted, offers ample scope. The performance evaluation interview focuses on the employee's work and the (near) future. The object is to solve any problems and improve the co-operative relationship. Performance evaluation interviews are divided into four phases.

In the first phase, the parties state the goal of the interview and indicate how long it will last. In the second phase, they take stock of the various points of discussion and draw up an agenda. In the third phase, they go through the various agenda items one by one. Listening is the most important skill when it comes to reviewing a problem. The parties should try to identify a solution that they can both accept. It is furthermore important that the superior responds constructively rather than defensively to the employee's objections and criticism. The interview should be rounded off by summarising the decisions taken and by making an appointment for a follow-up interview.

When conducted in this fashion, the performance evaluation interview can be a powerful means for improving both an employee's performance and relationship with the superior and/or colleagues.

REFERENCES

Egan, G. (1994) *The Skilled Helper* (5th edn), Brooks-Cole, London.

Emans, B., Kuijer, R., Postema, M. and Kuiper, P. (1995) 'Functie en functioneren van functioneringsgesprekken' [Function and Functioning of Performance Evaluation Interviews], *De Psycholoog*, 10, 401–7.

Gramsbergen-Hoogland, Y. and Van der Molen, H. T. (1992) *Gesprekken in organisaties* [*Interviews in Organizations*], Wolters-Noordhoff, Groningen.

Hoogstad, J. and Weststeijn, H. (1993) 'Beoordelen en beoordelingssystemen' [Appraisal and Appraisal Systems], in F. Kluytmans and C. Hancké, *Leerboek Personeelsmanagement* [*Textbook on Personnel Management*] (2nd revised edn), Kluwer Bedrijfswetenschappen, Deventer.

Kikoski, J.F. and Litterer, J. A. (1983) 'Effective Communication in the Performance Appraisal Interview', *Public Personnel Management*, 12, 33–42.

King, P. (1984) 'How to Prepare for a Performance Appraisal Interview', *Training and Development Journal*, 38, 66–9.

Kirkpatrick, D.L. (1986) 'Performance Appraisal. Your Questions Answered', *Training and Development Journal*, 40, 68–71.

Lang, G., Molen, H. T. Van der, Trower, P. and Look, R. (1990) *Personal Conversations. Roles and Skills for Counsellors*, Routledge, New York.

Likert, R. (1961) *New Patterns of Management*, McGraw-Hill, New York.

Maier, N. R. F. (1963) *Het gesprek als stimulans* [The Interview as Stimulant], Spectrum, Marka Boeken, Utrecht.

McGregor, D. (1957) 'An Uneasy Look at Performance Appraisal, *Harvard Business Review*, 35, 89–94.

Millar, R., Crute, V. and Hargie, O. (1992) *Professional Interviewing*, Routledge, London.

Pinder, T. H. (1986) 'How to Interview: The Appraisal Interview', *British Journal of Occupational Therapy*, 49, 293–4.

Roe, R. A. and Daniëls, M. J. M. (1984) *Personeelsbeoordeling: Achtergronden en toepassing* [*Personnel Appraisal: Background and Applications*], Van Gorcum, Assen.

Trower, P. and Van der Molen, H. T. (1995) 'Social Skills at Work', in P. Collett and A. Furnham (eds), *Social Psychology at Work. Essays in Honour of Michael Argyle*, Routledge, London.

Vrolijk, A. (1991) *Gesprekstechniek* [*Communication Techniques*], Bohn Stafleu Van Loghum, Houten.

18 THE COGNITIVE INTERVIEW

Amina Memon

INTRODUCTION

Effective interviewing skills can be described as one of the most useful tools a professional can possess. Although the aims may be diverse there are few practitioners who do not require to collect information of one sort or another using interviews. Those who work in the field of medicine rely on accurate case histories from patients, social workers rely on detailed case notes including family histories, market researchers rely on accurate information obtained from public surveys and therapists rely on eliciting accurate personal histories from their clients. We may be using the interview as a therapeutic technique (exploring an individual's current attitudes and emotions) or as an investigative technique (attempting to retrieve information from an individual's memory). This chapter examines one such investigative technique, namely the cognitive interview, which can serve to increase the quantity and quality of accurate information that can be obtained in an interview (Fisher and Geiselman, 1992).

The cognitive interview (or CI) is one of the most exciting developments in forensic psychology in the last ten years. The CI is a method that comprises a series of memory retrieval techniques designed to increase the amount of information that can be obtained from an interviewee. It can so help professionals obtain more complete and accurate reports from interviewees. The CI can only be used with a co-operative interviewee and so may be most suitable in interviews where the interviewee is not a suspect. The effectiveness of the CI in improving the quality and quantity of information from an eyewitness and as a way of improving the skills of interviewers has been empirically tested. To date, some forty-five studies have been conducted. This includes two studies conducted in the field using real-life witnesses and police officers trained in the CI technique.

The CI was initially developed by the psychologists Ed Geiselman (University of California, Los Angeles) and Ron Fisher (Florida International University) in 1984 as a response to the many requests they received from police officers and legal professionals for a method of improving witness interviews. The CI is based upon known psychological principles of remembering and retrieval of information from memory. Police detectives trained to use this technique enabled witnesses to produce over 40 per cent more valid information than detectives using their traditional interviewing techniques. Furthermore, university students using this new procedure obtained more information from witnesses than did experienced police officers who interviewed in their normal way! (See Fisher and Geiselman, 1992; Memon and Bull, 1991; Memon and Koehnken, 1992, for reviews).

This chapter will provide a critical review of research on the CI and will highlight methodological and theoretical issues. Two key questions will be addressed throughout: (1) Has the CI been adequately tested in laboratory research? (2) Does the CI work because of the cognitive techniques or are we seeing an effect of improved communication or rapport between interviewer and witness? Practical issues and implications for future research will be considered. Before describing the procedure and reviewing the empirical research, it is useful to understand *why* a procedure such as the CI is necessary.

WHAT LED TO THE DEVELOPMENT OF THE COGNITIVE INTERVIEW?

The ability to obtain full and accurate information is critical in an investigation – it may determine whether or not a case is solved, yet the eyewitness literature reveals that such recall is difficult to achieve (e.g. Goodman *et al.*, 1987; Ceci and Bruck, 1995). Much of the research has concentrated on variables which influence the input of information into memory, but comparatively little research attention has been devoted to the retrieval of information from memory.

An empirical study of the techniques used by untrained police officers working in a police department in Miami, Florida (Fisher *et al.*, 1987a) however, suggested that improving witness memory was only part of the story. There existed some fundamental problems in the conduct of police interviews that were leading to ineffective communication and poor memory performance. Fisher *et al.* (1987a) document several characteristics of the 'standard police interview' among which were constant interruptions (when an eyewitness was giving an account), excessive use of question–answer format and inappropriate sequencing of questions. More recently, George (1991) studied the techniques typically used by untrained officers in London and found a remarkably similar pattern among that group. This led to the characterisation of a 'standard police interview' as being one of poor quality and stressed the need for an alternative procedure for interviewing witnesses. Such calls have now begun to be answered and a number of innovative procedures have been developed for use by professionals who interview witnesses (Bull, 1992, 1995). However, the focus has tended to be on child interviews while there is much room for improving the quality of investigative interviews with adult witnesses (see Cherryman and Bull, 1995; Gudjonsson, 1994, for reviews).

The CI represents the alliance of two fields of study. The original version drew heavily upon what psychologists know about the way in which we remember things. Revisions of the procedure focused more heavily on the practical considerations for managing a social interaction and this was led by a desire to improve communication in police interviews and alleviate some of the problems described above. Obviously, the 'cognitive' and 'communication' components work in tandem. However, for the purposes of describing the procedure as it has been depicted in the published literature, the 'cognitive' and 'communication' components will be outlined separately.

WHAT IS THE COGNITIVE INTERVIEW

The 'cognitive' components of the CI draw upon two theoretical principles. First, that a retrieval cue is effective to the extent that there is an overlap between the encoded information and the retrieval cue (Flexser and Tulving, 1978) and that reinstatement of the original encoding context increases the accessibility of stored information (Tulving and Thomson's encoding specificity hypothesis, 1973). The second theoretical perspective that influenced the development of the CI was the multiple trace theory (Bower, 1967). This suggests that rather than having memories of discrete and unconnected incidents, our memories are made up of a network of associations and consequently, there are several means by which a memory could be cued. It follows from this that information not accessible with one technique may be accessible with another (Tulving, 1974).

Context reinstatement

The first technique is for the interviewee mentally to reconstruct the physical and personal contexts which existed at the time of the crime. Although this is not an easy task the interviewer can help witnesses by asking them to form an *image* or *impression* of the environmental aspects of the original scene (e.g. the location of objects in a room), to comment on their emotional reactions and feelings (surprise, anger, etc.) at the time, and to describe any sounds, smells and physical conditions (hot, humid, smoky, etc.) that were present. Geiselman and his colleagues (Saywitz *et al.*, 1992) have suggested that it may be helpful for child witnesses to verbalise aloud when mentally reinstating context. For example, to describe the room as the picture comes to mind, to describe smells, sounds and other features of the context. The following is an example of how the instructions to reinstate context were administered in a study where adult witnesses were interviewed about a photography session (Memon *et al.*, in press a):

Interviewer: First of all I'd like you to think back to that day. Picture the room in your head as if you were back there. . . . Can you see it? (*Pause for reply.*) Think about who was there (*Pause*). How you were feeling? (*Pause.*) What you could see? (*Pause.*) What you could hear? (*Pause.*) If you could smell anything (*Pause.*) Now I want you to tell me as much as you can about what happened when you came to get your photograph taken.

With child witnesses, the context of the original event can be recreated by explicitly requesting the child to think about the context and by asking specific questions that require them to think about it. The questions are asked slowly and deliberately with pauses. It is important to emphasise to the child that they must listen carefully to what the interviewer is saying. The instructions to reinstate context were administered as follows in a study where the witnesses were 8- and 9-year-old children being interviewed about a magic show (Memon *et al.*, in press b):

Interviewer: Put yourself back to the same place where you saw the magic show. Can you see the room now? (*Pause*) Tell me about the room. (*Pause*) Where were you at the time? (*Pause*) Tell me about your feelings. (*Pause*) Could you hear anything? (*Pause*) Could you smell anything? (*Pause*)

Report everything

A second technique is to ask the interviewee to *report everything*. This may well facilitate the recall of additional information, perhaps by shifting criteria for reporting information.

For instance, witnesses are encouraged to report in full without screening out anything they consider to be irrelevant or for which they have only partial recall (Fisher and Geiselman, 1992). The instruction to 'report everything' was used as follows in a study where the witnesses were 6- and 7-year-olds being interviewed about an eye test (Memon *et al.*, 1993).

Interviewer: Just try and tell me what happened, as much as you can remember. If you cannot remember all of it, just tell me what you can. Even little things are important.
Child: We had this ... even little things?
Interviewer: Even little things.

As well as facilitating the recall of additional information, this technique may yield information that may be valuable in putting together details from different witnesses to the same crime (see Memon and Bull, 1991). An eyewitness who provides more details is also judged to be more credible in the courtroom (Bell and Loftus, 1989), although the overall accuracy of these details rather than amount of information that is reported should be the major question in this context (see Koriat and Goldsmith, 1994, for a full discussion).

Change perspective

The third component is to ask for recall from a variety of perspectives. This technique tries to encourage the witnesses to place themselves in the shoes of the victim (if the witness is not a victim) or of another witness and to report what they saw or would have seen. Again the aim is to increase the *amount* of detail elicited. Geiselman *et al.* (1990) report that changing perspectives can be particularly helpful for children if the following instructions are given: 'Put yourself in that other person's body and describe what they would have seen.' However, there are several concerns about the use of the change perspective instruction, in particular the possibility that it could lead to fabricated details and confuse the witness as illustrated by the following example taken from the Memon *et al.* (1993) child witness interviews about an eye test.

Interviewer: What I'd like you to try and do is imagine that you are the nurse and that you can see the room from where she was standing, by the wall chart. Just tell me what you can see.
Child: Umm ... Did you see the letters, can you see the letters good and I said yes and that's all she said to me.

Evidence obtained using this particular technique may not be easily accepted in legal procedures where it is likely to be seen as subjective information or as an inference (see Memon and Koehnken, 1992).

Reverse order

The fourth component of the CI is the instruction to make retrieval attempts from different starting points. Interviewees usually feel they have to start at the beginning and are usually asked to do so. However, the CI encourages extra focused and extensive retrieval by encouraging witnesses to recall in a variety of orders from the end, or from the middle or from the most memorable event. Geiselman and Callot (1990) found that it was more effective to recall in forward order once followed by reverse order than to make two attempts to recall from the beginning. There is some doubt about whether young children can effectively use this technique, as illustrated by the following example from Memon *et al.*, 1993.

Interviewer: OK. What we are going to do now is tell the whole story backwards. Now the very last thing that you did is you went back up to your classroom.
Child: Well, I just walked back and nothing happened.
Interviewer: So what happened before you left the room to go back to your classroom?
Child: I'm not quite sure.

Tests of the original 'cognitive' CI procedure

Between 1984 and 1990 several 'simulation' studies of CI were undertaken employing staged and filmed scenarios of forensic relevance including Los Angeles Police Department training films which depicted 'realistic' criminal events. The interviews in some of these studies were conducted by trained and experienced police officers. For example, Geiselman *et al.* (1985) compared the cognitive interview with the interviews more usually conducted by experienced police officers (the 'standard' interview procedure described earlier). The participants (witnesses) were undergraduate students and the interviewers were experienced law enforcement professionals (e.g. police investigators, members of the CIA and private detectives). The training films used in this study were simulations of life-threatening situations which depicted a number of scenarios modelled on real-life events. Witnesses were interviewed by the interviewers (who had *not* seen the training films) approximately 48 hours after viewing the film. Three weeks prior to the interview the interviewers received instructions to follow one of two procedures: (1) *standard interview,* or (2) the *cognitive interview*: the procedure described earlier. There are several points that should be noted here: first, the means by which the CI group was trained is not specified; second, there were no apparent checks on whether or not interviewers and witnesses *understood* the CI techniques and the frequency with which the instructions were applied; and third, the control group was not trained and there was no monitoring of the techniques they used.

Geiselman *et al.* (1985) coded the witnesses' recall information as pertaining to information about 'persons' or 'objects' or 'events'. The 'persons' category included physical clothing, mannerisms and speech. The 'objects' category included guns, knives, etc. The 'events' category included movements, number of shots, etc. Each subject's transcribed report was then scored for: (1) number of correct items of information recalled; (2) number of incorrect items of information recalled (e.g. describing a person as having blue eyes when they were brown); and (3) number of confabulated items of information recalled (e.g. a description of the suspect's face when the suspect's face was not shown on the film). The CI elicited 35 per cent more correct information than did the standard interview but the two types did not differ on incorrect items or confabulations. Scoring of critical items from the film showed that the CI not only enhanced recall of ancillary facts but also key information. Subsequent studies extended the earlier findings based on student populations by employing more representative samples of the general public (e.g. Geiselman *et al.*, 1986a) and real-life victims and witnesses (Fisher *et al.*, 1989; George, 1991).

REVISIONS OF THE CI: IMPROVING COMMUNICATION AND RETRIEVAL

The original version of the cognitive interview resulted in substantial gains in the amount of correct information that was elicited from eyewitnesses without any apparent increases in errors. However, in order to be able to implement effectively the use of the 'cognitive' components of the CI, it is necessary to provide interviewers with the necessary social skills and communication strategies that are required in order to build rapport. As indicated earlier, research with police officers suggested this was something they lacked. The revised version of the CI (also referred to as the enhanced version because it is even more effective than the original version of the CI (Fisher *et al.*, 1987b) included the following techniques.

Rapport-building

This is an attempt to get to know the witness a bit, clarify what the expectations are and generally put the person at ease. An important component of rapport-building is for the interviewer explicitly to 'transfer control', (1) making it clear to interviewees that they have to do the work and (2) allowing them time to think and respond. This may facilitate the implementation of the instruction to reinstate context as described above.

Focused retrieval

The interviewer facilitates eyewitnesses using *focused* memory techniques (to concentrate on mental images of the various parts of the event such as the suspect's face and use these images to guide recall). Fisher and Geiselman (1992) draw a distinction between conceptual image codes (an image stored as a concept or dictionary definition) and pictorial codes (the mental representation of an image). The notion is that images create dual codes or more meaningful elaborations (Paivio, 1971). The 'imaging' part of the CI usually occurs in the questioning phase of the interview and assumes that the witness has effectively recreated the context in which an event occurred. The instruction could take the following form: 'Concentrate on the picture you have in your mind of the suspect, focus on the face and describe it.'

In order effectively to engage the interviewee in focused retrieval, the interviewer needs to speak slowly and clearly, pausing at appropriate points to allow the interviewee time to create an image and respond.

Interviewee compatible questioning

Finally, the timing of the interviewer's questions is critical (deemed interviewee compatible questioning). Following principles of encoding specificity and feature overlap, questions should be guided by the interviewee's pattern of recall rather than adhering to a rigid protocol. For example, if an interviewee is describing a suspect's clothing the interviewer should not switch the line of questioning to the actions of the suspect.

TESTING THE CI: AN EFFECTIVE CONTROL GROUP

From a practical perspective, it is important to show that the CI is more effective than the techniques currently in use by police officers and others. The selection of untrained police interviewers in the Geiselman *et al.* (1985) study was a sensible control. From a theoretical perspective, an experimental control is needed to demonstrate that the techniques themselves are causing the effects and not some aspect related to training such as motivation, quality of questioning, or rapport building skills. The use of the term 'standard' in earlier studies itself implies inferiority.

The issue of experimental control has become even more important in testing the revised version of the CI given that it combines the cognitive techniques with some general strategies for improving communication. What evidence is there that the gains in information elicited are not merely due to the improved communication?

More recent tests of the CI have addressed this question by comparing the CI with a procedure known as the structured interview (SI) procedure where the quality of training in communication and questioning techniques is comparable to the CI procedure. The training of the structured group follows a procedure that is recommended to professionals who interview children (the Home Office Memorandum of Good Practice, Home Office and Department of Health, 1992: see Bull, 1992, 1995). The essence of the Memorandum is to treat the interview as a procedure in which a variety of interviewing techniques is deployed in relatively discrete phases proceeding from general to open, to specific, closed-form questions. Rapport-building, through open questions and active listening, is also an important component.

So is it possible for an interviewer armed with a range of 'good' interviewing techniques and effective communication skills to achieve the same effects as a CI trained interviewer? This question was first addressed by Guenter Koehnken and colleagues in their studies conducted in Germany (Koehnken *et al.*, 1994; Koehnken *et al.*, 1995; Mantwill *et al.*, 1995). In these studies the cognitive interview was compared with a structured interview. The structured group received training of comparable quality and length in basic communication skills. This included instruction on rapport-building and use of various types of questioning. The training of the cognitive group also involved the use of the various cognitive techniques. The cognitive and structured interviewers received a sample of written questions and interview transcripts which were discussed and judged according to their appropriateness. Comments on the transcripts pointed out the retrieval aids used by the interviewer and the specific question type (CI group), while the SI group focused on questioning strategy and types of questions (open, closed, leading, forced-choice, etc.). The interviewers then watched a videotaped interview. Finally, each interviewer took part in a role-play and received feedback on their performance. The training session lasted between 4 and 5 hours.

In the German studies, the to-be-remembered event was a videotape showing a blood donation. Participants were tested a week after viewing the event. In the Koehnken *et al.*, (1994) study the participants (interviewees) and interviewers were non-psychology students without any prior experience in investigative interviewing. Each interviewer conducted one interview (n = 30). The CI resulted in an average of 52 per cent more correctly recalled information without increasing the number of errors and confabulated (made up) details. The interviewer's memory was also tested by asking them to prepare from their memory written accounts of the event. The superiority of the CI was noted in the interviewer accounts with an average of 42 per cent more correct details as compared to the structured interview group.

Koehnken *et al.* (1995) conducted a similar study. The interviews were conducted by students and adults served as interviewees. Again there was an increase in correct details with the enhanced cognitive interview, although this time a small increase in confabulated details was also noted. However, the overall accuracy (proportion of correct details relative to the total number of details reported) was almost identical in both interview conditions.

In the Mantwill *et al.* (1995) study a sample of fifty-eight interviewees was drawn from a variety of professional groups and were selected on the basis of their having experience of a blood donation (the to-be-remembered event) or having no experience. The interviewers were non-psychologists of various professions, none of whom had knowledge of blood donation. The number of details elicited in the cognitive and structured interview were compared. The enhanced CI yielded 25 per cent more correct information without any differences in errors and confabulations. The performance of experienced and inexperienced subjects did not differ significantly.

So far the evidence suggests that the enhanced CI effects are due to the use of the cognitive techniques rather than merely a result of enhanced communication. However, this does not fit with the results of a series of studies conducted in England as part of a project funded by the Economic and Social Research Council in the UK (Memon *et al.*, in press a, in press b, in press c). Memon *et al.* (in press b) directly examined whether the source of the CI advantage was due to facilitated communication arising from the use of the 'social' components of the enhanced CI (namely rapport-building and transfer of control) or a result of the 'cognitive' components of the enhanced CI (context, imagery, reverse order and reporting in detail). The structured interview in the Memon *et al.* studies therefore resembled the enhanced CI more closely than the structured interview used in the Koehnken studies due to a greater emphasis on 'transfer of control'. As in the Koehnken research, cognitive and structured interviewers received a similar quality of training. The interviewers were psychology students who had no previous experience of interviewing. Both groups were led to believe that they were using the superior interview technique. They were trained separately over a period of two days in basic communication techniques such as building rapport, in types of questions to ask and had the opportunity to conduct role-plays and receive feedback on practice interviews. Finally, Memon *et al.* introduced a 'second retrieval (SR) phase' in their CI/SI interviews. In the SR phase of the CI interview, the instruction to go through the event again in reverse order was administered. While in the SI group, the request was simply to try one more time. The purpose of this SR was to test directly the hypothesis that the various CI techniques merely increase the number of recall attempts and this accounts for the gains in new information (reminiscence), a well-documented effect (see Payne, 1987, for a review). These effects could be a result of retrieval practice (Roediger and Thorpe, 1978) or stimulus sampling whereby repeated attempts to access a memory will result in different samples drawn from a population of encoded details.

The studies conducted by Memon and colleagues showed that the cognitive interview is a highly complex procedure and that the advantage gained from the CI may be restricted to a rather narrow set of conditions. When these conditions are violated the CI appears no better than an effectively matched control group (Memon and Stevenage, 1996). This will be illustrated by considering the results obtained in the Memon *et al.* research in some detail.

In the Memon *et al.* (in press b) study where the interviewees were 8- and 9-year-old children, the CI was found significantly to increase correct and incorrect (errors) about a live event (interview two days after the event) while accuracy was unaffected. The increases in information were isolated to the questioning phase of the interview. The CI interviewers asked significantly more questions than the structured interviewers and when question number was partialled out there were no significant effects of the cognitive interview. Moreover, in another study where the structured interviewers were encouraged to ask more questions there were no CI/SI differences (Memon *et al.*, in press c). However, this does not necessarily mean that the CI does not yield more information than the SI. Memon *et al.* (in press b) argue that it is because the cognitive techniques (context reinstatement, imagery and reporting in detail) increase the amount of information that is elicited by interviewees that interviewers ask more questions. In other words, interviewers are simply following up details with more questions. It is well established in the literature that questions may serve as prompts and that they may also increase errors (e.g. Davies *et al.*, 1989; Gee and Pipe, 1995). In the Memon *et al.* (in press b) study further investigation of the errors revealed that they were associated with particular types of details, namely descriptions of persons. Again, previous research suggests children have difficulty with person details (Davies *et al.*, 1989). The results obtained by Memon *et al.* were replicated in an independent study conducted by Milne *et al.* (1995) and suggest that further investigation of interviewer behaviour in the questioning phase is required to identify possible confounds.

Memon *et al.* (1996) compared the cognitive and structured interview as described above with an untrained control group. The interviewers were graduate students and the interviewees (college students) viewed a videotaped event of a sequence in which a child is murdered. In this study, the cognitive interviewers and structured interviewers did not differ in terms of the overall amount recalled, the accuracy of recall, the number of errors or the number of confabulations. Both trained groups elicited more in the way of overall information and amount of correct information relative to an untrained group. However, this was offset by their producing a significantly higher number of errors and confabulations than the untrained group. These findings are important in themselves but they also raise the question of what is the appropriate control group. Clearly, if the cognitive interviewers are compared to an untrained group then they show some advantages. However, if the cognitive interviewers are compared to a group matched for everything but the cognitive techniques (namely the structured interview), then the advantage of the CI disappears. This finding is at odds with the studies conducted in Germany and suggests that the effects of the cognitive interview depend on the standard of comparison that is used. It is not clear where there is a discrepancy but it could be due to sampling differences and interviewer differences (Memon's interviewers were psychology graduates and were possibly more motivated). It should be pointed out that while the structured interviewers in the Memon *et al.* (1996) study were behaving like cognitive interviewers they did not use any of the cognitive techniques. Of course, this does not rule out the possibility that the interviewers were spontaneously using CI techniques. Memon *et al.* (in press a) found that college students frequently report the use of context reinstatement and imagery as aids to recall. Indeed, such techniques are also reported to be used by older participants drawn from the general population (Harris, 1980). Future studies may benefit from collecting data not only on the techniques that interviewers use but also on the techniques used by interviewees.

A second explanation for the results of the Memon *et al.* studies is that the primary effect of the CI is that it enhances communication. It is possible that the most effective component of the enhanced CI is the 'transfer of control' instruction. Transfer of control is achieved in three main ways. First, the interviewers explicitly tell the interviewee that they do not have knowledge of the event and that it is the interviewee who holds all the relevant information. This confers power and status to the interviewee. Second, the interviewers ensure that the interviewee is not interrupted when speaking and pause after interviewees have spoken in case they have more to add. This also confers to the interviewee that what *they* have to say is important. Finally, whenever possible the interviewers use open-ended questions so that it is the interviewee who does most of the talking. The effect of transfer of control may not only be improved rapport but also a more fruitful memory search (e.g. due to interviewers not interrupting) and possibly more effective use of context reinstatement. However, this explanation does not account for the lack of a significant difference between CI and SI group in the Memon *et al.* (1996) study and the increase in errors and reduction in accuracy when these techniques are used as compared to an untrained group.

It would be premature, however, to conclude from the Memon *et al.* (1996) study that untrained interviewers are the safest ones for a number of reasons. First, the study was limited in ecological validity. The interviewers were not police officers but college students. Moreover, they were intelligent and motivated students who had been asked by an authority figure to collect some data for a research project and they knew the interviews were being recorded. It is unlikely that they could be compared to typical police officers (Memon *et al.*, 1994). Indeed, the quality of interviews of the Memon *et al.* untrained group were opposite to what is found with police officers using the standard procedure. In other words, they tended to ask fewer questions, did not interrupt the interviewee when they were speaking and did not ask leading questions (cf. Fisher *et al.*, 1987a; George, 1991). The untrained student interviewers in the Memon *et al.* (1996) study also made fewer inaccuracies.

Finally, it should be noted that in the Memon *et al.* (1996) study and in the two earlier studies (Memon *et al.*, in press b, c) there was considerable variability in interviewer performance. The untrained interviewers in particular adopted quite different styles of questioning; they varied in how persistent they were and how frequently they interrupted an interviewee. This has to be taken into consideration in interpreting the results and suggests future studies should use more representative samples and collect some qualitative data on how interviewer background and motivation may influence their performance.

FIELD TESTS OF THE CI

To date, there have been only two field tests of the cognitive interview. The first was a project that enlisted the assistance of police detectives in Miami, Florida (Fisher *et al.*, 1989). The second was a study involving the Hertfordshire police in the UK (George, 1991).

The aim of the Fisher *et al.* (1989) field study was to examine the use of the enhanced CI by trained and 'control' police detectives when questioning real-life victims and interviewees. The pre-training phase of the study involved the collection of tape recordings of interviews from a sample of detectives using their usual, standard techniques. Half of the group underwent enhanced CI training over four 60-minute sessions. During this time they were given an overview of the procedure and the general psychological principles of cognition, training in specific interviewing techniques, communication techniques and advice on the temporal sequencing of the CI. After the fourth training session each detective tape recorded a practice interview in the field and received individual feedback from the psychologists on the quality of the interview. The detectives then followed the enhanced CI procedure or 'standard interview' procedure (as defined earlier) during the course of their interviews with real interviewees over a period of time. Two measures of the effects of training were taken. First, number of facts elicited before training (i.e. the tapes from the pilot phase) versus after training (thus a within-subjects comparison). Second, facts elicited by trained and untrained officers after some had undergone the training programme (between-subjects). The tapes were transcribed by trained research assistants who recorded all the relevant details. Opinionated and irrelevant statements were ignored. The statements included physical descriptions, actions and clothing.

The CI was found to be effective in the before/after comparisons (the within-subjects factor) and in the trained/untrained (between-subjects) comparison. The trained detectives elicited 47 per cent more information after training and significantly more information than detectives not trained in CI. Baseline measures showed that there were no differences between the groups prior to training. In order to examine the impact of CI on the amount of incorrect information recalled, it was necessary to examine corroboration rates. (In real crimes, of course, corroborating information from other interviewees' forensic evidence, and so on, is not always easily available.) When the corroborating source was another interviewee/victim, the corroborating interview was always conducted by someone other than the original detective (usually a uniformed officer). Some 94 per cent of the statements from the interviews in this study were corroborated and there was no difference in the corroboration rates of pre- and post-training interviews, so CI did not appear to increase the amount of incorrect information.

The results of the CI field study are promising. Six of the seven detectives who were trained improved significantly. However, given the relatively small sample size, the issue as to how representative the trained group were is questionable. The officers were selected for training rather than being randomly assigned to conditions and this is of some concern, especially in light of evidence that police officers may not be so open to the use of new techniques (Memon *et al.*, 1994, 1995). Finally, there was no trained control group in this field study and data are not provided on the techniques used by interviewers.

George (1991) reported a field study involving thirty-two experienced British police officers. They were randomly assigned to one of four conditions: CI, conversation management, CI and conversation management and a no training control group. Conversation management is a procedure which resembles the structured interview described earlier and includes training in planning the interview, listening skills, conversational styles, question types and summarising. Prior to training, each subject provided a tape recording of an interview they had conducted with a real-life interviewee or victim. Following training each police officer tape recorded three more interviews with victims or interviewees of street crimes. The tape recordings were transcribed and evaluated, among other things, for the amount of information provided by the interviewee. The results showed that the CI elicited significantly more information than the standard police interview (14 per cent more than the no training control group). A before and after training comparison showed an increase of 55 per cent. There were no significant differences between conversation management and the untrained control: in fact, the conversation management group fared worse.

At this stage, it is necessary to point out two things. First, the success of the CI depends upon adequate training of interviewers in the techniques described above. It is not clear how much training is needed. Some studies report effects with relatively brief training. Fisher *et al.* (1989) report benefits after four 60-minute sessions, while George (1991) trained officers over two days. Memon *et al.* (1994) trained officers over a more limited period of time (4 hours) and found this was insufficient to motivate officers to use the new techniques, while Turtle (1995) has evaluated several one-week training courses on the CI for Canadian police officers and found that training has relatively little effect on the use of CI techniques. Clearly, the effects of training are complex and depend not only on length of training, but quality of training, background of interviewer, attitudes towards training, and so forth.

Finally, it should be noted that the CI relies upon a co-operative interviewee. It has not as yet been established how useful a CI would be in the case of an interviewee who does not wish to remember (e.g. in the case of a traumatised interviewee) or an interviewee who does not wish to communicate information to the interviewer (e.g. a traumatised interviewee or one who is likely to be a suspect).

So far, the review of evidence has focused largely on studies using adult interviewees (with the exception of the Memon *et al.* ESRC research). One important question is to what extent can the CI be effectively used with child interviewees?

THE CI AND CHILD INTERVIEWEES

Research in this area has been timely given recent developments for child interviewees testifying in criminal trials (e.g. in Britain, the Criminal Justice Acts, 1988, 1991). Among the most significant changes in some countries is the use of video-recorded interviews with children as evidence in criminal trials and the admissibility of the evidence of children under the age of 7 years. A code of practice for the conduct of such interviews was provided by the British Home Office in the form of the Memorandum of Good Practice (1992), a document informed by the knowledge of psychologists and legal professionals (see Bull, 1992, 1995, for details).

There is reasonable evidence to suggest that younger children (ages 6 to 7) will often recall *less* information than older children (ages 10 to 11) (e.g. Davies *et al.*, 1989, Memon *et al.*, 1996). Given that the primary aim of CI is to increase the *amount* of information retrieved, it may be a most effective procedure to use with young children.

A first published attempt to apply the CI with child interviewees was reported by Geiselman and Padilla (1988). Children aged between 7 and 12 years viewed a videotape of a liquor store robbery and were interviewed three days later using a CI or a standard interview. The CI produced significantly more correct information (an increase of 21 per cent) as compared to a standard interview while the number of incorrect and confabulated details was not affected by the type of the interview.

In a more elaborate follow-up study, Saywitz *et al.* (1992) attempted to evaluate and refine the CI for children (7- to 8-year-olds and 10- to 11-year-olds) using a live event.

The event was a game where children dressed up, interacted with, and were photographed by, a stranger. The CI significantly increased correct facts recalled across both age groups by 26 per cent. In a second study, a 'practice session' was included, the aims of which were to familiarise the children with the cognitive interview techniques and to give feedback on their performance. The interviewers were experienced police officers who received written instructions and a 2-hour training session during which they were informed about child-appropriate language, rapport-building, interview preparation and procedure. The CI group received additional information on the use of the four original CI techniques. The standard interview group were instructed to use the techniques they would normally use. The CI led to more correct details being recalled than did the SI (20 per cent increase for the 8- to 9-year-olds and 44 per cent for the 11- to 12-year-olds). Furthermore, collapsing across age levels, a practice cognitive interview prior to the main interview improved performance by an additional 25 per cent. No increase in the amount of incorrect or confabulated details was observed. Thus it appears to be an efficient strategy to familiarise children with the CI before they are questioned about the event (cf. Memon *et al.*, 1996). Interestingly, it was the older children whose performance improved most with a practice interview which is the opposite to what we would expect based on our understanding of children's development of memory strategy usage (Ornstein *et al.*, 1985). An analysis was conducted to look at the frequency with which interviewers used the four CI techniques. It was apparent that the student interviewers were more likely to use each of the four techniques compared to the experienced detectives. For example, only half of the detectives used the 'change perspective' instruction as compared to 94 per cent of the student interviewers. George (1991) in the British field study and Turtle (1995) also found police officers did not use this technique even though they had been trained to do so.

The Saywitz *et al.* study provides a powerful demonstration of the effectiveness of a CI with children over the age of 8 years. There are, however, several concerns. First, the CI groups received training while the standard group did not: this may affect the motivation of the CI interviewers (Memon *et al.*, 1996). Second, while the authors of this study did attempt to correlate use of each CI technique with overall memory scores we have no information about the types of details elicited with the various CI techniques. A related point is that the details about errors are not provided. Third, while the CI practice group had an opportunity to practise and become familiar with the task of retrieval, the control group did not. Despite these shortcomings, this research has been supported by the findings produced in Germany by Guenter Koehnken and colleagues. Koehnken *et al.* (1992) investigated the effectiveness of the enhanced CI with fifty-one 9- and 10-year-old children who had been shown a short film. After a delay of three to five days, they were questioned by trained psychology students about the film using either an enhanced CI or SI (structured) interview. In this study, great care was taken to ensure that the SI interviewers were trained in the same way as CI interviewers save for using the special CI techniques. The enhanced CI produced a 93 per cent increase in the amount of correct information recalled compared to the SI. The number of confabulations (the reporting of details not present in the event) increased, however, and this has been found in several studies where the CI had been used with child interviewees (e.g. McCauley and Fisher, 1995; Mantwill *et al.*, 1995).

Memon and colleagues have attempted to isolate the effects of the individual components of the original CI (Memon *et al.*, 1996) and have tested the effectiveness of the CI with younger children (aged 6 to 7 years). In the Memon *et al.* (1996) study, each of the four mnemonic techniques of the CI (context, report in detail, change order and change perspective) was compared with an instruction to 'try harder'. Prior to each interview there was a practice session in which each child described a familiar activity using one of the four CI techniques (e.g. context reinstatement). There were no significant differences in correct recall or errors as a function of instruction condition; this suggested that the 'try harder' instruction could be as effective as each of the CI techniques. There were a number of interesting differences between the age groups, most notably that the younger children (5-year-olds) performed less well under the CI 'context reinstatement' and 'change perspective' conditions as compared to the 8-year-olds in the same conditions. A qualitative analysis of the interview transcripts suggested that the children did not fully understand all the techniques and had difficulty using the change perspective instruction. This suggests refinement of the CI is needed for children. As Ornstein (1991) points out, a good interviewer should tailor the interview so that it takes into consideration the cognitive and linguistic capabilities of an individual child.

Memon *et al.* (1993) interviewed thirty-two 6- and 7-year-olds about an eye test. The effectiveness of a CI, comprising the usual four mnemonic techniques was compared with that of a structured interview. The latter, like the CI, was a good interview procedure and one in which the interviewers used open-ended questions and did not interrupt the interviewee when he or she was speaking. Children's recall of the event was tested one week after the event and again six weeks later. As illustrated earlier, children had difficulty in understanding interviewer instructions to change perspective and to recall in reverse order such that they became confused about what was expected of them. This may have worked against the CI. Indeed, there were no significant differences in the types of information elicited between each type of interview with the exception of information about locations of objects and people which was significantly greater with the CI. This increase in location information was possibly a result of the language used to fulfil the context instructions (e.g. 'describe the room') rather than a direct product of memory improvement (one of the problems of the CI research has been the difficulty separating the two).

Finally, there has been some interest in whether the CI resembles procedures used by professionals (McCauley and Fisher, 1995). The interviewers in the latter study were McCauley, two undergraduates and two professional social workers. The social workers followed a standard protocol that they themselves had developed based upon their interviewing experience. The other interviewers served either in the CI or standard conditions. An important component of the interview procedure was a rapport-building or practice session, the aim of this being to prime the children to produce detailed responses. The children were asked to describe their favourite game in as much detail as possible. McCauley and Fisher only used that part of the CI procedure which comprised instructions to image and reinstate context and a series of prompts. There were then two CI instructions to focus on the central character in the interviewee event with a further CI instruction to form an image of the stranger. Specific prompts were also used. The standard group asked the children to generate a free report and then asked a series of mostly open questions. McCauley and Fisher found the CI significantly increased recall as compared to the standard, and the standard produced as much recall as did social workers using their own protocol.

LIMITATIONS OF THE USE OF CI WITH CHILD INTERVIEWEES

Several problems in applying the CI with children have been identified. First, younger children (6 to 7 years of age) have difficulty understanding the CI techniques in the form developed for adults (Memon *et al.*, 1993, 1996). Second, CI when used with children can increase errors (Memon *et al.*, 1995b; Milne *et al.*, 1995) and confabulations (Koehnken *et al.*, 1992). Third, the CI procedure may also increase demand characteristics in that children respond in a way they think may please the interviewer. This is illustrated in the following transcript taken from the Memon *et al.* (1993) child interviewee study.

Interviewer: OK, but what about the day the nurse came, can you tell me about that? I know you've told me already, but I need to find out more.
Child: Yes, just in case I am saying the right things.
Interviewer: Well no, not exactly, but just in case you remember any more.
Child: Yes, some different things that I forgot to say at all.
Interviewer: Yes. The best thing to do is to start again and tell me everything again.
Child: Well, I can't tell you the same things.

It is apparent from the above example that the success of the technique relies to a large extent on the interviewers' abilities effectively to communicate techniques to the children and this may in part be related to the quality of training received. Finally, the effective use of CI with child interviewees rests upon the interviewers' rapport-building skills. This conclusion is supported by data from Memon *et al.*'s ESRC studies with child interviewees where some interviewers emerged as more effective than others, regardless of interview condition (see the next section). At the same time individual qualities of the interviewee may also contribute to the successful use of the CI techniques and this is an area where there is a dearth of data.

Interviewer differences

It is generally accepted that interviewee performance varies with the quality of the interviewer and vice versa. There is evidence that interviewer performance will vary with interviewer expectations (Ceci *et al.*, in press) and with level of training (Memon *et al.*, 1994). Given that the CI is an interactive process between the interviewer and interviewee aiming to facilitate recall, it is surprising that such little attention has been paid to interviewer behaviour in the CI. It could be argued on the basis of the research of Fisher and Geiselman that the original CI procedure could be applied with relatively little training whereas the enhanced CI procedure, which places far greater demands on the interviewer, may well require more extensive training (Fisher *et al.*, 1987b). In addition, as the revised version places more emphasis on social skills it is reasonable to expect more variation between interviewers in their use of the techniques.

A quantitative analysis of interviewer behaviour (i.e. use of the various techniques and questioning style) in cognitive and structured (control) interviews was undertaken in the Memon *et al.* (in press b) experiment and some preliminary data were collected on interviewer variability. There were differences amongst the individual CI interviewers in the number and type of questions asked (e.g. open-ended versus closed). For example, one female interviewer asked significantly more open questions and one male interviewer asked the most closed questions. In addition to differences in questioning style, there were differences between the interviewers in the use of the various CI techniques. As an example, consider the context reinstatement instruction, applied prior to the free report by the CI interviewers. In the following examples, Interviewer A begins with an explanation followed by a series of questions about the context before requesting a free report, Interviewer B adopts a similar approach with slightly different prompts, while Interviewer C simply lists the questions.

Interviewer A: I am going to say loads of things to you and I want you to think about them in your head OK and I want you to try and picture all the things I am going to say and keep them in your mind. Where did you watch the magic show? (*Child replies*.) Think about what it looked like. (*Child replies*.) Where were you sitting? (*Child replies*.) Can you think about how you felt before watching the magic show? (*Child replies*.) When you are ready I want you to tell me everything you can about the magic show.

Interviewer B: I'd like to ask you some questions about the magic show you saw and I would like you to describe everything in as much detail as you can, OK? Before doing that can you describe to me how you felt when you knew you were going to see the magic show? (*Child replies*.) So you felt good, then. Can you remember whereabouts you saw the magic show? (*Child replies*.) Who were you sitting with? (*Child replies*.) What was the room like? (*Child replies*.) What was the temperature like, hot or cold? (*Child replies*.) So if you could put yourself back there, can you see inside your head that you are sitting down and watching the magic show all over again? Can you describe to me anything you can see?

Interviewer C: What I want you to do now is think back to the magic show, where were you sitting, what could you see, what could you hear, what could you smell, so in your own time can you describe to me the magic show?

Again it is possible that further training and practice may iron out some of these differences. However, as mentioned earlier, some flexibility in use of instructions is desirable given that some interviewees (i.e. young children) may require a fuller explanation of the techniques than others.

Analysis of the structured interviewers in the Memon *et al.* (in press b) study revealed that they were a more homogeneous group when it came to their use of questions and interview style, although there was some variability in performance. Again, it is important to note that the use of the techniques is likely to have varied with characteristics of the interviewee and this is something that could be systematically investigated in future research.

OVERVIEW

The cognitive interview (CI) emerges as probably the most exciting development in the field of eye interviewee testimony in the last ten years. It presents itself as a technique to facilitate recall, and initial tests show consistent gains in the amount of information that can be gathered from an interviewee with a cognitive interview. The early work, however, was limited in conclusions due the use of an untrained control group. In other words, it is not possible to conclude that the CI effects reflect the use of cognitive techniques or some aspect of interviewer behaviour that has changed as a result of training. More recent studies have remedied this by including trained control groups and at the same time have scrutinised revised versions of the CI to determine the effects of improved communication skills on interviewee memory performance. Such studies have yielded mixed results and suggest that the CI may be more effective than a structured interview under some conditions but not others. Of more serious concern is that under some conditions the CI may result in a less accurate report from an interviewee (Memon and Stevenage, 1996). Obviously, the benefits of any innovative technique need to be carefully weighed up against any costs. In a forensic investigation an increase in number of details could be especially helpful at the information gathering stage in providing new clues that could lead to a successful conviction. On the other hand, what if investigators are led up the wrong path? Previous researchers have argued that a relatively small increase in errors should be of no consequence provided overall accuracy rates are unaffected (Mantwill *et al.*, 1995). So far there are two studies which suggest the CI may result in a less accurate report (Memon *et al.*, 1994; Memon *et al.*, 1996). These studies have also identified a number of variables that may determine the outcome of a cognitive interview including the characteristics of the interviewee, quality of interviewer training and interview style (see Memon and Stevenage, 1996, for a more extensive list).

The implication for practitioners is that the cognitive interview will not always work; it will not always provide a significantly richer and more accurate account. What it seems necessary to do is to determine exactly when and why the cognitive interview will prove to be effective. In order to shed light on this question, further research is required and the effects of training need to be monitored over a reasonable period of time in order to assess the effects of feedback and experience in use of the techniques on performance. Furthermore, it is essential that researchers consider the effects of interviewer variables either by including interviewers as factors in the design of experimenters and/or by collecting baseline data on interviewer performance prior to training. Finally, a more detailed scrutiny of the techniques used in cognitive interviews is required in order to understand the relative contribution of cognitive and communication components of the procedure and the ways in which they may work together to facilitate memory search and retrieval.

REFERENCES

Bell, B. and Loftus, E. F. (1989) 'Trivial Persuasion in the Courtroom: The Power of a Few Minor Details', *Journal of Personality and Social Psychology*, 56(5), 669–79.

Boggs, S. R. and Eyberg, S. (1990) 'Interview Techniques and Establishing Rapport', in A. M. La Greca (ed.), *Through the Eyes of the Child: Obtaining Self-reports from Children and Adolescents*, Allyn & Bacon, Boston, pp. 85–108.

Bower, G. (1967) 'A Multicomponent Theory of Memory Trace', in K. W. Spence and J. T. Spence (eds), *The Pyschology of Learning and Motivation, Vol. 1*, Academic Press, New York.

Bull, R. (1992) 'Obtaining Evidence Expertly: The Reliability of Interviews with Child Interviewees', *Expert Evidence: The International Digest of Human Behaviour, Science and Law*, 1(1), 5–12.

—— (1995) 'Innovative Techniques for the Questioning of Child Interviewees Especially Those who are Young and Those with Learning Disability', in M. Zaragoza, J. R. Graham, G. C. N. Hall, R. Hirschman and Y. S. Ben-Porath (eds), *Memory and Testimony in the Child Interviewee*, Sage, Thousand Oaks.

Ceci, S. J. and Bruck, M. (1995) 'Amicus Brief for the Case of NJV Michaels Presented by Committee of Concerned Social Scientists', *Psychology, Public Policy and Law*, 1(2), 494–520.

Ceci, S. J., Leichtman, M. and White, T. (in press) 'Interviewing Preschoolers', in D. Peters (ed.), *The Child Interviewee in Cognitive, Social and Legal Context.* , Kluwer, Netherlands.

Cherryman, J. and Bull, R. (1995) 'Investigative Interviewing', in F. Leishman, B. Loveday and S. Savage (eds), *Core Issues in Policing*, Longman, London.

Davies, G., Tarrant, A. and Flin, R. (1989) 'Close Encounters of the Interviewee Kind: Children's Memory for a Simulated Health Inspection', *British Journal of Psychology*, 80, 415–29.

Fisher, R. P. and Geiselman, R. E. (1992) *Memory Enhancing Techniques for Investigative Interviewing: The Cognitive Interview*, Charles C. Thomas, Springfield, Ill.

Fisher, R. P., Geiselman, R. E. and Raymond, D. S. (1987a) 'Critical Analysis of Police Interviewing Techniques, *Journal of Police Science and Administration*, 15, 177–85.

Fisher, R. P., Geiselman, R. E., Raymond, D. S., Jurkevich, L.M. and Warhaftig, M. L. (1987b) 'Enhancing Eyeinterviewee Memory: Refining the Cognitive Interview', *Journal of Police Science and Administration*, 15, 291–7.

Fisher, R. P., Geiselman, R. E. and Amador, M. (1989) 'Field Test of the Cognitive Interview: Enhancing the Recollection of Actual Victims and Interviewees of Crime', *Journal of Applied Psychology*, 74(5), 722–7.

Flexser, A. and Tulving, E. (1978) 'Retrieval Independence in Recognition and Recall', *Psychological Review*, 85, 153–71.

Gee, S. and Pipe, M.-E. (1995) 'Helping Children to Remember: The Influence of Object Cues on Children's Accounts of a Real Event', *Developmental Psychology*, 31, 746–58.

Geiselman, R. E. and Callot, R. (1990) 'Reverse Versus Forward Recall of Script Based Texts, *Applied Cognitive Psychology*, 4, 141–4.

Geiselman, R. E. and Padilla, J. (1988) 'Interviewing Child Interviewees with the Cognitive Interview', *Journal of Police Science and Administration*, 16, 236–42.

Geiselman, R. E., Fisher, R. P., MacKinnon, D. P. and Holland, H. L. (1985) 'Eyeinterviewee Memory Enhancement in the Police Interview: Cognitive Retrieval Mnemonics Versus Hypnosis', *Journal of Applied Psychology*, 70, 401–12.

—— (1986a) 'Eyeinterviewee Memory Enhancement in the Cognitive Interview', *American Journal of Psychology*, 99, 386–401.

Geiselman, R. E., Fisher, R. P., Cohen, G., Holland, H. L. and Surtes, L. (1986b) 'Eyeinterviewee Responses to Leading and Misleading Questions under the Cognitive Interview', *Journal of Police Science and Administration*, 14, 31–9.

Geiselman, R. E., Saywitz, K. J. and Bornstein, G. K. (1990) 'Cognitive Interviewing Techniques for Child Interviewees and Interviewees of Crime', report to the State Justice Institute, New York.

George, R. (1991) *A Field Evaluation of the Cognitive Interview*, unpublished MA thesis, Polytechnic of East London, London.

Goodman, G. S., Aman, C. and Hirschman, J. (1987) 'Child Sexual and Physical Abuse: Children's Testimony', in S. J. Ceci, M. P. Toglia and D. F. Ross (eds), *Children's Eyeinterviewee Memory*, Springer, New York, pp. 1–23.

Gudjonsson, G. (1994) 'Investigative Interviewing: Recent Developments and Some Fundamental Issues', *International Review of Psychiatry*, 6, 237–45.

Harris, J. E. (1980) 'Memory Aids People Use: Two Interview Studies', *Memory and Cognition*, 8(1), 31–8.

Koehnken, G., Finger, M., Nitschke, N., Hofer, E. and Aschermann, E. (1992) *Does a Cognitive Interview Interfere with a Subsequent Statement Validity Analysis?*, paper presented at the conference of the American Psychology-Law Society, San Diego.

Koehnken, G., Schimmossek, E., Aschermann, E. and Höfer (1995) 'The Cognitive Interview and the Assessment of the Credibility of Adults' Statements', *Journal of Applied Psychology*, 80(6), 671–84.

Koehnken, G., Thurer, C. and Zorberbier, D. (1994) 'The Cognitive Interview: Are Interviewers' Memories Enhanced Too?', *Applied Cognitive Psychology*, 8, 13–24.

Koriat, A. and Goldsmith, M. (1994) 'Memory in Naturalistic and Laboratory Contexts: Distinguishing Accuracy Oriented and Quantity Oriented Approaches to Memory Assessment', *Journal of Experimental Psychology*, 123, 397–15.

McCauley, M. R. and Fisher, R. P. (1995) 'Facilitating Children's Eyeinterviewee Recall with the Revised Cognitive Interview', *Journal of Applied Psychology*, 80(4), 510–17.

Mackinnon, D. P., O'Reilly, K. and Geiselman, R. E. (1990) 'Improving Eyeinterviewee Recall for License Plates', *Applied Cognitive Psychology*, 4, 129–40.

Mantwill, M., Koehnken, G. and Aschermann, E. (1995) 'Effects of the Cognitive Interview on the Recall of Familiar and Unfamiliar Events', *Journal of Applied Psychology*, 80, 68–78.

Memon, A. and Bruce, V. (1985) 'Context Effects in Episodic Studies of Verbal and Facial Memory: A Review', *Current Psychological Research and Reviews*, Winter, 349–69.

Memon, A. and Bull, R. (1991) 'The Cognitive Interview: Its Origins, Empirical Support, Evaluation and Practical Implications', *Journal of Community and Applied Social Psychology*, 1, 291–307.

Memon, A. and Koehnken, G. (1992) 'Helping Interviewees to Remember More: The Cognitive Interview', *Expert Evidence: The International Digest of Human Behaviour, Science & Law*, 1(2), 39–48.

Memon, A. and Stevenage, S. V. (1996) 'Interviewing Witnesses: What Works and What Doesn't?', *Psycholquy*, 7, psyc. 96.7.06.witness.memory.1.memon.

Memon, A., Bull, R. and Smith, M. (1995) 'Improving the Quality of the Police Interview: Can Training in the Use of Cognitive Techniques Help?', *Policing and Society*, 5, 53–68.

Memon, A., Cronin, O., Eaves, R. and Bull, R. (1993) 'The Cognitive Interview and Child Intervieweees', in G. M. Stephenson and N. K. Clark (eds), *Children, Evidence and Procedure Issues in Criminological and Legal Psychology. No. 20*, British Psychological Society, Leicester.

—— (1996) 'An Empirical Test of the Mnemonic Components of the Cognitive Interview', in G. M. Davies, S. Lloyd-Bostock, M. McMurran and C. Wilson (eds), *Psychology and Law: Advances in Research*, De Gruyter, Berlin.

Memon, A., Milne, R., Holley, A., Bull, R. and Koehnken, G. (1994) 'Towards Understanding the Effects of Interviewer Training in Evaluating the Cognitive Interview', *Applied Cognitive Psychology*, 8, 641–59.

Memon, A., Wark, L., Bull, R. and Koehnken, G. (in press b) 'Isolating the Effects of the Cognitive Interview Techniques', *British Journal of Psychology*.

Memon, A., Wark, L., Holley, A., Bull, R. and Koehnken, G. (1996) 'Eyewitness Performance in Cognitive and Structured Interviews', manuscript submitted for publication.

—— (in press a) 'Context Effects and Event Memory: How Powerful are the Effects?', in D. Payne and F. Conrad (eds), *Intersections in Basic and Applied Memory Research*, Lawrence Erlbaum Associates, New York.

—— (in press c) 'Reducing Suggestibility in Child Witness Interviews', manuscript submitted for publication.

Milne, R., Bull, R., Koehnken, G. and Memon, A. (1995) 'The Cognitive Interview and Suggestibility', in G. M. Stephenson and N. K. Clark (eds), *Criminal Behaviour: Perceptions, Attributions and Rationality, Division of Criminological and Legal Psychology Occasional Papers, No. 22*, British Psychological Society, Leicester.

Ornstein, P. A. (1991) 'Putting Interviewing in Context', in J. Doris (ed.), *The Suggestibility Of Children's Recollections: Implications For Eyeinterviewee Testimony*, American Psychological Association, Washington DC.

——, Stone, B. P., Medlin, R. G. and Naus, M. J. (1985) 'Retrieving for Rehearsal: An Analysis of Active Rehearsal in Children's Memory', *Developmental Psychology*, 21(4), 633–41.

Paivio, A. (1971) *Imagery and Verbal Processes*, Holt, Rinehart & Winston, New York.

Payne, D. G. (1987) 'Hyperamnesia and Reminiscence in Recall: A Historical and Empirical Review', *Psychological Bulletin*, 101, 5–27.

Roediger, H. L. and Thorpe, L. A. (1978) 'The Role of Recall Time in Producing Hyperamnesia', *Memory and Cognition*, 6, 296–305.

Saywitz, K. J., Geiselman, R. E. and Bornstein, G. K. (1992) 'Effects of Cognitive Interviewing and Practice on Children's Recall Performance', *Journal of Applied Psychology*, 77, 744–56.

Tulving, E. (1974) 'Cue-dependent Forgetting', *American Scientist*, 62, 74–82.

—— and Thomson, D. M. (1973) 'Encoding Specificity and Retrieval Processes in Episodic Memory', *Psychological Review*, 80, 353–70.

Turtle, J. (1995) 'Officers: What Do They Want? What Have They Got?', paper presented at the first biennial meeting of the Society for Applied Research in Memory and Cognition, University of British Columbia, July.

Part V
The training context

19 Training in communication skills: research, theory and practice

Owen D. W. Hargie

This book has incorporated a detailed analysis of a wide range of communication skills. Although the focus throughout has been on interactions between professionals and clients, it is obvious that many of the elements of communication focused on also have direct applicability to everyday 'social' encounters. Thus, for example, while a knowledge of the skills involved in being assertive is important for most professionals in their work, such skills are also of relevance in more general encounters. In this sense it is hoped the content of this text will be both interesting and of wide utility for the reader. At the very least, the material contained herein provides a comprehensive language with which to analyse and evaluate interpersonal interaction. Without the necessary linguistic terminology to guide cognitive processes, it is not possible to conceptualise and deal effectively with complex problems. Since social interaction is undoubtedly a complex process, it is essential to have a language with which to describe, analyse and attempt to understand this milieu. At this stage, the reader should be familiar with a wide glossary of interactional terms, pertaining to verbal and non-verbal communication in group and dyadic contexts, which can be employed when observing, describing and evaluating interpersonal communication.

An increased knowledge of the nature of communication should, hopefully, be followed by an increase in social competence. This competence encompasses both an ability to perceive and interpret accurately the cues being emitted by others, and a capacity to behave skilfully in response to others. Therefore, it is vital that the information contained in this book be *used* by the reader, who should be prepared to experiment with various social techniques until the most effective response repertoire is developed in any particular situation. It is anticipated that such experimentation will, for many professionals, occur in the context of a skills training programme. For this reason, it is useful to examine briefly the rationale for the skills approach to training, and some of the criticisms which have been levelled at this approach.

TRAINING IN SOCIAL SKILLS

As discussed in the Introduction to this book, many professionals now undergo some form of specialised training in interpersonal communication as a preparation for practical experience. The most widely utilised method of training for professionals is the microtraining approach, which can be traced back to the development of microteaching in teacher education. Microteaching was first introduced at Stanford University, California, in 1963, when a number of educationalists there decided that existing techniques for training teachers 'how to teach' needed to be revised. In recognising the many and manifold nuances involved in classroom teaching, the Stanford team felt that any attempt to train teachers should take place in a simplified situation (Allen and Ryan, 1969). Attention was turned to the methods of training used in other fields, where complicated skills were taught by being 'broken down' into simpler skill areas, and training often occurred in a simulated situation, rather than in the real environment.

Thus, prior to the presentation of a play, actors engage in rehearsals when various scenes are practised in isolation until judged to be satisfactory. Tennis players in training concentrate on specific aspects such as the serve, smash, lob, volley and backhand in order to improve their overall game. Similarly, the learner driver learns to use various controls separately before taking the car on the road. The rationale in all of these instances is to analyse the overall complex act in terms of simpler component parts, train the individual to identify and utilise the parts separately and then combine the parts until the complete act is assimilated.

At Stanford this approach was applied to the training of teachers in a programme which comprised learning a number of teaching skills in a scaled-down teaching encounter termed 'microteaching'. In microteaching, the trainee taught a small group of pupils (five to ten) for a short period (5 to 10 minutes) during which time the focus was on one particular skill of teaching, such as using questions. This 'microlesson', which took place in college with actual pupils being bussed in, was video-recorded and the trainee then received feedback on the skill under review (e.g. effectiveness of the questioning techniques used), in the form of a video replay coupled with tutorial guidance. This procedure was repeated for a number of teaching skills, and was designed to prepare students more systematically for actual classroom teaching practice.

Research in microteaching found this to be an effective method for training teachers (Hargie and Maidment, 1979; McGarvey and Swallow, 1986). As a result, this training method was adapted by trainers in other fields to meet their own particular training requirements, leading to the introduction of the term 'microtraining', to describe the approach wherein the core skills involved in professional interaction are identified separately and trainees provided with the opportunity to acquire these skills in a safe training environment. More recently, the term 'communication skills training' (CST) has been widely employed to describe this microtraining method.

Hargie and Saunders (1983) identified three distinct phases in this form of CST, namely preparation, training and evaluation. At the *preparation* stage, the skills necessary for effective professional communication are identified (for a review of skill identification methods see Caves, 1988). Although most of the skills presented in this book are relevant to all professions, there will be important differences in focus and emphasis. For example, a classroom teacher will use a great deal of overt verbal reinforcement during lessons, whereas a counsellor will usually rely more heavily on non-verbal reinforcers. Thus, the application of skills to contexts is an important task during preparation.

The second stage is the implementation of *training*. The first part of training is devoted to what Dickson *et al.* (1997) referred to as the 'sensitisation phase', during which trainees learn to identify and label the communication skills. This involves guided reading, lectures, seminars and the use of video models of skills in action. Sensitisation is followed by practice, when trainees are given an opportunity to try out the skills, usually in a simulated encounter such as role-play. This practice is normally video-recorded and is then followed by the phase when trainees receive feedback on their performance in the form of comments from tutor and peers, together with discussion and analysis of the video replay.

The final element is the *evaluation* of the programme. This includes ascertaining the attitudes of trainees to the CST programme itself, charting changes in the performance of trainees and their ability to interact successfully in the professional situation, and monitoring the impact of the programme upon relevant client groups. Although a large amount of formal evaluation has been conducted in this field, trainers also should evaluate their programmes informally, in terms of feedback from trainees, other tutors and field work supervisors. Such information can then be used to guide future training approaches.

The CST training paradigm is clearly based on a 'reductionist' strategy for the study of social interaction. As was discussed in Chapters 1 and 2, this approach to the analysis of social skill evolved from work carried out in the field of motor skill where a similar *modus operandi* had proved to be successful. Thus, it was argued, just as a motor sequence, such as driving a car or operating a machine, can be broken down into component actions, so too can a social sequence, such as interviewing or teaching, be broken down into component skills.

CRITICISMS OF THE SKILLS APPROACH

This reductionist methodology to the study of interpersonal communication has met with some opposition from adherents of other theoretical perspectives. The opposition falls into two main areas. First, it is argued that the analysis of communication in terms of skills simply does not make sense, since the study of such component skills is totally different from the study of the whole communication. Second, there is the viewpoint that by analysing social interaction in terms of skilled behaviour, the spontaneity and genuineness of human interaction will be lost. It is useful to examine each of these criticisms separately.

The whole and the parts

Advocates of Gestalt psychology would reject the notion that it is meaningful to isolate small segments of an overall sequence, and study these in isolation from the whole. Gestalt psychology (the psychology of form) originated in Germany in the early twentieth century, and emphasised the concept of structure. A central tenet of Gestaltism is that the whole is greater than the sum of the parts. Once an overall structure is broken down into smaller units, it is argued, the original meaning or form is changed accordingly, since the study of each of the units in isolation is not equivalent to the study of the whole. For example, a triangle comprises three intersecting straight lines, yet the study of each of the lines in isolation is patently different from the study of the overall triangle.

Within Gestalt literature, however, there is confusion as to the nature of the relationship of component elements to the whole from which they are derived. Murphy and Kovach (1972) illustrated how, on the one hand, some Gestaltists argued that the component parts need to be studied in terms of their interrelationships in order to understand the whole structure. On the other hand, however, there is the view that there are no component parts with separate attributes, and that structures can only be studied meaningfully as total entities. Taking this latter, more extreme, interpretation, social interaction could be likened to a beautiful piece of pottery. The beauty and meaning of the pottery lie in its wholeness, and if the piece of pottery is smashed into smaller parts this beauty and meaning is lost forever. It does not make sense to study each of the smaller parts separately in order to understand the whole, and even if the parts are carefully put back together again, the original beauty is lost. *archeology wouldn't agree.*

But is social interaction broken down, in this sense, in CST? Proponents of CST would argue that the answer to this question is 'no'. Rather, social interaction is analysed in terms of clearly identifiable behaviours which are, at the same time, interrelated. Although emphasis is placed on one particular skill sequence of behaviours at a time during training, others will be present. Thus, for instance, while the focus may be on the skill of questioning, it is recognised that skills such as listening or reinforcing will also be operative when questions are being employed. No one skill is used in total isolation, and in this sense the 'parts' of social interaction differ from the 'parts' of a broken piece of pottery. Indeed, it can be argued that the piece of pottery as an entity represents only one component and that the analogy to interaction is therefore spurious. Taking a different example, in studying a motor car it is essential to understand the workings of the various elements which comprise the more complex whole in order to diagnose breakdown, effect repair, or improve performance. In similar vein, social interaction is a multifarious process which necessitates careful examination to ensure understanding. Just as it is possible to drive a car without understanding the mechanics of its operation, so it is possible to interact socially without being able to analyse the key dimensions involved in the process. However, to achieve greater comprehension and insight, identify areas of communication weakness, or train people to improve their social repertoire, a much more systematic and greater depth of analysis is required.

Obviously, each of the interpersonal skills studied can only exist in a social context. Social interaction, by definition, can never occur in a vacuum and this is recognised within the skills model which underpins the 'micro' approach to the analysis of interpersonal interaction (see Chapter 2 for a discussion of this model). In practice, the CST method can be described as one of *homing in and honing up*, where one aspect of social interaction is focused on at a time and trainees are encouraged to develop and refine their use of this particular aspect. Once the trainee has acquired a working knowledge of a number of skills of social interaction, the ultimate goal is to encourage the appropriate use of these skills in an integrated fashion.

It is also emphasised within the skills model that the overall process of social interaction is affected by a large number of both situational and personal factors which may be operative at any given moment (see Chapter 2). The study of skills *per se* is undertaken in order to provide some insight into this overall process of communication. It is recognised not only that should these elements be studied separately, but that consideration should also be given to the interrelationship between elements. This line of thought is consistent with the view of those Gestaltists who hold that the study of parts should be undertaken in terms of their interrelationships, in order to understand the overall structure.

Artificiality

Another objection which has been raised in opposition to CST is that, by teaching interpersonal skills, eventually social interaction will lose its natural beauty and become artificial and stilted. Everyone will become so aware of their own actions, and the actions and reactions of others, that this knowledge will inhibit their natural behaviour. In the final analysis, people will all end up behaving in the same fashion and individuality will be lost forever. This line of argument raises several important issues concerning the skills approach to training in communication.

During CST those undergoing instruction will become aware of the nature and function of social behaviour – indeed, the development of such awareness is one of the main objectives of training. As a result of such awareness, social actions will become more conscious and at times may even seem artificial. This also occurs during the learning of motor skills. For example, when one is learning to drive a car, one is conscious of all of the motor skills necessary to perform the act, namely turning the ignition key, depressing clutch, engaging gear, releasing clutch, depressing accelerator, and so on. When one is completely conscious of all of these motor skills the overall act becomes less fluent -- thus the learner driver experiences the 'kangaroo petrol syndrome'! With practice and experience, however, the motor skills involved in driving a car become less conscious, and eventually the individual will perform the actions automatically. It is at this stage that the person is said to be skilled.

A similar phenomenon occurs in CST. Once the individual receives instruction in the use of a particular skill, the cognitive processes involved in the performing of this skill become conscious. At this stage, a 'training dip' may occur, where the awareness of the skill actually interferes with its implementation and performance suffers accordingly. This is not a particularly surprising phenomenon and occurs not just with trainees undergoing programmes of CST, but with all students involved in the academic study of human behaviour, where, as noted by Mulholland (1994, p. xiv), 'there could be a period of awkwardness and self-consciousness, but once that stage has passed people would be left with an increase in knowledge about the communicative practices of their daily lives, and an enhanced potential to communicate successfully'. Following the training period, the use of skills will again become spontaneous, and the individual will lose this self-consciousness. However, if an interaction becomes strained we are more likely to become more aware of and focus upon actual behaviour. At such times prior training in communication skills should bear fruit, allowing us to reflect quickly on the likely consequences of certain courses of action, in relation to the probable reactions of the others involved. Training dips are also encountered in the learning of motor skills. Thus, someone being coached in tennis may find that having to focus on the component elements of, and practise separately, the serve, lob, smash, or volley actually interferes with the overall performance. It is only when the tennis player has a chance to 'put it all together' that performance begins to improve.

The initial emphasis in CST has been on identifying social behaviours and grouping these behaviours into skills in order to facilitate the training process. In this respect, CST has been successful and, as illustrated in this book, advances have been made into the identification and classification of a large number of skills in terms of their behavioural determinants. Once the behaviours have been mastered by the trainee, then the categorisation, by the individual, of these behaviours into more global skill concepts seems to facilitate their utilisation during social interaction. As discussed in Chapter 1, such larger skill concepts are assimilated into the cognitive schemata employed by the individual during social encounters. These are then used to guide responses in that they provide various strategies for the individual to employ in the course of any interaction sequence (e.g. ask *questions* to get information; provide *rewards* in order to encourage participation; be *assertive* to ensure that one's rights are respected; introduce *humour* to make the interaction more enjoyable). Just as the tennis player combines the separate motor skills, once these social skill concepts have been fully assimilated, they too are 'put together' in the overall social performance. Behaviour then becomes smoother and fully co-ordinated, with the individual employing the concepts subconsciously. In other words, the person becomes more socially skilled.

As mentioned earlier, the study of communication skills provides the individual with a language for interpreting social interaction. This is of vital import, since without such a language it would be extremely difficult to analyse or evaluate social behaviour. By studying interaction in terms of skills it is possible to discuss the nuances of interpersonal communication and give and receive feedback on performance. It also facilitates reflection on previous encounters, and the conceptualisation of these in terms of the appropriateness of the skills employed, and how these could be developed or refined. Indeed, this process of self-analysis is one of the most important long-term benefits which accrue from CST.

The argument that providing professionals with the opportunity to engage in CST will result in them all behaving in exactly the same way, can also be countered. This is analogous to arguing that by teaching everyone to talk, we will all eventually end up saying exactly the same things! Just as the latter state of affairs has not prevailed, there is absolutely no reason to believe that the former state of affairs would either. Individual differences will always influence the ways in which people behave socially. One's personality, home background, attitudes, values, and so on, will invariably affect one's goals in any given situation, and these will, in turn, affect how one behaves accordingly. Different professionals will develop different styles of behaviour in different contexts, and this is a desirable state of affairs. There is no evidence to suggest that, following instruction in interpersonal skills, everyone will conform to a set pattern of behaviour in any given situation. Rather, it is hoped that the individual will become more aware of the consequences of particular actions in given situations and will be able to choose those deemed most suitable.

The emphasis during CST is on the development of understanding of social interaction, in terms of the effects of behaviour. Any controls on this behaviour should come from within the individual, who is always the decision-maker in terms of choice of responses. It is intended that the individual will become freer as a result of such training, possessing a greater behavioural repertoire from which to choose. This is, in fact, evidenced by the finding that CST serves to increase the confidence of trainees in the professional situation.

The function of training

In terms of wider social and cultural concerns, another criticism of the CST approach pertains to the reason for offering this training, the actual purpose of the programme itself, and the meanings imbued in the process. For example, Elmes and Costello (1992) criticised CST in the business sphere, on the basis that it is an inherently manipulative means of strengthening management control within organisations. They argued that CST uses covert methods of control by creating emotional indebtedness (employees may conceive attendance as a form of paid vacation and so have their loyalty to the company increased); by transforming the training experience into a sophisticated type of social drama conducted by charismatic trainers in such a way as to create a form of mystification; and by changing the views of trainees about what constitutes effective communication. It should be noted that such criticisms could be applied to any form of communicaton training in the business sphere and not just to CST. However, the criticisms of CST made by Elmes and Costello were based primarily upon observations at one workshop, and have been countered by Hargie and Tourish (1994).

The 'time-off from work' argument could be levelled at any form of in-service training away from the work place wherein trainees are allowed to participate during working hours. The CST programme discussed by Elmes and Costello took place away from participants' work place, in a rather plush environment, and was undertaken by trainers wearing expensive apparel. But this would not be typical. While it is likely that inservice training can be best facilitated if people are away from the day-to-day pressures of work, little research exists to validate the exact location of training programmes. Yet removing employees from their work environment can also be viewed as mystification and manipulation – the interpretation proffered by Elmes and Costello. However, if it is accepted that training is necessary, decisions then have to be taken about its location. Training can, and does, occur in-house run by staff in the organisation's own training department and using the firm's facilities. Where these do not exist, then external consultants can be employed and such training normally occurs in modest hotels or conference-type locations. Typically, training is conducted by staff in normal business attire. In all of these senses, the CST course experienced by Elmes and Costello, with its palatial surroundings, is not typical. At the pre-service level, of course, CST normally occurs in college, conducted by far from mystifying lecturing staff, within a less grandiose setting!

Elmes and Costello did, however, raise the more important issue of CST being conducted primarily for the benefit of trainees. Of course, this can also lead to benefits for the employer in relation to job performance of employees. For instance, if a hospital pharmacist attends a training programme on the skills of interviewing, it would be reasonable for the employing authority to expect benefits to accrue, both for the pharmacist in terms of greater knowledge, awareness, insight and job satisfaction, and also for patients in terms of how they are dealt with during actual interviews. However, some of the central concerns highlighted by Elmes and Costello were, in fact, detailed by Pawlak *et al.* (1982) who, in recognising the tensions which may be inherent between the goals of organisations and those of trainees, pointed out that CST trainers 'may have to confront management with the incongruence if it is marked and likely to lead to low trainee motivation or dissatisfaction. In extreme circumstances, they may even have to refuse to offer the training program' (p. 379).

In their analysis of CST as manipulation, Elmes and Costello failed to distinguish between the *acquisition* of skill and how it is *exercised*. It is certainly the case that all skills are open to abuse. Children taught to write may later use the skill of writing to spray obscenities on walls or send poison pen letters, but this does not mean that they should not be taught to be literate. Likewise, people may use interpersonal skills learned during CST for devious Machiaviellian purposes. However, the possibility of such abuse does not *ipso facto* mean that people should be denied training in how to function effectively with others. What is the case is that ethical issues in CST should form an integral part of the training package and this would include how the knowledge learned should be used. For instance, Elmes and Costello contended that it is unethical to attempt behavioural change without individuals being aware that such an attempt is being made. This is true, and the aims and objectives of CST should be fully itemised by trainers at the outset of the programme, and discussed with trainees.

What Elmes and Costello did identify was that the wider phenomenological concerns regarding the backdrop within which training occurs have not been charted (although again this is true of most forms of training and not just applicable to CST). The social meaning of the process for trainer and trainee has not been a central area of focus. Skills theorists, while recognising the importance of situational context, have not grappled with the issue of how trainees conceptualise their involvement in training and what meanings are construed therein. Trainees probably bring a range of interpretations to the training process, some of which will be more positive than others.

Training does not occur in a vacuum and research into CST should consider the wider ramifications of the methodological and social dimensions which underpin this approach. For example, an organisation may wish employees to undergo CST simply to produce greater profits as a result of increased sales or influencing skills on their part. This would be an example of CST deployed as management control rather than for the personal development of the trainee. An ethical consideration of these issues would suggest that a CST programme should seek to address both the wider needs of the organisation and the individual needs of the trainee.

THE EFFECTIVENESS OF CST

A vast volume of research has been conducted into the effectiveness of the microtraining approach to CST. Part of the problem with comparisons of research in this field is that CST is not a unitary phenomenon. Rather, there are wide variations in approach within this paradigm, in terms of number of skills covered, time spent on each phase of training, nature and use of model tapes, type and length of practical sessions, numbers of trainees involved, total training time, and so on. Indeed, Dickson *et al.* (1989, p. 275) emphasised how 'Communication skills training is a technique the flexible use of which has resulted in the emergence of a plethora of specific programmes specially tailored to meet population requirements and circumstantial dictates. Its enormous potential can be more completely exploited by pursuing this versatility'.

This adaptability of CST may well be an important strength, since the main conclusion to be reached from an analysis of research investigations is that this system of training offers significant benefits. In an early review, these were summarised by Ellis and Whittington (1981, pp. 195–6) as follows:

1 Short-term effects are consistently reported;
2 Trainees' attitudes towards the experience are positive;
3 Results (short- and long-term) are at least as positive as most comparable interventions;
4 It engenders debate among theorists, practitioners and trainees about the nature and contexts of interaction;
5 It is a relatively short, inexpensive intervention strategy which proved viable across a wide range of trainees and settings;
6 The face-validity of the exercise is high. Other activities with similar face-validity are far more expensive and, to date, lack any comparably rigorous evaluation.

In a slightly later review, Hargie and Saunders (1983, p. 163) likewise concluded that:

'The general outcome from this research has been to demonstrate that microtraining is an effective method for improving the communicative competence of trainees; that it is often more effective than alternative training approaches; and that it is well received by both trainers and trainees alike.'

These findings have been confirmed in a whole host of studies across a variety of professional contexts, as detailed by, among others, Baker and Daniels (1989), Dickson *et al.* (1989), Baker *et al.* (1990), Cronin and Glenn (1991), Papa and Graham (1991), Ivey (1994), Irving (1995) and Tourish and Hargie (1995). For example, Dickson *et al.* (1989, p. 44), in relation to CST with health professionals, concluded that 'skills training is effective in improving communication performance, clinical practice and patient satisfaction'. Likewise, the conclusion reached by Baker and Daniels (1989, p. 218) in relation to counsellor training was that 'the microcounseling paradigm, as it has been used thus far, is an effective educational program'. In an evaluation of CST in the business field, Papa and Graham (1991, p. 368) found that 'Managers participating in communication skills training received significantly higher performance ratings on interpersonal skills, problem-solving ability and productivity' than those receiving no such training. Similarly, Cronin and Glenn (1991, p. 356), in their analysis of the effects of CST on the communicative competence of students in the higher education context, concluded that 'this approach holds significant promise for curricular development and improvement of student communication skills'.

Thus, there is overwhelming evidence that, when used in a systematic, co-ordinated and informed fashion, CST is indeed an effective training medium. As summarised by Ivey (1994, p. 17), 'a general conclusion is warranted that considerable validation of the microtraining model is found in the research literature'.

OVERVIEW

This book has been concerned with a comprehensive analysis and evaluation of interpersonal communication, with particular reference to the work of professionals in terms of: providing an understanding of many of the nuances of social interaction; increasing their awareness of their own behaviour and of its effect upon others; interpreting and making sense of the behaviour of others; and generally contributing to an increased social awareness and interpersonal competence.

The theoretical perspectives discussed in Part 1 are essential in that they provide an underlying rationale for the analytic approach to communication adopted in the remaining chapters of the book. The eight core communication skills covered in Part 2 are of direct application to all professionals. Likewise, in most occupations people spend a considerable proportion of their time working in groups, being assertive, negotiating and ensuring effective relationships are maintained with others, and so a knowledge of these specialised aspects, as covered in Part 3, is of vital import. Finally, the dimensions of interviewing included in Part 4 will be of relevance to most professionals, who will be involved to a greater or lesser degree in selecting, appraising, helping or using a cognitive approach to eliciting information.

Overall, therefore, this text should be a useful handbook for many professionals, both pre-service and practising. Ideally, it can be employed as a course reader during training programmes in communication, thereby facilitating the learning by trainees of interpersonal skills and dimensions. However, it can also be employed solely as a reference text by the interested, experienced professional. Either way, the coverage represents the most comprehensive review to date of communication skills. At the same time, it should be recognised that this is a rapidly developing field of study and, as knowledge increases, further skills and dimensions will be identified, and awareness of interpersonal communication expanded accordingly. As summarised by Riggio (1992, p. 4), 'It is likely that as we isolate and are able to measure more and more of these specific communication skills, that the skill approach to studying social interaction will become more common-place'.

REFERENCES

Allen, D. and Ryan, K. (1969) *Microteaching*, Addison-Wesley, Reading, MM.

Baker, S. and Daniels, T. (1989) 'Integrating Research on the Microcounseling Paradigm: A Meta-analysis', *Journal of Counseling Psychology*, 36, 213–22.

—— and Greeley, A. (1990) 'Systematic Training of Graduate Level Counselors: Narrative and Meta-analytic Reviews of Three Major Programs', *Counseling Psychologist*, 18, 355–421.

Caves, R. (1988) 'Consultative Methods for Extracting Expert Knowledge about Professional Competence', in R. Ellis (ed.), *Professional Competence and Quality Assurance in the Caring Professions*, Croom Helm, London.

Cronin, M. and Glenn, P. (1991) 'Oral Communication Across the Curriculum in Higher Education: The State of the Art', *Communication Education*, 40, 356–67.

Dickson, D., Hargie, O. and Morrow, N. (1989) *Communication Skills Training for Health Professionals: An Instructor's Handbook*, Chapman & Hall, London.

—— (1997) *Communication Skills Training for Health Professionals* (2nd edn), Chapman & Hall, London.

Ellis, R. and Whittington, D. (1981) *A Guide to Social Skill Training*, Croom Helm, London.

Elmes, M. and Costello, M. (1992) 'Mystification and Social Drama: the Hidden Side of Communication Skills Training, *Human Relations*, 45, 427–45.

Hargie, O. (1980) 'An Evaluation of a Microteaching Programme', DPhil thesis, University of Ulster, Jordanstown.

—— and Maidment, P. (1979) *Microteaching in Perspective*, Blackstaff Press, Belfast.

Hargie, O. and Saunders, C. (1983) 'Training Professional Skills', in P. Dowrick and S. Biggs (eds), *Using Video*, John Wiley, London.

Hargie, O. and Tourish, D. (1994) 'Communication Skills Training: Management Manipulation or Personal Development?', *Human Relations*, 47, 1377–89.

Irving, P. (1995) 'A Reconceptualisation of Rogerian Core Conditions of Facilitative Communication: Implications for Training', DPhil thesis, University of Ulster, Jordanstown.

Ivey, A. (1994) *Intentional Interviewing and Counseling: Facilitating Client Development in a Multicultural Society* (3rd edn), Brooks-Cole, Pacific Grove, CA.

McGarvey, B. and Swallow, D. (1986) *Microteaching in Teacher Education and Training*, Croom Helm, London.

Mulholland, J. (1994) *Handbook of Persuasive Tactics. A Practical Language Guide*, Routledge, London.

Murphy, G. and Kovach, J. (1972) *Historical Introduction to Modern Psychology*, Routledge & Kegan Paul, London.

Papa, M. J. and Graham, E. E. (1991) 'The Impact of Diagnosing Skill Deficiencies and Assessment-based Communication Training on Managerial Performance', *Communication Education*, 40, 368–84.

Pawlak, E., Way, I. and Thompson, D. (1982) 'Assessing Factors that Influence Skills Training in Organizations', in E. Marshall, P. Kurtz and Associates (eds), *Interpersonal Helping Skills*, Jossey-Bass, San Francisco.

Riggio, R. (1992) 'Social Interaction Skills and Nonverbal Behavior', in R. Feldman (ed.), *Applications of Nonverbal Behavioral Theories and Research*, Lawrence Erlbaum, Hillsdale, NJ.

Tourish, D. and Hargie, C. (1995) 'Preparing Students for Selection Interviews: A Template for Training and Curriculum Development', *Innovation and Learning in Education*, 1, 22–7.

Name index

Abelson, R. P. 214, 217
Abrami, P. C. 199
Adams, N. 206
Adams, R. 361
Addington, D. W. 92
Adorno, T. W. 262
Agarwala-Rogers, R. 139–40
Aiken, L. R. 52
Akert, R.M. 142
Alberti, R. E. 290–2
Alberto, P. A. 148
Albrecht, T. L. 174, 228
Alden, L. 305, 313
Alderfer, C. P. 393
Alexander, E. R. 243
Allen, D. 138, 146, 474
Allen, M. 213, 218
Allport, G. 70, 93, 262
Alpher, V. 175
Altman, I. 217—19, 364, 370–1
Anderson, J. 247
Anderson, N. R. 388, 396
Anderson, S. 175
Annett, J. 41
Antakis, C. 183–4
Apple, M. W. 155
Apter, M. J. 280
Archer, D. 142
Archer, R. L. 214, 219, 221–2
Arends, R. L. 146
Argyle, M. 9–10, 13, 15, 29–30, 50, 53–4, 70,
    72–3, 80, 85, 138, 140, 142–4, 148, 162, 309,
    358, 366–7
Arisohn, B. 310
Aristotle 19, 68, 188
Armento, B. J. 195
Armstrong, S. 194–5
Aronson, E. 53
Aronson, H. 91
Asch, S. E. 323–7, 329–30, 336

Ashford, S. 363
Askling, L. R. 332
Athey, T. R. 387
Atkins, M. 160, 183–207
Atkinson, M. 189
Auerswald, M. 161, 178
Ausubel, D. 188
Authier, J. 58, 161, 163–4, 168
Averill, J. 38
Axelrod, R. 334, 344
Ayer, W. 204

Babbitt, L. 113
Baccus, G. 177
Bach, B. W. 227
Bacharach, S. B. 341, 343
Bacon, Francis 68
Baddely, A. 242
Badler, N. I. 93–4
Bae, H. 85
Bagozzi, R. P. 13
Baker, D. D. 230
Baker, S. 481
Bakhtar, M. 198–9
Baldock, J. 160
Bales, R. F. 268
Balint, M. 203
Bamford, D. 206
Bandura, A. 19, 137, 306, 309, 379
Banks, S. P. 378
Banski, M. A. 213, 215
Bantz, C. 57
Banyard, P. 183
Barber, A. E. 386, 402
Barnabei, F. 164, 170, 177
Baron, R. A. 387, 401
Baron, R. M. 73
Baron, R. S. 332
Bartels, L. K. 388
Barth, J. M. 336

Bartlett, F. 70
Bateson, G. 376
Batstone, E. 352
Bauchner, J. E. 250
Baum, W. 168
Baumeister, R. 70
Bavelas, J. B. 226
Baxter, J. C. 67–96
Baxter, L. A. 214, 216–18, 220–1, 228, 371, 374, 376
Bayne, R. 162
Bazerman, M. H. 344–6, 353
Beard, R. 198
Beatty, M. 240
Beck, S. 296
Becker, M. H. 185
Becker, R. E. 11
Becker, W. C. 145, 155
Beecroft, J. L. 151
Beharry, E. 176
Beier, E. G. 88, 396
Beighley, K. 240
Bellack, A. A. 184, 192
Bellack, A. S. 16, 294, 296, 298–300, 309
Belle, L. W. 198
Belnap, N. 115, 124
Bem, D. 238
Ben-Yoav, O. 345
Benjamin, A. 160–3, 173
Bennett, N. 194, 197
Bennett, W. L. 351
Bentley, S. C. 36, 44
Bereiter, C. 145
Berg, J. H. 219
Berger, C. R. 33, 214, 220–2, 360–1
Bergmann, J. R. 202
Berliner, D. C. 193
Berlo, D. K. 139
Berlyne, D. E. 262, 269, 274
Berne, E. 7
Berry-Rogghe, G. 128
Berscheid, E. 37
Bhardway, A. 71
Biddle, B. J. 146, 192–3
Billsberry, J. 388
Bilodeau, E. 71
Bindra, D. 34
Bingham, S. G. 229–30
Binning, J. F. 225
Birdwhistell, R. 69, 142
Birnbrauer, J. S. 147
Bjork, R. 71
Blanck, P. D. 46–7
Blankenberg, R. W. 306

Blazer, D. G. 358
Blieszner, R. 361
Bligh, D. 198
Bloch, S. 265, 268, 276, 278
Blumberg, H. H. 7
Bobrow, D. 187
Bochner, A. P. 215, 220
Bochner, S. 201
Boden, M. 15
Bokun, B. 263
Bonachich, P. 335
Bond, C. 85
Book, W. 8
Booth-Butterfield, M. 244
Booth-Butterfield, S. 224
Borders, L. D. 410
Bordewick, M. C. 298, 305
Borisoff, D. 51
Bornstein, P. H. 298, 305
Bostrom, R. N. 236–54
Bourhis, R. Y. 269
Bourque, P. 299
Bovis, H. E. 346, 351
Bowen, G. L. 369
Bowen, S. P. 221
Bower, G. 453
Bowers, J. 37
Bracewell, R. J. 239
Bradac, J. J. 214, 221, 397
Bradburn, N. M. 111, 129–30, 252
Brain, L. 422
Braithwaite, D. O. 226
Braithwaite, R. B. 341
Brammer, L. 161–3, 167, 173–4
Brandes, P. D. 280
Brandt, F.S. 353
Brewer, M. B. 335
Bridge, K. 228
Britten, N. 201, 203
Broden, M. 147
Brody, N. 15
Brooks, L. 229
Brooks, W. D. 140
Brophy, J. 147–8, 193–4
Broverman, I. K. 312
Brown, A. L. 39, 58, 136
Brown, B. 343
Brown, D. 281
Brown, G. A. 146–7, 160, 183–207
Brown, G. W. 358
Brown, J. 240
Brown, L. 239
Brown, P. 376
Brown, S. 348

Brown, W. 352
Brown, W. J. 58
Brownbridge, J. 202
Bruce, V. 43
Bruch, M. A. 293, 296, 305–6
Bruck, M. 452
Bruner, J. 47, 187
Bryan, W. 8
Bryant, J. 22, 49, 242, 281
Bryman, A. 152
Buchli, V. 240
Buck, R. 35, 38
Buckwalter, A. 110–11, 115, 117, 120–1
Buehler, R. 238
Bull, R. 451–2, 454, 457, 462
Bullis, C. 227
Bulwer, J. 68
Burbeck, E. 387
Burgoon, J. K. 15, 159, 238, 244, 362
Burgoon, M. 365, 370
Burke, J. W. 151
Burleson, B. R. 229, 360
Burman, E. 183
Burns, C. L. 394
Busche, H. 242
Bush, L. E. 38
Buss, A. 169
Bussey, J. 243
Byrne, P. S. 202

Cairns, L. G. 134–55
Calabrese, R. G. 220
Calderhead, J. 194
Calhoun, K. S. 309–10
Callot, R. 454
Cameron, J. 148, 154
Cameron, K. 360
Campion, M. A. 389–90, 392, 394, 398
Canary, D. J. 215
Canter, S. 11
Cantor, J. 262, 268
Cantor, N. 364
Cappe, R. 305, 313
Cappella, J. N. 219
Carlisle, J. 343, 348, 353
Carlsen, R. 240
Carlson, D. S. 398–9, 401
Carlson, N. R. 32
Carnevale, P. J. 342–6, 354
Carre, C. G. 194
Carrell, S. 240
Carroll, J. S. 344
Carter, J. 167
Cartledge, G. 11

Carver, C. S. 364
Cash, W. B. 160, 225–6, 392
Cattell, R. B. 50
Caves, R. 206, 474
Ceci, S. J. 452, 465
Chaudhuri, A. 38
Chalmers, W. E. 346
Chang, T. 241
Chapman, A. J. 260–1, 267, 272, 274–5, 280, 401
Chapman, D. I. 346
Charisiou, J. 398
Chase, W. 23
Cheney, G. 227–8
Cherryman, J. 452
Chervin, D. D. 221
Chiauzzi, E. 307, 309–10
Chobor, K. 43
Chomsky, N. 153
Chrisoff, K. A. 311
Churchill, L. 123
Citkowitz, R. 178
Clair, R. P. 229–30
Clark, R. D. 326
Clementz, B. 296
Cline, R. P. 215, 221
Cline, V. 176
Clore, G. L. 38
Coakely, C. 244
Cobb, S. 360
Cockroft, R. 188
Cockroft, S. M. 188
Coddington, A. 341
Cody, M. J, 85, 172, 183
Cohen-Cole, S. 174
Cole, K. 150
Cole, P. 69
Coleman, M. L. 224
Collett, P. 73, 85–6
Collins, A. 242
Collins, B. E. 362
Collins, N. L. 219–20
Colman, A. 344
Combs, M. 10
Cook, D. J. 296
Cook, M. 44, 53, 72, 143
Cook, T. D. 205
Cooley, C. H. 363
Corah, N. 204
Cormier, L. 163–4, 168, 171, 173
Cormier, W. H. 147, 163–4, 168, 171, 173
Costanzo, M. 86
Costello, M. 478–80
Cournoyer, B. 161, 174

Cousins, N. 275
Covey, S. R. 152
Coward, Noel 16
Cowen, E. L. 213
Cowgill, S. 276
Cox, K. 200
Craighead, L. W. 306
Crane, D. P. 150–1
Cratty, B. 8
Crawford, J. 25
Crawford, M. 295, 312–13
Crittenden, K. S. 85
Crompton, P. 280
Cronbach, L. 125
Cronin, M. 481
Cronshaw, S. F. 385, 389–90
Crossman, E. R. 9
Crouch, E. 268
Crowhurst, S. J. 193
Crute, V. 206
Culley, S. 161–2, 173
Cupach, W. 10, 12, 25, 377
Curran, J. P. 11, 19, 149–50

Daines, J. M. 198
Dale, H. 242
Daniel, C. 391
Daniëls, M. J. M. 434
Daniels, T. 481
Danish, S. 161
Dansereau, F. 222
Darwin, C. 68
Davies, A. P. 280
Davies, G. 459, 462
Davis, J. 118
Davis, J. M. 265
Davis, M. 82
Davis, M. 125
Davis, M. S. 373
Dawes, R. M. 333
Day, J. D. 229
Day, W. 168
De Vito, J. 46
Dean, J. 73
Deaver, M. 248
Delamater, R. J. 311, 313
Delbecq, A. L. 329
Deluty, R. H. 310
Deming, W. E. 152, 154
DePaulo, B. M. 70, 81, 85, 89, 92, 95, 224
Derks, P. L. 276
Derlega, V. J. 213–14, 219–20, 222–3, 359, 364
Deutsch, F. 69
Deutsch, M. 327, 330

Dever, S. 296
Devine, E. C. 205
DeVito, J. 159
Dewey, J. 187, 289
Dickens, M. 240
Dickson, D. A. 16, 31, 48, 52, 159–79, 202, 205–6, 368, 379, 474, 480–1
Diehl, M. 328, 332
Diesing, P. 340–7
Dillard, J. 13
Dillon, J. 103–31, 173
DiMattia, D. 163–4, 178
Dindia, K. 213–30
Dipboye, R. L. 225, 385–7, 391–3, 396–402
Dittman, A. T. 73, 77–8, 89
Donahoe, C. P. 144, 149–50
Donahue, W. 378–9
Donohew, L. 250
Doob, A. N. 92
Dornan, H. C. 201
Dorsey, M. A. 92 92
Dougherty, T. W. 388, 391
Douglas, A. 345, 353
Douglas, W. 221–2
Draper, S. 191
Drash, P. W. 146
Dray, W. 190
Driesenga, S. A. 144, 149–50
Drucker, P. 353
Druckman, D. 67–96, 343
DuBrin, A. J. 399, 401
Duck, S. W. 53, 214, 358, 368, 371–2, 374–5
Duncan, S. D. 72, 74, 80, 91, 171
Dunkin, M. J. 146, 192–3, 198
Dunsire, A. 351
Dura, J. R. 296
Dutta, A. 8, 16
Dwyer, J. 151
Dzindolet, M. T. 329
D'Zurilla, T. J. 310

Earle, W. B. 214, 221–2
Ecker, J. 276
Eckes, T. 51
Edelstein, B. A. 311
Edgar, T. 221
Edwards, R. 21
Egan, G. 165, 167, 173
Ehrlich, R. 177
Eicher, J. 54
Einhorn, L. J. 397, 400–1
Eisenberg, E. M. 228
Eisenberg, E. W. 237

Eisler, R. M. 298–9
Ekman, P. 68–9, 72–3, 75–7, 79, 84, 89, 91, 95, 225, 299
Elcock, H. 353
Eldridge, C. 92
Elias, F. G. 227
Ellis, A. 106, 307
Ellis, R. 1–2, 11, 17
Ellison, C. 175
Elmes, M. 478–80
Emans, B. 437
Emmons, M. L. 290–1
Engelmann, S. 145
Ennis, R. H. 184, 192
Entwistle, N. J. 188
Entwistle, A. 188
Epling, W. 169
Epstein, N. 309, 311
Ernest, C. 240
Estes, R. W. 329
Etkin, D. 290
Evans, J. H. 224
Evuleocha, S. U. 398
Ewan, C. 200
Exline, R. V. 92

Farina, A. 265
Farrelly, F. 279
Faure, G. O. 85
Feigenbaum, W. 176
Feild, H. S. 389
Feinberg, S. E. 252
Feldman, M. S. 351
Feldman, S. 69, 223
Felson, R. 363
Fennell, M. L. 223
Ferris, G. R. 398–400
Ferwerda, M. 397
Festinger, L. 251
Fiedler, K. 46, 86
Finch, A. J. 148
Fink, L. S. 402
Firestone, I. 175
Fischetti, M. 301, 309
Fisher, C. B. 378
Fisher, R. P. 341, 343, 345, 348, 451–2, 455–6, 460, 462–5
Fiske, D. W. 72, 171
Fitch, K. 57
Fitch-Hauser, M. 244, 251
Fitts, P. 9, 42
Fitzpatrick, M. F. 215
Flanders, N. A. 193
Fletcher, C. 225, 399, 401–4

Flexser, A. 452
Foa, E. 368
Foa, W. 368
Fodor, I. G. 312, 314
Fogel, A. 367, 370, 372, 375
Foot, H. C. 259–82
Forabosco, G. 261
Forbes, R. J. 88, 396
Forgas, J. P. 38
Fouraker, L. E. 344
Fox, J. 335
Frank, R. S. 92
Frankenberg, R. 55
Freedman, J. 358
Freedman, R. 92
Freese, J. H. 188
French, P. 161–3, 173
Fretz, B. R. 87
Freud, S. 69, 136, 263, 270
Friedman, H. S. 70, 204, 346–7
Friend, J. K. 353
Friesen, W. V. 73, 75–7, 79, 89, 91, 95
Frijda, N. 39
Frisch, M. B. 296, 313
Froberg, W. 296, 313
Fry, J. 201–2
Fry, W. F. 259, 275, 282
Fry, W. R. 345
Fulk, J. 223
Furnborough, P. 395, 401
Furnham, A. 12, 31, 204, 314, 387
Fyock, J. 46

Gadlin, H. 230
Gage, N. L. 193, 195
Galassi, J. P. 291, 295, 298, 312
Gale, E. 204
Gallagher, M. 177, 206, 385–404
Gallois, C. 37, 291–3, 297, 300–1, 305–6, 312–13, 398–400
Gambrill, E. 291, 295, 297, 312
Gardner, H. 240
Garfinkel, H. 171
Garratt, G. 85–6
Garvin-Doxas, K. 214
Gatewood, R. D. 389
Gee, S. 459
Geiselman, R. E. 451, 453–7, 462, 465
Geller, E. S. 152
Gelso, C. 167
Genberg, V. 207
Gentner, D. 67
George, A. L. 344, 347
George, C. S. 150

George, D. 385–6, 389, 392
George, R. 452, 455, 460–3
Gerard, H. B. 138, 327
Gergen, K. J. 52, 312, 364
Gergen, M. 52
Gergen, V. 183
Gervasio, A. H. 295, 298, 302, 312
Giacalone, R. A. 225
Giannantonio, C. M. 393, 402
Gibbs, R. 68
Gilbert, P. 368
Gilbert, S. J. 215, 220
Giles, H. 51, 272–3
Gillett, G. 351
Gilligan, C. 306
Gilmore, D. C. 388, 398–400
Gilmore, S. 162–3
Glashow, S. 67
Glassnap, D. 241
Glenn, P. 481
Godkewitsch, M. 274
Goffman, E. 70, 74, 80, 376
Goldin, J. 289
Goldsmith, M. 454
Goldstein, A. P. 347
Goldstein, J. H. 261, 275
Golen, S. P. 225
Goltz, S. M. 393, 402
Good, T. L. 193–4
Goodale, J. G. 391–2
Goodall, H. L. 237
Goodchilds, J. D. 280
Goodenough, D. 172
Goodman, G. S. 452
Goodwin, R. 57
Gormally, J. 176, 178, 311
Graber, D. A. 247, 251
Graham, E. E. 481
Gramsbergen-Hoogland, Y. 438, 444
Graves, T. D. 84
Greatbatch, D. 124
Greene, D. 148
Greene, J. O. 36
Greenhalgh, L. 346
Greeno, J. G. 188
Greenwald, H. 276
Grewendorf, G. 125
Grieger, R. 307
Grier, T. B. 396–7
Griffin, D. 238
Grimes, T. 249
Gross, A. M. 296, 304, 313
Grossman, S. A. 277
Grotjahn, M. 270

Grudin, J. 67
Gruner, C. R. 272, 279–81
Grzelak, J. 214, 222
Gudjonsson, G. 452
Guetskow, H. 362
Gunter, B. 247–9, 251
Gutek, B. M. 229
Guyer, M. 335

Haase, R. 163–4, 178
Habeshaw, T. 200
Hackman, R. J. 332
Hackney, M. 392
Hager, J. C. 69
Hakel, M. D. 87, 92
Hale, J. L. 362
Hall, B. 228
Hall, E. T. 73, 83, 88
Hall, J. 161, 172, 201
Hall, L. 348
Hamburger, H. 344
Hamilton, M.A. 204
Handy, C. 152
Hare, A. P. 7
Hargie, C. T. C. 206, 358–80, 401, 481
Hargie, O. D. W. 2, 7–26, 29–60, 70, 138, 149,
    163–4, 177, 201, 205, 386, 391, 393, 398–9,
    473–82
Harkins, S. 335
Harn, T. J. 402
Harper, N. L. 332
Harper, R. G. 72
Harrah, D. 124
Harré, R. 350–1
Harrington, H. J. 153
Harris, J. E. 459
Harris, M. M. 223, 385, 402
Harris, R. 151
Harris, S. 108
Harris, T. 358
Harter, N. 8
Hartley, J. 198, 353
Hartley, P. 173
Hatton, N. 194, 207
Hauer, A. 161
Hautaluoma, G. E. 387
Hayes, N. 183
Hazan, C. 358
Heath, R. L. 22, 49
Heckel, R. B. 145
Heesacker, M. 412
Hegarty, E. J. 279
Hehl, F.-J. 261–2
Heimberg, R. G. 290, 298–9, 306–7, 309–10

Heisler, G. H. 293, 311
Hemsley, G. D. 92
Henbest, R. J. 202
Henderson, M. 366–7
Heneman III, H. G. 393, 402
Hequet, M. 226
Herbert, T. T. 329
Heritage, J. 171
Hermann, M. G. 92
Herold, K. 226
Herriot, P. 385–8, 394–5, 398, 401
Hertzler, J. O. 272–3
Hewitt, J. 171
Hewstone, E. 183, 190
Hickling, A. 353
Highlen, P. 177
Hildebrand, M. 198
Hill, C. 173, 175–6, 178
Hill, R. 410
Hillel, Rabbi 289
Hiller, J. 194
Hintikka, J. 125
Hinton, P. R. 44, 48
Hirsch, R. 244–5
Hitchcock, J. M. 224
Hobbes, T. 262
Hocker, J. L. 369
Hoffnung, R. 170, 178
Hollandsworth, J. G. 88, 292–3, 397
Hollin, C. R. 137, 147–50
Holsti, O. 347
Hoogstad, J. 430
Horenstein, D. 220
Horowitz, R. 250
Hosking, D.-M. 343, 347, 350–3
Hrelec, E. S. 267
Hrop, R. 314
Hsia, H. 240
Hudson, B. L. 206
Huff, A. S. 352, 354
Hughes, K. 51, 59
Hull, D. B. 313
Hummert, M. L. 52
Hung, J. H. 305
Hunt, J. G. 152
Hunt, R. G. 91–2
Hunter, M. 155
Hurt, T. 243
Husband, C. 271
Huston, T. L. 223
Hutcheson, S. 161
Hutton, W. 358
Hyman, R. 77, 85–6, 90, 95
Hyman, R. T. 184, 192

Iklé, F. C. 343
Ingham, A. G. 333
Irion, A. 8
Irving, P. 59, 166, 168, 481
Isen, A. M. 281, 345
Ivey, A. E. 57–8, 161, 163, 171, 174, 409–28, 481
Izard, C. E. 38, 68

Jablin, F. M. 113, 160, 224–5, 228, 361, 392, 402
Jacklin, C. N. 51
Jackson, D. A. 145
Jackson, E. 204
Jackson, J. 333, 336
Jackson, N. 225
Jackson, P. R. 88, 396
Jacobson, L. 47
Jacobson, N. S. 369
Jakubowski, P. 290–1, 294
James, W. 37
Janis, I. L. 328–30
Janz, N. K. 185
Janz, T. 224, 389
Jarboe, S. 230
Jaynes, J. 68
Jemmott, J. B. 358
Jepson, C. 204
Johnson, J. 21, 361
Johnson, M. 68, 123–4
Johnson, R. A. 346
Jones, D. C. 369
Jones, E. E. 45, 73–4, 82, 138, 359, 361–2
Jones, T. S. 230, 346
Joshi, A. 128
Jourard, S. M. 84, 215, 218
Jucker, A. 108, 126–7
Jungck, S. 155

Kacmar, K. M. 388, 398–401
Kafka, F. 203
Kagemni 1
Kahn, S. E. 312
Kahneman, D. 345
Kane, T. R. 264, 266
Kanfer, F. H. 305
Kanter, R. M. 352
Karass, C. L. 349
Karis, D. 95
Kasl, S. V. 92
Katz, J. 204
Kazdin, A. E. 135–7, 139, 145, 290
KcKersie, R. B. 342
Keely-Dyreson, M. 244
Keenan, A. 87, 387, 390, 397, 401–2
Keenan, P. A. 345

Kegan 410
Keith-Spiegel, P. 275
Kellerman, K. 16, 361
Kelley, H. H. 7, 367
Kelley, J. 54
Kelly, C. 240–1
Kelly, G. 410
Kelly, H. H. 344
Kelly, J. A. 11, 149–50
Kelly, J. D. 294
Kendon, A. 9–10, 68, 70, 80, 138, 148
Kennan, A. 225
Kennedy, A. J. 280
Kennedy, T. 170, 176, 178
Kennedy, W. A. 147
Kern, J. M. 311–13
Kerr, N. L. 332
Kerr, P. 8
Kessler, R. C. 358
Kestler, J. 108, 119, 121
Kikoski, J. F. 438
Kikuchi, T. 43
Killinger, B. 277
Kilpela, D. E. 280
Kim, M. 57–8
Kimmel, M. J. 334
Kimmel, S. K. 13
King, P. 432
Kintsch, W. 242
Kirkpatrick, D. L. 433
Kirschner, C. L. 298
Klein, S. S. 200
Kleiner, B.H. 392
Kleinke, C. L. 299
Kleitsch, E. C. 144
Klemmer, E. 239
Kline, P. 50
Klinzing, D. 240
Klonoff, F. A. 201
Klopf, D. W. 84
Kluytmans, F. 430–49
Knapp, B. 8
Knapp, M. L. 35, 70, 81–2, 161, 172, 238, 371, 374
Knapper, C. 44
Knouse, S. B. 400
Koch, J. J. 223–4
Koehnken, G. 451, 454, 457–8, 463, 465
Koestler, A. 67
Kohn, A. 148, 154
Kolotkin, R. A. 294–5, 298, 300
Kolt, R. 378–9
Komorita, S. S. 336
Konrad, A. M. 229

Konsky, C. W. 13
Koriat, A. 454
Kovach, J. 475
Kozma, R. B. 198
Kramer, M. W. 228
Kramer, R. M. 335, 343, 345, 347
Kravitz, D. A. 333
Kreetner, R. 151
Kreps, G. L. 35, 230
Krone, K. 160
Krone, K. J. 224
Krueger, D. L. 369
Kruglanski, A. 191
Krupat, E. 53
Ksionzky, S. 91
Kubie, L. S. 277
Kunda, G. 227
Kunimoto, E. N. 35
Kunkler, K. P. 410
Kuperminc, M. 306
Kurdek, L. A. 358
Kwan, J. L. 328

L'Abate, L. 149–50
Ladouceur, R. 299
LaFrance, M. 72, 85, 299
LaGaipa, J. J. 267–8, 272
Lakoff, G. 68
Lambert, B. 36
Lampton, W. E. 280
Land, M. L. 200
Landrine, H. 201
Lang, G. 174, 443
Lange, A. J. 290–1, 294
Langer, E. 15
Langston, C. A. 364
Larzelere, R. E. 223
Latané, B. 333
Latham, G. P. 14, 42, 151, 387, 389
Lavater, J. 68
Laver, J. 161
Law, S. A. T. 201, 203
Lawler, E. J. 341, 343
Leary, D. E. 67
Leathers, D. 244
Lepper, M. R. 148, 154
Levin, P. H. 354
Levin, R. B. 296, 304, 313
Levine, T. R. 243, 251
Levinson, S. 376
Levy, R. 39
Lewinsohn, P. 11
Lewis, P. N. 313
Ley, P. 192, 202–3

Leyens, J. P. 359
Libet, J. 11
Liden, R. C. 399, 401
Lieberman, D. A. 137, 170
Likert, R. 434
Linehan, M. M. 298, 311
Litterer, J. A. 438
Littlepage, G. E. 244
Livingston, J. A. 230
Livingstone, K. 361
Llewellyn, S. 192, 202–3
Locke, E. A. 14, 42
Lockhart, C. 339, 341, 343–4
Loftus, E. 117–18, 120, 242
Loftus, G. 242
Long, B. E. 202
Long, L. 106
Lopez, F. M. 395
Lowry, P. E. 385, 389, 391, 393
Lull, P. E. 279
Lundsteen, S. W. 37
Luthans, F. 151, 223
Lynch, M. 279

Maass, A. 326
Macan, T. H. 387
McArthur, L. Z. 73
McCall, G. J. 363
McCampbell, E. 311
McCartan, P. 138, 149
McCarthy, T. E. 151
McCauley, M. R. 463–4
McClendon, P. 240
McClintock, C. C. 91–2
McCloskey, M. 242
McComb, K. 113
McCord, C. G. 393
McCormack, J. 293, 311
McCroskey, J. 1
McDaniel, M. A. 385, 390
McDonald, J. L. 21
MacDonald, M. L. 312
McDougall, W. 13
McFall, R. 290, 299–300
McGarvey, B. 474
McGhee, P. E. 261, 271, 275–6
McGrath, J. E. 328
McGregor, D. 437
Machotka, P. 68, 70
McIntyre, D. J. 146
MacKay, D. M. 74
McKersie, R. B. 340–1, 343, 347, 353
McLaren, M. 34
McLaughlin, M. L. 171–2, 183

MacLeod Clark, J. 205
MacMillan, D. L. 137, 147
McNamara, J. R. 311, 313
MacNeil, M. K. 322
McNinch, G. 240
Madanes, C. 278
Mader, D. C. 51, 57
Mader, T. E. 51, 57
Magill, R. 8
Magliore, K. 358
Magnusson, D. 17
Maguire, P. 202, 204–5
Mahl, G. F. 72, 92
Maidment, P. 474
Maier, N. R. F. 437
Makin, P. J. 385
Mallinckrodt, B. 314
Mandler, G. 15
Mani, S. 223
Manning, P. 73
Mannix, E. A. 346
Mansell, R. E. 250
Mantell, M. 275
Mantwill, M. 457–8, 463, 467
March, R. M. 85
Marchioro, S. J. 388
Marengo, F. D. 347
Markham, S. E. 222
Markle, A. 11
Marsh, H. W. 198
Marsh, P. D. V. 351, 353
Marshall, P. 398
Marteau, T. M. 203
Marteniuk, R. 8
Martin, B. 333
Martin, G. 136
Martin, J. K. 184, 190, 192
Martin, R. A. 266, 282
Martineau, W. H. 268
Martinez, A. M. 221
Marton, F. 188
Maslow, A. H. 32–3, 152
Masters, J. C. 290, 292, 301
Mathews, A. 37
Matsumoto, D. 69, 77
Matthews, S. 279
Mawhinney, T. C. 153
Mayer, G. R. 147
Mayer, R. 245
Mayo, C. 72, 85, 299
Mead, R. 57
Meertens, R. 320
Mehrabian, A. 78–9, 81, 91–2, 142
Meichenbaum, D. 306

Meikle, S. 296–8
Meisels, M. 92
Mellinger, G. D. 223
Melody, W. H. 250
Memon, A. 451–67
Merbaum, M. 170, 177
Meredeen, S. 346–7, 353
Merrill, L. 51
Messer, D. J. 19
Messick, D. M. 343, 345
Mettee, D. R. 267
Metts, S. 25, 37, 377
Metzler, K. 108
Meuwessen, J. 202
Meux, M. O. 184, 192
Mey, J. 171
Michal-Johnson, P. 221
Michelson, L. 12
Middleton, R. 268
Midgaard, K. 346
Miell, D. E. 214
Miene, P. 52
Mikolic, J. M. 86
Milan, M. A. 149–50
Milburn, J. 11
Millar, R. 3, 16, 31, 35, 45, 366, 385–404,
    434
Miller, G. 127
Miller, G. R. 238
Miller, J. L. 364
Miller, L. C. 13, 39, 50, 214, 219–20, 225
Miller, R. L. 264
Miller, V. D. 224, 392, 402
Mills, C. 176
Milne, R. 459, 465
Milne, S. H. 223
Mindess, H. 270, 276
Minkin, N. 140, 144
Miron, M. S. 347
Mischel, W. 50
Mishler, E. 113
Moland, J. 268
Monsell, S. 242
Montgomery, B. M. 217, 369–71
Montgomery, J. 199
Monti, P. M. 149–50
Moore, Roger 134
Morehead 394
Morgan, G. 352
Morgenstern, O. 341
Morley, I. E. 339–54
Morris, D. 18
Morris, E. 354
Morrison, R. L. 309

Morrow, N. C. 13, 113, 201, 205
Moscovici, S. E. 321, 325, 327
Motley, M. T. 236
Motowildo, S. J. 389, 392
Mulac, A. 397
Mulholland, J. 477
Mullinix, S. B. 295, 312
Murdock, J. I. 13
Murphy, G. 475
Murstein, B. I. 368
Myers, D. W. 223

Nagata, D. 177–8
Nakamura, Y. 15
Nash, J. F. 341
Neisser, U. 36, 347
Nelson-Jones, R. 161, 163, 172
Nemeth, C. J. 327–8
Newell, S. 385
Newhagen, J. E. 249–50
Nezu, A. 310
Nicholas, R. 177
Nichols, R. 239–40
Nicholson, P. 162
Nicholson, W. S. 276
Nickerson, R. S. 188
Nimoy, Leonard 134
Nisbett, R. E. 82
Nofsinger, R. 171
Norman, D. 187
Norrick, N. R. 264
Northouse, L. 163
Northouse, P. 163
Norton, R. 40, 159

O'Connell, W. E. 276
O'Connor, P. 358
O'Farrell, M. 168
O'Hair, D. 85
O'Keefe, B. 36
O'Leary, K. D. 145, 147
O'Leary, S. G. 145, 147
O'Leary-Kelly, A. M. 229
Olinick, S. 122
Oppenheimer, R. 67
Orbell, J. 334–5
O'Reilly, D. A. 223
Ormerod, R. 351
Ornstein, P. A. 463–4
Orpen, G. 388
Orton, Y. A. 39
Ortony, A. 68
Osborn, A. F. 328
Oster, H. 69

O'Sullivan, M. 77, 84
Owen, J. W. 312
Oxford, G. S. 272–3

Padgitt, J. S. 229
Padgitt, S. C. 229
Padilla, J. 462
Paetzold, R. L. 229
Paivio, A. 456
Palamatier, R. 240
Palmgreen, P. 251
Papa, M. J. 481
Paquette, R. J. 311, 313
Parker, I. 183
Parkinson, B. 37
Parks, M. R. 20, 22, 215
Parsons, C. K. 399, 401
Pask, G. 188
Patterson, C. 160
Patterson, G. 378
Patterson, M. L. 79–81
Paulus, P. B. 328–9
Pavlov 168
Pawlak, E. 479
Payne, D. G. 458
Payne, S. 111, 240
Payrato, L. 76
Pear, J. 136
Pearce, W. 240
Pearn, M. 152
Pedersen, P. B. 427
Pellegrino, J. 242
Pendlebury, M. 204–5
Pendleton, D. 31, 192, 201–2
Pennebaker, J. W. 358
Pepper, G. L. 58
Pepper, S. 67
Perot, A. R. 229
Perreault, R. M. 281
Perret, D. I. 53
Perry, E. 388
Peters, T. 152
Peterson, J. L. 301, 309
Petrie, C. 240
Petronio, S. 218
Pettigrew, T. F. 359
Petty, R. 333
Pfeifer, K. 263, 271–3
Pharaoh Huni 1
Phares, E. J. 49
Phillips, E. 11
Phillips, G. M. 10, 13, 230
Piaget, J. 187, 410–11
Pierce, W. D. 148, 154, 169

Pinder, T. H. 435
Pineault, M. A. 244
Pinker, S. 237
Pipe, M.-E. 459
Pirianen-Marsh, A. 199
Pitcher, S. W. 296–8
Pittman, T. S. 361
Planalp, S. 214, 360
Plato 237
Plum, A. 24
Podell, R. N. 202
Polanyi, M. 70
Polzer, J. T. 343
Poortinga, Y. H. 76
Porter, E. 162
Posner, M. 9, 42
Poteet, G. W. 403
Potter, J. 183, 190
Poundstone, W. 341
Powell, G. N. 229, 402
Powell, W. 169–70, 176
Poyatos, F. 70
Presser, S. 111, 117–19, 130
Prior, D. 160
Proctor, R. W. 8, 16
Pruitt, D. G. 334, 342–6, 353–4
Pryor, J. B. 229
Ptah-Hotep 1
Putnam, L. L. 346, 350
Putnam, S. 172

Quay, J. 392–3
Quillian, M. 242

Rackham, N. 343, 348, 353
Rae, J. P. 190
Raiffa, H. 342, 349–50
Rakos, R. 289–315
Ralston, S. M. 402
Ramp, E. 146
Rankin, P. 239
Rapoport, A. 91
Rasmussen, K. G. 397
Rawlins, W. 217–18
Read, S. J. 214
Reardon, K. K. 236, 251
Redmon, W. K. 153
Reeves, B. 249–50
Reis, T. H. 358
Remland, M. S. 230
Reynolds, M. J. 147
Rhine, W. R. 145–6
Rhodes, S. C. 59
Rich, A. 290, 292–3, 308

Richmond, V. 53, 365
Ricoeur, P. 192
Ridge, A. 12
Rigazio-DiGilio, S. A. 409–28
Riggio, R. 482
Riley, M. S. 188
Rinn, R. 11
Risley, T. R. 147
Robb, M. 8
Roberts, K. R. 223
Robertson, I. T. 385–6, 396, 402–3
Robinson, A. 201–2
Robinson, W. L. 309–10
Rodgers, R. H. 410
Roe, R. A. 434
Roediger, H. L. 458
Rogers, C. A. 106, 160, 165–8
Rogers, C. R. 152–4
Rogers, E. M. 139–40, 236, 238, 251
Roloff, M. 16
Romanish, B. 155
Romano, J. M. 294, 296, 298–300
Rook, K. S. 360
Rose, Y. J. 298, 300
Rosen, T. H. 222–3
Rosenfeld, G. W. 147
Rosenfeld, L. B. 369
Rosenfeld, P. 225, 359
Rosenheim, E. 277
Rosenshine, B. 195
Rosenthal, R. 47, 70
Ross, L. 82
Rossiter, C. 240
Roter, D. 202
Roth, I. 43–4
Roth, P. L. 390, 398
Rothbart, M. K. 261, 270, 274
Rowe, M. 121
Rowe, P. M. 225–6
Royal, R. 110
Rozelle, R. M. 67–96
Ruback, R. B. 311
Rubin, J. Z. 343
Rubin, Z. 213
Ruch, W. 259, 261–2, 272
Rudy, T. E. 309
Rutte, C. G. 336
Rutter, D. R. 204
Ryan, K. 138, 146, 474
Ryle, G. 192
Rynes, S. L. 386, 402

Sackett, P. R. 225
Sacks, H. 171–2

Safadi, M. 76
St Lawrence, J. S. 290, 296, 304
Saks, M. J. 53
Salameh, W. A. 259
Salter, A. 290
Sampson, E. E. 363
Samuels, S. J. 250
Sanders, R. 57
Sarangi, S. 394–6
Sarason, S. B. 350
Saunders, C. 2, 138, 198, 206, 391, 474,
   480
Saunders, E. D. 198
Saywitz, K. J. 453, 462–3
Schachter, S. 324–5
Schafer, R. 69
Schank, R. C. 214, 217
Schefft, B. K. 305
Scheflen, A. E. 69, 80, 143
Schegloff, E. 172
Scheibe, K. 70, 95
Scheier, M. F. 364
Scherer, L. L. 230
Schiffman, H. 118
Schlenker, B. R. 70, 364
Schlosberg, H. 68
Schmandt-Besserat, D. 236
Schneider, B. E. 224
Schroeder, C. C. 305
Schroeder, H. E. 290–3, 296, 308, 310, 313
Schuh, A. J. 393
Schulman, H. 242
Schulze, G. 72
Schuman, H. 111, 117–19, 130
Schutt, S. 110
Schwartz, B. 148, 154
Scott, A. 51
Scott, R. R. 309
Searle, B. H. 248
Senge, P. M. 152
Serby, M. 43
Shackleton, V. J. 385, 388, 396
Shaffer, D. R. 393, 397
Shaver, P. 38, 358
Shaw, M. 147
Sherif, M. 321–3, 327, 329
Sherman, W. 169
Shotter, J. 190
Shumaker, S. A. 73
Shurcliff, A. 270
Shuter, P. 84
Shutes, R. 195, 197
Siefert, R. F. 311
Siegel, S. 344

Sigal, J. 312
Sigman, S. J. 213, 215
Sillars, A. 378
Silver, R. 175
Silvester, J. 401
Simmons, J. L. 363
Simon, H. 23
Sims, H. P. 152
Singelis, T. M. 58
Skinner, B. F. 135–6, 139, 150, 169, 237
Skipper, M. 59
Skopek, L. 202
Slaby, D. 10
Sletta, O. 7
Sloboda, J. 14, 22, 42
Smith, B. O. 184, 192
Smith, D. 207
Smith, M. 385–6, 389, 392, 396, 402–3
Smith, M. J. 251
Smither, J. W. 402
Smoliar, W. W. 94
Snyder, F. 239
Snyder, G. H. 340–7
Snyder, M. 37, 52, 70
Soloman, C. M. 223
Solomon, L. J. 296, 312
Sonnenstuhl, W. J. 223
Soyland, A. 68
Spence, S. 10
Spiegel, J. 68, 70
Spitzberg, B. 10, 12, 243
Spooner, S. 178
Sprecher, S. 369
Squire, L. 241
Stahelski, A. 344
Stahl, L. 247–8
Stang, D. J. 87
Stangor, C. 46
Stanislavski, C. 70
Starkey, K. 39, 58
Stasser, G. 328
Stauffer, J. 248
Stearns, P. 351
Steel, T. 115, 124
Steele, F. 222–3
Steiner, I. D. 331
Steinhauer, J. 251
Stenstroem, A.-B. 123–4
Stephen, T. 59
Stephenson, G. M. 343, 345–6, 353
Sterling, B. S. 312
Sternberg, R. 240
Stevenage, S. V. 458, 467
Stevens, D. C. 376

Stevens, G. E. 387, 393
Stevens, R. 121
Stewart, C. J. 160, 225–6, 392
Stewart, J. 34
Stewart, M. 202
Stewart, R. 53–4
Sticht, T. 241
Stiff, J. 127
Stiles, W. 172
Stokes, R. 171
Stokols, D. 73
Stolz, W. S. 140
Stone, R. J. 151
Street, R. L. 51, 160
Streeter, L. A. 244
Strickland, B. 203
Stroebe, W. 328, 332
Sudman, S. 111, 129–30
Sue, D. W. 427
Suls, J. J. 261, 264
Sulzer, B. 147
Summers, J. 8
Sushelsky, L. 88
Sutherland, S. 359, 364
Swallow, D. 474
Swann, J. 51
Swift, L. F. 184, 190–1
Sypher, B. D. 243
Szilagyi, A. D. 152

Tagalakis, V. 226
Tagiuri, R. 47
Tannenbaum, P. H. 140
Tanur, J. M. 252
Tardy, C. H. 213–30
Tayeb, M. 58
Taylor, A. 134
Taylor, B. C. 52
Taylor, C. 392
Taylor, D. A. 217, 364, 370–1
Taylor, D. M. 184, 190
Taylor, E. G. 68
Taylor, P. H. 280, 385, 391
Tempstra, D. E. 230
Tengler, C. 113
Tesser, A. 222
Tessler, R. 88
Thain, J. W. 245, 251
Thibaut, J. W. 7, 74, 367
Thomas, K. 378
Thomas, L. T. 243, 251
Thompson, B. 43
Thompson, D. 85
Thompson, E. 240

Thompson, L. L. 346
Thompson, T. L. 224
Thomson, D. M. 453
Thorndike, E. 168
Thorne, A. 364
Thorne, B. 165
Thornton III, G. C. 402
Thorpe, L. A. 458
Thyne, J. M. 187, 192
Ting-Toomey, S. 379
Tisher, R. P. 197
Titus, W. 328
Tolhuizen, J. H. 214
Tomkins, S. 68
Toulmin, S. 190
Tourish, D. 358–80, 399, 401, 479, 481
Trenta, L. 396–7
Triandis, H. C. 69
Troutman, A. C. 148
Trower, P. 137–8, 140, 143, 147–50, 291, 299–301, 305, 309, 434
Tryon, W. W. 298, 300
Tschan, F. 332
Tsoukas 350
Tsui, A. 363
Tucker, D. H. 226
Tuckett, D. A. 201–2
Tudor, R. M. 146
Tullar, W. L. 224, 391, 394–6, 399
Tulving, E. 452–3
Turkat, I. 175
Turner, T. J. 39
Turney, C. 138, 146, 184, 192–5
Turtle, J. 462–3
Tversky, A. 345
Twentyman, C. T. 296

Ugbah, S. D. 398
Uhlemann, M. 177
Underdal, A. 346
Ury, W. 341, 343, 345, 348

Valacich, J. S. 332
Valencia, S. 391
Valentine, C. A. 76
Van de Ven, A. H. 329
Van der Molen, H. T. 174, 430–49
Van Maanen, J. 227
Van Vianen, A. E. M. 388–9
Vangelisti, A. L. 213, 215, 371, 374
Vernon, P. 70
Verplanck, W. S. 140
Von Cranach, M. 14
Vondracek, F. 176

Vrij, A. 85
Vygotsky, L. 410

Wahler, R. G. 147
Wakeford, R. 201
Waldhart, E. S. 242–3
Waldron, V. R. 227–8
Walersee, R. 223
Walka, I. 86
Walker, R. O. 298
Wallace, R. F. 145
Waltman, J. L. 225
Walton, R. E. 340–3, 347, 353
Warr, P. B. 44, 346, 353–4
Washburn, P. V. 87, 92
Waskow, I. 178
Watson, D. 171
Watson, J. 168
Watson, O. M. 82, 84
Watzlawick, P. 159, 236, 410
Weaver, K. 241
Wedderburn, A. A. I. 390
Weick, K. 222
Weiner, M. 69, 74
Weiner, S. 172
Weingart, L. 14
Weintraub, E. R. 341
Weintraub, W. 91
Weisberg, J. 378
Weiser, A. 126
Weldon, E. 14
Welford, A. T. 8–9, 17, 29–30, 348
Welford, T. W. 281
Wellman, F. 121, 129
Wessler, R. 37
West, C. 112, 121
Weston, W. W. 201
Weststeijn, H. 430
Wetherall, M. 183, 190
Wethington, E. 358
Wheeler, D. D. 325, 329, 334
Whetten, D. 360
White, G. B. 388
White, M. J. 388
Whiting, H. 8
Whittington, D. 2, 17
Wiesner, W. H. 385, 389–90
Wiksell, W. 239
Wildman, B. G. 296
Wiley, J. W. 225
Wilke, H. A. M. 320–37
Wilkens, P. C. 267
Wilkinson, J. 11
Willcutt, H. S. 147

Willems, E. P. 73
Willemsen, T. M. 389
Williams, F. 240, 251
Williams, G. R. 344, 349–50
Williams, G. W. 198
Williams, K. D. 333
Willis, F. N. 85
Wilmot, W. W. 159, 218, 220–1, 364, 368–9, 371, 373, 375–6
Wilson, C. P. 268, 271
Wilson, G. L. 403
Wilson, H. S. 224
Wilson, K. 291–3, 297, 300–1, 305–6, 312
Wilson, S. R. 58
Wine, J. D. 306, 313
Winham, G. R. 346, 351
Winkel, F. W. 85
Winship, B. J. 294
Wit, A. P. 320–37
Witkin, B. R. 43
Witteman, H. 229
Wojnilower, D. A. 313
Wold, H. 242
Wolf, M. M. 290
Wolfgang, A. 71
Wolpe, J. 290, 298
Wolvin, A. 244
Wood, J. T. 229

Wood, P. S. 314
Woodbury, H. 106
Woods, J. 369
Woodworth, R. 68
Woodworth, R. S. 8
Woolfolk, R. L. 296
Wooliscroft, J. 113
Wortman, C. 74
Wragg, E. C. 193–7
Wright, D. S. 273
Wright, P. M. 389–90, 392

Yalom, I. D. 268, 277
Yamada, S. 120
Yardley, K. 24
Yeschke, C. 110
Yi Chao, E. 85
Yoder, D. 13
Young, D. M. 88, 396
Young, I. P. 393, 402
Youngman, R. C. 280
Yount, K. R. 230

Zajonc, R. B. 87
Zartman, I. W. 350
Zillman, D. 262, 268
Zimmer, J. 175, 178
Zollo, L. J. 306, 312

Subject index

adaptors 76
advertising 279, 281
adjacency pairs 171
affect displays 77
affect orientation 244
age 52
aligning actions 171
ambiguity axiom 351
anxiety management 269
appearance 53–4
appraisal interviews: defining features of 431–2; goals of 432–3; impinging features 433–5; the interview model 435–6
arbitration schemes 341
architects 183
arousal theory 34, 262–3
aspiration zone 340
assertion: and aggression 291–2; and gender 312; and philosophical beliefs 307–8; covert behavioural components of 304–5; cultural and racial variables 313–14; definitions of 290; in appraisal interviews 446; in selection interviews 399–400; non-verbal aspects of 297–301; overt behavioural components of 294–304; philosophical background to 289; response classes of 291; social validity of 311; stimulus control skills 304–5
assertion training 425
attitudes 39, 238
attractiveness 53, 388
attribution 48–9, 220, 359, 397, 401, 434
autokinetic phenomenon 321–3

backchannel behaviour 42, 142, 172
backchat (short and long) 243, 251
banter 267, 367, 392
bargaining: distributive and integrative 342; rational and irrational 347
behaviour modification 147
behaviour therapy 289

behaviourism 136, 168–70, 237
beliefs 39, 191, 305, 307, 326, 409
bids 344–6
brainstorming 328–9, 332
Brown–Carlsen Test 240
business process improvement (BPI) 153

central tendency 387
change 347
Chicken Game 341, 343, 344
children 451–66
CIA 455
closing of interviews 393–4, 436, 448
cognition 20–2, 36–9, 161, 187, 236, 245, 261, 304–5, 320, 339, 345, 347, 351, 409, 411, 414–15, 434, 461
cognitive complexity 176
cognitive interviews: and child interviewees 462–6; background to 451–2; defining features of 452–5; effectiveness of 457–65; field tests of 460–2; limitations of 465–6
cognitive restructuring 309
communication boundary management theory 218
communication skills training (CST): criticisms of 475–80; effectiveness of 480–1; rationale for 473–5
communication spirals 375
competence 12–13, 16
complaints (handling of) 443–4
conceptual complexity 305
conceptual image codes 456
concession-making 341, 344
concrete orientation 413–4, 417
confabulations 455–9
confirmatory bias 388
conflict in relationships 378–9
conflict management 409
conflict mediation 369
conflict resolution 293–4, 309, 379

conflict spirals 343
confirmation bias 46
conformity 321
conscious and sub-conscious performance 15
context reinstatement 453
contrast effect 387
contrient interdependence 330–2
conversation management 461
courtrooms 454
counselling, 160, 162, 164, 167, 171, 175–8, 183, 206, 387; *see also* helping interview
covering law model 190–1
Criminal Justice Acts 462
culture 33–4, 57–8, 84–6, 245, 313–14, 369, 395–6, 401, 423, 426–7, 439
cultural expertise 58
cybernetics 41

deception 85–6, 88–90, 92, 127, 250, 270, 299, 403
decision-making 353, 388
dentists 204–5
depression 358
Developmental Counselling and Therapy (DCT) 409–28
dialectic/systemic orientation 413–14, 417
discourse analysis 190, 202
discursive psychology 351
dissonance 251
doctors 111–13, 160, 172, 183, 184, 189, 201–4
doctor's surgery 18
drive theory 34
dual concern model 345

embarrassment 269, 274, 278
emblems 76
emotions 25, 37–9, 161, 361, 414–15
empathy 166–8, 309, 409, 415
employee assistance programmes (EAPs) 223
employment interview *see* selection interview
engineers 183
erklärung 189
ethics 402–4
expectancy confirmation 388
explaining: and teaching 193–7; definition of 184; in health contexts 200–6; in higher education 197–200; nature of 187–8; philosophical roots 188–9; tasks of 185–7; types of 184–5
expressiveness 195, 199
eye contact 299
eyewitnesses 451–8

face 25, 343, 376–7
facial expressions 299–300
family therapy 278
feedback 41–3, 134, 139, 187, 197, 200, 204, 359–60, 363, 435, 442
feminist counselling 425
first impressions 87, 387, 396
flattery 362, 399, 400
focused retrieval 456
formal orientation 413–14, 417
free riding (in groups) 333–5
friendliness 393
friendship 369

games theory 341
gender 50–2, 248, 299–300, 312, 388, 399, 423
Gestalt psychology 475–6
gestures 300
gist formulations 171
goals: and behaviour 8, 11, 14, 16; and motivation 31–4; and relationships 35; and self-disclosure 216–17; and situations 54–5; and social skills 13–16; in appraisal 435, 438; in counselling 417–18; in negotiation 345; in relationships 359, 366; in selection interviews 394, 398; short-term and long-term 14–15; theories of 13–14
goal conflict 35
goal expectation theory 334
groups: cognitive tuning in 321; conformity pressures of 323–5; co-ordination losses in 331–2; informational and normative pressures in 327–8; innovative minority pressures in 325–6; motivation losses in 333–5; norms 321–2, 334; overcoming dysfunctional pressures 328–30; tuning of interests 330–6
group interaction 268
group therapy 277–8
groupthink 328, 330
guilt 86

halo effect 387, 434
happiness 358
helping interviews: case example of 418–21; cognitive-developmental orientations 411–16; facilitating client development 416–18; theoretical assumptions 410–11
hermeneutics 190
hierarchical control theory 20–2
homosexuality 224
horn effect 434
humanistic psychology 153–4, 165
humour: and self-disclosure 265; arousal theories of 262–3; functions of 264–71;

definition of 261; in advertising 279; in teaching 280–1; in therapy 277; incongruity and developmental theories of 261; mental health applications of 275–7; psychoanalytic theories of 263; superiority theories of 262

identity 227
illustrators 76
immune function 358
implicit personality theory 47
impression formation 388
impression management 82, 87, 359, 389, 394, 398–401, 403
incentive theory 34
incentive values 362–3
incompleteness axiom 351
influencing 15–16, 329
information processing 247, 388
ingratiation 361–3, 400
inner speech 21
innovation 228, 321, 325–6
integrative agreements 345–6
intelligence 240
intentionality: and communication 236; and non-verbal behaviour 74; and skilled performance 8, 15; during explanations 192
interpersonal expectancy effect 46
interviewing 160, 171, 175
irrational beliefs 307–8

job satisfaction 358
jokes 270–1

kinesics 40, 72

laughter: and tension release 269; health benefits of 275; functions of 271–3; types of 263, 273–5
law of effect 169
lawyers 183
leadership 152, 351–2, 437
lesbians 224
life changes 416
listening: and behaviour 251; and memory 241–3; and reading 250; approaches to 242; attitude to 241; audio and video modalities of 247–50; in cognitive interviews 457; in negotiations 348; in selection interviews 393; interpretive 243–4; measurement of 239–41; research into 238–42, 252–3; schematic 244–7
locus of control 176, 203
logotherapy 425

marriage 358, 361, 367
matrix games 344
mediating factors 35–9, 369
mediation 230
Memorandum of Good Practice 462
memory 36, 241–3, 249, 280, 451–4, 456
memory strategy usage 463
mental health 276, 358
mentalism 168
mental metaphors 67–8
mental reinstatement 453
metacognition 37
metaperception 25, 309
micro-momentary expressions (MMEs) 95
microteaching 473–4
microtraining 474
mindful behaviour 15, 222
mindless behaviour 15, 238
minimal effective response (MER) 301
modelling 19, 219, 278
mood 387
mood disturbance 266
mortality rate 358
motivation: and behaviour 32, 35; and goals 31–4; and needs 32–4; and reinforcement 148; definition of 32, 35; losses in groups 332–4; theories of 34–5
motor skill: and social skill 7–26, 30–1; definitions of 8–9; elements of 7, 29
motor skill performance: analogy with social skill performance 22–25; models of 29–31
multicultural counselling 425
multiple trace theory 453

narrative models of therapy 425
needs: and motivation 32; hierarchy of 32–4, 237
negotiation: behavioural studies of 343–6; discursive models of 350–4; effectiveness in 349–50; information processing models of 346–8; strategic interaction models of 341–2; utility models of 399–41
networking 352
nominal group technique (NGT) 329, 332
non-directive counselling 425
non-verbal behaviour: and commitment 91; and health 91; as code 69; as communication 68–70, 75–81; as dramatic presentation 70; as ingratiation 362; as skilled behaviour 70–1; as style 70–1; encoding and decoding 73–4; functions of 79–81; in assertion 297–301; in context 73, 81–6; in relationships 365; in selection interviews 393, 396–7; scientific study of 71–5
nursing 205

opening of interviews 391–2, 436, 440
operant conditioning 169
operant psychology 135
organisational communication 222, 237
organisational culture 227
outcome expectancies 306

paralanguage 39–40, 72, 161, 297
paraphrasing 163, 165, 178
Pareto optimal 345–6, 353
participation model of interviewing 443
pay as an incentive 154
perception: accuracy of 45–6; and labelling 46;
    definitions of 43–4; elements of 44; in
    assertion 309; in relationships 359; in
    selection interviews 388; selective nature of
    43; theories of 47–8
performance evaluation interview: defining
    features of 431–2; example of 441–8;
    historical context 437; phases of 438–41;
    situating the interview 437
personality 50, 388–9
person-centred counselling 165–8
personnel management 430
person-situation debate 49–50
perspective taking 409
persuasion 188–9, 279, 327
pharmacy 17–18, 113, 205, 479
phenomenological field 166
physiotherapy 186
police–citizen interactions 82–5, 109, 117, 361
political propaganda 281
positive regard 166, 388, 403
positiveness 78
pragmatics 170–2
predominant orientation 411, 417
primacy effect 45
Prisoner's Dilemma Game 341, 343, 344
problem-solving 310, 344, 359, 409, 415, 435,
    437, 442
production blocking 332
promotive interdependence 330–2
propositional memory 249
prospect theory 345
prototypical interview candidates 388
proxemics 40, 72
psychoanalytic methods 425
psychotherapy 105, 160, 178, 267, 277
punishment 139

questions: answers to 123–31; assumptions
    behind 114–17; elements of 114; open/closed
    119–20; presumptions of 116–17;
    presuppositions of 115; wording of 117–19

questioning: and self-disclosure 220–1; in
    appraisal 442; in classrooms 103–5; in
    cognitive interviews 452, 457; in counselling
    416–18; in courtrooms 106–8; in
    interrogations 109–10; in journalism 108–9; in
    medicine 111–13; in personnel interviews
    113–14; in polling contexts 111; in
    psychotherapy 105–6; in selection interviews
    392–3

radiographers 206
rapport building 456–8
rating scales 433, 435
rational-emotive therapy 106
rational relabelling 309
reactance 176
reality therapy 425
recency effect 45, 434
reference group axiom 351
reflecting: and self-disclosure 176; behaviourist
    approach 168–70; defining features of 160–5;
    function of 172–4; humanistic approach
    165–8; in appraisal 442; in counselling
    418–19; linguistic approach 170–2; research
    into 174–8; theoretical perspectives 165–72
reflection of feeling 163, 165, 177
regularity model 190
regulation (skill of) 442
regulators 76
reinforcement: and feedback 134–5, 139–42;
    and learning 19; and social skills training
    148–50; criticisms of 153–5; definition of 135;
    in business and management contexts 150–3;
    in classroom contexts 146–8; non-verbal
    142–3; positive and negative 139; primary
    and secondary 136, 169; social 137, 169
reinforcers: hierarchy of 137; non-verbal 142;
    verbal 144
relational communication: and conflict 378–9;
    and impression management 359–60; as
    ingratiation 361–3; at the formation and
    dissolution stages 369–78; benefits of 358;
    dimensions of control in 365; interpersonal
    behaviour in 363–4; rules in 366–9;
    uncertainty reduction in 360–1
relationships 213–16, 238, 293, 352
relationship formation: stage model 370–2;
    continuous process model 372
reminiscence 458
repertoires of behaviour 55, 366
reporting (in interviews) 453–4
resistance point 340
response timing 301
retrieval practice 458

rewardingness 16, 367–8
rhetoric 68
roles 55, 359, 366, 394–5
role-taking 309
rules 55, 359, 394, 433

schemas 21–2, 244–6, 251, 387
scripts 7, 21, 245, 359, 368, 394–5
selection interviews 87–8, 113, 224–6, 359:
    definition of 385–6; errors in 387; functions
    of 386; impression management in 398–401;
    reliability and validity of 389–40; structure of
    386–91; the applicant's perspective 395–401;
    the interviewer's perspective 386–94
self-actualisation 166
self-concept 166–7, 358, 364, 415
self-disclosure: consequences of 218–20, 227–30;
    and humour 265; and relational maintenance
    215; and safe sex 221; in marriage 215–16; in
    personal relationships 213, 361–2, 364; in
    relational initiation and development 214–15;
    in selection interviews 397–8; in work
    environments 221–30; of stigmatising
    information 224; requests for 220–1, 224–6;
    strategic use of 214
self-efficacy 306–7
self-esteem 360, 415
self-fulfilling prophecy 46, 388
self-image 363
self-monitoring 37, 42, 304, 310
self-persuasion 238
self-presentation 360
self-reinforcement 137, 305
self-statements 306
sensation-seekers 250
sensorimotor orientation 412, 417
sequences of behaviour 18
Sequential Tests of Educational Progress
    (STEP) 240
Sesame Street 280
settlement range 340
sexual harassment 229–30, 265
situational interviews 389–90
social exchange theory 7, 219, 362, 367–8
social inadequates 20
social learning theory 19–20, 137, 379
social loafing 333, 335
social networks 358, 360
social penetration theory 217, 370
social situations 17–19, 54–6, 73
social skill: and behaviour 16–17, 39–41; and
    control 20–2; and learning 19; and motor
    skill 7–26; and situations 17–19;

appropriateness of 17; definitions of 10–12;
    elements of 12–22; model of 30–60; purposes
    of 479; sequential nature of 18; study of
    9–10; training in 473–480
social workers 160, 183, 206, 452, 464
speech fluency 298
speech intensifiers 397
speech rate 298
standard police interview 452, 455
standard theory model 190
status 362
stereotyping 46, 52, 271, 359, 387
stimulus sampling 458
structure of interviews 386–91
structured interview (SI) 457
style 40–1, 159–60, 350, 398
supplication 361
survey interviewing 111, 252–3
symbolic interactionism 237
symbolic processing 247
systemic counselling 425

tacesics 40
teacher–pupil interaction 104–6
teaching 160, 192, 193–7, 280–1
television news programmes 248
tendermindedness 262
theory of planned behaviour 14
theory of reasoned action 13
theory of self-regulation 14
theory of trying 14
tit-for-tat strategy 334, 344
total quality management (TQM) 152–3
touch 72
toughmindedness 262
track-checking behaviour 43
transactional analysis 7
transfer of control (in interviews) 458, 460
trust 360, 362
turn-taking 171, 395
Type A and Type B persons 293

uncertainty reduction 33, 214, 220–1, 360–1
upshot formulations 171
utilitarianism 403

values 39, 57, 228
verstehen 189
visual memory 249
vocal decoding 243–4
voice volume 298

witness testimony 452–65